Quest for Harmony

Quest for Harmony
Native American Spiritual Traditions

William A. Young
Westminster College

Hackett Publishing Company, Inc.
Indianapolis/Cambridge

For further information, please address:

Hackett Publishing Company, Inc.
P. O. Box 44937
Indianapolis, IN 46244-0937

www.hackettpublishing.com

Cover Art © Getty Images. Reprinted by permission.
Composition, Rachel Hegarty
Printed at Victor Graphics, Inc.

Library of Congress Cataloging-in-Publication Data

Young, William A., 1945–
    Quest for harmony : Native American spiritual traditions / William A. Young.
        p.   cm.
    Includes bibliographical references and index.
    ISBN-13: 978-0-87220-861-2 (pbk.)
    ISBN-10: 0-87220-861-3 (pbk.)
    ISBN-13: 978-0-87220-862-9 (cloth)
    ISBN-10: 0-87220-862-1 (cloth)
    1. Indians of North America—Religion.   I. Title.
    E98.R3Y68 2006
    299.7—dc22

                        2006021717

Contents

Part IV: Epilogue

Preface

IF THERE WERE an "endangered religions list," the spiritual traditions of Native American nations would be on it. As the twenty-first century begins, the survival of the traditional lifeways of American Indian nations and other indigenous peoples around the world is at risk. Why? The reasons include loss of ancestral lands, disappearance of indigenous languages, leveling of cultural differences as a result of spreading consumerism and technologies, attacks on traditional beliefs and practices by missionaries and native converts, and exploitation and trivialization of indigenous spiritual traditions by others.

If a losing battle for survival were the full story, *Quest for Harmony* would be little more than a sad eulogy for a few of the spiritual traditions of the more than 500 Native American nations. Indeed, many books on the lifeways of American Indians are written in the past tense, creating the impression that their traditional cultures have already died. Fortunately, despite the incredible pressures under which Native Americans today struggle to preserve and renew their spiritual traditions, reports of their demise are greatly exaggerated.

As the following pages make clear, not only are Native American spiritual traditions still very much alive, they are in the midst of a dramatic revival. The four nations on which this work focuses—the Lenape (Delaware), *Ani'-Yun'-wiya* (Cherokee), Lakota (Sioux), and Diné (Navajo)—each bear witness to the reality of Native American cultural and spiritual renewal and continuity amidst change. In addition, pannational spiritual movements, especially the Native American Church, remain strong and are growing stronger. The impact of Native American spiritual traditions beyond their own nations is also deepening, as is evident when we consider their important role in confronting the environmental crisis.

Should a nonnative author attempt to write a book about Native American spiritual traditions? That is an appropriate and important question, and the introduction will address it, providing both an account of the personal journey that has led me to write this book and an overview of the book's contents.

Although they appear at the beginning, these words are the last I am writing as I complete *Quest for Harmony*. As I do, I am very aware of all those who have inspired me to share the results of my research and reflection on Native American spiritual traditions with you, the reader. I think of my great-great-grandparents, Isaac and Lucy Hines Mundy, who lived and worked among the Lenape people in Kansas in the mid-nineteenth century. I think of my parents, Art and Rhoda Magers Young, who taught me respect for all spiritual traditions, even while they were deeply committed to their own Presbyterian heritage. I think of my wife, Sue, and children, Rachel and Matthew, who have shared my fascination with Native American cultures on a number of trips in Indian country, and have been patient and understanding when I became lost in my work. Without their encouragement and support, *Quest for Harmony* would not have been completed. I think of a Native American friend in high school who probably does not know how much he influenced me as he shared his pride in his own Ponca nation.

I think of my first Religious Studies professor, the late John Gammie of the University of Tulsa, who modeled for me a life of dedicated teaching and scholarship. I think of my doctoral advisor, Ken Kuntz of the University of Iowa, and a number of other graduate school instructors and fellow students who challenged and inspired me in my own first efforts at serious research. I think of my colleagues on the faculty at Westminster College, especially emeritus professor Chris Hauer. I can imagine no more rewarding career than teaching in a small, liberal arts college, where sharing questions and insights across disciplines and real collegiality are a daily experience.

I think of the thousands of students who have sat in classrooms with me during my twenty-five- year teaching career. Much of what is in this book (and more that did not survive the editing process) has been shared with students in various classes, including a seminar on Native American spirituality. Their genuine interest has deepened my own desire to pursue the study out of which this work has grown. In particular, I am grateful to Westminster College Religious Studies majors Zac Imel, who read through an early draft and made helpful comments from a student's perspective, and Rady Todorova, who assisted with bibliographical research.

I also think of the reviewers of various versions of this work, colleagues at other colleges and universities whose names I do not know. I have drawn on many of their excellent suggestions as I have revised and revised again. They are not responsible, of course, for the mistakes of fact or interpretation that remain in these pages.

I think as well of those scholars who overcame a heritage of cultural and spiritual arrogance to write with sensitivity and respect about Native American cultures. On their shoulders I stand. I think of the Native Americans who shared the stories of their people and their own stories in the hope that they would not only be preserved but have a lasting impact on their descendants and on others. Many of their words will be found in these pages.

Finally, I think of the Lenape, Cherokee, Lakota, and Diné people I have met in recent years, some only in passing, but a few who have become lasting friends. They have shown me true hospitality and have shared with me in word and deed what the spiritual traditions of their nations mean to them. To all of them, this work is dedicated.

Acknowledgments

1. [Material from] *I Have Spoken: American History Through the Voices of Indians,* compiled by Virginia Irving Armstrong (Ohio University Press/Swallow Press, 1971).

2. [Passages from] Paul Boyer, *Native American Colleges: Progress and Prospects* (Princeton, N.J.: Carnegie Foundation for the Advancement of Teaching, 1997). © 2000, The Carnegie Foundation for the Advancement of Teaching. Reprinted with permission.

3. [Excerpts from] Leonard Crow Dog, *Crow Dog.* Copyright © 1995 by Leonard Crow Dog and Richard Erdoes. Reprinted with permission from Harper-Collins Publishers, Inc.

4. [Passages from] Vine Deloria Jr., *God is Red: A Native View of Religion* (1994). Reprinted with permission from Fulcrum Publishing, Inc., Golden, Colorado.

5. [Passages from] Raymond J. Demallie and Douglas R. Parks, ed., *Sioux Indian Religion: Tradition and Innovation* (1987); Royal B. Hassrick, *The Sioux: Life and Customs of a Warrior Society* (1964); Frank G. Speck and Leonard Broom, *Cherokee Dance and Drama* (1983; 1951); and Omer C. Stewart, *Peyote Religion: A History* (1987). Reprinted with permission from University of Oklahoma Press, Norman, Oklahoma.

6. [Excerpt from] D.M. Dooling, *The Sons of the Wind: The Sacred Stories of the Lakota* (HarperCollins, 1990). Reprinted with permission from The Society for the Study of Myth and Tradition, Inc.

7. [Excerpts from] John R. Farella, *The Main Stalk: A Synthesis of Navajo Philosophy* (1984); and Leland C. Wyman, *Blessingway* (1970). Reprinted with permission from University of Arizona Press.

8. [Material from] Armin W. Geertz, *Invention of Prophesy: Continuity and Meaning in Hopi Indian Religion* (Berkeley: University of California Press, 1994). Copyright © 1994 Armin Geertz. Reprinted with permission from University of California Press.

9. [Excerpts from] Sam D. Gill, *Native American Traditions* (Belmont, Calif.: Wadsworth, 1983).

10. [Passages from] Donald A. Grinde and Bruce E. Johansen, *Ecocide of North America: Environmental Destruction of Indian Lands and People* (1995); Oren Lyons, et al., *Exiled in the Land of the Free: Democracy, Indian Nations, and the U.S. Constitution* (1992); Huston Smith and Reuben Snake, *One Nation Under God: The Triumph of the Native American Church* (1996); and Reuben Snake, *Reuben Snake: Your Humble Servant* (1996). Reprinted with permission from Clear Light Press, Santa Fe, New Mexico.

11. [Excerpts from] Hazel W. Hertzberg, *The Search for an American Indian Identity: Modern Pan Indian Movements* (1971); and Clyde Holler, *Black Elk's Religion: The Sun Dance and Lakota Catholicism* (1995). Reprinted with permission from Syracuse University Press, Syracuse, New York.

12. [Passages from] J. Donald Hughes, *American Indian Ecology* (1983). Reprinted with permission from Texas Western Press, El Paso, Texas.

13. [Passages from] M. Annette Jaimes, ed., *The State of Native America: Genocide, Colonization, and Resistance* (1992). Reprinted with permission from South End Press, Cambridge, Massachusetts.

14. [Excerpts] Reprinted by permission of the publisher from *The Navaho: Revised Edition* by Clyde Kluckhohn and Dorothea Leighton, Cambridge, Mass.: Harvard University Press, copyright © 1946 by the President and Fellows of Harvard College, renewed 1974 by Florence Kluckhohn Taylor and Dorothea Leighton.

15. [Excerpts from] William G. McLoughlin, *The Cherokees and Christianity, 1794–1870: Essays on Acculturation and Cultural Persistence,* ed. Walter H. Conser Jr. (1994). Reprinted with permission from University of Georgia Press, Athens, Georgia.

16. [Materials from] Irvin M. Peithmann, *Red Men of Fire: A History of the Cherokee Indians* (1964). Courtesy of Charles C. Thomas, Publisher, Ltd., Springfield, Illinois.

17. [Excerpts from] *A Different Mirror* by Ronald Takaki. Copyright © 1993 by Ronald Takaki. By permission of Little, Brown and Company (Inc.).

18. [Excerpts from] *Native North American Spirituality of the Eastern Woodlands,* edited by Elisabeth Tooker © 1979 by The Missionary Society of St. Paul the Apostle in the State of New York. Used by permission of Paulist Press.

19. [Passages from] Stephen Trimble, *The People: Indians of the American Southwest,* SAR Press, School of American Research, Santa Fe, New Mexico, 1993. Copyright © 1993 by Stephen Trimble. Reprinted by permission of the author.

20. [Excerpts from] C.A. Weslager, *The Delaware Indians: A History* (Rutgers University Press, 1972) and *The Delaware Indian Westward Migration* (Middle Atlantic Press, 1978). Reprinted with permission from Ruth H. Weslager.

21. [Material from] James Wilson, *The Earth Shall Weep: A History of Native America* (1999). Reprinted with permission from Atlantic Monthly Press.

22. [Passage from] Paul G. Zolbrod, *Diné Bahané: The Navajo Creation Story* (1984). Reprinted with permission of University of New Mexico Press, Albuquerque, New Mexico.

Introduction

"SHOULD NONNATIVE SCHOLARS study, write, and teach about Native American cultures and their spiritual traditions?" Those being asked the question were members of the Lakota Studies Department at Oglala Lakota College, on the Pine Ridge Reservation in South Dakota. Each is an enrolled member of one of the Lakota (Sioux) tribes. The setting was a special seminar being conducted by the department in May 1996, for students I had brought to the reservation to learn about Lakota history, culture, and spirituality.

The question was not just hypothetical for me. For a number of years, I had been teaching courses touching on the Native American nations and their spiritual traditions, and the previous year I had published a book with a chapter on Lakota spirituality. What right did I have as a nonnative to study, teach, and write about the spiritual ways of Native American peoples?

One of those conducting the seminar was Wilmer Stampede Mesteth, who not only taught Lakota language and culture at Oglala Lakota College, but is himself a traditional spiritual leader. He had already told us that he had closed the sun dance ritual he conducts to non-Lakota people. I also knew that Mesteth was one of the authors of a statement entitled a "Declaration of War against Exploiters of Lakota Spirituality." The declaration focused on the "New Age" movement and nonnatives who conduct rituals purported to be authentic representations of Lakota ceremonies. The statement, however, also listed as a form of exploitation of Lakota spirituality "academic disciplines . . . at colleges and universities institutionalizing the sacrilegious imitation of our spiritual practices by students and instructors" and the sale of "books that promote the systematic colonization of our Lakota spirituality" (Mesteth 1995). I was particularly concerned to hear what this educator and traditional spiritual leader would have to say.

Indeed, wide support exists today for the position that only Native Americans should study, teach, and write about their own cultures, especially their own spiritual traditions, and that nonnatives should refrain from any further research and publication. This viewpoint is held both by concerned Native Americans, especially traditional spiritual leaders, and by many nonnative supporters.

In general, the basis for this perspective is that publications about Native American cultures by outsiders are a continuation of the long exploitation of American Indians. In other words, it is a moral issue. Proponents of this position point out that land and autonomy have been taken from Native Americans; now outsiders are seeking to appropriate Indian cultures and spiritual teachings as well. It is time, they maintain, for such arrogant appropriation to cease.

Moreover, how can nonnative scholars possibly understand the lifeways of indigenous peoples? They simply lack the experiential basis for such study. Meaningful knowledge of native cultures, especially their spiritual traditions, cannot be transmitted through the means ordinarily used in research. Such knowledge can only be communicated to those who have been raised in the culture, who know the native language intimately, and who have experienced the ceremonial life of the people as their own.

Furthermore, the frame of reference of contemporary scholarship is so foreign to the traditional worldviews of native peoples that serious distortion is inevitable. Is it not better simply to avoid altogether trying to translate the spiritual traditions of Native Americans into a mode of discourse that sees the world so differently?

Indeed, for many native peoples in recent decades, the prospect of any books and open discussion of their spiritual traditions, whether by nonnative or native interpreters, is offensive. At a conference bringing together scholars of Native American spiritual traditions and native elders, a Cree elder from the Piapot Reserve in Canada refused to discuss some of the questions because, as he explained, sacred knowledge must be learned through personal discovery and intuition (Waugh and Prithipaul 1977, vi).

Some traditional Native American spiritual leaders have said that decline of their cultures in this century is due in part to the inappropriate dispersal of sacred knowledge by those who claim to want to preserve it. When reduced to writing, the sacred power of the songs, prayers, myths, and ceremonies is undermined.

These are compelling arguments. As I sat waiting for a response from Wilmer Mesteth and his colleagues, I rehearsed in my mind the reasons justifying the involvement of nonnative scholars in study of Native American cultures. J. Donald Hughes, author of a study of the ecological teachings of Native American cultures, states the fundamental rationale most simply: "It is possible for non-Indians to penetrate the cultural barrier by basic humanity, careful study, and sympathetic understanding" (Hughes 1983, 82).

It may be argued that concerned outsiders have not only the right, but the obligation, to study, teach, and write in this area. Perhaps worse than the misrepresentations inevitable when trying to understand and communicate about cultures other than one's own is the pall cast by prior censorship. Because some earlier studies by nonnative scholars have been damaging and distorting does not mean that no further studies should be attempted. Indeed, there is a need to work hard to undo the harm done by previous works.

In addition, learning depends on a variety of perspectives, and nonnative scholars add to the diversity of ways of understanding American Indian cultures. Furthermore, nonnative scholars may serve as bridges, helping nonnative audiences understand and appreciate native traditions and countering the still all-too-common prejudices against Native Americans.

To be sure, "scholarly objectivity" has been exploited, and nonnative interpreters have inappropriately published what they have learned from participating in and observing Native American ceremonies or talking with spiritual leaders and other native people. Despite a heritage of insensitive and demeaning studies, however, there are now careful works respecting the integrity and depth of sacred traditions, which do not cross the line into exploitation and/or exposure.

Today, despite some very strident opposition to the prospect of nonnative study of native cultures, the dominant view among native scholars seems to be that such a right should not be at issue. Hopi anthropologist Wendy Rose has observed:

> We accept as given that whites have as much prerogative to write and speak about us and our cultures as we have to write and speak about them and theirs. The question is how this is done and, to some extent, why it is done. . . . Many non-Indian people have—from the stated perspective of the non-native viewing things native—written honestly and eloquently about any number of Indian topics, including those we hold sacred. (Rose 1992: 415–16)

Indeed, Wilmer Stampede Mesteth and his faculty colleagues in the Lakota Studies Department of Oglala Lakota College affirmed this basic perspective at the meeting with my students. They saw nothing wrong with nonnative scholars researching, writing, and teaching about Lakota culture, so long as they did not try to pass off their work as *authentic* representations of Lakota traditions. In particular, Mesteth vigorously condemned nonnatives, whether scholars or not, presuming to conduct Lakota ceremonies such as sweat lodges, vision quests, or sun dances under any circumstances, educational or otherwise. He agreed, however, that nonnative interpreters had an important role to play in correcting the stereotypical understanding of Native American cultures that is all too prevalent today.

It is from this point of view that I offer this introduction to Native American spiritual traditions. The goal is a sympathetic and respectful portrayal of these traditions, without pretending that there is, in these pages, a "native" perspective. The work is one nonnative researcher's attempt to share the results of decades of study with readers who share his interest in and respect for Native American cultures.

Wherever possible, I have tried to present the views of Native Americans in their own words (at least as they have been recorded). I am also intensely aware, however, that my own perspectives and experiences limit my ability to appreciate and present these traditions and that, despite my best intentions, I will inevitably misrepresent and distort. No reader should depend on only one introduction to a subject so vast and deep. For that reason, an extensive bibliography is included so that particular topics of interest may be pursued.

Before clarifying the approach to be taken in this work, let me explain more fully the personal journey that has brought me to this project. I grew up in northern Oklahoma, near the home (since the late nineteenth century) of the Ponca Indian nation. Like many nonnative young people living near Indian communities in the twentieth century, I was exposed to an array of negative stereotypes as a boy. I began to see beyond these distortions when, in high school, I met a proud Ponca teenager who helped me begin to understand the rich heritage of his people and the immense challenges they had faced in the century since their forced relocation from Nebraska. He made me aware that the prejudices about Native Americans to which I had been exposed were not only wrong but terribly destructive. At that point, I vowed to do what I could do to challenge the perceptions which had, at first, caused me to have a distorted view of Native American peoples and their cultures.

For more than a quarter-century now I have pursued an ever-deepening interest in Native American spiritual traditions. In teaching introductory courses on the world's religions since 1975 at Westminster College in Fulton, Missouri, I have committed myself to include meaningful discussion of Native American traditions in my classes.

Uniformly, the response of my students to the study of Native American spiritual traditions has been encouraging. Throughout the years I have continued to read as widely as possible the substantive literature on Native American cultures and to visit Indian communities. Finally, several years ago I introduced an upper-level undergraduate course on Native American spiritual traditions. The students in the seminar and I joined together in researching a number of Native American cultures. In the process I broadened and deepened my own understanding of the rich variety to be found among the lifeways of Native American peoples.

When I accepted the challenge of writing a world religions textbook in 1992, drawing on my two decades of experience in teaching world religions courses, one of my first decisions was to include a chapter on Native American spiritual traditions. Unlike other textbooks that, if they addressed Native American spirituality at all, had only very generalized discussions, I decided to focus on a particular Native American culture and its spirituality. Therefore, *The World's Religions: Worldviews and Contemporary Issues* (Prentice Hall, 1995) features a chapter which introduces Native American spirituality, focusing on the Oglala Lakota nation.

In 1993 and 1994 I made trips to Lakota (Sioux) reservations in South Dakota. In 1994, while participating with my daughter in the Jimmy Carter Habitat for Humanity week-long "blitz" build of thirty houses at Eagle Butte on the Cheyenne River Sioux Reservation, I lived with the Lakota family on whose new home we were working. During that week, through our new friends, we met Stanley and Cecilia Looking Horse and their son Arval, the current Keeper of the Sacred White Buffalo Calf Pipe of the Lakota nation (see chapter 4). They welcomed us graciously to their homes at Green Grass.

The next year my daughter and I returned to Eagle Butte for another visit. In 1996, after a semester's study of Lakota history, culture, and spirituality, a group of Westminster College students accompanied me on a trip through Nebraska, Wyoming, Montana, and South Dakota, visiting places and areas of significance to the Lakota. The highlight was the special seminar conducted by the Lakota studies faculty of Oglala Lakota College, to which I have alluded. We also stayed with a Lakota family in Kyle and with my friends in Eagle Butte.

In 1997 I made a fascinating discovery about my own family history, revealing an association with another Native American nation—the Lenape (Delaware). I learned that my great-great-grandfather, a man named Isaac Mundy (1815–1858), had worked among the relocated Lenape (Delaware) people in eastern Kansas as a blacksmith and paymaster. When he was killed in a hunting accident, the Lenape leaders honored him as one of the only whites buried among their people at a place called White Church, in what is now Kansas City, Kansas. In April 1997 a rededication ceremony of the Lenape cemetery was held at White Church. The featured speaker was Curtis Zunigha, then the elected chief of the Delaware Tribe of Oklahoma. My decision to include the Lenape nation in this study of Native American spiritual traditions was sealed as Chief Zunigha talked about the importance of maintaining connections with one's ancestors (see chapter 2).

A sabbatical leave from teaching, generously granted by Westminster College during the 1997–98 academic year, provided me the opportunity to concentrate full time on this project. In recent years I have also been able to make brief study trips to the Diné (Navajo), Hopi, and Eastern Cherokee reservations.

Quest for Harmony is intended for anyone seeking a basic understanding of the cultures and spiritual teachings of Native American nations. It may be used as a resource for college classes studying Native American lifeways. It is equally suitable for individual readers who, like the author, find themselves drawn to a serious and sustained study of the spiritual traditions of the native peoples of the North American continent. *Native America* refers, of course, to the original inhabitants of both North and South America. In order to devote sufficient attention to the nations chosen for study, this work is limited to native *North* America. Unless otherwise indicated, throughout the book, the phrase *Native America* is understood to refer only to native North America. In keeping with current usage,

American Indian and *Native American* are used interchangeably (see chapter 1). When referring to particular cultures, the designations *nation* or *people* are preferred to the more problematic term *tribe*. As is discussed in the first chapter, according to both Native American traditions and United States law and custom, American Indian peoples are in fact sovereign "nations." However, since at present the U.S. government recognizes "tribes," not "nations," and since most nations have adopted the designation, *tribe* is used as well.

The term *religion* is ordinarily not used in this discussion. Native American languages typically have no word for *religion*, which as a descriptive term is most widely used today in association with the "major" faith traditions of the world, such as Hinduism, Buddhism, Judaism, Christianity, and Islam. Moreover, as an essentially European and Euroamerican concept, the term *religion* can easily distort the reality of Native American traditions. Instead, I speak in this work of Native American "spiritual traditions" or "lifeways," unless the term *religion* is being used in a cited source.

Let me now provide an overview of the work for readers searching for a particular people or topic. The first chapter establishes a context by providing an introduction to Native American history, beginning with a discussion of the contrasting views of "history" in Native American and European/Euroamerican cultures. It continues with an example of a Native American story of origins and a broad historical overview based on modern research, from the first scientific evidence of occupation of the Americas to the general situation of American Indians in the last decade of the twentieth century. In particular, it provides an understanding of the often tragic history of interactions between Native American nations and the Europeans who invaded the Americas in force after 1492. It ends by raising the question whether genocide is a proper term to use in relationship to this interaction.

Most introductory works in this area speak about Native American spirituality in general, drawing on diverse traditions for examples of basic themes. The effect is to create the erroneous impression that there is an overarching, collective spirituality shared by all American Indians. In fact, there are distinct spiritual traditions associated with each of the approximately 500 native nations. Common themes and shared myths and rituals are found, but the place to start a study of Native American spiritual traditions is with specific nations.

Therefore, the approach adopted here is to discuss separately the spiritual traditions of particular nations in chapters 2 through 5: the Lenape (Delaware), the *Ani'-Yun'-Wiya* (Cherokee), the Lakota (Sioux), and the Diné (Navajo). Why these four? In their traditional homelands, they represent four distinct "culture areas" in North America long identified by scholars: the Northeast (Lenape), Southeast (Cherokee), Plains (Lakota), and Southwest (Navajo). In addition, they represent the four cardinal directions (North, South, East, and West) prominent in most Native American traditions as a way of understanding the structure of the cosmos.

The format followed in each of these chapters is first to introduce the names by which the nation has been known, the traditional location(s) and present population, the language, and usually the traditional social organization. Then, at least one of the stories of origins of the people is presented. Next, there is a historical survey of the nation, from the earliest documented times until recent decades. In the heart of each chapter, the spiritual worldview and rituals of the nation are introduced, with sections on cosmology, gods and spirits, rituals, and particular issues related to the nation.

The discussion of each nation's spirituality is, of course, by an outsider and is intended for nonnative readers. The purpose is to promote basic understanding and appreciation, not to provide information for the conducting of ceremonies or to violate any restrictions on the revelation of sacred knowledge. My intent is not to cross the line between description helpful for an outsider's understanding and exposure of knowledge intended only for the people themselves. Each of these chapters concludes with a description of the situation of the nation at the end of the twentieth century.

Throughout, the discussion is as descriptive as possible, with a self conscious attempt to minimize the use of theoretical filters adapted from various Western scholarly traditions. The purpose of the work is not to test a particular scholarly method, but to allow, as much as possible, the spiritual traditions of Native Americans to speak for themselves to the reader.

These chapters on particular nations do not assume that there is a "pristine" spiritual tradition for each people. Native nations did not and do not live in total isolation from one another; there was and is a diffusion of myths and rituals, a sharing of them among nations, especially within culture areas. In addition, the reality of centuries of interaction with European cultures and religions, and the resultant adaptation of spiritual traditions must be acknowledged. In a phrase, a recurrent theme in this work is continuity amidst change. Determined native peoples have sought to maintain their own distinct ways, even as they have drawn on and adapted the material resources and spiritual traditions of their native neighbors and the Europeans who invaded their lands.

Only after seeking to appreciate distinct spiritual traditions, will we turn to spiritual traditions clearly uniting Native Americans across cultural boundaries. In chapter 6 we encounter the late-nineteenth-century movement known as the Ghost Dance. The Ghost Dance offered hope to Native Americans at a time when their traditional ways of life seemed doomed. This movement was revived by some Native Americans late in the twentieth century as a means of reaffirming tradition and expressing hope for the future.

In chapter 7 we encounter the Native American Church, whose ceremonial use of the buttons of the peyote cactus roots has spread widely among the indigenous nations of North America as a pannational spiritual movement. Most recently, the Native American Church and the use of peyote have been at the center of a fight to preserve religious freedom for Native Americans.

An entire chapter (chapter 8) is devoted to the relationship between Native American spiritual teachings and the current ecological crisis. Many non–Native Americans in the environmental movement have claimed American Indians as "ecological saints." Is this an accurate portrayal or simply another in the long line of stereotypes of Native Americans by outsiders? Are there teachings within Native American traditions that might help all humanity learn to live in harmony with the rest of nature? If so, how can they touch nonnative people in the modern, secular world? How are Native Americans themselves confronting the ecological challenges they face on their own lands? These and other questions are pursued.

The concluding chapter (chapter 9) looks to the future, highlighting some of the most significant signs of cultural and spiritual renewal among Native Americans and portraying honestly the significant obstacles threatening the survival of Native American spiritual traditions. Issues addressed include population, health care, education, language, the powwow movement, economic empowerment, treaty rights and other legal issues, art and literature, stereotyping, religious freedom, protection of sacred sites, return of sacred items, exploitation of traditional spirituality, and the emergence of a common Native American spirituality.

According to Native American scholar Alfonso Ortiz, from the Tewa point of view in which he was raised, life is a double quest for wisdom and the spiritual. To live, Ortiz said, is to seek both knowledge about the world and experiences of the sacred (Beck and Walters 1977, 6).

This work seeks to honor both dimensions of the quest Ortiz describes. As a book about Native American peoples and their spiritual traditions, it seeks knowledge that will lead to a greater understanding and appreciation among nonnative readers. It offers no direct guidance to the experience of the sacred, and it cautions against merely trying to imitate another people's spirituality. (For other perspectives on the academic study of Native American cultures, see Mihesuah 1998 and Thornton 1999.) Nevertheless, those readers willing to open their own hearts and spirits as well as their minds to the people whose spiritual traditions are being described and honored may be touched at a deeper level. By listening carefully and respectfully to the many Native American voices in these pages, they may find their own quests for harmony enriched.

Part I

Establishing a Context

Chapter 1

Native America:
A Historical Overview

America has much to learn about the heritage of . . . American Indians.
Only through this study can we as a nation do what must be done if our
treatment of the American Indians is not to be marked down for all time as
a national disgrace.

—President John Fitzgerald Kennedy

During a seminar on the history of the Hopi people, held on the Hopi Reservation in northeastern Arizona, the question arose: "What is the origin of the Hopi?" A noted anthropologist presented his theory that the Hopi people were among a group of hunters and gatherers in the western Great Basin who moved south to canyons (including the Grand Canyon), where they became agriculturalists, and then migrated from the canyons to live on the mesas they currently occupy. After the professor finished, a Hopi leader rose to take issue with this scholarly answer. He spoke of what all the Hopi present at the seminar knew, that the Hopi people had come from the worlds beneath the present world at a place called *Sipapuni*, through a reed. When they emerged from the Third World to the current Fourth World they already had corn. The Hopi clans, he said, came not only from the north but from the four directions. After long journeys the clans settled on the current mesas.

Which of these answers is correct? That, of course, depends on the context and community in which one is asking the question. Had the anthropologist been offering his theory at an academic gathering, his would have been the preferred response. He was speaking, however, among the Hopi people, for whom the traditional story is assumed as true. The Hopi leader was right to challenge the scholar's theory; it was clearly the less compelling answer for him and his people. The Hopi myths of emergence and migration were the stories appropriately affirmed as the truth about Hopi origins. These tell the Hopi who they are, what their purpose in life is, and how they are to live in harmony in this world.

In this work, both perspectives—that of the native insider and that of the nonnative outsider—are respected. The account of native nations and their spiritual traditions is *not* meant to challenge, and certainly not to replace, the stories of the people themselves. Indeed, stories of origins, as they have become known and available to outsiders, are presented in this chapter and at the outset of the discussion of each nation. These stories give a sense of the truth that must take precedence for native peoples themselves over the mere descriptions found in this work. However, if we who are outsiders seek understanding of Native American traditions, we must also be willing to draw on the wealth of scholarship available. Therefore, much of this work represents a synthesis of the best studies of Native American lifeways by anthropologists and historians.

The main purpose of this first chapter is to provide a narrative of the history of Native American nations, from the earliest evidence of occupation of the Americas to 1990, with emphasis on the impact of European invasion of North America. It establishes a broad context for the study of four particular Native American nations and their spiritual traditions and pannational spiritual movements in subsequent chapters.

First, to explore further the dilemma posed at the beginning of the chapter, the problems raised by the prospect of studying American Indian history are addressed. Next, I present excerpts from the stories of origins of the Hopi nation, to illustrate the ways in which native peoples have traditionally known who they are as distinct nations. Then I turn to the history of Native America, as constructed by modern scholars, beginning with a selective recounting of the archaeological evidence of early Native American settlements. Next, I consider the story of the 500-year invasion and conquest of North America by Europeans after 1492 and the varied responses of Native American nations, drawing as much as possible on the recorded words of native peoples. In keeping with the theme of this work, I emphasize the role of spirituality, especially the European and Euroamerican perceptions of and approaches to the spiritual traditions of the indigenous peoples of North America. Again and again, one can witness people struggling to maintain continuity with the ways of their ancestors as they adapt to the changing conditions in which they find themselves, incorporating into their cultures innovations that they believe will assist them to survive. The chapter concludes by exploring the question of whether genocide has been committed against Native American peoples.

"American Indian History": A Threefold Dilemma

The phrase "American Indian history" poses a threefold dilemma. First, the names *American* and *Indian* are, of course, foreign to the original inhabitants of the continent. These are labels assigned to the native peoples of North America by the Europeans who made first contact with them more than 500 years ago. The names are drawn from the European experience, *American* from Italian-born explorer Amerigo Vespucci (1454–1512) and *Indian* from the mistaken belief that the islands "discovered" by Christopher Columbus were part of India. The more widely accepted designation *Native American* does not, of course, avoid this problem of naming from an outsider's perspective.

The second problem is that there is no one people who are "American Indians" or "Native Americans." Rather, there are the diverse nations of peoples who, according to Western scientists, have lived on the continent called North America for thousands of years, or, according to many of the traditions of native peoples, always. Each nation of "Native Americans" has its own stories that trace its origins, passed on orally from generation to generation. As Hotinonshonni (Iroquois) scholar John Mohawk has observed:

> In effect, the European invented the term "Indian" to mean a kind of "other." The indigenous peoples of the Americas identified themselves as distinct peoples such as the Diné or Haudenosaunee [Hotinonshonni] or any of hundreds of other distinct peoples. (Mohawk 1992, 51)

The third problem is that the concept "history" itself is problematic. "History" understood as the recording of human events in progression (as in a "history of America from 1492 to the present") reflects a view of time not central to the traditions of most of the original inhabitants of the continent. Lakota scholar Vine Deloria Jr. has observed: "The western preoccupation with history and a chronological description of reality was not a dominant factor in any tribal conception of either time or history" (Deloria 1994, 98).

As is discussed later, it is more common among these native peoples to image time primarily as the rhythmic repetition of the cycles of nature rather than the singular accomplishments of humans (see Nabakov 1996). Nonnative author James Wilson expresses the conflict in this way:

> For Native American cultures, an experience gains its significance not from when it happens but from what it means. If Time is essentially cyclical there is no simple straightforward chain of cause and effect: events have to be seen not in chronological relation to each other but in terms of a complex, coherent understanding of the world, rooted in the origin story, in which time, space, spiritual entities, and living beings all interact. The function of history is to provide not a linear record, but a blueprint for living, specific to a particular people in a particular place. (Wilson 1999, 8)

Therefore, to tell the "history" of "American Indians" in general, or even the "history" of any particular Native American nation, is to impose an interpretive framework from the outside. Indeed, some interpreters have questioned whether outsiders can or should write about the histories of societies which do not place themselves in the historical trajectory (Martin 1987).

Many critics believe a deliberate attempt has been made to destroy Native Americans' history as part of the campaign to assimilate Indians into Euroamerican civilization. As part of the physical subjugation of Native Americans came the attempted annihilation of their past. Not surprisingly "the victors write the histories; the vanquished are rendered historyless" (Armstrong 1971, xii).

Native American scholar Alfonso Ortiz (Tewa) has called for a "new Indian history" that "would frame questions and inquiries using terms and categories that reflect Indian realities and are important to the Indians." Too often, he contends, "history" has been a celebration of Western civilization that has bred "a relentless linearity of thought and, sometimes, cultural arrogance." "History" has too often functioned as a machine that devours actual Indian peoples' own wishes and experiences, while emphasizing the attempts of Europeans to "civilize" Native Americans (Hoxie 1988, 1–3).

The solution to this dilemma is not to avoid the terms *Indian* and *Native American* altogether, for their usage has become pervasive and accepted among native as well as nonnative interpreters, as Ortiz illustrates. In this work these terms are used interchangeably to speak in general about the first inhabitants of this continent and their descendants. Nor can one ignore "history" as understood chronologically, for it is the dominant perspective in the contemporary world.

Perhaps the best we can do is to be constantly aware of the "filters" through which we are observing the realities we are attempting to understand. We can also try, as much as possible, to avoid explicit or implicit value judgments based on our own cultural biases. For example, in this book I eschew terms such as *wilderness*, *civilization*, and *frontier* except as they are used by those I am discussing or citing or when their Euroamerican context is clear. Although seemingly objective, these concepts have implications that reveal a prejudice about who native peoples are, where they are, and what their rights are. *Wilderness* usually has been used to place Indians not only spatially but ethically, with the implication that in the effort to bring the virtues of "civilization" to the areas which had been "wilderness," it was necessary to transform, remove, and even annihilate Indian peoples. Likewise, *frontier* creates a sense of boundary, with the Indians on one side and the bearers of "civilization" on the other. Beyond the "frontier" is where the "savages" dwelled. As "civilization" pushed westward, the "frontier" shifted. Especially since historian Frederick Jackson Turner's epic essay, "The Significance of the Frontier in American History" (1893), there has been a tendency to view American history in this way. The result has been either to demonize Indians as symbolic of the forces that opposed this process or simply to ignore them as irrelevant to the real story of America (see Limerick 1987).

Before There Was History: Origins of the Peoples

A Tewa is not so interested in the world of archaeologists. . . . A Tewa is interested in our own story of our origin, for it holds all that we need to know about our people, and how one should live as a human. The story defines our society. It tells me who I am, where I came from. (Ortiz 1991)

Although similarities among the creation accounts of the various Native American peoples are evident, each story is unique, tied to the land in which the particular people had its roots. Indeed, a nation is likely to have more than one story of origins, and variations in each story as it was adapted over time. Unlike the written scriptures of some cultures, the sacred narratives of the indigenous peoples of North America are oral. Creation accounts and other stories are adapted by storytellers as they are passed along. In subsequent chapters we will encounter the stories of origins of the four nations selected for study in this work. This chapter briefly introduces the stories of origins told among the Hopi people of the Southwest. (For other examples of Native American creation stories, see Coffer 1978; Erdoes and Ortiz 1984, 1–124.)

The Hopi are a pueblo nation and they have lived principally on three mesas in northeastern Arizona for about 1,000 years. Their current reservation, created out of part of the original Hopi homeland, is totally surrounded by the much larger Navajo reservation. This relative isolation has enabled the Hopi to maintain strong ties with their traditions. As with other native nations, there is no single Hopi story of origins. Rather, each Hopi clan has its own legend which tells how it came to be and how it came to live on the Hopi mesas. In the 1980s Armin Geertz identified twelve versions of origins stories on Third Mesa alone (Geertz 1984). These stories are transmitted orally and are part of the sacred lore of the clan. Their purpose is not to recall what once happened, but to teach clan members their place in the Hopi world. These stories are not intended for wider distribution. Therefore, traditional Hopi people are reluctant to speak of them publicly, although sometimes emergence narratives have been used to promote various political objectives (Geertz 1994, 343).

For Westerners, with their fundamentally chronological orientation, the question of origins relates to a point in time: When did the world begin? For the Hopi, and indeed other Native Americans, the fundamental issue is place, not time. Stories of origin relate their belonging in and to a land. The temporal framework of the stories is not fixed. The stories relate to the present as much as to any time.

All Hopi tales typically begin with the word *Aliksa'i*, which means something like "Attention!" or "Listen up!" What is told is not just to entertain, not just to tell a good story, although they are good stories. The tales relate who the Hopi are and instruct the Hopi on how they are to live in the land to which they came at the time of origin.

Since the publication of the bestselling, but controversial, *Book of the Hopi* in 1963, Frank Waters's rendition of the "Creation of the Four Worlds" and "Migrations of the Clans" (based on material gathered from thirty Hopi elders by Waters's Hopi collaborator, Oswald White Bear Fredericks) has been widely assumed by readers unaware of the rich variety of Hopi legends to be *the* Hopi account of origins. Unfortunately, in this and other areas Waters oversimplified and distorted the Hopi reality.

With these qualifications in mind, it is still possible to use modern compilations at least to identify basic patterns and themes of Hopi origins legends (see Geertz 1994, 343–421). What follows is a truncated synopsis, presented here to give a basic, but very limited, sense of how Hopi people understand their origins and their place in the world. Once again, it should not be confused with actual Hopi stories of origins, which belong to the various clans.

In the beginning there was only endless space. Only Tawa, the sun spirit, existed. With some of his own substance Tawa impregnated Mother Earth and created the First World. The First World was inhabited by insect-like creatures who fought with one another because they could not understand the meaning of life and fell victim to sorcerers.

Upset by the chaos, Tawa created Spider Grandmother. She led the inhabitants, who grew fur on their bodies and took the shape of dogs, wolves, and bears, to the Second World.

However, these beings still did not understand the meaning of life, so Spider Grandmother led them to a lighter and moist Third World where they became people. Spider Grandmother warned them that they must renounce evil and live in harmony. In the Third World they constructed villages and planted corn. They learned to weave and make pots. However, it was too cold to grow the corn or bake the pots. One day Hummingbird came to tell the people of another world, where the spirit Masauwu, the owner of fire and caretaker of the place of the dead, lived and ruled. The Hummingbird taught them how to make fire in the Third World, so they were able to make pottery and cook their meat. However, sorcerers (*powakas*) began to lead the people astray. Men gambled; women revolted. The rains did not come, and the corn failed. Once again Spider Grandmother warned them and said that the people with good hearts would soon leave the Third World for another, upper world.

After various tries the *Sipapuni* (opening) was found to the Fourth World. After prayers and proper preparation led by ceremonial leaders, the virtuous people climbed through a hollow reed into the Upper World—the current world. A witch succeeded in coming along but was allowed to stay when she showed the people that the dead would return to the Third World and be safe there. Thus, in the Fourth World both good and evil are present, in tension with one another.

In the Fourth World the people encountered Masauwu, who told them he was now their god and that if they worshipped him their dead would return safely to the Underworld. The two grandsons of Spider Grandmother, the warrior twins Pokanghoya and Polongahoya, hurled discs into the sky and they became the sun and moon. Racing around the land, wherever their feet touched the ground became firm and trees and grass sprang up. They piled up mud which became the mountains.

The mockingbird now sorted out the people into different language groups—the Hopi, Navajo, Ute, Zuni, whites, and so on. He then laid out different colors of corn and explained that with each type there was a different life plan. The Navajos took the yellow corn, which meant a full but short life. Then the other people made their choices, until only the Hopi and the blue corn, which meant a hard but long life, were left. Therefore, the Hopi began a life of adversity, but with the promise that they would survive and endure longer than other peoples.

When the various peoples departed for their different homes, the *pahanas* (whites) allowed the witch (a *powaku*) to accompany them since she had great knowledge. They went to the south. The Hopi leaders warned their people that the *pahanas* would learn evil as well as good; whenever Hopi encounter *pahanas*, they should be cautious. However, one day a *pahana* would come to the Hopi bringing peace and harmony.

Spider Grandmother told the Hopi people to respect the spirits: Tawa, the Sun; Masauwu; Muyingwa, the spirit of germination; Balolokong, the water serpent. Then the Hopi divided into the bands that would become the Hopi clans and began an eastward migration. On their journeys the bands had encounters which gave them their distinct identities. For example, one group came across a dead bear and became the Bear Clan. Another group took skin from the carcass of the bear and became the Bear Strap Clan. Yet another found a spider on a web in the bear's skeleton and became the Spider Clan. In similar ways other clans took their names.

When the Bear Clan arrived at the Hopi mesas, Masauwu told them to choose their own leader and to build the village named Shungopavi. When the other clans arrived, they were assigned lands and responsibilities by the Bear Clan. From the four directions the clans came, leaving marks on rocks (petroglyphs) they passed. The ruins of places they occupied during their migrations can still be seen (the so-called Anasazi ruins) and are visited on sacred journeys by Hopi today. Each clan brought to Hopiland a special talent or ceremony intended to bring harmony to all the people. As the story continues, clans joined together in villages, then split up and began other villages, in a continuing process of change expressive of the ever-present tension between good and evil.

Historical Overview

We turn now to a chronological framework, offering a brief overview of the history of Native America as constructed by modern scholars, from evidence of the earliest occupation to the last decade of the twentieth century. The situation of Native American nations at the end of the century will be described in the chapters on individual nations and in the final chapter.

The "Paleo-Indian" (Lithic) Period (ca. 50,000–4500 B.C.E.)

From the point of view of modern scholars, Native American history begins with the earliest material evidence of occupation of North and South America (see Jennings 1994). Archaeologists currently distinguish among four phases of the earliest period of documented Native American activity, called either the Paleo-Indian or Lithic period: the Pre-Projectile-Point stage (ca. 50,000–10,000 B.C.E.), the Clovis or Llano Point phase (c. 9500–8000 B.C.E.), the Folsom Point culture (ca. 8000–7000 B.C.E.), and the Plano Point culture (ca. 7500/7000–4500 B.C.E.). Population estimates for this period range up to 100,000.

According to the theory still most widely accepted among contemporary archaeologists, sometime between 20,000 and 12,000 years ago a "land bridge" (called Beringia) formed, connecting Asia and North America. In fact, it would not have seemed a land bridge at all to Ice Age hunters, but "a continuation of the rich hunting grounds of northeastern Asia" (Snow 1996, 130). It was probably a broad isthmus, 1,000 kilometers wide. Although this was probably not the first time humans had appeared in North America (see, for example, Gore 1997), it is thought that this period represented the beginning of the major flow of groups into the North American continent.

According to the dominant theory, there was very little human occupation of North America until the last glaciation ended about 16,000 B.C.E. According to the current archaeological record, significant numbers of Paleo-Indians were widespread in America by 10,000 B.C.E. when the rising waters created the Bering Strait, closing the land passage (Snow 1996, 131–33).

Sometime around 10,000 B.C.E., stone and flint spear tips appear in the archaeological record. Three distinct phases in the development of these points have so far been distinguished. The Clovis Point (so-named because the first such points were found near Clovis, New Mexico) was in use between about 9500 and 8000 B.C.E. These points have been found mostly lodged in mammoth and mastodon bones in various areas across the continent. The next phase, the so-called Folsom period (ca. 8000–7000 B.C.E.), is named after a projectile point derived from the Clovis Point.

During the Plano Point phase (ca. 7500/7000–4500 B.C.E.), people seemed primarily to have hunted now extinct forms of bison. Their economy, however, was more varied than the big game hunting of the earlier phases, and thus it is considered transitional to the Archaic period.

This brief summary reflects how tentative and limited understanding is of this earliest phase in the scholarly account of Native American history. Indeed, the "land bridge" theory has been vigorously challenged by Native American and other scholars who claim the evidence is far from conclusive and that oral accounts of native peoples offer the basis for a more convincing reconstruction (see, for example, Deloria 1997).

The Archaic Period (ca. 4500–1000 B.C.E.)

A drier and warmer climate led to the larger animals dying off. The Archaic Indians shifted their economy from exclusively hunting to more foraging and gathering nuts, berries, seeds, and shellfish. Pottery was introduced, and the small-game hunters made use of spears with stone points. Heated stones were used to boil water to cook food. In New Mexico domesticated corn (only 3–4 inches in length) is evidenced by 3300 B.C.E.

Archaic period burials have been discovered, with red ocher pigment observed on bones. In addition, some burials from this period contain copper spearheads, gouges, and other tools. These are indicators of burial ceremonialism, although the beliefs underlying them cannot be determined.

The Formative Period (ca. 1500/1000 B.C.E.–1000/1500 C.E.)

During the next major period, cities of up to 40,000 people existed, indicating that sophisticated agriculture was in use. Two of the most significant and best documented cultures during the Formative period were the so-called Anasazi of the Southwest and the Mound Builders of the East.

The name *Anasazi* is a Diné (Navajo) term that means "ancient ones" or "enemies of the ancient ones." Throughout the Four Corners area, where the states of New Mexico, Arizona, Colorado, and Utah meet, the Anasazi developed an

The ruins of Anasazi dwellings, such as the famous Cliff Palace at Mesa Verde, Colorado, dot the four corners region of the Southwest.

elaborate civilization. Early Anasazi lived in pit houses. Later they built elaborate cliff dwellings, like those on the famed Mesa Verde in southwestern Colorado. For a time, there was an Anasazi complex in Chaco Canyon in northwestern New Mexico. From Chaco Canyon a road system linked this center with settlements as far as seventy miles away. In many Anasazi settlements underground chambers (called *kivas* after the similar structures still used by the Pueblo peoples) give evidence of rituals most likely linked to myths of emergence of the people's ancestors from one or more underworlds. In each *kiva* a small hole probably provided symbolic access to these lower worlds. The largest Anasazi villages served as homes of up to 5,000 people.

Climatic changes apparently led the Anasazi to abandon these settlements and move. About 1160 C.E. a long drought began in the Southwest, and by 1300 the Anasazi disappeared from their stone dwellings. Most interpreters assume that modern pueblo dwellers to the south and east of the area the Anasazi occupied (such as the Hopi, Tewa, Laguna, and San Ildefonso) are the cultural descendants of the Anasazi. The causes of the Anasazis' disappearance and the precise contours of their sophisticated civilization are among the most tantalizing mysteries for North American archaeologists.

The Mound Builders of the Adena (ca. 1000 B.C.E.–200 C.E.) and Hopewell (ca. 300 B.C.E.–700 C.E.) cultures flourished in the eastern areas of the continent (see Smith 1996). Their mounds were mostly for burials. The so-called Temple Mound Builders (sometimes identified as part of an extensive Mississippian culture) occupied the Southeast from 700 C.E. until after contact with Europeans. Today, the evidence of these cultures can be found in widely scattered mound complexes located between the Great Lakes and the Gulf of Mexico. Ohio and Illinois each have more than 10,000 mounds. Extensive archaeological research has demonstrated a culture of elaborate city-states, with highly developed ceremonial traditions and extensive trade networks. One of the sites is Cahokia, located in Illinois, just across the Mississippi River from St. Louis, Missouri. It includes the largest humanly constructed mound north of Mexico in the prehistoric era. At Cahokia and other mounds there is evidence of elaborate rituals.

Another of the temple mound complexes is the Etowah Mounds near the present Cartlesville, Georgia. There evidence of elaborate clan systems has been discovered. The Cherokee, Creek, Chickasaw, and other contemporary Native American nations are the descendants of the sophisticated culture of these "Mississippians." From these peoples we know that the mound cultures followed a seasonal calendar of festivals to celebrate and maintain harmony with the earth. The Green Corn Dance, for yearly renewal, is still observed among these nations (see chapter 3).

North America in 1492

Population estimates for North America prior to the European invasion range from the low range of about 1 million proposed by James Mooney and A.L. Kroeber in the late nineteenth and early twentieth centuries to the highest calculations of 16 million north of Mexico (with 100–200 million Indians in the Americas in general around 1500) proposed by Henry Dobyns (Dobyns 1983). The Smithsonian Institution's early-nineteenth-century handbook suggests a range of 1.2 to 2.6 million. Russell Thornton has proposed 7 million (Thornton 1987). (See Stiffarm and Lane 1992, 23–28; Johansen 1993; Grinde and Johansen 1995, 44–52; Trigger and Swagerty 1996, 362–63; Wilson 1999, 18–20.)

The estimates of precontact population are not a matter of sterile demographics. As Henry Dobyns observed, "The idea that social scientists have of the size of the aboriginal population of the Americas directly affects their interpretation of New World civilizations and cultures." In particular, as Lenore Stiffarm and Phil Lane Jr. point out:

For a number of reasons, all of them associated with the advancement of post hoc justifications for Euroamerican hegemony over the continent today, it has been expedient for non-Indian experts to minimize the size of aboriginal Indian populations, while denigrating the level of socio-economic attainment that presumably resulted in such sparseness of human presence. (Stiffarm and Lane 1992, 23)

At least 200–300 different languages were spoken in North America in 1492. Anthropologists have identified about a dozen separate "culture areas," with variations within each. There were, in fact, approximately 600 autonomous societies, each with its own way of life. These societies were not, however, isolated or "frozen in time." They interacted, connected by an elaborate trade network, pragmatically borrowing new cultural practices from one another as they maintained their own sense of place and identity (Wilson 1999, 21, 28).

According to the reports of the first Europeans to make contact with the inhabitants, the indigenous people were remarkably free of serious illness. The diseases that later decimated the native peoples were all introduced by the invaders of the continent.

The "Discovery" of America by Christopher Columbus (1492–1504)

The famous trio of ships, the larger *Santa Maria* and smaller *Pinta* and *Niña*, with Christopher Columbus (1451–1506) and about ninety men, set sail from Palos, Spain, on 3 August 1492. They sighted land at 2:00 A.M. on 12 October and later that morning a party came ashore on a small island in the Bahamas, which Columbus named San Salvador. He "took possession" of what he always believed was an island of the "Indies" near Japan, hence the name *West Indies*. That made the Arawak people who greeted him peacefully "Indians." Here, in Columbus' own words from his diary, are his impressions of the Arawak people he met:

> They were well-built, with good bodies and handsome features. . . . They do not bear arms, and do not know them, for when I showed them a sword, they took it by the edge and cut themselves out of ignorance. They have no iron. Their spears are made of cane. . . . They would make fine servants. . . . With fifty men we could subjugate them all and make them do whatever we want. (cited in Harvey and Harjo 1994, 59)

From San Salvador, Columbus sailed on to Cuba, believing at first he had found China. He then established a fort on the coast of what is now Haiti (on the island he named Hispaniola). There he left forty men to search for gold. On 16 January 1493 Columbus and the rest of his crew sailed for home. His intention to win Indians to Christianity by compassion rather than coercion had not kept him from treating the native peoples as part of the booty to be taken back to his sponsors. On his return Columbus presented to the Spanish court gold nuggets, parrots in cages, and six Indians he had captured.

Upon receipt of reports of these native peoples, Pope Alexander I in 1493 issued a papal bull (*Inter Catera*) in which he stated that "in our times especially the Catholic faith and the Christian religion be exalted and everywhere increased and spread, that the health of souls be cared for and that barbarous nations be overthrown and brought to the faith itself" (Washburn 1995, 5).

Between 1493 and 1502 Columbus made three more voyages to the "new world." Until his death, he firmly believed that God had sent him on his voyages to spread Christianity.

The dominant version of history still taught to schoolchildren in the United States and Europe is that Columbus was a courageous "explorer" who "discovered" America. Words have power; the use of the terms *exploration* and *discovery* to name the activity of Columbus and those who came after him creates a picture that ennobles those who did the "exploring" and "discovering." The same words serve to make those who lived in the land before "contact" seem to be nothing more than part of the strange terrain in need of "exploring," even nonexistent until they were "discovered."

From the perspective of most of the descendants of the people who dwelled in the land Columbus "discovered," however, he is no hero (see Sale 1990; Stannard 1992). Rather than "exploring" and "discovering," he invaded and destroyed. When he arrived in Hispaniola, the population was at least 2 million, perhaps as high as 8 million. Thirty years later, it had fallen to 20,000 as a result of the diseases the Europeans introduced (Wilson 1999, 34).

Columbus made no serious effort to find out who the indigenous peoples were, how they lived, and what they believed. It was enough for Columbus to know that they were "inferior," and that "with fifty men" he could conquer them all. Because they were not Christians, he assumed they had no religion, and that they could easily be converted to the true faith. "They do not hold any creed nor are they idolaters," Columbus wrote in his diary (Berkhofer 1978, 6).

European Perceptions of Native Americans

The perceptions Columbus and other early European explorers formed of Native Americans shaped the way Euroamericans thought of Indians through at least the nineteenth century and, to a greater degree than many acknowledge, to the present day. The first European settlers commonly described the natives as living in a "New World Garden of Eden." From this perspective the Indians represented "the innocent childhood of humanity," which gave rise to the stereotype of what became known as "the noble savage" who lived in a "state of nature." This stereotype persists in the modern environmental movement (see chapter 8).

Other Europeans, however, considered the Indians "the products of degeneration" (Trigger and Washburn 1996, 64). The term *cannibal* was a derivative of *Carib*, the name of an Indian nation (from which the term *Caribbean* is derived). It came to mean any "savage" of America, or elsewhere. In 1525 the Dominican Tomas Ortiz, at the Council of the Indies, described Indians as hostile to religion, idle, dishonest, abject, and vile, in their judgments, without faith or law. He called them liars, superstitious, and cowardly as hares. In his words, "God has never created a race more full of vice and composed without the least mixture of kindness or culture" (Trigger and Washburn 1996, 6–7).

The most persuasive advocate of the "noble savage" stereotype in the early encounters was the priest Bartholomew de las Casas (1474–1566), who had accompanied Columbus. On the basis of his own nearly half-century among Native Americans, Las Casas argued that Indians were a noble people, highly developed in the arts, language, and government, and that they were eager and able to learn about Christianity. According to Las Casas, the Indians of Hispaniola were "capable of all good learning, and very apt to receive our Religion, which when they have but once tasted, they are carried on with a very ardent and zealous desire to make a further progress in it" (Gill 1983b, 6).

These two stereotypes of Indians—as living innocently in harmony with nature, or as depraved, hardly human, or nonhuman beasts—became deeply entrenched and persist today. As Vine Deloria Jr. has observed, American Indians have traditionally been stereotyped as either "a villainous warlike group that lurked in the darkness thirsting for the blood of innocent settlers or the calm, wise, dignified elder sitting on the mesa dispensing his wisdom in poetic aphorisms" (Deloria 1994, 25).

According to Cherokee artist Jimmie Durham, both stereotypes serve to dehumanize and trivialize Native Americans:

> The good Indian is no more real than the bad Indian. Both contribute to the common notion that Native Americans are vanished Americans who belong to some earlier stage that we have already passed through; either . . . a kind of anarchy that we have overcome (in nature, in ourselves) or an innocent Golden Age that we have forfeited through greed and destructiveness. (Wilson 1999, xxi–xxii)

Native Perceptions of Europeans

It is common to hear that the native peoples received the Europeans with friendship and hospitality. Such was often the case, since native cultures typically observed traditions of reciprocity in which acts of sharing and generosity would be returned.

When and where Europeans failed to return the friendship and began to exploit the natives, however, the reaction was predictable. Indians resisted what they considered encroachment into their lands and most often rebuffed attempts to impose foreign beliefs and practices. By the sixteenth century, native responses ranged from terror and flight to fascination and reverence to resistance.

The killer diseases introduced after contact include smallpox, measles, influenza, bubonic plague, diphtheria, typhus, cholera, scarlet fever, trachoma, whooping cough, chicken pox, and tropical malaria (Trigger and Swagerty 1996, 363–69; Stiffarm and Lane 1992, 31–34). As Hotinonshonni leader Oren Lyons has observed, "many areas were completely depopulated before Europeans encountered [native peoples]—by diseases that spread from group to group among the Indians faster than the invaders themselves" (Lyons 1992, 28).

The Invasion of North America Begins (1493–1600)

The European invasion of the Americas began in earnest in the sixteenth century. In 1493 Pope Alexander VI divided the world outside Europe between Spain and Portugal, with Spain receiving all the Western hemisphere except Brazil. The official policy of the Spanish court was that the native peoples were to be converted to Catholicism and Spanish culture. A royal decree called the *requerimiento* stated that when Europeans encountered a native group, they had to read a document informing the natives of their duty to the Pope and the Spanish Crown. Of course, since the indigenous peoples did not understand Spanish, and there were few interpreters, it had little effect.

The Doctrine of Discovery (and its attendant Rights of Conquest) governed the European occupation of North America. It gave European nations the right to enter and use the lands they "discovered," and it gave priority to the first nation to do so. As enunciated, however, it did not remove the sovereignty of the indigenous people over their land, but rather "was a mechanism of controlling competing European states in their negotiations with indigenous nations regarding territorial cession" (Morris 1992, 64).

The *encomienda* system, used by the Spanish in its colonizing efforts after it was sanctioned by the Crown in 1503, had the effect of destroying native cultures throughout the Caribbean, Mexico, South America, and Florida. In this system a grant was made to a Spanish landholder, with the right to both the land and the labor of the native population. In effect, the landholder owned the people. In return, the grantee had to pay a tax and promise to see that the Indians were cared for and converted to Spanish ways and to the Christian faith. This was the first in a long history of efforts to "protect" the interests of Native Americans, which unfortunately resulted in their enslavement and a campaign to extinguish their cultures.

Under the related *reduccion* system that replaced it, the Native Americans were entrusted to church authorities, who may have treated them more humanely but were also concerned with transforming the "savage heathens" into good "Christian" people. This system was introduced by Bartolomé de Las Casas and was adopted first by Catholic, then later Protestant missionaries (Tinker 1993, 18–20).

In North America the century after Columbus's encounter with the inhabitants of the Caribbean was dominated by the Spanish moving north from Mexico and along the eastern and western coasts. The most famous expeditions were those of Francisco Vasquez de Coronado into the Southwest and Southern Plains (1540–42), Hernando de Soto into what the Spanish called La Florida (1539–43), and Juan Rodriguez Cabrillo into California (1542–43).

In July 1536, after an eight-year trek, four survivors of a group of several hundred Spaniards who had come ashore in Florida in 1528 reached Mexico City. Their report of rich cities to the north convinced the Spanish authorities to send expeditions out to find the Seven Cities of Cibola, the cities of gold.

Six Franciscan priests accompanied Coronado on his search for the cities of gold. When Coronado and his men returned to Mexico City in 1542, they had left a trail of anger and hostility among peoples whose lands they had invaded. The two priests who stayed behind were probably killed. Coronado was tried by his Spanish superiors because of the atrocities his men committed, but he was acquitted. For the next fifty years, the Spanish did not return to the Southwest.

In 1598 Juan de Oñate led the next Spanish expedition into the Southwest. The pueblos that resisted the Spaniards were destroyed, with inhabitants either killed or enslaved. In 1598 Oñate's nephew Juan de Zaldivar was killed at the Acoma Pueblo. After a two-day siege, about 600 of the 6,000 Acomas were massacred. Pueblo warriors who surrendered were executed. Those who resisted were burned out of sacred *kivas*. Survivors were marched to Santo Domingo Pueblo. Males over the age of twenty-five had one foot cut off and were bound as slaves to the Spanish for twenty years. All girls under the age of twelve were turned over to priests.

The Spanish conquest had devastated the pueblos. Catholic churches were built, and though the pueblo dwellers converted to Christianity, they began a practice which continued in succeeding centuries of maintaining their traditional rituals in secret. While preserving tradition, they also adopted from the Spanish new foods including wheat and chilies; wood ovens; horses, cattle, sheep, mules, and chickens; and blacksmithing, weaving, and woodworking. These had a profound effect on pueblo life.

In the East, between Florida and Atlantic Canada, throughout most of the sixteenth century, Native Americans had contact only with explorers, privateers, and fur traders traveling between Newfoundland and Florida. Very early in the century, the Calusas of southern Florida became adept at recovering goods and live "Christians" (who were sometimes killed but more often held for ransom) from ships that ran aground in the Florida Keys.

From 1524 to 1527 French, Spanish, and English expeditions charted the eastern seaboard looking for a sea passage to the Orient. In 1535 French explorer Jacques Cartier discovered that the Gulf of St. Lawrence was merely an estuary of a vast river, and hopes of finding a passage to the Orient were dashed.

From 1539 to 1543 Hernando de Soto led an expedition into the Mississippi heartland. His party included twelve priests, but only a few conversions were recorded.

In 1565 a Spanish explorer named Menéndez established the first permanent European settlement at St. Augustine, Florida. Menéndez placed Jesuits in Indian towns, exchanging them for women and boys he believed could be Hispanicized and returned to convert the rest of their people to Spanish ways. However, unruly soldiers and intolerant priests alienated the people and garrisons were needed to protect the missions.

Throughout most of the sixteenth century, English contact with Native Americans was slight despite the voyages of John and Sebastian Cabot, John Rut, and others. Martin Frobisher's three voyages in search of a Northwest passage (1576–78) resulted in sporadic encounters. He lost men to the Inuit and was able at times to seize some natives himself. On one occasion his men brought on board an Inuit woman; they took off her sealskin clothes to see if she had the cloven hoofs of a demon (Trigger and Washburn 1996, 69–70).

Between 1584 and 1588 Sir Walter Raleigh made his famous voyages to "Virginia." He and his men were first greeted with friendship by the Indians of the Cape Hatteras area, but hostility soon followed. Attempts at settlement on Roanoke Island in 1585 and 1586 failed. The residents of the second colony disappeared, and their fate remains a mystery. During this colonization, settlers returning to England brought back one of the many Native American "gifts" to European culture—the potato (on the many such "gifts," see Weatherford 1988).

Cooperation, Accommodation, and Resistance (1601–1763)

As the seventeenth century began, England, France, and the Netherlands were poised to challenge Spain and Portugal by establishing their own American empires. The impact on Native Americans was significant.

In 1606 the Virginia Company was established by King James I of England. In 1607 the first permanent English settlement in the New World was established in Jamestown under the leadership of John Smith. The settlement was on land controlled by the Tsenacommacah (known as the Powhatan Confederacy) and could have been easily destroyed. The Powhatan leader Wahunsonacock (also called Powhatan) decided to make the new arrivals one more nation within the

Powhatan alliance, however, believing that the English trade goods would be useful in diplomacy with other nations. The English had a different idea. The King endorsed a plan "to propagate the 'Christian Religion to such people' who as yet lived in 'darkness and miserable ignorance of the true knowledge and worship of God'" (cited in Takaki 1993, 33).

The capture of John Smith and his famous "rescue" by Wahunsonacock's daughter Pocahontas was, beneath the romanticized surface, most likely an adoption ceremony in which the Powhatans entered into alliance with the English. After Wahunsonacock's "coronation" by the English in 1608, the settlers tried to make clear their superiority. The Powhatans resisted, and war resulted. As the English began to attack Indians and destroy their villages in Virginia, a native leader declared: "We hear you are come from under the World to take our World from us." During one raid, the commander reported that they marched the captured queen and her children to the river where they "put the Children to death . . . by throwing them overboard and shooting out their brains in the water" (Takaki 1993, 34). The warfare continued sporadically, and Jamestown was besieged in 1609 and 1610. In 1614 Wahunsonacock was captured and submitted to humiliating peace terms, including his forced conversion to Christianity.

Following the introduction of commercial tobacco in 1618, English immigration began to swell. A school opened in 1621, and Indian children were in the first class, because, according to a contemporary commentator, "it would be proper to draw the best disposed among the Indians to converse and labor with our people for a convenient reward that they might not only learn a civil way of life, but be brought to a knowledge of religion and become instruments in the conversion of their countrymen" (Boyer 1997, 7).

By 1624 only twelve hundred of the original 7,000 colonists sent by the Virginia Company remained in Jamestown. From the time of the killing of 300 English villagers in 1622 by Indians led by the brother of Wahunsonacock, Opechancanough, the policy of the English was to drive out or exterminate the Indians. That same year John Smith denounced the Indians as "savages" and "cruel beasts" who possessed "a more unnatural brutishness" than wild animals. Christopher Brooke called them the "very dregs, garbage, and spawne of Earth. . . . Sprunge up like vermine of an earthly slime . . . Fathered by Sathan, and the sonnes of hell" (Miller 1995, 118).

In 1623 Captain William Tucker negotiated a peace treaty with a Powhatan village. He persuaded the villagers to drink a toast, but he served them poison. About 200 died instantly. His soldiers killed another fifty and "brought home part of their heads" (Takaki 1993, 35–36).

The year after the English settled Jamestown, Samuel de Champlain established a permanent French trading post at Quebec. Jesuit priests accompanied the French fur traders now dealing with northeastern indigenous nations such as the

Micmacs, Huron, and Montagnais and sought to win the peoples away from their "pagan ways." From the perspective of the native peoples, they were successfully incorporating the French and other Europeans into their trade network.

In 1609 Henry Hudson led a Dutch expedition up the river that was to bear his name. He arrived in the fall, and the Mahican farmers he encountered gave him pumpkins, grapes, and more from their bountiful harvest. Hudson's expedition also traded with Mohawks, who obtained metal axes, knives, and arrowheads.

In 1615 Tisquantum (Squanto), a member of the Pawtuxet band of the Wampanoag nation of Massachusetts, was taken by an English captain to Spain as a slave. He was bought by an Englishman who transported him to England. In 1619 Tisquantum returned to his village, but it had been decimated by European disease.

Hence, when the Pilgrims arrived at this site and established Plymouth in 1620, they found a desolate land. Their "settlement" was, in fact, a "resettlement" of land laid waste by other Europeans (Wilson 1999, 77–82). One of the Pilgrims wrote that "the hand of God fell heavily upon [the natives], with such a mortall stroke, that they died in heaps" (Miller 1995, 55). Encouraged by Tisquantum, the Wampanoags welcomed and aided the Pilgrims in order to obtain protection against their enemies. It is unlikely the Pilgrims would have survived without the assistance of Tisquantum and the Wampanoags. According to legend, they taught the Pilgrims how to plant corn, using fish as fertilizer. In 1621 Tisquantum helped negotiate a treaty between the colonists and the Wampanoag leader Massasoit. He died a year later of the European-introduced smallpox.

By the 1620s Franciscan missions in Florida were making inroads, by presenting the sacraments as means of summoning supernatural power. Many Indians converted but refused to give up polygamy. Epidemics killed half of the 16,000 Indians in the southern Franciscan mission field between 1613 and 1617 (Salisbury 1996, 404).

In New England the stereotyping of Indians was well under way, fueled by the Puritan perception that Indians were lazy and unproductive and would have to be removed from the lands settled by the Puritans. Puritan leaders had a clearly religious rationale for their attitude toward Native Americans. The Puritans believed they were on a mission, an "errand into the wilderness" to create the "city upon a hill." To the Puritans the Indians were the manifestation of the evil which had to be "extirpated" so that this divine mission could be fulfilled (see Slotkin 1973; Jennings 1975; Tinker 1993, 21–41; and Vaughn 1979).

Harvard College, founded in 1636, stated among its purposes "the Education of the English and Indian youth of this country in knowledge and Goodness" (Boyer 1997, 7). A college-within-the-college was created at Harvard for twenty Indian students, but few enrolled.

During the Pequot War of 1637, between 300 and 700 Pequots were burned alive as they sought to defend their village near West Mystic, Connecticut, against a combined British and Mohegan force. A member of the British force used biblical language to interpret the massacre: "thus was God seen in the Mount, crushing his proud Enemies and the Enemies of his People, burning them up in the Fire of his Wrath. . . . It was the Lord's Doings, and it is marvellous in our Eyes!" (Wilson 1999, 91) The Puritan theologian Cotton Mather described the event simply as "a sweet sacrifice" (Hauptman 1995, 9). The Pequot William Apess ironically observed, "We might suppose that meek Christians had better gods and weapons than cannon. . . . But let us again review their weapons to civilize the nations of this soil. What were they: rum and powder, and ball, together with all the diseases, such as small pox" (Miller 1995, 67).

Realizing the need for cooperation among native nations, in 1642 the Narraganset leader Miantonomo called for pan-Indian unity to resist the European invaders, saying, "we must become one; otherwise we shall all be gone shortly" (Takaki 1993, 45).

Roger Williams (1603?–1683), founder of the Rhode Island Colony and a Baptist leader, is remembered in popular history as a friend of Indians. In 1643 he chided the Puritan colonists for their arrogance toward Indians:

Boast not proud English, of thy birth & blood,
Thy brother Indian is by birth as Good
Of one blood God made Him, and Thee & All,
As wise, as faire, as strong, as personall. (Gill 1983b, 8)

However, Williams was not as helpful to Native Americans as is often assumed. Even after he was banned from Massachusetts, he continued to cooperate with the Puritan leadership and was instrumental in destroying a potential alliance between the Pequots and Narragansetts which left these tribes unprotected (Jennings 1975, 213).

In 1644 the English joined the Dutch in waging war against Wappinger bands in the Hudson River area. A combined force of English and Dutch troops slaughtered 700 Wecquaesgeek Indians along the Connecticut River then bivouacked on the crimson snow (Miller 1995, 78).

In addition to wars to drive out or annihilate Native Americans, efforts to confine and assimilate them also continued. Beginning in 1651 the Puritan leader John Eliot (see Tinker 1993, 21–41; Cogley 1999) established a series of communities called "praying towns" in New England. The inhabitants of these communities were the remnants of the conquered Nipmuc, Pennacook, and Massachusetts nations who agreed to become "civilized and Christianitized." The praying towns seemed to succeed for several decades, but in the end the towns were abandoned and most of the people returned to their traditional ways. By 1674, of 1,100 "praying Indians" only 119 had been baptized.

The first reservations built by Europeans to confine Native Americans in small areas were established in 1666 on Long Island. The Shinnecock, Unquachog, and Montauk peoples at first responded favorably in the hope that they would at least retain a small portion of their ancestral homelands. Other nations began the migrations westward in a process which would continue for over two centuries. The first trans-Allegheny crossing by nonnatives was completed in 1675, opening a way through the mountains for European settlers.

By 1675, as a result of new diseases and war, the population of Indians in southern New England had declined from 65,000 to 10,000. As noted previously, in the Puritan view this was simply God making the land vacant for His chosen people.

When Metacom, son of Massasoit, became sachem (chief) of the Wampanoags, he led an unsuccessful effort to forge an alliance among the native peoples of the region. Called King Philip by the English, Metacom and the Wampanoags were left to fight alone. The result was the so-called King Philip's War (1675–76). In the war 1,000 English and 6,000 Indians were killed from combat and disease. In one incident English soldiers threw a chief's baby into the water to see "if young Indians could swim naturally like animals of the brute creation." Some residents of the "praying towns" discovered what many other Native Americans would learn over the years, that conversion to Christianity did not protect them from being attacked and killed. Fifteen Massachusett Indians from the praying town of Marlborough were paraded through Boston like galley slaves and hanged on the suspicion of complicity in the rebellion.

As a result of the war, the Wampanoags were all but exterminated. The few survivors were sold as slaves or associated with other native nations. Not surprisingly, Puritan theologians explained the King Philip's War as a conflict between God and the Devil. According to Increase Mather, the Indians were Devil-driven to start the conflict, "which issued in their speedy and utter extirpation from the face of God's earth" (Miller 1995, 71, 75; Takaki 1993, 41–43).

Some Europeans did take a more humane approach to the acquisition of Indian lands. William Penn (1644–1718), the Quaker leader who received from King Charles II the right to the land which is now Pennsylvania, advocated justice in the treatment of Native Americans and, like Roger Williams, warned against maltreatment. "Don't abuse them," he wrote in 1683, "but let them have justice and you win them." His goal was also to take the Indian lands and to convert them to European ways. He believed, however, that it should be done "fairly" (Gill 1983b, 9).

By the end of the seventeenth century it is estimated that as a result of diseases introduced by Europeans the precontact population had been reduced by about 95 percent. In other words, for every 100 natives alive in 1492, there were only five natives living 200 years later.

Throughout this period and into the eighteenth century native nations were caught up in the wars between the British and French. They were forced to choose sides, and the result was that Indian nations tragically turned against one another. Together these conflicts (King William's War [1689–97], Queen Anne's War [1702–3], King George's War [1744–48], and the Great War for the Empire [1754–63]) are known as the French and Indian Wars to English and Euroamerican historians.

In the Southwest the Spanish invasion had taken a toll on the pueblos by the mid 1600s. The number of pueblos had been reduced from about eighty when the Spanish first arrived a century earlier to about forty, and the population of the pueblos had fallen by a third, from 60,000 to 40,000. The *encomienda* system of the Spanish negatively affected the pueblo peoples. The overgrazing of Spanish cattle caused a deterioration in the soil quality making traditional agriculture more difficult.

In 1680 all but two of the remaining pueblos joined in the famous Pueblo Revolt. The actual rebellion, which according to tradition was led by a man named Popé of the San Juan Pueblo, lasted only several weeks, but about 400 Spanish were killed (including twenty-one missionaries), and the remainder of the Spanish were driven from the pueblos. The pueblo people burned the mission churches and began more overtly to practice the indigenous spiritual traditions that they had been observing mostly in secret during the century of Spanish rule.

Unfortunately, freedom did not last long. Apache and Diné (Navajo) raiders exploited the weakened condition of the pueblos, and within a dozen years the Spanish returned to reestablish their authority. In the next century the pueblos entered into military alliances with the Spanish in order to resist the marauders from other native nations. As a result, the pueblo people were able to maintain an autonomy which allowed them to preserve their own way of life. Their accommodation to Christianity was not at the expense of their own traditional beliefs and rituals.

Two successful confederacies demonstrated that Indian people could cooperate together to negotiate with and, when necessary, resist the European invasion. The most famous is the six-nation Hotinonshonni (Iroquois) Confederacy in the Northeast, including the Onondaga, Mohawk, Oneida, Cayuga, Seneca, and Tuscarora. Another was the Creek (Muskogee) Confederacy of the Southeast.

Located by the 1500s in what are now the states of Alabama and Georgia, the Creek Confederacy (as it was known to Europeans) included many nations, among them the Alabamas, Natchez, Shawnees, Yamasseea, and Yuchis. Because most members of the Confederacy spoke a Muskogean language, the league also carries the name Muskogee. The Confederacy grew as nations that had been forced out of their homelands by colonists joined the original member nations. By 1770 it encompassed approximately 20,000 people.

The Creek Confederacy was shielded from European influence until the eighteenth century, by the Choctaws to the south and west, by the Chickasaws to the northwest, and the Cherokees to the northeast. This allowed the member nations to maintain their culture and traditional spirituality while surrounding nations were rapidly assimilating to European ways. In 1733 their situation of insulation began to change. The state of Georgia exerted pressure on the Creeks, refusing to recognize the Confederacy's land claims. As a result of the Indian Wars of the early nineteenth century, the Creek peoples were defeated and forced ultimately to move to Indian Territory (later Oklahoma) where many reside today in and near the city of Muskogee. A Creek leader expressed what the loss of land meant: "The thing that was asked us to part with, was like asking us to cut ourselves in two" (Miller 1995, 140).

Separation and Removal to "Indian Country" (1763–1839)

Until the late 1700s Native Americans could not have imagined that any of the five European nations that invaded the continent would be triumphant over them. Based on their own experience, they foresaw the emergence of a balance of power with the Europeans, a new equilibrium of many nations, including their own (Spicer 1969, 11). As Europeans began to move westward, however, this attitude changed and Native American resistance grew more determined as nations and leaders realized that their ways of life were threatened.

In the 1760s an Odawa (Ottawa) chief named Pontiac organized the nations of the northern Ohio River Valley to resist the settlers beginning to flood into the region. Influenced by the message of the Lenape (Delaware) prophet Neolin (see chapter 2), Pontiac sought to drive out the English and lead a return to traditional ways. He said:

> It is important for us, my brothers, that we exterminate from our land this nation which only seeks to kill us. . . . When I go to the English chief to tell him that some of our comrades are dead, instead of weeping for the dead . . . he makes fun of me and of you. When I ask him for something for our sick, he refuses, and tells me that he has no need of us. You can well see that he seeks our ruin. (Miller 1995, 93)

A year later Pontiac's forces seized British posts from Lake Michigan to western New York and laid siege to Detroit for five months. Many historians believe that the British responded with the first use of germ warfare by a "civilized" nation. Blankets infected with smallpox were apparently spread among the allied nations. After distributing the blankets, Colonel Henry Bouquet of the British Army observed, "I wish we could make use of the Spanish methods, to hunt them with English dogs, supported by rangers and some light horse, who would, I think, effectually extirpate or remove that vermin" (Miller 1995, 95).

Pontiac's rebellion helped encourage the English to try to resolve what had became known as the "Indian question." In the Proclamation of 1763 the British government created a line along the Appalachian Mountains (the Appalachian Divide) and stated that no English settlers would be allowed to cross the Divide until the government had negotiated treaties and land purchases with the native peoples. The proclamation established two important principles: (1) that Indian nations were sovereign entities; and (2) that the best way to avoid conflict between settlers and Indians was to establish clear boundaries controlled by a central authority. These two principles governed relations with native peoples first for the British and then for the United States for the next century. Of course, the proclamation also assumed that the Indian nations living east of the Appalachian Divide no longer had claim to their ancestral lands.

In 1775 the Continental Congress instituted a Committee on Indian Affairs and Commissioners of Indian Affairs for three regions: northern, middle, and southern. During the Revolutionary War (1776–81) most Indian nations sided with the British for the simple reason that the British had entered into treaty relations with many of them and the colonists were the ones who were taking Indian lands. Indians fighting on the British side did commit atrocities against colonists, as did the Revolutionary army against Indians who supported the British. One result was a deepening of the stereotype that Indians were by nature "savages" who delighted in committing acts of barbarism against all whites. Nevertheless, the Continental Congress did continue the treaty-making policy of the British. In 1778 its first treaty was made with the Lenape (Delaware) nation (see chapter 2).

Without influence from Native Americans, would the colonists have been ready for the revolution of 1776 and the subsequent formation of a united nation? Some historians take the position that "without the steady impress of Indian culture, the colonists would probably not have . . . felt sufficiently Americanized to stand before the world as an independent nation." That is, "the Indian presence precipitated the formation of an American identity" (Axtell 1988, 222–43).

In general, the position is that it was with the Hotinonshonni (Iroquois) (and other Native Americans) that colonists experienced some of the basic concepts that undergird the creation of the new nation, including "unity, federalism, and natural rights that existed in American Indian governments." According to this point of view, political theorists such as John Locke and Jean Jacques Rousseau, who strongly influenced the colonial architects of the American democratic experiment, "derived much of their ideas about democracy in a workable form from traveler's accounts of American Indian governmental structures" (Grinde 1992, 231; Arden 1987, 370). In addition, advocates of this view argue that specific Hotinonshonni concepts had a direct influence on the American experiment in democracy: e.g., power in leaders resting on the consent of the governed and non-coercive policies in military service, policing, and taxation. Colonial use of the

Iroquois symbols of the council fire, tree of peace, and covenant chain can also be documented (Grinde 1992, 240, 250–54).

Some contact occured between colonial leaders and the Hotinonshonni. In 1754 Benjamin Franklin proposed his famous Albany Plan of Union. He had witnessed Iroquois ceremonies and was clearly impressed by the Iroquois League, and the Albany Plan plainly reflected that exposure (Johansen 1982). In 1751 Franklin had written (revealing both the racism of the time and his admiration for the Hotinonshonni):

> It would be a strange thing . . . if Six Nations of Ignorant savages should be capable of forming such a union . . . , and yet a like union should be impractical for ten or a dozen English colonies, to whom it is more necessary and must be more advantageous. (Grinde 1992, 242, 245)

The Albany Plan envisioned forty-eight representatives chosen unequally by eleven of the colonies. Although the Albany Plan was not adopted, it did help create the momentum that led eventually to the Articles of Confederation and finally the Constitution.

James Madison also visited and had many conversations with Hotinonshonni leaders. In addition, John Adams saw the advantage of the Iroquois model. He even wrote that it would be more valuable to study the Iroquois form of government as a window to premonarchic European government than to discuss theories of European philosophers such as Locke (Grinde 1992, 263).

The first attempt at a union of the former colonies, the Articles of Confederation, called for the formation of a league of friendship among sovereign states, very much like the Hotinonshonni Confederacy. To be sure, the Constitution did move away from the model of local sovereignty of the Iroquois League. In the devaluing of women and African Americans, and in its emphasis on the separation of church and state and private property rights, the drafters of the Constitution also departed from the principles on which the Iroquois League was formed. The Bill of Rights, however, reflects the Iroquois emphasis on life and liberty. Ironically, the Founding Fathers chose in the Constitution to adopt a form of centralized government based on European models, which they had fought to overturn (Venables 1992, 115–16).

These differences have caused a number of contemporary scholars to conclude that Hotinonshonni influence on the development of the United States has been overemphasized. For example, in his survey of Iroquois history, Dean Snow concludes that "[t]here is . . . little or no evidence that the framers of the Constitution sitting in Philadelphia drew much inspiration from the League." He is concerned that "such claims muddle and denigrate the subtle and remarkable features of Iroquois government" (Snow 1994, 154; see Hauptman 1995, 27–38, for the positions of other scholars).

A more moderate position is taken by Robert Venables, who points out that

> the revolutionary generation which won its independence from Britain and then formed a more perfect union under the Constitution, was itself a synthesis of the old and the new, the European and the uniquely American. Woven within the warp and weft of this synthesis were the philosophical threads of uniquely American Indian ideas. (Venables 1992, 78)

Indeed, the attitude of other "founding fathers" of the United States toward the Indian nations was mixed. As a war leader George Washington authorized attacks on Indian villages which resulted in the slaughter of innocents. He likened Indians to wolves, "both being beasts of prey, tho' they differ in shape" (Hauptman 1995, 124). Benjamin Franklin, in contrast, expressed outrage when settlers massacred Conestoga Indians in 1764. "This is done by no civilized nation in Europe," he wrote. "Do we come to America to learn and practice the manner of barbarians?" (Harvey and Harjo 1994, 103).

As governor of Virginia, Thomas Jefferson expressed the view that Indians were to be civilized or exterminated. By civilized he meant converting them from hunting to farming. He blamed the Indians for their own decline because of their refusal to adapt to white ways. In his words, "Indians must learn how a little land, well cultivated, was superior in value to a great deal, unimproved." Ultimately, for Jefferson "Indians as Indians would not be allowed to remain within the borders of civilized society" (Takaki 1993, 47–50; for a full discussion of Jefferson's attitude toward Native Americans, see Wallace 1999).

In 1781 Article IX of the Articles of Confederation gave the Continental Congress "sole and exclusive right of . . . managing all affairs with the Indians not members of any of the states." After the Revolutionary War the Secretary of War was charged with developing Indian policy. As a pariah state the new country needed the recognition of indigenous nations, more than the native peoples required the new nation's affirmation. Not surprisingly, the "founding fathers" decided to continue the European policy of treating the Indian nations as sovereign powers.

By the latter years of the eighteenth century, the phenomenon of Europeans voluntarily taking up Indians ways was well established. In 1782 Hector St. John de Crevecoeur wrote in Letters from an American Farmer: "Thousands of Europeans are Indians, and we have no examples of even one of these Aborigines having from choice become European!" (cited in Trigger and Washburn 1996, 75).

The view of Indians as "savages" who stood in the way of the advance of Christian civilization was found even among the most educated Euroamericans. In 1783 Yale University President Ezra Stiles asserted that the Indians were most likely descendants of the Canaanites, who fled to America at the time of Joshua's conquest. Like the Canaanites of old they would have to submit to the American "new Israel" which had been given the "promised land" by God, Stiles maintained (Washington and Trigger 1996, 77).

When the Treaty of Paris brought the American Revolution to an end in 1783 (without mentioning what was to happen to the native peoples of the colonies), the population of American Indians had decreased to only 600,000 (according to Russell Thornton; see Thornton 1987). The fundamental cause was the variety of diseases introduced by Europeans, but also alcoholism, war, dietary changes, and malnutrition. By this time European population in the colonies had skyrocketed to 5 million. What was perhaps most remarkable was the "persistence of Indian community life and cultural identity in the face of such overwhelming odds" (Salisbury 1996, 455–56).

When the Constitutional Convention was called in 1787, American Indians most likely symbolized for many of the "founding fathers" two of the principal values they wished to embody in the new form of government, namely life and liberty. For example, Gouverneur Morris was speaking of Native American cultures when he said, "liberty and life . . . they possess both in the savage state in the highest perfection" (Venables 1992, 75).

The U.S. Constitution (1787) stipulated in the Commerce Clause that the federal government would be responsible for regulating trade with "Indian Tribes" as it was with trade with other nations and between states. Article I, Section 2, defined "Indians not taxed" as a polity (or polities) separate from the United States. Article I, Section 10, stated that the federal government could enter into treaties only with fully sovereign national bodies.

The Northwest Ordinance of 1789 reaffirmed the principles of the Proclamation of 1763 and pledged that the United States would conduct its relations with Indian nations with "utmost good faith." In 1790 Congress began enacting a series of laws (called the Trade and Intercourse Acts) which codified the principles of the Constitution with regard to native peoples.

The pressure of western migration of Euroamerican settlers was becoming irresistible, however. The Louisiana Purchase of 1803 brought under U.S. authority virtually hundreds of new native nations, and it added weight to the idea of moving all Indian peoples still living east of the Mississippi River to a new Indian territory west of the Mississippi.

During this period campaigns of resistance to European encroachment continued to spread westward. In 1790, in an area of the Northwest Territory that became the state of Indiana, the Miami leader Little Turtle drove out the army. When troops returned a year later, a coalition had formed that included Shawnees and Ottawas. In August 1794, along the Maumee River in what is now Ohio, a force of 2,000 Indians met troops under General "Mad Anthony" Wayne. Near what is now Toledo, Wayne's command delivered a crushing blow to the coalition in a forty-minute confrontation known as the "Battle of Fallen Timbers." A year later the Treaty of Greenville opened southern Ohio to settlement.

Late in the eighteenth century there was growing preference for biologically based explanations of human behavior. This reinforced the view that Indians were inherently savage "redskins" and "could no more be civilized than an animal's nature could be fundamentally changed" (Trigger and Washburn 1996, 80). One self-acknowledged "Indian expert" of the period blamed the decline in Indian population on a "racial" characteristic, claiming that "some 'strong exciting' racial characteristic impelled native people to Their own ceaseless hostilities [which] have, more than any other cause, led to the melancholy depopulation" (Wilson 1999, 45).

At the same time, the Protestant "Great Awakening" of the late eighteenth and early nineteenth centuries resulted in new impetus to evangelize and civilize Native Americans. In 1802 Congress appropriated $15,000 annually to "promote civilization among the savages." Beginning in 1819 funds were apportioned among Christian groups dedicated to civilization of the Indians. The annual appropriation was not repealed until 1973 (Beck and Walters 1977, 152).

On 14 May 1804 Meriwether Lewis, William Clark, and forty-five other men left St. Louis on a two-year journey to the Northwest coast and back. Their assignment from President Jefferson was to explore the northwest area of the recently acquired Louisiana Territory and the Oregon region beyond, which no nation had yet claimed. In South Dakota the "Corps of Discovery," as Jefferson called the expedition, met Lakotas whose belligerence they found threatening (see chapter 4). The Mandans of North Dakota were more receptive, allowing them to build a winter fort near one of their villages. During the winter a French trader and his Shoshoni wife Sacagawea joined the expedition. Resuming the journey in April 1805, Lewis and Clark reached the Rocky Mountains the next month. Amazingly, they met the band of Shoshoni to which Sacagawea belonged. With her intervention, Lewis and Clark were able to acquire horses and supplies and receive guidance on how to cross the Bitterroot Mountains. They finally reached the Oregon coast in November and wintered there among the Clatsop. The next spring they began the journey home. They had brief skirmishes with Blackfeet and Crow bands but made it back to St. Louis by September 1806. Their successful expedition was a harbinger of the incursions to follow.

In 1809 the Shawnee leader Tecumseh and his brother, Lalawethinka, known as Tenskwatawa ("The Open Door") and to Europeans simply as the Shawnee Prophet, who had received a revelation calling for a rejection of white ways and a return to the traditional way of life (see Spicer 1969, 266–67), led an alliance against the westward expansion. They created a village called Prophetstown in Indiana, where people from various nations gathered in the hopes of restoring their old ways. Tecumseh traveled throughout the Midwest to recruit warriors among various nations. Tenskwatawa called the Euroamericans "children of the evil spirit" who "grew from the scum of great water" (Miller 1995, 187). On 7 November 1811 the Shawnee Prophet led an alliance of warriors against a militia force which had been raised by Indiana Territory Governor William Henry Harrison and was threatening an Indian village on the Wabash and Tippecanoe Rivers. After a vicious battle, the Indians withdrew, and the confrontation helped create a reputation for Harrison which carried him to the U.S. presidency in 1840.

Inspired by Tecumseh, warriors from the nations of the Creek Confederacy attacked Fort Mims in Alabama in 1813 and killed several hundred settlers. As terror spread through the South, Andrew Jackson (who also rode his Indian fighting reputation to the White House) raised a militia with the slogan "Remember Fort Mims." At the Battle of Horseshoe Bend in 1814 on the Tallapoosa River in Alabama, Jackson's forces were triumphant, and the Creeks surrendered a large area of land. Before the battle, Jackson wrote "I must distroy [sic] those deluded victims doomed to distruction [sic] by their own restless and savage conduct." Calling them "savage dogs," he bragged of preserving the scalps of those he had killed. During the battle 800 Creek men, women, and children were killed. Soldiers took strips of skin from the corpses to make bridle reins (Takaki 1993, 84–85).

One of the Creek nations, the Seminoles, continued the resistance in Florida. After Jackson marched into Florida in 1817, however, Seminole resistance was broken (until they again began to fight in 1835), and the Spanish were forced to cede Florida to the United States.

Secretary of War John C. Calhoun (1817–25) made the case for subordinating Native Americans to Euroamerican domination:

> By a proper combination of force and persuasions, of punishment and rewards, they [the Indians] ought to be brought within the pales of law and civilization. Left to themselves, they will never reach that desirable condition. (Jaimes 1992, 124–25)

In the midst of the growing pressure to force Indians from their lands, the Supreme Court ruled in *Johnson* v. *McIntosh* (1823) that the United States had the right to acquire native lands by virtue of the Doctrine of Discovery and Rights of Conquest long stated by European nations. The Court also ruled, however, that lands must be taken through treaties with native nations, which were recognized as the rightful owners of the lands on which they lived. Lands could be taken through wars, the ruling stated, only if natives engaged in unprovoked attacks on legal settlers, if they refused to engage in trade with them, or if they would not allow Christian missionaries to travel among them.

A few years later, responding to the lobbying efforts of settlers eager to seize all Indian lands in the Southeast, Congress passed the Indian Removal Act of 1830 (see Green 1982). It legalized the relocation of all Indians to the new territory west of the Mississippi River. In 1832 in *Worcester* v. *Georgia*, Chief Justice John Marshall of the Supreme Court wrote an opinion establishing the principle that native nations have a "quasi-sovereignty" as "nations domestic to and dependent on the United States." They were sovereign enough to enter into treaties with the federal government, but not to manage their own affairs. This established the Plenary Power Doctrine, which holds that "the federal government holds full and inherent power over Indian affairs and a concomitant 'trust responsibility' over all Indian assets" (Churchill 1992, 18).

Jackson justified Indian removal on the basis that efforts to civilize Indians had failed (see Satz 1975). As whites purchased their lands, they were forced deeper into "wilderness" areas. Efforts such as those of the Cherokees to become "civilized" were doomed to failure, because they attempted to set up independent nations within states (see chapter 3).

In 1832 the Bureau of Indian Affairs was established in the War Department, giving the Secretary of War jurisdiction over the removal of Indians from their ancestral homelands. The Trade and Intercourse Act of 1834 officially established an Indian Territory in what is now the state of Oklahoma.

Removal was carried out in two ways, indirectly through land allotments (the principal strategy for seizing lands from the Creeks, Chickasaws, and Choctaws) and directly through treaty (forced on the Cherokees). The first of the nations of the Southeast to be removed to Indian Territory was the Choctaw in the 1830s. They were followed by the nations of the Creek Confederacy, the Cherokees, and the Chickasaws. Each of these peoples has a tragic story to tell of the removal. The Cherokee "Trail of Tears," for example, is described in chapter 3. Ironically, together these nations were called the Five Civilized Tribes because of their eager adapting of European ways. Being "civilized," however, did not stop the seizure of their homelands and their forcible relocation, with an estimated 15,000 dying in the process.

Observing the removal of the Choctaws from Mississippi, Alexis de Tocqueville was struck by how the whites were able to deprive the Indians of their rights and exterminate them "with singular felicity, tranquilly, legally, philanthropically, without shedding blood, and without violating a single great principle of morality in the eyes of the world." (cited in Takaki 1993, 92).

The Struggle for Survival (1838–90)

By 1848 the removal of the Five Civilized Tribes to Indian Territory had been completed, with an estimated 70,000 Indians forcibly relocated from their homes east of the Mississippi. That same year the discovery of gold in California led Euroamericans to put their sights on what was known simply as the West. Wave after wave of settlers began to move westward along trails, creating friction which led to a protracted struggle for survival of the Indian nations of the Great Plains, a story that will be told in part in chapter 4.

In the Southwest, as a result of the Treaty of Guadalupe Hildago in 1845, the territory now included in the states of Arizona and New Mexico was ceded by Mexico to the United States. The efforts of the U.S. government to gain control of the area led ultimately to the tragic Long Walk in 1864 for the Diné nation (see chapter 5).

Within four years of the discovery of gold in California in 1848, a flood of about one-quarter million settlers had poured into the state. Within twelve years the Indian population of the state had been reduced from about 100,000 to 35,000. Fifty years later it was between 12,000 and 20,000. Although a reservation system to "protect" Indians was instituted in the area in 1853, "a systematic policy of extermination" designed to rid the state of the "Indian menace" continued. The effects of the policy were particularly evident in northern California where the Hoopa, Nisenan, Shasta, Yana, Yuki, Yurok, Wintu, Wiyot and other peoples were made targets of vicious campaigns of extermination (Hauptman 1995, 10–14; see also Heizer 1974).

In 1849 the Bureau of Indian Affairs was moved from the War Department to the Department of the Interior, where it is still lodged. Thus began the development of a bureaucracy which, in the view of most interpreters, has defied all efforts at meaningful reform. Two years later the Secretary of the Interior, recognizing that land was fast running out for the relocation of Indians, said "the only alternatives left are to civilize or exterminate them" (Wilson 1999, 289).

In 1855 a medicine man named Smohalla ("returned from the dead") reappeared after a four-year journey around the West. He returned to the area near the Middle Columbia River in what is now Washington and Oregon where he had lived. The Yakima, Cayuse, Wasco, and Wishram nations had the same year signed a treaty confining them to small reservations in exchange for a guarantee of protection against the settlers. Smohalla began to preach about visions he had received and conducted ceremonials based on the traditional Prophet Dance (see Spicer 1969, 275–76). Smohalla proclaimed that if Indians followed his new religion the whites would disappear. He taught that European agriculture defiled Mother Earth and urged Indians to maintain their traditional hunting-based lifestyle. Despite his use of some Christian symbols, he vigorously rejected Christian teachings. He continued to preach for twenty years, and the new religion spread among the Indians of eastern Washington and Oregon. Smohalla's teachings form part of the background for the more widespread Ghost Dance movements of the 1870s and 1880s (see chapter 6).

In 1850 Congress began to give federal land to the states to assist in the development of railroads which were to have a profound impact on the native nations of the west. When the first transcontinental railroad was completed in 1869, the river of migration became a flood, and the pressure to confine Indians to small tracts of second-rate land grew irresistible. By the end of the century there were five transcontinental lines in the United States and one in Canada.

On 29 November 1864, at Sand Creek in southeastern Colorado, an event took place which sent a chill throughout Native American nations and helped set in motion the so-called Plains Wars of the late 1860s (see chapter 4). The following description of the Sand Creek Massacre and the events leading up to it comes from native writer Simon Ortiz's *From Sand Creek*:

> On that cold dawn, about 600 Southern Cheyenne and Arapaho people, two thirds of them women and children, were camped on a bend of Sand Creek . . . The People were at peace. This was expressed two months earlier by Black Kettle, one of the principal chiefs of the Cheyennes, in Denver to Governor John Evans and Colonel John M. Chivington, head of the Colorado Volunteers. "I want you to give all these chiefs of the soldiers here to understand that we are at peace, and that we have made peace, that we may not be mistaken for enemies." The Reverend Colonel Chivington and his Volunteers and Fort Lyons troops, numbering more than 700 heavily armed men, slaughtered 105 women and children. . . . A U.S. flag presented by President Lincoln in 1863 to Black Kettle in Washington, D.C., flew from a pole above the lodge on that grey dawn. The People had been assured that they would be protected by the flag. (cited in Jaimes 1992, 1)

By mid–1865, the Cheyenne and Arapaho people had been driven out of Colorado. In response to growing concern over such atrocities, President Ulysses S. Grant adopted a so-called Peace Policy in 1869. Instead of military officers, Christian missionaries were entrusted with the responsibility of seeing to the welfare of Indians. President Grant gave twelve Christian denominations control of Indian agencies. Although the formal division of reservations among denominations ended in 1882, the churches have continued to play a major role on agencies and reservations. Increasingly, Indian agencies (composed of a combination of a government house, school, blacksmith, warehouse, and Christian mission) were an ever-present, intrusive fact in the lives of Native Americans.

Grant appointed his Civil War colleague and Seneca chief, Ely Samuel Parker (Doneghogawa), as Commissioner of Indian Affairs, with instructions to implement his Peace Policy. However, Parker proved too honest for the position and was driven out of office by political enemies. In a report on the failure of the new policy to effect needed change, he wrote:

> The white man has been the chief obstacle in the way of Indian civilization. The benevolent measures attempted by the government for their ad-

vancement [have] been almost uniformly thwarted by the agencies employed to carry them out. (Armstrong 1971, 94)

By this time the basic goal of government policy in the latter decades of the nineteenth century was all too clear. The strategy was to replace the collective nature of traditional Indian societies with the Euroamerican values of individual, private ownership and to replace the traditional spirituality of native nations with Christianity (see Hoxie 1984).

The reaction among Native Americans to this policy split in general between those who embraced the new ways, with enthusiasm or resignation, and those who rejected them and held with varying degrees of steadfastness to the traditional ways of living. The split has often been described as being between "full bloods" and "mixed bloods," although these terms are misleading. "The lines of cleavage were not biological but cultural. The 'mixed bloods' were those who tended to accept White customs more extensively, to speak English, adopt American house types and attitudes toward work and money-making" (Spicer 1969, 110). Nevertheless, the distinction between "full blood" and "mixed blood" became common, alongside terms used by government officials, such as "friendlies" and "hostiles." Traditionalists took to calling other Indians who they thought were too enamored with Euroamerican ways "hang-around-the-fort" Indians because of their tendency to live close to government agencies and their dependency on government handouts.

In 1871 Congress formally ended a century of treating Indian nations as sovereign entities with whom treaties must be made. The new law made American Indian nations wards of the United States government. The 371 treaties already concluded with Native American nations were not abrogated. The law stated that "nothing herein contained shall be construed to invalidate or impair the obligation of any treaty heretofore lawfully made with any such Indian nation or tribe." Despite this law, the government continued to send out treaty commissions to negotiate the taking of land from Native American nations until 1905.

In the spring of 1877 the Nez Percé (pierced nose) people, a name given to this northwestern nation by a French trader in 1805 who noticed that some of the people wore decorative shells in their noses, refused to leave the reservation established for them in the 1860s. That reservation was located in their traditional lands in the Wallowa Valley of Oregon. Prospectors had overrun the reservation after gold had been discovered, and the government was seeking to move the Nez Percé people to a smaller reservation in Idaho. Under Chief Joseph, the Nez Percé, influenced by the teachings of the prophet Smohalla, first fought the troops sent to move them, then left to join Sitting Bull and the Lakota people who had earlier fled to Canada after the Battle of the Little Big Horn (see chapter 4). During the thousand-mile retreat, Chief Joseph and the 800 Nez Percé men, women, and children with him skillfully evaded the U.S. military. They were finally captured by a force led by Colonel Nelson Miles near Bear Paw Mountain in Montana, forty miles from the Canadian border. In surrendering to Colonel Miles on 5 October 1877, Chief Joseph spoke these famous, fateful words: "From where the sun now stands I will fight no more, forever." In 1878 the Nez Percé were relocated to Indian Territory. In response to public pressure, in 1885 Chief Joseph and his band were allowed to live nearer their homeland, on the Colville Reservation in Washington.

In 1878 Congress authorized the employment of Indian policemen on reservations and in 1883 established Courts of Indian Offenses. The hope was that Indian judges and law enforcement officers would be able to enforce order on the reservations, while lessening the animosity caused by use of non-Indian policemen and courts. It was also anticipated they would assist in the abandonment of traditional ways on the reservations. In 1885 the Major Crimes Act, passed in response to a Supreme Court ruling which held that the federal government had no jurisdiction to prosecute one Indian for killing another on reservation land, extended for the first time the federal government's jurisdiction over the territories of Indian nations.

A victory for all Native Americans was won by the Ponca chief Standing Bear in 1879. The Poncas had been relocated in 1877 from their homeland in northern Nebraska to Indian Territory after a mistake in the 1868 Fort Laramie Treaty (see chapter 4) had effectively given the Ponca land to the Lakotas, traditional enemies of the Poncas. Standing Bear had led a funeral party back to the Poncas' homeland to bury his son, who had died after the relocation. Standing Bear was arrested for leaving the Ponca reservation without permission. From his jail cell in Nebraska, Standing Bear brought suit, claiming his habeas corpus rights. In April 1879 a U.S. District Court judge ruled in his favor after hearing Standing Bear say, raising his hand before the judge: "That hand is not the color of your hand, but if I pierce it I shall feel pain. The blood that will flow from mine will be the same color as yours. I am a man. The Great Spirit made us both" (Armstrong 1971, 123–24; see 164–78 for the full ruling).

Although many Indian nations had developed their own schools (and all nations had a traditional method of instructing children), by the late nineteenth century all tribal schools had been closed and replaced by Bureau of Indian Affairs and mission schools. Proponents saw the schools as a new campaign in the war against Indians. One put it this way: "We are going to conquer the Indians by a standing army of school-teachers, armed with ideas, winning victories by industrial training, and by the gospel of love and the gospel of work" (Wilson 1999, 311).

In 1879 Richard Henry Pratt, an army captain, opened the Carlisle Indian School in Pennsylvania, with the expressed purpose of assimilating Indians into Euroamerican culture. As he put it, "let us by patient effort kill the Indian . . .

and save the man" (O'Brien 1989, 76). He also said, "I believe in immersing the Indians in our civilization and when we get them under, holding them there until they are thoroughly soaked" (Boyer 1997, 11). The school's motto was "From Savagery into Civilization." Part of the regimen at Carlisle was nonsectarian Christian education. At Carlisle and other government and denominational schools, children were forbidden to speak their native languages or wear their traditional dress. Any sign of attachment to traditional Native American cultures was taken as a sign of defiance. Children often were not allowed to go home or receive visits from family members for long periods of time.

The Lakota Luther Standing Bear, a Carlisle student, describes the effect the school had on many Indian children:

> The change in clothing, housing, food, and confinement combined with lonesomeness was too much, and in three years nearly one half of the children from the Plains were dead and through with all earthly schools. In the graveyard at Carlisle most of the graves are those of little ones. (cited in Wilson 1999, 315)

Between 1880 and 1895 the Bureau of Indian Affairs (BIA) opened twenty off-reservation boarding schools and initiated or expanded day schools at every agency. By 1887 there were 227 BIA and mission schools, with about 14,000 Indian children attending. Between 1880 and 1930 an estimated 50,000 Indian youths were taken, with force if necessary, to off-reservation schools (Spicer 1969, 116; Hoxie 1996, 199). A directive from the Commissioner of Indian Affairs late in the century stated that teachers at the schools should "carefully avoid any unnecessary reference to the fact that [the students] are Indians" (Boyer 1997, 13). This was simply the culmination of a long process which had begun in 1611 when native youngsters were forced to attend Jesuit boarding schools. (For a fuller account of the history of the education of Native Americans and its effects, see Noriega 1992.)

As noted previously, beginning in the seventeenth century, Europeans had adopted the strategy of removing Native American peoples from their traditional lands and confining them to carefully supervised tracts of land called reservations (as they are designated in the United States) or reserves (the Canadian term). At first reservations were thought of as places where Native Americans could continue to practice their own way of life. With the development of the assimilationist perspective, however, the purpose of reservations shifted. They were considered "way stations" where Indians could be taught how to live "civilized" lives.

The dominant attitude among Euroamericans during this period was expressed clearly in the 1872 Report of the Secretary of the Interior:

The philosophy of the Carlisle Indian School—"kill the Indian" and "save the person"—is graphically illustrated in two famous "before" and "after" pictures of a Diné (Navajo) student. (AP/Wide World Photo)

> In our intercourse with the Indians it must always be borne in mind that we are the most powerful party. . . . We . . . claim the right to control the soil which they occupy, and we assume that is our duty to coerce them, if necessary, into the adoption and practice of our habits and customs. (Spicer 1969, 235)

During this period, however, a number of organizations formed in response to the increasingly desperate plight of the Native American nations. *A Century of Dishonor* by Helen Hunt Jackson chronicled injustices, broken treaties, and disregard for Indian welfare. Influenced by this and other portrayals of the dire situation facing Native Americans, groups such as the Indian Protection Committee, the Indian Rights Association, the Women's National Indian Association, and the National Indian Defense Association formed. Today, there is growing consensus among historians that although such groups may have had good intentions, their efforts to improve life for Indians was simply a more benign form of the plan to transform Indians on the basis of Euroamerican values.

At the same time, under pressure from the Christian churches with missions on reservations, the government began to restrict traditional Native American rituals. For example, in 1885 the sun dance, practiced by various Plains Nations including the Lakota (see chapter 4), was prohibited because it was considered "barbaric." Other "offenses" prohibited plural marriage, ritual practices of "so-called medicine men," destruction of property at a burial, and use of any intoxicants (Stewart 1987, 130).

In 1887 Congress passed and President Grover Cleveland signed the General Allotment Act (also known as the Dawes Severalty Act, after its sponsor, Senator Henry L. Dawes of Massachusetts). Under the provisions of the Dawes Act, the president was empowered to break up Indian lands (except for those of the Five Civilized Tribes, the Osages, and a few other nations in New York and the Southwest) and allot the parcels to individual Indians. The act also legally defined for the first time the "blood quantum" approach to determining federally recognized membership in tribes. Under the Act's original provisions, a "full blood" head of family received 160 acres and unmarried men and minors received lesser amounts, as little as forty acres. An 1891 amendment gave equal shares to all (including married women): eighty acres of agricultural land and 160 acres of grazing land. (For more on the Dawes Act, see Carlson 1981.)

In an effort to protect the new landholders from exploitation, the allotments were to be held in trust for twenty-five years. At the end of the trust period, all trustees were to become U.S. citizens. "Mixed-blood" Indians were forced to accept U.S. citizenship if they took allotments under the act. Any tribal lands remaining after the allotments to individuals were subject to sale to non-Indians, with the money to be held by the government for the use of the nation which had "owned" the land. The law specified that Congress could draw on these surplus funds to support efforts to educate and "civilize" Indians. The 1891 amendments also allowed for allotted lands to be leased by the owners.

The Dawes Act turned out to be, in the estimation of most Indian people, an unmitigated disaster. Before the Act there were approximately 160 million acres of Indian lands. In 1934, when an attempt was made to undo the damage caused by the Dawes Act, two-thirds of this land was gone, sold off as surplus or lost by individual landowners.

One of the principal objectives of the Dawes Act was to enable Indians to become farmers like their Euroamerican neighbors. This idea had two basic problems. First, the type of farming proposed was foreign to the traditions of virtually all the allottees. They had no experience and very little help in learning the new skills. Promised animals and equipment were either slow in coming or did not arrive. Second, most of the land allotted was not suitable for farming. The lands set aside for reservations had been in the least desirable locations for agriculture originally. Dividing up the land among individuals did not improve its quality.

Despite these obstacles Indian farmers did remarkably well. A recent study of thirty-three reservations shows that twenty-seven (82 percent) maintained rates of growth in the number of acres cultivated per person of more than 5 percent during this period (Hoxie 1996, 198).

Opposition to the Dawes Act was carried out by Indian leaders who saw it as a threat to their heritage, according to which no one individual "owned" land. They recognized that introducing the idea of private ownership of land would create friction among the people and lead inevitably to the weakening of the solidarity of native nations. They also understood the act to be part of the ongoing effort to turn Indians into whites and destroy traditional cultures. Many supporters of Indians objected to the act because they believed that it was really designed to open up Indian lands to settlement by non-Indians rather than to assist native peoples.

In some cases resistance to the unrelenting government pressure to civilize turned violent, and the response was vicious. For example, when in the 1880s Chiricahua and White Mountain Apaches fled their reservations and began hit-and-run attacks on those who had invaded their lands, they were relentlessly pursued across the border into Mexico by army troops. Even after their leaders, the famed Geronimo and Naiche, surrendered in 1886, worried government officials insisted on sending the "hostiles" to prisons in Florida and then Oklahoma.

The Ghost Dance movement, which brought hope for a renewal of traditional ways to a number of Native American nations, flourished in the 1880s (see chapter 6). The reaction by the government to the Ghost Dance on the Lakota reservations, which led to the 29 December 1890 massacre at Wounded Knee, is detailed in chapters 4 and 6.

Commissioner of Indian Affairs T.J. Morgan established in 1889 an "Indian policy" which can be summed up in a phrase from its report: "The American Indian is to become the Indian American" (Bailey and Bailey 1986, 106).

Forced Assimilation (1890–1934)

By the early twentieth century, the attitude that Euroamericans had an inherent right to displace Native Americans forcefully, if necessary, was the dominant perspective. In 1901 President Theodore Roosevelt wrote:

> Of course our whole national history has been one of expansion. . . . That the barbarians recede or are conquered, with the attendant fact that peace follows their retrogression or conquest, is due solely to the power of the mighty civilized races which have not lost their fighting instinct, and which by their expansion are gradually bringing peace into the red wastes where the barbarian peoples of the world hold sway. (cited in Churchill 1992, 139)

In 1903 the U.S. Supreme Court ruled in *Lone Wolf* v. *Hitchcock* that Congress had the authority to abrogate the provisions of any Indian treaty. This meant that the 371 treaties which had been negotiated with Indian nations could be arbitrarily revoked by action of Congress. Not until 1959 did Supreme Court rulings begin to move back in the direction of recognizing the sovereignty of Native American nations and the need to respect treaty rights. The Commissioner of Indian Affairs triumphantly reported to Congress that the ruling "will enable you to dispose of land without the consent of the Indians" (Hoxie 1996, 203).

In 1906 the sacred Blue Lake of the Taos Pueblo, people was appropriated by the federal government to be part of the Carson National Forest. For the people of the Taos Pueblo, Blue Lake was the source of all life and a place of retreat for the souls of ancestors. For the Forest Service the lake was in the midst of land designated for "multiple use," which meant recreation, extraction of raw materials, and scientific exploration. The struggle for Blue Lake, led by traditional spiritual leaders of the Taos Pueblo and their supporters, continued until 1971 when President Richard Nixon signed a law restoring Blue Lake to the exclusive ceremonial use of the Taos people.

During the first two decades of the twentieth century popular tribal and intertribal social gatherings grew rapidly. Powwows (see chapter 9), community festivals, and fairs were deemed nonthreatening secular events by government officials and missionaries who encouraged them. The Grass Dance, originally a Pawnee and Omaha ceremony for warriors, was adapted as a social dance by other Plains nations during this period and spread to other peoples. At such dances distributions of food and clothing were often made, continuing the giveaway traditions of many peoples. Added to the dances at powwows were drumming competitions and displays of traditional crafts. Attendance at such gatherings was facilitated by the expanding rail lines and roads for automobiles.

During World War I, 10,000 Native Americans served in the U.S. armed forces. In recognition of this sign of loyalty to the country (and to bring citizenship to Indians not already made citizens under the provisions of the Dawes Act), Congress awarded citizenship to veterans in 1919 and passed the Indian Citizenship Act in 1924. The act specified that Indians did not forfeit their tribal membership as a result of becoming U.S. citizens. Several nations, however—most prominent among them the Hopi, Diné, and nations of the Iroquois Confederacy—refused to accept citizenship on the grounds that to do so would be to subordinate their identity as members of sovereign native states.

By the 1920s non-Indians were becoming increasingly curious about Native American life. For example, the Boy Scout movement (which had come to the United States from England in 1910) incorporated many Indian traditions and lore, although these practices were removed from their cultural context and inevitably distorted.

By 1921 twenty-six Protestant churches were doing missionary work among tribal communities in the United States. There were 597 Indian churches and 268 Native American ministers serving congregations with a total membership of about 110,000. Approximately 336 Catholic churches, chapels, and schools served more than 61,000 communicants. Roughly half the 400,000 Native Americans in North America were at least nominal Christians (Hoxie 1996, 227)

At the same time, suppression of traditional Native American rituals continued. In 1921 Commissioner of Indian Affairs Charles H. Burke issued an infamous order which outlawed dances and ceremonial activities involving "mutilation," "give-aways," "immoral relations," and "the destruction of clothing or other useful articles" (Hoxie 1996, 224). Two years later he was urging Indians to spend less time in all ceremonies and devote themselves more to their stock, crops, gardens, and home interests.

Sympathy for the plight of Native Americans was increasing. Unfortunately, the transition to an urban, industrial economy in the United States had exacerbated the economic and other problems faced by Native Americans. In 1928 the Brookings Institution published the Meriam Report. It examined health, education, economics, family and community life, legal issues, and missionary activity. The report (see Spicer 1969, 243–46) documented that conditions for Indian people were deplorable. The annual income per capita for American Indians was about $100. The average life expectancy was only forty-four years. Infant mortality (190 per 1,000 births) was higher than for both Euroamericans (70.8) and African Americans (114.1). Medical care, housing, sanitation, and employment opportunities were all terrible. In short, the Meriam Report was evidence of the utter failure of the policies of assimilation and allotment that had dominated U.S. policy for more than a hundred years.

Restoration, Termination, and Renewal (1933–90)

In many ways the contemporary era for Native Americans began in 1933 with the appointment by President Roosevelt of John Collier as Commissioner of Indian Affairs (see Kelly 1983; Wilson 1999, 333–58). Disillusioned with "modern civilization," Collier had established himself as a champion of Indian interests and an admirer of Native American spirituality, believing it to be what "our sick world most needs" (Wilson 1999, 336). In 1923 he had founded the American Indian Defense Association, an organization committed to the preservation of Native American cultures. As an ethnologist he had done research among the pueblo peoples of the Southwest, had written glowingly of their spirituality, and had become involved in the fight for their rights. As a result of his direct involvement with native peoples, Collier was deeply committed to the principles of Indian self-determination, self-government, and self-preservation. The government, Collier wrote, should seek "to preserve the Indian's love and ardor toward the rich values of Indian life as expressed in their arts, rituals, and cooperative institutions" (Philip 1986, 118).

Under Collier's leadership, Congress passed the Wheeler-Howard Indian Reorganization Act in 1934. The overall purpose of the act was to draw on the strengths of traditional Indian cultures, rather than imposing values foreign to them. Collier recognized that the commitment to community in Native American cultures had served them well for centuries. The individualism the government and churches had been trying to implant in native peoples in order to strengthen them had not produced the expected results.

In the area of spirituality, the act stipulated that boarding schools could not force Indian children to attend Christian religious services. The rulings forbidding traditional practices such as the sun dance were overturned. Attempts to control the traffic in peyote were ended, thus allowing the Native American Church (see chapter 7) to conduct its ceremonies without fear of interference from the federal government, at least for a short period. Collier was determined to see that the right to religious freedom guaranteed in the First Amendment of the Constitution was not denied to American Indians. In a BIA circular he said simply, "No interference with Indian religious life or ceremonial expression will hereafter be tolerated" (Stewart 1987, 232). Unfortunately, as is discussed later, this battle has not yet been fully won. Called the "Indian New Deal," the act also created an Indian Civilian Conservation Corps. A separate Indian Arts and Crafts Act helped Indian artists market their work.

The Reorganization Act was so sweeping in its effects on government policy toward Native Americans that opposition to it was inevitable and immediate. Some missionary organizations opposed its endorsement of Indian "paganism." Conservative politicians claimed that its affirmation of communalism was a veiled endorsement of communism. They pointed out that there were no meaningful provisions to support economic development on reservations. Some Indians who had benefited from allotment objected to the act. From both Indians and non-Indians came complaints that a return to "tribalism" represented a policy of segregation of Native Americans from the larger society. They accused Collier of "romanticizing" Indian cultures. They said that the government should continue to try to help Indians become self-reliant Indian Americans, not simply return them to their separate status as American Indians.

In contrast, Indian traditionalists found the act's formula for new tribal governments too influenced by European-style constitutional, representative models. Subsequent history has seemed to prove correct their objection that the act would only exacerbate the factionalism on reservations. Fearing that Collier's type of tribal governments would undermine sovereignty, traditionalists favored a return to authentic self-government based on each nation's own traditions. When referendums were held on reservations to determine whether the act's provisions for elected governments would be implemented, 181 tribes (with a combined population of 130,000) endorsed it while 77 tribes (with a population of 86,000) did not (with 14 not voting and therefore subjected to the act).

This mixed result was in spite of intense pressure orchestrated by John Collier to win tribal endorsements. The Diné were the largest nation to reject tribal self-government. The Diné's opposition was in reaction to the efforts to reduce livestock on Navajo lands, which were by this time seriously overgrazed (see chapter 5). In any event, the entrenched bureaucracy and inertia of the Bureau of Indian Affairs ensured that whatever the act stated, implementation would be slow and controlled by BIA insiders.

During this period others echoed Collier's disdain for Western civilization and his high regard for Native American spirituality, although in the abstract rather than any particular nation's tradition. In *The Redman's Message* (1936), Ernest Thompson Seton wrote:

> The Civilization of the Whiteman is a failure; it is visibly crumbling around us. . . . We offer you the Message of the Redman, the Creed of Manhood. We advocate his culture as an improvement on our own, if perchance by belated repentance, remorse, restitution, and justification, we may save ourselves from Divine vengeance and total destruction. (cited in Wilson 1999, 344–45)

As in the first World War, during World War II Native Americans answered the call to arms in numbers greater than other ethnic groups in terms of their percentage in the population. By 1944 nearly 25,000 Indians were serving in the Atlantic and Pacific theaters. Twice that many worked in war-related industries. The famed Navajo Code Talkers (see chapter 5) are credited with helping win the war against Japan. The war introduced many American Indians to the world beyond the reservations, fostering a desire to reap the material rewards of American society. A new, pantribal lobbying organization, the National Congress of American Indians, was formed in 1944 to give tribes more political influence than they had separately.

Nevertheless, Indians who fought in defense of the United States in Europe and Asia were treated as second-class citizens when they returned from the war. The dilemma posed for Native Americans was dramatized in Kiowa author N. Scott Momaday's Pulitzer Prize–winning novel *House Made of Dawn* and in Laguna writer Leslie Marmon Silko's moving novel *Ceremony*.

After the war, the momentum to assimilate Indians into mainstream American life again picked up. John Collier resigned as Commissioner of Indian Affairs in 1945, and it was several decades before the principles of self-determination he favored returned to popularity. That same year a House of Representatives report asserted that "the goal of our whole program [of federal Indian education] should be . . . to develop better Indian Americans rather than to perpetuate better American Indians" (Hauptman 1986, 1). Plans were soon under way to cut the federal budget by withdrawing services and terminating the treaty relationships between the federal government and native nations.

The movement of Indians to the cities, stimulated by wartime employment opportunities, was enhanced by continuing unemployment and poverty on the reservations. "Relocation" became the dominant government policy, with programs to help Indians find new homes in urban centers such as Los Angeles, Denver, Salt Lake City, Portland, Chicago, Cleveland, and New York. Between 1949 and 1957 about 30,000 Indians had relocated from reservations and rural areas to cities. Some found their own version of the "American dream" and made new lives for themselves. The move to the cities did not improve life for most of those who relocated, though. Lured by promises of high-paying jobs and beautiful homes, they found only menial employment, substandard housing, and the racial discrimination that African Americans had long experienced. "Red nigger" became an epithet shouted at newly arrived Indians in the cities. The promise of extended BIA support usually evaporated after only a month in the city. Indian "ghettos" and the attendant social problems developed in most of the cities. Cut off from the extended families and elders so important in native cultures, many felt adrift and lost. "I was as distant from myself as the moon from the earth," wrote Native American novelist James Welch (cited in Mankiller 1993, 73). By the early 1960s about half of those who had relocated had returned to the familiarity and security of reservations.

One of the effects of relocation was a growing movement that brought together Indians from different nations. Such "pantribalism" had long been a byproduct of the boarding schools. Now as Native Americans from many nations gathered in the Indian centers created in cities, distinctions among cultures diminished while a sense of Indian solidarity in the face of their common plight grew. Throughout Indian country, powwows brought together people from various nations for dancing and socializing (see above and chapter 9). An "American Indian spirituality" was developing, which joined together Native Americans who either had lost contact with their own national spiritual traditions or were willing to supplement them in order to support Indian unity.

Although the Indian population of the United States had increased from the 1890 level of about 228,000 only to 343,000 in 1950, it then began a rapid rise, which has continued every census period since. The population increased to 523,000 by 1960, to 793,000 by 1970, to 1.6 million by 1980, to more than 2 million by 1990. The increase is due in part to a birthrate twice as high as that of the general population, but also to the heightened willingness of Indian people to identify themselves as Native Americans on census forms.

In part motivated by the exemplary war service of Native Americans and the irony of the Nuremberg Trials being held to bring to justice Germans who had engaged in wars of aggression and conquest, in 1946 Congress created the Indian Claims Commission to settle the claims of Indian nations against the government. The motivation, however, was not simply redress for past injustices. Many in Congress believed that if old claims were resolved, the federal responsibility for the welfare of Indians could be ended. The commission was not given the authority to return lost lands or award new lands to settle claims. Instead, the commission was to award monetary payments based on the market value of the land at the time it was taken.

The commission continued until it was dissolved in 1978. By then it had awarded $800 million in settlement of some 550 claims. The average interval between filing a claim and having it settled was fifteen years. Needless to say, this was not a popular approach to resolving the breaking of treaties and other injustices among most Native Americans.

Nevertheless, the commission did give native peoples "a forum in which they might clarify the factual nature of their grievances for the first time." The commission's research (if not always its decisions) "revealed the full extent to which the United States had occupied areas to which it had no lawful title." It showed that according to the last known rulings and legislative action, fully 35 percent of the continental United States was unceded native land! (Churchill 1992, 147–48)

Despite the appearance of a willingness to treat native nations more fairly, in the two decades after World War II, millions of additional acres of Indian land were lost as a result of federal water and dam projects. For example, six massive dams in the Missouri River Valley resulted in the destruction of 550 square miles of Lakota lands.

In 1948 Congress defined "Indian country," extending the legal concept not just to reservations but also to individual allotments and all enrolled members of federally recognized tribes.

The National Congress of American Indians, an exclusively Indian organization, worked hard to secure rights and benefits for native peoples guaranteed by federal and state governments, to promote better understanding of Indian people, and to preserve Native American cultural values. By 1992 NCAI represented 160 tribes and about 400,000 Indian people.

In addition to "relocation," government policy toward Native Americans from after World War II into the 1960s was characterized by a plan known as "termination" (see Fixico 1986). In 1949 the Hoover Commission on the Reorganization of Government had recommended the termination of Indian tribes. Relocation and the work of the Indian Claims Commission also contributed to the view that Indians would be better off if they no longer lived under the traditional tribal structures. Dillon Myer, who had been in charge of Japanese internment camps during World War II, was named Commissioner of Indian Affairs in 1950 and during his two-year tenure set in motion the policies of both relocation and termination (see Drinnon 1987).

In 1953 a resolution of Congress stated that the status of Indians as wards of the United States government should be ended and they should have the same privileges and responsibilities as other citizens. Between 1954 and 1962 Congress terminated the federal relationship with 109 separate native nations and other entities, totaling 13,263 individuals owning 1,365,801 acres of land. Although large nations such as the Diné and Lakota were able to resist termination, smaller nations like the Menominee of Wisconsin and the Klamath of Oregon were not. The policy of "termination" was cloaked in the language of "civil rights for Native Americans" and "dignity not dependency," but the clear purpose of the policy was a return to the attempts to "acculturate" and "civilize" Indians which had dominated Indian policy in earlier times.

In 1956 the Relocation Act financed the moving of Indian families to urban areas, establishing job training centers. It also cut off funds for similar programs on reservations in order to encourage Indians to move to cities. Those who left had to sign agreements that they would not return to their reservations. The law set in motion a migration which by 1980 resulted in the spreading of about half the nation's 1.6 million Indians throughout the country.

Although the policy of termination was not formally ended during the presidencies of John Kennedy and Lyndon Johnson, it was curtailed. In its place, President Johnson's War on Poverty introduced new programs in housing, health care, education, and employment on reservations. Most bypassed the Bureau of Indian Affairs and were under the auspices of the Office of Economic Opportunity, which theoretically (if not very well in practice) advocated Native American self-determination in developing programs.

During the 1960s Red Power became a rallying cry for young Indians on, but especially off, the reservations. In 1960 the National Indian Youth Council (NIYC) was founded by a new generation of Native American leaders, among them Vine Deloria Jr. and Clyde Warrior. Warrior, a Ponca, expressed a sentiment shared by other young Native American leaders:

> If there is one thing that characterizes Indian life today it is poverty of the spirit. . . . [W]e are poor in spirit because we are not free—free in the most basic sense of the word. We are not allowed to make those basic human choices and decisions about our personal life and about the destiny of our communities which is the mark of free mature people. (Wilson 1999, 370)

In 1968 the American Indian Movement (AIM) was formed in Minneapolis by Ojibwas Dennis Banks, Clyde Bellecourt, and several others. During the next decade AIM became the most significant political organization for activist Native Americans and, according to its supporters, was often the target of government and corporate efforts to reduce its influence (see Weyler 1984; Churchill and Van der Wall 1988). It first attracted alienated Indian youths in big cities, most of whom knew little about their own heritage. Few spoke their native languages.

Gradually, however, AIM's influence spread to reservations. (For more on AIM, see Weyler 1984; Crow Dog 1995, 159–243; and chapter 4 of this book).

Groups such as NIYC and AIM are heirs of the nineteenth-century pantribal movements intent on reclaiming Native American pride and self-determination. As James Wilson puts it, quoting an NIYC leader:

> Like Tecumseh before them, the young radicals tried to forge a pantribal coalition based on "high principles" derived from the values and beliefs of our ancestors' but adapted to new conditions; like him they used bellicose rhetoric and assertive tactics which provoked alarm and opposition among the more "accommodationist" elements in their own community. (Wilson 1999, 389)

They denounced these "accomodationist" leaders, who had collaborated with the government, as "apples" (red on the outside, white on the inside) and "Uncle Tomahawks." Their heroes were the traditionalists in each nation, especially spiritual leaders, who had shunned assimilation and lived in relative isolation, clinging to their language, myths, and rituals.

In 1968, as part of an effort to reverse the more extreme provisions of termination policy, Congress passed, and President Johnson signed, the American Indian Civil Rights Act. The law extended the provisions of the Bill of Rights of the U.S. Constitution to Indians on reservations, stipulating that states could not take jurisdiction for law and order on reservations without the consent of the affected tribes, and placed the same restrictions on tribal governments that federal and state governments have. Unfortunately, the impact of the Civil Rights Act was to restrict more the ability of traditional governments to function. It in effect further incorporated tribal governments into the federal system.

In 1969 Vine Deloria Jr., who in 1964 had become executive director of the National Congress of American Indians, published *Custer Died for Your Sins: An Indian Manifesto*. The book defined the Indian activist agenda in an engaging and satirical manner that caught the attention of the media and a wide reading audience.

In his campaign for the presidency in 1960, Richard Nixon had committed himself to policies in keeping with the traditional values of Native American cultures. When he became president in 1968, he formally ended "termination," declaring it both legally and morally reprehensible, and developed a new approach to guaranteeing Indian self-sufficiency. President Nixon also gave his support to the Indian Education Act of 1972, which sought to give Indian people control of their own educational institutions and called for increased funding for Indian education. One result was the creation of tribal colleges (see chapter 9).

Encouraged by this new recognition of their right and responsibility to chart their own course and inspired by the growing activism of the anti–Vietnam War movement, some Indians began a campaign of direct action. On 18 December 1968 Mohawks blockaded the Cornwall Bridge as a protest against the Canadian government's refusal to honor the Jay Treaty of 1794. On both sides of the border Mohawk militancy in defense of sovereignty and traditional ways continues to this day.

Beginning in November 1969, Alcatraz Island in San Francisco Bay, site of the then-vacant famous federal prison, was occupied for nineteen months by a group calling itself "Indians of All Tribes" who proposed that the island be turned into an Indian cultural and educational center. The lasting effect of the occupation was to call national attention to the problems of Native Americans. As one leader put it, "Now the nation knows we Indians are still here." (For a full account of the Alcatraz occupation, see Smith and Warrior 1996.)

In 1970, on the 350th anniversary of the landing of the Pilgrims, a group of AIM members, led by Russell Means (Lakota), boarded the replica of the Pilgrim ship, the *Mayflower*, and raised an AIM flag. They covered Plymouth Rock with a truckload of sand. This was but one of a host of AIM-sponsored rallies and demonstrations throughout the country.

Two other interrelated events in this era of activism, the Trail of Broken Treaties march on Washington, D.C., in 1972 and the reoccupation of the site of the 1890 Wounded Knee Massacre in 1973, are discussed in chapter 4.

In 1973, under the leadership of leaders such as Ada Deer and the organization she formed (Determination of Rights and Unity for Menominee Shareholders [DRUMS]), the Menominees of Wisconsin were able to reverse the termination of their nation that had occurred twenty years earlier.

During the rest of the 1970s, the movement toward self-determination gained momentum, but also experienced judicial obstacles. The International Indian Treaty Council (AIM's "diplomatic arm"), created in 1974, brought the plight of Native American nations to the attention of the United Nations and the world press. Under the provisions of the Indian Self-Determination and Educational Assistance Act (1975), Native American nations were allowed to administer all federal programs on their reservations (including schools, law enforcement, health care, social service, and community development) and to adopt any governing structure they saw fit (rather than just the one set forth in the 1934 Reorganization Act). Once again, however, the law further imbedded tribal governments in federal agencies (Churchill 1992, 16–17).

In 1934 the land base for American Indians was 2.6 percent of all U.S. lands south of Canada: 51 million acres. By 1974 this land base was decreased by 1.8 million acres, including nearly 500,000 acres in dams, reservoirs, and other water projects. Two-thirds of the 400 Indian reservations in the United States were smaller than the 24,000 acres of Walt Disney World in Florida (Vecsey and Venables 1980, xix–xx).

In 1977 American Indians joined with indigenous people from Central and South America to present their grievances to the International Treaty Rights Conference. The Indian International Treaty Council was given the status of a nongovernmental organization (NGO) by the United Nations, providing Native Americans a continuing forum to call world attention to their struggle to have the provisions of treaties observed by the U.S. government.

In 1978 the Indian Child Welfare Act responded to the tragedy of up to 25 percent of Indian children being taken from their homes and given to non-Indian families for adoption or placed in government institutions. Many Indian leaders saw this practice as a continuation of a policy of cultural genocide. The act gave tribes authority over child custody proceedings and stated that parental rights for Indian children could not be terminated by state courts without proof that they would suffer serious emotional or physical harm if they continued with their biological parents. Implementation of the provisions of the act have proven difficult, and opponents have alleged that Indian children have been arbitrarily removed from non-Indian families where they were being well nurtured and returned to desolate situations. Recent court decisions have weakened tribal rights in adoption proceedings.

The American Indian Freedom of Religion Act (AIFRA), also enacted in 1978, recognized that "the religious practices of American Indian (as well as Native Alaskan and Hawaiian) are an integral part of their culture, traditions and heritage, such practices forming the basis of Indian identity and value systems." The act provided that

> henceforth it shall be the policy of the United States to protect and preserve for American Indians their inherent right of freedom to believe, express, and exercise the traditional religions of the American Indian, Eskimo, Aleut, and Native Hawaiians, including but not limited to access to sites, use, and possession of sacred objects, and the freedom to worship through ceremonies and traditional rites.

The act also directed federal departments and agencies to evaluate their policies and procedures related to the practice of traditional Native American religions in consultation with traditional spiritual leaders of the various nations.

After the adoption of the Act a struggle ensued to assure its implementation (see Michaelsen 1983). The act itself lacked enforcement provisions, and a series of court decisions in the 1980s and 1990s have in effect denied "any practical content in indigenous spiritual rights." For example, in 1980 the Supreme Court refused to apply the act to a joint Diné-Hopi effort to protect a site of spiritual significance called Rainbow Bridge. Efforts to force the return by museums and educational institutions of ceremonial objects and the remains of Indians removed from burials to tribes are continuing, with mixed results. The difficulty in obtaining legal protection for members of the Native American Church in their ritual use of peyote is examined in greater detail in chapter 7.

The 1978 Supreme Court ruling in *U.S.* v. *Wheeler* held that Indian tribes had not given up full sovereignty and that unless Congress specifically acts to limit them, tribes retain their sovereign powers under the Constitution. This represented a tremendous victory in the long effort to reassert what had been recognized at the outset of the formation of the United States, that Indian nations were indeed sovereign political communities.

Also in 1978 an intertribal coalition sponsored another event to raise public awareness of the plight of Native Americans. Called the Longest Walk, it began on the West Coast of the United States in the winter of 1978 and continued across the continent until the walkers reached Washington, D.C.

In the early 1980s the U.S. Commission on Civil Rights issued a report entitled "Indian Tribes: A Continuing Quest for Survival." The report, written principally by Native American lawyers, urged Congress to recognize Indian tribes on the same basis as states. It concluded that denial of Indian rights was based on public ignorance of those rights and by the failure of governmental agencies to respond properly when rights were violated. The report made clear that Indian tribes have a unique political and legal status based on treaties, confronting the public misconception that Native Americans were claiming special rights based on race (Silko 1996, 73–79).

During the rest of the 1980s, self-determination for Native Americans continued to be the basic principle guiding federal policy. In 1982 the Supreme Court recognized the right of native nations to levy taxes on minerals extracted from their lands. In 1983 President Ronald Reagan announced in a policy statement his administration's support for a "government-to-government" philosophy of relationships among tribal, state, and federal governments. Part of the policy was to transfer to states more responsibility for dealing with Native American nations.

Unfortunately, cutbacks in federal budgets (although about $3 billion was still being appropriated annually for Indian programs) and continued inertia and corruption in the Bureau of Indian Affairs made meaningful implementation of the self-determination principle difficult. In addition, in an effort to increase the funds generated on reservations, the controversial Indian Mineral Development Act (1982) "encouraged" native nations to dramatically increase the mining on their lands, often with waivers of environmental regulations.

At the same time, however, increasing numbers of Native Americans were taking advantage of better educational opportunities, including those offered by the tribal colleges (see chapter 9), and many accepted the challenge of applying their knowledge and skills in the service of their people.

At two points this historical overview of Native America up to 1990 may appropriately be brought to a close. Both are symbols of a determination among Native Americans to face tragedies of the past, and to look to a more hopeful future.

The first occurred on 6 October 1989 at the University of Colorado in Boulder. On that date, in a simple rededication ceremony, a building named Nichols Hall was renamed Cheyenne-Arapaho Hall. Nichols Hall had honored David Nichols, one of the early business leaders of the Boulder community and a regent of the university. As a captain in the Colorado Volunteer Calvary Regiment, however, Nichols was one of the leaders of the massacre of Cheyenne and Arapaho women and children at Sand Creek in southeastern Colorado on 29 November 1864 (see above). The renaming of the hall was the culmination of a twenty-year struggle to remove Nichols's name from the campus dormitory. As one observer noted, "for at least one brief moment, the light of truth shone upon a fragment of the real history of the conquest of Native America" (Jaimes 1992, 1–2).

The second event took place on 20 December 1990 at Wounded Knee on the Oglala Lakota Pine Ridge Reservation in South Dakota. For four years groups of riders had recreated the tragic journey of Big Foot's band from the Cheyenne River reservation through the Badlands. On the morning of 29 December 1890, Big Foot and at least 200 of the people traveling with him were massacred by U.S. army soldiers at Wounded Knee Creek (see chapters 4 and 6). The four-year Big Foot Memorial Ride, which culminated in 1990, was intended not only to honor the memory of those who had died but to begin a new day for the Lakota people. It was meant to "wipe the tears of the seven generations" and "restore the sacred hoop," that is, to rebuild the unity of the Lakota people. For the riders it was a spiritual experience, both connecting them to the past and preparing the Lakota people for the future. As one of the ride's leaders said, "The spirits join us . . . you see them, you hear them, travel with them, they tell us things towards the future and the past. For us we call it the hoop, the understanding . . . it's all one; it exists within what's called the sacred hoop" (Wilson 1999, xix).

Conclusion: Genocide?

In recounting the history of Native America, should the word *genocide* be used? *Genocide* is a term coined in 1944 in light of the attempted extermination of Jews and other ethnic groups in Europe by the Nazis before and during World War II. Although the term has been applied to a host of incidents of violence against groups, most historians agree that it should be reserved for the implementation of a planned and systematic policy of elimination of a racial, ethnic, religious, or (although some would dispute this) political group. Strictly speaking, not *every* instance of mass killing should be called genocide.

Historians have been engaged in a lively debate over whether genocide is an appropriate label for the treatment of Native Americans by European and Euroamerican authorities since 1492. According to James Axtell, "[g]enocide, as distinguished from other forms of cruelty, oppression, and death, played a very small role in the European conquest of the New World." Axtell contends that to use to the term is to place an unfair moral onus on Euroamericans, who should not be compared with the Nazis (Axtell 1992, 260–63).

Other scholars such as Laurence Hauptman and George Tinker have maintained that genocide is an appropriate term to apply to particular times, places, and events in American Indian history. Hauptman cites as examples the treatment of the Pequot people in the so-called Pequot War of 1637 (see above) and the actions taken against the Indians of northern California after the gold rush of 1848 (Hauptman 1995, 3–14; see also Wilson 1999, 227–40; Churchill 1994; Stiffarm and Lane 1992, 34–36; Todorov 1982).

In general, the treatment of Native Americans we have described in this chapter might fall under the heading *ethnocide* or *cultural genocide*. Although only in specific instances such as those Hauptman cites was there literal, physical genocide, the widespread and entrenched policy of "civilizing" Native Americans was an attempt to exterminate their lifeways. Cultural genocide is "the effective destruction of a people by systematically (intentionally or unintentionally in order to achieve other goals) destroying, eroding, or undermining the integrity of the culture and system of values that defines a people and gives them life" (Tinker 1993, 6). Tinker identifies four aspects of the cultural genocide visited upon Native Americans (6–8):

1) Political—as in the crippling treaties forced them and the breaking of these treaties, and ultimately confining the people to reservations where their traditional political structures were broken down;
2) Economic—as in the eradication of the buffalo and the destruction of the agriculture of the Diné people;
3) Religious—as in the outlawing of traditional ceremonies and the imposition of another religion (Christianity); and
4) Social—as in the imposing of the ideology of individualism and the nuclear family on native peoples.

Not all Euroamericans have agreed with General Philip Sheridan's famous statement that "the only good Indian is a dead Indian," but throughout most of the period since 1492, the notion that in order to "save the person" you must "kill the Indian" has been the widely accepted assumption. To try to extinguish the American Indians' language, rituals, dress, and ways of living with one another and with the rest of nature was to attempt to terminate them as distinct peoples. Even Christian missionaries, whose goal was "saving" Native Americans and who often genuinely cared for Indian people, were agents of cultural genocide. At least as far as most Native Americans are concerned, the intended effect was the same as physical killing. It was (and some would maintain, still is) genocide. That it was not successful is a tribute to the depth and vitality of the spiritual traditions of Native American nations.

PART II

The Spiritual Traditions of Four Native American Nations

CHAPTER 2

The Lenape (Delaware): The Grandfather Nation

When we come into this house of ours we are glad, and thankful that we are well, and for everything that makes us feel good that the Creator has placed here for our use.
    —Charles Elkhair, a leader of the Lenape Big House ceremony

NEAR THE SMALL TOWN of Dewey in northeastern Oklahoma is a cemetery, a resting place for some of the Lenape (Delaware) people who were among those relocated to Indian Territory from Kansas after the Civil War. In the fall of 1997 I had been taken to this spot by Curtis Zunigha, then elected chief of the Delaware Tribe of Indians, headquartered in nearby Bartlesville. I had met Chief Zunigha earlier that year, at a ceremony rededicating another Lenape cemetery at White Church in Kansas City, Kansas.

My great-great-grandparents, Isaac and Lucy Mundy, had lived among the Lenape people in eastern Kansas during the 1840s and 1850s. In April 1997 other descendants of the Mundys and I had been invited to participate in the re-dedication of the Lenape cemetery in which Isaac Mundy was buried amidst the Lenape with whom he worked. Now Chief Zunigha had taken me to another Lenape cemetery, a sacred place, he said, where he could feel the presence of his ancestors. Among the names on the traditional Lenape gravemarkers in this cemetery was Charles Elkhair, a leader of the traditional Lenape Big House ceremony in the late nineteenth and early twentieth centuries. He was buried alongside Lenape members of Christian churches, suggesting a mutual respect among Lenape people who kept alive their own spiritual traditions and those who had embraced the Christian faith and no longer practiced the traditional ways.

At the cemetery that day and in our conversations afterward, Chief Zunigha helped me to understand the economic, political, cultural, and spiritual challenges this small nation was facing at the end of the twentieth century. He spoke with pride about the heritage of the Lenape people, once respectfully identified by neighboring native nations in their northeastern homeland as a grandfather nation. He shared his dreams for the spiritual rejuvenation of his people, and his awareness of the obstacles to be overcome if that renewal was to continue. Later, at a small cafe in Bartlesville, Chief Zunigha introduced me to Leonard Thompson, the ceremonial chief of the Delaware Tribe and several other Lenape elders. I was moved by their warmth and openness to an outsider, as well as their obvious concern for one another and the well-being of their tribe and its future.

The Lenape (Delaware) nation is not as well known as the others included in this work. Nevertheless, theirs is a story important to tell. Forced to relocate from their original homeland in what is now New Jersey and Delaware, the Lenape were moved six more times in their trek to Indian territory. Theirs is a story of survival in the face of seemingly insurmountable odds. It is also a story of hope, as contemporary Lenape people work together to find ways to keep alive and pass to a new generation their cultural and spiritual heritage.

Motivated by my own ancestors' association with the Lenape people more than a century ago and the determination and pride of the modern Lenape people I have been privileged to meet, I offer this chapter in the hope that it will promote respect among nonnative readers for the "grandfather nation."

Who Are the Lenape?

The Lenape (Delaware) are an Algonquian-speaking people whose forced migration westward from their ancestral homeland on the East Coast of the United States during the eighteenth and nineteenth centuries has left them widely scattered. Today there are Lenape peoples in northeastern and southwestern Oklahoma, Wisconsin, Ontario (Canada), and a few other isolated locations. The present total Lenape population is about 13,000, with the largest concentration living in and near Bartlesville, Oklahoma.

Traditional Lenape speak dialects of two related Algonquian languages, Munsee and Unami. *Lenape* means "real or common people," and was used by each linguistic subgroup to refer to itself. So, for example, Munsee speakers might speak of themselves as Lenopi and, in addition, distinguish as a separate people the Unami. This gave rise to the sometimes-used phrase *"lenni lenape,"* which means something like "the *real* real people." Like other native nations, the Lenape have adopted as their own the name by which others knew them, in this case "Delaware." In our discussion, the names Lenape and Delaware will be used interchangeably. The Lenape were known to other Algonquian-speakers as a "grandfather" of the nations, an indication of respect.

By 1661 the designation Delaware for the Lenape was in use among the English settlers in Maryland. "Delaware" derives from Sir Thomas West, Lord de la Warr (1577–1618), the first governor of Virginia, for whom the Delaware River was named. The name was first used formally in a treaty made with the British in 1736. Ironically, Sir Thomas never met the people named for him.

A Lenape story of the derivation of "Delaware" for their nation is somewhat different. According to this tradition, the first European who encountered the Lenape people could not pronounce their name correctly. When he finally did, a Lenape said, *"Nal ne ndeluwen!"* which means, "That's what I said!" The European, however, heard *duluwen,* and said, "I see. You are called Delawares!"

Lenape Creation Legends

As in most Native American cultures, a number of traditional stories of creation exist among the Lenape. For example, the traditional Delaware history known as the *Wallam Olum,* to be analyzed below, begins with the following account of creation:

Book One

1) At the beginning,
    The sea everywhere
    Covered the earth.
2) Above extended
    A swirling cloud,
    And within it,
    The Great Spirit moved.
3) Primordial,
    Everlasting,
    Invisible,
    Omnipresent—
    The Great Spirit moved.
4) Bringing forth
    The sky,
    The earth,
    The clouds,
    The heavens.
5) Bringing forth
    The day,
    The night,
    The stars.

6) Bringing forth all
    Of these
    to move in harmony.
7) Stirred to action
    Strong winds blew,
    Cleansing
    The sky
    In rapid streams.
8) Pure as snow
    Arose the lands
    To be inhabited.
9) Again,
    The Great Spirit
    Created:
    The creator spirits,
10) Living beings,
    Immortals,
    The Souls [for]
    Everything.

11) Then the Spirit
    Ancestor,
    Grandfather
    Of Men,
12) Gave
    The First Mother,
    Mother of Life,
13) [Who] gave the fish,
    Gave the turtles,
    Gave the beasts,
    Gave the birds.
	14) But the bad spirit
	    Brought forth
	    Bad creatures:
	    The snakes and
	    Sea monsters.
	15) It brought forth
	    Flies;
	    It brought forth
	    Mosquitos.
	
	    (McCutchen 1993, 52, 54)

One of the better known Delaware creation stories (Bierhorst 1995, 28) says that Creator brought up a turtle from the depths of the water, which was everywhere at the time of creation. As the water fell from his back, a tree took root on it. The tree sent out a sprout, and the sprout grew into a man. A second sprout appeared on the tree which became a woman. The Lenape people descended from this couple. The turtle is a symbol for Mother Earth; in fact, the turtle was life itself, and its breathing caused the waters to ebb and flow (hence the tides). The twelve plates of its shell became a sacred number incorporated into the Big House ceremony, the most famous Lenape ritual (see below).

In some stories, the Creator, also called Great *Manito* (Spirit), assigned the four quarters of the earth to the four powerful *Manitowuk* (lesser spirits): the North, West, and East (assigned to the Grandfathers) and the South (who was under guardianship of *Koo-hum-mun-nah,* Our Grandmother). The Great *Manito* gave the duty of providing light to the sun. The sun and moon are addressed as Elder Brothers (Weslager 1972, 66–67).

A Lenape story recorded by the ethnologist M.R. Harrington in eastern Oklahoma early in this century speaks of a stranger who came to the Lenape, before the white man had arrived. From foam on a stream the stranger created the white man, who was strong and multiplied rapidly. The white people became boisterous and mean, and their creator could not control them. The stranger finally turned the palefaces over to his brother, who taught them mechanical trades and industries. The whites became successful, but their creator learned that his brother was evil. The informant, reflecting the Christian influence on the Lenape, told Harrington that this story explained why there was so much evil in the world and that the evil brother must have been Satan (Bierhorst 1995, 48, 101–2).

Another story of origins popular among the Lenape describes the creation of the seven stars of the Pleiades constellation from seven boys who are transformed (Bierhorst 1995, 34, 47, 53, 57, 62, 98–99).

The Traditional History: The Wallam Olum ("Red Record")

The Lenape are unique among Native American peoples in claiming a version of their national epic committed to writing. It is called the *Wallam Olum*, which translates as "Red Record."

The *Wallam Olum* is composed of 183 symbols combined with words that tell the story of the Lenape before the Europeans came. It begins with the Lenape account of Creation recorded above and a story of a great flood. It then tells of the Lenape people coming from Asia into the "New World" and their encounters with people already dwelling here. It next speaks of the journey of the people south and eastward across North America, and the succession of nearly 100 generations of Lenape leaders, creating "an unbroken chain of names and deeds stretching over thousands of years and thousands of miles" (McCutchen 1993, 4).

The people survive schisms, droughts, and wars until they reach the beautiful Delaware River valley. It ends with a description of the arrival of European ships on the Delaware River in the 1620s with the enigmatic verse: "Friendly people, in great ships; who are they?" (V:60). The symbols telling this story were written on wooden or birch bark strips. The strips themselves have not survived, but a record of them has.

A "fragment" appended to the *Wallam Olum* in the Rafinesque manuscripts (Rafinesque 1836) tells in its twenty verses the story of the Lenape from their first encounter with Europeans in 1620 until 1820 when the main body was about to depart Indiana for Missouri (see below). According to the fragment, the Lenape soon recognized that the "friendly people" who had come from the Sea were Snakes who would rob them of their land. Nevertheless, the Delaware treated the Europeans with hospitality and helped them survive. They traded with them and acquired new tools and weapons. The Europeans' guns and the liquor brought destruction, however. Events known from other sources, which will be described in the historical overview below, are then hinted at in the fragment. It ends with another question and a hope: "Shall we be free and happy there [in Missouri]? We want rest and peace and wisdom."

Is the *Wallam Olum* authentic, or was it, as some modern interpreters argue, either a fake produced by Euroamericans sympathetic to the Lenape or the work of a nineteenth century Lenape trying to inspire a revival of Delaware culture during a time when it was dying out? Doubts about the authenticity of the *Wallam Olum* are raised by the manner in which it was first made known. A Transylvania College professor named Constantine Rafinesque claimed to have obtained an original copy from a Dr. Ward, a physician who claimed he obtained it in 1820 from a Delaware record-keeper named Olumpees, who lived on the White River in Indiana. Dr. Ward said he cured Olumpees during an epidemic and received as payment Olumpees's most prized possession, the wooden strips of the *Wallam Olum*. Rafinesque says that he received by 1822 either the wood sticks with the glyphs on them or a record of them and a manuscript with the accompanying verses in the Lenape language. By 1833 he had translated the verses into English and copied the pictographs in two small notebooks. In 1836 he published his translation of the verses (and the twenty additional verses claiming to carry forward Lenape history until 1820). His division of the *Wallam Olum* into five sections, often called books, has been followed in subsequent translations (see, for example, Indiana Historical Society 1954).

After Rafinesque's death in 1840, his notebooks passed through several hands until the pictures were published in 1884 by Dr. Daniel Brinton (Brinton 1884), along with translations of the verses as well as the Lenape words translated. Brinton and other serious students of Lenape culture, including Frank Speck, C.F. Voegelin, C.A. Weslager, Gregory Schaaf, and David McCutchen, are convinced that the *Wallam Olum* is authentic, if not fully accurate in all its details. The most recent study has shown that the symbols and words are remarkably accurate in their description of a journey eastward out of Asia and across the continent. Research has also shown a close correspondence between the *Wallam Olum* and Lenape oral tradition. (McCutchen 1993, 19–44; Weslager 1972, 88–94).

David McCutchen best sums up what seems to him the most responsible position:

> We may never know how much of the Wallam Olum is fact and how much is fiction; how much is accurate and how much might have been garbled or lost in transmission. What is important is for the Wallam Olum to be acknowledged as a possible, if shadowy, beginning of our written history, like the Norse saga of Leif Erikson's voyages to America. (McCutchen 1993, xiii)

It should be noted that many Native Americans are concerned about use of the *Wallam Olum* to support the theory of a migration across the Bering Sea. Their reason is that this theory has long been used to support the contention that Native Americans are an "immigrant" people without aboriginal rights. As noted, however, the Red Record recognizes that before the Lenape came to North America, there were other native peoples already here.

Historical Overview

Because of seven forced migrations and the scattering of Lenape peoples, the history of the Lenape nation is quite complex. To understand the situation Delawares face at the end of the twentieth century, however, it is a story that must be recounted in some detail. Two twentieth-century scholars, Ives Goddard and

C.A. Weslager, have researched Lenape history most carefully. I am especially indebted to their studies in this overview.

Prior to Contact with Europeans

The Lenape people encountered by the earliest Dutch explorers of the Delaware River valley in the sixteenth century lived in small, dispersed villages along the banks of the river and its tributaries. They were politically separate communities, adapted to a variety of habitats ranging from open coastal plains to rolling, forested hills.

Some interpreters take the view that the Lenape at this time were found as far north as the Hudson River. The dominant view, however, is that Munsee speakers occupied what are now the five boroughs of New York City and the southwest corner of Nassau County, Long Island. They also occupied an area demarcated by the Connecticut–New York line to the southwest corner of Massachusetts, and then west to the northeast corner of Pennsylvania and from there south to the vicinity of Scranton; from Scranton to the Delaware Water Gap and across the present state of New Jersey to the Atlantic Ocean southeast of Staten Island. The rest of New Jersey to the south, the Philadelphia area, and the northwestern two-thirds of Delaware was the homeland of the Unami speakers (Bierhorst 1995, 4).

The Munsee and Unami dialects were different enough that the two groups would have had some difficulty understanding each other. They may be even be considered related, but separate languages.

A number of subgroups have been identified for both the Munsees and Unamis. It is estimated that the the main body of the Delaware people resided in about forty village bands, each with a few hundred members and may have grown from around 8,000 in the early 1600s to a peak of as many as 11,000–12,000 in total (Goddard 1978, 213–16).

Within each autonomous village a leader was selected from a particular lineage as a first among equals. The chieftain had little more than persuasive powers, however, and acted principally as a mediator if disputes arose, and as a ceremonial leader. Chieftains also organized collective hunting, on trips that might range a substantial distance from the villages. Families might have their own hunting grounds, but there was no sense that they "owned" these areas.

The autonomous villages probably collaborated in matters of mutual defense, negotiations with neighboring nations, fishing areas, and intermarriage. Cooperating villages in the same area might be called bands, and the most influential village chieftain was recognized as the titular head of the band. These bands were often given names by Europeans based on a geographical feature. For example, those living on Rancoca Creek were known as the Rancocas. The best analogy for Euroamericans might be a group of politically separate but culturally related rural villages, with many family connections, who collaborate with one another in matters of common concern.

Key decisions on issues of importance to villages or bands were made in a general council of elders and those deemed particularly wise. Succession of chiefs seems to have been mostly, if not exclusively, matrilineal. In some groups there were priests, but it was more likely for chiefs to function as ritual leaders. There were also war chiefs, who took office on the basis of demonstrated fighting and leadership ability. These chiefs came to be known also as war "captains," and eventually the title *captain* was associated with these Delaware leaders. Europeans would later make the mistake of calling band leaders "kings," imposing terminology from their own political structure on a people who had a very different kind of government.

Before contact with Europeans, the Lenape people led a subsistence lifestyle. They lived in small, one-room bark huts along the river or creek banks. They practiced year-round hunting, with fall as the principal hunting season, followed by summer. Hunting parties as large as 200 were organized. Deer was the main game, but a variety of small animals were also hunted. Fires were intentionally set both to trap game and to clear land for cornfields.

In addition to corn, crops included beans, squash, and tobacco. Berries and nuts were gathered. Spring was a time of visiting, trading, fishing in the ocean, and gathering shellfish. Travel on waterways was by dugout canoe. Trails linked villages and led to hunting areas. After the fall harvest there was the greatest concentration of population in one place. It was also the main time for the important harvest festivals. As with other northeastern peoples, purple and white wampum was in ceremonial use. Small sweat lodges were also used ritually for purification.

The notion of "owning" land would have been foreign to the Lenape at this time. Like the air, sunlight, and water, land was a gift of the Creator intended for the use of all. People took what they needed to survive, usually without depleting the resources. Like other animals, people had territories that they might defend against others of the same species who enter it. Unlike the European "right of discovery," however, occupying an area did not mean ownership. To grant someone else the right to take resources from the land on which you lived did not mean you were giving up your own right to hunt, fish, and grow crops on it. Europeans would exploit this different perspective in their relations with the Lenape and other native peoples.

During times of war there is some indication that the Delaware villagers stayed in multiple-family longhouses surrounded by stockades. Unlike the Hotinonshonni (Iroquois) villages to the north, however, they typically did not have palisades. Warriors wore wooden helmets and carried decorated wooden war clubs and wooden or hide shields. Fighting was usually in small groups, with few fatalities. As with the Iroquois, captives were either adopted to replace killed kinsmen or, less commonly, tortured and executed.

Both men and women applied paint to their faces and displayed tattoos, usually in the shape of animals. Men also painted their thighs, legs, and breasts. Colors were symbolic, with white representing happiness, and black, grief or mourning. Men wore soft deerskin aprons or loincloths in the summer and robes thrown over one shoulder and leggings in the winter. Women wore knee-length skirts in the summer, and in the winter covered their breasts and shoulders with animal pelt shawls and robes of turkey feathers. Women wore bands of wampum beads on their foreheads; and both men and women wore various types of jewelry made from stones, shells, and animal claws and teeth.

Babies were tied to cradleboards for their first year, and women carried them with straps attached to their foreheads. They were typically nursed for their first two years. As soon as they were able, children were given gender-distinguished tasks: boys were sent to fish and hunt, while girls were given tasks around the home or garden. Men hunted, fished, traded, and made tools and weapons. Women gardened, cooked, and were responsible for the care and moving of the household.

After a period of separation during the time of initial menstruation, girls wore special wampum and headdresses to indicate their readiness for marriage. Suitors indicated their interest with gifts of wampum. A year-long betrothal was marked by a feast but there was no special marriage ceremony. Divorce was by common consent and occurred rather frequently. Premarital sexual activity was not forbidden, but adultery (except by consent) was not permitted.

Early Interaction with Europeans (1524–1700)

When Giovanni da Verrazano's ship entered New York Harbor in 1524, the natives on the shore greeted the sailors warmly. A legend known to the Lenape relating this first encounter of coastal Algonquians on Manhattan Island with the Dutch gives a good sense of their suspicion toward Europeans and an awareness of the repercussions of the liquor the outsiders brought. According to the story, the Dutch arrived on a "large house" on which the Indian people believed *Kee-shay-lum-moo-kawng* (Our Creator) lived. Preparation was made to greet him. But as the "house" approached, they saw it was full of strangely dressed men, with faces of white color, and a leader in a red coat. They were afraid he was *Kee-shay-lum-moo-kawng* in disguise. When the Dutch came ashore, their leader passed around a glass of liquor, which the people at first refused, until one chief harangued them for their lack of respect for the Creator. He drank it and started staggering around, until he fell down on the ground as though dead. After a while he jumped up and declared his happiness. Soon the whole assembly was drunk.

The Dutch brought gifts and after a time asked for a piece of land no bigger than that which the skin of a bull would cover. But they cut the skin into a rope and extended it until it was a quite large piece of land. The Lenape were surprised at their deception but did not complain because they had more land than they needed. (The story was recorded by the Moravian missionary John Heckewelder in 1762. See Heckewelder 1876, 71–75, 77. It is reproduced in McCutchen 1993, 140–44; see also Weslager 1972, 104–6; Bierhorst 1995.)

During the rest of the sixteenth century, the Lenape traded with Portuguese and Spanish ships sailing along the Atlantic coast. Information about these contacts is quite sketchy, however.

In 1609 Henry Hudson, the Englishman hired by the Dutch East Company, began trading with Delaware people south of Staten Island. Early encounters were not all friendly, and Hudson continued up the river later named after him to establish relations with the Mahicans.

In 1624 the first Dutch colonists began to settle on Burlington Island in the Delaware River. Two years later, Fort Amsterdam was established on Manhattan Island. In an event romanticized by tradition and learned by every American school child, the island had been purchased by the Dutch for only a few dollars worth of trade goods. As noted above, in native tradition the right to use did not mean ownership. Those who "sold" the island did not accept the outrageous idea that by accepting such a token gift they had somehow given up their right to use the land.

The purpose of the Dutch settlements was to create centers for the growing fur trade. The Lenape hunters quickly depleted the beavers along the coast and were soon making extended inland hunts to trap beaver for the trade. The goods the Delaware traders received in exchange had a profound impact on their culture. For example, by the 1650s muskets were being received as payment for pelts and for land. Liquor was also popular. Cloth replaced skins in the making of skirts, coats, leggings, and shirts. Pumpkins, watermelons, pigs, and chickens were introduced from Europe into Lenape agriculture.

From Hudson's discovery of Delaware Bay in 1609 to the first Swedish settlements along the Delaware in 1638, the Dutch had trade along the river largely to themselves. By 1643, evidence suggests some activity of Lutheran pastors among the Delaware. They soon began compiling lists of Lenape words and translated Lutheran documents. Resentment against Swedes grew as they began to use their colonies among the Delaware to trade with the longtime enemy of the Lenape, the Minqua.

In the early 1640s tension between the Lenape and the Dutch (probably due to the different views of land tenure), as well as between the Lenape and other native nations, resulted in outbreaks of revenge killings. Although peace was negotiated in 1645, the friction continued into the 1660s. By 1663 Hotinonshonni raiding parties were roaming in Delaware lands, terrorizing settlers.

Dutch leaders thought they had purchased ownership of Manhattan Island with their token gifts, but the native peoples who hunted and fished on the island understood their acceptance of the gifts as a simple acknowledgment of the newcomers' right also to hunt and fish there. (© Bettmann/CORBIS)

In order to give the English authority over all land between New England and Virginia, in 1664, Charles II of England gave his brother the Duke of York (later King James II) a patent for land in America, including the Delaware Valley. The Duke sent forces up the Delaware River and took control over Dutch, Swedish, and Finnish settlers. The vagaries of European politics left the Delaware people confused. It made no sense to them that Dutch promises were now void, with the English in charge.

Despite this confusion with the Europeans' ways, Lenape leaders tried to explain to those entering their lands that they would not wage indiscriminate warfare. As one said:

> We are minded to live at Peace. If we intend at any time to make War upon you, we will let you know of it, and the Reasons why we make War with you, and if you make us satisfaction for the Injury done us, for which the War is intended, then we will not make War on you. (Wilson 1999, 54)

Lenape population steadily declined through the century, largely as a result of exposure to diseases introduced by Europeans. By the end of the seventeenth century, only about 3,200 Lenape, well below the peak population of 11,000–12,000, remained.

The First Migration:
To The Susquehanna River Valley in Pennsylvania (1700–42)

By 1700 the Lenape people were caught between the settlers spreading throughout the Middle Atlantic area and the Hotinonshonni Confederacy. Their 150-year odyssey of displacement and relocation began when the combined pressure of the Quakers and the Iroquois caused Delaware bands to move to central Pennsylvania along the Susquehanna River, about 100 to 150 miles from their Delaware River homeland. In 1709 a small group settled at a place they called Paxtang (within the present city of Harrisburg). The gradual migration continued for three decades.

From the outset William Penn, who had received a patent that covered most of the Delaware lands, determined to treat Indians as brothers deserving of love and respect. Most important, he understood the different conception of land tenure among Indians. Penn often paid a second time for lands already purchased by the Swedes and the Dutch, but, when he did, he made it clear that the conveyance was permanent. Of negotiations with the Lenape, Penn wrote, "Nothing of Moment is undertaken be it War, Peace, Selling of Land or Traffick, without advising with them; and which is more, with the Young Men too. 'Tis admirable to consider how Powerful the Kings are, and yet how they move by the Breath of their People" (Weslager 1972, 166).

The romanticization of Native Americans by Europeans is also evident during this period. A Delaware leader named Tamany became known as "King" Tamany among Europeans and was "canonized" as St. Tamany. The St. Tamany Hall was created in New York in 1798. It was dedicated to independence and liberty, with annual celebrations on 1 May. Later, the chief's name was transferred to the infamous New York political machine—Tammany Hall. Tamany was not recognized as "king" or "chief" by other Delaware bands, but the pressure of Europeans to install a central leader with whom they could negotiate was growing.

After Penn's death in 1718, the situation for the Delaware people began to deteriorate. Hunters had to travel ever greater distances to find game and thus stay away from villages longer. "Brother Onas" (the name used by the Lenape for all Pennsylvania officials after Penn's death) tried to make "King" Sassoonan the central Delaware leader. The reduced Lenape population began to be more concentrated, into just three areas: Tulpehocken, Brandywine, and the Forks.

The infamous Walking Purchase Deed was signed on 25 August 1737, essentially cheating the Delaware out of land in the Forks area. According to the deed, the boundary of purchased land was to be as far as a man could walk west into the woods in a day and a half. A path was cut in advance and three specially trained men were recruited. Crowds lined the route, cheering the walkers on. Two of the walkers died from the exertion, but one covered more than sixty miles, essentially all of the Delaware's land. Further deception was used in measuring the land so it became a triangle from the Delaware River to an apex at the end of the "walk." When the Lenape refused to leave, Pennsylvania officials called upon the Iroquois to move them. As the Lenape leader Teedyuscung said, "this very ground that is under me was my land and inheritance, and is taken from me by fraud" (Miller 1995, 85).

The growing domination of the Hotinonshonni nations over the Lenape people was graphically demonstrated in 1742, when the Iroquois proclaimed that the Delaware warriors were "women," a metaphor for their dependent status. The Iroquois made the Delaware men symbolically take up corn-pounders and wear women's "petticoats" and forbade them to go to war or sell land. In 1744 the Iroquois forced a number of the Lenape bands to relocate to the Susquehanna buffer zone. The Cayuga and Oneida nations were specifically designated as responsible for the subordination of the Delaware.

The Second Migration: To the Allegheny and Ohio Rivers (1742–59)

Soon, groups of young Lenape men followed the lead of the Shawnee, moving westward. On the Allegheny River they established a village known as Kittanning ("Place on the Big River"). More Delaware people soon followed, and some settled on the Ohio River at Logstown (eighteen miles south of the junction of Allegheny, Monongahela, and Ohio Rivers). They were still under the watchful eye of their Hotinonshonni overlords.

Evidence suggests that by this time the Lenape were organized into three distinct clan groupings (sometimes called phratries): Wolf (*tukwsit*), Turkey (*pele*); and Turtle (*pukuwango*). Each clan had a chief, with one of the three serving as spokesperson for the people as a whole. These clan groupings continue and are still important in the life of the Delaware. At the 1997 encounter in Bartlesville, Oklahoma, mentioned above, a Lenape elder spoke to the author with a glimmer in her eye about her search to find her clan-group identity. "I was always told I was Turtle," she said. "But I have recently learned I am Wolf. I always thought in my heart I was Wolf . . . not that there is anything wrong with being Turtle!"

By 1752 Shingas was named "King" of the Delaware people on the Ohio by the Iroquois with the assent of the English. Intent on restoring the reputation of his people and exacting revenge against the colonists, he became known to frontier families as "Shingas the Terrible" for the ruthless raids he conducted in alliance with the Shawnees. In response to a British offer of peace Shingas sent the following message:

> It is told us, that . . . the French and English intend to kill all the Indians, and then divide the land among themselves. . . . Look now, my brother, the white people think we have no brains in our heads; but that they are great

and big, and that makes them make war with us: we are but a little handful to what you are; but remember, . . . when you hunt for a rattlesnake, you cannot find it; and perhaps it will bite you before you see it. (Armstrong 1971, 20)

In the meantime, "King" Teedyuscung (see Wallace 1949), a Jersey Lenape, became (at the urging of Quakers) leader of the Susquehanna Delaware group. He had been baptized by the Moravians at the Gnadenhütten ("Tents of Grace") settlement near Bethlehem. At first Teedyuscung tried to remain neutral in the conflict between the French and English. Delaware warriors took matters into their own hands, however, and began attacking English farms in eastern Pennsylvania. Teedyuscung reluctantly joined the conflict and soon proved himself an effective strategist. According to tradition, the English general governor of North America responded by urging that the blankets given to Indians be infected with smallpox and that every possible method be used "to extirpate this execrable race" (Weslager 1978, 20).

By 1753 the French (who called the Lenape *Loups*, "wolves") were pressing south into Ohio, intent on linking French Canada with Louisiana. The same year George Washington was sent west to warn the French that they were treading on land claimed by Virginia (and the King of England). He met Shingas, whom he called "King of the Delawares." In 1754 the French established Fort Duquesne, and Washington was forced to surrender to them, before withdrawing.

On 9 July 1755 the French decisively defeated the General Edward Braddock's British force, which was pressing a campaign against Fort Duquesne. The Delaware war parties might have made a difference in the outcome of what turned into a rout of the British, but they remained neutral after Braddock showed disdain for them. On 24 November 1755 a group of Susquehanna Delaware warriors attacked the village of Gnadenhütten and murdered eleven unarmed Moravians.

In April 1756 Governor Robert Morris of Pennsylvania declared war on the Lenape. At first, he promised cash bounties for Lenape scalps, but he withdrew the offer after Quakers protested. On 8 September 1756 a group of armed Pennsylvanians under Colonel John Armstrong attacked the Lenape village at Kittanning. The intent was to liberate Euroamerican prisoners being held in the village, but they had been taken from the village before the battle. Many of the prisoners freely chose to remain with their captors.

The Delaware left behind in New Jersey had become the object of Presbyterian missionary activity. In 1745 David Brainerd came to New Jersey and began to attract a few converts among Lenape women. One Delaware man told Brainerd he was having little success because the Lenape people had far more vices since Christianity had been brought to them. In the view of many Lenape leaders, Brainerd spread more tuberculosis than Christianity. Brainerd did succeed in creating a Delaware community near Cranbury called Bethel. After his untimely death the Brotherton Reservation was created by his brother. This group joined the "Stockbridge Indians" near Oneida Lake in New York in 1802. In 1824 they moved to a tract near Green Bay, Wisconsin, where some of their descendants still reside and form one community in the Lenape diaspora.

Beaver replaced his brother Shingas as chief of the Ohio River Lenape. Beaver entered into a peace treaty with the British at Fort Pitt (which had been built on the site of Fort Duquesne when the French fled). At the same time Teedyuscung was negotiating with the British in eastern Pennsylvania. Other Delaware groups denounced him, however, claiming they had never selected him as chief. Pressured by settlers moving from Connecticut into the fertile land along the Susquehanna, most of the remaining Lenape joined the Ohio Delaware. A few moved north into Canada and settled on the Grand River (where their descendants still live).

The Third Migration: To Southeastern Ohio (1759–1800)

As the pressure increased from settlement west of the Alleghenies, the main body of the Lenape people once again relocated, this time into what is now southeastern Ohio. They took advantage of the willingness of the Wyandot nation to allow them to settle in lands the Wyandots had claimed. By 1759 a Delaware village had been established at the site of the present city of Cuyahoga Falls, Ohio. Other Delawares moved into small settlements at or near what is now Lancaster, Zanesville, Chillicothe, and Youngstown. By 1775 about 3,000 Delawares were living in eastern Ohio.

Dedicated Unity of Brethren (better known as Moravian) missionaries had followed the Delaware westward. Along the Susquehanna and Ohio Rivers they had created villages separate from other Delaware communities so that their Lenape converts could better observe the new way of living they had adopted. There the Moravians taught the new converts to practice monogamy, avoid alcohol, be obedient to their teachers, not contract debts, and treat Sunday as a day of rest. They required them to abstain from idolatry, witchcraft, "deceits of Satan," murder, lying, scolding, wearing traditional attire, idleness, and taking long hunting trips without informing the minister. They also insisted the converts attend daily services, honor their parents, erect fences on their property, and (in keeping with the Moravians' pacifism) refuse to go to war. They also taught the Lenape converts to read and write.

By 1772 the Moravians had arrived in Ohio and had begun to build villages on the Tuscarawas River. One of them was called Gnadenhütten, named after the community in Pennsylvania where Moravians had been killed by Delaware warriors seventeen years earlier.

At this stage, the Moravians were usually well received even by the Delaware people who did not convert. They were impressed by the general kindness of the missionaries, their willingness to learn the Lenape language, and their assistance in various everyday matters. Some Lenape leaders, however, considered the Moravians a danger to the people. Their pacifism was of particular concern to war captains. When traditional chiefs converted to Christianity, the issue of whether they should be allowed to stay in the General Council was raised. The council allowed them to keep their offices, stating that liberty was given the Christian religion, which the council advised the entire nation to adopt. A Moravian pastor was even allowed to sit on the Great Council as an adopted Munsee (although many traditionalists objected). This dominance of Christian Lenape leaders in the General Council of the main body of the Delaware continued through the years.

At the same time that many Delawares were embracing Christianity and the accompanying Euroamerican culture, others were seeking to purge themselves of these influences. In 1762 a spiritual leader named Neolin, often called simply the Delaware Prophet, began to preach a nativist message of return to the traditional ways. Under the influence of supernatural revelation, he prepared a fifteen inch square "map" which he carried as he preached. Neolin vigorously renounced European culture and proclaimed a return to a way of life before Europeans arrived. The way to that restoration, he preached, was rejection of European trade. He wept as he spoke of the "Path," a direct route to a better, heavenly land. The people, the Prophet proclaimed, must rid themselves of domestic animals and adhere to special rituals revealed to him (Spicer 1969, 251–52; see chapter 1).

Quoting the Prophet, a Moravian missionary recorded the following message Neolin claimed to have received for the people:

> Hear what the Great Spirit has ordered me to tell you! . . . put off entirely from yourselves the customs which you have adopted since the white people came among us; you are to return to that former happy state, in which we live in peace and plenty, before these strangers came to disturb us . . . . (Mooney 1896, 666–67)

He called for Indians to "drive from your lands those dogs in red clothing [the British]; they are only an injury to you" (Wilson 1999, 126).

The Prophet's call to arms was heard by Pontiac and other warriors, who in 1763 united Algonquian nations in an effort to drive out the British (see chapter 1). Many Lenape warriors joined Pontiac because the promises made to them—that there would be no settlement west of the Susquehanna, then west of the Alleghenies,—had not been kept. "Pontiac's War," as it was called by the British, failed, and the Lenape people were forced in 1765 to renounce all land rights and accept the influx of Euroamericans.

A split occurred among the Lenape during the Revolutionary War. The Continental Congress tried to influence the Delaware people to remain neutral. In 1775 a treaty was signed in Pittsburgh in which the Lenape signatories pledged their neutrality in exchange for a commitment that the Ohio River would be the permanent western border for Euroamericans. Some Lenape leaders, however, including Hopokam (known to the British as Captain Pipe) sided with the British as did their hosts, the Wyandots. They moved to northwestern Ohio. Those who sided with the colonists were concentrated near Pittsburgh. Others who favored the American cause left for Indiana, responding to an invitation from the Miami nation, and settled near the White River. More Lenape people came to this area after the Treaty of Greenville in 1795.

On 17 September 1778 the Continental Congress ratified a treaty entered into with the Delaware and signed by the leaders White Eyes, Captain John Killbuck Jr. (Gelelemend), and Captain Pipe. It is often described as the first treaty made by the United States with a Native American nation. In the treaty the Delaware agreed to allow the Americans safe passage through their territory in Ohio so that they could attack the English fort at Detroit. The Americans agreed to erect a fort to protect the Delaware against retaliation from the English and their native allies. Article VI of the treaty included the following endorsement of the the concept of working toward an American Indian state, headed by the Delaware, as part of the planned United States:

> And it is further agreed on between the contracting parties should it for the future be found conducive for the mutual interest of both parties to invite any other tribes who have been friends to the interest of the United States, to join the present Confederation, and to form a state whereof the Delaware nation shall be the head, and have a representative in Congress. (cited in Venables 1992)

A U.S. army officer present during the negotiations called the treaty conference "improper" and "villainous" because the Delaware negotiators were given liquor, and the terms of the treaty were misrepresented to them. Two months later, White Eyes, who had been commissioned as an officer in the U.S. Army, was murdered while serving as a guide for an American force. In addition, the material assistance promised to the Delaware by the Continental Congress failed to come. Captain Pipe, whose sympathies had long been with the English, seized the opportunity and convinced the Lenape General Council to switch their allegiance to the British. He led war parties against Americans on the frontier.

In retaliation, a group of settlers from Pennsylvania raided the Moravian village of Gnadenhütten, Ohio, in March 1782. Ninety Moravian Indians (fifty-six adults and thirty-four children) were killed, although, as pacifists, they had not been involved in the fighting. A Delaware chief responded to the massacre in these words:

> And yet these white men would be always telling us of their great Book which God had given them. They would persuade us that every man was bad who did not believe in it. They told us a great many things which they said were written in the Book; and wanted us to believe it. We would likely have done so, if we had seen them practice what they pretended to believe—and acted according to the good words which they told us. But no! While they held the big Book in one hand, in the other they held mur-derous weapons—guns and swords—wherewith to kill us poor Indians. Ah! And they did too. They killed those who believed in their Book as well as those who did not. They made no distinctions. (Armstrong 1971, 33)

In 1783 Delaware leaders met with representatives of thirty-five other native nations to form a confederacy against invaders of the lands on which they were living. Two years later the Delaware and Wyandot nations effectively withdrew from the confederacy and signed the Fort McIntosh Treaty which opened settle-ment west of the Ohio River but which guaranteed these two peoples protected lands in Ohio Territory. The leader of the confederacy, the Mohawk Joseph Brant, ridiculed the Lenape by holding a ceremony in which he invited them to remove their petticoats, reminding them of their earlier humiliation. Settlers entered these areas, however, and the Delaware responded with raiding parties. Delaware warriors were among the alliance soundly defeated in 1794 by General "Mad Anthony" Wayne at the Battle of Fallen Timbers in Indiana.

In the midst of the turmoil, in 1789, a group of Lenape people moved to land near Cape Girardeau in southeastern Missouri that had been offered to them by the Spanish governor. In 1792 a group of Moravian Delawares moved to Canada, where they settled on a river now known as the Thames, thirty miles from an existing Munsee settlement.

On 3 August 1795 the Lenape joined with eleven other native nations in sign-ing the Treaty of Greenville (Ohio). The Delaware and the other nations agreed to end hostilities against the settlers, give up prisoners taken, accept the protection of the United States, and leave their residences in eastern Ohio (although they could still hunt there). In exchange, the treaty gave these nations the right to occupy land between the Cuyahoga and Mississippi Rivers (including western Ohio and all of what is now Illinois and Indiana). Importantly, this treaty clearly recognized the Lenape and the other signatories as sovereign, foreign nations. The United States also promised to deliver goods worth $9,500 each year "forever after" to these nations (for the Delaware a share of $1,000 for about 2,000 people). In an effort to encourage the Indians to take up European-style farming, the government offered to pay annuities with domestic animals and farm implements.

The Fourth Migration: To Indiana (1800–1820)

By 1801 Delawares were well established in a series of nine or ten villages along a forty-mile stretch of the West Fork of the White River, between what are currently Muncie and Indianapolis. They included Munsee Town (within what is now the city of Muncie) and Wapenminskink ("Chestnut tree place"), home of William Anderson of the Turkey group, now known as Anderson, Indiana. Each of these towns had council houses where the important Big House ceremonies were conducted (see below).

At the invitation of the council, a small group of Moravian Delaware moved to Indiana in 1801, along with their missionary pastors. The main body of the Lenape in Indiana were openly hostile to the Moravians and other Christian missionaries, though. The memory of the Gnadenhütten massacre was still vivid, and the attitude that the Moravians had pacified the Lenape so they could be killed was prevalent. The traditionalist leader Buckongahelas warned the Lenape not to forsake their ancient customs and never to trust Euroamericans. Many of the people adopted bark huts as a sign of their commitment to return to the traditions of the past. A number of Moravian Delawares gave up Christianity, and the Moravian pastors closed the mission and left in 1806.

This reaction may have been in part a result of increasing efforts to entice the Delaware into European-style farming with fenced fields. To help implement this policy of assimilation an Indian Agency was established at Fort Wayne for the Delaware, Miami, and other relocated nations.

Most Delaware did not adjust well to their new home. Alcoholism was rampant, and food and other essentials were constantly in short supply. Once again they were in effect, living as guests of another native nation. Moreover, Euroamericans were still pressing westward. In 1802 Lenape and other Native American leaders went to see President Thomas Jefferson to complain about the encroaching settlers. Jefferson, who by this time had given up his dream of settlers and Indians living and farming side by side, now favored (after the Louisiana Purchase of 1803) the removal of the Indians to a land further west where they could live as they chose.

The Fort Wayne Treaty of 1803 ceded some of the land in Indiana Territory for settlement. More treaties followed, which shrank the land available for the Delaware people. By 1805 the territorial governor, General (later President) William Henry Harrison, had succeeded in arranging cession of more than 56 million acres. The Miami were angry with the Delaware because Delaware leaders had signed an 1804 cession without Miami permission. More deeply frustrated than ever, some young Lenape began to talk about going west to hunt buffalo.

The situation stabilized somewhat in 1809 when the Miami signed a treaty recognizing the rights of the Lenape to land on the White River. Yet another perpetual $500 annuity was promised to the Delaware under this treaty.

Nevertheless, traditionalist sentiments continued to grow. One chief sarcastically responded to the missionary teaching that the Lenape people must give up their traditional ways and adopt Christianity in order to avoid going to hell by saying that there were no Indians in hell, only whites. Floods on the White River were interpreted by Delaware shamans as warnings against living like the Euroamerican settlers.

When the Shawnee Prophet Tenskwatawa, brother of the famed leader Tecumseh, preached in White River towns, his message of rejection of white ways and a return to tradition was enthusiastically embraced by many traditionalists. The Delaware council, however, voted not to support Tecumseh's effort to mount a military campaign against the settlers and the government. Chief William Anderson, himself a traditionalist, convinced the council that armed resistance was futile and would be disastrous for the Delaware people. No authorized Delaware warriors were among the force that attacked General Harrison's troops at the ill-fated battle at Tippecanoe on 7 November 1811. Undoubtedly, however, some renegade Lenape warriors joined the coalition.

Meanwhile, the Delaware continued to receive allotments of $1,600 to $1,800 worth of goods as part of their annuity payment, including powder, lead, gun flints, calico and linen, brass kettles, blankets, knives, thread, vermilion face paint, scissors, rifles, and one-square-yard cotton shawls. These items had become virtually essential to their culture, but they were completely dependent on the government and traders for them. Cash payments of the annuities came later.

When the War of 1812 broke out, the Miami and other nations sided with the British, while the Delaware were among the nations that sought neutrality. At General Harrison's urging, the Delaware group moved a hundred miles from their White River villages to Piqua so that they could be protected by U.S. forces. The agent at Piqua, James Johnston, completed a questionnaire prepared by Lewis Cass, governor of Michigan Territory, which provides information on Lenape culture during this period (Weslager 1978). Captain Ketchum was one of several leaders commissioned in the American army to lead Delaware and other Indian volunteers during the war. When the war ended, the Delaware returned to their White River villages.

With their Indiana land increasingly infiltrated by settlers, the time had come for the Delaware to continue their westward trek. On 3 October 1818, the Treaty of St. Mary's (Ohio) was signed. The Lenape gave up occupancy rights in Indiana. In exchange, the government agreed to supply lands of equal worth west of the Mississippi River. The treaty made a lump sum payment of $13,300 and added another $4,000 in annuities for improvements made by the Delaware to the lands on the White. The treaty gave the Lenape three years to prepare for removal. According to the treaty, the government would arrange for the move and provide a blacksmith at their new home. The reluctant signers included Captain Ketchum, who would play a significant leadership role later. The granting of private annuities to the leaders who signed, although kept secret at the time, has since been confirmed. Probably about 2,000 people were in the main body of Delaware at this point, a total of about 1,200 Lenape in the three Canadian groups, less than 100 among the Stockbridge Indians, about the same number still in Ohio, and the small group in Missouri.

The Fifth Migration: To Southwestern Missouri (1820–29)

In the summer of 1820, records show, 1,346 Delaware from Indiana and their 1,499 horses were taken across the Mississippi River by ferry boat at Kaskaskia, Illinois. One group, led by Chief Anderson, camped along the Current River in southern Missouri and planted corn, but the crop was killed by an early frost. A large number were still on the Current in the summer of 1822. Another group was delayed and had to spend the winter of 1820–21 near Vincennes, Indiana. Both groups were short of food to the point that a number starved.

The separate groups converged on the James River, a tributary of the White River in southwestern Missouri. They were joined there by emigrees from the Cape Girardeau group, responding to an invitation from Chief Anderson to join the main body. Territorial Governor William Clark (one of the co leaders of the Lewis and Clark expedition) assigned them to a seventy by forty-four mile tract in southern Missouri Territory. The main settlement, Delaware Village, was on James Fork near Wilson's Creek, about ten miles south of the present city of Springfield, Missouri.

Game was not plentiful, and by 1824 the Lenape were in desperate conditions. Although the Osage nation had ceded this land in an 1808 treaty, they still hunted in the area. Lenape hunters had to go west to the plains and prairies where buffalo passed. There they encountered Pawnee warriors who attacked them. The Lenape also engaged in conflict with the Miami, who had also been relocated in Missouri.

The Sixth Migration: To Eastern Kansas (1829–67)

On 24 September 1829 Lenape leaders agreed to a treaty cancelling their rights to lands on the James Fork and allocating to them land at the junction of the Kansas and Missouri Rivers in what was to become the state of Kansas. The designed land included the area known as the "Outlet," a ten-mile-wide, 150-mile-long strip reserved as passageway to buffalo hunting grounds. Chief Anderson hoped that his dream of reuniting all the scattered Lenape groups in one area could be achieved.

The United States pledged in the 1829 treaty "the faith of the government to guarantee to the said Delaware Nation forever, the quiet and peaceable possession and undisturbed enjoyment of the same against the claims and assaults of every other people whatsoever" (Weslager 1972, 169). The government also pledged farm implements, one year's provisions after the Delaware arrived, and a gristmill and sawmill within two years. Another annuity of $1,000 was added to others already paid. The amount realized from sale of the best Lenape land in Missouri was to be applied to the support of new schools to educate Delaware children.

The Delaware leaders would not sign the treaty until a group had been sent to examine the lands. They reported that it was a good land on which the people could productively live. Isaac McCoy, a Baptist minister who had worked among Lenapes in Indiana, surveyed the lands and found nearly 2 million acres (924,160 in the reserve and the rest in the outlet).

The Kansas land was good for agriculture and cattle raising and many of the Delaware made a commitment to establish European-style farms. They were unwilling to, however, give up their tradition of holding land in common. By 1834 about 1,000 Delawares were living in Kansas. When Euroamericans began to move through the Delaware lands, Delaware men were hired as guides across the plains and through the mountain passes. In 1832 the author Washington Irving, on a visit to the Great Plains, made the following observation in his journal about the Lenape people he met:

> The bravest and finest race is the Delaware. They are called the
> [grand]fathers—all the others give them preference. . . . They are clean,
> neat, civil, generously obliging, light hearted, gay, fearless—go to the
> Rocky Mountains in bands of 20 men—have frequent skirmishes.
> Excellent hunters—when they go out to kill a deer, you may be sure of
> their succeeding. (cited in McCutchen 1993, 166–67)

The government did make good on its promise of providing a blacksmith for the Lenape in Kansas. From 1845 until 1858, Isaac Mundy, a migrant from Virginia (and great-great-grandfather of the author), served as a blacksmith and paymaster among the Lenape. When he died in a hunting accident, Mundy's wife, children, and several slaves they had brought with them from Virginia were cared for by the Lenape. When it became unsafe for slaveholders to remain in Kansas territory, their Lenape friends assisted the Mundy family in crossing over the Missouri River to Weston, Missouri.

At the mouth of the Kansas River where it joined the Missouri, on the north bank, was a Wyandot settlement on land purchased from the Delaware. Just as the Wyandot had allowed the Delaware to live on their land in Ohio, the Lenape reciprocated by playing host to them.

By 1859 the annuities, now paid in cash, amounted to $83 for each of 941 men, women, and children. When the annuities were paid near "Delaware Crossing," on the banks of the Kansas River, traders set up stands of all types to take advantage of the sudden influx of cash. A house built by the trader Moses Grinter in the 1850s at Delaware Crossing still stands and has been renovated as a Kansas historic site.

A Baptist Mission had been opened near Delaware Crossing and a Methodist Mission was located several miles north. The White Church, as the Methodist mission eventually became known, still stands as a functioning congregation (now of the Christian Church, Disciples of Christ). It is the site of a recently refurbished and rededicated Delaware cemetery where Captain Ketchum (who served as principal chief for eight years until he was replaced by John Conner) and other prominent Lenape leaders (as well as their Euroamerican blacksmith Isaac Mundy) are buried.

In 1833 five whites and twenty-seven Indians were listed as members of the Methodist Church. By 1844 the Methodists had 108 Delaware converts, among them Charles and James Ketchum, both ministers. As they had for more than a century, the Moravians also had a mission among the Delaware. In assessing the work of Christian missionaries among the Lenape, a contemporary Lenape leader has said, "This is a difficult matter to discuss because in one way they were attempting to bring a good belief to the Lenape, but by trying to make it be the only belief, and by strict rules forbidding many activities that were our native ways, a lot of harm was done" (Zunigha 1997).

After the creation of the Territory of Kansas in 1854, the process of the taking of Delaware lands began anew. To assist in the extinguishing of Lenape land rights, the Delaware Agency was established in 1855. Yet again a once secure, relatively isolated area in which the Lenape were living peacefully had become a destination for white settlers. The controversy over whether slavery should be allowed in Kansas and the warfare arising from this issue also impacted the Delaware nation. Perturbed that so much good land was set aside for so few Indians, settlers began moving in, and Delaware horses and the trees on the land were considered free for the taking.

An 1854 treaty created a "diminished reserve" for the Delaware. About 558,000 acres were sold for more than $1 million, and that amount was put into a "national fund" for the Delaware. The Kansas outlet was the next to go, with the government paying only $10,000 for land the Claims Commission a century later said had an 1850s value of $617,980. In 1860 the government agreed to pay the Delaware nation $30,000 for timber and $9,500 for ponies and cattle taken from their land.

Since the Delaware people were not American citizens, they did not have recourse to the courts. These treaties were secured with the continued practice of secret payments to the chiefs who signed them (including the revered Captain

Ketchum). Unfortunately, much of the money paid to the Delaware in these agreements was dispersed to families instead of going into the national fund and was quickly spent.

In 1858 the Delaware council wrote to President Buchanan asking for apportionment of the diminished reserve since many Delawares has ceased hunting and were adopting the "manners and customs of our White Brothers." By 1860 the council was also discussing whether to move to the Rockies, the Far West, or the Southwest. As part of this process, a delegation went to inspect lands among the Cherokees and Choctaws in Indian Territory.

In a May 1860 treaty the government agreed to the request to allot the reserve to members of the nation—eighty acres per person. Further treaties in 1860 and 1861 permitted the sale of surplus Delaware lands to the several railroads building lines in the area. Many Lenape complained to President Lincoln that the 1860 treaty was signed with chiefs who had purposefully been made drunk and who were given various incentives to sign. Despite anger at the treaty process, 170 out of 201 eligible Delaware males from Kansas volunteered for service in the Union Army. (Reflecting the divided loyalties in the region, some Lenape men elected to serve with the Confederacy.) Estimates of the Delaware population in Kansas in 1866 range up to 1,200.

During their stay in Kansas, traditional Delaware people were still gathering for Big House ceremonies. One was located six miles east of Lawrence. In contrast, prominent families such as the Journeycakes (who were Baptists) were outspoken assimilationists who urged that the old ceremonies be abandoned. In the middle were families like the Ketchums, Youngs, and Adamses, most of whom were Christian converts who still advocated respect for tradition and may have taken part in Big House ceremonies.

Lenapes who had gone to Texas from southeastern Missouri, instead of joining the main body in Kansas, allied with the Texans against the Comanches and in 1854 were given a reservation (with Shawnees and Wichitas) along the Brazos River. They gave up farming and took up buffalo hunting. In 1859 most were relocated again to the Washita River where they joined other Delawares already in Indian Territory.

The Seventh Migration: To Indian Territory (1867–?)

In the winter of 1865–66 chiefs of native nations in Kansas were summoned to Washington to convince them to sell their homes and move to Indian Territory or further west. Under the terms of a treaty finalized on 4 July 1866, the Delaware were allowed to select a tract of land in Indian Territory equal to 160 acres for every man, woman, and child who moved from Kansas. For the land they would pay the price the government had to pay Indians from whom this land was taken, with money to come from the sale of the "diminished reserve." The government also agreed to reimburse the Delaware in cash for land sold to railroads. The monies were to be put into the Delaware national fund, with annuities paid twice yearly from the interest. The 1866 treaty also allowed Delawares to leave tribal membership and become U.S. citizens if they wanted to remain in Kansas. A small number of assimilationists did.

After Delaware leaders had selected Cherokee land in northeastern Indian Territory, the government instructed the Delaware and Cherokee to work out an agreement, under which the Delaware could choose to give up their own independent government and affiliate with the Cherokees. According to a Lenape legend, the Delaware had long ago dominated the Cherokees and also had aided them when they were besieged by the Osage (Adams 1905, 72–75). A Delaware/Cherokee agreement was reached on 8 April 1867. Although the U.S. government was not a party to the treaty, government agents pressured Lenape men to sign. The Cherokees agreed to sell the Lenape people land equal to 160 acres for each of the 985 enrolled members. (An epidemic which struck the Delaware in Kansas, shortly before the migration, had reduced the population.) The agreed-on price was $1 per acre for 157,600 acres (within a thirty-by-ten-mile-area along the Caney River). By payment of $123 for each enrolled Delaware, those covered by the agreement became full members of the Cherokee nation. Children of these Delawares were to be regarded as native Cherokees.

The Lenape understood that this agreement meant that although they were purchasing the right to be considered Cherokee citizens for the sake of the privileges associated with citizenship, they were not relinquishing their national sovereignty and identity. They never intended that their action be interpreted as a dissolution of the Delaware Nation.

This seventh Lenape migration began in December 1867 and continued through the summer of 1868, with each family traveling at its own expense. It was completed in 1869. For most of the elderly among the immigrants, it was the fourth relocation they had personally experienced.

Traditionalists and assimilationists chose different areas in which to live. The Christian Delawares settled in what are now Nowata, Rogers, and Craig Counties. More traditional Lenape people stayed among the Peoria people east of Neosho, Missouri, for a few years, then relocated in 1873, mostly in the present Washington County. There they built a Big House and continued a traditional Lenape ritual life well into the twentieth century (see below). Traditionalists typically opposed the assimilation into the Cherokee nation and the giving up of the traditional chiefs. They continued to recognize Delaware chiefs and war captains for ceremonial purposes and the authority of shamans like Delaware Charley (*Chah-la-wees*), a mystic who conversed with the spirits of the departed and was called on to perform the traditional naming ceremonies.

Assimilationists, in contrast, accepted the new political arrangement, and soon Delawares were serving on the Cherokee national council. Both Baptist and Methodist Delawares actively opposed the Big House ceremony, denouncing it as just the sort of paganism the people must reject if they were to be successful in their new situation.

The adjustment was not easy. Money from the sale of the Kansas land was delayed, leaving many in dire straits, forced to live in squalid log cabins. Militant Cherokees and Osages (whose reservation was located to the west of Delaware land) harassed their new neighbors, but innovative resolutions to the conflicts were found. According to one story, after a Delaware man had been killed by Osages, leaders of both peoples agreed to hold an annual "smoke" so that they could interact socially rather than fighting. This event and the gatherings for the payment of annuities were the precursors to the tribal and intertribal powwows that continue today.

In 1867 a small tract of land was set aside in southwestern Oklahoma, next to the larger Kiowa, Kiowa Apache, and Comanche Agencies, for the Caddos, Wichitas, and Delawares, who had been associated in Texas at the ill-fated reservation on the Brazos River. In 1876 only eighty-six Lenapes were listed among this group. After 1878 these Delawares agreed to merge with the Caddos and sacrifice their political identity. These two groups of tribes were administered as the Kiowa-Comanche agency headquartered in Anadarko. As a result, the Lenape in Indian Territory were divided between the Registered (or Cherokee) Delawares in what was to become northeastern Oklahoma and the Western (or Absentee) Delawares in Caddo County, on the reservation shared with the Wichitas and Caddos. They also are known as the Delaware Tribe of Western Oklahoma, while the Lenape of northeastern Oklahoma are called the Delaware Tribe of Indians. Cultural and other exchanges between the two groups continue to the present.

In 1875 Jacob Bartles, who had come to Indian Territory from New Jersey and had married the daughter of Delaware leader Charles Journeycake, built a mill on the Caney River, which later developed into the village of Bartlesville. In 1876 a $27 annuity was being paid semiannually to each of the 786 registered Delawares in northeastern Indian Territory. The Lenape were actively protesting, however, that monies realized from the sale of the Kansas lands were being withheld.

Angered by the low annuities, many Delawares demanded that all the money held by the government be dispersed to enrolled members. The government agreed and in 1891 paid $508 to each of 836 Delawares. Two years later another disbursement of $527 was made. Thereafter, according to the government, no money was left in the Delaware national fund.

In the meantime, relations between the Delaware and Cherokee were growing sour. In 1883 the Cherokee leadership denied the right of Lenapes to share in proceeds from the sales of cattle leases and grasslands west of the Arkansas River.

Journeycake, Baptist minister and chief as far as assimilationist Delawares were concerned, was hired to recover money owed to the Delaware. In 1886 Journeycake, reflecting his Lenape pride and his Christian convictions, spoke of the Lenape situation in these words:

> We have been broken up and moved six times. We have been despoiled of our property. We thought when we moved across the Missouri River and had paid for our homes in Kansas we were safe. But in a few years the white man wanted our country. We had good farms. Built comfortable houses and big barns. We had schools for our children and churches where we listened to the same gospel the white man listens to. The white man came into our country from Missouri. And drove our cattle and horses away and if our people followed them they were killed. We try to forget these things. But we would not forget that the white man brought us the blessed gospel of Christ. The Christian hope. This more than pays for all we have suffered. (Armstrong 1971, 127–28)

In the light of statements such as this, traditionalists considered Journeycake a fully assimilated preacher who had no interest in preserving Lenape culture. They looked upon Charles Elkhair (*Kaw-wul-lup-poo-x-way*, "One who walks backward") as their chief, for he led the Big House ceremonies. In 1895 the first Delaware Business Committee (in effect replacing Chief Journeycake) was selected.

On 19 November 1894 the United States Supreme Court decreed that under the 1867 agreement the Delaware were entitled to equal rights with all other Cherokee citizens. This, however, did not resolve the dispute. Soon there was controversy over oil, gas, and coal rights, as Cherokees and Euroamericans acquired mineral leases on Delaware lands. This time the federal Court of Claims ruled against the Delaware, saying that they did not have perpetual title to the land. The ruling was upheld by the Supreme Court in 1904.

In the meantime settlers were pouring into Indian Territory in anticipation that they would soon be allowed to homestead on unoccupied Indian lands. In 1902 the Cherokee voted to accept land allotments under the provisions established by the Dawes Commission and dissolve the Cherokee government. Under the provisions of the Dawes Allotment Act, Delawares on the 1867 list were to receive 160 acres each, and their descendants were to be treated as any other Cherokee citizens. As it turned out, an allotment of only 110 acres was made, and 157,600 acres which the Delaware believed they owned were released. Some Delawares sold their allotments to Euroamerican settlers and spent the money. Others wisely held their allotments, and their descendants continue to live on them today. In an attempt to wipe the slate clean, an additional $415,000 was awarded in 1904 to the Lenape people to settle any outstanding claims.

In 1907 renowned ethnologist James Mooney accepted an assignment to research and publish a bulletin on the Delaware for the Bureau of American Ethnology. After an extensive search, he estimated the Delaware population at about 1900. In 1907, when Oklahoma became a state, the Delaware living in Oklahoma became citizens of the United States and were, theoretically, to be treated as individuals, like any other citizens. Nevertheless, a Delaware Business Committee for the Eastern Delaware continued to function through modern times to conduct the affairs of the tribe.

The Stockbridge-Munsee Community of Wisconsin was recognized by the Department of the Interior as an official tribe under the provisions of the Reorganization Act of 1934. In the early 1970s there were about 1,400 registered members, but the number of Munsee Lenapes in the tribe was impossible to determine. They had become a fully assimilated community; most of the families attended Presbyterian or Lutheran churches.

In the 1970s there were 60–70 individuals with identifiable Munsee ancestry, descended from among those who settled with a band of Chippewas near Ottawa, Kansas, in 1836. They had been absorbed into the general population (Weslager 1972, 16–17).

In the early 1970s there were about 250 registered Delawares among the 5,300 Indians on the Six Nations Reserve in Ontario. These Lenape are descendants of a group who had taken refuge among the Cayuga. The last fluent Delaware speaker died in 1956, and the last of the traditionalists died in 1969, lamenting that "the younger generations couldn't care less" (Weslager 1972, 17–20).

During this period 300 Delawares were living 125 miles west of the Six Nations Reserve on a reserve called Moraviantown on the Thames River in Kent County, Ontario. Thirty miles up the Thames, near Melbourne, about 100 Munsies were living on another reserve. These are the groups Mooney identified in 1907 as the "Moravians on the Thames" and the "Munsies of the Thames" (Weslager 1972, 20–24).

When the Indians Claims Commission was created after World War II to resolve outstanding land claims of native nations, petitions were filed on behalf of the 6,446 Delawares descended from those on the 1867 roll in northeastern Oklahoma and the 1,480 who had ancestors in the Anadarko group. In 1963 $1.6 million was awarded for land ceded in Indiana under the terms of 1818 treaty and $1.4 million for lands sold in Kansas under the 1854 treaty. By 1969 these amounts were raised to $9 million to reflect the interest which would have accrued. That same year $458,000 was awarded for the Delaware Outlet in Kansas. In 1971 another $1.5 million was awarded for the Indiana lands. By 1978 more than $14 million had been awarded to the Oklahoma Lenape, with cases still pending. Checks for $1,339.59 were mailed to each of the 9,608 approved as eligible descendants of the registrants in 1867. Ten percent of the funds were reserved for use by the nation as a whole.

In 1979, during the period in which "termination" was a guiding principle in U.S. Indian policy, federal recognition of the Delaware Tribe of Oklahoma was withdrawn by the stroke of a bureaucrat's pen, at the request of the Cherokee Nation of Oklahoma. The issue was control over millions of dollars still due the Delaware. Almost immediately legal action was initiated to challenge this arbitrary ruling. This chapter returns to this issue and to the situation of the Delaware at the end twentieth century after an overview of the traditional spirituality of the Lenape people.

Traditional Lenape Spirituality

From the seventeenth into the nineteenth centuries there was remarkable continuity in the ritual life of traditional Lenapes. Nevertheless, the impact of Christian missionaries, who had been active among the Lenape since first contact, and the incredible pressure to assimilate to Euroamerican ways, led ultimately to the decline and ultimately the virtual disappearance of traditional Lenape spirituality. Among the nations studied in this work, contemporary Lenape people have the least contact with the spiritual beliefs and rituals of the past. Today, however, a commitment among Delaware people to revive the spirit of their traditions, if not the ceremonies themselves, is growing.

Ethnologists M.R. Harrington and Frank G. Speck are responsible for reporting most of what is known to outsiders of traditional Delaware spirituality. Harrington visited Oklahoma and Canadian Lenapes between 1907 and 1910. The Canadian Delawares had already given up the traditional rituals as a result of their conversion to Christianity, but Harrington was able to gather information about the Big House ceremony and other rituals in Oklahoma. Speck worked among the two groups of Delawares between 1928 and 1938. Both came to believe that at the heart of traditional Lenape spirituality was a belief in dreams and visions and personal guardian spirits (Weslager 1972, 67–68).

Cosmology

Traditional Delaware cosmology recognizes twelve heavens, each presided over by the Creator. "Our Creator" dwells in the highest of the heavens (Weslager 1978, 113). The intricate Lenape cosmology is discussed below in the context of the Big House ritual.

Gods and Spirits

In the traditional Lenape pantheon, the supreme god is *Kee-shay-lum-moo-kawng* ("Our Creator"). Our Creator "is everything and everything is God." The subordinate spirits are called *manetuwak*, the plural of *manitou*, often written simply as "manitous." Our Creator is sometimes also addressed as Great *Manitou* (Spirit).

Nature is addressed with kinship terms, such as Our Mother Earth and Our Old Brother the Sun. According to a Delaware informant in 1822 (Weslager 1978, 109), the Sun is a deity who causes the vegetation to grow when the Sun returns under the ground to the east each night. The Moon is a deity equal in rank with the sun who regulates the night and divides the year. This informant explained that twelve subordinate deities are placed in different ranks, with the lowest on earth among the people but invisible. This deity reports to the next highest deity, and so forth, until the word reaches the Creator. This is why petitioners repeat a prayer twelve times (Weslager 1978, 113).

Thunderers are winged men who protect the world from the Great Horned Serpent, a powerful though not entirely evil spirit (in contrast to the Christian Devil). In the woods live the benevolent but mischievous Little People.

Mesingw, the Mask Being, is guardian spirit of all game animals such as deer and bear. He helps the Lenape have success in hunting. He sometimes appears riding on the back of a deer. Mesingw's face, half red and half black, was carved on the center pole of the Big House. His face also appears on the modern seal of the Delaware Tribe of Indians. Mesingw appeared at Big House ceremonies in the form of a man wearing a bearskin costume and a large, oval, wooden mask. When the Big House ritual was being observed, he functioned as as a disciplinarian. Because of his frightful appearance, the mere mention of Mesingw by a traditional Lenape parent is enough to correct a child behaving badly.

Some spirits are more powerful than others; in some good dominates, in others evil. The emphasis is on human frailty, for "without guidance from the Great Manito and the other Spirit Forces life [is] futile" (Weslager 1972, 66).

Although Europeans sometimes called Delawares devil worshippers, the concept of a devil or Satan was actually introduced to them by Christian missionaries. A Moravian missionary in the late eighteenth century reported that "they seem to have had no idea of the devil until in modern times preachers arose among them who proclaimed that there was such a being, having secured their knowledge from the whites" (Weslager 1978, 113).

Healers

In traditional Lenape society, healing practitioners "are the media through which the Creator sends his healing power" (Tantaquidgeon 1972, 12); they may be either men or women. Curers are one of two types: One is an herbalist who prescribes herbal medicines. Another, called "powerful one," functions more as a shaman, empowered by supernatural powers to call upon spirits to mediate in a situation of distress. Sometimes these healers were called "sweat doctors" because of their practice of calling spirits during rituals in the small Lenape sweat lodges.

Herbal healers are consulted not just for cures of sickness but also to assist in family problems or to win the favor of a lover. Those with supernatural powers might be called upon to locate a lost person or object, to communicate with the dead, or to foretell coming events.

When an herbalist is called upon to cure someone, the request is initiated with a tobacco offering. The healer then seeks an appropriate plant. When found, another tobacco offering is made to the spirit of the plant before it is taken for use in the healing. Here is an example of a medicine-gathering prayer:

> Grandfather, I come now for medical treatment. Your grandson needs your aid. He is giving you an offering here of tobacco. He implores you that he will get well because, he, your child, is pitiful. And I myself earnestly pray that you take pity on him the sick one. . . . For with you alone rests the spiritual power sufficient to bless anyone with. . . . (Tantaquidgeon 1972, 13).

Medicine Bundles

As in other Native American nations, traditional Lenape might carry their own "medicine bundles," in which are found charms of particular potency for that individual. The items are assembled in accord with instructions given by one's guardian spirit. For example, a boy dreamed of a horned toad, and knowing that the toad was to be his guardian spirit he ritually obtained a horn from a toad for his medicine bundle. The items in the bundle may include pieces of root, feathers, bird claws, pieces of bone or horn, an animal's tooth, or a magic stone. The medicine stone is a particularly cherished item, known in Lenape as an "emergency gift." It might be rubbed on a snake bite or a war wound and is known to have healed wounds deemed fatal. An elder might choose to bestow his or her medicine bundle on a younger person, but only if the youth has shown spiritual and physical purity (Tantaquidgeon 1972, 24–27).

Tobacco

From the earliest recorded times, tobacco has been used ceremonially among the Lenape.

The blend of powdered leaves may be used in divination, in curing diseases, in treaty councils, and in social gatherings. Pinches of dried tobacco are also thrown into fires during ceremonies and are offered to trees when they are cut down as an offering to the spirits of the tree.

Clippings from cedar leaves are also burned to create a purifying smoke. Eagle feather fans are used to fan smoke to take prayers to heaven.

Death Rituals

Before contact with Europeans, Lenape burial rituals were as follows: Several days after death, the corpse was buried in a grave surrounded by a stone fence. Over a man's grave a post with carved images indicating his abilities and accomplishments might be placed. Old Lenape cemeteries have been found, but burial could just as easily be isolated. Food, utensils, tools, and wampum were placed with the body. During the funeral, feasts were held. At the time of death, the bereaved painted their faces black. Women might make demonstrative displays of grief, crawling and weeping on the grave of a husband or burning their hair on the grave of young people or those killed in war. Graves were traditionally visited annually. Mentioning the names of the dead was taboo. Souls of the dead rightly honored were thought to go to a place of abundant game.

Some of these practices continued after contact, well into the nineteenth century. The European custom of spending the night before the burial at a wake was adopted. As recently as the 1820s, the post placed over the graves of males had images on them, although the practice of placing a cross over a woman's grave had become common. The funeral feast took place four (or among some groups eleven) days after the burial. Annually, for four years, a special meal was held.

Among traditional Delawares in Oklahoma the following practices were still observed in the 1970s: purification by the burning of cedar, painting the face of the deceased, a processional to the cemetery, a hole cut in the coffin with reddened edges for the escape of the spirit, food served in a prescribed manner at the grave, and distinctive markers for men and for women (Weslager 1978, 100). The markers for graves (*kee-keen-he-kun*, "identifying thing") were made by friends (never family members) of the deceased. The marker for males was straight, with the top carved in a diamond shape. Female markers had crosspieces (Weslager 1972, 441).

According to Chief Zunigha, those dedicated to renewing their commitment to Lenape tradition today go to the cemetery near Dewey mentioned above to find inspiration from the ancestors and to experience the spiritual power of a sacred place.

Visions and Guardian Spirits

According to ethnologist Mark Harrington, "[t]he most vital and intimate phase of Lenape religion is the belief in dreams and visions, and in the existence of personal guardian spirits or supernatural helpers" (Harrington 1921, 61). At about age fifteen Lenape young people traditionally acquired a spirit guide, typically an animal or bird, during the rite of passage into adulthood. The boy or girl would receive the vision or dream while searching for one. The guardian spirit took a special interest in the person and became his special protector from this point on.

It was thought that Our Creator and the higher spirits were too busy to concern themselves with individuals. Those who were visited by a guardian spirit often kept a symbol of the spirit in clay, wood, or stone. Dreaming of the spirit guide was deemed indicative of future success. Not everyone had a spirit guide.

Although receiving an original vision during youth was most common, it also might come later in life at a time of sadness or trouble. Sometimes a later vision would come to clarify the meaning of an earlier one.

Occasionally, the vision would give a person power to become a healer. While a student at the Chilocco Indian Boarding School, about eighty miles from his home, *Wi-tapanoxwe* ("Walks with Daylight") received his first vision during a serious sickness. The summer before, he had converted to Christianity when an evangelist came to the school. In his vision, however, he was shown by a man speaking Lenape the traditional ceremonies of his people, some of which he had never seen before. He was puzzled by this until years later when visions returned and he learned that he had been chosen to heal the sick and to lead the Big House ceremony (Tantaquidgeon 1972, 8–11).

Harvest Festival

The main ceremony recorded before the nineteenth century is a circle dance, which took place once or twice a year, most frequently in October after the corn harvest. It lasted for several evenings and was accompanied by feasting. Two men sat in the center, drumming and singing. The rhythmic movements of the dancers were punctuated with shouts and jumping. Around the dancers were observers who kept time by beating sticks on the ground. Those in attendance were expected to present gifts of wampum, with some thrown down for the "poor and fatherless."

Big House Ceremony

By the eighteenth century the annual harvest festival which had been observed among the Lenape in the Delaware Valley had apparently evolved into a fall ritual known as the Big House Ceremony (*Xingawikaon*). Its name comes from the structure in which it was celebrated, a rectangular house made from hewn logs, with one door on the west and one on the east and two fires inside. The house had a center post extending through a hole in the roof. On the center post and on the wall and door poles, twelve faces of Mesingw, Keeper of the Game, were carved, painted half black and half red.

The Big House ceremony (or Big House Church as it is sometimes called) was the most important traditional communal ritual of the Lenape. Although apparently no longer actively performed, it still stands as a powerful symbol of the people's spiritual identity. The ceremony shows humility of spirit, and through it the people seek divine guidance. During the suffering and hardship of the Lenape migration, the Big House sustained and renewed the people.

The legendary origins of the ceremony may trace to the period described in the *Wallam Olum* as a time of corruption and rebirth (McCutchen 1993, 91).

According to a story recorded by Speck (Speck 1931, 80–85), the Big House was created at a time in which the earth ("our mother's body") quaked and the animals were frightened. Huge crevices appeared in the earth, and dust and smoke and a black fluid came from these crevices. A council was held to determine what to do. Aware that they had angered Our Creator, the people shared their dreams and recognized spiritually that the Big House structure should be built. They received precise instructions for how it should be constructed. They also were told to select three men and three women, one each from the Turtle, Turkey, and Wolf clan groupings. According to James C. Webber, the Lenape leader who told the above story to Speck during a 1928 interview, the people were told the ceremony should last twelve days. An informant in 1822 reported that the ceremony "keeps the world from coming to an end" (Weslager 1978, 114).

According to another story (Adams 1904, 8–17; Bierhorst 1995, 39), at this time of upheaval a mistreated boy was sent to dig wild sweet potatoes. He returned with many potatoes, but he received none when they were cooked. The starving boy cried out to the Great Spirit and heard twelve echoes. While he slept, a spirit with a face half red came to him and showed him how to construct the Big House with a center post with four faces carved on it. The spirit also instructed him in the details of the Big House ceremony. (See Bierhorst 1995, 51, 66, 107–9; Speck 1945, 41–42; Harrington 1921, 127–28, 147–51 for still other legends of the origin of the Big House.)

A map of the Lenape village at Kittanning, Pennsylvania, drawn by a Euroamerican in 1756, shows a thirty-foot longhouse, with the note that it was used for "frolickes and War Dances." One can assume that it was a ceremonial Big House (Weslager 1978, 7). A 1776 description of a Lenape council house by a Presbyterian missionary as a longhouse with two fires has been interpreted to support the theory that the Big House evolved from the earlier council houses (Weslager 1972, 292–93). Whether the Big House reflects influence from the Iroquois longhouse is a matter of speculation.

The symbolism of the Big House is clearly cosmic. The floor is the earth; the walls represent the quarters of the world; the roof is the vault of the sky. On the center pole are carved the two faces, one facing east, the other west. The center pole pierces the sky through twelve levels to the top level that forms the abode of the Creator. He holds the top of the pole in his hand. Therefore, the pole symbolizes the connection between the Creator and the Earth. The faces of Mesingw on the center pole and door and wall posts are painted half black, half red to symbolize the balance of life and death in the world. Their foreheads are incised to indicate wrinkles, perhaps to suggest wisdom. It may be that the faces carved on the support pillars on each wall manifest the *manitou* or spirits of these cosmic regions. They watched the ceremony and carried prayers to the Creator. According to Nora Thompson Dean:

We do not worship or pray to these faces. These are *manewuwak* (lesser spirits), and like the Lenape people they were created by *Kishelemakong* (the Creator). The doors on east and west symbolize the rising sun (beginning of things) and the setting sun (end). Beneath the floor are the underworlds. (Philbrook 1993)

According to the present ceremonial chief of the Delaware Tribe of Indians, Leonard Thompson, the Big House ceremony formally began when someone came out from the Big House and said *Temikekw* (Come In!). Participants entered the Big House by the east door, moving in a circular direction to the north around the center pole. This movement was the "white path," the cycle of life. Within the lodge were specified places for people in the three clan groupings—wolf, turtle, and turkey—and for men, who sat apart from the women. The ceremonial attendants who supervised the ceremony were called *ash-kah-suk*. Among other things, they lit the fires, swept the floor twelve times with turkey wings to brush clear the path to heaven, and passed out the prayer sticks at the appropriate time.

Once assembled, the people listened to a speech by the ceremonial leader of the sponsoring clan group. Here is an excerpt from an opening speech given by a famous early-twentieth-century Big House leader, Charles Elkhair:

We are thankful that so many of us are alive to meet together here once more, and that we are ready to hold our ceremonies in good faith. Now we shall meet here twelve nights in succession to pray to Our Creator, who has directed us to worship in this way. And these twelve mesingw are here to watch and carry our prayers to Our Creator in the highest heaven. The reason why we dance at this time is to raise our prayers to him. . . .

When we come into this house of ours we are glad, and thankful that we are well, and for everything that makes us feel good that the Creator has placed here for our use. We come here to pray to him to have mercy on us for the year to come and to give us everything to make us happy; may we have good crops, and no dangerous storms, flood, or earthquakes. . . . We are thankful to the East because everyone feels good in the morning when we awake, and sees the bright light coming from the East, and when the Sun goes down in the West we feel good and glad we are well; then we are thankful to the West. And we are thankful to the North, because when the cold winds come we are glad to have lived to see the leaves fall again; and to the South, for when the south wind blows and everything is coming up in the spring, we are glad to live to see the grass growing and everything green again. We thank the Thunders, for they are the manitous that bring the rain, which the Creator has given them power to rule over. And we thank our mother, the Earth, whom we claim as mother because the Earth carries us and everything we need. When we eat and drink and look around, we know it is Our Creator that makes us feel good that way. (quoted in Harrington 1921, 88–90)

Then, according to Nora Thompson Dean, the ceremony proper began. Her description of the beginning of the ritual, included in the commentary accompanying the Big House exhibit at the Philbrook Art Center, is as follows:

The Temiket (head man) picked up the turtle rattle which was on the ground in front of him and placed his fingers under the two buckskin thongs on the back of the rattle and he shook it strongly. The two Talekaok (singers) who were sitting across from him in the Church [Big House] answered by two hard beats upon the long deerhide drum. He began to Wenjikanei (recite and sing) his vision song. All this time the Talekaok kept the same rhythm as his song. The visionary danced about ten feet and then said KWIH! There was never any whooping as things were not boisterous but were gentle and dignified. During the dance, any adult could join in. Then the visionary, still standing, stopped to recite more of the vision's words and then the remainder of the song. He continued on in this manner, reciting and dancing, until he had made the entire round of the two fires. Then, he raised his hand saying, Hoo, Hoo and took his seat. (Philbrook 1993)

The whole assembly repeated the recitation of the dream after the dancer. Once one recitation was finished, another would begin. Recitations were preceded by prayers (repeated twelve times) and exhortations from the chief of the sponsoring clan and were followed by feasting.

Charley Elkhair's recitation, which he offered in the ceremony held annually in the northeastern Oklahoma Big House, told of a vision which came to him when he was grieving over the death of his younger brother. He described a red-looking being who came to him to reassure him saying, "Do not think that you are not cared for; I do, my friend!" As the being appeared in the north and south, it repeated the phrase:

It goes off,
The worship
Of the Delaware,
All over the world.

In his recitation, Chief Elkhair spoke to those present, saying:

We have danced up to where stands this grandfather [mesingw] of ours. All together there are twelve of our grandfathers, by whom every *manitou* alike is represented: Here is our grandfather Fire, and here is our mother Water, and all the food that supports our life. It is enough, my kindred, to make us happy when we are given all the things that are growing. All of that is what our Father, the Great *Manitou*, has provided, which is why it is possible for us to see it. (Tooker 1979, 109–14)

In the recitations the dancers typically spoke of their sense of inadequacy in performing the ceremony as the long-departed ancestors had. They also acknowledged their need for the support of the community in the recitation, "for that has been the strict rule since the beginning of the world, that people should help each other. For even a little child may suddenly remind people of something" (Tooker 1979, 116).

On the fourth day of the ceremony hunters departed to find meat; they returned on the seventh night. During the ceremony someone dressed in bear skins might look for improper conduct among the participants and have the doorkeepers expel any found acting inappropriately.

On the ninth night the fires were rekindled and new hay was put out for people to sit on. Purifying cedar was burned on the renewed fire. The sponsor offered a prayer and spoke again of the meaning of the ceremony (see Tooker 1979, 117–19). According to Lucy Parks Blalock (Philbrook 1993), also on the ninth night, drumsticks (*Pahkandikana*) with small faces of Mesingw on them were brought out and used through the rest of the ceremony.

The wampum beads were passed out the same nights. As they were distributed, a woman attendant painted everyone's face with ochre and bloodroot. The faces of Mesingw were also painted. Everyone was given some hominy and meat, and those who wished to spend the night in the Big House were allowed to do so. Dean said that when the time came for wampum to be given out, some was scattered between the center post and the fire on the east. The attendants were told to go get them and put them in their mouths as fast as they could, all the while making a humming noise. At times some would be dropped and the sight of this was amusing. This was called *Mawensin* (gathering of beads).

According to Dean (Philbrook 1993) on certain nights of the ceremony *mahtehikan* (prayer sticks) were used. The attendants passed these out while the drum was at a fast beat and these sticks had to be passed on "one on each side while the drum was being beat. That was the time you were to lift up your prayer stick in prayer to the Creator inside this Church."

On the final night of the ceremony women and younger men recited in a different format. The next morning the people struck their camps and left for home. The sponsor bade them farewell.

The twelve nights of the Big House ceremony may be interpreted as symbolizing the twelve moons or lunar months and the ceremony itself represents the transition through the year. In 1822 the months were named as follows:

- January—Squirrel Moon
- February—Frog Moon
- March—Bass Moon
- April—Shedding of the Hair of the Deer Moon
- May—Moon Between Spring and Summer
- June—Moon when the Vegetation is in Blossom
- July—Moon when the Vegetation Blooms
- August—Moon when the Deer begin to turn grey
- September—Moon previous to the falling of the leaves
- October—Moon that the leaves fall
- November—Moon when the snow begins to fall
- December—Moon when the severe cold begins (Weslager 1978, 108–9)

Dancing that followed the white path reflected the east to west movement of the sun as well as the passage of life from birth to death. In the early nineteenth century, the reciter still performed the animated dance of earlier times, but a quarter-century later it had disappeared. Other minor changes were introduced. Observers stood during the recitation and danced, and instead of beating time, the sticks (called prayer sticks) were simply waved.

In 1903 Senators Matthew Quay of Pennsylvania and Clarence Clark of Wyoming, supporters of the Delaware nation in Congress, were invited to participate in a Big House ceremony. They described the participation of the Lenape as "solemn and sincere" and said they were deeply moved by it (Weslager 1978, 233).

In 1921 Harrington published the words of Charles Elkhair, reflecting on the meaning of the ceremony, at a time when many Delawares thought the time had come to give up the annual celebration:

The Delaware meeting helps everybody in the world, for they pray for good crops and everything good, even wild fruits. About ten years ago the people thought they would give up holding these meetings, and the following year they had high winds and big rains, and everyone was frightened. Then grasshoppers came in swarms, but they came in the fall a little too late to get all the crops. So the people held a council and talked about the Big House again. They finally decided to resume it, before any more bad luck came .. . . Then it seemed as if all the trouble stopped. Of late there has been talk of again giving up the meeting, but if we do give it up we are likely to have a tornado or maybe dry weather to ruin the crops. . . . When the Creator looks down from Heaven, he sees but a very few Delaware peo-

ple, and the reason for this is that they cannot follow the Big House ceremonies now. . . . The people could get along fine, if they followed the rules
of the meeting—not only the Delaware, but the other people round about.
For when the Delaware prays, he prays for things that will benefit everybody; he prays for the children as well as for himself; he prays for a future
time. But if anything comes to destroy the world, it will be too late to
think of starting the Big House then. (cited in Tooker 1979, 123–24)

Elkhair's warnings were not heeded. The last Big House ceremony was celebrated among the Eastern Delaware in Oklahoma in 1924. A few years later a
drought came and decimated the crops. The demise of the ceremony, however,
was probably inevitable. Established visionaries were too old to recite their
visions. Children could no longer receive new visions, as the land where visions
were sought was no longer part of the Delaware lands. Moreover, many young
people had stopped believing in the traditional ways.

Before the last remaining Big House fell down and the land on which it was
located was put to other uses, the Mesingw faces were cut off in 1939 and were
taken to the Philbrook Art Center in Tulsa for safekeeping. Later the prayer sticks
and other ritual objects used in the ceremony were sold to the same institution.

Improvised Big House ceremonies were held on several occasions during the
Second World War (in 1944 and 1945). Some of the elders remembered the prophecy which said that if the annual ceremony was ever discontinued, the world might
come to an end. They were anxious to renew the ceremony. They also wanted to
ask the Creator to grant victory to the United States in the war and the safe return
of their young people in the armed forces. The wartime ceremonies were held in a
temporary bark structure near Dewey, Oklahoma, but they were hampered by the
absence of ceremonial objects such as white wampum beads. In addition, young
people did not come because they considered the ritual superstitious or because
they did not understand the language (Weslager 1972, 14).

Traditional Lenape elders today say the Big House ceremony will never return as
it was known. No one is left with the proper knowledge to lead the ceremony. Without knowledge of the traditional songs and prayers and the actions of the ritual, any
attempt to revive it would, they say, be artificial and disrespectful. But the elders also
say the sacred objects from the Big House remain powerful (Zunigha 1997).

In 1993 the tribal council of the Delaware Tribe of Indians worked with other
Delaware groups and the Philbrook Art Center to create a Big House exhibit.
With the leadership of the elected chief, Curtis Zunigha, the council and tribal
elders agreed to an exhibit which would enable the Delaware people to experience
once again the power of the ritual objects. According to Chief Zunigha:

Under the provisions of the American Indian Freedom of Religion Act of
1978, we could have insisted the mesingw masks and other sacred items

be returned to us. But they would have simply been placed in storage, for we have no place at present to properly present them. Through an exhibit at the Philbrook Art Center our people could remain in touch with this essential part of our traditional heritage. My hope is that someday the Big House objects will become part of the National Museum of the American Indian. For now the Philbrook staff is doing an excellent job of preserving and respectfully exhibiting the items. Through this exhibit other people can also learn about Lenape culture and its spiritual essence. (Zunigha 1997)

The Philbrook exhibit opened on 13 November 1993. Tribal singers offered a deer hunting song. Ceremonial chief Leonard Thompson recited traditional prayers. The elders who remembered the Big House ceremony wept as its ambience was recreated. The exhibit, with explanatory texts and an introductory video approved by the council, is divided into two areas. One is for items from the daily lives of traditional Lenape people, including jewelry, a corn pounder, and other objects. The inner area has a large photograph of the inside of the last Big House. In the middle is the center post with the carved red and black face of Mesingw. Two door posts are also carved with Mesingw faces. In display cases are ritual objects (turtle rattles, prayer sticks, drum sticks, and wampum) with quotations from elders who remembered the ceremony.

Whether this is an appropriate way to preserve and renew traditional spirituality, when the ceremonies themselves have been lost, is an issue on which Lenape people today have differing views. Some believe strongly that it is inappropriate and dangerous to display objects of such meaning and power in a public, non-Lenape setting. Others hold that this is the only way to maintain any continuity with traditional spirituality. (For more on the Big House ceremony, see Wyckoff and Zunigha 1994; Philbrook 1993; Tooker 1979; Weslager 1978, 114–16; Prewitt 1981; Dean and Miller 1977; Müller 1968; McCracken 1956; Speck 1931.)

Sweat Lodges

Some evidence suggests that Lenapes used sweat lodges in the Delaware Valley. Sweat houses large enough for two or three persons were built near running water, with coverings of branches sealed with clay. Throughout the years, Lenape families have continued to use sweat lodges for purification and renewal (Tantaquidgeon 1972, 20–24).

The practice continues among those Delaware people seeking to maintain the traditional ways. Bigger lodges, built with twelve poles to symbolize the twelve levels of heaven leading to the abode of the Creator, were found in Oklahoma earlier in this century (Speck 1931, 74). Curtis Zunigha (Zunigha

1997) would like to have space for a communal sweat lodge, available for use by the Lenape people, at a new Lenape cultural center.

Family Feasts

Every year or two, a traditional family conducted a special ceremony in fulfillment of an obligation passed down from an ancestor. Typical were grease-drinking ceremonies in which a bear (later a hog) was eaten and the grease was drunk. Doll dances were also popular. In these social dances, women, then men, carried a doll on a stick as they danced around the fire in alternate rows.

Other family ceremonies mentioned include first-fruit offerings, green-corn rituals, war dances, and, as mentioned, curing rituals conducted by healers.

Naming

Names are traditionally not bestowed on Lenape children at birth but later, when the children are believed to be firmly established on this earth. At that time a ceremony is held in which a name received by vision (either by the parents or by a visionary called *way-huh-wée-huh-lah*, "one who gives names over and over") is bestowed on the child. From this time on the person and his/her "real name" are one and the same. At death, the real name of a person is avoided, lest the spirit of the deceased be inadvertently called. Traditional Lenape people are reluctant to reveal their names given by vision outside a narrow circle lest enemies use the names to bring evil on them. Like other native peoples, Lenapes have adopted European names to use in lieu of their traditional names.

The Native American Church

The void left by the disappearance of the Big House ceremony and other traditional rituals was filled for some Lenapes by the introduction of the peyote ritual of the Native American Church. (For a full discussion of the history and rituals of the Native American Church, see chapter 7; also Petrullo 1934; Wallace 1956; Newcomb 1956b; Stewart 1987, 95–96.) A Lenape/Caddo man named John Wilson had brought the first peyote to the Western Delawares in about 1880. In the mid–1880s he introduced peyote to the Eastern Delawares.

Charles Elkhair, the ceremonial chief previously mentioned, was also an active peyote missionary. Elkhair had turned to the Half Moon peyote ritual when his wife had become desperately ill and he had become deeply depressed. He claimed it cleansed his mind and prepared the user's soul for death.

Another Lenape peyotist explained why he had embraced peyotism in place of the traditional spirituality:

The old Delaware religion is too heavy for us who are becoming few and weak. It is too difficult; Peyote is easy in comparison. Therefore we who are weak take up this new Indian religion. This is the very objection raised by the old men, taking it up. But Peyote knows that the Indian's burden of becoming educated and at the same time keeping up the old religion is too heavy, for he said that to the old woman who was the first to discover our new religion. Peyote is to be the Indians' new religion. It is to be for all the Indian people and only for them. (Petrullo 1934, 76)

Despite the evidence in these testimonies, peyotism was not widely embraced. In the early 1970s Weslager found only a few Delawares who admitted to participating in peyote rituals. Since then, however involvement has increased.

The Lenape Today

Today more than 13,000 Delawares live in all fifty U.S. states and in other countries. In addition to the ancestors of the main body in northeastern Oklahoma, small communities exist in southwestern Oklahoma, Canada, Wisconsin, Kansas, and New York. In Oklahoma and elsewhere Lenape have assimilated economically into the mainstream of American life, but there remains a widely shared pride in Lenape culture and a commitment to keep alive Lenape language, customs, and traditional spiritual values. Although only a few fluent Lenape speakers are still alive, many Lenapes of all ages are studying the language.

In 1992 the Delaware Nation Grand Council of North America was created to represent all the Lenape peoples and to preserve Lenape culture. Its headquarters are in Ohio, near where the Delaware lived in the late eighteenth century.

The annual powwow during Memorial Day weekend continues to attract hundreds of Delawares to northeastern Oklahoma in a celebration of Lenape heritage and as a continued expression of commitment to a living Lenape nation.

After a seventeen-year struggle to regain federal recognition, Assistant Secretary of the Interior for Indian Affairs, Ada Deer, ruled on 26 September 1996 that full federal recognition be restored to the Delaware Tribe of Indians. She called the 1979 action terminating recognition "illegal" and "immoral." The Cherokee Nation of Oklahoma has challenged Deer's decision, and, at this writing, the situation is not resolved, although the ruling was upheld by the U.S. District Court in Washington, D.C., in October 1996. The Court of Appeals has returned the case to the District Court for further argument. According to then-Chief Curtis Zunigha, "despite the difficulties now posed by the [Cherokee Nation's] challenges, we as a tribe intend to move forward with our cultural and economic growth . . . We intend to pursue the re-establishment of Delaware control over Delaware affairs with as much vigor as we fought for the return of our rights."

With restored recognition of its sovereign status, the Delaware Tribe of Indians will have the same rights and responsibilities as any other Native American nation, including the right to determine its own membership. As Chief Zunigha put it, "The restoration of federal recognition shows very clearly that [this] small tribe, numbering about 10,000, has not lost either its negotiating and diplomatic skills, or its ability to fight for justice."

Approaches have been made to the leadership of the Cherokee Nation by the Delaware Tribal Council, but so far t/he Cherokee have not shown a willingness to settle the dispute through direct negotiation. Chief Zunigha said in October 1997:

> Instead of letting this be decided by white lawyers before white judges who don't really know us, we should settle our dispute nation to nation as was done traditionally. Let's redefine the terms of the 1867 agreement in a way that makes sense for the twenty-first century. We should look to the future instead of the past. (Zuniga 1997)

In the meantime, the Delaware Tribal Council is trying to ratchet up the pressure on the Cherokee nation so that its leaders will eventually recognize the inevitable—that the Delaware are indeed a sovereign nation.

In addition to fighting efforts to overturn the recognition of restored tribal sovereignty, in 1997 the Delaware Tribe of Indians was debating whether and how quickly to move toward the pursuit of tribal-sponsored gambling as a way to earn money for tribal projects. Chief Zunigha opposed considering the question of gambling until other issues are resolved. Other Delawares who have seen the success of Indian gambling across the country were mounting an effort to move more quickly toward the development of Delaware-sponsored casinos and/or other forms of gambling in northeastern Oklahoma.

Reflecting the commitment to honor Lenape tradition, Chief Zunigha wrote in the April 1997 edition of *Delaware Indian News*:

> In the Indian way, the new year begins now, with spring and warmth and growth. I have welcomed the new year with prayer and ceremony, with cedar smoke and tobacco asking for guidance and blessings as I bear this awesome responsibility as your Chief. I prayed for the ancestors in whose name and memory we continue to carry the name Lenape. I prayed for our elected leaders who are charged with representing our legal and political interests and championing tribal sovereignty. I prayed for our elders who must pass on the wisdom of their life's experience and inspire us to keep our cultural traditions strong. I prayed for our children that they will always know of their Lenape heritage and keep it with pride. I prayed for the peo-

ple, Lenapeok, as we venture forth to growth and prosperity. I prayed for the Creator to change the thoughts of those who would keep our tribe from realizing its destiny and make them champions for our cause.

Several months later, in a conversation with the author (Zunigha 1997), Chief Zunigha expressed his commitment to devote himself to the renewal and revitalization of Lenape culture. Standing in the traditional Lenape cemetery near Dewey, Oklahoma, he stated that it is up to his generation and younger Lenape people to show that they are living by the principles and values of Lenape tradition, to become fluent in the Lenape language, and to learn the prayers and songs. The elders have said that the Big House ceremony cannot be revived as it was. Nevertheless, Chief Zunigha said he hoped that as the people demonstrate that they are living in a spiritual way, there might be a divinely inspired (the only way it can come) renewal of this traditional ceremony, not as it was, but in a new way appropriate for a different era. A new Big House could then be built for new ceremonies, he explained. He acknowledged that the Delaware cannot expect other people to respect their sacred rituals, if the Lenape themselves are not living in the spirit of the traditions themselves. The essence of the Big House ceremony is not dead, he said, even though it is no longer practiced. It will be renewed if the people walk the right path.

Efforts are ongoing to work more closely with Delawares in western Oklahoma and Ontario to renew the Lenape culture. In August 1997 representatives of the Delaware Tribe of Indians met with representatives from other Lenape communities gathered in Anadarko, Oklahoma, for a meeting of the Grand Council. The Cultural Preservation Committee of the tribe sponsors social dances once a month and other events to foster appreciation for Lenape language and customs. As a Lenape leader phrased it in an April 1997 challenge to her fellow tribal members, "The uniqueness of Delaware culture must be treasured, shared and preserved. What are you doing to see that we never lose it?"

CHAPTER 3

The *Ani'-Yun'-wiya* (Cherokee): Keeping the Eternal Fire Burning

The Fires kept burning are merely emblematic of the greater Fire, the greater Light . . . . I realize now as never before it is not only for the Cherokee but for all mankind.
— Redbird Smith, Cherokee traditionalist

In . . . the language of my people, there is a word for land: Eloheh. This same word also means, history, culture and religion. This is because we Cherokees cannot separate our place on earth from our lives in it, nor from our vision and our meaning as a people.
— Jimmie Durham, Modern Cherokee leader

CHEROKEE, NORTH CAROLINA, is a small village nestled in a valley in the beautiful mountains on the border between Tennessee and North Carolina. The town is the headquarters of the Eastern Band of Cherokees, for whom, as we shall see, these mountains were a place of refuge when most other Cherokees were forcibly removed to Indian territory in the 1830s on the infamous Trail of Tears. At the beginning of the twenty-first century, the town of Cherokee is an increasingly popular tourist destination. As the southern terminus of the Blue Ridge Parkway and the eastern gateway to Great Smoky Mountains National Park, Cherokee bustles with activity, especially during the summer months. A garish casino now draws in thousands of visitors eager to strike it rich, and curio shops line the streets, offering for sale "Indian souvenirs," an array of items mostly foreign to the traditional culture of the Cherokee people.

For those willing to take the time to look, however, modern-day Cherokee, North Carolina, also witnesses to the proud heritage and living tradition of this branch of the Cherokee people. For example, the recently renovated Museum of the Cherokee Indian tells the story of the Eastern Cherokees, from the time of mythic origins to the present economic and spiritual renewal. A display of dance masks gives a sense of the traditional ceremonial life of the Cherokee, and a moving exhibit re-enacts the beginning of the Trail of Tears. Nearby, the Qualla Arts and Crafts Mutual offers for sale authentic works by contemporary Cherokee artists skilled in basketmaking, mask carving, and other traditional crafts.

Standing at the edge of the dance circle during the 4 July 1998 intertribal powwow in Cherokee, listening to the rhythmic drumbeat and watching the colorful dancers, I felt a growing desire to learn more about the fascinating and tragic history of this people and their struggle to keep alive their culture and their spirituality.

This chapter first identifies and locates the Cherokee people, then shares a few of the stories of origins passed orally through the generations. Next it traces the Cherokee history from the earliest evidence of their presence in the southeastern United States until the early 1990s. The discussion of traditional Cherokee spirituality includes descriptions of the Cherokee understanding of the cosmos (including the sacred fire), gods and spirits, healers and healing, rituals (including the six traditional calendric ceremonies, and especially the still-practiced Green Corn Festival), the nineteenth-century Ghost Dance movements, the traditionalist Keetoowah Societies, and the popular Stomp Dances. The chapter concludes with a portrayal of the situation of the Cherokee people at the end of the twentieth century.

Who Are the Cherokee?

Like each of the other nations we are encountering, the Cherokee have a self-designation: *Ani'-Yun'-wiya*, translated as Principal or Real People. Several possibilities exist for the derivation of the more widely used *Cherokee*. It may, for example, be a corruption of the Cherokee term *Tsa lagi* ("cave people"). *Chalaque* appeared as a reference to the Cherokee in the Portuguese description of De Soto's expedition into Cherokee lands, published in 1557. It then was written as *Cheraqui* in a 1699 French document, and in English as *Cherokee* in 1708 (Mooney 1900 [1982], 15–16). In this chapter we use *Ani'-Yun'-wiya* and *Cherokee* interchangeably.

Today three bands of *Ani'-Yun'-wiya* have federal recognition. The largest is the Cherokee Nation of Oklahoma (CNO); next is the Eastern Band of Cherokees of North Carolina; the third and smallest is the United Band of Keetoowah, which has its headquarters in Oklahoma but is seeking to relocate to Arkansas. The history resulting in these three branches of the Cherokee is recounted below.

By 1990 the enrolled Cherokee population had reached nearly 120,000, with at least twice that number self-identifying as Cherokee on the census. Because of an inclusive policy on tribal membership, the *Ani'-Yun'-wiya* are today the fastest growing Native American nation.

The Cherokee language is a branch of the Iroquoian linguistic family. Of the three original dialects, only two have survived: the Middle or *Kituhwa* dialect spoken among the Eastern Band in North Carolina and the Western (*Otali*) or Upper dialect spoken in Oklahoma.

Ani'-Yun'-wiya Creation Legends

The Floating Island

The most often repeated *Ani'-Yun'-wiya* story of cosmic origins comes from the myths collected by ethnologist James Mooney between 1887 and 1890 during fieldwork among the Eastern Cherokees:

> In the beginning, before Mother Earth was made, there was only a vast body of water that was both salty and fresh. There were no human beings, only animals. They lived in the heavens above the sea. They were secure in a solid rocky sky vault called *Galunlati*. As the animals, birds, and insects multiplied, the sky became more crowded and there was a fear that some creatures would be pushed off the sky rock. All the creatures called a council to decide what to do.
>
> At last "Beaver's Grandchild," the little Water-beetle called Dayunisi, offered to leave the sky and investigate the water below. Water-beetle darted in every direction over the water's surface, but could not find any place to rest. So the beetle dived to the bottom of the sea and returned with soft mud, which began to grow and spread until it became known as earth.
>
> The earth eventually became a great island floating in the sea of water. It was suspended from the heavens at each of the four principal points by cords which hung from the sky vault. The myth keepers claimed that when the earth grows old and wears out, the cords will become weak and break and the earth will sink into the ocean and everything will die. All will be water again.
>
> After the Water-beetle returned to the sky rock and told the others about what he had done, the creatures sent out the Great Buzzard, grandfather of all buzzards, to find a place for them to live. The new earth was wet and soft and flat. The Buzzard soared low, searching for a suitable place. He grew tired, and as his huge wings dipped and struck the pliable earth, deep valleys were created. When the bird rose in the sky, his flapping wings formed ridges and mighty mountains. This is what would become Cherokee country.
>
> At last the earth dried and the creatures came down, but it was still dark, so they convinced the sun to move overhead every day from east to west. But

the sun was so hot that Tsiskagili, the Crawfish, scorched his shell a bright red, and his meat was spoiled. Then the conjurers moved the sun higher in the sky, and at last they positioned it seven handbreadths high, just below the sky arch. This became what the soothsayers called "the seventh height," or the highest place. To this day the sun moves along below this arch, and then returns every night on the upper side to the starting point.

When all the animals and plants were created, they were told to stay awake and keep a vigil for seven nights. They tried their best to do this, and nearly all of them remained awake the first night. But the next night several dropped off to sleep, and by the third night even more were asleep. This continued until the seventh night, when only the owl, the panther, and a few others were still awake. Because they did not succumb to sleep, they were given the power to see in the dark. Of the trees, only the pine, the spruce, the cedar, the holly, and the laurel remained awake seven nights. They were allowed to remain always green and were considered to be the best plants for medicine. Unlike the other trees, they were also allowed to keep their hair throughout the winter. This was their gift.

Human beings were created after the animals and plants. There were several versions of the story of how the first humans were made. It was said by some of the old Cherokees that in the beginning there were only a brother and sister, and that the man touched the woman with a fish and told her to multiply. In seven days she bore a child. She continued to do this every seven days until the earth became crowded. Then it was deemed that a woman should have only one child each year. (Mankiller 1993, 16–17; cf. Mooney 1900 [1982], 239–40; Perdue 1989, 13–14; Peithmann 1964, 12–13; Erdoes and Ortiz 1984, 105–7)

Mooney's collection of Cherokee myths (Mooney 1900 [1982]) includes a number of other accounts of creation, including stories about how the first fire was brought to the cold world by Water Spider (240–42), Kanati (Lucky Hunter) and Selu (Corn Woman) and the origin of game and corn (242–49), the origin of disease and medicine (250–52), the daughter of the sun (252–54; cf. Erdoes and Ortiz 1984, 152–54), how the *Ani'-Yun'-wiya* brought back tobacco (254–55), the origin of the Pleiades and the Pine (158–59), the origin of strawberries (259–60), and a flood story (261).

The Creation of Humans: Red, Black, and White

After contact with Euroamericans and with Africans brought as slaves, new stories developed which took note of the diversity of ethnicities and the conflicts among them. One such Cherokee myth states that when the Creator brought humans into existence, some were red, some were black, and some were white:

To the red people the Creator gave the bow and arrow, putting them in America amidst the game; to the black people the hoe and axe, placing them in Africa to work in the fields; to the whites a book, depositing them in Europe where they would discover many secrets. Trouble resulted when these separate peoples and their ways of life were combined together. (McLoughlin 1986, 177)

Another myth tells the story of how the Creator made humans out of clay and baked them in an oven over a hot fire (McLoughlin 1986, 178; 1994, 195). The first clay image was baked too long and turned out black. The second was not heated long enough and remained pale. The third try got it right, as the baked image was a handsome red.

The Crystal and the Silver

Another of the creation myths reflective of cultural interaction reveals the view of Euroamericans held by many traditional Cherokees:

At the time of creation, an *unlunsuti*, or crystal was given to the white man, and a piece of silver to the Indian. But the white man despised the crystal and threw it away, while the Indian did the same with the silver. In going about, the white man afterward found the silver piece and put it in his pocket and has prized it ever since. The Indian, in like manner, found the crystal where the white man had thrown it. He picked it up and has kept it since as his talisman, just as money is the talismanic power of the white man. (Mankiller 1993, 117; cf. Mooney 1900 [1982], 35–51)

Historical Overview

As with other Native American nations, the history of the *Ani'-Yun'-wiya* includes forced relocation and scattering. Therefore, it too is a complex story, one which must be told fully, if we are to understand the contemporary situation of the Cherokee people. (For the basic historical information in this overview, I am particularly indebted to Mooney 1900 [1982], 14–228; Woodward 1963; Perdue 1989; Mankiller 1993; and Wilson 1999).

Prior to Contact with Europeans

The *Ani'-Yun'-wiya* have existed as a distinct people for at least 1,000, perhaps 2,000 years (Thornton 1990, 8; see Dickens 1979). Before they developed their successful culture in what was to become the southeastern United States, the Cherokee may have lived in the Great Lakes area and then migrated southward through western Virginia and the Carolinas, a route later followed by European settlers. This view is based largely on the fact that the *Ani'-Yun'-wiya*, like the Hotinonshonni (Iroquois) nations of the north, speak an Iroquoian language, and must, therefore, have a common origin.

Another theory proposes that the Cherokee migrated northward from South America. A legend associated with the traditionalist Keetoowah Society (see below) links the peoples' origins to islands off the eastern coast of South America. The similarity between *Ani'-Yun'-wiya* basket and pottery styles and those of South American and Caribbean peoples has been cited to support this view. Yet another story claims they came from the Southwest.

Some interpreters believe that the Cherokee were native to their southeastern homeland, basing their view on the fact that aspects of *Ani'-Yun'-wiya* culture have been shown by archaeologists to be at least a millennium old in their Appalachian homeland (Fogelson 1978, 10; King 1979, x).

Regardless of where the *Ani'-Yun'-wiya* came from originally, it is certain that when Europeans arrived in the Southeast in the sixteenth century, the Cherokee had been there for centuries.

With the high Appalachians as a center and stronghold, the *Ani'-Yun'-wiya* spread over the adjoining lowlands. At their peak in precontact times, there may have been about 30,000 Cherokees (Thornton 1990, 18) living in about sixty-five autonomous villages scattered throughout a 40,000–square–mile area in what is now North Carolina, South Carolina, Kentucky, Tennessee, Georgia, Alabama, Virginia, and perhaps a portion of West Virginia (Mooney 1900 [1982], 14).

The original nucleus in the *Ani'-Yun'-wiya* homeland may have been the sacred Kituwha settlement near the present Bryson City, North Carolina. The sacred town of Nikwasi was located near the contemporary city of Franklin, North Carolina. The first national capital was Echota, just above the mouth of the Tellico River, near the present Cartlesville, Georgia. Echota was known as the "white town" or "peace town," a place of refuge where someone who had committed a crime would be safe from revenge for as long as the person stayed there. At one time each Cherokee region probably had such a town of refuge. Town populations ranged up to 600 but averaged about 250–300. Houses were built from logs, even before the arrival of the European axe.

Larger towns were built around a central council house and a plaza for stickball games (similar to modern lacrosse) and ceremonial activities (see below). A council house was a large circular building, sometimes built on top of an earthen mound. It had benches along the walls and a critically important central fire.

Like their southeastern neighbors, the Cherokee were agriculturalists, cultivating maize, beans, melon, tobacco, and other crops. They also drew on the abundance of turkey, deer, bear, nuts, and berries in the lush hills and valleys surrounding their stockaded villages.

Seven clans composed the *Ani'-Yun'-wiya*: Kituwha (or Blind Savannah), Wolf, Deer, Bird, Holly, Paint, and Long Hair. Each village had households representing the various clans. Families were matrilineal; a child's clan was determined by the clan of his or her mother, and families lived in the household of the mother. As in other nations, marriage was exogamous, with members of a given clan forbidden to marry one another.

Clans were charged with the responsibility of avenging the breaking of the social code. For example, when a clan member was killed, the person's clan was expected to retaliate. The Cherokee believed that the spirit of a dead kinsman could not enter the "darkening land" where souls dwelled after death until revenge had taken place. The clan of the person killed in revenge took no further action because harmony had been restored. An unavenged death left a state of disequilibrium, causing disease, drought, or other calamity.

Each town had a council composed of all adults, but dominated by three groups of older men: the priest-chief and his assistants; seven elders (one from each clan); and the "beloved men," the rest of the senior men (Persico 1979, 93). Deliberations were continued, with anyone allowed to speak, until a unanimous decision was reached. Those who remained opposed simply withdrew from the discussion. Each town also had a mutual aid society called the *gadu:gi*, later the Free Labor Society, which oversaw agricultural work. After European contact the Society took the responsibility of providing for those in need. No higher authority existed above the town level.

No records show towns going to war against one another. In times of war against outside enemies, younger war (Red) chiefs assumed leadership. In peacetime administrative authority was in the hands of the older peace (White) chiefs.

Women played key roles in the leadership of *Ani'-Yun'-wiya* society. They had a voice in daily councils and voted in elections. The Cherokee assumed that any "civilized" society would follow the same practice. As one Beloved Man pointedly asked a British governor, "It is customary among [us] to admit women to our councils. . . . [Since] the white people as well as the red, are born of women, is not that the custom among them also?" (Wilson 1999, 138–39).

Women of each clan also selected their own leaders who formed a Women's Council. The Women's Council would challenge the Chiefs' Councils when they thought the welfare of the people was at stake. The head of the Women's Council was a powerful woman called *Ghigau*, or Beloved Woman (or perhaps Red or War Woman). She was considered to be the voice of the Great Spirit, who spoke through her. Women were known to go to war, probably serving as cooks and water carriers.

According to former chief of the Cherokee Nation of Oklahoma, Wilma Mankiller, the Cherokee during the precontact period were "profoundly religious, believing that the world existed in a precarious balance and that only right or correct actions kept it from tumbling. Wrong actions could disturb the balance" (Mankiller 1993, 20). In the view of many Cherokee traditionalists, this is what happened as a result of acculturation, and one result may have been the subordination of women.

First Contact with Europeans (1540–1776)

In March 1540 the Spanish explorer Hernando De Soto marched out of Florida with 600 men, heading northeast. As De Soto's expedition approached the Blue Ridge mountains, it was met by 500 *Ani'-Yun'-wiya* warriors, probably near the ancient town of Etowah. This is the first recorded contact between Europeans and the Cherokee. After a short visit in which they were treated with hospitality, and having noted the military prowess of the Cherokee, De Soto's party continued to the west in search of gold.

About thirty years later another group of Spaniards led by Juan Pardo arrived in *Ani'-Yun'-wiya* country. By this time the Spanish had introduced diseases that had already swept through some Cherokee villages. Medicine men said that the horrors brought by the Spanish invaders were a result of the world being out of balance. The fleeting encounter with the Spanish, however, did not dramatically change Cherokee culture.

Interaction with English settlers, beginning in 1654, had a more lasting impact. By the late 1600s English traders were coming from Virginia and South Carolina to trade with the *Ani'-Yun'-wiya*. In 1684 a treaty between the Cherokee settlements of Toxawa and Keowa and the English colony of South Carolina was negotiated at Charleston. The colonists promised to help the Cherokee resist their enemies, who had sold Cherokees into slavery.

The growing threat posed by the English settlers caused the *Ani'-Yun'-wiya* to unite and, with pressure from the English, elect their first principal chief in 1721, creating the united Cherokee nation. A National Council met to select peace and war chiefs. The English called the principal chief "emperor of the Cherokee nation." The same year the Cherokee Nation agreed to its first land cession to the English, in the expectation that in this way peace could be achieved between the two peoples. On a visit to England a Cherokee leader observed, "[t]hough we are red and you are white, yet our hands and hearts are joined together" (Wilson 1999, 144).

During the eighteenth century European traders began to take Cherokee wives, realizing that this was a way to gain acceptance among the *Ani'-Yun'-wiya*. In a matrilineal society, children were deemed Cherokee if they were born to a Cherokee mother. This practice created a significant mixed blood class that would come to distance themselves from traditional Cherokee ways and eventually become a ruling elite. Children of such mixed unions typically took their fathers' names and inherited from their fathers, upsetting well-established customs.

According to Chief Mankiller, "the purebloods and traditionalists tried to hold on, aware that the balance of our world was going awry. . . . It seemed as if the spiritual and social tapestry they had created for centuries was unraveling. Everything lost that sacred balance. And ever since, we have been striving to return to the harmony we once had" (Mankiller 1993, 26, 29).

Many *Ani'-Yun'-wiya* became increasingly dependent on traded goods, lived in colonial-style cabins, took up European-style farming, and developed a taste for European food and drink. According to the traditionalist perspective, one of the signs that the balance was broken was that more animals than were necessary for the peoples' sustenance were taken to trade for European goods.

As part of their trade with the English, some Cherokees took up slavery. By the late eighteenth century a Cherokee elite mimicked colonists by maintaining black slaves as field workers and servants. From the outset, however, African slaves were treated with respect by their *Ani'-Yun'-wiya* masters (Perdue 1979).

In 1720 the population of the Cherokee had already declined to an estimated 10,500–11,500. In 1738 a smallpox epidemic brought by slave ships killed up to half the remaining people. Other epidemics through the rest of the eighteenth century caused declines in population offsetting natural growth, keeping the population between 8,000 and 12,000 (Thornton 1990, 21, 30). The failure of traditional healers to halt the spreading diseases caused many *Ani'-Yun'-wiya* to question their powers.

During the 1750s a number of *Ani'-Yun'-wiya* turned to a ceremony called the Booger Dance (see below). It was adapted from a dance in which the Cherokee parodied the peculiarities of their traditional enemies, like the Creeks, Chickasaws, and Choctaws, and was applied in the new context to the threat posed by European incursion.

When war broke out between England and France in 1754, the *Ani'-Yun'-wiya* sided with the British, who promised to build forts to protect Cherokee towns from the French. The alliance broke down when drunken British soldiers raped the women of a Cherokee town they were ostensibly protecting and Cherokee veterans returning from fighting the French were killed by Virginia frontiersmen. Honoring the tradition of blood revenge, their clansmen attacked settlers near to them in Carolina. A peace delegation of Cherokees was taken into custody in 1759 and held until several Cherokees accused of murdering settlers were turned over for execution. Enraged Cherokees mounted a campaign that led to the surrender of Fort Loudoun in 1760. The next spring an English militia devastated *Ani'-Yun'-wiya* settlements. Cherokee leaders, returning from a trip to England in 1762, warned their people that further resistance against so powerful a nation was futile.

Treaties in 1770 and 1772 resulted in the loss of Cherokee hunting grounds in Virginia and West Virginia and territory east of the Kentucky River. In 1775 the English obtained control of virtually all of the present state of Kentucky in the Sycamore Shoals treaty. In a prophetic speech the Cherokee chief *Tsu-gun-sini* (Dragging Canoe) warned the council of chiefs present for this treaty council that the insatiable appetite of the Europeans for land would not be satisfied. "Finally," he said, "the whole country which the Cherokee and their fathers have so long occupied, will be demanded and the remnant of *Ani'-Yun'-wiya*, The Real People, once so great and formidable, will be compelled to seek refuge in some distant wilderness" (Peithmann 1964, 30).

Growing Hostility and the Cherokee Renascence (1776–1830)

By 1776 the Cherokee had already ceded 50,000 square miles to the expanding colonies. During the Revolutionary War the *Ani'-Yun'-wiya* again sided with the British, because they viewed containment of the colonists to be in their interest. In June 1776 Cherokee warriors joined with the British in an attack on Charleston, South Carolina. In less than a year fifty towns had been attacked by retaliating colonists and hundreds of Cherokees killed, including women and children. For many settlers the *Ani'-Yun'-wiya* and other Indians were viewed simply as a "vermin" to be exterminated so that they could take the Cherokee's land.

On 20 May 1777 the Cherokee entered into the first of a series of treaties with the colonists, giving up all remaining land claims in South Carolina. Dragging Canoe refused to acknowledge these treaties and led his Lower Town followers to the western frontier where they established five towns and continued to resist the Americans until late in the century. They were known as the Chickamaugans, after the Chickamauga Creek where he located his settlement of Running Water (near the present Chattanooga, Tennessee).

In 1785 the *Ani'-Yun'-wiya* entered into their first treaty with the new United States government at Hopewell, South Carolina. According to the treaty, the Cherokee were to receive protection from the United States "and no other sovereign" in exchange for yet another cession of land.

The ambiguity of early American leaders in their reactions to the *Ani'-Yun'-wiya* is perhaps best exemplified by the attitude of Thomas Jefferson. He said to the Cherokee in 1808:

> My children, I shall rejoice to see the day when the red man, our neighbors, become truly one people with us, enjoying all the rights and privileges we do, and living in peace and plenty as we do. . . . But are you prepared for this? Have you the resolution to leave off hunting for your living, to lay off a farm for each family to itself, to live by industry, the men working that farm with their hands . . . ? (Takaki 1993, 48)

Jefferson obviously was deeply conflicted in his attitude toward the Cherokee and other Native Americans (Wallace 1999). On the one hand, he called the *Ani'-*

Yun'-wiya the equal of Europeans in body and mind and advocated intermarriage. On the other hand, he said they were "a useless, expensive, ungovernable ally." Although he opposed forced relocation, he was, as noted, the first architect of the policy of removal of Indians to the west of the Mississippi River.

After the so-called Massacre at Muscle Shoals, when Chickamauga warriors attacked a group of settlers, a group of about 1,200 (out of 12,000) *Ani'-Yun'-wiya* traditionalists, at the invitation of the Spanish, moved from Alabama across the Mississippi River under the leadership of *Diwa-li* (the Bowl). After the earthquake of 1811, they moved to Arkansas and settled between the White and Arkansas rivers in what was known as Cherokee Nation West. After a disputed treaty in 1817 that ceded large tracts of land in Georgia and Tennessee, 2,000 more *Ani'-Yun'-wiya* came from the East to join the Arkansas Cherokees, who also became known as the Old Settlers. Some of these western Cherokees went on to Texas in 1819 and 1820. They lived there until their grant of land was nullified when Texas declared independence. By 1828 the rest were forced by settlers into western Oklahoma, where they were slated to be joined by the main body of Cherokees during the period of removal described below.

Many Cherokees in the East had by now fully assimilated to European ways. In 1789 William Bartram wrote, "if adopting the manners and customs of the white man is to be termed civilization, perhaps the Cherokee have made the greatest advance." By the 1820s mixed-bloods with names like Adair, Ward, Rogers, Vann, Lowery, and Ross, many with blue eyes and light hair, had acquired most of the wealth of the Cherokee nation and held at least four of every ten Cherokee government posts (Woodward 1963, 120). Many followed the example of their English neighbors and owned slaves.

Assimilated leaders gave full approval in 1801 for the establishment of missionary churches and schools (built by Moravians, Presbyterians, Baptists, Methodists, and Quakers), saying, "our very existence depends on it" (Mankiller 1993, 79). Until this time Christian missionaries had had relatively little success among the Cherokee. Even after approval, conversion went slowly. The Moravians were first to receive permission to evangelize in 1801. They adopted a strategy that was followed by other churches. Recognizing the desire of Cherokee leaders for education for their children, they built schools. The Moravians began accepting pupils at their first school in 1804. In 1817 they were joined by northern Presbyterians and Congregationalists under the auspices of the American Board of Commissioners for Foreign Missions.

One of the more successful schools, Brainerd Mission, was established by the board at present-day Chattanooga, Tennessee, in 1817. Soon Baptists and Methodists were at work among the *Ani'-Yun'-wiya*. The missionaries continued to focus their efforts on children, hoping that by bringing the "blessings of Christianity and civilization" to the children, they would become leaders of a transformed, Christianized Cherokee society (Perdue 1989, 41–43; Perdue and Green 1995, 43–45).

It is important to realize that like other native peoples, the Cherokee adapted Christianity to their own situation and traditions. As ethnohistorian William McLoughlin has noted:

> Increasingly they practiced a form of Christianity that they had adapted to many of their own values and beliefs. . . . They believed that Adam, the first man, was red. Because God protected the weak against oppression, they claimed him as their savior against the whites who were trying to destroy their nation. (McLoughlin 1994, 4)

Cherokee traditionalists, however, continued to resist acculturation and "Christianization." During the treaty negotiations of the 1780s, a leading "Beloved Man" of the Cherokee, Old Tassel, said:

> Many proposals have been made to us to adopt your laws, your religions, your manners, and your customs. We do not see the propriety of such a reformation. We should be better pleased with beholding the good effect of these doctrines in your own practices than with hearing you talk about them . . . You say, "Why do not the Indians till the ground and live as we do?" May we not ask with equal propriety, "Why do not the white people hunt and live as we do?" (Spicer 1969, 254)

By the end of the eighteenth century, the Cherokee seemed "a ruined people." "Disorder was everywhere-between old chiefs and young chiefs, between one town and another, between parents and children, between man and the retreating animals" (McLoughlin 1986, 4). The harmony that had sustained them from the time of origins had seemingly been lost. From the perspective of Cherokee traditionalists, the reason was clear: The *Ani'-Yun'-wiya* had embraced the materialistic culture of the invaders and the occupiers' religion and had turned from their own spiritual way of life.

By the early 1800s the Eastern Cherokee population had declined to about 12,000 (Thornton 1990, 47). About half were mixed-bloods (Littlefield 1971, 404). The people lived in about seventy-five towns and villages east and north of the Creek nation in eastern Tennessee, northwestern Georgia, and northeastern Alabama (see Finger 1984). A large number had already migrated westward.

In 1802 the federal government entered into an agreement with the state of Georgia to extinguish the land claims of Cherokees and Creeks as soon as possible. Cherokee leadership was now dominated by those who felt that hope for the future lay in assimilating to European ways. "If we follow the customs of our old people, we will never do well," a group of leaders (including the future chief John Ross) said to President Jefferson in 1808 (McLoughlin 1986, 177).

In 1810 Upper and Lower Town factions reunited and established a National Committee, beginning a process of centralization that would culminate in the formal creation of the Cherokee nation a few years later. When the Shawnee chief Tecumseh tried to enlist the *Ani'-Yun'-wiya* for his campaign against the Americans in 1811 (see chapter 1), the council of chiefs (dominated by the assimilationists) turned him down.

The friction, however, between "traditionalists" and "progressives" continued. One traditionalist leader warned that the Mother of the Nation (Selu, Corn Mother) would abandon the people if they turned from the ways of their ancestors and adopted the milling of corn. The grinding, he said, "breaks her bones" (Wilson 1999, 159–60). The tension led to the Cherokee Ghost Dance movement (see below), an attempt to come to terms with the now obvious gap between old and new. During the War of 1812, the pressure on the Eastern Cherokees to join the group in Arkansas grew, as did friction between the two Cherokee factions.

In an effort to show their loyalty to the United States, some Eastern Cherokees allied themselves with General Andrew Jackson in his 1813–14 campaign against the Creeks. At the battle of Horseshoe Bend, the Cherokee warrior Junaluska (who later expressed regret for his action) saved Jackson's life.

According to the terms of the treaty of 1819, Cherokees within ceded territory could elect to register for individual reservations of 640 acres and become U.S. citizens. Forty-nine families in North Carolina chose to accept these terms instead of moving into the reduced boundaries of the Cherokee nation. They were, for the most part, traditionalists who had resisted assimilation and wanted only to pursue their own way of life in peace. The land had already been sold by the state, however, and they had to settle on a tract of land on the Oconaluftee River (hence they were known as the Oconaluftee Cherokees). A Euroamerican orphan taken in by this group, William Holland Thomas, helped them consolidate their holdings by purchasing land as it became available. His efforts helped them avoid removal to Indian Territory.

Despite the continuing loss of land, the period between the early 1800s and the mid–1830s has been labelled the Cherokee Renascence because of the economic, cultural, and political achievements of the era (see McLoughlin 1986). In Georgia a number of large estates were owned by highly educated Cherokees.

In 1820 the Cherokee Nation in Georgia formally became a republic, with its own legislature, judiciary, and police force. By 1821 Sequoyah, motivated by a desire to preserve Cherokee traditions in a permanent form, had developed an alphabet, so the Cherokee had a written language. Seven years later the first issue of the first Native American newspaper, the bilingual *Tsa la gi Tsu lehisanunbi* (*Cherokee Phoenix*), was published.

Many acculturated leaders were by this time openly dismissive of traditional spiritual practices. For example, John Ridge wrote in 1826 that those Cherokees claiming supernatural powers "are generally living monuments of fun to the young and grave Ridicule for those in maturer years." He then spoke glowingly of the Christian missionaries who had, in his view, converted from error and sin "many a drunken, idle & good for nothing Indian" turning them into "useful Citizens" (Perdue and Green 1995, 39–40). Once again, however, traditionalists rejected acculturation.

The White Path Rebellion was one such expression. In 1825 the old, traditional chief White Path was expelled from the National Council for rejecting the Christianization of Cherokee country. Other *Ani'-Yun'-wiya* concerned that the new constitution would turn the Cherokee nation into a Christian republic rallied around White Path. They resented the dominance of an acculturated elite bent on imposing Christian morality on their fellow Cherokees and dismissing *Ani'-Yun'-wiya* tradition as "backward."

The rebellion, which actually began in March 1827, was not violent. Rather, it followed the traditional Cherokee practice of dissidents withdrawing from a council whose decisions they rejected. Cherokee healers played a key role in the movement by reviving traditional dances and other ceremonies.

Dreams and visions also were particularly important, and miraculous occurrences were noted. On one occasion a Cherokee woman gave birth to triplets, all born with a full set of teeth. The first one born chastised his mother for her godless (i.e., nontraditional) way of life. The point, of course, was that a generation was coming that would rebuke its elders for their rejection of the traditional way of life.

Many missionaries (including the famous Reverend Samuel Worcester) and proconstitution leaders dismissed the rebellion as, in Chief John Ross's word, "noise." Moravian missionaries, however, warned of dire consequences for Christianity among the Cherokee as a result of the traditionalist revival.

On 26 July 1827 a Cherokee constitution, modeled after the United States Constitution, was adopted and an independent Cherokee Nation declared. The old clan system was replaced with a representative form of government. The constitution's principal author was John Ross (*Kooweskoowee*), who served as elected principal chief from 1828 to 1866. Although only about one-eighth Cherokee (and probably seven-eighths Scottish), Ross was, in the opinion of many Cherokee today, "one of our most remarkable chiefs," the "hope of the Cherokee as the whites swept over our people" (Mankiller 1993, 85–86; see Moulton 1985).

During the 1830s, however, Ross's strategy of accelerating acculturation to European ways failed. In July 1828 gold was discovered in the heart of *Ani'-Yun'-wiya* country, and a flood of new settlers was unleashed. In December 1828 the Georgia legislature annexed Cherokee lands within its charter. The same year President Andrew Jackson promised in his inaugural address a speedy implementation of the policy to remove the Eastern Cherokee and other native nations to the West.

Some Christian theologians were contributing to the growing fervor to force out the Cherokee. They argued that removal or even worse was preordained by God, who had a plan to bring the Europeans to this new land. For example, Reverend John Thompson suggested that "[i]t may be part of God's plan in promoting the interests of His church to destroy the majority of the Cherokee" (McLoughlin 1994, 48). Others said that since Indians were not endowed with the same human feelings as Europeans, they would not be hurt by such a policy.

In part because of such attitudes, the missionaries' efforts to convince the Cherokee of the truth of the Bible did not always meet with success. When told the story of the sin of Adam and Eve in the Garden of Eden, a Cherokee chief offered the opinion that if the Europeans' God had simply put a fence around the tree he did not want Adam and Eve to eat, "you would not be bothered by this Evil you call sin and you would not be living in fear of your God" (Peithmann 1964, 45, 50). Another leader, Chief Yonaguska, said, after listening to a reading of several chapters of the Gospel of Matthew, newly translated into *Ani'-Yun'-wiya*, "Well, it seems to be a good book—strange that the white people are no better, after having had it so long." (Mooney 1900 [1982], 163).

The Policy of Removal and The "Trail of Tears" (1830–40)

With the passage of the Indian Removal Act in 1830, the fate of the majority of Eastern Cherokees was sealed, although their skillful defiance would draw out its implementation for nearly a decade (see Anderson 1991).

In 1831 the Supreme Court ruled in *Cherokee Nation* v. *State of Georgia* that the Cherokee were a "domestic dependent nation" who could not be subjected to state law. Only the federal government, the court determined, could enter into relations with the Cherokee and other native nations.

The missionaries working among the Cherokee tended to side with the Cherokee in defending Cherokee sovereignty and opposing removal. When two missionaries, Congregationalists Reverend Samuel Austin Worcester (see McLoughlin 1994, 50–90) and medical missionary Dr. Elizur Butler, refused to swear allegiance to Georgia, they were sent to prison. This brought to a head the issue of the sovereignty of the *Ani'-Yun'-wiya*. The Cherokee National Council mounted a campaign in defense of their cause, appealing to Christian teaching. "Let Americans remember the great law of love," the Council said in 1830, "'Do unto others as ye would that others would do unto you.' Let us remember that all nations on this earth are under the greatest obligations to obey this law" (Peithmann 1964, 61).

The missionaries appealed their conviction, and in 1832 the case reached the U.S. Supreme Court as *Worcester* v. *State of Georgia*. The Cherokees' lawyers warned that mistreatment of the *Ani'-Yun'-wiya* was a disgraceful stain on the nation that must be removed. In an opinion written by Chief Justice John Marshall, the Court ruled that the federal government had exclusive jurisdiction within the boundaries of the Cherokee nation and state law was void. But state officials ignored the ruling, and President Jackson refused to intervene. "John Marshall has made his law," he said, in an often quoted remark, "now let him enforce it."

The role of Andrew Jackson, widely heralded by historians as a champion of democracy, in the removal of the Cherokee and other southeastern nations is still debated. Robert Remini is among the historians who have sought to absolve Jackson from guilt. According to Remini, Jackson was simply trying to move Indians to a "safe haven" west of the Mississippi. He saw "removal as a humanitarian means of preserving Native American life and culture." The problem was in the unscrupulous implementation of the policy by subordinates. Most other historians, however, now maintain that Jackson "was responsible for the criminally negligent homicide of thousands of American Indians" (Hauptman 1995, 41, 48).

A Cherokee faction sometimes called the Treaty Party, led by Major Ridge, Elias Boudinot (editor of the *Cherokee Phoenix*), and Stand Watie, broke from the elected leadership and sought to negotiate the removal to the West. President Jackson's representative, a Dutch Reformed minister named J. F. Schermerhorn ("a sly politician in the garb of a Christian minister"; cf. Hauptman 1995), drew up terms of a treaty binding the *Ani'-Yun'-wiya* to surrender their whole territory and move to the West. The vast majority of Cherokees, however, remained loyal to Chief Ross, who skillfully led the opposition to removal. On 29 December 1835, only a few hundred of the 17,000 Cherokees met at New Echota to approve a treaty that relinquished all land east of the Mississippi in exchange for a payment of $5 million.

The treaty was denounced as fraudulent by Chief Ross and the entire Cherokee council, and nearly 16,000 Cherokees signed a petition opposing it. On the same day the treaty was approved, the following memorial was submitted to the U.S. Congress by the *Ani'-Yun'-wiya* opposed to removal:

> In truth, our cause is your own. It is the cause of liberty and justice. It is based upon your own principle which we have learned from yourselves; for we have gloried to count your Washington and your Jefferson our great teachers.
>
> We have practiced their precepts with success and the result is manifest. The wilderness of forest has given place to comfortable dwelling and cultivated fields.
>
> Mental culture, industrial habits, and domestic enjoyment have succeeded the rudeness of the savage state. We have learned your religion also. We have read your sacred books. Hundreds of our people have embraced their doctrines, practiced the virtue they teach, cherished the hopes they awaken.

We speak to the representatives of a Christian country; the friends of justice; the patrons of the oppressed; and our hopes revive, and our prospects brighten, as we indulge the thought. On your sentence our fate is suspended, on your kindness, on your humanity, on your compassion, on your benevolence, we rest our hopes. (Peithmann 1964, v)

Many famous Euroamerican leaders, including Davy Crockett, Sam Houston (who married a Cherokee woman), Daniel Webster, and Henry Clay, and a number of Christian ministers, rallied in support of the majority of the *Ani'-Yun'-wiya*, but to no avail. Clay called the removal policy "unjust, dishonest, cruel, and shortsighted in the extreme" (Peithmann 1964, 68). Nevertheless, in May 1836 Congress ratified the treaty by one vote, and the Cherokee were given two years to vacate their homeland.

With the majority of Cherokees following Chief Ross's policy of passive resistance, the removal went slowly. By spring 1838 only about 2,000 had left voluntarily, including Ridge and many of his Treaty Party supporters (see Wilkins 1986). An angered President Martin Van Buren sent General Winfield Scott and 7,000 troops to carry out removal by force. Stockades were built, and *Ani'-Yun'-wiya* were rounded up and placed in what today would be called concentration camps. In the nineteenth-century equivalent of ethnic cleansing, troops seized whole families and dragged them away to the camps. Their houses and property were left to be plundered by Euroamerican settlers. The troops passed mixed-blood girls from soldier to soldier like bottles of whiskey.

About 1,400 *Ani'-Yun'-wiya* avoided the roundup and escaped into the mountains. According to a story colored by the passage of time (Mooney 1900 [1982], 131; King 1979, 165–66) and now recreated each summer for tourists in an outdoor pageant near Cherokee, North Carolina, one of the escapees was a man named Tsali (the Cherokee pronunciation of Charley). According to the legend, he had fled into the mountains with his family after killing a soldier in a fight that broke out when his wife had been prodded with a bayonet. General Scott agreed to leave the rest of those hiding alone if Tsali and his sons were captured or surrendered. They did so, probably with "encouragement" from the Oconaluftee Cherokees, who feared they would be subjected to removal if they did not cooperate, and were ordered shot. After the execution, General Scott kept his word and did not attempt to capture the others in hiding. The legend of Tsali served to unify disparate groups. The Eastern Band continues to this day to live in western North Carolina in and near the Great Smoky Mountains (on the boundary of Great Smoky National Park) on lands designated as the Eastern Cherokee Reservation (also called the Qualla Boundary). The 56,000 acres of the reservation are on land purchased in the nineteenth century by Will Thomas, the adopted Cherokee.

Another legend told by those who hid in the mountains describes the Immortals, the *Nuñnehi* (see below), appearing and telling the people to come and join them in the mountains and under the water. Those of Anisgayayi town were taken to the top of Lone Peak near Cheowa and became solid rock. Those of Hiwassee were taken under the water and can still be heard talking below when the wind ripples the surface.

On 1 August 1838 the Cherokee National Council met at Red Clay, Tennessee, for the last time in its homeland. The following resolution was adopted:

> The Cherokee people have existed as a distinct national community for a period extending into antiquity beyond the dates and records and memory of man. These attributes have never been relinquished by the Cherokee people, and cannot be dissolved by the expulsion of the Nation from its own territory by the power of the United States Government. (Peithmann 1964, 80)

With *Ani'-Yun'-wiya* dying in the squalid conditions of the detention camps, Chief Ross asked General Scott to allow him to organize the migration to the West in contingents of 1,000 each. Scott agreed, and the Eternal Fire was lit from the sacred hearth of the council house, to be taken westward. The first of 645 wagons left in August 1838; the last departed in December.

The tragic story of the "Trail of Tears" (*Nunna daul Tsunyi*), literally "the trail where we cried," cannot be fully recounted here (see Ehle 1988). It should be noted, however, that before the last of the *Ani'-Yun'-wiya* reached Indian Territory in 1839, about 4,000 had died. Among the dead were elders who carried to their graves many of the ancient traditions of the people and the wife of Chief Ross, who had given her blanket to a sick child. It is estimated that at least 10,000 more Cherokees "would have been alive in 1840" if removal had not taken place (Thornton 1990, 76). Fifty years later James Mooney interviewed survivors of the death march and provided the most reliable account of the ordeal. One, a Georgia volunteer who later served as a colonel in the Confederate army, said: "I fought through the civil war and have seen men shot to pieces and slaughtered by the thousands, but the Cherokee removal was the cruelest work I ever saw" (Mooney 1900 [1982], 130).

It was, in the words of Chief Wilma Mankiller, "our holocaust" (Mankiller 1993, 49). Interestingly, on the trail little friction arose between traditional healers and the few Christian ministers who accompanied the deportees, as "each allowed the other the consolations of the religion of his or her choice" (McLoughlin 1994, 101).

Life in Indian Territory (1840–1907)

The *Ani'-Yun'-wiya* in Indian Territory were divided into three groups: the Old Settlers, who had moved from Arkansas to Indian Territory under a form of government all their own; the Ridge or Treaty Party; and the National Ross Party.

The forced march of thousands of Cherokees from their southeastern homeland to Indian territory in the winter of 1838–39 is remembered by Cherokees as "the Trail of Tears." Four thousand Cherokee men, women, and children died along the way. (© Baldwin H. Ward and Kathryn C. Ward/CORBIS)

The first two joined forces against the majority Ross group, insisting that the Old Settlers rule until an election in the fall of 1839. Six thousand Cherokees of all factions met on 10 June 1839. After twelve days of heated debate, no agreement was reached. A day after adjournment three of the leaders of the Treaty Party (Major Ridge, John Ridge, and Elias Boudinot) were killed to avenge their alleged betrayal of the Cherokee nation.

Tahlequah became the Western Cherokee capital, and a new constitution similar to the original one (with three branches of government and property held in common) was adopted on 6 September 1839. Except for the band in the mountains of North Carolina, all *Ani'-Yun'-wiya* were now reunited under the leadership of Chief John Ross. In 1841 approximately 14,000 Cherokees were living in Indian Territory (Thornton 1990, 82).

Despite continued tension among factions, Cherokee society was revived. A new newspaper, the *Cherokee Advocate*, began publication in 1844, with the motto "Our Rights, Our Country, Our Race." A public school system was instituted in 1841, and by 1844 there were eighteen schools. Male and Female Seminaries were opened by 1851. The Female Seminary was modeled after Mount Holyoke Seminary (later College) and was a sign of the commitment of the *Ani'-Yun'-wiya* to the education of women.

In part because of their continuation of slavery, mixed-bloods again became a wealthy class. By 1860, although they constituted less than 10 percent of the *Ani'-Yun'-wiya* population, mixed-blood planters owned 4,000 slaves. The rest of the Cherokee in Indian Territory were non-slave-owning subsistence farmers and most of them were full-bloods (Mankiller 1993, 122–23; Perdue 1989, 72–73; McLoughlin 1994, 225).

Removal had also taken a toll on Christian missions. Many *Ani'-Yun'-wiya* converts had rejected Christianity after the treatment they received at the hands of a "Christian" nation. Such missionaries as Baptist Evan Jones, however, had accompanied the Cherokee on the Trail of Tears and strongly supported Cherokee autonomy and respected Cherokee tradition (McLoughlin 1994, 91–108).

Between 1840 and 1860 missionary activity was more subdued and gradually trust was rebuilt. In the 1850s the Bible was translated into the Sequoyan syllabary. Gradually Cherokee converts were ordained as Christian ministers and they challenged the traditional healers (*adonigisi*). Traditional practices such as the "going to water" ritual (see below) were blended with Christian rituals (in this case, the sacrament of baptism). In addition, more tolerant missionaries such as Jones and the new Cherokee clergy made the healers feel welcome in the church, so many continued their healing practices while participating in Christian rituals. Baptist and Methodist churches proved themselves much more willing to adapt to the traditional practices, and therefore grew rapidly, while the missionary churches less willing to modify dogma and/or ritual (especially Moravians and Congregationalists) declined. Although by 1860 only about 15 percent of the Cherokee in Indian Territory were formal members of Christian churches, many more had adopted a syncretic worldview that bridged Christianity and traditional spirituality (McLoughlin 1994, 188–218).

With the help of Evan Jones, the Keetoowah Society (see below) was formed in the late 1850s to defend Cherokee autonomy and tradition and to counter the influence of wealthier slaveholders.

During the Civil War the Treaty Party supported the South, viewing the war as an opportunity to unseat Ross. Full-bloods favored the abolition of slavery and supported the North. John Ross, though he owned slaves, leaned toward the North (because of the role of southerners in the forced removal of the Cherokee), but he tried to remain neutral.

After federal troops withdrew from the Cherokees' territory, Chief Ross reluctantly signed a treaty with the Confederacy in 1861. Cherokees were now fighting on both sides of the conflict. Stand Watie rose to the rank of Brigadier General in the Confederate Army and, with Ross in Washington trying to repair relations with the Union government, Watie was elected chief. When the war ended he was the last Confederate general to surrender.

The Civil War took a terrible toll on the Cherokee. About one-fourth of the Cherokee in Indian Territory perished (reducing the population from 21,000 to

14,000 [Thornton 1990, 94]), and thousands of others fled to Kansas. In 1863 the council voted to abolish slavery and to abrogate the treaty with the Confederacy.

After the Civil War the Cherokee and the other "five civilized tribes" were punished for supporting the South. In an 1867 message to Congress, President Andrew Johnson said, "If the savage resists, civilization, with the Ten Commandments in one hand and the sword in the other, demands his immediate extermination" (Mankiller 1993, 128). New treaties were forced upon the Cherokee and the others, which freed the remaining Cherokee slaves and opened Indian Territory to other native peoples, including, as we have seen in the previous chapter, the Lenape. The treaties also granted rights-of-way to railroads.

Once again, however, the *Ani'-Yun'-wiya* rose from the ashes. Ross was reelected principal chief and served until his death in 1866. In 1867 full-blood Baptist minister and leader of the Keetoowah Society Lewis Downing was elected chief. His election was the result of an effective coalition among full-blood traditionalists and converts to Christianity to take power away from the mixed-blood elite. The population rebounded by 1871 to about 18,000 (Thornton 1990, 103). Tahlequah became a thriving center of Cherokee culture. The *Cherokee Advocate*, which had ceased publication in 1850 due to a shortage of funds, resumed in 1870. Livestock herds were replenished, and new homes, stores, and schools were built.

By 1872 the lines of the Missouri–Kansas–Texas railroad ran across *Ani'-Yun'-wiya* lands, causing the value of land to skyrocket and bringing Euroamerican settlers to Indian Territory. Soon the Territory was flooded with a host of gamblers, prostitutes, cattle thieves, and whiskey peddlers, all intent on taking advantage of the fact that the Cherokee had no jurisdiction over white people on their lands. To raise money the Cherokee government was forced to lease land to ranchers in the Cherokee Outlet, a strip of land in what is now north central and western Oklahoma that had been reserved for Cherokee use.

At this point the *Ani'-Yun'-wiya* in Indian Territory reached a crossroads. Many Cherokees continued on the path of assimilation and mixing with Euroamericans which had been underway for so long. Increasingly, they became a group who spoke of their "Cherokee ancestry" rather than calling themselves Cherokees. They also became known as "white Cherokees." Another group withdrew when Euroamericans began rushing into Indian Territory. The result was "a geographic partitioning of the Cherokee Nation" with one faction confining themselves to the Ozark hollows where they sought to perpetuate their traditional culture. These Cherokees mostly refrained from intermarriage and thus maintained full-blood families. The other faction intermarried with whites and became the power structure of the rejuvenated Cherokee nation and part of the Oklahoma political establishment (Wahrhaftig 1979, 226–28).

In the early 1880s Senator Henry Dawes visited the Cherokee nation and reported that the people were flourishing under their own system of government.

Still, he found a fatal flaw: individual Cherokees did not own their own land. And among them, he wrote, "there is no selfishness, which is at the bottom of civilization." Until their lands were divided up, they would make no real progress, he concluded (Hendrix 1983, 32).

In 1889 Oklahoma (from the Choctaw phrase for "Red People") Territory was created out of the western half of Indian Territory. The action created 2 million acres of "surplus lands," which were opened to settlement, and soon the famous Oklahoma "land runs" were underway. With the homesteaders came pressure for statehood.

A 5 October 1892 letter to the *Cherokee Advocate* expressed the point of view held by many *Ani'-Yun'-wiya*, whose tradition was common ownership of land:

> The term "allotment" as used among us is simply another word for title in severalty to our lands. If the system of owning land in severalty has the effect to exclude so many people among the whites from the enjoyment of a home, it seems to me that the same system among the Cherokee would soon have the effect to render many of them homeless. Business knows no pity, and cares for justice only when justice is seen to be better policy. If it had power to control the elements, it would grasp in its iron clutches the waters, sunshine and air and resell them by measure, and at exorbitant prices to the millions of famished men, women, and children. I do not want to see our Cherokee people without homes. The title in common to our lands is the strongest guarantee against the homelessness of many of our people. (Mankiller 1993, 167)

Despite being exempted from allotment in the original Dawes Act (see chapter 1), the Cherokee nation and the other "Five Civilized Tribes" were subjected to the practice. The 6.5–million–acre Cherokee Outlet, which the Cherokee had ceded under duress to the government for use in settling Native American nations being forced off their homelands, was opened for settlement under the provisions of the 1862 Homestead Act. On 16 September 1893 the largest land run in U.S. history began. In payment, the Cherokee received $1.29 an acre. In 1894 the funds held in trust for the Cherokee by the U.S. government totalled $2.7 million (Debo 1984, 7).

The principal resistance to the allotment plan came from the intertribal Four Mothers Society (which had as many as 24,000 members at its height) and the *Ani'-Yun'-wiya* Keetoowah Society (see below). Redbird Smith, a leader of the Keetoowah Society, was imprisoned for refusing to enroll for the land allotment. Some members were among those who had withdrawn to the hills to practice traditional Cherokee spirituality in isolation. They hoped to consolidate large tracts of land to be held in common in accord with the tradition of shared ownership.

Others dreamed of a new purified Cherokee society in Mexico (Littlefield 1971). Smith, however, sought reconciliation among the various Cherokee factions. "I have always believed," he wrote, "that the Great Creator had a great design for my people, the Cherokee. . . . [W]e must now get together as a race and render our contribution to mankind" (Mankiller 1993, 170). By the closing of the allotment roll in 1907, nearly 42,000 citizens of the Cherokee nation had been enrolled (including 4,300 freedmen); only about one-fourth were full-bloods (Thornton 1990, 123).

Between 1891 and 1970 the holdings of the Cherokee would be reduced from 19,500,000 acres to only 146,598. The story of what happened to the Cherokee and the other "Civilized Tribes" is, in the words of historian Angie Debo, "an orgy of plunder and exploitation probably unparalleled in American history" (Debo 1984). Her award-winning work, *And Still the Waters Run*, graphically documents the tragedy through the 1930s.

In 1898 a law named after Charles Curtis, a Kansas congressman of Kaw descent who later became vice president of the United States, was passed. It effectively ended tribal rule by abolishing Cherokee tribal laws and courts, making Cherokees subject to federal courts.

It had long been a dream of John Ross and other *Ani'-Yun'-wiya* leaders to have an independent Cherokee state as one of the United States. In 1905 a convention was called to consider a constitution for an Indian state to be called Sequoyah in the eastern half of the original Indian Territory. The proposal was rejected by Congress, however, amid growing pressure to create a non-Indian state dominated by Euroamericans in Indian and Oklahoma Territories. In 1906 the government of the Cherokee which had functioned so well since 1839 was finally ordered dissolved by an act of Congress.

In 1907, after a convention that involved few native people, Indian and Oklahoma Territories were joined and recognized as the forty-sixth state. A mock wedding between an Indian princess and a cowboy was held to symbolize the union of the two cultures. One of the first Oklahoma senators was an assimilated Cherokee, Robert Latham Owen. In the opinion of many Cherokees today, however, it was then, and remains to this time, a sad day for the Cherokee people.

The Cherokee Nation in the Twentieth Century (1907–95)

By the time Oklahoma became a state, many Euroamericans in Oklahoma and elsewhere believed that the Cherokee had been fully assimilated into their culture and were prosperous. President Theodore Roosevelt called the Cherokee "a bright intelligent race, better fitted to 'follow the white man's road' than any other Indians" (Mankiller 1993, 168). While this was true for the small ruling elite, it was not the case for the majority. As a result of the land grabbing which followed allotment, many Cherokees were now destitute. Even when oil was discovered, little of the revenue found its way to the Cherokee most in need.

By 1914 the Bureau of Indian Affairs was attempting to run the Cherokee nation as an "administrative dictatorship" through the last elected chief, W.C. Rogers, who at that point was serving only a token role. In 1976 a federal court said that BIA's policies had been "bureaucratic imperialism." From the time of Rogers's death until the 1930s, a Cherokee chief was appointed by the federal government only when one was needed to endorse government policies. During this period Cherokee lands were greedily taken and pressure to assimilate grew ever stronger. Cherokee schools were closed and children were sent to boarding schools to be "cleansed" of any remaining Cherokee ways. Nevertheless, the Keetoowah Societies continued to resist, and Keetoowah members and other traditionalists perpetuated ceremonial dances (see below). By 1930 Cherokee population had grown to more than 45,000, with Cherokees in forty-two states besides Oklahoma and North Carolina (Thornton 1990, 129, 131).

In 1936 the Oklahoma Indian Welfare Act created the opportunity for the Cherokee and other native nations in Oklahoma to adopt constitutions and secure corporate charters. It provided for the federal government to buy land to be held in trust for incorporated nations and to make loans available for development projects. Unfortunately, the Cherokee were too scattered and divided to take advantage of this opportunity.

By the 1940s and 1950s the mistaken impression was even stronger that all Cherokees were happily assimilated and doing well. In fact, many *Ani'-Yun'-wiya* who followed the more traditional ways lived in extreme poverty on their family allotments in small communities scattered through the hills and hollows of Eastern Oklahoma. In these areas many spoke only Cherokee, and the all-night ceremonial dances described below were common. Those who participated in the dances often kept their involvement largely to themselves, however, because of the disdain many Christian Cherokees now had for these "pagan" dances.

In 1950 the United Keetoowah Band (UKB) of Cherokee Indians was formally recognized by the federal government. The roll of the UKB was dominated by full-bloods, and the band emphasized Cherokee tradition.

In 1961, in settlement of a suit before the Indian Claims Commission, the Cherokee were awarded $14.7 million for the Cherokee Outlet (for which they had received only $1.29 per acre in 1893).

According to the 1970 census, the Cherokee population had grown to 66,150 (reflecting the new census policy of using self-identification to determine ethnicity), with 27,197 in Oklahoma, 6,085 in North Carolina, and 32,878 in other states, especially California, Texas, and New Mexico. This made the Cherokee the second largest Native American nation after the Navajos. Only 12,000 were officially enrolled as members of the Cherokee nation, however (Thornton 1990, 136, 138).

Not until 1971 were the Cherokee in Oklahoma allowed to elect their own chief. A new Cherokee constitution, with executive (principal and deputy chiefs), legislative (fifteen-member tribal council), and judicial (three-member appeals tribunal) branches, was adopted in 1976. Under this system the chief had responsibilities comparable to the head of a small nation and chief executive of a large corporation. The Cherokee began to be known for their growing ability to manage their own institutions. Without a land base to provide unity, the Cherokee were able to preserve and extend Cherokee identity at a time when it might otherwise have been lost, through their new constitution's inclusive policy toward tribal membership and affiliation.

By the 1980 census 232,344 (17 percent) of the 1,366,676 Americans who self-identified as American Indians claimed the status of Cherokee, making the Cherokee the largest Native American nation (with the Navajo second). Of these, only 78,781 were enrolled members: Eastern Band (8,381), Cherokee Nation of Oklahoma (63,400), and United Keetoowah Band of Cherokee Indians in Oklahoma (7,000). By 1980 many more who did not self-identify as Cherokees were claiming Cherokee ancestry, and that number certainly continues to grow (Thornton 1990, 143, 145, 157, 170, 172–74, 199–200).

In the late 1970s a Cherokee spiritual leader had a vision of the Red Lady of the Eternal Flame, one of the ancient deities of the people. He interpreted it to be a prophecy of the coming of a woman as principal chief of the Cherokee. In 1983 the prophecy came a step closer to realization when Wilma Mankiller became deputy chief under Ross Swimmer. She had left her ancestral home in Oklahoma as a child and moved to California during the relocation program of the 1950s (see chapter 1). There she had become active in the Red Power movement of the 1960s and 1970s. Mankiller moved back to Oklahoma, where she worked for the Cherokee nation and achieved recognition for her work as a community organizer and development specialist. Mankiller also sided with traditionalists in their efforts to preserve Cherokee language, culture, and spirituality.

In 1984 a reunion of the Eastern Band of Cherokees and the Cherokee Nation of Oklahoma was held in Red Clay, Tennessee, the first since removal. Since 1984 a series of meetings of the two councils has been held to consider issues of common concern. An eternal flame still burns at the site of the meeting.

In 1987 Congress passed a law creating the "Trail of Tears National Historic Trail." The National Park Service's plan called for interpretive centers and historical markers as well as hiking trails at points along two of the routes followed by the Cherokee in 1838 and 1839. A decade later, however, not very much money had been appropriated to implement the plan. State and private efforts have resulted in sites at the restored New Echota capital in northern Georgia as well as at Red Clay.

When Cherokee Chief Ross Swimmer was named head of the Bureau of Indian Affairs by President Ronald Reagan in 1985, Wilma Mankiller assumed the office of principal chief of the Cherokee nation. She was elected in her own right in 1987 and, in a landslide, to a second four-year term in 1991.

Chief Mankiller, whose name probably came from the tradition of a group who were charged with protection of the village, brought world attention and much needed grant money to the Cherokee nation and succeeded in increasing the self-sufficiency of the *Ani'-Yun'-wiya*. In 1979 and 1980, after an automobile accident almost took her life and a rare disease further weakened her, Mankiller underwent a spiritual awakening in which she committed herself to the age-old Cherokee way, to what elders of the people call "being of a good mind." In Chief Mankiller's own words, "[i]ndividually and collectively, Cherokee people possess an extraordinary ability to face down adversity and continue moving forward. We are able to do that because our culture, though certainly diminished, has sustained us since time immemorial. The Cherokee culture is a well-kept secret" (Mankiller 1993, xix).

The notion that all Cherokees had fully assimilated to Euroamerican culture was still misleading in 1990. More than 10,000 Cherokees still lived in about fifty settlements in northeastern Oklahoma where they spoke mainly Cherokee and lived traditional lives, keeping alive at least some of the Cherokee ceremonies we will discuss below. Whether Chief Mankiller's policy of economic development and cultural renewal was of benefit to such traditionalists or subtly increased pressure on them to assimilate is a matter of continuing dispute. When Chief Mankiller declined to stand for reelection in 1995, Joe Byrd was elected principal chief, the first full-blood, bilingual leader of the Cherokee nation in nearly 200 years.

This chapter returns to the present situation of the Cherokee people after considering the traditional spirituality of the *Ani'-Yun'-wiya*.

Traditional *Ani'-Yun'-wiya* Spirituality

Traditional *Ani'-Yun'-wiya* spirituality focuses on preserving the harmony that exists in the human relationship with the rest of creation, and restoring that equilibrium when it has been disrupted (Perdue and Green 1995, 4). The world as created is in balance. First woman and man, Selu and Kana'ti, balanced one another as providers of vegetables and meat. Following that model, traditional Cherokee women and men have followed complementary roles of farming and hunting. Indeed, all daily activities must be performed in a manner respecting the basic harmony. When they are not, and harmony is disturbed, rituals must be conducted to restore the balance.

A good bit of our knowledge of traditional Cherokee spirituality is a result of the decision of several healers of the Eastern Cherokees to share their knowledge of myths, legends, rituals, and sacred formulas with ethnologist James Mooney in the late 1880s. Mooney published much of this material in two classic volumes, which were reprinted in a single work in 1982 (Mooney 1891 and 1900 [1982]). These works remain essential both for *Ani'-Yun'-wiya* striving to renew their own unique sense of spiritual identity and for non-Cherokee seeking to understand and appreciate the rich Cherokee spiritual tradition.

An Eastern Cherokee who worked with Mooney, Will West Long, also played a critical role in the preservation of Cherokee spirituality. Long's Big Cove band was a "settlement that resisted European cultural intrusions and preserved its ceremonial heritage more effectively than other groups or towns of the Eastern band" (Speck and Broom 1983, xxiii). He collaborated first with Mooney, then with the noted ethnologist Frank Speck and Speck's student Leonard Broom in the 1920s and 1930s. Long's meticulous gathering of information about the ritual life of the Big Cove band is one of the most important sources for our understanding of the traditional spirituality of the *Ani'-Yun'-wiya.*

Long's ambivalence about sharing this information represents the attitude of many native informants:

His attitude toward the tradition and ritual he revealed to ethnologists was clear, but caused him considerable difficulty. He believed the knowledge he carried was of very real power, and its potentiality for good or evil strong. On the one hand, he wanted to see it preserved and interpreted, and he needed the wages he received for his work; on the other, he was always afraid of exposing himself and his people to ridicule, and he was never sure that the people who hired him did not use his information for commercial, and perhaps even antisocial, purposes. He saw the men for whom he worked prosper, while he remained impoverished. (Witthoft 1948, 359)

The principal reason that our knowledge of traditional *Ani'-Yun'-wiya* spirituality is limited is because of the active assault on it by Christian missionaries. As we have seen, missionaries began their work in earnest among the Cherokee in the early nineteenth century. From the outset they regarded the traditional rituals of the Cherokee "as competitive systems and treated them as curious practices of ignorant savages to be derided, as symptoms of idolatrous behavior to be challenged, or as a system of decadent revelry and a focus of infection for the forces of sin equated with the forces of intemperance" (Speck and Broom 1983, 6). This attitude spread to assimilated Cherokee leaders such as Elias Boudinot, editor of the *Cherokee Phoenix.* Such pressure caused traditionalists to withdraw into isolated areas to observe rituals. While it might have extinguished the observance of ceremonies altogether, those committed to keeping alive the tradition in such communities as Big Cove believed strongly that if they stopped the dances, the harmony on which their lives depended would be lost. Not only would they suffer, but the *Ani'-Yun'-wiya* people as a whole would also. In fact, the earth and all its inhabitants would be endangered.

Cosmology

According to traditional Cherokee cosmology, as evidenced in the origin legend recounted above, the earth is suspended from the sky by cords at the four cardinal points. It is the place of humans. Above the earth is the Upper World, the realm of order and peace, the place of origin of the animals, who transcend humans. It is also where benevolent and guiding spirits reside. Under the earth is the water, where disruptive spirits dwell. They come to the earth through caves, springs, and deep lakes.

Both guiding and disruptive spirits are necessary to the balance of life, for without either harmony will be lost. Traditional Cherokee life focuses on observing the pattern in all areas of life that will maintain the harmony of these three levels of reality. There is no division between the secular and sacred areas of life, the supernatural and natural. All of life is sacred and spiritual. Everything is imbued with spiritual significance.

Symbols

Sacred Fire. Central to the rituals of the *Ani'-Yun'-wiya* (and other southeastern nations) is the sacred fire. In the Cherokee homeland a sacred fire on a mound at the center of the special ceremonial plaza was addressed as "Ancient and Honorable Red Person" and "Grandfather" (Campbell and Sam 1975–76, 466–67). The sacred fire "is more than just a symbol of deity, it is the living manifestation of God" (Hendrix 1983, 76). It protects the people, and its smoke bears prayers upward to the heavens.

Periodically, in the context of the traditional festivals (see below), the sacred fire is extinguished and rekindled. It is also a symbol of the unity of the people, which has a particular importance in the renewal of Cherokee national unity today.

Cardinal Directions, Colors, and the Number Seven. As in other native spiritual traditions, the six cardinal directions (north, south, east, west, skyward, and down toward the earth) are important symbols. According to Mooney (1891 [1982], 342–43), each of the directions was associated with a color and a particular power: east (red, success and triumph), north (blue, defeat and trouble), west (black, death), south (white, peace and happiness), skyward (brown, uncertain but propitious), and toward the earth (yellow, defeat and trouble). In modern parlance, these directions determine "where one is at" and help a person become centered (Mankiller 1993, 113).

As is evidenced below, the number seven is recurrent in Cherokee spirituality. For example, the nation comprises seven clans, and the sacred fire is kindled from seven types of wood. Seven, of course, is a universal symbol of wholeness and harmony.

Gods and Spirits

Although Christian missionaries identified a Great Spirit in the Cherokee pantheon, which they associated with the Biblical God, traditional *Ani'-Yun'-wiya* apparently did not put emphasis on a central deity. Although some Cherokee myths speak of three superior beings called "Creators," "Masters of Life," and "Givers of Breath," who gave life to human beings, the original myths associated with these deities are now lost and references to them are found only in the syncretistic narratives of the early nineteenth century. None of the stories collected by Mooney or other anthropologists mention a central Creator or "Great Spirit" (McLoughlin 1994, 160). It seems likely that *Ani'-Yun'-wiya* use of the term "Great Spirit" came as a result of the effort to blend Cherokee tradition with Christian monotheism. The threesome may also show the influence of the Christian belief in the trinity.

According to Mooney, the Cherokee "pantheon includes gods in the heavens above, on the earth beneath, and in the waters under the earth, but of these the animal gods constitute by far the most numerous class, although the elemental spirits are more important" (1891 [1982], 340–42). The principal animal deities he identified are *uktena* (a mythic great horned serpent), the rattlesnake, the terrapin, the hawk, the rabbit, the squirrel, and the dog. The spider is also a particularly important spirit.

Principal "elemental" deities are fire, water, and sun. Sun is addressed as *Unelanuhi*, the "apportioner" of day and night. According to Mooney, missionaries mistakenly associated the Sun with the Great Spirit, apportioner of all things. Water, especially rivers, is invoked as "Long Person." Principal inanimate deities are Stone, Flint, and Mountain. Personal deities include Red Man (or Woman) and Little Men. Important also is Selu (Corn Woman), from whose blood the life-giving gift of corn comes.

Certain people can change themselves into owls and travel through the night to do evil. For example, Mankiller describes a man who shot an owl and learned the next day his most bitter enemy had died (Mankiller 1993, 37). *Estkene*, the Owl, can change shape and appear in almost any form. The transformed owl is a *dedonsek*, "one who makes bad medicine." If owls come close to your house, it may mean bad news. On the night before her near-fatal car accident, Chief Mankiller writes that her house was surrounded by owls (Mankiller 1993, 221).

The *Nuñnehi*, the Immortals or "people who live anywhere," are a spirit people said to live in the highlands of the original Cherokee homeland (Mooney

1900 [1982], 330–31). They are invisible until they wish to be seen, and then they appear as *Ani'-Yun'-wiya.* They are fond of music and dancing, and hunters often hear them in the hills. They take in Cherokees who are lost and care for them, and at times of crisis *Nuñnehi* warriors may appear to aid the Cherokee in defeating enemies. But they do not like to be disturbed and will throw a spell on anyone who does not leave them alone.

According to tradition, the Cherokee were visited long ago by a number of little beings from another planet in the sky. These *Yunwi Tsunsdi,* the "Little People," are spirits who live in rock caves. According to Mooney's informants (Mooney 1900 [1982], 333), they are "little fellows, hardly reaching up to a man's knee, but well shaped and handsome, with long hair falling almost to the ground." They love music, spending half their time drumming and dancing. The Little People taught the Cherokee such crucial values as sharing, not taking more game than was needed, and not desiring the possessions of others. They also punish wrongdoers. When a child is disobedient, he might be told that the Little People are watching, for they see everything. They are thought to function also as guardians and may be called on to help find a lost object. When a person is injured or killed, it might be said that his Little People are resting (Peithmann 1964, 15–17; Mankiller 1993, 41; for other stories of encounters of Cherokees with Little People, see Kilpatrick 1964, 77–95).

Healers and Healing

In the precontact period becoming an *Adawehi* was a high honor. An *Adawehi* was a man or woman skilled in the secrets of medicine and ritual. To become a "medicine man or woman" (as they were called by Euroamericans) required years of apprenticeship with an accomplished *Adawehi.* The sacred knowledge they learned was to be carefully protected and not shared with anyone. Some *Adawehi* were the mythkeepers of the village.

A young woman was recognized as especially sacred through the performance of a particularly heroic deed. She was known as a "wise woman" and, thereafter, she was looked upon as an equal of the male counselors and sat in council with them. She was often called upon to decide whether prisoners should be killed or adopted into the village (Peithmann 1964, 9).

Legend says there was once an hereditary secret society called *Ani-Kutani,* which controlled sacred knowledge, but which became too powerful and was overthrown by the people.

Today there are two types of *Ani'-Yun'-wiya* healers (known collectively as *adonigsi*): those who use herbs, roots, and other gifts of creation for curing and those who draw on ancient tribal rituals and customs, including songs, incantations, and various actions. Sometimes medicine may be used to harm or settle scores (Mankiller 1993, 220–21).

According to Cherokee tradition, when the harmony of the world is out of balance, *adonigsi* (either men or women) can call upon the spirits of the Upper World to restore balance. They counter the activities of spirits that have caused the imbalance. For example, sickness traditionally has been assumed to result from a failure to observe the way of harmony, as when a hunter neglected to seek forgiveness from an animal he was about to take or a woman failed to observe the rules of female purity. Many *adonigsi* are skilled in the use of herbs, in conjunction with special songs, prayers, and dances. They might also "suck out" an offending spirit, often manifest in the form of a small stone or stick.

Among the plants used by Eastern *Ani'-Yun'-wiya* healers in the later nineteenth century were the following: Virginia or black snakeroot, wild senna, milkweed, skullcap, maidenhair fern, liverwort, tassel flower, ginseng, ladyslipper, and cone flower. Tobacco was also used, the smoke carrying petitions to *Ye-Ho-Wa*, "The Master of Life," who had given tobacco to the Cherokee (Mooney 1891 [1982], 324–27).

The formulas used by healers (Hurtevant 1979; Mooney and Olbrechts 1932; Mooney 1891 [1982]) were traditionally "owned" by each healer and sometimes were sold to one another (and later to ethnologists who wished to record them). They had been passed down orally over the centuries until the invention of the Cherokee syllabary in the early nineteenth century, when they were put in writing (Mooney 1891 [1982], 308). They served to cure maladies or misfortunes already experienced. Ceremonial dances, in contrast, served to ward off illness or misfortune.

One of the formulas collected by Mooney among the Eastern Cherokees in 1887 and 1888 was the following used in treating rheumatism:

> Listen! Ha! In the Sun Land you repose, O Red Dog, O now you have
> swiftly drawn near to hearken. O great adawehi, you never fail in anything.
> O, appear and draw near running, for your prey never escapes. You are
> now come to remove the intruder. Ha! You have settled a very small part of
> it far off there at the end of the earth. (Mooney 1891 [1982], 346–49)

In the formulas the disease is personified as the intruder, here the spirit of a slain animal who visits vengeance on a hunter. It can be driven out only by a more powerful animal spirit, here Red Dog, called the great healer (*adawehi*). These animals live at the ends of the earth, beyond the seventh heaven. The Sun Land is the east. The formula continues to call on other spirit animals from other cardinal points: Blue Dog of the Frigid Land (north), the Black Dog of the Darkening Land (west), and White Terrapin of *Wahala* (south).

Mooney believed that though these healers still had much influence among traditional Cherokees in the late nineteenth century, "they [were] daily losing ground and [would] soon be without honor in their own country" (Mooney 1891

[1982], 308). The perpetuation of traditional healing among Cherokees a century later has proven him wrong.

In modern times many *adonisgi* engaging in the ancient healing practices also "consider themselves to be good Christians and feel that their work is completely consistent with Christian doctrine" (Fogelson 1961, 219–20; McLoughlin 1994, 188).

The Six Traditional Rituals

In preremoval days, until pressure from Christian missionaries caused the full traditional ritual calendar to fade, the head men and ritual specialists of Cherokee towns planned a series of six communal rituals to be observed throughout the coming year (see Speck and Broom 1983, 7–8; Campbell and Sam 1976–77, 467–71; Hudson 1976, 317–75).

The songs associated with the ceremonies originated, according to Cherokee legend, with the sacrifice of a monster called Stone Coat:

> A creature named Stone Coat lived among the people in human form. In truth he was a monster covered completely with scaly armor which made him invincible to attack. When he took human form the people did not know his identity, and he could become invisible whenever he chose. He roamed the earth killing people so that he could eat their livers. When he approached a victim, he would take the shape of an old woman and puncture the victim's skull with a sharp and crooked forefinger.
>
> Once Stone Coat took the shape of a little orphan boy, a Cherokee took pity on him and brought Stone Coat to his home. After a series of children died, and their livers were found to be gone, suspicion fell on the orphan boy because he was not hungry after each of the deaths. In council a plan was developed to entrap him. Along the path he trod in search of victims, seven menstruating women lay in wait. As he passed the women, he became weak and began to vomit blood. Knowing he was about to die, Stone Coat told the people to build a fire around him and burn him up. As he was consumed, Stone Coat sang a series of songs and told the people that this was his gift to them, that they should teach them to their children and preserve them forever. He said that they must learn the meaning of suffering and the joy of release from suffering. If they did, they would value the songs. His death, he said, would unleash disease in the world, but the songs he taught them would cure it. He also said he would leave a powerful medicine made from the stone forming his stone coat. It would remain in the fire after his body was consumed. All night they burned his body and watched the flames. Stone Coat sang songs as he perished, which the people learned. Some songs were for dancing, others were to be used

for hunting, war, or to heal sickness. When the fire died down they found the pieces of stone about which Stone Coat had spoken. Each man took a piece of stone and decided whether to become a hunter of bear, deer, or buffalo or to be handsome for women. Whatever they chose as their life's calling applied to them and their descendants. (Speck and Broom 1983, 13–16; cf. Mooney 1900 [1982], 319–20)

First New Moon of Spring. This festival was celebrated at about the time the grass began to grow, during the month of March. On the first day social dances were held through the night, including a friendship dance of seven women. At dawn a sacred stone or crystal was consulted to determine the success of the season's crops.

"Going to the Water," a purification ritual, was held on the second day. The whole town went into the nearest running water, where the people removed their old clothes and allowed them to float away. They dipped themselves into the water four times, pointing to each of the cardinal directions. They resolved to live with a clean heart and with friendship toward their neighbors during the new year.

Dried tobacco flowers and a deer's tongue were placed as an offering on the sacred fire, and a feast and another all-night dance were held. A fast was held on the third day.

Seven days later, the sacred fire was rekindled. The firekeeper extinguished the perpetual fire, and then using goldenrod blossoms and a fire rod, ignited a new flame, using branches from seven species of trees: blackjack oak, post oak, red oak, sycamore, locust, plum, and redbud. Women took new embers from the rekindled sacred fire to ignite the fires in their own homes.

A series of steps that marked the beginning of each of the subsequent festivals was initiated in association with the First New Moon ceremony. Seven messengers were dispatched to announce the date of the festival; seven hunters were sent out to bring meat for the accompanying feast; seven attendants prepared the ceremonial altar; and seven others gathered firewood from the trees.

Preliminary or New Green Corn. Also called "roasting ears time," this ceremony occurred in August, when the corn ripened and was fit to taste. Eating corn was forbidden until this ritual had taken place. Seven ears, taken from the fields of different clans, were taken to be blessed by the priest. On the seventh day, after a six-day fast, the ceremony itself began. The sacred fire of the village was rekindled, with tobacco and corn offerings. Then the villagers feasted on the roasted corn.

Mature or Ripe Green Corn. This important festival, which is still celebrated in modified form in many Cherokee communities today, is discussed in some detail below. At one time it followed the New Green Corn festival by forty or fifty days, being held in late September. Its purpose was to encourage fertility and mark the beginning of a new ritual cycle.

Before removal each town began the ceremony by scrupulously cleaning the plaza as well as all houses and streets. Participants "went to water" to purify themselves. A process of renewal, including fasting, continued for four (sometimes eight) days and was broken by four days of feasting, dancing, and the rekindling of household fires from the sacred, central fire.

In the dance, the principal male dancers, carrying evergreen boughs, came single file into the ceremonial plaza and circled a tree in the center seven times. To one side the chief's assistant danced on a platform held on the shoulders of a group of men. This dance was repeated on each of the days of the festival. In the evenings social dances were held, in which women participated.

Great New Moon. This two-day ceremony, also called "Big Medicine," was held in October when the first new moon appeared in in early autumn. Each family brought food from their own fields to share with others whose harvest had not been good. The ritual began with a dance performed by women. At sunrise, participants "went to water," dipping themselves seven times at a place in the river where it was believed that fallen leaves had added a special curative power. The fates of individuals for the coming year were divined. Those with favorable readings joined in a communal feast, while those with more ominous forecasts fasted and sought another, hopefully more positive reading.

Reconciliation/Propitiation. This five-day ritual, literally *Atahuna* or "Friends Made Ceremony," followed the Great New Moon Festival by ten days. Its purpose was to overcome hostilities, remove impurities and disease, and renew friendships. Debts were paid, injuries forgiven, and disputes reconciled.

At this ritual "the Cherokee tried to wipe out any disorder that had crept in during the year and begin anew" (Perdue 1989, 25). This would involve cleaning houses thoroughly and discarding old clothes, broken items, and surplus food. These would be burned in a communal fire on the plaza. The color white was used in the ceremony. For example, walls of the council house were whitened. The sacred fire was rekindled, and a ritual medicine made from bits of cedar, white pine, hemlock, mistletoe, greenbrier, heart leaf, and ginseng was prepared on the fire.

Women then presented new corn for a village feast. Seven men went through the pavilion striking buildings with rods made from white sycamore and chanting a sacred formula to drive away evil spirits. Seven white gourds were dipped into the sacred medicine and given to the headmen of each of the clans. Ritual bathing, a feast, and a friendship dance were then held. The festival ended with the secret storing of the basket in which the medicine had been prepared.

One of the effects of this ritual was to underscore the belief that accumulating wealth was not in harmony with the order of things. You should keep only what you need for daily living, not accumulate things.

Bounding Bush. Also known as the Pigeon Dance, this four-day ceremony was held in December. A special dance was held on three evenings, and on the fourth evening the dancing continued through the night. As dawn approached, the year was closed with a fire offering.

THE COMMON FEATURES of these six annual observances include the lighting of the sacred fire, ritual sacrifice, purification rites, and all-night dances. The dances included the music of drums, flutes, and tortoise-shell or gourd rattles. Both men and women participated. According to Speck and Broom (1983, 19–24), the Big Cove dances which kept alive elements of these traditional ceremonies in the early twentieth century generally had the following characteristics:

Dances were sponsored by a host, who appointed a "driver" to serve as master of ceremonies, announcing leaders for dances and the sequence of dances, preserving order as necessary, and urging participation in the dances. Lead singers danced at the head of the line of dancers.

The traditional Cherokee ceremonial instruments were a hollowed wooden water drum, hand-held gourd rattles, and tortoise-shell leg rattles (worn by the woman partner of the dance leader). Water was used to stretch the drum head and kept in the drum to remoisten the head as needed.

Song units began and ended with a vigorous shaking of the rattles or rapid beating of the drum. Each dance unit typically had four periods: a walking period in which the leader beat his rattle in a tremolo, walking once around the circle, and shaking a tremolo once more; the initiation of the dancing, with each song repeated seven times; the leader signaling with his rattle, and one or two women with leg rattles entering behind the leader, who held the rattle elevated, with the songs sung four times; with rattle held aloft the leader shaking it in a tremolo and the dancers facing the center, stomping heavily in place. At this point the men whooped or yelled and the dance broke up.

As the leader began the dance, walking once clockwise around the circle, he shook his rattle and announced the songs he would perform. The animal dances usually lasted ten to fifteen minutes, while the duration of Booger Dances depended on how many masked performers appeared. It could be as long as an hour and a half.

The style of dancing was in a simple, alternating shuffle, with knees bent and the body relaxed. The dancers stayed close behind one another. At times the leader might turn sideways to his left and the rest of the company followed suit. The dancers let their arms hang limp at their sides unless they were imitating the motions of the leader.

Once every seven years the *Uku* Dance replaced the Great New Moon Ceremony in October (Campbell and Sam 1975–76, 471–72). The White chief of the capital town ("First Beloved Man") was reconsecrated as the high priest in an elaborate ceremony.

The Green Corn Festival: A Continuing Tradition

Among the six annual festivals, the Green Corn Dance is the one still observed regularly in many traditional *Ani'-Yun'-wiya* communities among both the Eastern Band and the western Cherokees.

As observed at Big Cove, North Carolina, in the 1930s, the Green Corn Dance had four periods (Speck and Broom 1983, 45–54, 77). In the first stage male dancers gathered a distance from the dance ground and there danced through the morning, accompanied by the discharge of guns. At the same time, women dancers gathered at the dance ground. The lead woman dancer wore tortoise shell leg rattles. When the separate dances were concluded, the men proceeded to the dance ground in a shuffling trot, two abreast. They surrounded the women dancers in a large circle, drawing closer until they merged with the women's line.

Then a feast open to all, including visitors, was held, before the dancing resumed just before sundown. In this stage, the male and female dancers again began separately, then merged. During the night, animal dances (with the exception of the Bear and Eagle Dances) and other dances (not including the Booger Dance) were held, beginning with the Friendship Dance and ending just before dawn with the Round or Running Dance. Just before the Round Dance, the Green Corn Dance itself was performed (symbolizing the planting of the corn in the early spring and preventing illness associated with the eating of green corn).

Another ritual action associated with the traditional Green Corn Ceremony (and found among other southeastern nations) was and is the lighting of the new fire. In the center of the town, four logs are laid to form a cross, facing each of the four cardinal directions. At dawn the firemaker faces the rising sun and strikes a piece of flint, lighting a bundle of dry grass. It bursts into flames and he places it in the center of the four logs. As the people dance around the new fire, songs are sung. In keeping with tradition, each woman is given an ember to take home to rekindle her hearth.

The Cherokee Green Corn Dance commemorates the gift of maize to the people by Selu (Corn Woman), whose blood has the power to cause crops to grow. In one version of the story, Selu is killed as a witch by her sons, and the corn grows from the spot where her blood fell. In other versions, she asks to be killed and have her body dragged across a field, where corn springs up. In any event, the Green Corn Ceremony was traditionally deemed essential to Selu's continuing to give the gift of corn to the people.

During the late eighteenth and early nineteenth centuries the Green Corn Dance was one of the few traditional ceremonies that retained its vitality in the face of the onslaught of European culture. Elements of other traditional festivals, such as the Renewal Ceremony, were incorporated into it, making the Green Corn Dance the central ritual in traditional Cherokee spirituality. Even so, it became in some communities "a plaything for federal agents," who worked with chiefs to schedule it at a time convenient to them. The government distributed provisions and whiskey at these times, to "put the Indians in a good mood for bargaining" (McLoughlin 1984a, 11).

At the conclusion of the dancing, a feast was held, often with games such as tug-of-war and football. Men and women opposed one another, and if the men lost, the feast was of meat; if the women lost, the food would be cornbread or meal.

The Booger or Mask Dance

As noted in the historical overview, the Booger (also called Mask) Dance in its earliest known form parodied the traditional enemies of the Cherokee people. It was subsequently adapted to respond to the threats posed by the introduction of European culture. According to Speck and Broom, "by relating the invasion of the white man to the spiritual forces of nature with which the Cherokee aboriginally learned to cope, the potency of the threat is somehow lessened. . . . With the white invaders as men they cannot deal, but with the white invaders disguised as mythical animals and frivolous demi-men they feel competent to deal" (Speck and Broom 1983, 3).

In this ritual dancers wore elaborate masks portraying terrifying spirits. (The name *Booger* is probably an adaptation of the English *bogey*, signifying "ghost.") They shouted and frightened children with their aggressive ways, perhaps in order to scare them into obedience and to highlight the dangers of adopting non–*Ani'-Yun'-wiya* attitudes.

In the Booger Dances of the Eastern Cherokee Big Cove settlement during the 1930s (Speck and Broom 1983, 25–39), the dancers wore masks with exaggerated human features and ragged European clothes, sheets, and quilts. There were four to ten male dancers (sometimes with a couple of women as companions), with masks to represent "outsiders": Germans, French, Chinese, blacks, or other Indian nations. The "European" masks had exaggerated features: mustaches, big noses, bald heads, bushy eyebrows, and so on. Some carried an imitation phallus made from a gourd neck (sometimes filled with water and released to simulate ejaculation) or wrapped cloth, and some distorted their figures. They typically had obscene names (like Big Testicles, Sooty Anus, or Burster [Penis]) and spoke in languages other than *Ani'-Yun'-wiya*.

The Booger Dances were included in night dance series and were not independent rituals. They were typically preceded by social dances that built up anticipation among the participants. When the first dancer arrived and his identity and nationality were questioned, he might respond by breaking wind.

When the whole company of dancers arrived, in their first action they might fall on the floor, strike the participants, or chase the girls. In their second action,

Wild potato clan mask by a contemporary Cherokee artist.

the host of the dance whispered with the leader of the troop, determining who the dancers were, where they came from, and where they were going.

In the third action, the singers began to sing while a dancer took awkward and grotesque steps, as though he was a clumsy European trying to perform an Indian dance. When the dancer's Booger name was sung, the spectators applauded and yelled. Each Booger performed a solo dance in this way. The dancers did not themselves speak but engaged in obscene pantomimes, thrusting their buttocks or displaying their large gourd "phalli" hidden underneath their clothes. The Boogers then chose one of the animal dances to perform, followed by an interlude in which a pipe was ritually smoked.

The fourth action of the Boogers was their distinctive dance. It was performed with woman partners who dressed nicely in *Ani'-Yun'-wiya* style. "Their entry is a symbol of the submission of the Indians to the will of the invader, the gratification of his carnal desires" (Speck and Broom 1983, 34). When the women entered, the Boogers began to engage in pseudo-intercourse with them. Having completed their dance, the Boogers left, some trying to drag women spectators with them.

The Booger Dances portrayed the traditional Cherokees view of the European invaders as "awkward, ridiculous, lewd, and menacing." They functioned to weaken "the harmful powers of alien tribes and races, who, as living beings or ghosts, may be responsible for sickness or misfortune" (Speck and Broom 1983, 36–37).

Other Dances

At the Big Cove settlement, two other winter dances were common in the 1930s, the Eagle Dance and the Bear Dance.

Eagle Dance. Called the most spectacular of the Eastern Cherokee dances, the Eagle Dance symbolized victory or peace. Its purpose was "to stimulate in the minds of the young growing people the spirit of war." As a victory dance, it had once included dancers carrying enemies scalps, but it largely fell into disuse in the late eighteenth and early nineteenth centuries, as a result of the transformations of Cherokee society noted earlier.

The Eagle Dance has, however, been revived by traditionalists at various times. In the Big Cove version, pairs of male and female dancers faced one another in opposite lines. The eagle-feather wands used in the dance as emblems of peace were never allowed to touch the ground, lest the dancer who violated this taboo die as a result. The touching of the wands to the ground by dancers when performing the dance for tourists in the 1940s was probably an intentional violation of the taboo, showing either bravado or disregard for the power of the dance. A distinctive step in the dance was a stooping or crouching movement with one knee lowered. The dance was conducted in the winter because it could cause a late frost or destruction of the crops if performed in other seasons, or perhaps arouse snakes. (See Speck and Broom 1983, 39–44, 64; Campbell and Sam 1975–76, 472.)

Bear Dance. In this winter dance, male dancers shuffled and swayed their bodies, following the example of the leader, who growled like a bear (Speck and Broom 1983, 44–45). They were joined by female partners, who were potential mates, suggesting the dance had sexual significance. At one point the dancers tore the air, mimicking a dance believed to be performed by bears. It was believed that old bears danced around a tree, leaving tooth marks on the bark. The decline of hunting in the late eighteenth century made both the Buffalo and Bear dances obsolete (McLoughlin 1984a, 11), but they have been kept alive by traditionalists apart from the hunting context.

Ballplayers' Dance. This summer dance was performed to strengthen and purify players in preparation for the stickball games that were an integral part of traditional Cherokee life (Speck and Broom 1983, 55–62). It may originally also have been conducted in preparation for war. The dancers carried the sticks used in the ball game, at one time with pendants made from feathers suspended from them. The dance was often performed near a body of water so that the dancers might "go to water" during the ritual.

During the decline of traditional Cherokee culture in the late eighteenth and early nineteenth centuries, the Ballplayers' Dances became "spectacles for white visitors and scenes of wild orgies of gambling, drunkenness, and brawling, . . . a symptom of despair, not of vitality" (McLoughlin 1984a, 11). They have been revitalized in traditional communities, however, and continue in modified form to this day.

Friendship Dance. This dance, still observed in some traditional communities, occurs regularly during the Green Corn Ceremony as well as at other times. In its most traditional form, men and women dance holding hands and make other gestures of intimacy. For example, the dancers, paired face-to-face, first symbolically greet one another. They also place their hands on one anothers' shoulders or put their palms against their partners' palms.

Although not typically part of the Friendship Dances observed today, in secluded, traditional settings, male dancers might touch their female partners' breasts while dancing side by side, and finally the dancers touch one anothers' genitals while dancing paired. In this context, the dance acted out the course of intimacy between men and women, beginning with the getting to know one another, developing through the various stages of familiarity and courtship, culminating in intercourse. (See Speck and Broom 1983, 65–68; Campbell and Sam 1975–76, 473–74.)

Round or Running Dance. This dance began with women dancing slowly, led by a woman wearing leg rattles and a singer with a drum. As the song quickened, men joined in, coming between the women as their partners. Songs were ended with shouts. The dance was a culminating action in a night series and involved all the dancers. (See Speck and Broom 1983, 68.)

Animal Dances. A series of animal dances were observed by Frank Speck and Leonard Broom at the Big Cove settlement in the 1930s: the Beaver Dance, a simulated hunt of this animal much valued in the early fur trade; the Buffalo Dance, simulating an animal found in the Smoky Mountains until the late eighteenth century; the Pigeon Dance; the Partridge Dance; the Groundhog Dance; the Horse Dance; the Chicken Dance; the Spring Frog or Knee-Deep Dance; the Pissant Dance; the Raccoon Dance; and the Gizzard Dance (Speck and Broom 1983, 69–80). The popular Mosquito Dance was used to liven things up. Women dancers softly hummed in unison and simulated mosquitos in flight. At intervals designated by an accented drumbeat, dancers would "bite" observers who had nodded off during all-night dances, using a pin to prick them (Campbell and Sam 1975–76, 475).

Sweat Lodge

Like most other native nations, traditional Cherokees used sweat baths, typically in small sweat houses with sunken floors (Mooney 1891 [1982], 333–36), although not with the same accompanying ceremonies found, for example, among the Lakota (see chapter 4).

Hunting Formulas and Rites

A number of *Ani'-Yun'-wiya* traditions associated with the ritual of hunting have been noted (Mooney and Olbrechts 1932; Speck and Broom 1983, 84–96; Mooney 1891 [1982], 369–75). These included wooden decoy masks representing deer, buffalo, or bear, to be worn by hunters (along with the skin of the animal) during preparatory dances, while approaching the prey, and after a successful hunt. In addition, formulas appropriate for the desired animal (those listed above, as well as turkeys and eagles) could be purchased from specialists. For example, a bear formula included these words: "And now surely we and the good black things, the best of all, shall see each other."

The Ghost Dance Movements (1811–13, 1867)

The term *Ghost Dance* was coined by ethnologist James Mooney to describe the apocalyptic revitalization movements that swept across Indian country in the late nineteenth century (see chapter 6). As Mooney noted, however, similar movements had begun earlier in other native nations, including the Cherokee Ghost Dance movements of 1811–13 and 1867 (McLoughlin 1984a). They emerged out of the tension between Cherokee traditionalists and assimilationists and envisioned a purging of Euroamerican influences and a renewed *Ani'-Yun'-wiya* nation.

The first of these two movements "was not directed against the missionaries or even against the young chiefs [the assimilationists]. It was a spiritual struggle to reconcile the old myths and the new ways" (McLoughlin 1986, 178). It was not merely a return to the past, as was the case with other nativist movements. Rather, the Ghost Dance of the early nineteenth century sought to retain *Ani'-Yun'-wiya* identity as the Cherokee adopted the new ways necessary for survival. It was a search for order, rooted in a belief that the *Ani'-Yun'-wiya* had a special relationship with the spirit world. Some of its leaders spoke of a peaceful emergence of harmony; others described it in more ominous and apocalyptic terms.

In 1811 a series of calamities and portents occurred: a severe famine, an epidemic that killed many horses, a comet that blazed across the sky for weeks, and a series of earthquakes. It appeared that "the Cherokee people and Mother Earth were dying together under the strain of acculturation and the confusion it caused" (McLoughlin 1984a, 118).

At such times of social breakdown and natural catastrophes, it is not uncommon for people to receive visions that point to a way out of the chaos and promise a new age of hope. In January 1811, according to a report given by Moravian missionaries, two Cherokee women and a man had a vision near a place called Rocky Mountain of a band of Indians coming down from the sky on black horses. They told the Cherokee that the Creator was upset with the Cherokee for allowing so many whites into their lands and for their taking up the European method of farming. As a result, they said, "The Mother of the Nation" had allowed the game to move away from the Cherokee. If they would return to their traditional practices and keep the whites out of their lands, Mother would bring the game back, the messengers said. At the same time, the emissaries told them to build houses in their villages for those whites who treated them well and who would teach them useful skills such as writing (McLoughlin 1984a, 142–43).

This vision exemplifies much, if not all, of the movement: reaffirmation of tradition and rejection of many things European, but with a recognition of the value of learning some aspects of European culture from whites willing to help them. This was certainly different from the militant rejection of European society associated with the visions of the Shawnee prophet Tenkswatawa and his brother, Tecumseh (McLoughlin 1986, 179–81; McLoughlin 1984a, 121–22).

About the same time, a prophet named Charley (*Tsa-li*) claimed to have received a message from the Creator, expressing displeasure because the Cherokee had taken up white ways such as clothing, cattle, plows, spinning wheels, featherbeds, fiddles, cats, and books (McLoughlin 1984a, 149–51). He wanted them to return to their traditional dances and feasts, to a time when they listened to the Creator speaking to them through dreams, and he warned that if they did not, they would face death.

Specifically, he said that a terrific wind and hailstorm would come and annihilate all the white men, their cattle, and all their works. In order to escape the devastation, the people must withdraw to a holy spot in the mountains. After the storm, true believers would return home to find that the game that had disappeared had returned (McLoughlin 1984a, 113). When death did not come, his prophecy was discounted. But, as Wilma Mankiller has speculated, perhaps the death of which he spoke was not physical, but spiritual (Mankiller 1993, 257).

In March 1812 the purificatory "going to the water" was engaged in anew by many who had given it up. Renouncing the Virginia reels that had replaced ceremonial dancing and burning the European clothes they had adopted were other signs of the renewal of tradition. A number of Cherokees in Alabama and Georgia "abandoned their bees, their orchards, their slaves, and everything that had come to them from the white man, and took up their toilsome march for the high mountains [of Carolina]" (Mooney 1900 [1982], 88).

The *Ani'-Yun'-wiya* Ghost Dance movement of 1811–13 did not give rise to a dominant, charismatic prophet such as Handsome Lake of the Senecas or Tenkswatawa of the Shawnees. Nor did it result in a new moral code, as revitalization movements often do. The enthusiasm of many who left their homes for the mountains faded, and they returned to their European ways ashamed.

The Cherokee Ghost Dance movement of 1867 was largely an attempt by acculturated mixed-bloods to manipulate traditionalists by duping them into joining a nonexistent intertribal military alliance supported by European powers (assisted by Mormons) to drive whites back across the Mississippi River (McLoughlin 1994, 293). Fearful of the rise of traditionalist political power (through the Keetoowah Society), these leaders succeeded in whipping up some enthusiasm but not in inspiring an insurrection. The movement failed, but it may have played an unintended role in renewing traditional ceremonies.

The Keetoowah Societies and the Renewal of Tradition (1859–present)

The first recorded Keetoowah Society was, as previously noted, organized before the outbreak of the Civil War, sometime between 1856 and 1859. *Keetoowah* (also spelled Kituwha, Kituwah, Ketoowa, and Ketowa; cf. McLoughlin 1994, 332, n. 1) most likely refers to the ancient city of Kituwha, northernmost town in the

Ani'-Yun'-wiya homeland in the East. Kituwha defended the Cherokee people against invaders from the north (Hendrix 1983, 23–24).

Another possibility is that the society had its roots in the *Ani-Kutani*, the ancient medicine society that defended the sacred traditions of the Cherokee people (Woodward 1963, 7–8). From that perspective, the Keetoowah Society of the 1850s was a reorganization of the original movement and an effort to reclaim the "Kituwha spirit" that drew Cherokees together across clan boundaries in response to external threats.

In the words of the "Keetoowah laws," drafted by "Head Captain" Bud Gritts and adopted in 1859:

[O]ur Keetoowah forefathers . . . loved and lived as free people [who] never surrendered to anybody. They loved one another for they were just like one family, just as if they had been raised from one family. They all came as a unit to their fire to smoke, to aid one another and to protect their government with what little powder and lead they had to use in protecting it. (McLoughlin 1994, 245)

Because of its secretive beginnings, the early years of the society are not clearly understood (McLoughlin 1994, 220–22). One of the principal controversies among historians is whether it was an organization dominated by those committed to traditional *Ani'-Yun'-wiya* spirituality or by Cherokee Christians who saw it as a political movement. As evidenced below, it was most likely a movement that drew together both traditionalists and Christians in defense of Cherokee autonomy and the traditional Cherokee way of life. It provides a model many contemporary Cherokee leaders are attempting to follow. The Keetoowah Society was probably also founded as an alternative to the proslavery societies such as the Knights of the Golden Circle, which were led by mixed-blood slaveowners.

Among the society's organizers were Baptist missionary Evan Jones, who had walked the Trail of Tears, and his son, Reverend John B. Jones. They were noted for their dual commitment to the evangelizing of the Cherokee and to the preservation of *Ani'-Yun'-wiya* tradition. They probably worked with a group of full-blood Cherokee leaders in initiating the society (McLoughlin 1994, 227–34; cf. also 30–32, 50–126; McLoughlin 1990).

Although Keetoowah Society meetings apparently opened and closed with a Christian prayer, "the society accepted as equals any traditionalists committed to their goals." Meetings were held in the woods at night, like traditional ceremonies, and followed "the ceremonial and consensual procedures of ancient Cherokee councils. Ancient dances were performed; tobacco was smoked for its spiritual powers" (McLoughlin 1994, 119).

The traditionalists in the society undoubtedly considered it an important instrument in their effort to preserve traditional rituals and ceremonies.

(McLoughlin 1984b, 468). Nevertheless, "[t]here is no evidence the Keetoowah Society was either pro-Christian or pro-traditionalist but rather that it tolerated both in a syncretic blending of their shared values" (McLoughlin 1994, 223). In any event, from the outset it was viewed as dangerous by assimilationist, mixed-blood leaders on both political and religious grounds.

The "Legend of the Keetoowah" suggests the attitude probably common among traditionalists in the society. The story, recalled in 1930 by Levi B. Gritts, recounts how the *Ani'-Yun'-wiya* came originally from islands in the Atlantic Ocean near the eastern coast of South America. According to the legend, they lived in large cities with tall buildings. They were attacked by seventy nations, but the attackers withdrew when they were shown that the Cherokee were a particularly holy people. The mysterious power with which the people were blessed was to be used for the good of all the people, but over time some leaders began to use the power for selfish reasons.

It was then that they migrated to other countries (including Asia, India, and North America) from their island home. The cities were destroyed, and the islands sank beneath the ocean. The people who migrated to North America were entrusted with wisdom and power, but the time came again when they turned from the true way. The seven clans began feuding, and revenge killings were common. They sought divine guidance and were told that from then on they would be called Keetoowah. Their future was prophesied, and they were warned that they would be driven westward by an enemy from the East and that they would divide into different factions. Families would split against one another, and traditional leaders would be ignored. If the younger people at that time would return to tradition, however, there would be a chance that they could return to the East, and, if not, to the western coast, where a boat would take them away.

There are indications that the society renewed the *gadugi* heritage of Cherokees coming to one another's aid at times of crisis. An 1860 resolution states that "[i]f any Keetoowah should get sick, or unable to take care of himself, all members of Keetoowah society who live nearby, shall look after him and visit him" (McLoughlin 1994, 241; Fogelson and Kutsche 1961).

In 1867 the society was instrumental in electing Lewis Downing, a native Baptist pastor, as chief, reestablishing full-blood control over the Cherokee nation. He was the first of several full-blood chiefs who were either members of or sympathetic to the Keetoowah Society. Under President Grant's "Peace Plan," in 1870 John Jones was appointed federal agent for the Cherokee nation, the first missionary and the first citizen of the Cherokee nation to hold the post. In the latter decades of the nineteenth century, the society, no longer secret, was able to relax its vigilance and militancy and become more a social and cultural group than a political organization (McLoughlin 1994, 279).

By the late 1800s, however, a split had developed between those members of the Society who accepted Christianity and traditionalists who rejected Christianity. The former continued under the name Keetoowah Society Incorporated and put more emphasis on political and cultural issues than on spiritual concerns. They were recognized as a distinct entity under a federal court order in 1905.

The latter group was led by Redbird Smith, a Natchez-Cherokee who is credited with keeping alive commitment to the traditional ceremonies and "keeping the sacred fire burning" (Hendrix 1983, 22; Thomas 1961). At a time when the traditional ceremonies were all but extinct, he renewed them and taught a philosophy which put them in the context of traditional *Ani'-Yun'-wiya* values. He taught that Cherokees must follow the White Path, the path of peace and good will. "If you follow the White Path," he said, "God will give you protection." He believed that the traditional medicine should only be used for positive ends, not for injuring others. He also reintroduced the traditional Cherokee wampum belts, believing them to have been made by the ancient Keetoowahs as a way of passing their sacred beliefs on to later generations (Hendrix 1983, 76–79).

After 1907 the movement called itself the "Original Keetoowah Society," but it is more widely known as the "Nighthawk Keetoowahs" or the "Redbird Smith movement." These traditionalists tended to live in the isolated, rural Cherokee settlements in northeastern Oklahoma. Redbird Smith dreamed of a full-blood utopia in which land would once again be held in common and the people would be self-reliant. He did not oppose Euroamerican education or modern modes of business and farming, but he felt that they should be used for the welfare of the community, and for self-sufficiency, not for individual gain and the accumulation of wealth (Littlefield 1971, 424; Hendrix 1983, 83).

Smith kept alive the traditional ceremonies at *Nu-wo-ti* ("Medicine Spring"), one of the five traditional towns or "fires" among the western Cherokees. From the Nighthawks' perspective, here they kept alive the "mother fire" of the Cherokee ignited in North Carolina and carried to Indian Territory after removal (Campbell and Sam 1975–76, 463–64). In all, as many as twenty-two separate traditionalist "fires" spread throughout the Cherokee nation (Hendrix 1983, 80–81).

Shortly before he died, Redbird Smith wrote to an Indian agent to explain his beliefs about traditional *Ani'-Yun'-wiya* spirituality:

> This religion as revealed to me is larger than any man. It is beyond man's understanding. It shall prevail after I am gone. It is growth like the child—it is growth eternal. This religion does not teach me to concern myself of the life that shall be after this, but it does teach me to be concerned with what my everyday life should be. The Fires kept burning are merely emblematic of the greater Fire, the greater Light, the Great Spirit. I realize now as never before it is not only for the Cherokee but for all mankind. (Hendrix 1983, 85)

Redbird Smith's son, John Smith, continued to make prophetic utterances about what would happen to the Cherokee people if they abandoned tradition.

He also introduced a Seven-Clan Council (modeled after the ancient form of Cherokee governance) to replace leadership by a "chief" (Hendrix 1983, 82).

Over time the Nighthawks divided into factions, focusing on different ceremonial grounds. Two were associated with Redbird Smith's family: the Redbird Smith grounds and the Stokes Smith grounds. Others were the Going Snake "Seven Clans" Fire (under the leadership of Eli Pumpkin), which stressed common ownership of land, and the Medicine Springs Fire (or Medicine Society), which was led for many years by Archie Sam.

Together the Nighthawks numbered about 3,000 by the early 1960s. From the perspective of many Cherokee traditionalists and their supporters, the Nighthawks are "the conservators of the traditions and the stable center from which the tribe gains its strength and retains its unique identity" (Hendrix 1983, 73). They continue to hold all-night ceremonials on stomp grounds near Gore, Oklahoma.

Similar to the Nighthawk Keetoowahs as a movement committed to keeping alive the traditions of the southeastern nations is the Four Mothers Society (see above), a "religious organization in the Southeastern tradition with its main ceremonial ground at Abeka in the Creek Nation" (Hendrix 1983, 75). In the late 1970s the Four Mothers Society gathered on the first Saturday of every month, April to October, for stickball, food, and ceremonial dances which sometimes lasted until sunup.

On the political side, under the terms of the 1934 Indian Reorganization Act, the United Keetoowah Band (UKB) was organized as a distinct Cherokee body. The UKB today considers itself the Third Band of Cherokees and maintains a political structure separate from the Cherokee Nation of Oklahoma. It also rejects the Nighthawk Keetoowahs as a splinter group, while the Nighthawks claim the UKB is the group that split off from the original intent of the Keetoowah Society. Since 1979 the Cherokee nation has formally disputed the UKB's sovereignty. The UKB in 1995 claimed 7,700 enrolled members and said it was the largest full-blood Cherokee body. At this writing the UKB is actively seeking to relocate to Arkansas as the Third Band of Cherokees.

Stomp Dances

The best-known Cherokee ceremony today is the Stomp Dance. In many traditional communities there are central meeting places, the *gatiyoti*, called the stomp grounds. Here the Mature or Ripe Corn Dance (see above) is kept alive, symbolizing continuity with traditional Cherokee spirituality. In addition, reminiscent of the traditional social dances, simplified all-night Common or Stomp Dances are held at these stomp grounds. Stomp dancing had faded almost completely by the late nineteenth century, but beginning in 1896 it was revived by Redbird Smith and the Nighthawk Keetoowahs in association with traditionalists of the

Creek nation. By this time "[o]nly the old people knew how to dance, and one of the elders had to tie turtle shells on his own legs and teach the women the art of shell shaking" (Hendrix 1983, 76).

Archie Sam, long-time leader of the Nighthawk Keetoowahs and the Four Mothers Society, describes typical, modern Stomp Dances (Campbell and Sam 1975–76, 473). They are led, he says, by a head dancer, followed by a single file of other dancers. The men enter and walk around the central fire several times. Sometimes a "medicine" drum is used to signal the beginning of the dance. Women wearing rattles then take their places between the men, and the leader initiates the dance by singing short stanzas repeated by the male dancers. The tempo is set by the head dancer and the women wearing turtle-shell shackles filled with pebbles on their legs. The sound of the shells creates a syncopated rhythm for the dance as the women stomp their feet on each step (hence the name of the ceremony).

In a Wind Up Dance the participants interlock hands and follow the lead dancer, winding their way around the ground, creating confusion which is greeted by laughter from the observers. This dance is repeated at any time the leader senses the dancers lagging in enthusiasm. As dawn nears, a series of three dances conclude the observance. In a Morning Dance the women remove their rattles and whoop and sing with the men. In a Drunk Dance dancers stagger but show their exhilaration in dancing the night through despite their fatigue. Then the more solemn Olden or Grandpa Dance is repeated four times. Elders who have not been able to dance through the night, but who have observed the other dancers, join in this final dance. The ceremony ends as the first light of day appears in the east. After the last dance, firekeepers tend the fire so that its ashes can be rekindled for the next dance.

In Stomp Dances today men usually wear everyday clothing as they dance, but the women wear dresses or long skirts (never jeans or pants). The adults dance near the fire, with children on the outside. Sometimes the dance starts an hour before sunset with a Buffalo Dance, a traditional hunting ritual. After dark the "long" dance began, with participants asking for strength to continue dancing through the night. Most of the dancing is open to all, but only members of the particular grounds perform the three stomp dances accompanied by special chants. Animal dances, especially popular among children, are also held, with dancers imitating horses, foxes, alligators, and other animals.

Traditionally, Stomp Dances have been held at the Redbird Smith grounds at Medicine Springs, east of Gore, Oklahoma, every third Saturday. On the weekend nearest 19 July each year, a ceremony has been held in celebration of Smith's birthday.

Another widely known ceremonial grounds in recent times has been the Stoke Smith grounds at Pin Hook Corner near Vian, Oklahoma. Stoke Smith was the youngest son of Redbird Smith. After Stoke Smith's death the grounds

were under the leadership of his son William. They have become the most widely recognized Nighthawk Keetoowah group among the Cherokee people. Each
summer, Stomp Dances are held every second and fourth weekend. On alternating weekends, traditional stickball games are played. During the rest of the year,
a meeting is held at the grounds at least once a month, and a Stomp Dance is
held, weather permitting.

On Labor Day weekend, a Green Corn Dance (see above) is held at the Stoke
Smith ceremonial grounds. This three-day ritual is the high point of the year spiritually. During the ceremony the healers and ritual leaders recount the history of
the Keetoowahs and admonish the people to remain committed to the Cherokee
way. Stickball games are played during the day and Stomp Dances are held at
night. A great feast is held on Saturday.

In recent decades Stomp Dancing has been revived among other originally
southeastern nations as well. For example, the Seminole peoples of Oklahoma
and Florida have renewed their own Green Corn Dance tradition (Beck and
Walters 1977, 259–66).

The *Ani'-Yun'-Wiya* Today

The Three Bands

In 1990 some 90,000 members were enrolled in the Cherokee Nation of
Oklahoma, 8,500–9,000 in the Eastern Band of Cherokees in North Carolina, and
about 7,500 in the United Keetoowah Band of Oklahoma (Thornton 1990, xvii).
The 232,344 Americans who self-identified as Cherokees in 1980 had grown to nearly 300,000 by 1990. This number does not account for the hundreds of thousands
of other Americans who claim Cherokee ancestry. Each time the author asks students at his Missouri college if they have Native American ancestors, in a class of
thirty at least a few invariably say they "have Cherokee blood."

The annual budget of the Cherokee Nation of Oklahoma in the early 1990s
was $75 million, with a staff of 1,200 employees. The area encompassed by the
CNO covers 7,000 square miles. By most accounts it was the most successful
Native American nation in developing economic self-sufficiency. The large
Cherokee Heritage Center near Tahlequah, Oklahoma, features a reconstructed
traditional nineteenth-century Cherokee village. This "reconstruction" of tradition has been criticized by some Cherokee traditionalists.

Friction arises among factions within the nation, which in the late 1990s was
boiling over into demonstrations and threats of violence. In addition, tension continues between the Cherokee Nation of Oklahoma and the Lenape (see chapter 2)
and other Native American nations in Oklahoma, principally over sovereignty issues.

By 1997 the number of registered members of the Eastern Band of Cherokees
had risen to about 11,000, with most living in the Qualla Boundary, the Cherokee

Indian Reservation. Capitalizing on its beautiful location on the slopes of the Great Smoky Mountains (the "Land of the Blue Mist"), as noted, the Eastern Cherokee Reservation has become a thriving tourist attraction visited by millions annually.

As noted, dialogue has been opened between the Cherokee Nation of Oklahoma and the Eastern Band, and relations are cordial. Much ground remains to be covered, however, in order to renew a strong sense of *Ani'-Yun'-wiya* unity. The smallest of the three bands, the United Keetoowah Band of Oklahoma, continues to press its campaign to return to Arkansas, the state to which their ancestors, the Old Settlers, had migrated in the early nineteenth century (see above).

Traditional Cherokee Spirituality Today

Although the vast majority of Cherokees today are members of Christian churches, with most either Baptists or Methodists, more and more Cherokees, including many fully assimilated mixed-bloods, have reawakened to their *Ani'-Yun'-wiya* spiritual heritage. It is difficult to document at present, but people speak of the growing enrollment in Cherokee language classes, increasing attendance at traditional Stomp Dances, and expanding utilization of traditional herbal remedies and consultation with healers. Like other native peoples today, many Cherokee Christians see no conflict in participating in traditional rituals while they continue to attend Christian worship services.

There is, Chief Mankiller notes, "an old Cherokee prophecy which instructs us that as long as the Cherokee continue traditional dances, the world will remain as it is, but when the dances stop, the world will come to an end. Everyone should hope that the Cherokee will continue to dance" (Mankiller 1993, 29).

The seal of the Cherokee nation suggests an ongoing commitment to traditional spirituality. In its center lies a seven-pointed star to symbolize the sacred number of seven and the seven traditional matrilineal clans of the Cherokee. A wreath of oak leaves, surrounded by the name of the Cherokee Nation in English and Cherokee, signifies strength and eternal life. Oak is used in the sacred fire kept burning perpetually (Mankiller 1993, 130).

According to Chief Mankiller, the traditional Cherokee way is

being positive, accepting things as they are and turning it into a better path. Sometimes in a traditional prayer, a leader will ask that everyone remove all negative things from the mind, to have a pure mind and heart for the ceremony ahead. That is the spirit with which *Ani'-Yun'-wiya*, the Real People, are looking toward the future, confident that the same powers that enabled the ancestors to find harmony, even in times of tragedy, and to be "of good mind." (Mankiller 1993, 226)

A traditional story holds out the hope that if the Cherokee people remain committed to their heritage, they will not struggle alone:

> Once while all the warriors of a certain town were off on a hunt, or at a dance in another settlement, one old man was chopping wood on the side of the ridge when suddenly a party of the enemy came upon him. . . . Throwing his hatchet at the nearest one, he turned and ran for the house to get his gun and make the best defense that he might. On coming out at once with the gun he was surprised to find a large body of strange warriors driving back the enemy. It was no time for questions, and taking his place with the others, they fought hard until the enemy was pressed back up the creek, and finally broke and retreated across the mountain. When it was over and there was time to breathe again, the old man turned to thank his new friends, but found that he was alone—they had disappeared as though the mountain had swallowed them. Then he knew they were the *Nuñnehi*, the Immortals, who had come to help their friends, the Cherokee. (Mooney 1900 [1982], 337)

CHAPTER 4

The Lakota (Sioux):
The Way of the Sacred Pipe

We are like prisoners of war on these reservations. But we are also survivors.
We have our culture and it is intact.
—Wilmer Stampede Mesteth, Lakota spiritual leader and Lakota
Studies instructor at Oglala Lakota College, 1996

We're gonna make it as we go along, generation to generation, addin' on and
addin' on.
—Dawson No Horse, at a Yuwipi ceremony, 1981

THE VAN BOUNCED ALONG A RUTTED TRACK as we approached the group of houses
and mobile homes located at a remote settlement called Green Grass on the
Cheyenne River Sioux Reservation in north-central South Dakota. We sat for a
while, as is the custom when arriving at someone's home on the reservation, soak-
ing in the rugged beauty of the sloping hills. The first to greet us was Cecelia
Looking Horse and a young girl whom Cecelia and her husband Stanley had res-
cued after the girl had been abandoned during a cold winter several years earlier.
Cecelia spoke with pride about how well their new daughter was doing in school.

Our small group (including my daughter and me) had come to meet Arval
Looking Horse, Stanley and Cecelia's son, the present Keeper of the Sacred Buffalo
Calf Pipe of the Lakota Nation (see below). We were on the reservation for the
Jimmy Carter Habitat for Humanity work project, building thirty new houses in
Eagle Butte, South Dakota. We had been brought to Green Grass by one of the
new Habitat homeowners, a friend of the Looking Horse family.

Arval Looking Horse soon joined us and, after accepting our offering of tobacco, led us to the site of his family's sweat lodge on a creek bank. As a fire was built
to heat the rocks for the lodge, Arval Looking Horse prepared us to enter, speak-

ing of the meaning of this ceremony of purification and renewal. He said that the lodge would be a deeply spiritual experience, cleansing us and filling us with a new commitment to walk in a holy manner.

There are honest differences as to whether, as non-natives, our group should have participated in a Lakota sweat lodge ritual, and whether Arval Looking Horse should have invited us into his lodge. Was our presence in the lodge intrusive and insensitive? Were we interlopers in a ritual we could not possibly comprehend? These are questions I considered then and have pondered often since. I do know that the time I spent in the lodge at Green Grass that night was one of the most moving experiences in my life. It confirmed my already growing desire to learn as much as I, an outsider, could about the spirituality of the Lakota people. This chapter is the product of that search. I offer it with gratitude to the Looking Horse family and the other Lakota people I have been privileged to meet in recent years.

The chapter includes an orientation to the Lakota nation, a description of traditional Lakota social organization, an account of the Lakota story of origins, a historical overview from the earliest evidence of the arrival of the Lakota on the Great Plains to the 1990s, and an introduction to traditional Lakota spirituality. Included in that introduction is discussion of the legend of the gift of the sacred pipe by White Buffalo Calf Woman, Lakota cosmology and symbols [the sacred pipe, the Black Hills, the "sacred hoop"], gods and spirits, sacred men and women, ritual clowns, the seven "classical" Lakota rituals [with emphasis on the sweat lodge, vision quest, and sun dance], and other rituals [especially the *yuwipi* ceremony]). The chapter continues with a case study focusing on the controversy surrounding the famous Lakota holy man Black Elk and a discussion of the contemporary renewal of Lakota spirituality. It concludes with a summary of the situation of the Lakota people at the end of the twentieth century.

Who Are the Lakota?

The Lakota (also called the Western or Teton Sioux) are among the largest and most influential (as well as best documented) of the native nations of the Great Plains. Events such as the Battle of the Little Big Horn in 1876, the massacre at Wounded Knee in 1890, and the reoccupation of "the Knee" in 1973 have had a profound impact on American history and the situation of Native Americans to the present. All principally involved the Lakota nation. For the non-Indian public, Lakota leaders Tashunka Witko (Crazy Horse; see Ambrose 1975, Sandoz 1992) and Tatanka Totanka (Sitting Bull; see Vestal 1957, Utley 1993) are probably the two most famous Native Americans.

Black Elk Speaks, the story of a Lakota holy man as told by poet John Neihardt, may be the single most widely read book touching on Native American spirituality. The Lakota have also been the subject of many Hollywood movies, mostly quite stereotypical treatments ranging from the vicious savages of the westerns of the 1940s and 50s to the noble savages of the 1990 Oscar-winning *Dances with Wolves.*

In addition, elements of traditional Lakota spirituality such as belief in the "Great Spirit" and rituals such as the sweat lodge, vision quest, and sun dance are today widely known and imitated, but also often misunderstood and exploited.

In short, the Lakota are arguably the most influential Native American nation spiritually in the late twentieth century. Most recently, the 1994 birth of a white buffalo calf in Wisconsin has been linked to a Lakota prophecy with universal implications. It would be hard to imagine a work intending to introduce readers to representative Native American spiritual traditions without thorough discussion of the Lakota.

The Lakota ("allies") are among a people better known as the Sioux. The word *Sioux* is a French corruption of the Algonquian term *nadowesiih* ("little snakes"), but the name has long been adopted by Lakota people themselves, particularly when speaking to non-Lakota, despite its originally pejorative connotation.

The Lakota are one nation among those who speak the Siouan language. The Lakota dialect is closely related to Dakota and Nakota. The political designation of those who speak the Lakota dialect is Teton or Western Sioux (or *Tetonwan*), while those who speak Nakota are called the Yankton (Yanktonai) Sioux. Dakota speakers are the Santee (or Eastern) Sioux. According to the 1990 census, the total number of Sioux in the United States was 103,253.

According to their own traditions of origins, the people known today as the Lakota/Nakota/Dakota are in fact *Ikce Oyate* (the "real or common people"), descendants of the *Pte Oyate* (Buffalo People). All other peoples are *Unma Oyate* ("other people") (Walker 1982, 3).

As is discussed later, the number seven has special significance in Lakota spirituality. According to tradition, the Lakota, Dakota, and Nakota together are composed of "seven fireplaces": the Mdewkanton, Wahpeton, Wahpekute, and Sisseton (Dakota or Santee); Yankton and Yanktonai (Nakota or Yankton); and Teton (Lakota) (Powers 1977, 13, 21–23).

Within the Lakota nation are seven historically verifiable subdivisions (*ospaye*):

- Oglala—"they scatter their own"
- Sichangu—"burned thighs," also known by the French term *Brule*
- Hunkpapa—"end of the circle"
- Mnikowoju—"planters beside the stream," often transliterated as Mineconjou
- Sihasapa—"black feet," not to be confused with the separate Blackfeet people of Montana

- Oohenunpa—"two boilings," better known as the Two Kettle
- Itazipcho—"without bows," better known by the French *Sans Arc*

By the mid-nineteenth century, Dakota bands lived in forested areas from the upper Mississippi and Minnesota Rivers westward onto the prairies of Minnesota and North and South Dakota. The Lakota bands roamed freely on prairies and plains, mostly west of the Missouri River. Between these two peoples were the Yankton and Yanktonai Sioux (the so-called Nakota), who lived on the prairies of Minnesota and eastern North and South Dakota.

Fifty years later, all of these peoples had been confined to reservations/reserves in Minnesota, North and South Dakota, Montana, and Canada. A century later, the reservations in central and western South Dakota and southern North Dakota are the locus of a profound revival of Lakota tradition. Where the Lakota *ospaye* are in the majority they include Pine Ridge (Oglala), Rosebud (Sichangu), Lower Brule (Sichangu), Cheyenne River (Mnikowoju, Sans Arc, and Two Kettle), and Standing Rock (Hunkpapa and Blackfoot).

Because we cannot do justice to all seven *ospaye* in this chapter, we focus here principally on the Oglala Lakota, whose principal home now is the Pine Ridge Reservation in southwestern South Dakota, near the Black Hills.

Traditional Social Organization

The Lakota "password" *mitakuye oyasin* ("all my relations"), heard frequently in rituals, expresses the Lakota perspective that "relationships [spin] outward like a giant web from the extended family to the band, to the *ospaye*, to the tribe, to the land, plants, insects, animals, to the universe and to the Great Mystery (*Wakan Tanka*)" (Price 1996, 2–3). In this section this circle is described as it extends to the Lakota people. The fuller extent of the sense of kinship is explored in the context of the traditional spirituality of the Lakota.

Ideally, each of seven subdivisions of the Lakota (e.g., the Oglala) was itself divided into seven "bands" (*tiyospayes*) of migrating groups of several hundred. In the memory of traditional Lakota today, each *tiyospaye* was "like a warm womb cradling all within it" (Crow Dog 1991, 13). A movement is underway on the Pine Ridge and other Lakota reservations today to renew the role of the *tiyospaye* system in social, political, and ceremonial life (see discussion below). Indeed, in the more remote areas the *tiyospaye* system has remained influential throughout the reservation period.

Within each larger band were traditionally one or more camps (*wicoti*) of twenty-five or more persons each. Two or more camps could associate if they chose, and a number of camps usually came together to form a winter camp.

Each camp (or band if it was not large enough to divide into camps) typically had a council of indeterminate size, leaders chosen by the majority of the camp to be responsible for overseeing day-to-day life: the headman (*itancan*); the chief (*blotahunka*), who took charge at times of armed conflict; and enforcers (*akicita*), who maintained order and discipline within the camp and served as messengers to other camps, bands, *ospaye*, or even other Plains nations. Each spring a group of camp administrators (*Wakiconza*, "one who determines") was selected "to organize the movement of camps and the communal buffalo hunt, to arbitrate disputes, umpire games, and supervise all wagers" (Price 1996, 13). They also appointed the enforcers and assigned locations in the camps to families.

Each camp typically had one or more *wicasa wakan* and/or *wicasa winyan* (sacred men or women) to conduct the traditional ceremonies, serve as healers, and in general act as intermediaries between the spirit world and the people (see below). They would often serve as storytellers for the camp, although anyone who knew the lore of the people could fulfill that critical role.

Leaders remained in their positions as long as they could provide for the needs of the group related to their office. Leadership roles were not necessarily confined to men, as evidence has shown that there were women leaders, women's societies, and even women warriors.

The lodges (tipis) in a camp were set up in a circle with an opening to the east, toward the rising sun. The places near the entrance, the "horns" of the circle, were reserved for the lodges of leading families. A large tipi (*tiyotipi*) erected opposite the entrance to the circle was used for councils. All deliberations took place around a central fire, and coals from it were used to light the sacred pipe. When the camp moved, coals from the previous council fire (symbolic of the sun, the god *Wi*) were carefully saved and used to rekindle a new fire at the new campsite.

Anyone could speak in a council, including senior women. Council sessions always began with the sacred pipe being offered to the six directions (the four cardinal directions, the sky, and earth) and passed around the circle. This practice was applied when government commissions came to forge treaties with the Lakota. Decisions in the council were by consensus, and they were often delayed until consensus could be obtained.

Traditional Lakota society tends to be matrilineal, although not rigidly so. A man customarily lives with his wife's extended family for a time after marriage. Uncles on the mother's side still often play a critical role in the education of young people, as they did historically.

Traditional Lakota kinship terms are complex, reflecting gender, generation, and birth order. Lakota children address their father's brothers and mother's sisters as parents and their father's sisters and mother's brothers as aunts and uncles. Therefore, the children of one's father's brothers and one's mother's sisters are addressed as brothers and sisters.

Appropriate behaviors are determined by the nature of one's relationship with another. For example, in traditional settings daughters and sisters-in-law carefully observe an avoidance taboo, which dictates that they may not look at or address brothers-in-law or fathers-in-law. This is in part because if the woman's husband should die, a close relative of her husband would be expected to take her as a companion.

To be drawn into the Lakota circle, outsiders were traditionally given kinship designations. For example, an agent on a reservation was named "father" so that he could interact with his charges. Being so named, he was expected to act as a good father, as a generous provider and protector of his "children." And the "Great Father," the President of the United States, was expected to maintain a paternal relationship with all Indian peoples. (See Walker 1982, 57–58, 46–50; Hassrick 1964, 114–20; Powers 1986a, 62–65, 79–81; Price 1996, 3–4.)

On the prairie, wealth was measured principally in terms of the number of horses a man owned (or could give away). Guided by the four basic Lakota virtues of bravery, fortitude, generosity, and wisdom, men were expected to devote themselves to the well-being of the people even while they proved their individual courage (Hassrick 1964, 32–39). Boasting about one's exploits was also a demonstration of commitment to the people. Men were hit particularly hard by the relocation of the Lakota to reservations in the late nineteenth century, as their traditional roles of hunters, warriors, and, in general, protectors of the people were largely taken from them (Powers 1986a, 3; Macgregor 1946).

The virtues by which Lakota women sought to live have been characterized as bravery and generosity, like those of the men, but also truthfulness and childbearing (Hassrick 1964, 39–41). Women were in charge of the household activities, and they owned not only the tipi skins but all the cooking implements and other domestic items. They did the tanning, sewing, and gathering of food. In other words, like the men, women had roles to play that were essential to the harmony of the camp. On the whole, Lakota women more successfully adapted to reservation life because they continued to function in their traditional roles as wives and mothers, and, in general, nurturers (Powers 1986a, 3).

When anthropologists began their study of the Lakota on the reservations, they were told of a variety of men's and women's societies. One such group was the men's "dream" or "medicine" society, which was composed of men who, in their vision quests, had seen the same animal, such as a Buffalo, Elk, or Bear. With the help of the animal spirit guide, they were given special healing powers. Those who received the vision acted it out in special dances (Hassrick 1964, 277–79; Powers 1977, 57–59; Mails 1991a, 226–27; Black Elk 1972 [1932], 173–81).

Other men's societies have been classified by outside observers as civil, police, and war. They cut across band lines. The societies were still active on the reservations in the early twentieth century and undoubtedly reflected the organization of Lakota life in prereservation times. The civil societies were the "Big Bellies," White-horse Owners, Tall Ones, and Owl Feather Headdresses. The war societies were the Kit-fox (*Tokala*) (cf. Deloria 1988, 95–99), Crow Owner (*Kangi Yuha*),

Brave Heart (*Cante T'inza*), Badger (*Ihoka*), Plain Lance Owners (*Sokta Yuha*), and Packs White (*Wicinska*). It was estimated that half the young men were members of the war societies. They took the lead in defending the people from enemy attacks and going on raiding parties.

All societies were expected to sponsor ceremonies, and to hold feasts, give-aways, and social dances, although there were also feast associations charged with planning these events. They were also expected to provide for the needy in the camp.

Two men who formed a particularly close bond, usually as members of the same society, and pledged exclusive devotion to one another were called *kolas*, and they addressed one another with that name.

Although not actual members, women were invited to participate in leadership of the rituals held by the men's societies, typically as singers. There were also women's societies (Powers 1986a, 73–74, 86–87), among them the Tanners (who made lodge covers), the Praise-worthy women (virgins), the Owns Alone (women over forty who had known only one man), and the Medicine Societies (women who had seen visions, who made war medicine and shields for warriors). The Strike Dead Society was a women's warrior society made up of women whose male relatives had accomplished acts of bravery.

Most early study of the Lakota was dominated by the assumption that women were subservient and limited to "domestic" tasks, but modern researchers are recognizing that "traditional Lakota society was not 'male dominated' but rather was much more complementary, with women and men performing quite different but equally valuable roles (*okicicupi*)" (Price 1996, 19; Deloria 1944, 26; cf. Powers 1977, 63–64; Albers and Medicine 1983; Powers 1986a, 5–6). Unfortunately, stereotypical portrayals of Lakota women as inferior have continued even into modern anthropological and historical studies (Powers 1986a, 7–18).

According to distinguished Yankton Dakota linguist Ella Deloria (see Rice 1992), the aim of traditional Sioux life is simple: "One must obey kinship rules; one must be a good relative." Everything else is secondary—"property, personal ambition, glory, good times, life itself. Without that aim and the constant struggle to attain it, the people would no longer be Dakota in truth. They would no longer even be human" (Deloria 1988, x).

Lakota Creation Legends

In 1895 Dr. James Walker came to the Pine Ridge Reservation as a physician, at a time of crisis. Only five years had passed since the tragedy at Wounded Knee (see below), and a tuberculosis epidemic was decimating the Oglala population. Unlike other Euroamerican doctors, Walker worked cooperatively with Lakota healers in combatting the diseases he encountered. As a result, some of the elders took him into their confidence and taught him the lore of their people. Between 1896 and 1914, encouraged by anthropologist Clark Wissler, Dr. Walker transcribed and translated what he was told, and his records are among the principal sources for our understanding of Lakota mythology, including stories of origins (Walker 1980, 3–54).

Walker was apparently puzzled by the fact that there seemed to be no single creation narrative among the Lakota comparable to the Biblical account of creation in the first chapters of Genesis (Jahner 1987). He found only fragments of stories, depending for his material principally on a Christian informant named George Sword (Walker 1983, 41–100). From these fragments Walker constructed a unified Lakota narrative about initial creation (Walker 1983, 17, 206–45). It was available only in mimeographed form until 1983, when Elaine Jahner edited it, together with other myths Walker had gathered.

Here is a short excerpt from the beginning of the intricate origins narrative drawn together by Dr. Walker, and paraphrased by D.M. Dooling:

In the beginning was *Inyan* [stone], who had no beginning, for he was there when there was no other, only *Hanhepi*, the Darkness. *Inyan* was soft and shapeless, but he was everywhere and he had all the powers. These powers were in his blood, and his blood was blue. His spirit was *Wakan Tanka*.

Inyan desired that there be others so that he might exercise his powers. But there could be no others unless he created them from himself. To do so he would have to give part of his spirit and part of his blood, and the powers that were in the blood. So he decided to create another but only as part of himself, so that he could keep control over the powers. He took part of himself and spread it over and around himself in the shape of a great disk. He named the disk *Maka*, the Earth, and he gave *Maka* a spirit, *Maka-akan*, Earth Spirit, and she is part of *Inyan*. But in creating her, he took so much from himself that his veins opened and all his blood flowed from him, and he shrank and became hard and powerless.

As *Inyan's* blood flowed, it became the blue waters which are on the earth. Because powers cannot live in water, they separated themselves and became a great blue dome whose edge is near the edge of *Maka*. This blue dome of the powers of the blood of Inyan is now the sky and is not material but is the spirit of *Taku Skanskan*, the Great Spirit. When these powers assumed one shape, they said a voice spoke, saying: "I am the source of energy, I am *Skan*." This was the beginning of the third of the Sacred Beings who is the highest of all because he is spirit. *Inyan* and *Maka* are material, and the world of matter has no powers except what are given by *Skan*.

[*Skan* then creates Light (*Anpetu*) and the fourth Sacred Being, *Wi*, the sun. He gathers the other Sacred Beings and says to them:]

I, *Skan*, and you, *Inyan*, *Maka*, and *Wi*, are four, but we are only one, and that one is *Wakan Tanka*, which no one can understand. Each of us is part of *Wakan Tanka*, which is the Great Incomprehensible. (Dooling 1990, 3–5; cf. Powers 1986a, 36–38)

Each of the Sacred Beings is given a color and a realm. *Wi* (red) is the chief of the Sacred Beings, because she is above all. *Skan* (blue) is the source of all power and spirit and has domain over all. *Maka* (green) has dominion over all the lands except the mountains and high hills. *Inyan* (yellow) is given the mountains, rocks, and high hills. Each of the beings creates a companion: *Wi* creates the Moon; *Maka* creates Passion, but throws her into the waters because she became jealous of her; *Skan* creates Wind; *Inyan* makes Thunderstorm. From a huge egg made by Thunderstorm and fertilized by *Skan* comes *Ksa* (Wisdom), who invented language, told stories, and gave names to all creatures and things.

The elaborate tale continues with the story of *Pte Oyate* (the "Buffalo People"), the animals, four times and directions. Finally comes the story of the emergence of the *Ikce Oyate* (the "Real People"), which, as noted, is a Lakota self-designation (Walker 1983, 197–205, 245–381). This story of emergence is usually cited by contemporary Lakota as their "creation story," for it is the narrative of the beginning of life on the surface of the earth. The emergence story sets the stage for the story of White Buffalo Woman and the gift of the sacred pipe to which we return later.

Also discussed later are the implicit cosmology and some of the gods and spirits mentioned in this rich narrative. At least a touch of circularity in a discussion of the Lakota nation and Lakota spirituality seems appropriate!

Historical Overview

The traditional Lakota manner of recording events is known as *waniyetu yawapi* (winter counts). Composed of pictures drawn typically on buffalo or deer skins, the winter counts were a sort of visual shorthand, portraying the most significant event in the life of the particular band for whom the winter count was being kept. There was at least one count keeper in each camp, and the skins were passed from generation to generation. For example, the winter count of No Ears, which begins with an entry dated to 1759, the year "the people scattered during the winter," concludes with 1912, the year "White Wold died during the winter" (Walker 1982, 124–57; cf. Iron Shell's count in Hassrick 1964, 346–51).

Nowhere in any of the extant winter counts is there mention of battles with the U.S. Army, not even the great victory at the Little Bighorn in 1876; the counters were more interested in recording events of more immediate significance to their camps (Hassrick 1964, 10). According to Raymond DeMallie, the functions of the counts were to locate events in time (each Lakota could identify the picto-graph of the year of birth) and to teach and instruct, using the pictographs as the basis for stories about the life of the camp (Walker 1982, 112). According to Lakota scholar Vine Deloria Jr., the winter counts represent the "psychic life of the com-munity" (Nabakov 1996, 41).

For the Lakota all history is sacred history, with the gods and spirits ever-pre-sent realities. From a traditional Lakota perspective, "history is never simply the past, but the past as it relates to the present" (Walker 1982, 113). Therefore, although we relate the history of the Lakota in chronological fashion, from a Lakota perspective, the events described continue to "live" just as do the events of the time of origins.

The Arrival of the Lakota on the Plains (1650–1830)

According to some theories, the ancestors of the Lakota migrated to Minnesota after being forced out of their original homelands on the East Coast, perhaps in the Carolinas, sometime before the 1600s. Evidence for this movement is at best hypo-thetical, however, and is based on the fact that there are Siouan-speaking peoples such as the Catawba in the East. By contrast, according to some Lakota traditions, the people had lived in the region of the Black Hills for 10,000 years and spread out from there (Lazarus 1991, 417). Some winter counts can be interpreted to support the view that the Lakota were living near the Black Hills since at least 900 C.E.

Regardless of their prior history, most modern historians hold that by the 1600s the ancestors of the Lakota had settled in semisedentary villages in the forests of Minnesota. They gathered wild rice, hunted, practiced limited horti-culture, and engaged in trade with other native Americans (Hassrick 1964, 62).

By the seventeenth century European goods, including guns as well as knives, cooking pots, needles, and glass beads, had been introduced, resulting in cultural adaptation which continues to the present. In 1665 the Sioux had their first record-ed contact with Christian missionaries, when Jesuit missionary–explorers Claude Allouez and Jacques Marquette met the Eastern Sioux. This initial encounter was followed by sporadic visits from Roman Catholic missionaries throughout the sev-enteenth and eighteenth centuries (DeMallie and Parks 1987, 9).

Modern historians also take the position that the Lakota then moved on to the plains of what is now South Dakota from Minnesota. The movement began in the mid-seventeenth century as Crees and Assiniboines began to push the Lakota out of central Minnesota, forcing them westward. In turn, the Lakota (and the Yanktons and Yanktonais) pressured the Iowa, Oto, Missouris, Ponca, and Cheyenne people, forcing them to move to the south and west.

According to this reconstruction, by the 1740s the Lakota had reached the Missouri River. They attacked Mandan, Hidatsa, and Arikara villages, and by the late 1770s were dominant in the upper Missouri area. The Lakota acquired guns from the Santees at trade fairs in western Minnesota and eastern South Dakota and from British traders.

The Lakota adapted well to the prairie environment. During most of the year they lived in camps of tipis alongside rivers and streams, which could be moved quickly to follow the buffalo herds. The buffalo provided the basis for a subsistence, but adequate, lifestyle. Every part of the buffalo could be put to use: hair for ropes and pads and ceremonies; horns and hoofs for implements; bones for soup and various articles; sinews for thread, cords, and bowstrings; skins for robes, tipi coverings, ordinary clothing, ceremonial dress, thongs; the flesh and viscera for food; and the skull in ceremonies (Walker 1982, 74).

In the winter the Lakota established camps in more sheltered areas. In the spring they moved along rivers to trade with and/or raid other people. In the early summer they gathered with as many other Lakota bands as possible in a camp circle, during which the annual sun dance would be celebrated.

Before the introduction of the horse, Lakota and other nomadic plains hunters used dogs to move their belongings as they followed the buffalo during the warm months and wintered in semipermanent villages in the winter. By 1750 the Lakota had obtained their first horses (probably from raids on and/or trading with Arikara villages), increasing their mobility for hunting and warmaking. They called these strange new beasts "sacred dogs." Acquisition of the horse required more frequent movement, as horses grazed out an area rapidly. The increased efficiency in hunting allowed young men to spend more time raiding neighboring peoples' camps and villages for horses. The raids occasioned revenge attacks, and bravery in raids became critical in determining prestige and leadership for men.

A hunter-warrior could show his valor and earn "coup points" by riding into a buffalo herd and striking the lead animal a blow on the nose, or into an enemy camp and hitting a foe with a glancing blow. Rather than being concerned with their own glory, however, the warriors were dedicated to the well-being of the people. Lakota families with larger herds were expected to share their horses and the meat taken in hunts with those less fortunate in the band. By 1780 the Sioux were the largest of the peoples of the Plains, numbering perhaps about 25,000 (Mails 1991a, 226).

By 1795 the Lakota were dealing with French traders who were traveling up the Missouri river in keelboats and pirogues. They often harassed French traders trying to reach the Arikara villages upstream, demanding payment for the right of passage.

In September 1804 the Lakota encountered the "Corps of Discovery," the official U.S. government expedition commissioned by President Thomas Jefferson and led by Meriwether Lewis and William Clark, making its way up the

Missouri River from St. Louis, seeking a water route to the Pacific Ocean. In a dramatic encounter, Lakota leaders demanded that the expedition pay more than Lewis and Clark were willing to pay for the right to pass through Lakota territory. Lewis and Clark and their men escaped without casualty, but not without developing a healthy respect for the power of the Lakota and their refusal to be intimidated by the American intruders into their lands.

In addition, the perilous encounter only served to harden the stereotype of the Lakota as ruthless. Clark wrote in his journal that the Sioux were "the vilest miscreants of the savage race." Lewis and Clark reported that the Lakota were the "pirates" of the Missouri, who would remain so unless and until the government made them dependent on Euroamerican trade goods. Unfortunately, their ability to intimidate the expedition may have caused the Lakota to overestimate their ability to prevent the Euroamericans from entering their territory (Ambrose 1996, 165–75).

The traders who followed the Corps of Discovery sold utensils that made life easier for the Lakota, but they also offered alcohol, called "the water that makes men foolish" by the Lakota. The traders also brought smallpox, cholera, and venereal disease. One Lakota winter count called 1818 "the year many died of cramps."

In 1825 another expedition entered Lakota lands and made treaties with several bands, promising to protect the Lakota and their lands from "wrongdoers." At one treaty-making ceremony a young army lieutenant named William Harney read aloud to the Lakota the Declaration of Independence. This same year the Great Plains were designated by the U.S. Government Permanent Indian Country, reserved for the sole use and occupancy of the original inhabitants (Lazarus 1991, 10, 13).

Prosperity on the Plains (1830–55)

By the mid-nineteenth century the Lakota were the power to be reckoned with in the northern Great Plains. Lakota hunting and raiding parties moved across a large stretch of land from the Missouri River in the east to the Yellowstone River and Bighorn Mountains in the west, from above the Canadian border in the north to the Republican River on the Kansas-Nebraska border in the south. The buffalo and other game were in abundance, and the Lakota nomadic culture was flourishing.

The Lakota particularly regarded western South Dakota as their land, with the sacred Black Hills at the center of their universe (see below). They aggressively attacked any people who ventured into an area they had come to regard as their original homeland.

During the 1830s trading companies built forts among the Plains peoples and began to use the recently invented steamboats to speed the movement of furs to market. Fort Tecumseh (later Fort Pierre) was built in central South Dakota. By the 1840s French Jesuits had established missions among the Dakota to the east. In 1847 Father Auguste Ravoux visited Lakota who were trading at Fort Pierre (DeMallie and Parks 1987, 9).

In *The North American Indians,* George Catlin wrote about his encounters with the Lakota during the 1830s. His impressions of their values and their spirituality, although tinged with ethnocentrism, challenge the more common, stereotypical portrayal of the Sioux as dangerous savages:

> I have found these people kind and honourable, and endowed with every feeling of parental, of filial, and conjugal affection, that is met in more enlightened communities. I have found them moral and religious; and I am bound to give them great credit for their zeal, which is often exhibited in their modes of worship, however insufficient they may seem to us, or may be in the estimation of the Great Spirit. (Gill 1983, 13)

In the 1840s "westward expansion" began in earnest with the annexation of Texas in 1845, the acquisition of Oregon in 1846, the taking of lands in California after the defeat of Mexico in 1848, and the discovery of gold in California in 1849 (which unleashed a flood of 90,000 fortune-seekers). Newspaper editor John O'Sullivan coined the phrase "manifest destiny" to justify the movement of Euroamericans westward.

The first Euroamerican wagon trains to cross Lakota country left Missouri in 1842. The road west moved through Nebraska along the south bank of the Platte River, where the travelers encountered the Lakota. The Oregon Trail, as it was called, crossed through prime hunting grounds of the Lakota and their allies. The stream of Euroamericans fouled the land with broken wagons, rotting corpses, and discarded belongings and drove away the buffalo and other game. The buffalo, who had ranged up to 15 million in the northern Plains before the migration began, divided into herds north and south of the Platte and kept their distance from the trail. The travelers also brought more cholera, smallpox, and other diseases to the native peoples.

At first the American travelers were merely harassed by the Lakota and other Plains groups, who, as was their custom, insisted on the payment of tolls in exchange for the right of travel. Friction increased, however, and the Lakota became convinced that the buffalo were being driven away and diseases intentionally introduced in order to exterminate them. In turn, the government sought to protect the emigrants and placate the native peoples through treaties. From this point on different strategies were developed among the Lakota in responding to the invaders, with some leaders committed to armed resistance while others favored negotiation.

In 1846 historian Francis Parkman spent three weeks with the Oglala and came away with a view of them as savages. He called Oglala women "shrivelled hags" and spoke of "swarms" rather than bands of Sioux. Since he was a respected historian and his views were widely reported, these stereotypes were widely accepted (Trigger and Washburn 1996, 85).

At this point the official government strategy was to placate the Lakota. When Colonel S.W. Kearney arrived in 1845, he carried alongside the Stars and Stripes a flag with two hands clasped in friendship, calling it the "Sioux flag" (Lazarus 1991, 14). But Kearney's expedition also purchased from the American Fur Company a post in the heart of the Lakota's lands, in what is now eastern Wyoming, and renamed it Fort Laramie.

According to the 1851 Fort Laramie treaty, representatives of the Lakota and other Plains nations and the government entered into "a lasting peace." The Indians promised not to molest travelers on the Oregon Trail, to stop harassing the forts and outposts, and to end the conflicts among themselves. Boundaries were established for the hunting grounds, taking away lands the Lakota had won in conflicts with the Crows and Kiowas. In exchange, the government agreed to pay the Lakota and other nations an annual annuity of $50,000 for ten years (reduced by Congress from the fifty-year period specified in the negotiated treaty) in the form of food, domestic animals and agricultural implements. By implication the treaty recognized the Lakota and other nations as having sovereign status.

The Plains Wars and the Lakota Victory (1855–76)

When a lame cow strayed from (or was abandoned by) a Mormon wagon train near Fort Laramie in 1855, a young Sichangu warrior killed it and shared it with his hungry friends. It was hardly a serious or unique incident, but when the cow's owner angrily protested to the army post at Fort Laramie, a young lieutenant named Grattan was sent to the camp where the Sichangu man had taken refuge. When the Lakota refused to hand over the young man, Grattan's troops opened fire, killing several Lakota outright. In retaliation, Grattan's contingent of thirty was wiped out, and the so-called Plains Wars had begun.

The next summer a contingent of 1,300 troops led by then-Colonel William Harney attacked a Lakota camp, killed eighty-six, and took the rest captive. Thereafter, Harney was called "Hornet" by the Lakota because of his rapid and painful sting. Years later the highest of the sacred Black Hills, the center of the Lakota world, would be named Harney Peak by the government in his honor.

Other unprovoked attacks by army patrols on Lakota hunting parties followed. As a result, a number of other Lakota, including the Sichangu leader Spotted Tail, surrendered. Spotted Tail became convinced of the insurmountable power of the military forces aligned against the Lakota, and thereafter he was a leader in the Lakota faction arguing for accommodation rather than resistance.

Other Lakota leaders refused to be intimidated and committed themselves to fight in defense of their right to continue their nomadic lifestyle in the hunting grounds as protected by the 1851 treaty. These "hostiles," as the government called the resisters, began to ridicule those who favored accommodation as "Laramie loafers (*wagluhe*)" or "hang-around-the-fort" Indians.

During the rest of the 1850s, small war parties of "hostiles" mounted sporadic attacks on wagon trains, army patrols, and trappers. In 1857 the largest gathering of Lakota bands ever recorded (estimated to be from 5,000 to 7,000) came together at the sacred Bear Butte north of the Black Hills to plan how to drive out the intruders. Among them were young warriors soon to be known for their leadership in the struggle: Red Cloud, Crazy Horse, and Sitting Bull. Fortunately for the Lakota, when the American Civil War began in 1861, large numbers of army troops were withdrawn and the hostilities decreased.

After the Santee Sioux uprising in Minnesota in 1862, however, Santee refugees who had been expelled from Minnesota fled west and joined with the Lakota in resistance to immigrant pressure. The massacre of a peaceful Cheyenne village at Sand Creek in Colorado in November 1864 by a militia force led by Colonel John Chivington (see chapter 1) also convinced many Lakota and their allies that peace with the invaders would not be possible.

The post–Civil War exodus of Euroamericans from the East put increased pressure on the Lakota and other Plains nations. Civil War hero General William Tecumseh Sherman, who had earned fame for his ruthless "March to the Sea" in Georgia, was named army commander in the West. One of his principal tasks was to defend the new Bozeman Trail, which split off from the Oregon Trail west of Fort Laramie and cut through the prime Powder River hunting grounds of the Lakota and their Plains allies. It led to Montana, where gold had been discovered in 1862. In 1866 Sherman ordered the construction of a series of forts to protect the Bozeman Trail.

Red Cloud led the Lakota and their allies in a campaign to protect the hunting grounds, destroy the forts, and close the trail (Larson 1997, 74–104; on Red Cloud's life see also Lazar 1995). Red Cloud called the Euroamerican incursion "an insult to the spirits of our ancestors." He asked his fellow Lakota, "Are we to give up our sacred grounds to be plowed for corn? . . . I am for war" (Lazarus 1991, 36).

In December 1866 a force led by Captain William Fetterman (who had boasted he could ride through the entire Sioux nation with eighty men) was sent out from Fort Phil Kearney near what is now the Wyoming/Montana border to protect a wood cutting party. Fetterman led his eighty men into an ambush, and his entire contingent was killed.

When he learned of the debacle, General Sherman called for a vindictive response against the Sioux, "even to their extermination, men, women and children" (Andrist 1993 [1964], 124). Sherman's recommendation, however, was not immediately followed. Instead, the "Fetterman Fight" inspired yet another re-examination of Indian policy, in which those who favored negotiation prevailed. The sentiment was that "it was much cheaper to feed the Indians than to fight them, cheaper to kill a culture than a people" (Lazarus 1991, 43).

A Peace Commission, which included General Sherman, was formed, and another Fort Laramie treaty was eventually signed in 1868, promising that all of present-day South Dakota west of the Missouri River, including the Black Hills, would be "for the absolute and undisputed occupation of the Sioux." This area would be known as the Great Sioux Reservation. The intent of the government was to shrink this large reservation gradually as the Lakota began to adapt to farming. The Lakota were also guaranteed the right to hunt outside the reservation in a vast "unceded Indian territory," "so long as buffalo may range there in numbers sufficient to justify the chase." It also stipulated that no future land cessions would be valid unless three-fourths of all adult Lakota males signed the agreement.

Only after the forts along the Bozeman Trail were abandoned did Red Cloud agree to "touch a pen" to the treaty, but he insisted he had no intention of becoming a farmer. According to the treaty, the Lakota and other nations who signed it agreed to stop their attacks, and despite the failure of the government to keep its promises, Red Cloud never again took up arms (although he remained a wily and determined negotiator and zealous defender of the Lakota's remaining land and rights). He later cynically told other Lakota that to become wealthy like the Euroamericans: "You must begin anew and put away the wisdom of your fathers. You must lay up food and forget the hungry. When your house is built, your storeroom filled, then look around for a neighbor whom you can take advantage of and seize all he has" (Deloria 1994, 198).

Some Lakota leaders, including Crazy Horse and Sitting Bull, and their people, stayed to the west beyond the Black Hills, coming to the agencies only to get supplies. Others went north into Montana and shunned the agencies altogether.

In the 1869 Supreme Court ruling that undermined the well-established principle that the Lakota and other native nations had sovereignty (*United States* v. *Lucero*), one of the justices wrote:

> The idea that a handful of wild, half naked, thieving, plundering, murdering savages should be dignified with the sovereign attributes of nations, enter into solemn treaties, and claim a country 500 miles wide by 1,000 miles long as theirs in fee simple, because they have hunted buffalo or antelope over it, might do for beautiful reading in Cooper's novels or

Longfellow's *Hiawatha*, but is unsuited to the intelligence and justice of this age, or the natural rights of mankind. (cited in Mankiller 1993, 132)

In 1870 Red Cloud, Spotted Tail, and other Lakota leaders were taken to Washington to marvel at the magnificence and power of the government. At Cooper Union in New York City, Red Cloud spoke to an enthusiastic audience, and said:

My Brothers and my Friends who are here before me today: God Almighty has made us all, and He is here to hear what I have to say to you today. The Great Spirit made us both. He gave me lands and He gave you lands. You came here and we received you as brothers. When the Almighty made you, He made you all white and clothed you. When He made us He made us with red skins and poor. When you first came we were very many and you were few. Now you are many and we are few. . . . We do not want riches, but we want to train our children right. Riches would do us no good. We could not take them with us to the other world. We do not want riches, we want peace and love. (Armstrong 1971, 91–92)

As part of the national "peace policy" instituted by President Grant (see chapter 1), Christian churches were given oversight of the various agencies established after the 1868 treaty. Episcopalians were given responsibility for the the Red Cloud (later to become Pine Ridge) Agency, among others. Roman Catholic orders received jurisdiction over other agencies. (Demallie and Parks 1987, 11).

In 1874 General Philip Sheridan (famous for his remark that "the only good Indian is a dead Indian") sent an exploratory expedition led by George Armstrong Custer (known to the Lakota as "Long Hair") into the Black Hills, in clear violation of the 1868 treaty (Jackson 1972). He acted with the tacit approval of President Grant, who had secretly decided to open the hills to miners. The trail they cut into the hills was called by the Lakota the "Thieves Road." As predicted, Custer's party (which had taken along reporters and photographers in anticipation of a "big story") discovered gold in the Black Hills, "right under the roots of the grasses," he boldly announced. Euroamericans flooded into the Black Hills in search of "the metal that makes white men crazy" despite perfunctory efforts by the army to keep them out. In 1876 government agents fraudulently obtained an agreement for the Lakota to relinquish their permanent right to the hills (see below). In response Crazy Horse is reputed to have said simply, "One does not sell the earth upon which the people walk" (Miller 1995, 244).

These events set the stage for the last great Lakota victory at the Little Big Horn in southern Montana (see Utley 1963; Andrist 1964, 252–300; Black Elk 1972 [1932], 88–109; Ambrose 1975, 435–47; Welch and Stekler 1994). A large army force was sent out to confront the "hostiles," including many who had left the agencies because of the government's deceit in the Black Hills matter. In June thousands of Lakota came together along the Little Big Horn River for a sun dance. On 25 June 1876 Custer's Seventh Cavalry foolishly attacked the large village of about 1,500 lodges. Custer had claimed that he could whip all the Indians on the continent with the Seventh Cavalry. Assured of success by the Hunkpapa spiritual leader Sitting Bull, Crazy Horse and other Lakota warriors repulsed the assault and killed Custer and all 225 men under his direct command. As they prepared to ride into battle, Crazy Horse spurred on the Oglala warriors with the cry "Ho-ka hey! It is a good day to fight! It is a good day to die! Strong Hearts, brave Hearts to the front! Weak hearts and cowards to the rear!"

The Breaking of the Sacred Hoop (1876–90)

The Lakota could not celebrate the Little Big Horn victory for long. Whipped up by distorted press accounts of the bravery of Custer and the savagery of the Lakota, the public demanded revenge (see Greene 1994). A winter campaign beginning in November 1876 forced almost all of the Lakota and their remaining allies to the agencies. Sitting Bull led a flight to Canada but returned in 1881. Some Lakota, however, stayed in Canada and in 1913 were given a reserve at Wood Mountain.

Sitting Bull explained why he did not surrender in these words:

> Because I am a red man. If the Great Spirit had desired me to be a white man he would have made me so in the first place. He put in your heart certain wishes and plans, in my heart he put other and different desires. Each man is good in his sight. It is not necessary for eagles to be crows. (Armstrong 1971, 112)

In August 1876 Congress created a Sioux Peace Commission to negotiate the acquisition of the Black Hills and other territories. The commission acknowledged that the Lakota had been the victims of gross injustices, saying "our country must forever bear the disgrace and suffer the retributions of its wrongdoing" (Wilson 1999, 297). As one Lakota leader put it in his remarks to the commission: ". . . since the Great Father promised that we should never be removed we have been moved five times. I think you had better put the Indians on wheels and you can run them about wherever you wish" (Armstrong 1971, 105).

Nevertheless, the 1876 commission succeeded in visiting even more inequities on the Lakota, reducing the Great Sioux Reservation established by the 1868 Fort Laramie treaty by more than half and winning the Black Hills by staging a fraudulent "election." Its actions remain at the heart of the continuing legal attempts to force the government to abide by the terms of the 1868 treaty.

The Pine Ridge Reservation was established east of the Black Hills and south of the Badlands of South Dakota in 1878 for the Oglala Lakota bands. Although it had only one small area of farmable land (which was excised from the reservation in 1911), the Oglalas were told to become self-sufficient farmers, following the Euroamerican model. Some government leaders recognized what this meant to the Lakota. Thomas J. Morgan, U.S. commissioner of Indian affairs under President Benjamin Harrison, wrote:

Sitting Bull was a warrior and holy man who is remembered for never surrendering his pride as a Lakota. (© CORBIS)

> The buffalo had gone and the Sioux had left to them alkali land and government rations. . . . Suddenly, almost without warning, they were expected at once and without previous training to settle down to the pursuits of agriculture in a land largely unfitted for such use. . . . Under these circumstances it is not in human nature not to be discontented and restless, even turbulent and violent. (Mooney 1896 [1965], 70)

Deceived by the promise that he could have his own reservation in the Powder River hunting grounds and because his band was starving, Crazy Horse surrendered in 1877. He was imprisoned and murdered at Fort Robinson, Nebraska. According to tradition, Crazy Horse had this to say to the Euroamericans before he died:

> Now, you tell us to work for a living, but the Great Spirit did not make us to work, but to live by hunting. You white men can work if you want to. We do not interfere with you, and again you say, why do you not become civilized? We do not want your civilization. We would live as our fathers did, and their fathers before them. (Lazarus 1991, 51)

In 1883, at the insistence of Secretary of the Interior H.M. Teller, who said that the Lakota sun dance was "hindering the civilization of the Indians" (Holler 1995, 119–20) and stimulating the violent tendencies of young warriors, a concerted effort to annihilate traditional Lakota rituals began. According to Bureau of Indian Affairs regulations:

The "sun dance," and all other similar dances and so-called religious cere-monies, shall be considered "Indian offenses" and any Indian found guilty of being a participant in any one or more of these offenses shall . . . be punished by withholding from him his rations for a period of not exceed-ing ten days; and if found guilty of any subsequent offense under this rule, shall be punished by withholding his rations for a period not less than fif-teen days no more than thirty days, or by incarceration in the agency prison for a period not exceeding thirty days. (Echo-Hawk 1991, 8)

As a result, the traditional rituals described below were forced underground. The ban effectively ended the annual sun dances near the agencies until the 1960s, but not the more remote dances (Holler 1995, 133).

Modern tribal historian Charlotte Black Elk, granddaughter of Nicholas Black Elk, speaks of the effect of the ban and other measures designed to strip the Lakota of their traditional way of life:

All of a sudden we were told: "Not only will you not be able to practice your religion, but you shall also bring all of your sacred objects—sacred pipes, spirit bundles, everything that we had that was sacred—into the agency and there we shall have a great bonfire." . . . every thing about our culture was systematically to be destroyed. (Wilson 1999, 309)

By the early 1880s the buffalo, which had once roamed on the Plains in herds tens of miles long, had been virtually exterminated. Government leaders recognized that with the buffalo gone, the Lakota and other nomadic plains peoples would have to accept a settled life. Coins circulated in the West stamped with the phrase: "One dead buffalo: One dead Indian: One dollar" (Hughes 1983, 112). By the late 1880s devastating droughts were scorching the northern plains. To make matters worse rations were cut just when the droughts were at their worst. For the Lakota these were "years of thin grass and little rain" (Crow Dog 1995, 41).

Still, Lakota resistance continued. During the 1880s traditional leaders such as Sitting Bull, Gall, and Red Cloud successfully held off two separate attempts to reduce the size of the reservation. Their struggle was not violent, but it was effective. They insisted that the generous boundaries of the 1868 treaty be recog-nized. Determined to break all resistance, the government disbanded the *akicita* societies and created Lakota police forces who answered to the reservation agents rather than the people (Powers 1986a, 29).

In June 1880 both Red Cloud and Spotted Tail visited Carlisle Indian School in Pennsylvania (see chapter 1) where many Lakota children had been taken to be educated. Both were shocked at what was happening to the Lakota youngsters. When Spotted Tail saw his own children in military uniforms with their hair cut and heard how they were being taught to despise their Lakota heritage, he abruptly removed them from the school.

In 1885 German Jesuits began work on the Pine Ridge and Rosebud Reservations, at the invitation of Red Cloud and Spotted Tail, who considered them to be more respectful of the Lakota people than the Episcopalians who had been assigned to the reservations. The Jesuits were willing to learn Lakota, while the Episcopalians did not seem interested in doing so. The Jesuits and sisters of Saint Francis founded Holy Rosary Mission and Boarding School at Pine Ridge (now renamed Red Cloud School).

Despite their willingness to learn Lakota, the Jesuits were enthusiastic advocates of the government's assimilationist policies. They hoped that by following a stringent regimen the Oglalas could be "advanced from 'savagery' to 'civilization' in one or two generations" (Markowitz 1987, 121). Half the day children attended classes in such subjects as reading, composition, and math. The rest of the day boys were taught the essentials of agriculture, animal husbandry, shop repair, carpentry, and painting. Girls were taught how to milk cows, sew, cook, wash, and manage a home. Children were punished for speaking Lakota. Home visits were prohibited after the first year, when it was discovered that many Lakota children would not come back to school after holidays and those who did had reverted to their "savage" ways (Powers 1986a, 109–16). The schools continued to follow the assimilationist policy until the 1960s, as is evident in the experience of Mary Crow Dog at the Catholic school on the Rosebud Reservation (Crow Dog 1991, 28–41). One Lakota elder reflects on her boarding school days with bitterness: "We never received any good from these Christians, their teaching, their beatings, they don't understand what they done to me was really made me unsure of myself. . . . it's left a permanent scar, I'll never forget it. . . . It still influences how I live every day" (Wilson 1999, 321–22).

The traditional men's and women's societies were transformed into the Saint Joseph and Saint Mary sodalities. These and other measures aimed at replacing "Sioux heathenism" as rapidly as possible. "Given such a perspective, missionaries rejected the notion that a Lakota could participate in traditional Indian ceremonies and simultaneously be a Catholic" (Markowitz 1987, 124).

During the 1880s "Buffalo Bill" Cody and other entrepreneurs enticed Lakota men and women into joining "Wild West" shows, where they participated in mock battles and, in the end, dutifully "surrendered" to the victorious cavalry (Black Elk 1972 [1932], 181–89). The point was to dramatize the successful subjugation of once proud warriors. Even the defiant Sitting Bull traveled for a short time with Cody's show throughout the United States and Europe.

In order to implement the provisions of the Dawes Allotment Act (see chapter 1) among the Lakota, in 1889 Congress passed the "Sioux bill," which divided the Great Sioux Reservation into smaller tracts, opening millions of acres to settlement by Euroamericans. A sixty-mile corridor was opened so that settlers could reach the Black Hills without having to pass through a Lakota reservation. The Great Sioux Reservation was reduced to six smaller reservations, from north to south: Standing Rock, Cheyenne River, Lower Brule, Crow Creek, Pine Ridge, and Rosebud (Greene 1970).

One effect of the implementations of the Dawes Act was the weakening of the *tiyospaye* system, as families were required to set up independent households evenly divided among the reservations' districts (Powers 1977, 109). As one Lakota leader put it, the government "made us many promises, more than I can remember, but they never kept but one; they promised to take our land and they took it" (Larson 1997, 263). When asked what Indians thought of the 1889 law, Sitting Bull replied indignantly, "Indians! There are no Indians left now but me" (Mooney 1896 [1965], 108).

The Ghost Dance movement that spread among a number of Native American nations, including the Lakota, in the 1880s is discussed in chapter 6. Here, however, it is important to note the tragedy that occurred amidst the frenzy of that movement and the overreaction of the government to it near a settlement called Wounded Knee on the Pine Ridge Reservation on 29 December 1890. After Sitting Bull and several of his followers were killed on 15 December by Lakota police trying to arrest him on orders from the army, a band of about 350–400 Hunkpapa and Mnikowoju Lakota led by an elder named Big Foot had fled from the Cheyenne River Reservation. Big Foot's band was trying to reach Pine Ridge, where they hoped to find food and shelter, but late in the afternoon of 28 December, a contingent of 7th Cavalry troopers (Custer's unit) caught up with Big Foot's band and encircled them.

On the morning of the 29th, after a night of drinking and boasting of revenge for the death of Custer and his men at Little Big Horn, the soldiers were attempting to disarm the Lakota warriors in the group when a scuffle broke out, and the infamous Wounded Knee massacre began. Four Hotchkiss cannons capable of firing two-inch explosive shells at a rate of fifty shells per minute opened up on the camp. Within minutes, some two hundred Lakota men, women, and children were dead (along with about thirty soldiers, most of whom were killed by other soldiers in the crossfire). Women and children who tried to flee through the ravines were pursued and slaughtered; the line of bodies extended two miles from the camp. In all, about three hundred Lakota died, two-thirds of them women and children.

Leonard Little Finger tells a story he heard from his grandfather, a survivor of the Wounded Knee massacre:

> After the shooting in the ravine ceased, soldiers went around kicking the
> victims. If they moved, the soldiers shot them again. A woman with a baby

in her arms sat on the ground rocking back and forth. A soldier grabbed the baby out of her arms and threw it on the ground and fired two shots. The woman leaped to her feet and ran for the baby; with the barrel of the pistol, the soldier hit her on the back of the head and knocked her down. Then he pressed his boot against her throat. Then he fired the pistol four times into her body. (Beasley 1995, 131)

Although the army commander on the scene was charged with misconduct, twenty-three members of the Seventh Cavalry were awarded the Congressional Medal of Honor, the nation's highest military honor, for their "heroic action" at Wounded Knee. (For other Lakota accounts of the massacre, see Crow Dog 1995, 186–87; Mooney 1896 [1965], 138–40; Jensen, Paul, and Carter 1991; Walker 1982, 157–68; Danker 1981; Black Elk 1972 [1932], 217–23; McGregor 1946.)

Today, a simple stone marker stands beside the mass grave where the murdered Lakota were dumped a few days after the massacre, without Lakota, or even Christian, prayers. As is discussed below, they were finally memorialized properly during the Big Foot Memorial Ride in 1990. At this writing, an effort to create a "Chief Big Foot National Memorial Park" to be run by the National Park Service at the site of the Wounded Knee massacre has been stalled. It has been adamantly opposed by the Wounded Knee community, which would be swallowed up in the park, and by other Lakota concerned that turning Wounded Knee into a tourist attraction run by the federal government would desecrate sacred ground and undermine Lakota sovereignty.

The Struggle to Survive (1890–1968)

Until 1890 many Lakota maintained the belief that somehow their traditional way of life on the plains could be revived. The suppression of the Ghost Dance and the massacre at Wounded Knee, however, caused even the most hopeful to accept the inevitable. They would have to do their best to adapt to life on the reservations.

By 1900 another spiritual movement that was uniting Native Americans reached the Lakota. A Winnebago named John Rave brought the Native American Church and its peyote rituals to South Dakota (see chapter 7). He ordained another Winnebago, Henry White, who introduced the church to the Pine Ridge Reservation. By 1924 an organized branch of the Native American Church with ministers had been established on the Pine Ridge reservation (Spider 1987, 189).

By 1905 Dr. James Walker reported that there remained only "five holy men among the Oglala and three of these were very old." During this period Long Knife (George Sword), a respected elder and captain of the Oglala police who had converted to Christianity, convinced other holy men that unless they shared what they knew with Walker, "soon they would go from the world and all their sacred lore would pass with them" (Walker 1983, 3). Until he left the reservation in 1914, Walker dedicated himself to collecting whatever the holy men were willing to share. Most of Walker's work has now been made available for study (Walker 1980, 1982, 1983).

In 1911 the Black Hills Council was formed, as representatives from nine communities (including the Lakota reservations and the Northern and Southern Cheyenne agencies) came together. The council began to plan a legal strategy to prosecute a case for recovery of the hills, basing the claim on the Fort Laramie treaty of 1868. A dozen years later, a suit was filed to reassert the Lakota right to the hills. The legal efforts to reclaim the Black Hills continued for the rest of the century, without a resolution acceptable to the Lakota. (For the complete story of the Lakota's struggle for the Black Hills, see Lazarus 1991; Churchill 1992, 162–69.)

Despite the 1883 ban, public sun dances were held for Lakota soldiers in World War I, and in 1917 four men were pierced (Steinmetz 1990, 28). In 1921 the ban on the sun dance was reaffirmed by Commissioner of Indian Affairs Charles Burke, who said in a circular letter on Indian dances that "it is not right to torture your bodies." Nevertheless, large sun dances (without piercing) were held in 1928 on the Rosebud Reservation and in the following year at Pine Ridge. Although the ban was effectively lifted in 1934 when John Collier became commissioner of Indian affairs, the first public sun dance with piercing was not held until 1952 (Holler 1995, 137–39).

In 1930 Father Eugene Buechel, the superior at both St. Francis and Holy Rosary Missions and a scholar responsible for producing an excellent Lakota-English dictionary, wrote of the Lakota as the "wee little brother" of the white man, "just crawling from the cradle days of civilization." He said that in time the new infant Lakota too would be well-educated and would be just as efficient as his elder brother. He blamed on "external factors" the failure to accomplish the assimilation of the Lakota in a couple of generations as the first missionaries had predicted. These factors included anthropologists who idealized the primitive Indian and showmen who exploited them for Wild West extravaganzas, but most of all the "nonprogressive" or "blanket" Lakota, especially among them the medicine men who he said were in "partnership with the Devil by blinding the Lakota people to the first glimmers of true religion" (Markowitz 1987, 125–28).

Despite efforts by traditionalists to defeat implementation of the Indian Reorganization Act (see chapter 1), in 1934 majorities on the Lakota reservations (but only by 94 votes out of over 2,200 cast on Pine Ridge) voted to accept the constitutional, tribal council form of government. The traditionalists objected because the electoral districts further broke up the *tiyospaye* structure of Lakota society (Powers 1986a, 33). The new system included no provision for traditional leadership.

Unfortunately, the Black Hills case stalled. In 1956 the Court of Claims affirmed an Indian Claims Commission ruling declaring that, after seventy years of benefits paid by the government, the Lakota people had been "paid in full" for the admittedly illegal seizure of the Black Hills.

The Renewal of the Lakota Nation (1968–90)

Lakota were involved in the formation of the American Indian Movement (AIM) in 1968, and they participated in the occupation of Alcatraz Island between 1969 and 1971 (see chapter 1). In 1971 AIM members led by Russell Means, himself an Oglala, organized a one-day occupation of Mount Rushmore in the Black Hills, demanding that the 1868 treaty be honored (see Means 1995).

In 1971 Oglala Lakota College (OLC) opened its doors on the Pine Ridge Reservation as one of the first American Indian tribal colleges. It has grown into a four-year institution, with a curriculum that combines classes in Lakota language, history, culture, and spirituality with preparation in the skills and aptitudes needed for a variety of careers. In 1993 OLC began to offer a Managers as Warriors program based on Lakota values, spirituality, and language. Now most of the OLC administrators, faculty, and staff are themselves Lakota. (For more on the tribal colleges, see chapter 9.)

In February 1972 five white men beat to death Raymond Yellow Thunder, a fifty-one-year-old Lakota from the community of Porcupine on the Pine Ridge Reservation, in the nearby "whiskey" town of Gordon, Nebraska. At the request of Yellow Thunder's relatives, the American Indian Movement became involved. For several days up to 1,400 Indians from over eighty Native American nations descended on Gordon to demand justice. As a result, the two brothers who had attacked Yellow Thunder were charged with manslaughter, convicted, and imprisoned (Lazarus 1991, 298–99; Crow Dog 1995, 165–68; Smith and Warrior 1996, 117–18).

The response to Yellow Thunder's death, as well as the unsolved killings of other Native Americans, led AIM to call for a march on Washington to confront the government. Called the Trail of Broken Treaties and Pan-American Native Quest for Justice, the march started at various points around the country and converged on Washington, D.C., on 2 November 1972. A twenty-point proposal for government action in response to the situation faced by Native Americans was drafted, calling for the reopening of the treaty process with native nations. Frustrated by a lack of response from the government, the marchers occupied the hated Bureau of Indian Affairs building. A sign left by the occupiers in the building read:

This is the beginning of a new era for the Native American people. When history recalls our efforts here, our descendants will stand with pride knowing their people were the ones responsible for the stand taken against tyranny, injustice, and the gross inefficiency of this branch of a corrupt and decadent government. —Native American Embassy

Still, no action was taken on the occupiers' demands. (See Smith and Warrior 1996, 166; Deloria 1985; Crow Dog 1991, 84–91; Lazarus 1991, 299–301; Crow Dog 1995, 171–76.)

Returning to South Dakota, emboldened AIM members, in coalition with Lakota traditionalists, formed the Oglala Sioux Civil Rights Organization (OSCRO). In February 1973 the Lakota full-bloods and their AIM supporters were becoming increasingly frustrated by harassment from Oglala tribal chairman Dick Wilson, who called the Trail of Broken Tears supporters "hoodlums, commies, and radicals" (Crow Dog 1995, 179). His infamous "GOON (Guardians of the Oglala Nation) Squad" was supported by a special force of federal agents who equipped them with weapons. Challenged by older Lakota women to take some action, and encouraged by traditional spiritual leaders and elders such as Frank Fools Crow and Pete Catches, AIM leaders spontaneously decided to reoccupy the site of the 1890 Wounded Knee massacre.

A group of young traditionalists, leaders of OSCRO, led a two-month occupation, which has become known as Wounded Knee II or simply "the Knee." AIM's leaders were Dennis Banks, Russell Means, and several others. The spiritual leaders of the group were Sicangu Lakota medicine men Leonard Crow Dog and Oglala Wallace Black Elk (see Crow Dog 1995; Black Elk 1990). Crow Dog had inspired the occupation by comparing the militants to the warriors in Big Foot's band (Zimmerman 1976, 127). He was the occupiers' doctor, using traditional herbal remedies. There were daily sweat lodges and frequent *yuwipi* ceremonies, and Crow Dog renewed the Ghost Dance for the first time in eighty years (see chapter 6).

The occupiers succeeded in focusing national, indeed international, attention on their demands. One poll showed that 93 percent of the American people were following the occupation, and 51 percent supported the Indians. Despite this public support, as Mary Crow Dog, who gave birth during the occupation, put it, "We always had the moral edge, but they had the hardware" (Crow Dog 1991, 137).

Wounded Knee II ended when the White House promised to send a delegation to discuss violations of the 1868 Fort Laramie treaty. The government failed to keep either this promise or a commitment to prosecute the members of GOON who had engaged in attacks on AIM supporters on the reservation, but a well-orchestrated campaign to follow through on prosecutions of AIM members helped to cripple the organization. Nevertheless, the occupation gave many in the Oglala Lakota Nation a renewed sense of pride. As Vine Deloria Jr. observed, watching an audience to whom AIM leader Russell Means was speaking after the occupation, "Almost every face shone with a new pride." It was, he said, "a beatific vision of the tribe as it should be, not as it had become through a century of betrayal" (Smith and Warrior 1996, 273). (For full accounts of Wounded Knee II from a variety of perspectives, mostly supportive of the occupation, see Smith and Warrior 1996, 194–279; Crow Dog 1995, 185–209; Deloria 1994, 243–45; Crow Dog 1991, 111–69; Lazarus 1991, 301–11; Lyman 1991; Kehoe 1989, 71–91; Catches 1997, 150–171; Zimmerman 1976; Burnett and Koster 1974).

During the two years following Wounded Knee II, a reign of terror was carried out on the reservation by supporters of Dick Wilson. AIM supporters' homes were shot at, and some were found dead, dumped by the roadside in remote areas of the reservation. It is estimated that nearly 100 people were killed on the reservation.

On 26 June 1975 two FBI agents and one Oglala Lakota teenager were killed in a confrontation near Oglala, in the northwest corner of the Pine Ridge Reservation. A massive manhunt followed, and several trials were held for AIM members charged with the killings of the FBI agents. All but one resulted in acquittal; a Lakota/Ojibwa AIM member, Leonard Peltier, was convicted and sentenced to life in federal prison. At this writing he remains incarcerated, despite an extensive international campaign to secure a new trial or a presidential pardon based on the revelation that fraudulent evidence was used against him in the original trials (Matthiesen 1992; Crow Dog 1995, 213–16; Messerschmidt 1984).

Amid the turmoil, a transfer of power from the Bureau of Indian Affairs to the elected tribal council was under way. Between 1965 and 1975 the annual budget of the Oglala tribal government rose from $10,000 to $6 million. Efforts began in earnest to decentralize the government, to reaffirm Lakota language and culture, and to give a greater voice to the disenfranchised traditionalists (Gagnon and White Eyes 1992, 23).

In 1976 Frank Fools Crow, one of the most highly respected Lakota holy men of modern times, testified before a congressional committee on the Lakota's understanding of the Black Hills, declaring, "The Black Hills is our church, the place where we worship. The Black Hills is our burial grounds. The bones of our grandfathers lie buried in those hills. How can you expect us to sell our church and our cemeteries for a few token white-man dollars? We will never sell" (Mails 1979, 212; see also Lazarus 1991, 349–55).

After these hearings Congress nevertheless voted to allow the Black Hills claim to proceed, and in 1980 the Supreme Court awarded the Lakota $106 million in compensation for the Black Hills, in return for Lakota abandonment of their legal claim (see Lazarus 1991, 381–402). The various Lakota tribal councils and the vast majority of Lakota people refused, however, to accept the financial settlement and to renounce their claim. Leonard Crow Dog expresses a widely held sentiment among Lakota today (Crow Dog 1995, 161):

> *Paha Sapa* [the Lakota name for the Black Hills] . . . wears *Wakan Tanka's* ornaments and jewels—the pines, the aspens, the cottonwoods. The Black Hills are not for sale. The government stole them from us. Now they want to ease their bad conscience by paying us a little money. No! The Hills, the home of the sacred thunderbirds, are not for sale. (Crow Dog 1995, 161)

In the mid–1980s, the Black Hills Steering Committee drafted legislation that called for giving the Lakota title to 1.2 million acres in federal lands (excluding Mount Rushmore) in the original Great Sioux Reservation, in addition to the Supreme Court's award (which had risen to $160 million with interest). It called for a Sioux Park and Black Hills Sioux Forest to protect the sanctity of the hills. Senator Bill Bradley of New Jersey introduced the bill in Congress in 1985 and once again in 1987. Disputes arose among the Lakota, however, about whether to seek an even bigger settlement, especially since the value of the minerals taken from the Black Hills since the 1870s was by then estimated to be as much as $40 billion. In any event, lobbied by non-Lakota landowners who were afraid they would lose their property in a settlement, the entire South Dakota congressional delegation opposed the bill, and it went nowhere (Lazarus 1991, 403–28). At this writing, the value of the settlement for the Black Hills has risen to about $500 million, and the Lakota are still refusing to accept the financial award.

On 24 August 1980 a ceremony was held at Green Grass on the Cheyenne River Reservation, where the Sacred Pipe of the Lakota nation (see below) is kept. The keeper of the Buffalo Calf Pipe had been instructed by the spirits to put it away following the tragedy of Wounded Knee II in 1973 and the subsequent conflicts among the Lakota. During the meal after the ceremony, an old woman harangued those gathered, saying that the putting away of the sacred pipe was "the fault of those who had strayed from their Indian ways, that the people must have proper respect for the old traditions if they expect to live as Lakota and maintain their dignity and integrity in the whites' world" (DeMallie and Parks 1987, 3–5).

In the 1980s the economic situation of the Lakota remained desperate. Two of the poorest counties in the United States were on Lakota reservations; one was Shannon County, part of the Pine Ridge Reservation. At the same time, coal and uranium deposits on the reservations were being exploited (Churchill and LaDuke 1992, 250–55; see chapter 8 for more on mining on the Lakota and other reservations).

Medically, the situation was little better. Alcoholism was rampant, with the cleaner Lysol a commonly consumed drink. On Standing Rock an estimated half of the adult population were suffering from the disease of alcoholism. Health care was barely adequate. In one year half of those who died on the Rosebud reservation were under the age of forty-five (Lazarus 1991, 420).

In the 1980s, however, a spiritual revival was also under way. Its full effects are still unfolding. In 1985 a Lakota holy man, Curtis Kills Ree, went on a vision quest and returned with precise instructions for a ride to follow the route of Big Foot and his followers from the Cheyenne River Reservation to the site of the massacre at Wounded Knee in 1890. He said there should be a ride each December for four years, climaxing in a ceremony at the grave of the victims of the massacre on the 100-year anniversary of the tragedy. Kills Ree said the ride would be a ceremony in fulfillment of Black Elk's prophecy that seven generations after Wounded Knee the sacred hoop of the Lakota would be mended. Inspired by Kills Ree's vision, a group of Lakota leaders planned a four-year ritual re-enactment to be called the Big Foot Memorial Ride (*Sitanka Wokiksuye*). Hopeful that a spiritual revival was under way, seven years after the Buffalo Calf pipe had been put away, its keepers, the Looking Horse family, unveiled it once again (Beasley 1995, 149).

The Big Foot Ride culminated in December 1990, when some 300 Lakota riders traveled through the intense cold of a South Dakota winter to Wounded Knee. This event was a time to remember those who had been massacred and to heal the wounds of the past (to "wipe the tears of the seven generations"), but it was also intended to bring the Lakota people together to work for the future well-being of the nation. In 1990 serious problems remained. For example, the 1990 population on the Pine Ridge Reservation was about 20,000 (including about 17,000 Lakota), but only about 2,500 regular jobs were available. At the time of the ride, unemployment stood at 85 to 90 percent (Beasley 1995, 155; Gagnon and White Eyes 1992, 5).

The leaders of the Big Foot Ride (Birgil Kills Straight, Arval Looking Horse, Ron McNeill, Alex White Plume, and Jim Garrett) represented various segments of the Lakota population. Each of the four days of the 1990 ride was dedicated to a different segment of Lakota society: orphans, the elderly, the sick and infirm, prisoners, and women (Beasley 1995, 150).

Ron McNeill put the ride in historical context on the last day of the event, claiming that the government had carved up the Great Sioux Reservation in order to destroy the Lakota people's cohesiveness and dilute their power. "By our actions this week," he said, "we have taken a small but significant step toward bringing these different factions back together again." Alex White Plume said, "One of the lessons we can all learn from the ride is how to be humble, how to be a follower, how to be a common person, how to make ourselves worthy of the spirit of the sacred pipe." He also pointed out the superiority of women in Lakota culture.

The memorial ride culminated in a special service on the morning of 29 December 1990. In the graveyard in front of Sacred Heart Catholic Church, where the Lakota killed in 1890 had been dumped in a common grave without a Lakota or Christian ceremony, a Wiping of the Tears ceremony was held (Beasley 1995, 149–50, 153, 159–60; Wisecarver 1990). The dead had finally been laid to rest.

The Big Foot Ride as a whole was an enactment of a traditional Lakota *washigila* (death wake). As one commentator has observed,

> The rhetoric which emerged from this ritual-in-the-making honored the endurance of the commemorators (much as relatives commiserate with the suffering pledgers in a modern Lakota sun dance), their efforts to complete the proper mourning, and their recommitment to Lakota values. (Nabakov 1996, 38)

The contemporary renewal of Lakota culture is discussed more fully below, after a focused examination of the traditional spirituality of the Lakota nation.

Traditional Lakota Spirituality

As has been mentioned in discussions of other nations, no pristine "traditional" spirituality exists in any Native American nation. The term *traditional* as used here refers to modern indigenous people who are seeking to restore their culture as much as possible to the way they imagine it was before Euroamerican contact. In a Lakota context, "the category 'traditional' encompasses all the cultural artifacts and behaviors that are perceived to have existed before the coming of the white man" (Powers 1986a, 2). "Traditional Lakota spirituality" represents an attempted restoration of the myths and rituals of the Lakota nation in existence on the Plains in the late eighteenth and early–to–mid-nineteenth century. "Traditionalists" believe that these myths and rituals have been passed down from generation to generation orally and thus can be recreated if there is the will to do so.

Scholars must be more cautious, however. As they study "traditional spirituality," they inevitably find elements that reflect developments over time and, in the case of the Lakota, changes in the cultural situation brought on by, among other things, contact with Europeans. Nevertheless, as an idealized category, "traditional" has merit, because although never fully realized in practice, it is a goal toward which practice is oriented. Thus, traditionalists may actually be committed to maintaining what they perceive to be the essence of Lakota spirituality, even if the forms of its expression change over time. In short, traditional Lakota spirituality is not "a monolithic system, for it reflects the blending of many strains of ideas over the past centuries" (DeMallie and Parks 1987, 7–8).

This study begins with the foundational story for Lakota spirituality, the legend of the Sacred White Buffalo Woman, before proceeding to describe some of the fundamental features of the understanding of the structure of the world (cosmology) as reflected in Lakota tradition. Next, a discussion of the Lakota sacred pipe, its cosmic symbolism and its central role in all Lakota rituals, is followed by brief introductions to some of the basic symbols recurrent in Lakota spirituality: the sacred hoop, the Black Hills, and cardinal directions and numbers. Next come sections introducing the rich pantheon of Lakota gods and spirits, beginning with the mysterious *wakan* and *Wakan Tanka*, and then the holy men and women who are critical to the proper conduct of the many rituals and to the harmony of the nation, with a special section on the Lakota "ritual clowns" (the *heyoka*).

Following this overview, the study turns to the seven "classical" rituals many Lakota believe were brought to the nation by White Buffalo Woman (the sweat lodge, the vision quest, the sun dance, making a girl into a woman, making relatives, throwing the ball, and soul keeping), as well as some other rituals beyond these seven that deserve the name "traditional"—for example, the *yuwipi* ceremony. The discussion of traditional rituals concludes with an examination of life-cycle rituals. A case study in the context of traditional spirituality examines the various interpretations of Nicholas Black Elk, the holy man made famous by John Neihardt. Finally, this section surveys the various ways in which traditional Lakota spirituality is active in the contemporary scene, especially on the Pine Ridge Reservation.

The Sacred White Buffalo Woman (Ptesan Win) and the Gift of the Sacred Pipe

The single most important story in the Lakota spiritual tradition is the legend of the sacred White Buffalo Woman and her gift of the sacred pipe. As noted above, this tale is woven together in the full complex of Lakota origins legends. As is the case with other sacred narratives among native peoples, there is no one single version, for different storytellers and spiritual teachers relate somewhat different accounts (see, e.g., Mooney 1896 [1965], 297–99; Hassrick 1964, 257–60; Brown 1971, 3–9; LaPointe 1976, 23–26; Powers 1977, 81–83; Mails 1979, 142–45; Powers 1986a, 43–49; Pickering 1997, 16–19).

Still, the basic storyline remains much the same, as in the following paraphrase of the story as recounted by contemporary holy man Leonard Crow Dog:

> White Buffalo Woman appeared to two hunters out of a cloud that turned into a hill. She "walked the hill in the shape of a white buffalo calf who turned herself into a beautiful maiden dressed in white buckskin." She carried in her hands sage and the *chanunpa*, the sacred pipe. Four days before she came the hunters had foreseen her coming in a dream. In the dream she told them to prepare a tipi and the fire without end, *peta owihankeshni*. When she appeared four days later, they treated her with awe. They went back to the village without meat, but with spiritual food. The wind filled up their bellies like buffalo hump. At this time the people knew little about

hunting. They had stone axes and wooden spears; they hunted mammoth and other now extinct animals. Their language was rude and they did not know how to pray. They knew nothing about *Tunkashila*, Grandfather Spirit, the Creator. When the woman appeared, she wore her hair loose, on the right and tied with buffalo hair on the left. She carried the stem of the pipe in her left hand and the bowl in her right. She sang the song:

> *With visible breath*
> *I am walking.*
> *Toward this nation*
> *I am walking.*

Those who assembled saw she was beautiful beyond words. She also carried a sacred stone, into which seven circles had been carved. She also brought *chanshasha*, red willow bark tobacco. In the sacred lodge, she took the place of honor. The chief was *Tatanka Woslal Nazin*, Buffalo Standing Upward. She told them she had been sent by the buffalo nation to instruct them in the ways of *Wakan Tanka*, the Creator, whom she called *Tunkashila*, the Grandfather Spirit. She taught them how to pray with the sacred pipe and the sacred songs. She also taught them how to perform the seven ceremonies [see below].

She then instructed men and women in their separate roles. She taught the men to guard and provide for women and children. She told the women that they were life-givers. She taught them how to bear children and how to do quillwork. She also told them to avoid men and sacred things during menstruation. "She taught the people how to live like human beings, how to put things together, and to understand *Tunkashila*'s holy ways. She made the Lakota into the people of the sacred pipe."

White Buffalo said she would return after four years [although in some versions the timing of her return is left open]. As she left the people saw her turning into a *ptesan ska win*, a white buffalo calf, and also into a *tahca win*, a deer woman, and a *hehaka win*, an elk woman. They also said she turned herself into buffalo of four colors—black, dark brown, light yellow-brown, and finally white, as she disappeared into the clouds.

After she came the people split into the Seven Council fires (Oceti Shakowin). After her came four chiefs—a medicine man, a man of knowledge, a warrior, and a hunter. They lived together in the Black Hills. They taught the people how to live in the world and the language. They taught them to go by the four winds—snow from the north, rain from the west, sun in the east, warmth from the south. "Above the sky, between the earth and moon, the Great Spirit roams," they said. (Crow Dog 1995, 2–5)

What is the significance of the coming (and promised return) of White Buffalo Woman? Some have called her a goddess (Powers 1990a). According to Leonard Crow Dog, "It was *Ptesan Win*, the sacred White Buffalo Woman, who made our people holy and taught them how to live. She was the spirit of *waonshipla*, mercifulness. She was grace. She was beauty" (Crow Dog 1995, 2).

Cosmology

As in other indigenous cultures, there is no abstract Lakota teaching on the structure of the universe. Instead, Lakota cosmology is implicit in the stories of origins and other myths passed orally. Here only a brief sketch of the implied Lakota cosmos is provided.

The Lakota universe consists of four levels: sky, the place between the sky and clouds, the earth, and the underworld. Time and space as the Lakota understand them began when the Buffalo People emerged from their harmonious underworld to the earth's surface, where they encountered the vicissitudes of a world that is ordered but can also be unpredictable and dangerous, a world in which learning to live in harmony is a daily challenge.

The Lakota concept of the structure of the cosmos is perhaps best expressed in the image of a "sacred hoop," which is typically symbolized as a circle inscribed by a cross (Powers 1986b, 35). In various contexts the hoop encompasses the Lakota nation, all peoples, the life of an individual, the structure of a Lakota home, the sweat lodge, the space demarcated for someone on a vision quest, the sun dance circle, and much more. The cross symbolizes the four winds or directions.

Like *Wakan Tanka*, the circle has no end:

> The Power of the World always works in circles, and everything tries to be round. In the old days when we were a strong and happy people, all our power came to us from the sacred hoop of the nation, and so long as the hoop was unbroken the people flourished. The flowering tree was the living center of the hoop and the circle of the four quarters nourished it. . . . Everything the Power of the World does is done in a circle. The sky is round, and I have heard the earth is round like a ball, and so are the stars. The wind . . . whirls. Birds make their nests in circles, for theirs is the same religion as ours. The sun [moves in a circle as does the moon]. Even the seasons form a great circle [and so does the life of each human being]. (Black Elk 1972 [1932], 164–65)

As noted, when the Lakota lived freely on the Great Plains, in the early summer of each year, they gathered for a "camp circle," reflecting the symbolism of the nation as a sacred hoop. In the middle was an area for dances, with a tree at the center. The entrance to the circle was always at the east, nearest the rising sun. During the camp circle the sun dance (see below) was performed.

On the plains the Lakota home, the tipi, also manifested the circle symbolism. Viewed from above, a tipi forms a circle, in which the crossed poles mark a center, with the four cardinal directions manifested.

In the traditional Lakota reckoning, time relates to natural phenomena: the sun, moon, and seasons. In contrast to the Western perspective, which objectifies and quantifies time (measuring, saving, wasting, spending it), in the traditional Lakota world "time more fundamentally expresses qualities and relationships, not quantities" (Walker 1982, 111).

The "moons" (months) were named on the basis of what was occurring naturally or the peoples' response to nature:

- January—Tree Popping
- February—Sore Eyes
- March—Grain Comes Up
- April—Birth of Calves
- May–Thunderstorms or Ripening Strawberries
- June—Ripe Juneberries
- July—Cherry Ripening
- August—Ripe Plums
- September—Yellow Leaves
- October—Falling Leaves
- November—Hairless Calves
- December—Frost in the Tipi
                                            (Hassrick 1964, 174)

Like many other indigenous peoples, the Lakota regard the four cardinal directions (west, north, east, south) and the two central directions (sky and earth) as important symbols. According to Fools Crow, "in these six directions is found everything needed for renewal, physical and intellectual growth, and harmony." The sacred powers given by the directions include, he says, "joy, good health, growth, endurance, wisdom, inner peace, warmth, and happiness." In the pipe ceremony, the pipe is smoked and pointed with its stem out in a clockwise circle, to the west, north, east, and south; then down to Grandmother Earth, up to Grandfather, and "in an almost imperceptible higher movement to *Wakan-Tanka*" (Mails 1979, 58).

The four cardinal directions are representative of the Lakota use of the number 4 to express "all persons, places, and objects in nature—the four directions, the four seasons, the four stages of life, four kinds of living things, four phases of a plant." Seven is another special number, as it is in many cultures, with social and political divisions in sevens (Powers 1977, 47–51; 1986b, 127–44; Lapointe 1976, 27).

Also evident in modern Lakota cosmic symbolism are the "two roads" crossed within the sacred hoop: the black road of destruction, which stretches symbolically from west to east, and the red road of goodness, which goes from north to south. Black Elk, in particular, made reference to the two roads in his conversations with John Neihardt and Joseph Epes Brown (e.g., DeMallie 1984, 118–23; Brown 1971, 7). The roads may, in fact, be an example of a concept introduced to the Lakota by Christian missionaries, for a dualism of good and evil, truth and error, is a more typically Christian concept than would have been found among the Lakota before Christianity was introduced. Black Elk used the road symbolism in the manner of a Catholic catechist as he tried to explain the basic Christian teaching in terms of a choice between good and evil, drawing on the Lakota symbol of the sacred hoop and four directions.

The Black Hills (*Paha Sapa*). For Lakota traditionalists, within the Black Hills lies *Wamaka Og'naka Icante*, "the heart of everything that is," the center of the sacred hoop of the universe. The hills are called the Black Hills, *Paha Sapa*, because from a distance the dark pines that cover the slopes and peaks make them appear to be black in color. The hills are full of life, with wood, water, and game in abundance. Despite more than a century of exploitation by miners and other visitors, including millions of tourists each year, the Black Hills retain beauty and mystery today.

As noted, the Lakota tales of origins relate that beneath the Black Hills live the Lakota ancestors, the Buffalo nation. At a place now called Wind Cave, some of the people who lived beneath the earth emerged. At the opening to the cave (called *Washun Niya*, "the breathing hole"), air rushes in and out, because, according to Lakota belief, the Black Hills are the lungs of the earth. To the east of Wind Cave is *Pte Tatiopa* ("doorway of the buffalo"), a gorge created by animals rushing from out under the earth. It is known today as Buffalo Gap.

The hills are also called *Wita Paha*, Island Hill, with the surrounding prairie considered a vast sea. The granite outcroppings in the center of the Black Hills, today called the Needles, are known to the Lakota as *Wakinyan hinapa Paha* ("Hills like Thunder Clouds"). The hills are considered the home of the powerful Thunder Beings.

According to a popular Lakota legend, at the time of origins all the animals of the earth gathered at the site of the Black Hills for a race. The purpose was to bring order to the world and separate the animals according to their species. As the animals raced in a great circle, the earth "quivered and groaned like a huge animal in pain," and with a thunderous roar it burst open, rocks covered the earth, and the Black Hills were born. The remnants of the racetrack can be seen in the depression that encircles the hills (LaPointe 1976, 17–20).

The tallest of the hills is *Hinhan Kagha Paha* ("Evil Spirit Hill"), so named because a hideous and cruel phantom that looked like an owl with ugly, yellow eyes was said to live atop it. The monster delighted in capturing animals and children and bringing them back to the peak to torture and eat them. According to legend, warriors made an unsuccessful assault on the peak to attempt to kill the monster and rescue children (LaPointe 1976, 87–92). Today, as noted earlier, it is known as Harney Peak, named after General William ("Hornet") Harney, the army officer who led troops against the Lakota during the Plains Wars and served on the commission that negotiated the 1868 Fort Laramie treaty.

At the northern edge of the Hills is Bear Butte (*Mato Paha*), still a sacred site for Lakota and other Plains people, especially the Cheyenne. According to Lakota tales, the butte was created when a huge bear sat down on the site after combat with a monster. The bear died in that position, and Bear Butte was created. Today it is a state park, accessible to the public, with trails to the top of the butte, despite the fact that it is still used for vision quests and other pilgrimages and prayers by modern Lakota and other native people. Frank Fools Crow, who came to Bear Butte seeking and receiving visions (Mails 1979, 181–84), joined with other traditional leaders in filing suit to force the South Dakota government to protect Bear Butte as a sacred shrine, but they met with only limited success. Areas are reserved for traditional sweat lodges and vision quests, but the stream of tourists (rising from 9,000 in 1986 to nearly 100,000 a year in the late 1990s) has created a "fish bowl" atmosphere for Lakota and others attempting to conduct their traditional ceremonies.

Another Lakota sacred site near the Black Hills is Devil's Tower in northeastern Wyoming, a spectacular lava formation (now also a national park). It is called *Mato Tipilia* ("Bear Lodge") by the Lakota, on the basis of a legend that relates how the tower once saved Lakota girls from hungry bears. It was also called sun dance Mound in the belief that a young man once descended from the tower to instruct the Lakota in how to perform the sun dance ritual (LaPointe 1976, 65–70). The large formation is popular among rock climbers, although the Lakota and other Plains people for whom the tower is sacred have asked that climbers be restricted from desecrating it. As one Lakota spiritual leader put it, "Let them climb the Empire State Building!" At present, a voluntary ban is observed by many, but not all, climbers during the month of June, when sacred ceremonies are often held at Bear Lodge. In 1996 it was the site of a prayer service for people from all nations.

The Sacred Pipe. Like many other native American peoples, the Lakota make ritual use of a long-stemmed pipe. For the Lakota, however, the pipe is at the heart of their national identity and their sense of the meaning of life itself. In Lakota the pipe is the *cannunpa* (also *chanunpa*) *wakan,* or sacred pipe (see Powers 1977, 81–83, 86–88; Brown 1971, 3–10; Looking Horse 1987; Paper 1988, 50–51; Black Elk 1990, 49–67; Steinmetz 1984, 1990, 53–57; Lewis 1990, 44–47; Mails 1979, 55–59; Powers 1986a, 42–43; Powers 1986b, 42–49; Stolzman 1986, 1–12; Crow Dog 1995, 133–40; Kaiser 1984). The sacred pipe is used in all corporate Lakota rituals and by individuals when Lakota pray. It also symbolizes the universe as a whole.

The central symbol of traditional Lakota spirituality became known to Euroamericans as the "peace pipe" because it was smoked during treaty negotiations with U.S. government representatives. (© Layne Kennedy/CORBIS)

When the descendants of the chief to whom White Buffalo Calf Woman had given the pipe died out, the Buffalo Calf Pipe, as it was known, passed to the Elk Head family. Then it passed to the Looking Horse family at Eagle Butte, on the Cheyenne River reservation, where it remains today.

The pipe is so brittle it can no longer be smoked. It is, therefore, no longer actively used in rituals, "but when you touch it, power flows into you like an electric current. The power is so strong that you burst into tears" (Crow Dog 1995, 5). A holy man or woman might bring his/her own *cannunpa* to touch the original Calf Pipe Bundle, even though the pipe itself is kept from view except on the most special of occasions as determined by a vision given to the Pipe Keeper.

In presenting the pipe, White Buffalo Calf Woman said, according to Black Elk, "With this sacred pipe you will walk upon the Earth; for the Earth is your Grandmother and Mother, and She is sacred. Every step that is taken upon Her should be a prayer" (Brown 1971, 5–6). She told the people that the pipe bowl, made from red catlinite stone, represented the earth. Carved in the stone was a buffalo calf, representing all four-legged animals. The wooden stem symbolized all that grows on the earth. The twelve feathers stood for the Spotted Eagle and all the winged creatures. Those who smoke the pipe are joining themselves with everything in the universe. "When you pray with this pipe," she said, "you are praying for and with everything" (Brown 1971, 7). Whether this "universalism" reflects a general Lakota understanding, Black Elk's unique perspective, which was shaped in part perhaps by his encounter with Christian teaching, or the personal point of view of Joseph Epes Brown is a matter debated today by interpreters (see below).

Each Lakota's pipe is, in a sense, potentially an extension of the Sacred Buffalo Calf Pipe. When honored properly, any Lakota's pipe may become a manifestation of the holiness of the original pipe. When a sacred pipe is to be used in a ceremony, it is taken from its special pouch by the sacred person to whom it has been entrusted. The *wakan* person raises the pipe in both hands, above his/her head, or points the stem of the pipe in the direction to be invoked. Tobacco, sealed in the bowl of the pipe during its consecration, is then lit. Those smoking the pipe sit in a circle, each repeating the pointing of the pipe in the four directions and puffing on it four times. Smoking or even touching a sacred pipe in any but the prescribed manner, or by any but those of the highest integrity, is taboo. Nonspecialists, however, may use their own individual sacred pipes, praying with them in the four directions.

Gods and Spirits

The general name for gods and spirits in Lakota is *Taku-wakan*, "that which is sacred or mysterious." Lakota gods and spirits may be called on by everyone at times of hardship, but holy people who have been "chosen" by the supernaturals must supervise the rituals in which they are invoked.

Wakan. The Lakota term *wakan* is usually translated as "sacred" or "holy," but it also implies that which is inexplicable, mysterious, or awesome (Powers 1986b, 109). *Wakan* is certainly not confined to "deities." According to Dr. James Walker, "when an Oglala is amazed by anything he may say that it is *wakan*" (Walker 1980, 74).

Everything has *wakan* or spirit. Birds and animals have spirits, just as humans, so they too are called "people" (*oyate*): the "winged people (or nation)" and the "four-legged people" to distinguish them from the human "two-legged people." Other animals are the people who crawl or swim. Humans must learn to humble themselves before the smallest ants, for the ant people are especially *wakan*.

From a traditional Lakota perspective, every being potentially has a sacred influence, so humans must humble themselves and learn to be attentive before everything and everyone. That is the motivation behind the important Lakota ritual known as the vision quest, as we shall see.

Sometimes holiness is spoken of as an impersonal force (*wakana*), which is everywhere potentially present. The Lakota also speak of *wakan* beings, spirits of ancestors and other ghosts, which, though invisible, the Lakota believe are present with them and can appear to sacred persons or others during visions. As described below, these sacred persons are themselves known as *wakan* persons, because of their special powers.

Wakan Tanka ("The Great Mystery"). To Euroamerican observers conditioned to look at the spiritual from a monotheistic perspective, there would seem to be a central deity in the Lakota pantheon, *Wakan Tanka* (also written *Wakantanka*) to whom Lakota people pray. When addressed in prayer or song as "Grandfather (*Tunkashila*)," *Wakan Tanka* is not manifest; when invoked as "Father," *Wakan Tanka* is manifest, as for example through the sun. The feathers of the highest flying bird, the eagle, also symbolize *Wakan Tanka*. While the conception of *Wakan Tanka* as a sovereign, personal God ("The Great Spirit") is common among Lakota today, it is likely that this understanding of *Wakan Tanka* did not develop until Christian missionaries began to influence Lakota beliefs, using *Wakan Tanka* to speak of the one Christian God (Walker 1983, 8; Powers 1986b, 118).

In Lakota tradition, the single name *Wakan Tanka* represents "sixteen important supernatural beings and powers, half of which existed prior to the creation of the earth, half as a result of it" (Powers 1987, 436). In the sacred language of *wakan* persons, *Wakan Tanka* is called *Tobtob* ("four times four"), symbolic of the fact that all sacred things come in fours (Powers 1977, 49–50; 1986b, 121–25). As one interpreter has suggested, "rather than a single being, *Wakan Tanka* embodied the totality of existence" (DeMallie and Parks 1987, 28). It might also be said to be "the sum total of all that is sacred in the universe" (Powers 1986b, 119). Although *wakan* means "sacred" and *tanka* is "great or big," according to Frank Fools Crow, the best translation of *Wakan Tanka* into English is not the common "Great Spirit," but perhaps "Holiest of Everything" (Mails 1979, 120).

It is important to note that most Lakota themselves do not typically translate *Wakan Tanka* when speaking English (Powers 1986b, 118), out of respect for the incomprehensibility of the name. This study follows that convention.

Other Gods. As noted in discussion of the Lakota story of origins, a rich pantheon of deities is all bound up in *Wakan Tanka*. They comprise the "four times four." The following hierarchy, developed principally by Walker from his Lakota informants, undoubtedly reflects too much his penchant for classification, but it does identify the principal deities in Lakota mythology (Hassrick 1964, 247–48; cf. Powers 1977, 53–55):

The first of the four sets issuing from *Wakan Tanka* are the "superior gods": *Inyan* (the Rock) was the ancestor of all gods and all things; *Maka* (the Earth) is the mother of all living things; *Skan* (the Sky) is the source of all force and power; and *Wi* (the Sun) is defender of virtue.

Linked with each of these deities is the second group, the "associate gods." The counterpart of the Sun is *Hanwi*, the Moon. The Wind, *Tate*, is associated with Sky, controlling the seasons and admitting spirits to the Spirit Trail. *Wohpe*, the daughter of Sun and Moon, the Beautiful One, is linked to Earth, serving as "the Great Mediator, patron of harmony and pleasure." She is the "Falling Star," who, according to some interpreters, was transformed into White Buffalo Woman when she appeared on earth. Associated with Rock is *Wakinyan,* considered singularly as the Winged, or in the plural as the Thunder Beings, who speaks through the sound of thunder and is manifest in lightning strikes. A red zig-zagged fork is the symbol of the *Wakinyan.* Their mythic home, as noted above, is in the Black Hills.

The third group, the "subordinate gods," issuing from the "associates" are Buffalo (*Tatanka,* Buffalo Bull, and *Pte,* Buffalo Cow), patrons of fertility, generosity, and ceremonies; Bear, patron of wisdom and medicine; the Four Winds, controller of the weather; and the Whirlwind, patron of games and courtship. The Buffalo was known both as the People of the Sun and as an associate of the Sun. The fourth level are the *Wanalpi,* or Gods-like: the Spirit, the Ghost, the Spirit-like, and the Potency.

In addition to the "four times four," there are a number of other deities. Among them are a host of disrupters of order, including *Iya* (see below); *Waziya,* the Old Man; his wife *Wakanaka,* the Witch; and their daughter *Anog-Ite,* Double-faced Woman. Demons such as water spirits and forest dwelling spirits are also part of the traditional Lakota world. *Gnaske,* the Crazy Buffalo, may bring paralysis or insanity. *Untktehi* can capture humans and turn them into beasts. *Nini Watu* are maggots which cause aches and spoiling. *Gica* cause accidents and *Can Oti* lead people to lose their direction. (Hassrick 1964, 255).

Inktomi (Spider, the Trickster) and Iya (the Giant or Glutton).   The subject of many tales that serve to teach children basic Lakota values (e.g., LaPointe 1976, 93–114, Powers 1977, 83–84; Walker 1983, 166–74), *Inktomi* (also often transliterated as *Iktomi*) also plays a critical role in the Lakota stories of origins. As the first son of *Inyan, Inktomi* has named all things and brought culture to the people. Like the spider, he moves through the four levels of the Lakota universe: sky, the place between the sky and clouds, the earth, and the underworld. As a trickster, he can change his identity into anything or anybody to deceive people. Usually, "in his quest to deceive, he winds up being deceived, an apt moral story to tell young children."

The younger brother of *Inktomi* is *Iya,* "the giant who gorges himself on humans periodically and has to be killed and roasted to make him disgorge the humans so that they can populate the earth" (Powers 1986b, 155). He is associated with the cold of the north and appears during winter (Powers 1977, 55).

Animals, Birds, Insects.   The importance of the spider, as an animal that moves through the cosmic planes, has already been noted. Other beings (including ants, wolves, coyotes, moles, and snakes, to name a few) are considered especially sacred because of their ability to burrow to the lower worlds. Other beings (including, of course, birds, but also frogs, turtles, and lizards who fall to earth during rainstorms) are also revered as sacred.

A Lakota saying reflects the well-known attitude toward the buffalo as sacred:

The buffalo is our brother.
He gives his flesh so that
the people may live.
The buffalo is sacred. (Crow Dog 1995, 11)

Traditional Lakota people typically make food offerings to the animals, especially when they have given of their own sustenance for the well-being of the Lakota. For example, Ella Deloria describes the practice of returning food to mice when a cache of earth beans is taken from their nests (Deloria 1988, 9–10).

Wicasa wakan and winyan wakan (Sacred men and women). A traditional Lakota spiritual leader is known as *wicasa wakan* (literally, sacred or holy man) or *winyan wakan* (sacred or holy woman). The terms are usually rendered in English as "medicine man" or "medicine woman," but in a discussion of spiritual leaders the terms "medicine men and women" should probably be reserved for one type of *wicasa* or *winyan wakan* (see below). (On sacred men and women, see Hassrick 1964, 253–57; Lame Deer 1972; Powers 1977, 55–63; 1986b, 164–95; Black Elk 1990; Lewis 1987, 173–87; Lewis 1990, 39–42, 178–84; Catches 1997, 47–55; Lame Deer 1992; Crow Dog 1995.)

In general, Lakota sacred men and women are intermediaries for the people to the spirit beings and their powers. The holy people can speak with animals. They are able to call on the power of *wakana* for healing individuals as well as for the well-being of the people as a whole. Before the near-annihilation of the buffalo, they could determine where buffalo would be found through mystical means. They could also predict the outcome of wars.

The process of becoming a sacred person usually involves overcoming some misfortune, receiving instruction from another *wakan* person, crying for a vision, serving an apprenticeship, and finally "ordination." According to a Euroamerican physician who worked with healers on the Pine Ridge Reservation in the 1960s, each *wakan* person develops "a sense of personal and ritual competence, the garnering of spiritual helpers, the belief that one can safely represent the spirit world to humankind, and the accumulated confidence and assertiveness to present oneself as effective" (Lewis 1990, 40).

Powers suggests that there are four types of Lakota sacred men: curers, performers, wizards, and transvestites (Powers 1986b, 181–89). Among the curers are those who derive their power from a particular spirit helper who has come to them in a vision (e.g., bear curers). A *"yuwipi"* man (see below) is also a type of curer, as is a "bone sucker," who sucks the sickness out through a bone placed on the patient's body. A fourth type of curer is the *pejuta wicasa*, literally the "medicine man" who uses sacred herbs in curing and has the knowledge to wrap wounds and set fractures (see Lewis 1990, 106–12, 124–39; Hassrick 1964, 290–92).

The most famous of the sacred performers are the ritual clowns (*heyoka*), a group that is considered separately below. Another is the "elk performer," who has dreamed of a man who turns himself into a female elk and instructs the performer in medicines to use in healing rituals. He then acts out his dream in a ritual (Black Elk 1972 [1932], 173–80). There are also wolf and bear performers.

Wizards are holy people who can call upon the power to make people ill or depressed. They are blamed for accidents and other inexplicable events. Their harm can be reversed by another holy person through the proper prayers.

The final group consists of the Lakota *winkte*, usually translated as transvestite, but more properly as "would-be woman." They are men who, after a vision from "Double Woman," vow to live a life modeled after women. They wear women's clothes and follow women's rather than men's pursuits. They are considered especially sacred. For example, having a child named by a *winkte* has traditionally been considered very desirable (Hassrick 1964, 133–35).

Among sacred women Powers identifies three types of specialists (Powers 1986b, 189–92; cf. Powers 1986a, 96–98): curers, performers, and witches. Among curers, the most typical specialist is the medicine woman, who collects herbs and uses them to cure Lakota illnesses such as kidney and liver diseases, gall stones, urinary problems, and venereal diseases. Women performers traditionally took part only in *heyoka* ceremonies. Witches are similar to wizards.

The early response to Lakota holy men and women among Christian missionaries is expressed in an 1854 essay by Gideon Pond:

> Each in particular, and all together, as *wakan*-men, they are not only useless, but a decided and devouring curse to their nation, on whose neck, mentally and morally, they have firmly planted the iron heel of priestly despotism: and until they are put down by the might[y] operations of the Divine Spirit, through the word of Christ, they will effectually baffle any effort to elevate and civilize the Dacota [sic]. "O Lord, how long!" (cited in Holler 1995, 113)

This attitude continued for a century or more, making it very difficult for Lakota holy men and women to function. They were also severely limited by the bans on traditional rituals that began in the 1880s. It is a testament to the depth of spirituality of generations of *wicasa* and *winyan wakan* that they continued to fulfill their sacred calling in the face of hostility, and even imprisonment.

Heyoka (Ritual Clowns). Traditional Lakota spirituality includes an important role for "ritual clowns," called by the Lakota *heyok'a* (Lewis 1990, 140–52; Walker 1980, 14, 155–57; DeMallie 1984, 232–35; Black Elk 1972 [1932], 159–63). They are also known as the "contraries." By systematically breaking the accepted customs and taboos of the society, they relieve the pressure that builds up in normal life. No one chooses to be a "contrary." A *heyoka* is designated by a vision of Thunder Beings and is thereafter obligated to do everything in reverse, to ward off the dangers of lightning and storm.

On dance days *heyoka* are likely to engage in disorderly, even deviant behavior. The effect is a comic relief, especially appreciated at times of stress and despair, balancing the solemnity of the occasion. For example, a masked contrary might wear a costume with an exaggerated penis-like nose and feign lewd, even disgusting behaviors. Contraries sometimes urinate on their clothes, throw excrement on the crowds, and pretend ejaculations. Their deviant behavior is thought to be a source of curative power, and they are considered potent healers.

It may very well be that the more extreme behaviors of the *heyoka* were in response to the attacks by European missionaries and others on what they regarded as a pagan perversion of gender roles. In any event, *heyokas* are accepted and valued in traditional Lakota society.

Traditional Lakota Rituals

As noted, according to some traditions, with the sacred pipe White Buffalo Woman gave the Lakota people seven rituals. There are a number of other important rituals—as Lakota spiritual leader Wilmer Mesteth has put it, "The seven sacred rites are just the tip of the iceberg" (Mesteth 1996). A full survey would include discussion of other important Lakota rituals, such as the Kettle Dance, the Horse Dance (see Black Elk 1972 [1932], 136–48), and the Buffalo Dance, among others (see Fools Crows' description in Mails 1979, 60–82). Healing rituals like the Eagle ceremony (Lewis 1990, 93–105) could also be discussed.

It is possible that Nicholas Black Elk's now widely-reported formulation of a group of seven classical rituals (Brown 1971) was influenced by the Roman Catholic Church's seven sacraments (Holler 1984a; 1990, 140–41). Black Elk, who had been an Episcopalian since the 1880s, had converted to Catholicism in 1904. As observed above, however, the number seven has its own Lakota roots, and the recognition of a group of seven Lakota rituals is not limited to Black Elk.

These seven traditional rituals provide a sense of the types of rituals performed during the nineteenth century as well as an introduction to traditional Lakota spirituality today. The seven ceremonies remembered as given by White Buffalo Woman are the following:

- *Inikagapi*—sweat lodge
- *Hanblecheya*—vision quest
- *Wiwanyang wachipi*—sun dance
- *Ishnati awicalowapi*—making a girl into a woman
- *Hunkapi*—making relatives
- *Tapa wankayeyapi*—throwing the ball
- *Wanagi yuhapi*—soul keeping

The first three are very much a part of traditional Lakota spirituality today. The remaining four are not as frequently performed, although "soul keeping" has been adapted in another ceremony called the Memorial Feast, and the "making relatives" ritual continues to some degree in the popular naming ceremony. (On the seven traditional ceremonies, see Crow Dog 1995, 141; Wissler 1912; Brown 1971; DeMallie 1987.)

Utilized in virtually all Lakota ceremonies are tobacco (offered to the spirits directly or in small "tobacco ties" and smoked in the sacred pipe), sweet grass, and sage. All are pleasing to the spirits being called on in the rituals and contribute to the cleansing and harmony being sought. A typical practice (often called "smudging") is to cause the purifying smoke of burning sweet grass (or dry sage or cedar) to waft over a person or area. Sage is often used to make beds upon which participants may sit or recline. Sometimes an eagle wing is used to cause the smoke to pass over a person being healed (Brave Bird 1994, 29). Flags or banners in the sacred colors are also commonly used.

A buffalo skull manifests the presence and power of the Buffalo, whose importance has already been noted. Other "medicines" such as special roots express the power of the Bear and other spirits. As is discussed below, rocks also play a central role in the rituals.

Sweat Lodge (*Inikagapi*, "to renew life"). This ritual of purification or renewal, similar to those found in a number of another Native American nations, is often conducted in preparation for participation in other rites or to ready oneself for a great endeavor. It may also be enacted as a ceremony in itself, as a means of petitioning for a need or offering thanksgiving for a blessing. Both men and women may participate in the sweat lodge ritual, but not together in traditional lodges. (See Hassrick 1964, 266–69; Brown 1971, 31–43; Powers 1977, 89–91; Mails 1979, 95–102; Stolzman 1986, 13–30; Catches 1997, 77–91; Lewis 1990, 47–49; Crow Dog 1991, 202–7; Brave Bird 1994, 96–100; Crow Dog 1995, 83–87; Bucko 1999.)

The sweat lodge itself is a domed structure, typically made from sixteen bent willows, traditionally covered with buffalo robes and other skins (although today canvas tarps or blankets are often used), with hot stones in the center. The lodge symbolizes the cosmos, and the rocks are Grandmother Earth. The fire is the life-giving power of *Wakan Tanka*. A bed of sage is often put on the floor of the lodge, since the spirits are attracted by its smell. The hissing water symbolizes the Thunder Beings, who come fearfully but bring goodness. The round pit in the center of the lodge is the center of the universe where *Wakan Tanka* comes to the worshippers.

The door of the lodge faces west, unless it is a *heyoka* lodge, which has its door on the east side. From the entrance of the lodge, a path of eight paces is made, running east and west. During the ritual this path is not to be crossed. At the eastern end is a mound of earth dug from the pit inside the lodge. The mound is an altar, called "grandmother." Two paces further is the "fire without end," in which the stones are heated. The worshippers leave behind in the lodge (sometimes called the Stonepeople's Lodge) all that is impure.

Entrance to the lodge is on all fours, to show that one is are related to the four-legged people. On entering the lodge, the worshipper says *mitakuye oyasin* ("all my relations"). Traditionally, participants enter the lodge without clothes, because it is Grandmother's womb, earth womb, a place of spiritual birth and rebirth (although in modern mixed lodges, bathing suits are typically worn). Entrance is clockwise around the lodge, led by the one conducting the lodge. Last is the doorkeeper, who assists the leader.

Once all have entered, rocks are brought in, traditionally using antlers to move them from the "fire without end" (although today a pitchfork or shovel is more common). The first seven rocks symbolize the four directions, sky, earth, and the center. Sage and cedar are sprinkled on rocks to make them whisper, like a spirit voice.

According to traditional Lakota Henry Crow Dog, "The *inipi* uses all the powers of the universe. The fire, the water, the earth, the air are here, within the sacred lodge. Feel the power of *inyan wakan*, the sacred rock. All living things are in here." The leader pours water on the rocks and the lodge fills with steam, the purifying breath of the Creator.

A typical lodge has four "doors" or "rounds." Rounds consist of songs and prayers, with periods of sitting in silence. During one or more of the rounds, a sacred pipe is passed. After each round, the door is opened by the doorkeeper to let the lodge cool. Water may be passed so that those participating can drink. Then the door is closed and the next round begins. In some contemporary lodges, worshippers might be asked to offer their own prayers, in Lakota or English, with the understanding that everything spoken in the lodge remains there and is not to be revealed outside.

A lodge may be in response to a particular need, such as an illness or family crisis, which becomes the focus of the prayer. If the lodge becomes unbearable, it is understood that a participant may say "*Mitakuye oyasin!*" at which time the doorkeeper will open the door so that the person may leave.

At the completion of the lodge, the participants may plunge into a nearby stream or body of water. It is also typical to have food together after the lodge, since fasting before the lodge is common. The pipe may again be smoked, and joy expressed at the renewal and purification experienced in the lodge.

Vision Quest (*hanblecheya*, "crying for a vision"). Under the guidance of a *wakan* person, any Lakota may seek to experience communication with spirits by undertaking a vision quest, or "going on the hill" as the Lakota often describe this ritual. (See Hassrick 1964, 271–77; Brown 1971, 44–66; Powers 1977, 91–93; Stolzman 1986, 31–54; Catches 1997, 92–104; Lewis 1990, 49–51.)

By humbling oneself before the spirits, the one "crying or lamenting for a vision" may receive their power. A young person might "go on the hill" in order to receive guidance for his or her life. In earlier times, a warrior might go before a battle. A vision quest might also be undertaken in preparation for a sun dance. A family member might go to request healing for a sick or dying relative. A person might also "cry for a vision" as a way of giving thanks to *Wakan Tanka* for some special blessing. From a Euroamerican psychiatrist's perspective, "the vision quest answers the recurrent question 'What do I want to be, to devote myself to?'" (Lewis 1990, 51).

After purification through fasting, typically lasting four days, and participation in the sweat lodge ritual, the person seeking a vision is led by his guide to a sacred hill. The only thing taken is a blanket; no food or water is allowed. The seeker is given a sacred pipe to hold throughout the ritual. A pit is dug in the ground at the center. At times the worshipper will climb into this pit, covered with brush. The four cardinal directions are marked, with flags (first red, then yellow, white, and black) placed at each corner. The four flags may be connected with 400 *chanli* (tobacco ties), often made by the seeker as part of the preparation for the ritual. The person walks to each of the points, returning to the center, crying for a vision, all day long.

The ritual typically lasts from two to four days. The seeker may neither eat nor drink while lamenting. When the person finally lies down exhausted, a vision may come. The seeker may be spoken to by animals or visited by the Thunder Beings. One of the animals or forces may become the quester's "spirit guide," although this aspect has been overemphasized in New Age versions of the vision quest. Often the vision simply reinforces the seeker's sense of "nothingness" in comparison to the holiness of *Wakan Tanka* and the universe.

Sometimes visions come to persons spontaneously, often during a time of illness, as was the case with the famous "Great Vision" of Nicholas Black Elk (Black Elk 1972 [1932], 17–39). These "visions without crying" or "power visions" are usually commissions to a special leadership role.

Keeping of the Soul (*wanagi yuhapi*). When a Lakota dies, his or her "ghost" (*wanagi*) normally travels south along the "ghost road" or "spirit trail" (the milky way) until an old woman decides its fate, either sending it on its way to the spirit world or returning it to the earth where it lives as a shade. (See Hassrick 1964, 302–8; Brown 1971, 10–30; LaPointe 1976, 123–67; Powers 1977, 93–95; Deloria 1988, 141–47; Crow Dog 1995, 142–46.)

At times, however, the family may elect to "keep the soul," particularly if the deceased is a beloved son. The ghost is kept for a specified period, now usually six months to a year, then it is ritually released. The ritual assures that the ghost will make it to the spirit world when released and keeps the family and band mindful of the fragility of life. Several families may join together to conduct the ritual for deceased children.

In the ritual itself, a *wakan* person cuts a lock of hair from the dead person and wraps it. The hair is put in a buckskin bag and rolled into a bundle with a sacred pipe. The soul has its own tipi, and it is placed on a special tripod opposite the entrance.

On the final day of the ghost keeping, when the spirit is released, the family holds a great feast. Specially made gifts are given and the families' possessions are shared with the needy to honor of the departing ghost.

A White Buffalo Ceremony, honoring White Buffalo Calf Woman, may be held on the day the spirit is released. This rare ritual requires a white buffalo robe, on which are placed the gifts to be distributed.

Sun Dance (*Wiwanyang wachipi*, "dancing while gazing at the sun"). As early as 1700 the Lakota were observing an annual ceremony that became known as the sun dance (Holler 1995, 39). During the nineteenth century the Lakota sun dance was always held during the moon of the ripening chokecherries (June or July). Today, sun dances are held throughout the summer on Lakota reservations and beyond. Sun dances have also long been observed by other Plains nations. In modern times, the sun dance has spread beyond the Plains to other Native American nations and, in some places, has become a pannational ritual. A particular controversy today is whether to allow the participation of nonnatives in the ritual or even to allow them to be present as observers. (See Walker, 1917; Densmore 1918; Deloria 1929, 1988, 113–34; Hassrick 1964, 279–88; Brown 1971, 67–100; Jorgensen 1972; Powers 1977, 95–100; Mails 1978, 1979, 118–38; Amiotte 1987; Lewis 1990, 52–70; Catches 1997, 105–24; Crow Dog 1991, 252–60; Brave Bird 1994, 110–18; Holler 1995).

When the Lakota still lived freely on the prairie, the sun dance typically occurred when the bands gathered for a national "camp circle" in preparation for a communal buffalo hunt. In the 1870s so many Lakota gathered for the ceremony that the diameter of the encampment was up to four miles, with forty groups ranging from six to twelve dancers, each with a holy man. At a sun dance led by Red Cloud in 1880, 700 lodges were pitched, in a circumference of six miles (Steinmetz 1990, 27).

In general, the sun dance is a national ritual, undertaken for the well-being of the Lakota people as a whole, so that they may live in harmony. Individual participants may also have their own particular motivations, however. Typically, a man (and today a woman) takes a sun dance "vow," promising to participate in the sacrificial ritual in return for spiritual help at a time of danger. For example, a soldier might take a sun dance vow before leaving for battle, promising to participate in the ritual upon safe return. Or a family member might take a vow on behalf of a sick relative.

The manner in which any particular sun dance is conducted is determined by the "intercessor," the holy man chosen to lead it, and may therefore vary considerably from other enactments. Therefore, no two sun dances are the same, although there are common elements. The following description is a composite of a "traditional" sun dance of the early reservation period, drawn from a variety of sources. (For a thorough discussion of descriptions of sun dances and the developmental history of sun dances since 1866, see Holler 1995, 39–203.)

At its fullest duration, the dance itself is preceded by up to eight days of preparation, with four days for gathering and socializing and four for final instruction of the dancers. Contemporary dances tend to compress these aspects into the period of the dance itself, which is usually four days (or less).

In the four days of the dance proper, the first day is devoted to preparation of the area for the sun dance. A hole is dug in the center of the camp circle, and a large arbor is built around it. To the east a special lodge has been constructed for the participants, with one or more sweat lodges in the vicinity. An appropriate cottonwood tree, to become the sun dance pole, is symbolically "hunted" and a Buffalo Dance is held.

On the second day the cottonwood tree is ritually captured as an enemy would be, but by a selected group of virtuous women rather than warriors. A procession makes its way to the tree, which is then marked with red paint. The holy man officiating at the dance conducts a pipe ceremony before the tree is cut.

Then eight specially chosen young people, four boys and four girls, strike the first blows. Strong men "count coup" on the tree and finish the task, felling the tree without its touching the ground. The procession, with the people garlanded in leaves, stops four times before entering the sun dance circle.

On the third day the tree, shorn of most of its branches below a fork, is raised at the center of the sun dance lodge. It is painted red on the west side, blue on the north, green on the east, and yellow on the south. At the base of the pole a buffalo skull is placed. A bundle of chokecherry brush, the home of the *Wakinyan,* is placed in the tree, as are sweetgrass, sage, bison hair, and a red cloth banner. Rawhide effigies of a buffalo and a man with exaggerated genitalia (representing the chaotic gods *Iya* and *Gnaske*) are also hung from the pole. Arrows are shot until the effigies are hit.

During these three days those who have taken a vow to participate in the dance make their final preparations under the guidance of a *wakan* person. In the year or longer leading up to the dance, and especially in the days immediately before the dance, they have been engaged in fasting, sweating, giving away things, holding feasts, and making offerings to the spirits. They have been receiving instruction from elders in the traditions the sun dance represents. They are expected to embody in their participation in the dance and in their lives the Lakota virtues of integrity, generosity, bravery, and endurance.

On the morning of the fourth day the male pledgers enter the circle, naked from the waist up. Their hands and feet are typically painted red, with blue symbols of Sky on their shoulders. Other symbols related to the manner in which the participant has vowed to dance and the dancer's animal mentor are also painted on his body. In the nineteenth century dancers wore two white deerskins around the waist; in more recent times, dancers have worn long red kilts. Each man also typically wears a strip of rabbitskin around wrists and ankles, armlets of bison hair, and a rawhide "sun-flower" disk suspended about the neck, painted blue and notched around the rim. A single downy, pure-white feather may dangle from the disk. Dancers usually carry sprigs of sage in their right hands and wear wreaths of sage, perhaps with four deco-rated sticks pinned into their hair, crossed to represent the four sacred directions. They may carry blue willow hoops symbolic of Sky. In their mouths they hold eagle bone whistles, wrapped in porcupine quills with downy feathers attached, which they blow to call spirits while they dance. They are led into the circle by the sun dance intercessor, who carries a buffalo skull and places it to face the pole.

At the altar across from the tree, a pipe ceremony is held to bring harmony to the participants. Sweetgrass is placed on a fire of buffalo chips to purify the scene and the participants. A Buffalo Dance may also be held, as some of the dancers circle the buffalo skull, imitating an enraged buffalo bull while gazing intently at the skull.

At this point, children who have been selected to have their ears pierced lie down on sage beds. This act, performed on boys and girls, is a symbol of the com-mitment of their parents to raise them in a manner consistent with Lakota val-ues; it manifests the opening of their ears to the voices of the spirits.

The dancers and others supporting or fulfilling their own vows then may elect to give flesh offerings, taken by an elder qualified to do so. In her novel *Waterlily* Ella Deloria describes a young man fulfilling a vow of giving flesh offer-ings after his father has been spared from death:

> The old man rubbed cold water over Lowanla's shoulders and down his arms. Then, using a strong cactus spike, he pricked the skin and pulled it out while with the sharp knife he quickly snipped off a tiny piece and laid it on the hide spread out to receive it. Starting near the neck and alternat-ing from one side to the other, he made a line of cuts along the shoulders. Blood trickled down in parallel streams, but the youth only bit his lip and frowned and did not flinch nor utter a sound. (Deloria 1988, 127)

The dancers are now symbolically "captured" by those who have previously fulfilled a sun dance vow. With guidance from their spiritual mentors, the dancers have vowed to dance gazing at the sun, pierced and attached to the pole, sus-pended in the center of four smaller poles, or dragging buffalo skulls. In the lat-ter three forms, the dancer is pierced by a sacred person, as skewers are inserted in the openings, and rawhide thongs are attached to the skewers.

While special sun dance songs are periodically sung to the rhythm of drums, the dancers who have chosen to gaze at the sun do so throughout the day. The pierced dancers continue until the pressure causes the thongs to break free. During intermissions the dancers have their wounds cleansed and rest. If they are having trouble breaking free, friends and family may help them by increasing the pressure on the thongs. The dance ends when the last dancer has succeeded in breaking the hold of the thongs or the intercessor declares it over. All the dancers are then honored. The pole is left in place, until it deteriorates and returns to Mother Earth.

As James Walker recognized in 1908, describing what happens at a sun dance is not as difficult as understanding what it means in terms of Lakota spirituality (Walker 1983, 6). Among Lakota interpreters there are differing views.

Perhaps the most straightforward view was given to Frances Densmore by Red Bird, who was bemoaning the ascendancy of Christianity among the Lakota and the banning of the sun dance: "There is a mysterious power greater than all others, which is represented by nature, one form of representation being the sun. Thus, we made sacrifices to the sun, and our petitions were granted" (Densmore 1918, 86).

According to Nicholas Black Elk (as expressed by Brown), the sun dance was introduced as a rite of penance, when the people had begun to forget *Wakan Tanka*. At the conclusion of the dance, the dancers are told: "By your actions you have strengthened the sacred hoop of the nation. You have made a good center which will always be with you, and you have created a closer relationship with all things of the universe" (Brown 1971, 99–100). The dancers have voluntarily subjected themselves to suffering for the sake of well-being with everything and everyone (*mitakuye oyasin*, "all my relations"). The universalism implicit in this statement, however, may be less Black Elk's than Brown's.

According to Holler, the sun dance that Black Elk described to Brown and the themes he emphasized were a product of his "religious imagination," and especially his engagement with Catholicism and the Ghost Dance. Black Elk apparently intended to inspire a revival of the sun dance, but with overtly Christian themes— such as the overcoming of "ignorance" and suffering "so that the people may live" and the soul may be liberated from the body (Holler 1995, 141–53).

According to Frank Fool's Crow (as understood by Mails), the sun, like the sacred pipe and the cardinal directions, is an instrument of *Wakan Tanka*. Fools Crow also may reflect to some degree his experience with Christianity when he says, "We respect [the sun] and pray to it because it watches over the world and sees everything that is going on. It also serves God by bestowing special gifts that it has upon the world. But the sun is not God" (Mails 1979, 119). During the ritual, dancers are able to see the sun with their eyes open (although they do not stare constantly at the sun, as sometimes is reported).

Holler suggests that with the demise of the traditional life on the Plains the sun dance "became the memorial of a life no longer lived rather than the celebration of life as it was lived." In his opinion the sun dance became (and continues to be) "the

focus of Lakota cultural identity maintained against the pressure toward acculturation brought to bear by the dominant culture." Today, he maintains, the dance is
principally "a ritual of renewal for the traditional community." He credits Black Elk
with being the catalyst of this theme (Holler 1995, 181–83).

As noted above, the sun dance was officially prohibited by the Bureau of
Indian Affairs during the 1880s. It did not end, however, for on most, if not all,
reservations people went to hidden places in the hills where sun dances were conducted by courageous intercessors, who were risking their freedom.

According to one Lakota observer, "beginning as early as 1924, and developing especially during the 1960s and seventies, we had the revival of the ceremony
proper, gradually moving out of its transitional phase where it was part powwow
and part sun dance and part annual fair." For example, an annual sun dance fund-
ed by the Oglala Tribal Council was held during the 1960s east of the community of Pine Ridge, attracting tourists (see Lewis 1990, 55–70, for a description).
Rodeos, baseball games, and the selection of a "sun dance princess" suggest the
shift toward a secular observance, although some elements of the sacred ritual
persevered. One pamphlet distributed at a Tribal Council–sponsored sun dance
declared that the dance was intended to recall the Sioux past and was not a religious observance (Feraca 1963, 13).

Native Americans and Euroamerican supporters came to participate in or at
least observe these dances. According to Bea Medicine, a Lakota scholar:

> Today the sun dance has assumed an almost intertribal character as a
> nativistic movement. We see more and more native participants returning
> from urban areas, or coming from non-Lakota reservations, to take part in
> the ritual. . . . There are many Lakota who say, "*Inse skatapi*," "They're only
> playing (at the ritual)." (Medicine 1987, 164)

The approach of the new millennium also heralded a renascence "in which the
sun dance has returned somewhat to its formal, intensely sacred character, with
many of the same restrictions and dimensions that it had in its historical setting"
(Amiotte 1987, 75–76; for a description of a traditional dance conducted in 1983 at
Fool's Crow residence near Kyle, see Holler 1995, 169–78). At a meeting with
Lakota educators at Oglala Lakota College in Kyle in May 1996, this author was
told that more sun dances are now closed to non-Lakota, or at least nonnative,
observers, not to mention participants, and the emphasis is increasingly on the
intensely spiritual nature of the ritual, in continuity with Lakota tradition.

Making of Relatives (*Hunkapi*). This ritual creates a special bond between
two people that is stronger than kinship. The two promise to die for one another, if necessary. One of the two is always older and is referred to as "*Hunke* father."
As with the other rituals, this event occurs in a specially erected structure and is

presided over by a *wakan* person. (See Hassrick 1964, 297–300; Brown 1971, 101–15; LaPointe 1976, 135–39; Powers 1977, 100–101; Catches 1997, 125–34; Powers 1991; Crow Dog 1995, 153–57.)

Another type of *hunkapi* might also be held to honor a beloved child (Deloria 1988, 73–80). Ceremonial singer William Horn Cloud describes such a ritual: "There are two singers. An eagle plume is put on the person. It is to affirm that he is loved. An adopted child, for example, had this ceremony" (Lewis 1990).

After a fifty-year decline in observance, the *Hunka* ceremony was revived in the 1970s and in the early 1990s was continuing to grow in popularity. It has become a rite of initiation into the Lakota nation, a time at which a young person is given a special name. Hence it is known today as the "naming" ceremony or "tying on a feather" (Powers 1991, 1).

Preparing a Girl for Womanhood (*Ishnati awicalowapi*, "they sing over her menses"). This puberty ritual occurs after a young woman's first menstruation, and it marks her coming to be a woman. It is also called the Buffalo Ceremony or Sing, because of the belief that the buffalo guards a woman's chastity and fertility and because it was traditionally conducted by a holy person who had dreamed of a buffalo. In addition, as the mothers of Lakota society, women are equated with buffalo, who give life to the Lakota people. Finally, the Buffalo is the spirit who watches over all ceremonies. (See Hassrick 1964, 300–301; Brown 1971, 116–26; LaPointe 1976, 129–32; Powers 1977, 101–3; Powers 1986a, 67–71; Crow Dog 1995, 147–52).

In the ceremony the young woman is told that like Mother Earth she will be able to bear children. She is also instructed that during her menstruation she possesses an especially potent sacred influence that must be carefully guarded. She is taught the rituals of purification in which she will need to engage during her menstrual cycle throughout her period of fertility.

This ritual has rarely been conducted in modern times. Unlike in southwestern nations like the Diné, it has not yet become part of the revitalization of traditional spirituality among the Lakota and other northern Plains nations. According to some scholars, however, "lack of the girl's puberty ceremony creates dissonance in the present ritual revitalization because it was during this ceremony that women were instructed in their social roles, procreation, and the care of children" (Medicine 1987, 168–69).

Throwing of the Ball (*Tapa wankayeyapi*, "throwing the ball upward"). In this ritual, a young girl stands in a field surrounded by many people standing at the four directions. She throws a ball made from buffalo skin (symbolizing the universe and *Wakan Tanka*) to each of the four directions, and persons standing at each direction attempt to catch it. The ball also represents knowledge, and whoever catches it is considered fortunate. (See Hassrick 1964, 301; Brown 1971, 127–38; LaPointe 1976, 117–21; Powers 1977, 103; Powers 1986a, 59).

Other Ceremonies

In addition to the seven classical rites, other Lakota rituals are observed. One in particular, known as *Yuwipi*, is quite prevalent today and is thought to be very old. Another traditional ceremony still practiced in an adapted form is the give-away ceremony. It is also important to mention, at least in passing, some of the life-cycle rituals of traditional Lakota culture.

Yuwipi. According to anthropologist William Powers, most *yuwipi* ceremonies are performed to cure someone "who is suffering from an illness deemed to be Indian, that is, not brought to the Indians by whites" (Powers 1986b, 71). They may also be held to find a lost person or object (Lewis 1990, 73). (For full descriptions and analyses of *yuwipi* ceremonies, see Mails 1979, 93–95; Powers 1982, 1986, 113–16; Stolzman 1986, 55–67; Lewis 1987, 173–87; 1990, 71–105; Steinmetz 1990, 18–26, 63–77; Crow Dog 1991, 207–12; Brave Bird 1994, 104–9; Crow Dog 1995, 118–24).

The person who is suffering or who has lost something, or a member of the family of a person who has disappeared, approaches a holy man qualified to conduct a ceremony (often called a "*yuwipi* man") with a pipe. If the holy man takes the pipe and the two smoke together, he is agreeing to conduct the ceremony. The ritual itself is conducted in a house cleared of all furniture, with windows and doors covered. When an altar has been constructed in the center of the room and a bed of sage prepared for the *yuwipi* man, the sufferer and his family and friends gather around the edge of the room.

The *yuwipi* man is then wrapped in a quilt tied with seven knots and is laid face-down on the bed of sage. The room is darkened and the spirits are called. Tobacco offerings have been placed for the spirits. Announcing their coming with hammering on the floor and walls, the spirits enter the room, take the tobacco, and tell the healer what must be done to cure the patient. They may also make their presence known by emitting a blue spark. Sometimes they cause objects to fly across the room. Sudden bursts of air indicate the presence of the *Wakinyan*, the Thunder Beings.

When the lights are turned on, the *yuwipi* man has been untied by the spirits. The altar has been removed, and the patient has been cured or the location of the lost person or object identified. A feast is held, the sacred pipe is smoked, everyone greets one another, and all say *mitakuye oyasin*.

The songs of a *yuwipi* ceremony are taught to the *yuwipi* man by the spirits (typically during a vision quest). He teaches them to the singers who perform them during the ceremonies, with all present encouraged to join in (Powers 1986b, 72). Each *yuwipi* man has his own set of songs for the ceremonies he conducts, and they are, in effect, his property. Powers has been criticized for inappropriately publishing songs shared with him by *yuwipi* men (Powers 1982; 1986, 78–102).

When conducted by *yuwipi* men who accept Christianity, the ritual can take on syncretistic overtones. For example, Fools Crow said that the offerings in the ceremonies he conducted went "to the departed spirits of friends and relatives, to the grandfathers who go to Heaven with Jesus our Father, to the grandmothers who lay in the ground until they are remarried in the future" (Lewis 1990, 76).

Giveaway Ceremony. The traditional "giveaway ceremony," similar to a ritual found in a number of indigenous groups worldwide, deserves mention (cf. Hassrick 1964, 297). To avert some misfortune or to seek renewal and to offer thanksgiving after one, or to prepare for some special occasion, a Lakota family may give away some, even all, of its most valued possessions to others. Economically, this practice allowed for a ritualized avoidance of concentration of wealth in one family and stressed the positive values of sharing and concern for the well-being of the group as a whole.

Frank Fools Crow describes a giveaway ceremony he and his wife Fannie held in 1928, after the death of his daughter Grace:

> We . . . invited the poorest people in our district. Of our 183 horses, we gave away nearly half. We had 42 cows, and we gave half of them away. We gave away all of our poultry. We gave away our clothing. . . . All we kept of our furniture was the kitchen stove and the cooking utensils. (Mails 1979, 117)

After the safe return of Lakota men and women from service in the armed forces, a giveaway might be held to honor them and to give thanks to *Wakan Tanka.* Giveaways may also be held in association with *hunka* or "naming" ceremonies.

Other Life-Cycle Rituals. A few other rituals deserve mention. (See Hassrick 1964, 310–38; Powers 1986a, 53–103.)

To bear a child is a particular joy for a Lakota woman, who in doing so is fulfilling the admonition of White Buffalo Woman that the people be fruitful. During pregnancy the mother-to-be makes two amulets in the form of a lizard or tortoise. One is used for the child's umbilical cord, with the other serving as a decoy. The amulet is worn by the child on the hair braid when it begins to walk (Crow Dog 1991, 24, 158). At birth the baby is invested with *tun*, the aspect of the human soul that lives forever. *Tun* comes from the sky to the newborn child, and after a birth it is said, "A baby-traveler has arrived" (Powers 1986a, 53).

Lakota children have traditionally been named after "some important natural event, for a deceased relative or important person in the tribe, or for a historical occasion judged important to the *tiyospaye*" (Powers 1986a, 60). Naming feasts are held soon after the birth, with the child invested with a ritual name to be used at ceremonies. A *winkte* (see above) name may be given to a boy to ensure long life. At the next sun dance after the child starts walking, the ear-piercing ceremony is held. During their first year children are considered especially *wakan.*

For boys in the nomadic culture of the 1800s, the "rite of passage" to adult-hood was participation in a raiding party, and, if so honored, initiation into a men's society. The puberty rites for women have been discussed above. For both sexes, the transition usually involved vision quests. Today vision quests as rites of passage from adolescence for young men and women are increasingly common.

At death, depending of the status of the deceased and the family's stature, the insertion of pegs through the flesh, cutting hair short, flesh offerings, and give-aways were once common. It was also considered appropriate and respectful for the women and men of a camp to wail during the time of bereavement and bur-ial. The corpse was ceremoniously dressed, with "spirit moccasins" on the feet. After a four-day mourning period, the body was traditionally placed on a scaf-fold. If the deceased were a person of status, a favorite horse might be killed. A burial bundle, with the dead person's shield, medicine pouch, drum, and lance, might be placed on the scaffold. Lower-status people were buried in shallow graves near the crest of a hill.

Today most Lakota, including traditional spiritual leaders such as Frank Fools Crow, receive a "Christian" burial, which is combined with a pipe ceremo-ny, tobacco offerings, and traditional Lakota songs and prayers.

When a person dies, it traditionally falls to the older women to prepare the body and actually conduct the burial. The destination for spirits (*nagi*) which successfully navigate the spirit trail is said to be the "Land of Many Lodges," where one is reunited with ancestors and where one finds plentiful buffalo and other animals. In popular understanding, this has been distorted into the stereo-typical "happy hunting ground."

A Case Study: Black Elk and His Interpreters

According to a recent study, Nicholas Black Elk (ca. 1863–1950) was "an authen-tically American religious genius, the greatest religious thinker yet produced by native North America" (Holler 1995, 1; 1984b). He has been called a prophet like Wovoka, the founder of the Ghost Dance movement (see chapter 6) and has been credited with creating "a universal religion grounded in Lakota beliefs and res-onating with Christian symbols" (Kehoe 1989, 66). Whether these are reasonable assessments, or distortions of the role of this fascinating Lakota *wicasa wakan*, is a matter for consideration. First, however, one must ask, "Who was Nicholas Black Elk and why has so much been made of him?"

Black Elk first gained notoriety as a result of *Black Elk Speaks* (1932), a book by poet John Neihardt, based on interviews conducted in 1931 at Black Elk's home near Manderson on the Pine Ridge Reservation. Presented as "the life story of a holy man of the Oglala Sioux," *Black Elk Speaks* is actually a romanticized narra-tive based on the premise that Black Elk felt he had failed to live up to the role he had been given by the spirits in a "great vision" received when he was a young boy in 1873. This vision, which came to him from the Thunder Beings, revealed that he would restore the sacred hoop of the nation after it had been broken and cause the tree at the center of the hoop to flower once again (see Black Elk 1972 [1932], 17–39; DeMallie 1984, 111–42). Neihardt's Black Elk keeps returning to the vision as he tells of his life as a boy growing up during the time the Lakota were under intense pressure to leave their nomadic life on the Plains and accept confinement on the reservations. (See DeMallie 1984, 3–93, for an excellent summary of Black Elk's life and his interaction with Neihardt.)

Black Elk was present at the Battle of the Little Big Horn in 1876, and he observed firsthand Red Cloud, his cousin Crazy Horse, Sitting Bull, and other great Lakota leaders. Like Sitting Bull, he toured in one of Buffalo Bill Cody's Wild West shows. *Black Elk Speaks* ends with the tragedy at Wounded Knee in 1890, as Black Elk laments that in the bloody mud "a people's dream died" and that "I, to whom a great vision was given in my youth . . . have done nothing, for the nation's hoop is broken and scattered. There is no center any longer, and the sacred tree is dead" (Black Elk 1972 [1932], 230).

Recent studies have shown clearly that while it was Neihardt's belief that traditional Lakota culture and spirituality died at Wounded Knee, Black Elk did not share this view himself. Nor was Black Elk in 1932 simply a broken old man who lived in total despair, tragically yearning for a glorious past. In short, the message of *Black Elk Speaks* is Neihardt's, not Black Elk's (Holler 1995, 7). Despite the fact that the book is faithful to the interviews Neihardt conducted with Black Elk (DeMallie 1984, 120), it should certainly not be used uncritically as a source for traditional Lakota culture and spirituality (DeMallie 1984, 77–80). Unfortunately, for enthralled readers around the world, *Black Elk Speaks* (now translated into a number of languages, though not Lakota!) is the only source for understanding the Lakota people and their traditional ways. Modern Lakota and other Native American readers, especially those outside the reservations, seeking to reconnect with their own heritage, have also been drawn to it.

Some judgments of Neihardt's portrayal of Black Elk have been particularly harsh. Julian Rice, for example, has argued that Neihardt was a Christian racist (although not of the "virulent type") who believed that Native Americans had to be crucified in order to be redeemed by God's chosen instrument, the Aryan race (Rice 1991, xi, 17, 34–35). According to William Powers, in his "Black Elk" Neihardt deliberately molded a distorted character who conformed to Neihardt's Judeo-Christian assumptions of worldliness, suffering, and salvation (Powers 1990b, 137).

Any interpretation of Nicholas Black Elk and his own understanding of spirituality, however, must take into account the fact that for most of his life Black Elk was a practicing Christian. Sometime between 1881 and 1886 Black Elk became an Episcopalian. He would have had to be a Christian to be allowed to join Buffalo Bill's Wild West Show. He then converted to Catholicism, receiving the Sacrament of Baptism on 6 December 1904 (the Feast of St. Nicholas), being known thereafter as Nicholas (or Nick) Black Elk (DeMallie 1984, 10, 14). Between 1907 and 1930 Black Elk "was almost totally consumed by his duties in the Catholic church" as a member of St. Joseph's Society, a confraternity of catechists who served as custodians of local chapels and led prayer services when priests could not come (Powers 1990b, 137–39, 142–43; cf. Steinmetz 1980, 158–59). He continued to participate actively in the Catholic church until his death in 1950.

At the same time, after he had converted to Christianity, Black Elk apparently continued to lead traditional Lakota rituals as a *wicasa wakan*, although the evidence is admittedly slight (Holler 1995, 16–17; DeMallie 1984, 87; Steltenkamp 1993, 60–61, 117). He would naturally have kept his involvement secret from the priests he worked with as a catechist as well as from reservation agents, since leading, or even participating in, traditional rituals was illegal when he spoke with Neihardt. Participation by Lakota Catholics was anathema to the missionaries on the reservation until after his death. He would have endangered his freedom and his livelihood had he acknowledged openly leadership of or even presence at the rituals with which he had grown up. It seems likely, however, that while he was leading Catholic prayer services and trying to win converts to Catholicism, he was also serving as a *yuwipi* man and leading, or at least attending, underground sun dances and other rituals (Holler 1995, 18–20).

After his retirement from active church work in the 1930s, Black Elk showed his familiarity with the pipe ceremony and the sun dance in his role in an annual summer pageant held for tourists near Mount Rushmore (DeMallie 1984, 71), although his willingness to use the pipe in this secular show may also be interpreted as evidence that he had renounced traditional Lakota spirituality in favor of Catholicism (Kehoe 1989, 67). Finally, when Black Elk spoke to Joseph Epes Brown in 1948, he displayed an intimate knowledge of and commitment to the sacred pipe and the traditional rituals, which, according to Brown, he wanted to show had equal validity with the Christian sacraments (Brown 1971, xix–xx).

How can this seeming contradiction be reconciled? Was Black Elk a Lakota traditionalist who feigned conversion to Christianity for social and political reasons, as Rice suggests (Rice 1991, xi; cf. DeMallie 1984, 47, 92)? Was he a committed, progressive Lakota Christian who maintained only a "cultural" attachment to the Lakota tradition, as Steltenkamp argues (Steltenkamp 1993)? Or was he a "religious genius," the founder of a new "universal" religion that synthesized traditional Lakota spirituality with Christianity (Kehoe 1989, 68–69)? What, if anything, can be learned about Lakota spirituality in the reservation period from the story of Black Elk and about the interpretation of Lakota spirituality by the scholars seeking to understand him?

According to DeMallie, Black Elk's conversion to Catholicism was sincere, and he renounced the traditional rituals in 1905, never taking them up again

(DeMallie 1984, 14). In DeMallie's view, however, when Black Elk met Neihardt, the old man experienced a "reconversion" to Lakota tradition. As he told Neihardt about his vision and his life, according to DeMallie, "it was as if something long bound up inside the old man had broken free at last, an impulse to save that entire system of knowledge that his vision represented and that for more than twenty-five years he had denied" (DeMallie 1984, 28). But this is only one of several, sometimes conflicting perspectives on Black Elk's own spirituality offered by DeMallie in *The Sixth Grandfather.*

Paul Steinmetz offers yet another interpretation of Black Elk, suggesting that in Lakota spirituality Black Elk saw "foreshadowed" the truths of Christianity (Steinmetz 1990, 187–88). In other words, Christianity was for Black Elk the natural fulfillment and perfection of Lakota spiritual tradition. This was the approach taken by Steinmetz in his role as a priest on the Pine Ridge Reservation; to claim that it was also Black Elk's perspective seems farfetched.

The problem with all these interpretations of Black Elk's spirituality is that they insist on placing Black Elk in a single category at any given time: dedicated Lakota traditionalist, sincere Christian who left behind his tradition, committed Christian who reconverted to Lakota tradition late in life, prophet who envisioned a universal religion, or Christian who saw Christianity as the fulfillment of traditional Lakota spirituality. This penchant for classification reflects modern, Euroamerican interpreters' need for clarity more than the likely perspective of Black Elk himself. What seems most probable is that Black Elk, like thousands of other Lakota people throughout the reservation period, successfully blended Christianity with traditional Lakota spirituality, not to create a new religion but to use spiritual power from various sources to persevere in a difficult time.

Despite the pressure he would have received from missionaries on the one hand and a few traditionalists on the other, Black Elk almost certainly saw no contradiction in participating actively in and drawing on both traditional Lakota and Christian manifestations of spiritual power. Like his nephew Frank Fools Crow in the next generation, he was probably committed to both the way of the cross and the way of the pipe without homogenizing them (Steinmetz 1990, 86; but see Mails 1991b,12, who discounts Fools Crow's allegiance to Christianity). "The real Black Elk was not either a traditionalist or a Catholic; he was both at the same time" (Holler 1995, 22, 37, 204–23).

Black Elk was most likely a spiritual pragmatist who drew on those rituals that at a particular time and in given circumstances were spiritually powerful for him and the Lakota people to whom he was dedicated. Like many other Lakota spiritual leaders, Black Elk turned to the traditional rituals, as well as the teachings of Christianity, to help meet his own and the people's daily needs. Indeed, the fact that others on the Pine Ridge Reservation have tended to consider Nick Black Elk "just another Oglala," rather than a spiritual genius, shows that rather than being unique, Black Elk actually reflects the spiritual symbiosis that many Lakota have found both comfortable and comforting in the situation in which they have found themselves on the reservation. "The idea of focusing on one medicine man as some paragon of Lakota virtue is strictly a white man's idea" (Powers 1990b, 140, 146). It is interesting to note that *Black Elk Speaks* has never been translated into Lakota and that "there is no interest in Black Elk on the [Pine Ridge] reservation as a philosopher or spokesman for the traditional way of life" (Powers 1900, 148; but see Holler 1995, 183–85, 220, who maintains steadfastly the view that it was Black Elk who is largely responsible for the "creative reconciliation" of Christianity and Lakota tradition, and thus deserves recognition as a theologian and "religious genius").

Instead, as Steltenkamp rather sarcastically observed, this opinion of Black Elk as a unique theologian or philosopher is held by

> environmental activists, Indian militants, anthropologists, historians, religionists, students of Americana, and others [who] have gleaned from Black Elk passages that bolster or refute whatever conventional Native theme they choose because, it appears, his representation has become the conventional stereotype par excellence. (Steltenkamp 1993, xv)

As Albert Schweitzer suggested in *The Quest of the Historical Jesus* (1906), interpreters have looked deep into the well of history and rather than seeing the actual person (in this case Black Elk), have observed and portrayed in their descriptions of a spiritual leader their own most cherished assumptions and perceptions. Black Elk cannot be neatly fit into any of them!

The Renewal of Lakota Spirituality

Today it seems clear that, as Black Elk hoped, the "sacred hoop of the Lakota Nation" is being preserved and renewed in several ways (see Stead 1987). The first is revitalization of distinctive myths and rituals. This effort apparently began in earnest as early as the 1930s, when Black Elk told his story to John Neihardt and Fools Crow recognized, after a vision quest on Bear Butte, that "our only hope was to fall back upon our traditional way of life. It was the only foundation we had that would give meaning and purpose to us" (cited in Beasley 1992, 39).

The sacred lore of the Lakota, as told by *wakan* persons, recorded and translated earlier in the century, is now being published (e.g., Walker 1983) and preserved, but, much more importantly, it is being shared by elders with Lakota children orally, in their own language. Four of the traditional rites are now widely practiced, including the memorial feast (inspired by the "keeping of the soul" ritual), the sweat lodge, the vision quest, and especially the annual sun dance (Powers 1986a, 195–99; 1977, 131–41). In addition, the *yuwipi* ceremony is as popular as it ever has been (Powers 1977, 143–54; 1986a, 199–202). The *hunka* "naming ceremony" and giveaways are also increasingly observed (Powers 1991). More and more, women are participating in all the traditional rituals, including vision quests, a ritual once reserved for men.

It is estimated that about one-third of the Lakota people today participate actively in traditional ceremonies, and the number is growing. According to one contemporary spiritual leader, in the 1980s and 1990s traditional Lakota spirituality once again became the focus of the culture (Mesteth 1996).

While the increased participation in rituals is encouraging, the decline in fluency in the Lakota language threatens the renewal of traditional spirituality. As with other indigenous cultures, Lakota spirituality and language cannot be separated. Without knowledge of the language, the vibrancy of the ceremonies declines and the traditional way of life withers. As recently as the 1950s, most children on the Pine Ridge Reservation were fluent in Lakota and learned English in school, but that is no longer the case. By the 1990s, almost without exception, only the elders were fluent Lakota speakers. People in their forties spoke some Lakota, while men and women in their twenties and thirties could understand Lakota to some degree but could hardly speak it. If this trend continues, the Lakota language as a living reality may be dead within another generation or two. The hope is that a renewed commitment to traditional spirituality will inspire more Lakota people to commit themselves to their language as well. With increased control over educational curricula, students who come to school not knowing Lakota will have to be taught the language at ages young enough to develop fluency. A number of Lakota families are homeschooling their children until they become fluent in Lakota, and only then allowing them to go to reservation schools (Lone Hill 1996; Mesteth 1996).

The sun dance clearly embodies the challenges facing the Lakota today (Powers 1977, 139–43; Steinmetz 1990, 29–32; Lewis 1990, 52–70; Holler 1995). In 1960, with the permission of the Bureau of Indian Affairs, the Oglala Sioux Tribal Council allowed the practice of piercing to be reinstituted (although Fools Crow had been doing it since the early 1950s), although some traditionalists accuse the council of trying to stress the macabre aspects of the ritual in promoting it to tourists. The council even paid some Lakota to participate in the dance on a yearly basis. Despite this commercialization, the sun dance continues to help give the Lakota a sense of identity and unity. It also contributes to intertribal understanding, since many Native Americans from other nations participate in open dances.

The sun dance has proliferated in recent years, with as many as fourteen held on the Pine Ridge Reservation in 1987. (For descriptions of recent sun dances, see Steinmetz 1990, 77–82, and Holler 1995, 169–78.) Most of the dancers are young, in their late teens or early twenties. The numbers of men and women dancers have been approximately equal in the past few years, with a tendency toward more people being pierced. The trend in recent years has been toward dances closed to non-Lakota or at least to non-Indians.

Another way traditional Lakota spirituality is being renewed is through the growth of rituals that are rooted in the tradition though not part of the "seven classical rites," such as the *yuwipi* (see above).

The third method of renewal involves Christianity's role as a vehicle for the expression of traditional Lakota beliefs and rituals. Many Oglala Lakota converted to Christianity in the last century—most, like Nicholas Black Elk and Red Cloud, to Roman Catholicism (the "black robes") or Episcopalianism (the "white robes"), whose missionaries first reached the Pine Ridge Reservation (Deloria 1987). By the 1970s nearly 45 percent of the Oglalas on the Pine Ridge Reservation were Catholic; 38 percent were Episcopalian. There is also a small Presbyterian presence on the reservation and a smattering of other traditional Protestant denominations. Evangelical Christianity has come to the reservation in the form of the independent, pentecostal Body of Christ Church (Steinmetz 1990, 153–62, 174–76; Lewis 1990, 119–23; Poor Man 1987). In the mid–1990s thirty-four separate Christian denominations were represented on the Pine Ridge Reservation (Mesteth 1996).

Except for the fundamentalist churches, most included at least some aspects of Lakota tradition in their services, including use of the Lakota language. Since 1961 the Lakota Catholic Church in Pine Ridge, for example, has been decorated with a mural representing the Christian trinity with Lakota mythological symbols. The Holy Spirit is represented by an eagle with twelve tongues of fire. Beneath the crucifix is the sacred pipe, symbolic of the human offering to the trinity. Beginning in 1965, the priest of the Our Lady of the Sioux Church, Father Paul Steinmetz, prayed at funerals and other services with a sacred pipe, claiming that the pipe is Christ. Father Steinmetz contends that Christ is the pipe in the sense of the pipe symbolizing the source of all life and functioning as a Mediator among the Lakota (Steinmetz 1990, 35–39; 1998). Lakota members of the congregation, including several traditional holy men, were glad the priest had finally seen the light! (Powers 1977, 116)

The Christian aspects of the sun dance have also been emphasized. For example, Edgar Red Cloud, a descendant of the famed Chief Red Cloud, said that the wreath worn by the dancers was like the crown of thorns Jesus wore; the piercing of the chest is a reminder that Jesus was pierced on the cross (LaPointe 1976, 115). In addition, White Buffalo Calf Woman has been linked with the Virgin Mary. And some Catholic priests, like Steinmetz, have argued for a "fulfillment theology," which holds that Christianity simply completes what is implicit in traditional Lakota theology.

As noted above, most Lakota find no contradiction in practicing Christianity and traditional rituals (Parks and DeMallie 1987, 14; Powers 1986a, 188–89, 191; Stolzman 1992), and find no need to say that Christianity "fulfills" Lakota ways. Many Lakota may also see Christianity as a matter of institutional membership and the native ways as a powerful spiritual source to be turned to in times of need (Powers 1977, 129; 1986a, 193). Growing numbers of Lakota, however, are questioning their association with the Christian church. For example, Wilmer Mesteth, a traditional spiritual leader, was baptized as an Episcopalian when he was twenty-five at the request of his father; now he says that he felt uncomfortable and did not understand the ritual, and declares that Christianity is not his religion (Mesteth 1996).

Finally, some Lakota have joined the Native American Church, a syncretistic religion with its roots in the sacramental use of the peyote cactus (see chapter 7). In 1919 approximately 367 (5 percent) of the 7,340 Oglala on the Pine Ridge Reservation were using peyote (Stewart 1987, 175). Throughout the years, the Native American Church has remained active on Lakota reservations, despite opposition from some Lakota who consider it "foreign to Teton culture and against the pipe and against true Sioux religion" (Powers 1986a, 189–90; Lewis 1990, 116; Steinmetz 1990, 87–152). Today, some traditional spiritual leaders are members of the Half Moon division of the church, recognizing it as an authentic intertribal religion, into which they can incorporate distinctive Lakota traditions (Mesteth 1996).

In May 1996 at the Red Cloud School near Pine Ridge, during a meeting with the author and a group of Westminster College students, a Lakota educator commented that he participates in traditional Lakota rituals and Native American Church ceremonies, while he remains an active member of the Catholic church. He explained that for him all these associations and rituals contribute to his personal quest to live in harmony with "all his relations."

The Lakota Today

Return of White Buffalo Calf Woman?

On 20 August 1994 a female white buffalo calf was born on the Heider farm in southern Wisconsin. Word of the birth of the calf, whom the Heiders named Miracle, quickly reached the Lakota reservations, and many Lakota elders related it to the promise of the White Buffalo Woman to return at a time of great need, a prophecy noted by earlier generations of Lakota holy men such as Nicholas Black Elk (Brown 1971, xix–xx).

Had the prophecy of the return of White Buffalo Woman been fulfilled? Had the power of the Buffalo to bring life returned? That is, of course, not a question for a descriptive study such as this, but it is clear that many Lakota people and others believe it to be the case. They are convinced that White Buffalo Calf Woman has returned to offer not only the Lakota but all humanity an opportunity (perhaps the last) to learn the way of harmony she first came to teach.

Some elders interpret the black, brown, red, and white colors into which the White Buffalo Calf Woman in the legend (and Miracle after her birth) changed to represent all the colors of humanity. Lakota elder Floyd Hand "claims that Miracle was born to non-Indians to show that her message was meant for all people, not just Native Americans." Keeper of the Sacred White Buffalo Pipe Arval Looking Horse respects such teachings but believes that Miracle's birth especially represents a call for Lakota people to return to their traditional spiritual ways (Pickering 1997, 46–49, 66–72). Since her birth he has worked with other indigenous spiritual leaders to make people aware of the plight of indigenous peoples around the world and to call for a return of native peoples to their traditional ways. At the same time, he has joined in days set aside to pray for world peace, such as a gathering at Devil's Tower in June 1996.

According to another Lakota legend,

> at the beginning of time a buffalo was placed in the west to hold back the waters. Every year the buffalo loses one hair, and every age he loses one leg. When all his hair and all his legs are gone, the waters will rush in and the cycle will end. It is believed that the buffalo currently stands on one leg and is very nearly bald. (Powers 1977, 85)

The combination of these two prophecies creates a sense of urgency for those who believe that the renewal of the sacred hoop of the Lakota nation, and perhaps the hoop of all life, depends on a reawakening of traditional spirituality. As noted, however, there is no such thing as a pristine Lakota traditional spirituality (any more than there is a "pure" Christianity unaffected by its interpretation over time). There are ongoing efforts to reaffirm tradition in the context of new challenges and opportunities. Throughout history the Lakota have shown themselves fully capable of adapting their traditions to changing circumstances. There is no reason to believe that will not continue to be the case in the twenty-first century.

The Return of the Buffalo

In addition to excitement over the prophesied return of White Buffalo Woman, there is the reality today of the reintroduction of the buffalo to the Lakota nation. As the result of the work of the Intertribal Buffalo Cooperative, a number of the Lakota and other Native American reservations now have tribally-owned buffalo herds. For example, on the Pine Ridge Reservation in 1996 there was a herd of 4,000 owned by the Oglala Sioux Tribal Council. In addition to serving as a new opportunity for economic revitalization, the herds are critical for the spiritual renewal of the people. For example, students in Lakota culture classes at Oglala Lakota College have participated in a traditional killing and preparation of buffalo, learning first-hand how each part of the buffalo was used by the people.

As explained above, according to Lakota mythology the Lakota people are the descendants of the Buffalo nation. Buffalo skulls are used in the sun dance and other Lakota rituals, and the life-giving symbolism of the buffalo is a critical dimension of the Lakota perspective. Lakota people now have the opportunity to reconnect with the buffalo and, in so doing, to reclaim their identity.

A large statue of Crazy Horse is being carved in the Black Hills, although it is controversial among the Lakota because of the great warrior's insistence that no images be made of him. (AP/Wide World Photos)

Renewal of the Tiyospaye System

Another important feature of Lakota life today is the movement to revitalize the traditional *tiyospaye* (band) system. Until the creation of the reservation system and especially the implementation of the system of allotting land to families, Lakota life centered in the groupings of extended families into bands called *tiyospayes* (see above). The adoption of centralized tribal government after the 1934 Indian Reorganization Act (see chapter 1) further weakened the *tiyospayes*.

Despite the efforts of the federal government to undermine the traditional system, many Lakota have practiced a studied disdain for the centralized system of government imposed on them. Many Lakota "communities" (such as Porcupine on the Pine Ridge Reservation) have maintained the essence of the *tiyospayes* despite the odds against them.

Today, educated "progressive" Lakota leaders, who in many ways are committed to the development of the Lakota people in order to meet the economic challenges of a changing world, are joining "traditionalists" in urging a return of as many decisions as possible to the level of the *tiyospayes*. They believe that it is in *tiyospayes* that Lakota people will best take responsibility for themselves and show concern for the well-being of the community and the Lakota nation. This is one indication that the tension between "traditionals" and "progressives," which has plagued the Lakota since the nineteenth century, is moderating, if not disappearing.

Exploitation of Lakota Spirituality

In recent years concerned Lakota spiritual leaders have sought to address a serious problem—the exploitation of Lakota spirituality by self-appointed "medicine men." Some are Euroamericans who fraudulently claim ritual knowledge they are willing to share with others—for a price. Others are Lakota and other Native American entrepreneurs who are willing to take advantage of a hot "market" in alternative spirituality. The pipe ceremony, sweat lodge, vision quest, and sun dance, in particular, have become fads subject to exploitation.

Authentic Lakota holy men and women do not charge for rituals, although they will accept gifts from those for whom they are performed. For a fee of $750, however, an impersonator will take you into a sweat, or for $1,000 will put you "on the hill." For $2,500 you can even become a "Lakota Medicine Man" yourself, after a weekend workshop (Brave Bird 1994, 236).

In a 1995 "Declaration of War Against Exploiters of Lakota Spirituality" (Mesteth, Standing Elk, and Swift Hawk 1995), three traditional Lakota spiritual leaders (Wilmer Stampede Mesteth, Darrell Standing Elk, and Phyllis Swift Hawk) express outrage at this state of affairs. "For too long," they write, "we have suffered the unspeakable indignity of having our most precious Lakota ceremonies and spiritual practices desecrated, mocked and abused by non-Indian 'wannabies,' hucksters, cultists, commercial profiteers and self-styled 'New Age shamans' and their followers." They also cite programs at academic institutions that engage in "the sacrilegious imitation of our spiritual practices by students and instructors under the guise of education programs."

The declaration includes a call to "our Lakota, Dakota and Nakota brothers and sisters from reservations, reserves, and traditional communities in the United States and Canada to actively and vocally oppose this alarming take-over and systematic destruction of our sacred traditions." They assert that the highest duty of Indian people is "to preserve the purity of our precious traditions for our future generations, so that our children and our children's children will survive and prosper in the sacred manner intended for each of our respective peoples by our Creator."

Would the authors of this statement consider this chapter, indeed this book, a contribution to the exploitation they decry? In May 1996 I had the opportunity to meet and listen to Wilmer Stampede Mesteth, who teaches classes in Lakota culture and spirituality at Oglala Lakota College. He pointed out that as long as the issue the Lakota people face is cultural survival, they must zealously protect their right to teach their own way of life themselves. As long as the Lakota are struggling to protect the tradition from being obliterated, Mesteth said, there will be a tension between sharing the culture with others and preserving it for themselves. For him it is a matter of the freedom of religion, in this case the survival of traditional Lakota spirituality. For that reason, he has closed the traditional rituals he conducts to outsiders and is working with other spiritual leaders on a tribal ordinance to protect the traditional sites and rituals (Mesteth 1996).

As noted in the Introduction, however, many traditional leaders such as Wilmer Mesteth do affirm a role for non-Lakota scholars who are sympathetic to the traditional ways. These scholars can teach and write about what they have learned, he said, as long as they do not claim to have the perspective of someone within the tradition and as long as they are willing to learn from those who actually practice Lakota spirituality. If they do so with humility and respect, they can provide non-Lakota audiences with sources that will help them develop an appreciation for Lakota spirituality based on what is actually happening. That is the intent in this chapter, as it is in all the chapters; whether it has been realized is for others to determine.

CHAPTER 5

The Diné (Navajo):
Walking in Beauty

The Navajo religion is being Navajo. Religion is something that you live every day.
> —Jennie Joe, Diné educator and medical anthropologist

The Navajo are . . . changing in order to remain "traditional."
> —John R. Farella

MY INTRODUCTION TO Navajo Country was by way of U.S. 160, which cuts across the Big Reservation, from the Four Corners (where Arizona, Utah, Colorado, and New Mexico meet) to Tuba City, near the Grand Canyon. My wife and I stopped in Kayenta and drove north amid the spectacular formations of Monument Valley. Then we headed south, feeling that at any moment Joe Leaphorn or Jim Chee of the Navajo Tribal Police would speed by us, off the pages of a Tony Hillerman novel. Even along a major highway, one gets a sense of the expanse of the Navajo Reservation and the relative isolation in which most of the Navajo people still live.

We spent a day in Tuba City, mostly feeling as though we were being examined by the Navajo (Diné) residents we encountered. The Navajo people were polite and friendly when they had reason to speak to us, but their quiet observation while we shopped in the grocery store or walked along the street was a bit unsettling. In a store full of shoppers one afternoon we noted remarkably little noise. Only a young Diné boy, eager to guide us to the site of dinosaur tracks near Tuba City, broke this pattern of detachment.

That experience piqued my curiosity. How much could I learn and communicate about the Diné and their traditional spirituality, when the people themselves seemed so circumspect? Since the Navajo are the largest Native American nation, including them in a study of Native American spirituality seemed inevitable as I planned the project, but would my attempt to learn something of the tradition-al lifeways of this private people prove only frustrating? After studying Navajo history and spirituality, and listening on several occasions to Diné themselves speak about their worldview, my initial concern has been replaced by a growing fascination with the amazing intricacies of the Navajo way of life. In this chapter, I can provide only a glimpse of the complexity and depth of the Navajo culture, and I have learned enough to realize how limited my knowledge is. But having come to appreciate and admire greatly the "beauty way," I hope to communicate something meaningful of the Diné quest for harmony.

The chapter includes an orientation to the Navajo (known in their own lan-guage as Diné [the people]), an introduction to traditional Diné social organiza-tion, a sampling of the rich Diné origins legends, an historical overview from the likely migration of the ancestors of the Navajo to their present homeland from the far north to the situation of the Navajo in 1990, and an attempt at a mean-ingful description (for non-Navajo readers) of traditional Diné spirituality, begin-ning with the concept of *hozho* and including Navajo cosmology, gods and spir-its, hogans, dry [or sand] paintings, and medicine bundles. The heart of the chapter is the discussion of the intricate Navajo ceremonials conducted by skilled singers, with an overview of a number of the sixty-or-so rituals and emphasis on the Blessingway and Nightway ceremonials. The section on spirituality also includes brief descriptions of daily rituals, naming ceremonies, attitudes toward death, witchcraft, weaving, Christianity among the Diné, the Navajo branches of the Native American Church and their use of peyote, and contemporary chal-lenges to Navajo spirituality. The chapter concludes with remarks on the situa-tion faced by the Diné at the end of the twentieth century.

Who Are the Diné?

In 1996 the Diné numbered more than 200,000 (Towner 1996, 3), making them the largest reservation-based Indian nation, second in total population to the Cherokees. Most Navajo live on a 24,000-square-mile reservation on rugged, arid land in the states of Arizona, New Mexico, and Utah. Navajoland, as the reser-vation is known, is about the size of West Virginia.

The Diné world is the land within the four sacred mountains: to the east, *Sisnaajini* (White Shell Mountain–Blanca Peak in the Sangre de Cristo Range in central New Mexico); to the south, *Tsoodzil* (Blue Bead Mountain–Mount Taylor in north central New Mexico); to the west, *Dook'o'ooshiid* (Abalone Shell Mountain–the San Francisco Peaks near Flagstaff, Arizona); and to the north, *Dibvé nitsaa* (Obsidian Mountain–Hesperus Peak in the La Plata Mountains in southwestern Colorado near the modern town of Durango). These demarcate what the Navajo call *Diné Bikeyah* (Navajo Country).

The first Diné homeland in the Southwest is known as *Dinetah* ("Among the People" or "Land of the People"). *Dinetah* is a region of what is now northwestern New Mexico in the Chama Valley and part of the San Juan Basin (Underhill 1953, 15–16). The term has also been used, however, to speak of the larger land the Navajo came to occupy, the land between the four sacred mountains.

The people popularly known as the Navajo call themselves Diné (or Dineh), which means simply "People" or perhaps "Earth People." *Navajo* (sometimes written phonetically as "Navaho") is an English rendition of a Spanish term perhaps derived from a Tewa designation meaning "great planted fields." It was first used by the Spanish to describe the region the Diné called *Dinetah*, and eventually was applied to the People. The first recorded English use of the term is in the accounts of the 1805–7 Zebulon Pike expedition (Brugge 1983, 496).

Linguistically, the Diné are grouped with the Apaches as Apacheans, speakers of an Athpaskan language. Since Athpaskan is spoken in Canada, in Alaska, and along the Pacific coast, the Navajo language is the primary evidence cited to support the theory that the Diné are descendants of a people who migrated from the north.

Traditional Social Organization

The importance of kinship ties within Diné society can scarcely be overemphasized. One of the worst things one Navajo can say about another is "He acts as if he didn't have any relations." In contrast, a high compliment is to say, "You act as though everybody was related to you" (Kluckhohn and Leighton 1974, 100).

About sixty matrilineal clans compose the Navajo. A child becomes a member of his mother's clan. The mother-child bond is the closest and strongest of traditional relationships. Clans are exogamous, so the child's father is a member of another clan. When meeting other Navajo, a Diné identifies herself or himself as "born in or of" his or her mother's clan and "born for" her or his father's clan. Thus someone might identify himself as "I am Bitter-Water, born for Salt." The reality of different peoples being absorbed into the Diné is evident in the names of clans such as Mexican clan and Zuni clan.

The women of the mother's clan are known as "mothers" and the men of the father's clan as "fathers." Those whose fathers are of the same clan consider themselves "brothers" or "sisters." A man considers all those born for his clan as his "children." A woman considers those born for her clan as "paternal grandchildren" or "cross-cousins." Physical contact is avoided between adult brothers and sisters.

All those born into any of these categories are considered "my relatives" by virtue of *k'é* (kindness, love, cooperation, friendliness, and peacefulness). *K'é* is "the ideal that orders all social relations." Among Navajo outside this kinship circle, there is to be reciprocity (Witherspoon 1983a, 524–25).

The marriage relationship is reciprocal, with exchange expected. When a husband is irresponsible or a woman is barren, the relationship is often ended. Within a family a woman owns the hogan, the children, the sheep and other livestock, and whatever they produce. Men own what they bring from their families and whatever is produced by their own work. The Diné have no conception of joint property ownership by husband and wife.

The primary social unit for traditional Navajo is the residence group, organized around a head mother, a sheep herd (and other livestock), a land-use area, and perhaps an agricultural field. All are known as "mother" (Witherspoon 1983a, 525–26). Traditionally, an "outfit" was a group of relatives who cooperated for work or a ceremony or to settle disputes; it might include two or three extended families. Today outfits continue only on a social level (Kluckhohn and Leighton 1974, 109–11).

Diné Creation Legends

There is no one "official" Navajo story of origins because there is no authoritative written text. Creation stories are told differently by individual "singers" in the context of a particular Diné ceremonial (see below). Each creation story, however, seems to follow a basic pattern and storyline: "a journey ascending through several worlds below the surface of the earth followed by a cosmic ordering process once the earth surface is reached" (Gill 1983, 502).

Reproducing a version of a complete creation story is not possible here, but a brief summary of its three distinct stages is provided (Gill 1981, 49–58; see also Parezo 1996, 4–6; Page 1995, 27–34; Zolbrod 1984; Gill 1983a, 503–5; Klah 1942; for other versions, see Haile 1981a, 1981b, 1943a; Wyman 1965, 1970; O'Bryan 1956; Wheelwright 1949; Spencer 1947; Matthews 1897).

The Era of Emergence

The story begins with a subterranean domain of from two to fourteen worlds, stacked like platters one on top of the other. Each world is numbered and has a distinct color. These worlds are inhabited by insectlike "air-spirit people." They speak and live and act as Diné. They have been placed in these worlds to live in harmony, but give in to jealousy and quarreling. Although the air-spirit people are continually warned by the powers that reside at the four directions, their behavior (including incest and adultery) leads to violence.

In frustration, the powers unleash the oceans around them. As the people see the waters (or, in some instances, fire) approaching, they flee, seeking a way to ascend into the next world. A helper shows them the opening to the next realm, and they emerge to join others already living there. Once again, they pledge to live ordered and peaceful lives, but the cycle repeats itself and this world is destroyed.

One result of the chaos is the separation of men and women. The men move across a river, leaving the women behind. After a series of failed attempts to get along, the two genders attain a new understanding of their relationship and reunite.

In these lower worlds First Man and First Woman and other creatures who will take part in the creation of the Navajo cosmos come into being, along with the sacred medicine bundle (Farella 1984, 78–93).

The Era of Cosmic Creation

Finally, there is the last emergence, to the place of the "earth-surface" people, often called the "Fifth World." This world is covered with water controlled by water birds. When the water birds are vanquished, the waters recede and the winds of the four directions dry the earth, revealing a barren landscape.

First Man and First Woman discuss how this new world shall be. They open the sacred medicine bundle and transform the objects in it into holy figures in human form. Then they build a hogan in which they create the Navajo world. Standing at the place of emergence, the hogan is a microcosm of the world. Its four support pillars at the four cardinal directions are personified spiritual forces. In a manner resembling a sand painting, First Man places the objects from the medicine bundle on the floor of the hogan and arranges them in human shape. They are the life forms of all the living beings of the Navaho world: plants, animals, and all others. The months, the heavenly bodies, and the living landscape are also created.

All of this takes place in a ceremony that lasts through the night, with actions performed as songs describing the deeds are sung (the model for the Blessingway ceremonial). At dawn the world is complete; smoke carries the forms to their assigned places. A prayer is the transforming power which gives birth to the earth.

Dawn and evening twilight tour the new world. Climbing to the top of each of the four sacred mountains, they see a world of beauty and harmony, which stands in contrast to the chaos of the prior worlds. The most common version names the four sacred mountains, but some indicate as many as seven.

Into this world Changing Woman is born. Her parents are two of the sacred powers from the medicine bundle, thought and speech. She is raised by First Man and First Woman, and she inherits the medicine bundle. Her twin sons are Monster Slayer and Born for Water; their father is the Sun. The sons slay the monsters that had been born as a result of the adultery of Sun and others. Changing Woman then creates corn. From residue rubbed from her body mingled with cornmeal she creates the first four pairs of Navajo. They are the founders of the four original Navajo clans, from whom all the Diné come.

The Holy People depart from their own spiritual realms. Some return to the lower worlds, where they are associated with witchcraft, death, and other chaos-causing forces. Other Holy People say they will never again appear in their human form, but they will continue to watch over and guide life in the Navajo world.

The Era of the Heroes and the Origin of Ceremonials

The scene shifts from the rim of the place of emergence to the boundaries of the world. Introduced now are the impending threats to the harmony and beauty of the creation. If harmony is to continue it must be maintained. In this era heroes and heroines enter forbidden territories or violate the way things are to be. As a result, they suffer and are unable to escape the dilemma until the Holy People come to their aid by performing ceremonials. The ceremonials restore the heroes/heroines and initiate them into the knowledge of the ceremonials. The heroes/heroines return home to teach the ceremonials to a successor, but they must return to live among the Holy People. These myths of origins of the ceremonials become the patterns for the performance of the ritual complexes examined later.

The principal theme of the Navajo story of origins is the attainment, maintenance, and restoration of *hozho*, a fundamental Diné concept meaning beauty, balance, and harmony. A central feature in creating *hozho* is the relationship between genders (Haile 1981a; Farella 1984, 132–44), represented by First Man and First Woman, and then by Changing Woman and the Sun. The failure of First Man and First Woman to establish a good relationship causes evil by bringing about the birth of the Alien Gods. The union of Changing Woman and the Sun leads to the destruction of the evil monsters. Total harmony cannot be realized, however, until Changing Woman and the Sun reach a fully equitable relationship. Only then does the actual creation of the Navajo people occur. Everything that happens throughout the creation story relates directly or indirectly to the notion of delicate balance between male and female. This complementarity of the genders is a recurrent emphasis in the Navajo way of life.

The following excerpt, taken from the end of the section of the creation story in which the monsters are slain, gives a sense of its poetic quality, the relationship between the tale and the geography of Navajoland, and its importance in contemporary life:

> After the Changing Woman had departed to go with her husband the Sun, her son the Monster Slayer and his brother the Water Born went as they were bid by their father to [the place] where two rivers come together in the valley of the San Juan.

There they made a dwelling for themselves, and there they live to this very day. There we may sometimes see their reflection when, after a summer rain which brings the rainbow, the mist rises from the water as the sky clears. The bright colors shimmer in the moist light and the forms of the monster-slaying twins materialize.

To this very day the Navajo people go there to pray. But they do not pray for rain at that place, and they do not pray for good crops. They do not pray for their livestock to flourish or for success in hunting. They pray only for victory over their enemies at that place. They go there to pray only when they recognize the need to restore order and harmony in the world, it is said.

All of these things happend [sic] a long, long time ago, it is said. (Zolbrod 1984, 277–78, with Diné words omitted)

The story of creation is very much a living reality among virtually all Diné today. For example, during World War II, Navajo "gained their grasp of Hitler by associating him with the voracious monster (*Yé'iitosoh*)." They also point to landmarks made prominent by episodes in the story. The black lava deposits scattered among the western foothills of Mount Taylor (visible from Interstate 40 between Albuquerque and Gallup) are for Navajo the dried-up blood of Big Giant. As a recent commentator on the Navajo creation legends has observed:

If Navajo relate to their landscape in a special way it is because one version or another of the creation cycle is immediate and familiar to them, whether they are young or old, modern or traditional. . . . To this day the narrative gives individual Navajo an important ethnic identity that elders are anxious to preserve. It defines a meaningful relationship between each member of the community and between the community and the whole surrounding cosmos. Such a relationship is still very real among traditional Navajo, and it is very important. (Zolbrod 1984, 22–24)

As in other peoples' stories of origins, the Navajo myth defines the nature of the world and the place of human beings in it. The responsibility of maintaining *hozho* falls upon the Diné. Their everyday activities–planting, herding, and caring for their children–are essential to the continuation of harmony. To restore harmony once broken, at times of sickness or suffering, or to establish harmony at times of birth and transition, the ceremonies discussed below are necessary (Gill 1983a, 505).

While the first two eras deal with "the establishment of proper places and relationships for things in the world," the era of the origin of the ceremonials is concerned with how one lives in the world, the Navajo way of life. It deals with the "relationships which are necessary for life, such as the relationships between hunter and game, between a man and wife and women who are not his wife, between in-laws, between the living and the dead, between a Navajo and a non-Navajo, between a person and the plants and animals in his environment, between Earth Surface People and Holy People." Navajos use the analogy of a tree. The stories of cosmic creation are the trunk, and the adventure stories of heroes and heroines are the branches (Gill 1981, 56–57).

Historical Overview

The Migration from the North (ca. 1000–1500 C.E.)

At least 1,000 years ago (and perhaps as early as 500 C.E.), bands of Athpaskan-speaking people began a migration from the north which brought them eventually to a territory bounded on the north by the La Plata mountains in Colorado; on the east by the Sierra Blanc range in Colorado and the Pelado Peak near what is now Jemez, New Mexico; on the south by Mount Taylor and the Zuni mountains in the center of New Mexico; and on the west by the San Francisco mountains near Flagstaff, Arizona. According to modern historians, they were the ancestors of the Navajo people. (Major sources for the basic information in this overview are Bailey and Bailey 1986; Brugge 1983; Kluckhohn and Leighton 1974; Locke 1992; Page 1995; Roessel 1983b; Tome 1983; Iverson 1990; and Trimble 1993.)

Linguistic evidence suggests that the ancestors of the Diné, and their relatives, the Apaches, came south from western Canada and perhaps Alaska. In addition, Diné stories are remarkably similar to legends of the northern Athpaskan speakers.

When these Athpaskan speakers arrived in the Four Corners area, perhaps beginning about 1300 C.E., the land was most likely still occupied by the magnificent pueblo culture known today as the Anasazi (see chapter 1). According to Diné tradition and recent archaeological findings, the immigrant ancestors of the Navajo and Apaches did not arrive as one large wave that swept aside the Anasazi peoples, but in small, poverty-stricken bands. The Anasazis dispersed, and their descendants most likely became the pueblo-dwelling peoples of the Southwest.

The Diné settled around the mesas on which these pueblo people lived and adopted aspects of their culture, but they also continued their own distinctive ways. Indeed, although there have been periods of significant enmity between the Navajo and the pueblo peoples, peaceful interaction probably dominated the early relationship and has been common since.

At this early stage, and continuing throughout most of Navajo history until the twentieth century, each Diné band had a headman, a *naa'taanii*, who mobilized the people at times of threats. They would either negotiate for their band or lead warriors in battle. Headmen could not negotiate for other bands, however. Until it was imposed by the federal government in the twentieth century, there was no central Navajo organizational structure. Rather, the Diné were united by common stories and rituals as well as a shared material culture (Kluckhohn, Hill, and Kluckhohn 1971).

The Spanish Come to Dinetah (1598–1750)

In 1541 the Spanish explorer Coronado Entrada camped near the Rio Grande and encountered seminomadic bison hunters living on the eastern plains of what is now New Mexico. One group of these peoples he called the Querechos. They were Athpaskan speakers who lived in skin tents and used dogs to move from camp to camp. They were probably part of the people who became known to the Spaniards as the Navajo.

In 1583 Antonio de Espejo met Querechos near Mount Taylor. Fifteen years later Juan de Oñate and three hundred colonists arrived in what is now New Mexico to settle the land for Christ and Spain. He assigned a priest to minister to the "Apaches," showing that Apacheans were living near the pueblos east and west of the Rio Grande by this time (Towner 1996, 4).

According to Diné legend, the light-skinned god of the moon, *Klehanoai*, created the Mexicans as well as the sheep as subjects for the divine gambler *Nohoilpi. Nohoilpi* came to *Dinetah* in the person of Juan de Oñate to punish the Navajo for ignoring him. Although this first effort ultimately failed and Oñate returned to Mexico, the influence of Spanish culture on the Navajo was set in motion. The Spanish at first focused their attention on subduing the pueblo peoples and the Navajo were able to withdraw to the canyons and mesas of *Dinetah*.

By 1600 the Spanish put the enslaved pueblo dwellers to work herding their horses, sheep, and cattle. It is likely that escapees introduced the Spanish livestock to the Navajo soon thereafter. A hundred years later Navajo culture had evolved into a way of life dependent on these animals.

By 1606 the Diné were probably raiding the Spanish *encomiendas* and the enslaved pueblos for horses. The Spanish at first grouped all the nonpueblo people of the Southwest as "Apaches." In 1626 there was the first specific Spanish reference to the Navajo, when the priest at Jimez Pueblo described a group he called "Apache del Nabaxu," who lived up the Rio Chama, east of the San Juan River. According to Spanish accounts, they were "a semisedentary people who planted maize and perhaps other crops but moved to areas distant from their fields for hunting; traded meat, hides, and mineral products, primarily salt and alum, to the Puebloans" (Brugge 1983, 491). In addition, they had many local headmen, were skillful in war, and practiced polygamy (Brugge 1983, 491).

Throughout the rest of the century the Navajo continued their raids against the Spanish, with periods of truces. It is likely that some Navajo warriors participated in the 1680 Pueblo Revolt against the Spanish.

The Spanish reasserted control after the revolt and subdued the Pueblo peoples. Many Pueblo refugees fled from the Spanish and joined the Navajo in Dinetah. By the end of the seventeenth century, only the Navajo were strong enough to challenge the Spanish.

As with other cultures, the Navajo undoubtedly adapted aspects of the cultures they encountered when they arrived in the Southwest, including mythic and ritualistic elements. From the Pueblo peoples, the Diné may have borrowed "ceremonial masks, altars, prayer sticks, use of corn meal, sand paintings, the origin myth, and perhaps even selected aspects of the Pueblo matrilineal clan system" (Vogt 1961, 301). Interestingly, the Navajo did not adapt the underground ritual chamber (*kiva*) so typical of Pueblo peoples. Instead, they continued to use the ancient dwelling that became known as the hogan as their ceremonial chamber (see below).

For the next 150 years, except for a period of relative truce between 1720 and 1775, there was almost constant conflict between the Diné and the Spanish invaders from the south and the traditional Ute and Comanche enemies of the Navajo to the north and east. So fearsome were the Navajo that the Spanish called them *Los Dueños del Mundo*, the Lords of the Earth. The Diné increased their herds dramatically through their continual raiding, while losing many captives to the Spanish and their native enemies.

A tradition developed in which Spanish men would capture Indian slaves and present them to a woman when she was married so she would have her own household servants (Locke 1992, 182). The Spanish rationalized the seizing of slaves by claiming that they were being taken so that they could be converted to the true faith—Christianity. The first recorded baptism of Navajo captives was in 1705.

Conflict with the Spanish and Mexicans (1750–1846)

During a Navajo-Spanish truce in the mid-eighteenth century, Franciscan priests established two missions near Mount Taylor. They hoped to entice the Navajo into taking on the way of life of the pueblo peoples, and several hundred did. These "mission" Navajo and their descendants became known to the majority of the Navajo as *Dinehanaih*, the People who are Enemies. After only a decade the missions were abandoned, and raiding resumed.

When Spanish ranchers sent their herds onto Navajo lands to graze, the Navajo retaliated and the cycle of conflict resumed. Allied with the Comanches, the Spanish pushed many Navajo westward and seized the vacated lands. In 1818 a coalition of the Navajo with their sometime allies (as well as enemies) the Utes, united under the leadership of Narbona, mounted an offensive against the Spanish until another treaty was signed the following year. Two years later, however, hostilities resumed when a large force of New Mexicans entered *Dinetah* and hundreds of Navajo captives were taken.

Mexico achieved independence in 1821, and during twenty-five years of Mexican domination there was nearly constant warfare. The New Mexicans were now trading with the Anglo-Americans and raided Navajo areas for captives to be sold in the slave trade. They also sought to expand into the Navajo's territory. In 1822 twenty-four Navajo peace emissaries were murdered in Santa Fe.

During the hostilities that continued through the 1830s the Mexicans resorted to paying bounties for Navajo scalps. By the 1840s the Navajo had made ten treaties with the Spanish and Mexicans, seeking return of Navajo captives in exchange for the release of prisoners, but there had only been token returns of Diné captives. Thousands of Navajo women and children had been taken as slaves and were never returned.

Conquest by the Americans (1846–64)

When the United States annexed Texas in 1845, Mexico refused to negotiate the sale of what is now the western and southwestern United States, and a war with Mexico soon followed. A U.S. force under Colonel Stephen Kearny entered New Mexico and declared it a possession of the United States in August 1846. The "New Men," as Navajo called the Anglo-Americans, were yet another foreign group with whom the people had to contend.

Kearny soon sought to enter into a treaty with the Navajo. The eighty-year-old Narbona and other older leaders were amenable, but his wife and younger leaders, including Narbona's son-in-law Manuelito, resisted. Nevertheless, the Treaty of Ojo del Oso, which promised "a firm and lasting peace and amity between the American people (which specifically included the New Mexicans and Pueblo Indians) and the Navajo 'tribe of Indians'" (Locke 1992, 211), was signed in November 1846. The treaty was not popular with New Mexicans who wanted the government to crush the Navajo. The Diné also ignored the treaty when they deemed it necessary to conduct raids. Between 1846 and 1850 Navajo and Apache raiders took about 450,000 sheep from Spanish American settlements.

Yet another treaty was signed in 1848, again promising the return of Navajo captives, a promise which yet again was not kept. However, until the Americans mounted a new offensive the next summer, the Diné kept the treaty. On 31 August 1849, Narbona and six other Navajo were shot in the back and scalped. In retaliation, under the leadership of Manuelito, the Navajo conducted successful raids against American ranches.

Several headmen (deceptively claiming to speak for the Navajo nation as a whole) did sign another treaty at Canyon de Chelly on 9 September 1849. The warring Navajo paid no attention, however, and struck settlements in the Rio Grande Valley near Albuquerque. They continued their attacks the next year. In January 1851 the newly appointed governor of New Mexico called for the extermination of the Navajo who persisted in their raids and authorized civilians to organize their own raiding parties into *Dinetah*.

During this period One Blind Prophet dreamed that the Diné would perish and a new race would occupy their land. Medicine men went to the Meeting Place of Waters (*Tohe-ha-glee*) and consulted the Shining Sands of Prophecy. There a message drawn by the Holy People pointed to a time of floods and death and a journey to a distant land (Newcomb 1964, 27–29).

To try to bring the Navajo under control, Fort Defiance was constructed in the heart of Navajo' territory in 1851, within yards of sacred springs. About the same time serious discussion began with the objective of creating a reservation in which to place the Navajo. A new treaty caused a cessation in hostilities during the winter of 1851–52. Complaining that treaties only seemed to result in the Navajo keeping their promises while the Americans ignored theirs, the headman Armijo asked, "Is it American justice that we must give up everything and receive nothing?" (Locke 1992, 271)

A sympathetic agent, Henry Linn Dodge ("Red Sleeves" to the Diné), began his service in 1853 and soon earned a good reputation among the Navajo. He was convinced that if the government would support the development of Navajo agriculture, they would stop their raids.

In July 1854, Congress appropriated funds to negotiate treaties with the Navajo and surrounding nations with the objective of allotting twenty to sixty acres per adult. Of course, the idea of individual land ownership was as foreign to the Diné as it was to other native peoples.

Hoping to end the warfare that threatened to decimate them, the Navajo on 18 July 1855 reluctantly signed a treaty that reduced their territory considerably. Despite the treaty's guarantee of protection against raids from their neighbors, Ute and Comanche raiding parties were able to attack at will. In 1856 Dodge was killed by Apaches while deer hunting, and Manuelito was growing increasingly enraged at the failure of the United States to observe the 1855 treaty.

The Diné call the period between 1857 and 1864 the "Fearing Time." In 1858, with American settlers demanding access to more grazing lands in the Navajo lands, war broke out. When yet another treaty was forced on the Navajo late in 1858, Zarcillos Largos described to other headmen a vision: "Our sacred mountains were covered with black clouds, billowing so not even the Holy Ones could see the peaks." He said there was a deathly silence broken only with "the howl of wolves and the wail of black wind, death" (Locke 1992, 318). He reluctantly agreed to peace. Manuelito, however, urged that the Diné come together to drive the hated *Bilagaana* (whites) from *Dinetah*.

A year later, in January 1860, Navajo warriors under Manuelito laid siege to Fort Defiance. In April they attacked the fort directly and won a decisive victory. Retaliation inevitably came, however, and the Americans ravaged the Navajo homeland, leaving the Diné impoverished. Another treaty brought hostilities to a halt in February 1861, promising again to protect the Navajo from raids. With the army's contingents withdrawn from Fort Defiance as the Civil War began, however, civilian raiding parties again invaded Navajo territory to capture slaves.

When the Navajo responded defensively, a volunteer force from California under General James Carleton, recruited to drive Confederate troops out of the Southwest, turned its attention to the Navajo instead. Carleton's plan was to kill as many Diné as possible and drive the rest into a restricted reservation where they would be taught Christianity and agriculture. He justified his genocidal plan with this observation: "The races of the Mammoths and Mastodons, and the great sloths, came and passed away: The Red Man in America is passing away" (Hauptman 1995, 124).

Carleton selected an isolated and desolate strip of land called Bosque Redondo 175 miles southeast of Santa Fe for a joint Navajo and Apache Reservation. He recruited Christopher "Kit" Carson, called by the Diné the "Rope Thrower," to lead the volunteer force to round up the Navajo and Mescalero Apaches and drive them to Bosque Redondo, also called Fort Sumner after an earlier fighter against the Navajo who was known for his viciousness. Carson was at first reluctant to go to war with the Navajo, believing that they could be subjugated peacefully (Trafzer 1982).

By early 1863 as many as one-third of the estimated 15,000 Diné had been taken as slaves and those that remained in Navajo territory were physically impoverished. In June 1863 Carleton issued an order which said that the Navajo had to be moved because "[f]or a long time past the Navajoe [sic] have murdered and robbed the people of New Mexico." In September he said, "Go to Bosque Redondo, or we will pursue and destroy you."

Carleton placed a bounty for the seizing of Navajo livestock, and Carson led his troops on a scorched earth campaign. Many Diné desperately tried to avoid capture by hiding in the canyons deep in the rugged country. The roundup went slowly and continued until early 1864 when an assault on Canyon de Chelly trapped the last sizeable group of Diné. In all, about 3,000 Navajo had been captured, and General Carleton triumphantly declared the end of the 180-year-old "Navajo War" and promised a speedy solution to the "Navajo problem."

The "Long Walk" and Captivity at Bosque Redondo (1864–68)

In late February 1864 about 1,500 Diné were marched out of Fort Wingate, beginning the Navajo "Trail of Tears," known to history as the "Long Walk." Several days later a group of 2,400 left Fort Canby (as the reoccupied Fort Defiance was called). By the second day coyotes followed the contingent and hawks and crows circled overhead, waiting for Navajo to die. New Mexicans followed the convoy to pick off stragglers to sell as slaves. If a woman went into labor, she was killed. Those too weak to continue were also shot (Roessel 1973, 103–4). Nearly 200 from this group died on the Long Walk to Fort Sumner, located on the Pecos River in the plains of eastern New Mexico. From a group of 950, 110 died later in the month.

By July 1864 about 6,000 Navajo were in Bosque Redondo, 1,000 were at Fort Canby waiting to be marched there, and, according to General Carleton's estimates, only 2,000 were left on the loose. Without adequate building materials for hogans, those at Bosque Redondo were forced to live in makeshift shelters. They were convinced that the Holy People had deserted them, punishing them for leaving *Dinetah*. With 9,000 Navajo and 400 Apache at the new reservation by the end of the summer, cutworms destroyed the crops. Of the $100,000 appropriated for supplies at the reservation, only $30,000 worth of goods reached Bosque Redondo, and it was not nearly enough to support the people. Comanche and New Mexican raiding parties descended on Bosque Redondo, decimating the small herds.

Because there was no central Navajo political organization, the army organized twelve bands at Fort Sumner, with a "chief" appointed for each. Barbonocito was named "principal" chief of the Navajo.

The next year the situation was no better. Some Diné started slipping away to return to Dinetah, and the army was ordered to kill any Indian who left the reservation without a pass. By leaving Bosque Redondo the escapees hoped that the Holy People would restore them to harmony.

As word filtered out about the situation at Fort Sumner, critics began to mobilize, accusing the government of treating the Navajo as slaves. Although he was no supporter of the Navajo (accusing them of "wild religious superstitions"), Dr. Michael Steck, Superintendent of Indian Affairs in New Mexico, criticized Carleton for the cost of running Fort Sumner (Roessel 1983b, 515). Indeed, the annual cost of well over $1 million for maintaining Bosque Redondo was increasingly seen as prohibitive (Thompson 1976, 165).

Manuelito and his small band finally surrendered on 1 September 1866, and were taken to the reservation. In September 1866 Carleton was relieved of his duties, and control over the Navajo was transferred from the Army to the Bureau of Indian Affairs. A November 1867 report recommended that the Bosque Redondo experiment be abandoned and the Navajo relocated.

When negotiations were opened for a "final" treaty with the Navajo in May 1868, the commission was told that 7,000 Navajo were still at Bosque Redondo; 2,000 had died from diseases during their stay there; and 900 had escaped. The plea of Barboncito, principal spokesman for the Navajo at the treaty conference, that his people did "not want to got to go to the right or left, but straight back to our own country" was finally heard (Roessel 1983b, 517). Against General

William Tecumseh Sherman's recommendation that the Navajo be moved to Indian Territory, a decision was reached to return them to their own lands and there establish a permanent reservation.

The treaty, signed on 1 June 1868, established a reservation of 3.4 million acres, about one-tenth of the land they had occupied. It excluded the desirable eastern grazing lands and the best water resources. According to the treaty, the Diné agreed to accept allotment of land to individual families and promised to send their children to government schools. The government agreed to provide the livestock and supplies necessary to re-establish Navajo in their homeland. Pressed by the Navajo leaders, the government negotiators also agreed to work for the return of the estimated half of the nation taken by this time as captives.

According to the Navajo it was not the treaty but ceremonies (such as one called "Put a Bead in Coyote's Mouth") that secured their release. In that ritual Barboncito "captured" a coyote and put a piece of white shell in its mouth. When he released the coyote, it walked toward the west (Roessel 1983b, 518).

The impact of the four years at Bosque Redondo had been profound, almost unimaginable to outsiders. "One can no more understand Navajo attitudes. . . without knowing of Fort Sumner than he can comprehend Southern attitudes without knowing about the Civil War" (Kluckhohn and Leighton 1974, 41). The Diné had been forced from the land the Holy People had given to them. They had passed over three rivers their legends warned them never to cross (Roessel 1983b, 518). And they had endured horrendous suffering at Bosque Redondo. It could have destroyed them as a people, but it did not. (For the full story of the Long Walk and the Bosque Redondo "experiment," see Thompson 1976; Roessel 1973; Bailey 1970; Newcomb 1964, 55–62.)

Return and the Renewal of the Nation (1868–1968)

The first group of Diné left Bosque Redondo for their homeland in a ten-mile-long column, only two weeks after the signing of the treaty. When they returned home they largely ignored the boundaries of the treaty and went to the homesites they had left four years earlier. When the promised sheep and supplies failed to arrive, some Navajo resumed raiding. In addition to the returnees there were three to four thousand Diné who had avoided deportation. They did not consider the Bosque Redondo treaty binding on them.

Late in 1869, the promised sheep and other livestock began to arrive and tensions lessened. With their fields destroyed by Kit Carson's campaign, livestock became the center of the Navajo economy. Until irrigation practices were introduced in the mid-twentieth century, this continued to be the case.

Thomas Keam (who later became a trader at what is now Keam's Canyon on the Hopi Reservation) organized a Navajo police force under Manuelito. He also advocated expanding Navajo land and helped the Diné resist efforts to take land from the northern portion of the reservation. When railroads were granted rights-of-way through prime Navajo grazing lands, about 900,000 acres were added to the reservation to the west.

Keam tried to do what he thought best for the Diné, but other government agents were either corrupt, incompetent, or religious zealots committed to the stamping out of Navajo "paganism." One was Thomas Arny, whose moralistic approach to the Diné was particularly onerous. He finally left the reservation in 1875 when Manuelito suggested that he would kill him if he did not.

As the years went on, life slowly improved for the Diné as they successfully adapted to the new circumstances. In 1875 the population on the reservation was about 12,000; by 1892 it had risen to nearly 18,000. An additional 1.2 million acres were added to the reservation by President Hayes in 1880.

In 1882 a rectangular 2.4-million-acre reservation was created by another executive order just to the west of Navajo lands "for the use and occupancy of the Moqui [as the Hopi where then called], and such other Indians as the Secretary of Interior may see fit to settle thereon." The Navajo living within the bounds of this new reservation considered themselves the "other Indians," and the seeds were planted for a land dispute which continues to this day (see below).

Ten more additions of land to the Navajo reservation between 1884 and 1934 brought it (with some minor changes) to its present 24,000 square miles (still roughly one-third of the original Navajo homeland). In addition, there are three noncontiguous areas of Navajo reservation land.

As a result of President Grant's "peace policy" (see chapter 1), the Presbyterian Church was given the responsibility of evangelizing and "civilizing" the Navajo. Presbyterian missionaries began to arrive in 1869, and a school was established. Only a few Navajo attended during its first years, however, the school was closed; the effort to educate the Navajo seemed to be a rather dismal failure.

When Manuelito sent his son to Carlisle Indian School in Pennsylvania in 1882, support among the Navajo for having their children "learn paper" increased. Manuelito said, "It is as though the whites were in a grassy valley, with wagons, plows, and plenty of food, we Navajo up on a dry mesa. We can hear them talking, but we cannot get to them. My grandchild, school is the ladder. Tell our people this" (Trimble 1993, 145). But the boy became ill, died shortly after returning home, and Manuelito's enthusiasm for the white man's education turned to anger. He tried to escape his grief through whiskey and died a broken man in 1893.

In 1885 one of the first trading posts on the reservation was opened at Round Rock. In the next century, trading posts owned by non-Navajo (such as those run by Lorenzo Hubbell) played a key role in the developing Navajo society. By 1900 there were nearly eighty trading posts, and by the 1930s that number had grown to 150. The trading posts had largely replaced the traditional, subsistence barter economy (Page 1995, 72). The posts were gathering spots for the spread-out people. They gave the Diné access to goods they needed and served as an outlet for the sale of rugs, silverwork, and other crafts.

Some traders kept their Navajo customers in perpetual debt, reducing them to a state to effective peonage. Many traders treated the Navajo with respect, however, and became strong supporters of the Navajo people and their culture. Hubbell was a crucial buffer for the Navajo with the outside world throughout much of the first half of the twentieth century. His trading post near Ganado, Arizona, is now a national monument.

In 1887 Congress passed a law mandating education for Indian children, and boarding schools were built at Fort Wingate, Chinle, Crown Point, Toadlena, Shiprock, Tuba City (a town established by Mormons just west of the Hopi Reservation), Leupp, and Tohatchi. At first they were run by Presbyterians and other missionaries.

The prevailing idea that Navajo children should be sent to boarding schools in order to prepare to enter Euroamerican society took a terrible toll on the Diné, as it did on other native nations. In a pattern repeated throughout Native American nations, Navajo children were forbidden to speak their own language and beaten if they did, were required to dress in Euroamerican clothes, and were forced to convert to Christianity. Those who resisted or tried to escape were beaten, denied food, and chained or locked up. In order to fill the schools, children were taken from their families, forceably if necessary. Many Navajo children remained in the schools four to eight years with minimal visits to their families. More than 95 percent of the Navajo students who went to boarding schools returned home, "only to find themselves handicapped for taking part in Navaho life because they did not know the techniques and customs of their own people" (Kluckhohn and Leighton 1974, 141).

Although a number of missionaries were kind people committed to providing the children with a sound education, and clinics were established that provided good health care to any Navajo who came seeking treatment, the fact remains that until recent decades their principal objective was to eradicate traditional Diné culture.

During the 1880s the physician at Fort Defiance, Dr. Washington Matthews, became convinced that the traditional Navajo way of life would soon vanish. With several Diné assistants, he carefully recorded as many ceremonies and legends as he could. His collection remains a critical resource for study of the traditional spirituality of the Diné (e.g., Matthews 1902; 1897; 1887).

Despite the assault on their culture, the People as a whole refused to yield their pride and sense of dignity. Gradually, the nation began to recover economically. Traders who came to the reservation gave the Diné an outlet for the wool their sheep were producing. the Navajo became more prosperous than they had been at any previous time in their history. During the rest of the decade, however, this was followed by a period of economic collapse brought on by drought, overgrazing, and the economic turmoil throughout the United States (Bailey and Bailey 1986, 94).

In 1900 the Navajo population had grown to about 21,000, but the ratio of humans to sheep and goats had fallen from 1:95 in 1892 to 1:19, with about 1:40 or 50 necessary for subsistence (Bailey and Bailey 1986, 104). As a result of the expanding population but declining resources, most Navajo had no choice but to shift from subsistence herding to participation in the market economy.

In the first decades of the twentieth century, the government began to exert more control over Navajo affairs. Because of their relative prosperity, however, the Navajo had to endure less oversight than other nations. By 1909 six separate agencies had been established on the reservation (Hopi, Western, Leupp, Northern, Southern, and Eastern). Each agency had a superintendent, boarding and day schools, at least one physician and medical facilities, and specialists assigned to help with the development of farms and herds. Navajo councils were established in most of the agencies, but there was no central tribal government, in keeping with the national Indian policy of dealing with Indians as individuals and not as tribes.

Missionary activity also increased after 1900 (Warner 1970). For example, Presbyterians opened a mission, a school, and a hospital at Ganado. The government made land grants to churches and interdenominational mission agencies. By 1914 forty-eight missionaries were active among the Navajo, but the difficulty in winning Diné converts continued. In 1926 one agency superintendent observed that the reservation was "infected with missionaries," but he could vouch for only about twenty-five converts among both the Navajo and Hopi in his area (Bailey and Bailey 1986, 171–72).

Although Navajo did not serve in significant numbers in World War I, viewing it as a white man's war, they were impacted economically by the war, with serious inflation the major result. The 1918 flu epidemic struck the Diné harder than any other population group in the United States, causing about 1,600 deaths.

The same year the first successful oil well was tapped on the reservation, and exploration for oil and natural gas began in earnest in the 1920s. Under pressure for energy companies, the federal government forced a new tribal government on the Navajo. At first, the plan was to let general councils in various jurisdictions have authority to lease lands for mineral extraction. It soon became apparent, however, that a centralized tribal government was needed to negotiate leases, with representatives from all jurisdictions. As more roads were built to service leases, the isolation that had kept many Navajo from much meaningful contact with non-Navajo decreased.

With increased external pressures, Navajo traditionalists reacted with hostility, spurred on by a 1920 prophecy by Navajo healers that the world would soon end with a flood (Bailey and Bailey 1986, 222). Other factions were led by Henry Chee Dodge, who had converted to Catholicism and cooperated with the Bureau of Indian Affairs, but who also was rooted in traditional Diné values, and Jacob Morgan, a fundamentalist Christian who favored total assimilation.

By 1930 nearly 40,000 Navajo were living on the reservation, and a serious overgrazing problem had developed in the opinion of government agents. The general economic situation on the reservation was grave. An effort to increase direct involvement of the Navajo people in the governing of the reservation led to the creation in 1927 of chapters, averaging 500 persons each. In chapter meeting houses the people could speak directly with government officials. Today local chapters number around 100 and are organized into eighteen districts.

When John Collier became Commissioner of Indian Affairs he first tried to implement his reforms (see chapter 1) on the Navajo Reservation (Parman 1976). Working through a centralized Tribal Council (before the 1934 Reorganization Act introduced them to other native nations), Collier had initiated public works projects, had increased the number of day schools (to replace the boarding schools), and had begun a program to protect the soil and other natural resources through an aggressive livestock reduction effort (focusing primarily on goats).

The strong and consistent resistance to livestock reduction programs by many Navajo was and is not so much economic as it is spiritual. When animals are allowed to die or are actively killed simply to reduce their numbers, it is, from a Diné perspective, barbarism. Animals have as much right to live and not be subjected to wanton killing as do humans. According to most Navajo, "Stock was given to them by the supernaturals. If they cared for their stock, the supernaturals would provide rain and thereby, pasture. . . . When the livestock were taken away, the supernaturals also withheld the rain. Hence pasture also declined" (Aberle 1982b, 200). As one Navajo leader put it, "Before stock reduction it rained all the time. . . . Then, when John Collier put a blockade on livestock, the rain ceased altogether (Grinde and Johansen 1995, 115).

Despite such objections, the livestock reduction program did have an impact. When it began there were about 760,000 goats and sheep, or about 100 per family of five. By 1949 only 414,000 were left—about 44 per family, many fewer than the number necessary for the traditional subsistence lifestyle. For the first time many Diné were forced into the labor market.

Not since the days of Bosque Redondo had the government tried to exercise such total control over the Navajo. Convinced that most of this was another effort to destroy their way of life, the majority of Navajo opposed Collier's reform efforts. He was vigorously opposed both by traditionalists who objected to what seemed to them an assault on their way of life and by assimilationists such as Morgan, who considered Collier's policy a return to "tribalism." Diné voters rejected the implementation of the 1934 act and forced the termination of the chapter program (although it was eventually reintroduced in the 1950s). Collier persisted, and in 1935 the six districts were consolidated into a single Navajo Agency, headquartered in Window Rock (which continues today as the administrative center of the Navajo nation).

In 1938 a new constitution and Tribal Council (with an elected chairman, vice chairman and seventy-four delegates) were adopted without Navajo consent. Morgan rode his resistance to Collier to election as tribal chairman in 1938.

A centralized Navajo government flies in the face of the traditional Diné belief that "unanimity is the only basis of collective action." In other words, a group may not impose its will on individuals, and an individual may not impose his or her will on a group. Despite the imposition of majority rule by the federal government, the principle of unanimity continues to dominate Navajo life in significant ways (Witherspoon 1983a, 533).

During the 1930s Navajo began to join the Native American Church (Aberle 1966; see chapter 7). By 1940 there were centers of peyote ceremonialism in the north around Shiprock and further south near Window Rock. Both traditionalists and Christian converts and missionaries expressed opposition, claiming that the Native American Church sanctioned "sexual orgies." The Tribal Council adopted an anti-peyote resolution in 1940, but Commissioner Collier prevented the tribal police from enforcing it (Bailey and Bailey 1986, 226–27).

During World War II services on the reservation deteriorated while 3,600 Navajo men responded to the call to arms (Underhill 1956, 242). Some 450 famed Navajo "code talkers" used the complex Diné language to create a code that was critical to the success of the war in the Pacific (Begay 1977; Paul 1973). About 12,000 other Navajo left the reservation during the war, lured by the need for workers.

By the end of the war the population on the reservation had risen to about 65,000. Due to the shortage of schools, during the 1950s many Navajo young people were sent to boarding schools throughout the western states. This marked the first wide exposure of many reservation Diné to other Native Americans beyond their immediate neighbors, and it led to some friction. While many members of other native nations were now emphasizing their common identity as Indians over their tribal heritage, "[t]he Navajo. . . did not think of themselves as members of a larger Indian community. They considered their history to be unique and their culture, unlike that of many tribes, to be very much alive" (Bailey and Bailey 1986, 6).

Health care services after the war were also inadequate—there were fewer than 500 hospital beds for the entire reservation—and Navajo were not allowed to receive state welfare payments. Their per capita income was $82 a year, compared to $579 for the United States as a whole.

In the immediate postwar period the federal government was still committed to "civilizing" the Navajo. A famous study, commissioned by the Bureau of Indian

Affairs and published in 1946, called the Navajo "the nation's foremost Indian problem" and justified its attempt to understand the Navajo way of life with the contention that "to change a way of life you must change people," and "before you can change people you must understand how they have come to be as they are." The "Navaho problem," the report asserted, was that "there are already too many people for the resources; the people are increasing steadily and the principal resource (land) grows steadily less productive. How are the People to live?" (Kluckhohn and Leighton 1974, 24, 27, 53). The implication was that a federal government enlightened by anthropologists' insights could paternalistically provide the solutions.

Many Diné leaders, however, were convinced that the Diné must help themselves by utilizing the resources on the reservation. Oil, gas, timber, and uranium were (and continue to be) the principal natural resources used to raise revenues. In support of these self-development efforts, Congress appropriated $90 million in 1950 for the combined use of the Hopi and Navajo nations.

In 1952 the Navajo Tribal Council entered into a mineral extraction agreement with the Kerr-McGee Corporation. In return for access to uranium deposits near Shiprock, Kerr-McGee agreed to hire 100 Navajo workers. But they were paid only $1.60 an hour, two-thirds of the off-reservation wage, and the working conditions were dangerous. The uranium tailings polluted the San Juan River, and the level of birth defects related to radiation exposure rose dramatically (Churchill and LaDuke 1992, 247).

The Navajo Tribal Council used the capital to develop other industries on the reservation in an effort to improve the desperate employment situation. Instead of allotting earnings to individuals, the Navajo Tribal Council committed itself to a strategy of using income for programs deemed beneficial for the Diné as a whole. For example, a scholarship fund was created in the 1950s to ensure that any qualified Navajo student who wanted to pursue a higher education would be able to do so. Of course, not all Navajo think that their elected officials have always acted in the general interest of the entire nation!

The Navajo (or at least the leaders) were seizing control of their own destiny, decreasing the influence of the Bureau of Indian Affairs, reorganizing the tribal government, reinvigorating the chapter system, and improving the system of Navajo courts. As Peter Iverson put it, "The 1950s . . . witnessed the birth of the Navajo Nation" (Iverson 1981, 82).

The 1950s also witnessed the acceptance of nontraditional religions by Navajo in increasing numbers—especially Protestant Christianity, the Church of Jesus Christ of Latter-day Saints (the Mormons), and the Native American Church. The development of a Navajo clergy was crucial to the growth of the Protestant churches. The Mormons, who had suspended missionary activity among the Navajo in the late nineteenth century, resumed it in the 1940s and by the 1970s claimed 20,000 Navajo converts.

The most dramatic growth was experienced by the Native American Church. By 1951 there were as many as 9,800 Navajo peyotists, up to 14 percent of the nation. By 1960 about 30,000 Navajo, one-third of the population, were members of the Native American Church, despite efforts of the Tribal Council to repress it (Bailey and Bailey 1986, 278; Aberle 1982a, 110). In 1963 Raymon Nakai was elected tribal chairman, in part because of his promise to stop persecution of peyotists. In 1967 the Tribal Council passed an act assuring human rights for Navajo, including freedom of religion.

Despite these gains traditional Navajo spirituality remained strong. Indeed, it has been argued that rituals of the various churches were simply absorbed into the traditional Navajo ceremonial systems as new rituals (Wyman 1983a, 536). Other interpreters have suggested, however, that peyotism is becoming an effective substitute for traditional spirituality among the Diné (see Aberle 1982a, xlvii).

By the late 1960s there was a growing effort to draw tourists to the Navajo Reservation. Several tribal parks had opened, with Monument Valley the first in 1958, but the situation of the Navajo was still problematic by the 1970s in the eyes of those who focused on economic improvement. The total Navajo population had grown to 120,000, but 40,000 were illiterate in English. Per capita income was still only one-third the national average. These signs of "deprivation," however, were evaluated differently by those Diné committed to maintaining the traditional way of life. The persistence of Navajo who maintained their own language and refused to become "productive" American citizens was a sign to traditionalists that a large segment of the People still wanted nothing to do with the dominant materialistic culture.

Self-reliance continued to be the dominant theme on the reservation. In 1968 the Navajo Community College opened as the first institution of higher education in the United States established and administered by Native Americans (see chapter 9). Supported by both progressives and traditionalists, Diné College, as it is now known, remains today a dominant institution in the struggle to preserve and renew Navajo culture. In 1969 the Tribal Council officially declared the existence and sovereignty of what they now called the Navajo Nation.

The Peter MacDonald Era and the Hopi-Navajo "Land Dispute" (1970–90)

In 1970 Peter MacDonald, a college-educated engineer and a World War II code talker, was elected chairman of the Tribal Council and pursued a policy of self-sufficiency, replacing all non-Diné working in government positions on the reservation with qualified Navajo. In his first inaugural address, he said, "We must create for ourselves" (Trimble 1993, 168). In addition, he aggressively pursued contracts with energy companies, allowing more than forty uranium mines and four coal-stripping operations to be opened (Churchill and LaDuke 1992, 248).

MacDonald continued in office until 1982, when he was replaced by Peterson Zah. MacDonald was re-elected in 1986 but had to leave office in 1989 when he was accused of profiting personally from a huge land deal. MacDonald appealed to the American Indian Movement, which staged protests on the reservation. In 1992 MacDonald was found guilty in Tribal Court of abusing his office and also by a federal jury on charges of fraud, bribery, and conspiracy. (On the early MacDonald administrations, see Iverson 1981, 125–212; for MacDonald's view of the challenges faced by the Navajo nation and how he was influenced in his chairmanship by traditional Navajo spirituality, see MacDonald 1993.)

After MacDonald's conviction, the Tribal Council was restructured. The chairmanship was renamed the presidency, with curtailed powers. The legislative role of the council (which now has an elected speaker) was strengthened, and the independency of the judiciary was clarified.

In addition to the conflict over Peter MacDonald's leadership, most controversial during the 1970s and 1980s was the leasing of Navajo lands to energy companies. For example, in the 1960s Peabody Coal Company had signed a thirty-five year lease to mine coal on the reservation at a price of less than 38 cents per ton. By the 1980s the company had paid only $5.9 million in royalties on coal valued at more than $311 million. In 1968 the Navajo and Hopi Tribal Councils agreed to allow Peabody to take water from Black Mesa in order to pump slurry coal to power plants. The price of the water was $7.50 for ten-acre feet, compared to $500 for the same amount purchased in Los Angeles. In addition, the relentless sucking of the water was causing wells to dry up in a region that had no water to spare. Moreover, uranium mines were causing both environmental and health problems. More and more Navajo were angry at their Tribal Council for failing to protect the lands and for selling resources much too cheaply.

In 1974 Congress passed Public Law 93–531, the now infamous "Relocation Act." It was ostensibly an attempt to resolve a land dispute dating from the 1882 executive order that created a reservation for Hopi and "other Indians." Despite the fact that Hopi and Diné (mostly traditionalists) had been living amicably in the region for centuries, the 1974 law partitioned the region and mandated the relocation of 10,000 Navajo and 109 Hopi from what had become known as the "Joint Use Area" (or simply JUA). It was the largest forced relocation of Americans since the World War II Japanese internment program. The legislators tried to mollify Navajo in the region by creating "life estates" for those Navajo who wished to stay on their traditional land. It would not revert to Hopi control until the holder died. Navajo called this provision "death estates," and only one Navajo family applied. The law also offered a $5,000 cash payment and a new house in Gallup, Flagstaff, or Winslow to families who agreed to relocate at once.

The law was passed in response to a 1962 federal court ruling, in the case of *Healing* v. *Jones*, which ignored the land use settlement worked out among the people living in the region in the 1880s. At that time a line marked by an Indian agent and the trader Thomas Keam (called the Parker-Keam line) was drawn around the Hopi mesas and surrounding farmlands, an area of about 600,000 acres. The Navajo agreed not to cross over into the Hopi areas and the Hopi agreed to recognize the right of Navajo to continue to live outside the Parker-Keam line, but within the 1882 area. Despite this agreement, the court ruled that the Hopi had never formally accepted it, so it was invalid. The ruling gave the Hopi exclusive right to the mineral rights in District Six and said the remaining 1.8 million acres in the 1882 reservation belonged to both the Hopi and Navajo and that they must share equally any profits from mineral leases. Hence, neither Hopi nor Navajo were satisfied with the court's decision. While the situation remained unresolved, a freeze on government-funded improvements in the disputed area went into effect.

Those living in the JUA were increasingly isolated. They survived by practicing the subsistence lifestyle of their ancestors and dedicating themselves to the spiritual traditions handed down to them. For many it was the life they preferred. Only the Peabody Coal Company was allowed to continue its work in the area.

A U.S. Court of Claims ruling in 1976, which tried to settle the matter, resulted in a settlement offer of $5 million to the Hopi. Hopi traditionalist leaders opposed it, however, and the Hopi Tribal Council took no action. The money sat untouched in an Albuquerque bank and the dispute continued. Despite the tension there was very little violence between the Navajo and Hopi living in the contested area.

From the perspective of most Navajo traditionalists and their supporters, behind the so-called Hopi-Navajo Land Dispute was a well-orchestrated campaign by an alliance of the Hopi Tribal Council (dominated by a "progressive" faction) and the Peabody Coal Company to obtain access to the rich Black Mesa coal deposit in the JUA. A Utah lawyer named John Boyden had convinced the Hopi Tribal Council to file the suit and lobby for passage of the Relocation Act. His payment depended on resolution of the dispute and a payoff to the Hopi. Not surprisingly, he had urged the Hopi Council to accept the earlier $5 million offer. A public relations firm was hired by the Hopi Tribal Council to portray the Navajo as interlopers on Hopi lands and bullies who had no respect for Hopi culture and religion. The Navajo failed to counter this image, and the disastrous relocation program was implemented.

Many Hopi traditionalists, who do not recognize the authority of their own Tribal Council, have sided with the traditionalist Navajo in this dispute. They are adamantly opposed to the desecration of Black Mesa and have repeatedly said that whatever land dispute exists should be settled through direct negotiation among the peoples affected. Traditional Hopi have stated that "we want no interference from outside people until we come up with a solution among ourselves as the First People on this land. We do not want any more cutting on our Sacred Homeland" (Locke 1992, 469). In 1974 a Hopi-Navajo Unity Committee was formed, calling for a reservation for traditional Hopi and traditional Navajo (Clemmer 1995, 198).

In 1977 a few Navajo women chased off fencing crews sent to implement the relocation ruling from the Big Mountain area in the JUA. That was followed by a sustained campaign of resistance, which has brought thousands of sympathizers to the Big Mountain region to join the protest. *Broken Rainbow*, a documentary film sympathetic to the Navajo resisting relocation, spread the word about the situation. In a show of intertribal support, sympathetic Lakota came from the Dakotas and began to hold an annual sun dance at Big Mountain. World attention was brought to bear on the issue, and it was identified by various international agencies, including the United Nations, as a human rights concern, alongside apartheid in South Africa.

The relocation program has been, in the judgment of impartial observers, an unmitigated disaster. Or as one Big Mountain Diné elder put it, "There is no word for relocation in the Navajo language. To relocate is to disappear and never be seen again" (Trimble 1993, 172).

By 1993, records show, 2,216 Navajo households and 26 Hopi households had been relocated. The cost of relocating these 10,000 Navajo and 109 Hopi had risen from the original estimate of $34 million to more than $500–700 million. Five years later all of the remaining eligible Hopi and almost all of the Diné had been moved. Despite the promises of new housing, those relocated were often given substandard houses in the larger communities on the reservation or in cities off the reservation. Others had lost their new homes to loan sharks. Extended families were broken up as the program focused on moving "nuclear" families. Since they were typically traditional people who had chosen to live apart from the excessive materialism of the modern world, the adjustment of those relocated did not go well. About half of the Navajo relocated by the mid–1980s had died, of "broken hearts" in the estimation of their families.

At this writing, a few Navajo remain in the Big Mountain area, determined to resist relocation, and a worldwide campaign to inspire public pressure to reverse the relocation decision continues. (For analyses of the Navajo-Hopi "Land Dispute" from various perspectives, see Clemmer 1995; Brugge 1994; Benedek 1992; Mander 1991, 265–86, Washburn 1989; Feher-Elston 1988; Redhouse 1985; Kammer 1980.)

In 1985 a new judicial system was instituted on the Navajo reservation. It included "peacemaker" courts which drew on the traditional method of resolving disputes through the mediation of a respected elder. The goal of this traditional system was to restore the harmony of the community broken by the conflict. Peacemaker courts are now settling disputes over such matters as land, vehicles, livestock, divorce, and children (Page 1995, 79).

The contemporary situation of the Navajo nation is discussed below, after an examination of traditional spirituality of the Diné.

Traditional Diné Spirituality

As is the case with other native nations, the Diné language has no word for "religion." The Navajo world is a unity; no separate sphere of life denoted by a word equivalent to *religion* exists (Kluckhohn and Leighton 1974, 179). In fact, as one nonnative interpreter has put it, "there is no such thing as religion in Navajo culture because everything is religious. Everything a Navajo knows—his shelter, his fields, his livestock, the sky above him and the ground upon which he walks—is holy." (Locke 1992, 45, 5). For traditional Navajo, there is no distinction between "natural" and "supernatural."

Introduction: The Way of Beauty (hozho)

The key concept in the traditional Navajo way of life is *hozho*, a term that defies easy translation (Witherspoon 1983b; Matthews 1897, 266; Farella 1984, 153–87; Page 1995, 35). The purpose of life, from a traditional Diné perspective, is expressed in the phrase *sa'ah naaghai bik'eh hozho*, whose words convey the notion of "the ideal completion of the life cycle at a ripe old age as a part of the active continuing recurrence of this life cycle among people and all other things, according to the dictates of *hozho*." The phrase has been distilled into English most commonly as expressing the goal of life as to "walk in *hozho*."

Hozho is usually translated as "beauty" or "beautiful." Other English words used to describe *hozho* include "perfection, harmony, goodness, normality, success, well-being, blessedness, order, ideal, do for us" (Wyman 1970, 7). It means whatever brings harmony as opposed to that which causes disorder and evil. *Hozho* is perfection insofar as humans can obtain it, the end toward which all reality is oriented (Reichard 1970, 45). Or it is "the positive or ideal environment," or the state of health that "involves a proper relationship to everything in one's environment, not just the correct functioning of one's physiology" (Witherspoon 1983b, 573). "A Navajo uses this concept to express his happiness, his health, the beauty of his land, and the harmony of his relations with others. It is used in reminding people to be careful and deliberate, and when he says good-bye to someone leaving, he will say. . . 'may you walk or go about according to *hozho*'" (Witherspoon 1983b, 570). *Hozho* appears in the names of two of the principal Navajo ceremonials: Blessingway and Beautyway (see below).

At the end of ceremonies, the phrase "It is finished in *hozho*" is said, in the certainty that the ceremony rightly conducted has been effective in restoring participants to the state of beauty/harmony. As one contemporary Diné teacher explains, "When we pray, we say 'It is finished in beauty.' We don't say, 'I hope it will be finished in beauty.' We say, 'It is'" (Trimble 1993, 128).

The opposite of *hozho* is *hocho*—the evil, disorderly, ugly (Witherspoon 1983b, 575). The dualism of these two should not be overemphasized, however;

they are not conflicting opposites as much as complementary aspects of the process that makes up the universe (Farella 1984, 31–38).

Among Native American nations, the Diné have perhaps been the most successful in retaining their traditional spirituality. Today most Navajo remain committed to the traditional ceremonials and the accompanying myths even if they have affiliated with Christian churches, the Native American Church, or other religious communities such as the Baha'i Faith. Some reasons for the persistence of traditional Diné spirituality are suggested in the conclusion to this section.

Attempts by outsiders to understand Diné spirituality have long been plagued by the biases of the observer. In 1855 a surgeon at Fort Defiance sent observations about Navajo culture to the Smithsonian Institution, writing, "[o]f their religion little or nothing is known, as, indeed, all inquiries tend to show they have none; and even have not, we are informed, any word to express the idea of a Supreme Being" (Locke 1992, 45–46).

Although other interpreters since have been less obviously prejudiced, they have continued to see and describe Navajo spirituality from their own points of view (Faris 1990, 6–24). In their study of Navajo culture, Clyde Kluckhohn and Dorothea Leighton, for example, sought to distill a Navajo "philosophy of life" with nine "premises" such as "nature is more powerful than man" and "like produces like and the part stands for the whole" (Kluckhohn and Leighton 1974, 303–14). Their work also reflects the trend characteristic of modern social scientific analysis of religion, seeking the "meaning" of Navajo myths and rituals by speculating about their social function (Kluckhohn and Leighton 1974, 224–52).

All who seek to understand Diné spirituality would do well to try to appreciate more "the richness and integrity of each individual action, practice, and ceremonial detail" (Faris 1990, 14). Hopefully, at least some of this beautiful concreteness glimmers through the following attempt to describe what to the People is not "traditional spirituality," but simply "the way of life," or the "Beautiful Rainbow" (Locke 1995, 13; Luckert 1977).

Cosmology

As James Faris has observed, the Diné

> regard the universe as an orderly, all-inclusive, unitary system of interrelated elements. The tiniest object, being, or power, even minute insects; the most stupendous, the great mountains that bound the Navajo country and the thunder and lightning that crash above them; and man himself–all have their place and significant function in the universal continuum. (Faris 1990, 14)

As an all-inclusive unity, both "good" and "evil" are part of the universe in a complementary way, as the harmonious and orderly and the disharmonious and the chaotic. Every human being has both good and evil, and the evil becomes a dangerous ghost after death. With the exception of the always benevolent Changing Woman, the Holy People are also both good and evil. Many otherwise benign aspects of the universe can become evil if they are not properly controlled. Some things—ghosts of the dead; animals such as snakes, coyote, or bear; or natural phenomena such as lightning or whirlwinds—have greater potential for evil. It is important to realize, however, that such phenomena are not evil or dangerous per se but "only if there is a sacrilegious attitude toward them, or misstatement of them, or in failing to observe the proper relationship toward them" (Faris 1990, 14). The Holy People do not cause maladies. It is human violation of the prescribed order that brings distress.

The price humans pay for disharmony (as, for example, when they have improper contact with dangerous powers or engage in prohibited behaviors such as illicit sexual activity) is illness. In his autobiography, a Navajo known as Left Handed described how he became ill after he had touched an ancient pot he had found in a cave (Dyk 1967: 64–65). Disharmonious acts by a parent can cause an unborn child to experience sickness later in life. Maintaining and restoring the harmony (*hozho*) of the universe, especially when disharmony is causing illness, is the primary purpose of the Navajo ceremonials discussed below (Wyman 1983a, 536; Witherspoon 1983b, 575; Locke 1992, 46–47; Faris 1990, 14–15).

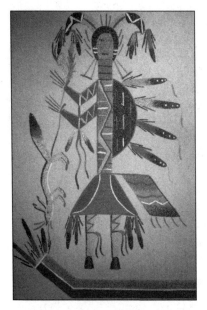

Sandpaintings (or drypaintings) are central to Diné (Navajo) healing ceremonies. (© Buddy Mays/CORBIS)

According to the Navajo conception, the universe is inhabited by two types of "people," the "Holy People" (*diyin dine'é*) and the "earth-surface people." The latter are those with five fingers and are divided into the Diné (Navajo) and non-Navajo. Non-Navajo are divided into the various native nations and nonnatives (Witherspoon 1983a, 524).

All beings (including "natural" phenomena such as earth, water, and mountains) have inner and outer forms. The inner form animates the being. These forms are humanlike in character and appearance, having independent wills. In humans the inner form is the "wind soul." The inner forms are independent of the bodies, or outer forms, they occupy. At death they leave the body and, some Navajo believe, inhabit another body (Witherspoon 1983b, 573–74).

Each being—including plants and animals—has a right to live, eat, and act for itself. "Only real and immediate human need justifies the killing of an animal or the cutting down of a tree. On such occasions a prayer should be said to the plant or animal explaining one's need and asking for the pardon and indulgence of the soul of the animal or plant" (Witherspoon 1983a, 533).

The power of thought and speech are particularly important in the Navajo worldview. As we have already seen, the world was brought into being when the Holy People thought it into existence. In the origins legend recounted in the Blessingway ceremonial, the Holy People sing, "I plan for it, when I plan for it, it drops nicely into position just as I wish" (Wyman 1970, 115) . In general, the People believe that "if one thinks of good things and good fortune, good things will happen. If one thinks of bad things, bad things will be one's lot. Among the Navajo it is believed that planning for a 'rainy day' would bring about "rainy days."

Thought (as an inner form), however, is not actualized until it is spoken (as an outer form). Behind thought (as an outer form) lies knowledge (as an inner form). Therefore, from a Navajo perspective, "knowledge is power, and the greatest power to transform or restore various conditions comes from the knowledge of various rituals acquired from the Holy People" (Witherspoon 1983b, 573, 574). Thus, at the center of the traditional Navajo worldview are the rituals, the ceremonials essential to the maintenance and restoration of *hozho*.

Gods and Spirits

The universe for the Navajo is full of spiritual beings and powers. So-called natural phenomena such as mountains and thunder have "souls," as do "material objects" such as arrows. Animals such as snakes, ants, and deer also are spiritually alive and powerful, as are plants. There are also "mythological powers" such as Water Monster, Big Snake, and almost innumerable others. The Holy People are not aloof and without emotion. Indeed, "[t]hey are described as feeling things like worry, jealousy, desire, anger, fear, and joy" (Farella 1984, 25). All are a part of and necessary for the harmonious balance of the world.

Although not central or most powerful, the most beloved Navajo "deity" is Changing Woman. As shown above, with her sons, the Hero Twins (Monster Slayer and Born of Water), and her mate, the Sun, she is prominent in Navajo origin myths. These "gods" are also pervasive in Navajo ceremonials. Changing Woman is often equated with White Shell Woman, and she is strongly associated with Earth Woman, Turquoise Woman, and Salt Woman. She is the nurturer, the provider. She has the responsibility for giving birth, and thus the increase of humans, sheep, corn, plants; almost everything is dependent on her. Changing Woman is often referred to as "my mother" or "my grandmother." She is responsible for the change of seasons, as a young girl in the spring and an old woman in the winter. Most interpreters consider her always helpful (Farella 1984, 62–64).

The first Holy People who emerged from the underworlds were First Man (Farella 1984, 39–51), First Woman, First Boy, and First Girl, who, with their companion Coyote (First Scolder), are also important. Coyote appears in some of the most beloved Navajo stories, as the "agent of disorder who arouses the need to keep things in their place." Coyote objected to allowing people to live forever, because "with perfect immortality, nothing would change and people and all other beings would cease to strive" (Willink and Zolbrod 1997, 4).

Besides Changing Woman, the other predominantly helpful Holy People include Sun, Racing Gods, First Man, First Woman, Salt Woman, Talking God, and House God. Although they are primarily helpful, First Man and First Woman also control witchcraft and can be called on by a witch to injure a victim.

The Holy People known as *Yeis*, led by Talking God, bridge the gap between the Holy People and the earth surface people (humans). They are impersonated by masked dancers in some of the ceremonials, especially the Nightway (see below).

Holy People are "holy" in the sense of powerful and awesome, not in terms of virtue. Some are mostly helpful to humans, but many are indifferent to humans and must be persuaded or coerced into helping a person who is out of harmony to restore balance.

There are also monsters (*nayéé*) in the Navajo pantheon. They are known as the Fearful or Dreadful Ones. *Nayéé* may be anything that gets in the way of a person living his/her life–old age, poverty, disease, worry, fear, jealousy, depression, paranoia. Some Diné seem to believe quite literally in the "monsters" who appear in the myths used in curing ceremonies, while others see them in a more metaphorical way as life "processes" (Farella 1984, 51–53).

Nilch'i (Holy Wind) is another key Navajo spiritual being. "Suffusing all of nature, Holy Wind gives life, thought, speech, and the power of motion to all living things and serves as the means of communication between all elements of the living world" (McNeley 1981, 1). According to the recorded origins legends, "Wind has existed as a holy being from near the beginnings of the Navajo universe, being endowed with the power to give life and movement to other beings and possessed of knowledge which it conveyed to the Holy People" (McNeley 1981, 7). As one myth puts it:

> The mists came together and laid on top of each other, like intercourse,
> and Supreme Sacred Wind was created. . . . Supreme Sacred Wind lived in
> light and black clouds or mists in space. (Fishler 1953, 9)

The Holy Wind emerged into the present world with the other Holy People and continues to provide life, thought, movement, and communication to the natural phenomena of this world (Earth, Sky, Moon, animals, and plants) and to the earth-surface people. In the words of an origins legend, speaking of the Holy Wind:

> It is the very same wind that gives those of us who dwell in the world today the breath we breathe. The trail of that very same wind can actually be seen in our fingertips to this day. The very same wind has likewise created our ancestors ever since. The very same wind continues to blow inside of us until we die. (Zolbrod 1984, 287)

Therefore, through Holy Wind the natural phenomena provide guidance and instruction to the Navajo and other earth-surface people (McNeley 1981, 14–31). From the four cardinal points, the Holy Wind joins with the winds of the two parents and enters earth-surface people during the reproductive process. It must be acknowledged, as well, that harmful winds foster bad thinking and behavior (McNeley 1981, 32–49).

Hogans

The traditional Navajo dwelling, the hogan, is "a major religious and social integrating force among the Navajo" (Cooper 1990, 71). Hogans serve as both ordinary dwellings and sacred chambers. They are a microcosm of the world. Their form came about at the beginning of creation, for creative acts took place within the "creation hogan." The area within and around a hogan is a virtual map of the Navajo worldview (Gill 1983b, 28).

Traditionally there have been two types of hogans, considered male or female depending on their shape. The conical of "forked-stick" hogan (constructed from three forked poles covered with logs, mud, and brush) is male, and the dome-shaped or cribbed-roof hogan is female. It is circular or six-sided and is made from logs or stones. The round hogan is a symbol of the sun. The door faces east so that the first thing the family sees when it arises is the sun. A smoke hole is in the center.

The conical hogan was the first construction of the present world, the home of First Man. From it radiates the creation of the entire world (Wyman 1970, 10–16). Traditionally, ceremonies were held only in conical hogans, but the Holy People blew the walls further apart to allow more room, and humans follow this example by building round hogans. The construction of a new hogan necessitates a performance of a Blessingway ceremony (Cooper 1990, 70–71).

The south side of a typical, traditional hogan is the women's; the north, the men's. The male head of the family and distinguished visitors sit on the west side facing the doorway. A hogan struck by lightning is considered *chindi* (bewitched) and is abandoned. When someone dies in a hogan, it is also deserted, and the body is removed from a hole broken on the north wall—the direction of evil.

Sweat hogans are small replicas of the conical, male hogan. At the sweat hogan the Holy People are invited to join in the bath. The bather throws dirt on the roof of the hut in order to prevent poverty (Kluckhohn and Leighton 1974, 206).

Drypainting/Sandpainting

The famous Navajo ritual art popularly known as "sandpainting" is called "drypainting" by most interpreters to reflect accurately the technique used. Most Navajo speakers, however, refer to "sandpainting" when using English (Faris 1990, 132 n. 1).

Sandpaintings are created in virtually all the ceremonials discussed below. From 500 to 1,000 separate designs have been identified by non-Navajo artists. There are thirty-five in a Red Antway ceremonial alone and as many as 100 in a Shootingway ceremonial.

The singer conducting the ceremonial (see below) directs the sandpainting but does not participate in most of it. The singer has learned the design by memory, since the keeping of permanent copies is forbidden. The painting itself is done by any men with proper knowledge of the technique. The painting is created on sand, cloth, or buckskin with sand, corn meal, flower pollen, powdered roots, stone, and bark. The painters trickle the dry pigments, holding them between their thumbs and forefingers, on a background of tan sand.

Sandpaintings are usually begun, finished, and destroyed within a twelve-hour period. The "patient" identifies with and absorbs the power of the Holy People portrayed by sitting in the midst of the painting. As Gladys Reichard put it, on the basis of her years of study of Diné spirituality, the drypaintings are "ceremonial membranes" (Trimble 1993, 152). At the completion of the sandpainting ceremony, the singer scatters the painting in the six directions and takes the remnants out of the hogan for disposal.

The paintings show the Holy People in pairs or larger multiples (to increase their power) standing on rainbowbars, which allow them to move from place to place, or on black bars, symbolic of the earth. To the experienced Navajo eye, the paintings are dynamic rather than static. The Holy People may be in human form or in the form of animals, plants, natural phenomena, or material objects. Standardized figures are used for natural phenomena, heavenly bodies, and mythological beings. There is a basic symbol of orientation, either the center in radial paintings or a foundation bar in linear paintings. In linear compositions the figures are arranged in rows; in radially oriented paintings there is a cross pattern. Sequences of color have particular meanings, and there is an encircling guardian spirit evident with an opening to the east to allow good to enter and evil to leave.

Sandpaintings outside ritual settings have "mistakes" intentionally made to avoid summoning the Holy People unnecessarily and risking their negative response. Since the 1950s Navajo artists have made permanent drypaintings for sale. Typically, only subjects that stress the attraction of good are depicted in these paintings. (For further analyses of Navajo sandpaintings, see Griffin-Pierce 1992; Parezo 1983; Wyman 1983b; Faris 1990, 109–39; Gill 1979a; Reichard 1977; Newcomb and Reichard 1975.)

Medicine Bundles (Jish)

The Navajo term *jish* may be translated as "bundle" or "pouch" (Frisbie 1987). Specifically, a "bundle" refers to "all the concrete objects that a Navajo singer uses in carrying out a ceremonial and that he usually keeps in a buckskin bag or even a commercial sugar or flour sack." "Pouch" is "a package of equipment specific for a given ceremonial" (Wyman 1983a, 548). The articles must be made in the context of a ceremonial, so the development of a complete "bundle" by a singer takes a long time. A singer's bundle is either bequeathed to his or his sister's children or buried with him.

The Ceremonials

Unlike their pueblo neighbors, the Diné have no annual ritual calendar, no religious societies, and no organized "priesthoods." Many, but not all, of the Diné ceremonials are curing rituals, for diseases actual or anticipated, performed for individuals (Spencer 1947, 12), although the community is present and the rituals affirm shared values (Cooper 1990). The central individual for whom the ceremonial is conducted, the "patient," is actually called "the one sung over." There may also be one or two secondary "patients," usually relatives of the central person. The rituals are typically performed by specialists known as *hataalii*, translated usually as "singers."

In keeping with accepted practice, the term "ceremonial" is used here to describe each ritual complex, while "ceremony" refers to the individual rites which together constitute the ceremonial. It is important to note that the numerous publications by scholars of Navajo ceremonials (e.g., Matthews, Wyman) have been shaped by their own views of reality and knowledge and must be considered "representations" rather than merely presentations of them (Faris 1990).

As discussed above, the fundamental purpose of the ceremonials is to maintain or restore *hozho* (harmony, beauty). The language of ceremonials is not descriptive; it is performative (see Gill 1981). That means the language is powerful. "It commands, compels, organizes, transforms, and restores. It disperses evil, reverses disorder, neutralizes pain, overcomes fear, eliminates illness, relieves anxiety, and restores order, health, and well-being" (Witherspoon 1983b, 575).

In general, the pragmatic purposes of the ceremonials are to restore and maintain health; to obtain wealth, the well-being of home, flocks, and fields, the security of relatives; and to acquire ceremonial property such as turquoise beads to wear as protection from dangerous powers such as lightning and snakes (Wyman 1983a, 537).

With each ceremonial there are elaborate myths of origin enacted in the songs and ritual actions. In general, there is a cosmic origin myth including the story of emergence from the underworlds and a myth related to the beginning of the particular ceremonial. Typically, the latter story relates how a hero or heroine gets himself/herself into predicaments requiring assistance from the Holy People. Often there is an injury or illness for which a ritual is necessary to restore the hero or heroine. The hero acquires the ceremonial knowledge and teaches it to the people.

Diné talk of the ceremonial system as a corn plant. The "roots" are in the underworld and refer to the stories of origins prior to emergence. The "branches" are the various ceremonials, given to the Diné by the Holy People after emergence. The main stalk, or the "backbone," is *hozho*, harmony, ceremonially expressed in the Blessingway (Farella 1984, 20).

According to Leland Wyman, one of the pre-eminent modern nonnative authorities on Navajo ceremonials, whose observations form the principal basis for this discussion:

> The Holy People, . . . attracted to the ceremonial by invocatory prayers and offerings, judge the correctness and completeness of the performance and if satisfied they are compelled by the ethic of reciprocity to come and "set things right"—to cure the patient, to restore universal harmony. Prayers and offerings in Navajo ceremonials are not for the purpose of glorifying or thanking the holy ones but are invocatory and compulsive, to attract and obligate them. (Wyman 1983a, 537)

A performance of one of the groups of ceremonials known as chantways is called a *hatal* or "sing." The term *sing* has become a general term in English for the ceremonials. The most common duration for a sing is two, five, or nine nights.

The "singers" learn ceremonials (typically only one or two, but sometimes as many as eight) by studying with older specialists, most frequently a kinsman from the father's clan, over an extended period (Newcomb 1964, 101–12). To perform a ceremonial a singer must learn "hundreds of songs, long prayers, plant medicines, material properties, symbolic drypaintings, and ritual acts" (Wyman 1983a, 538). A singer's "validation" comes when he performs the ceremonial properly with his/her teacher as a patient (Aberle 1982b, 45). Although no rule forbids it, there are few female singers, probably for fear of harming an unborn child by making a mistake in the performance of a ceremony.

In a study in the 1930s two singers spent five days out of fourteen leading ceremonials, and nearly 150 ceremonials were conducted during a six-month period on the Navajo Reservation. Adult men devoted one-fourth to one-third of their time to ceremonials and adult women one-fifth to one-sixth. People spent an average of 20 percent of their annual incomes on ceremonials (Kluckhohn 1938). While ceremonials are not as widespread today, they continue to play a significant role among the Diné.

The point has often been made by interpreters that for the ceremonial to be effective, each of the actions of the particular rites in the ceremonial must be performed without significant error. Making a mistake brings harm such as paralysis or loss of sight or hearing to the singer or to the patient(s). Indeed, when Washington Matthews, the first outsider to record ceremonials, who learned the Nightway himself as a singer, suffered a paralysis, his Navajo friends assumed that it was because he had made an error in singing the chant (Aberle 1982b, 197).

The point is not that every element must be exact, however, for "there is plentiful evidence that continual change is common" in ceremonials (Faris 1990, 104) and that singers "have considerable latitude in how they tell the story in terms of both style and content" (Gill 1981, 57). Deviations are dictated by the particular circumstances. Singers often use humor in the recitation, pausing for laughter and sometimes repeating the point for more. The creativity within Navajo ceremonials may be compared to the creativity in music or language. The notes and words are finite and principles of composition are followed. Despite these constraints, however, both music and language are open to infinite constructions, (Gill 1981, 180).

Although singers are paid by the families who hold a ceremony (up to $1,000 or more for a long ceremonial), the length of study required and fear of being accused of witchcraft has limited the number of singers.

To determine the appropriate ceremony for a particular patient's malady, when the cause is not obvious, divination is often used, through hand trembling, star gazing, and/or listening while in a trance state (Kluckhohn and Leighton 1974, 209–12). The diviners (usually women) are consulted to determine the needed ceremony or ceremonies. Tony Hillerman's novel, *Listening Woman,* describes a diviner going into a trance state to determine a proper set of ceremonials for a patient. "It was," he writes, "as if she had gone into the rock, and through it into the Black World at the very beginning—when there were only Holy People and the things that would become the Navajo were only mist" (Hillerman 1978, 11).

The causes of an illness may include natural phenomena such as lightning, wind, and thunder; animals such as bears, deer, coyotes, porcupines, snakes, eagles, and fish; coming into contact with ceremonial objects at the wrong times; ghosts of dead Navajo, foreigners, or witches (Wyman and Kluckhohn 1938, 13–14). If the illness results from a direct attack, the "weapon" or "arrow" may still be lodged in the patient. The "in-standing one" or wind of a dangerous animal, a natural phenomenon, a witch, or a ghost may have entered the person's body and become the "wind within one." In that case the curing will involve the removal of the "ugly things."

After the divination, the recommended singer is contacted, typically four days in advance of the ceremonial, and the family of the patient prepares for the sing: cleansing the hogan where the ceremonial will be performed; and securing firewood, medicinal plants, materials for the dry painting (sand, sandstone, etc.), grinding stones, baskets, buckskins, calico, and food. The singer is paid in advance. The patient is ritually prepared so that he/she can be identified with the deity whose help is sought to restore him/her to harmony with the universe. On the last night of the ceremonial, 100 or more friends may show up. Most of the patient's family are present each night.

In addition to singers, there is a class of specialists known as "curers," who perform shorter, less formal ceremonies. A special "sucking" ritual, similar to that found in other Native American spiritual traditions, may be conducted by such a curer to remove an offending object which is causing someone not to be in a state of harmony (Page 1995, 144–45).

Nearly sixty complex ceremonials, with variations, have been recorded, with about half that number performed in recent decades. Different interpreters have classified the ceremonials in several ways (see Gill 1981, 199–209) with little consensus. The pattern followed in this discussion is to distinguish three types of ceremonials, depending on how they maintain, ensure, or restore *hozho*: the Blessingway ceremonials, which maintain and reinforce *hozho* "by attracting the good and power of benevolent Holy People"; the Holyway ceremonials, which deal with potentially malevolent Holy People by transforming harmful, dangerous power into powers for good, and which are, in fact, the dominant category of the grouping of ceremonials that Wyman calls Chantways (Witherspoon 1983b, 575; Wyman 1983a, 539); and Enemyway ceremonials, which have been used "to respond to the infection caused by contact with foreigners at times of war but more recently . . . for any infection thought to be caused by foreign contact" (Gill 1981, 101).

Blessingway. The ceremonial complex known as Blessingway is, according to the Navajo singer Long Mustache, the "backbone" of traditional Navajo spirituality (Wyman 1970, 5). "One cannot overestimate its centrality in Navajo thought. It is for the Navajo synonymous with the continuation of their way of life" (Farella 1984, 32, 189). The Blessingway follows the pattern established at the time of origins (Wyman 1983a, 539–41; 1970; Gill 1981, 61–85; Mitchell 1980).

A Blessingway ritual begins at sundown and continues to dawn of the second day, thereafter and thus it is one of the shortest of Navajo ceremonials. In general, it is a ceremonial for maintaining harmony and averting evil. In other words, it is intended to assure or prevent, not to react to, a malady or misfortune.

All of the various types of rituals associated with Blessingway are designed to bring positive blessings and ensure a long, happy, and good life. Blessingways are conducted at times of new beginnings. For example, a Blessingway might be held for an unborn child to assure a good birth and a happy life for the baby.

One of the most common occasions for a Blessingway is when a young woman reaches puberty. At that time a *kinaalda* is held (cf. Frisbie 1967; Page 1995, 152–56, 160–69). During the *kinaalda* the young woman is identified with Changing Woman. Blessingways are also conducted to bring good fortune to a couple at the time of their marriage, to consecrate a new hogan, or to bless the term of a newly elected tribal officer.

A Blessingway begins with the spreading of cornmeal to consecrate the ceremonial hogan in which it is to take place. While the person being sung over holds a mountain soil bundle (a buckskin containing pinches of soil from the summits of the four sacred Navajo mountains and stone objects; cf. Wyman 1970, 20–24) in front of his/her chest, the singer offers prayers and songs. The next day begins with a ritual bath before noon, perhaps sandpaintings, and more songs and prayers. The ceremony continues through the second night with singing and closes at dawn. The one sung over leaves the ceremonial hogan, and, moving toward the east, "breathes in the dawn," which means "to become one with it" (Gill 1981, 65).

Here is an excerpt from the beginning of the Blessingway account of origins, related to First Man and First Woman's plan for creation, from the version sung by Slim Curly and recorded by Father Berard Haile:

> You see, yonder at the rim of the Emergence Place the waters had drained off, then the Winds had dried the surface of the mud. First Man and First Woman, out of earshot of everybody, were whispering to each other which they continued for four nights and days, they say. Then it seems somebody proposed to build a sweathouse. This they did, then entered the sweathouse. "Wonder what First Man and First Woman are discussing," somebody remarked, "does anybody happen to know?" It was Little Wind, one like those twister winds that speed around here, who answered, "What would they talk about but conditions as they'll be in the future?" he said. "As nights pass on there will be inner forms of all things, by which they will be living, the two say as they discuss things," he said. (Wyman 1970, 109)

At the end of every Holyway chant, and even at an Enemyway ceremonial, the following, oft-quoted final Blessingway song is sung to correct any errors made and assure the performance's effectiveness:

> *Before me may it be blessed,*
> *behind me . . . , below me . . . , above me . . . ,*
> *in all my surroundings may it be blessed,*
> *may my speech be blessed!*
> *It has become blessed again,*

It has become blessed again,
It has become blessed again,
It has become blessed again! (Wyman 1970, 337)

Holyway (Chantway). By far, the largest group of ceremonials, conducted to cure or prevent particular maladies, is called collectively chantways by many interpreters. Twenty-four chantway complexes have been catalogued, but in modern times only eight to ten are performed with any regularity (Wyman 1983a, 541–55; Locke 1992, 49–50; Gill 1981,127–37).

Diseases are in general believed to be caused by improper contact with animals, natural phenomena (especially lightning, thunder, and winds), ceremonials or the Holy People associated with them, ghosts, the dead or their possessions. In addition, witches may cause illnesses.

The Chantways still performed are dominated by the Holyway, Evilway, or Lifeway ritual patterns. Because the Holyway is the most dominant pattern in the group, it is appropriate to associate the name with the whole collection. The Holyway ritual pattern is either a Peacefulway in which the Holy People are summoned and goodness is invoked or Injuryway (also called Angryway, Fightingway, or Weaponway) in which something evil is exorcized. Virtually all Chantways include Holyway elements. Therefore, as Holyway chants those rituals still actively performed may be classified according to the following subgroups:

- Shooting Chant – Shootingway, Red Antway, Big Starway, Flintway
- Mountain Chant – Mountainway, Beautyway
- God-Impersonators – Nightway, Plumeway
- Wind Chant – Navajo Windway (Newcomb 1964, 149–52), Chiricahua Windway
- Hand-Trembling Chant – Hand-Tremblingway (Wyman 1983a, 545)

Shooting Chants are the most elaborate, using more drypaintings than other ceremonials. The symptoms usually associated with these chants are lung troubles and gastrointestinal diseases, but almost any symptom may be taken as an indicator.

The Mountainway (Wyman 1975; Matthews 1887), literally a chant towards (a place) within the mountains (Matthews 1887, 385), is associated with animals that live in the mountains: bears, porcupines, weasels, turkeys, and squirrels, to name a few. Arthritis and mental disturbances may indicate bear sickness. For example, a woman complaining of pain in her shoulder called upon a Mountainway singer because she believed she was suffering from "bear does-it-way" (Wyman 1975, 17). Kidney or bladder problems suggest porcupine disease. Skin diseases point to turkey illness, and coughing may imply squirrel disease.

The Mountainway is best known for the Dark Circle of Branches phase (Fire Dance, Corral Dance), which may take place during the nine-night performance.

This phase has been likened to "a great sacred vaudeville show" (Wyman 1975, 15) in which teams representing various Chantways put on a specialty ceremony from their ceremonial (25). The nine-night form cannot be performed before the first killing frost in the fall or after the first thunderstorm in the spring.

Beautyway (Wyman 1957) is related to snakes, lizards, frogs, and toads. Rheumatism, stomach trouble, bladder and kidney ailments, or virtually any malady may be symptoms of the need for a "snake chant," as the Beautyway is known.

The Nightway (Faris 1990; Matthews 1902; Gill 1979a; Newcomb 1964, 110–27; Kluckhohn and Leighton 1974, 207–9, 304–5, 310–11) is widely known because the last-night dances of this ceremonial have been performed publicly, outside the ceremonial context, and because the Nightway is held frequently. It has been called the crown jewel of Navajo ceremonials (Faris 1990, 79). Although a complete Nightway is nine days, shorter forms are increasingly performed.

The Nightway is "a healing practice by which human beings attempt to re-harmonize and re-order and re-balance their relationships with one another and with the Navajo universe." Compared to the Blessingway "[i]t is corrective (rather than creative), it is curative and re-establishing (not affirming and assurative), it is unchanging and remarkably rigid over time" (Faris 1990, 235–36).

The Nightway is the most demanding ceremonial for a singer to learn, with hundreds of songs, scores of prayers, dozens of sacred paraphernalia to manage, and several very complex sandpaintings. The Nightway medicine bundle is particularly difficult to put together, since it includes the God-Impersonator masks and perfect ears of corn when females are initiated (Faris 1990, 157–68). Improper behavior can lead to "*yeibichai* sickness." Only the most promising apprentices are allowed to attempt to learn it, and it is typically the last ceremonial a singer learns in his career.

The diseases cured in Nightways (emphasizing ailments of the head, including ear, eye, and mental problems, as well as paralysis) are initiated by the *Yeis* in response to some impropriety. Like the Mountainway, a nine-day Nightway may only be given between the first frost and first thunderstorm, when snakes are hibernating and there is no danger from lightning.

In the God-Impersonator chants, masked dancers impersonating the group of Holy People known as *Yeis* take part in the last night of nine-night ceremonies. The leader of the *Yeis* is Talking God, their maternal grandfather and great-uncle. In addition to Talking God, a recent study identified seventeen other Nightway holy persons (Faris 1990, 243–44). Talking God's Navajo name has been popularized as *Yeibichai*, a designation loosely applied to all the masked impersonators and to the Nightway ceremonial itself.

Navajo parents sometimes tell their children that the *Yeibichai* will come to snatch them away if they are disobedient. Left Handed remembered his parents telling him that the *Yeibichai* "have a sack into which they put the children who have disobeyed their fathers and mothers" (Dyk 1967, 34).

Against this background, on the last night of the Nightway, boys and girls, sometime between ages seven and thirteen, are initiated into ceremonial life. Two masked figures representing two of the *Yeis*, Grandfather of the Monsters and Female Divinity, appear. Each of the boys, naked to the waist, is led to the fire-light, where sacred pollen is placed on his shoulders by one of the masked beings, while another strikes him with a bundle of reeds. The girls are also marked with corn pollen. The masks are then removed and placed on each child so that the child can see the world through the eyes of the *Yei*. Then the dance begins and lasts all night. At dawn participants face the rising sun.

The most famous Nightway prayer, the Dawn Prayer, from which N. Scott Momaday drew the title for his Pulitzer-prize winning novel, *House Made of Dawn*, gives a sense of the mystery of this important ceremonial:

> *House made of dawn.*
> *House made of the dark cloud.*
> *House made of male rain.*
> *House made of dark mist.*
> *House made of female rain.*
> *House made of pollen.*
> *House made of grasshoppers.*
> *Dark cloud is at the door.*
> *The trail out of it is dark cloud.* (Gill 1983, 55–56)

The Evilway pattern (also called Ghostway or Uglyway; cf. Gill 1981, 119–25) is conducted when the patient has been struck by lightning, has been bitten by a snake, or has experienced some other type of "attack." It also serves to treat ill-nesses caused by ghosts or witchcraft. This ceremonial pattern involves such procedures as blackening the patient or blowing ashes. The Shootingway (Haile 1950 and 1947), Red Antway (Wyman 1965; Page 1995, 119–21, 127–37), Big Starway, and Hand-Tremblingway are among the particular rituals where some of the chants may be performed according to the Evilway pattern. The indications for ghost sickness or suffering from a witch's action include "bad dreams, insomnia, fainting, nervousness, mental disturbances, feelings of suffocation, loss of appetite, loss of weight or other alarming disturbances" (Wyman 1983a, 542).

In Evilway ceremonies participants divide into two main groups: those organized around the main patient and those around the "stick-receiver." Within the two groups there is *ké* (kindness, love) and a sharing of the costs of the ceremonial. Between the two groups there is reciprocity, with an exchange of gifts (Witherspoon 1983a, 524–25).

Elements of Shootingway chants are performed according to the Lifeway ritual pattern (Gill 1981, 87–99). Lifeway "is concerned with restoration or recreation on the occasions when imbalance and disorder result from the dynamic life processes" (Gill 1981, 98). At one time, these chants were sung for patients who suffered injuries received from lightning, arrows, or snakes. Today they are indicated by any type of accidental injury, and they include elements of all three ritual patterns (depending on circumstances). A chant with Lifeway elements is the Flintway (Haile 1943). In the Lifeway ritual pattern the patient is painted red, to symbolize a return to health and life.

A chant that has cured a person should be given for him a total of four times, usually in alternate five-night and two-night forms. This is reflective of the traditional Navajo belief that "repeating something four times will cause it to occur" (Witherspoon 1983b, 572).

Enemyway. Traditionally, the primary purpose of the Enemyway has been to protect Navajo warriors from ghost sickness they may have contracted while engaging in battle and killing enemies. For example, Enemyways were used extensively for Navajo members of the U.S. armed forces returning from the Persian Gulf War in the early 1990s (Page 1995, 122). They may also be conducted in relationship to any exposure to non-Navajo people or anything foreign. For example, Diné who marry non-Navajo sometimes are sung over with this ceremonial (Haile 1938a; Gill 1981, 101–17; Kluckhohn and Leighton 1974, 222–23).

In the Enemyway ceremony for the purpose of exorcizing alien ghosts, a female virgin carries a special staff. This rite became known to outsiders as the Squaw Dance, because in the evenings of the ceremonial girls choose male partners for a dance. Today the "Squaw Dance" portion of the Enemyway has become a popular social occasion, observed by many non-Navajo.

Daily Rituals

In addition to the array of complex ceremonials, most traditional Diné engage in what might be called daily rituals. For example, the day begins for them with the sprinkling of corn pollen and a morning prayer. After the evening meal, family members rub their limbs and say, "May I be lively. May I be healthy." More pollen may be offered and a Blessingway song performed. Throughout the day, each activity is accompanied by appropriate songs, prayers, and actions. A squirrel's tail may be tied to a baby's cradle, for example, to protect it in case of a fall (Kluckhohn and Leighton 1974, 203).

Naming

After birth a Navajo baby is called "baby boy" or "baby girl" until the child exhibits a distinguishing characteristic or an unusual mark is noted on the baby's body. This is used as a nickname throughout the person's life, or until another name takes its place.

Shortly after birth a formal naming ceremony is held. At that time, a ceremonial or "war" name is given. It is generally kept secret, known only to the person's immediate family.

Traditional Diné consider it bad manners to address a person by his name in his presence, using instead kinship terms. Since World War II all Diné children have been given English names (Kluckhohn and Leighton 1974, 114–17).

Death

It is a mistake to say that the Navajo fear death, a comment often made by outside observers. For example, Kluckhohn and Leighton claimed that "[d]eath and everything connected with it are horrible to The People" (Kluckhohn and Leighton 1974, 184). Rather, Diné "have a tremendous respect for life, and an avoidance of the dead, not a fear of death" (Witherspoon 1983b, 571).

At death the breath or wind of life departs the body. The body is buried as quickly as possible, and there is no coming together of the family. Precautions are taken, for, if not, the dead return as ghosts. For example, as noted, when someone dies in a hogan, a hole is opened in the north side of the hogan for the removal of the body, and the hogan is sealed up. It is a violation of a taboo to enter a "death hogan."

Since life is seen as a cycle that reaches a natural conclusion with death in old age and is renewed with each new birth, premature death is thought to be unnatural. It must have been caused by some evil force (Witherspoon 1983b, 571).

It is accurate to say that there is no glorious afterlife in the Navajo worldview. The afterworld is a shadowy place, located to the north, below the surface of the earth. It is reached after a four-day journey, down a trail. The dead may return to the earth as ghosts to avenge an offense or neglect. They appear at night "in human form or as coyotes, owls, mice, whirlwinds, spots of fire, or indefinite dark objects." They may change forms. Their appearance is an omen of something bad about to happen (Kluckhohn and Leighton 1974, 184–87).

Witchcraft

"The Navahos believe that by witchcraft evil men and women, acting separately or in a group, can obtain property and produce the illness or death of those who they hate" (Kluckhohn and Leighton 1974, 187). Witches are called "wolves," because they often wear the hide of a wolf or a coyote. Hence, they are also called "skinwalkers." The primary motivations for becoming a skinwalker seem to be the acquisition of personal wealth and/or obtaining revenge.

Even the most assimilated Navajo are likely to maintain a belief in (or at least caution about) the efficacy of witchcraft. They are concerned about both witches and the possibility of a charge that they are themselves skinwalkers.

Navajo witches may use any of four techniques against their victims: (1) a "corpse poison" made from powdered human flesh, fed or blown into the victim's face; (2) spells, particularly over something associated with the victim; (3) magically shooting a small object like a bone from a corpse or bit of ash from a hogan where someone has died into the body of the victim; or (4) a narcotic plant, used primarily in seducing women, in gambling, or in trading. The symptoms displayed by a victim of witchcraft include fainting, seizures, sudden pain, emaciation, or a lump where a foreign object has been implanted (Kluckhohn and Leighton 1974, 187).

Traditional Navajo take care with such personal items as nail clippings, hair, feces, even their real Navajo names, lest they fall into the hands of a witch who might use them as the one sung over in an evil use of the rituals. One should be careful about shaking hands with a stranger, because you do not know if he or she is a witch. Even a footprint in the snow can be used by a witch (Page 1995, 123).

While certain herbs may be used to treat an illness brought on by witchcraft, the principal antidote is a ceremonial such as the Enemyway (see above). If the victim is successful in resisting the witch's techniques, the evil will backfire on the witch, who will die within a year.

According to Clyde Kluckhohn, Navajo witchcraft has served as a social sanction on undesirable activities and a check on leaders who are afraid of acting as despots lest they be accused of being witches and have witchcraft directed against them (Kluckhohn 1962, 112–21; Kluckhohn and Leighton 1974, 240–52). It has also served as a levelling device. The poor are treated with generosity lest they bewitch those who do not share, and the rich act with generosity lest they be accused of being witches.

Weaving

Diné weavers believe that the Navajo were first taught the art of weaving and shown basic patterns by two Holy People, Spider Woman and Spider Man. Spider Woman, who lives on Spider Rock in Canyon de Chelly, taught the women how to weave on a loom made by her husband, Spider Man. She is "a symbol of the tradition of passing on knowledge from mother to daughter" (Parezo 1996, 20).

Like other ritual activities there are special songs, prayers, and taboos associated with weaving. Until traders refused to buy such blankets, Navajo weavers often left a hole in the middle of their weavings following the example of the Spider People (Willink and Zolbrod 1997, 38, 40).

Diné weavers, who are by tradition women, represent myths of the people in an abstract manner. (© The Purcell Team/CORBIS)

Diné weavers believe that in their work they are re-enacting the creation of earth and sky, which proceeded upward from the underworlds. Many rugs reflect elements of the creation story (Willink and Zolbrod 1997, 2, 14–15, 42–45).

Some weavers still include a "spirit outlet" in their patterns, usually a thin line from the center of the blanket to the outer edge. Those who do this believe that leaving it out would cause them to contract "blanket sickness" by weaving cobwebs in their heads.

After the Spanish introduced sheep to the Diné, wool was used in weaving. Navajo rugs became, and continue to be, a principal trade item for the Diné. The classic period of weaving was during the mid–1800s. During and after the Long Walk and captivity at Bosque Redondo, Navajo weavers began incorporating their historical experiences into the symbolism of their rugs. In some rugs mythic themes such as the perilous journey of the warrior twins were combined with the suffering of the Long Walk (Willink and Zolbrod 1997, 47–57).

The use of traditional designs declined late in the nineteenth century when traders introduced chemical dyes and bought weavings by the pound, resulting in less careful workmanship. In the 1930s, however, Navajo weavers returned to the use of traditional dyes, designs, and techniques. Diné College teaches weaving to women who did not learn it from their elders. Each blanket or rug is unique, reflective of styles related to particular communities and the imagination of the artists.

A traditional prayer that often accompanies weaving expresses the spiritual understanding Navajo weavers have of their work:

*With me there is beauty (*hozho*),*
in me there is beauty,
from me beauty radiates. (Willink and Zolbrod 1997, 8)

The making of the rug is itself an act of *hozho*. As Louise Lincoln has observed, "The piece is merely the vehicle whereby beauty, *hozho*, is transmitted from an artist, who is himself or herself in a state of beauty, to a recipient or audience, who will in some measure be brought into a state of beauty through viewing, wearing, or appreciating what the artist has been doing and made" (cited in Parezo 1996, 20).

Christianity among the Diné

By the mid-twentieth century the following major Christian denominations had active missions in Navajoland: Presbyterians, Episcopalians, Methodists, Baptists, and Roman Catholics (Franciscans). In addition, the Church of Jesus Christ of Latter-day Saints had long been present. Other, independent Christian churches were also seeking converts. By 1942 there were 300 Christian workers on the reservation, and the number grew rapidly after World War II (Kluckhohn and Leighton 1974, 132).

Diné have made extensive use of the various social services provided by Christian churches, especially hospitals and schools. As noted in the historical overview, however, the success of Christian missionaries in terms of numbers of converts has been limited. Those Navajo who did convert were mostly dependent on the missions for their livelihood. Christianity seems to most Diné a "part-time" religion, where God is available only for a few hours a week in a house where his spirit dwells. It also speaks of a faraway holy land, whereas the Navajo are living in the midst of a land they know to be holy. Christian missionaries describe God as male to Navajo, who know one of their principal deities to be a woman (Changing Woman). The idea that God is wholly good is also troublesome to Navajo who grow up believing the Holy People to have both good and evil tendencies. Indeed, the idea of a single, all-powerful God is not easy for Navajo to grasp.

The exclusivism of some Christians has bothered many Diné. Until fairly recently most Christian missionaries tried, subtly or more overtly, to suppress the ceremonials. Some Christian schools sought nothing less than to exterminate traditional Navajo culture.

Many Navajo who have become Christians continue to observe traditional spiritual practices and see no inconsistency in doing so. A study of religious affiliation in a portion of the western Navajo Reservation (Wood 1982, 177) found that only a few households listed a single religious affiliation; 53 percent gave two or more, and about 14 percent listed three. Many Navajo see no contradiction in being a traditionalist and a peyotist and a Christian all at the same time. Susanne and Jake Page describe an eighty-year-old hand-trembler being baptized as a Roman Catholic. The Navajo they have met prefer to add religions rather than switch (Page 1995, 147).

Native American Church (Peyote Religion)

The historical section of this chapter touches on the influence of and controversy over the use of peyote among the Navajo. Chapter 7 explores more fully the peyote movement that has spread across Native America in the past century and has taken institutional form as the Native American Church. In this chapter are described the particular characteristics of "peyote religion among the Navajo," as its primary interpreter, David Aberle, has called it, especially in relationship to traditional Diné spirituality.

Aberle takes the position that among the Navajo "peyote religion" is a nativistic movement originating in "the relative deprivation engendered by the domination of one group by another which possesses an alien and more powerful culture" (Aberle 1982a, 23). In his major work he outlines the deprivations experienced by the Diné and tries to explain how the peyote movement enabled thousands of Navajo to cope with this situation. He has been criticized for putting too much emphasis on "deprivation theory" and overlooking the role of peyotism in the "acculturation" of the Navajo in the past half century (e.g., Voget 1968).

In the early 1970s the approximately 60,000 Navajo who used peyote ritually were members either of the Native American Church of Navajoland (associated with the international Native American Church of North America) or the Native American Church of the Four Corners or the Northern Navajoland Native American Church Association. Some belonged to more than one. The purpose of the organized peyote churches has principally been to stand in opposition to attempts to make peyote illegal. They make no effort to impose a particular form of worship, nor do they "ordain" the Roadmen who conduct peyote services (Aberle 1983, 558–59).

There are indications of peyotists drawing on aspects of traditional Navajo spirituality in their rituals. For example, Navajo peyotists use the Navajo term for medicine, *azee*, when they speak of peyote (Aberle 1983, 559). "Medicine" is the entire complex of ritual that is brought to bear to use supernatural power for the benefit of the sick. Like all peyotists, they consider peyote, and the ritual in which it is used, to be "medicine," and, as such, a gift from God.

Aberle concludes, however, that "[t]here is little indication that traditional Navajo religious belief and ritual have had any major influence on Navajo Peyotist belief and ritual, or that the reverse has occurred" (Aberle 1983, 563).

Navajo peyote meetings typically focus, like traditional ceremonials, on a particular "patient," for whom the ritual is held. Someone sponsors the meeting, typically the family of the patient. Aberle's study has suggested, however, that Navajo peyote meetings follow the typical pattern of peyote meetings in other nations (Aberle 1983, 559–62).

The rapid spread of peyotism among Navajo in recent decades has come, in Aberle's assessment, as a result of disruption in the natural and social order. The natural order has been disrupted by rapid population growth and the federal government's pressure to decrease livestock. Social disruption occurred as a result of a breakdown of kinship reciprocity (although this assertion has been challenged by other researchers), mostly in response to external pressures such as the need to turn to wage labor as herds were reduced. There was also a rise in alcoholism. In Aberle's view, peyotism helped people cope with these disruptions; he asserted, for example, that peyotism "permitted men to feel a little less bound by kinship and a little more responsible for their own immediate affairs" (Aberle 1982a, 202). He moderated this claim in the second edition of the work, however, in response to critics. Peyotism also provided a morality rooted in individual commitment and experience at a time when the moral influence of tradition was declining.

On the basis of his research, Aberle concludes that many Navajo—both traditionalists and modernists—oppose the use of peyote because it "represents something utterly alien—something that neither perpetuates the old nor aligns them usefully with the new. It is a threat to Navaho religion as Christianity is not, because it is a curing religion. It is a threat as well because it introduces something Indian but not Navaho" (Aberle 1982a, 223). It also has been actively opposed by some missionaries and Navajo Christians, who see it as a form of paganism, and by physicians, who see it as a threat to their medical work.

Noted above are some of the actions of the Tribal Council against the use of peyote during the 1940s and 50s and the gradual turn toward support of the rights of Navajo members of the Native American Church in the 1960s. The spread of fundamentalist Christianity on the reservation has also resulted in opposition to peyotism (Dologhan and Scates 1978).

At present, a significant number of Navajo (perhaps a majority) are either active members of the Native American Church or participate sporadically in peyote rituals. As Aberle has put it in the conclusion to his decades of research on peyotism among the Diné:

> The beautiful ritual of the Native American Church, its moral code, its effort to maintain community against the corrosive atomization of Indian groups, its significance as a vehicle for Indian identity, and its ways of reacting to Indian deprivation are likely to make it appeal to Navajo people and to give meaning to the lives of tens of thousands of Navajo for many years to come. (Aberle 1982, xlviii)

Challenges to Traditional Diné Spirituality

Although the vast majority of Navajo remain committed to their traditional spirituality (even if they are members of Christian churches or the Native American Church), until recently there was a declining number of Diné willing to study to become singers. "Learning a traditional ceremony is a long and financially burdensome affair which does not carry the same high reward and status as it did in the past" (Cooper 1990, 78). Without trained singers the ceremonials essential to the continuation of traditional spirituality are in jeopardy.

Thirty years ago a survey of Navajo students showed that while most believed in the importance and effectiveness of the ceremonials, very few were willing to commit to the long process necessary in becoming a practitioner. Readers of Tony Hillerman's popular novels set on the Navajo Reservation have been introduced to that dilemma in the character of Jim Chee, a Navajo tribal policeman struggling to find the time to learn to become a singer while continuing his career in law enforcement (e.g., Hillerman 1978, 1989).

Some signs, however, suggest that the situation is improving. In response to the threat to the continuation of the ceremonials, programs to educate Navajo singers were introduced, to supplement the more informal apprenticeship system. Most noted was the apprenticeship program sponsored by the Rough Rock Training School for Medicine Men and Women (Bergman 1973). Although it is no longer functioning, it did produce a number of apprentices. Today Diné College has a Native Healing program which potential singers may attend. At best, these programs have introduced young people to the traditional prayers and songs, and have connected aspiring singers with experienced practitioners.

As a result, the Blessingway is still popular and widely practiced, as are the Nightway and Enemyway. It was estimated that in the late 1980s there were as many active Nightway singers as at any time in Navajo history. In the mid–1980s there were at least eighteen active singers. Some Nightways were being scheduled as much as two years in advance. God-Impersonator teams were busier than ever, traveling throughout Navajoland to dance at Nightway final night ceremonies. It is still difficult to attract Nightway apprentices, however, because the monetary rewards are not great given the commitment necessary (Faris 1990, 80–101, 237).

In order to attract more singers, the suggestion has been made "to shorten and simplify the ceremonials and to use some learning aids such as taking notes of ceremonial songs or using tape recorders" (Wyman 1983a, 536). Whether that can be done without undermining the power of the ceremonials is an issue being considered by experienced Diné singers. Because there is no formal regulating authority, change will come if it is accepted and considered in continuity with tradition.

The demise of traditional Navajo spirituality has been erroneously predicted many times. Early in this century missionaries claimed that the ceremonials were all but extinct. As recently as 1964 the vanishing of most, if not all, Navajo ceremonialism was believed to be near (Wyman 1965, 7). And a 1990 study suggested that "the number of traditional ceremonials practiced will decrease" (Cooper 1990, 78).

Today it is clear, however, that not only are a significant number of ceremonials very much alive, but also the worldview on which they rest. One of the principal reasons is the persistence of the Navajo language. Until World War II, English had not been extensively adopted by Navajo, and a half century later Navajo was still the principal language among most Diné. Although the percentage of Navajo who speak Navajo fluently is declining, in 1987 there were still 125,000 fluent speakers on the reservation (Trimble 1993, 126). As in all cultures, language relates to the ways the Diné perceive and construct reality (Witherspoon 1977). It continues to serve as a unifying force among the Diné (Cooper 1990, 70).

In addition, the continued use of the hogan, which, according to Navajo mythology, is a microcosm of the universe and is located at the center of the world, ties Navajo to their traditional spirituality. Finally, for each native nation, spirituality is rooted in the land, and the fact that most Navajo still live within the sacred mountains ties them together and roots them in their identity.

As noted, Navajo do not speak of religion; rather, they talk of "the way," the "beauty way." It is still a path most Navajo are seeking to walk in their own quest for harmony. The prayer offered at the close of many ceremonials still echoes across Navajoland:

> *In beauty may we dwell.*
> *In beauty may we walk.*
> *In beauty may our male kindred dwell.*
> *In beauty may our female kindred dwell.*
> *In beauty may it rain on our young men.*
> *In beauty may it rain on our young women.*
> *In beauty may it rain on us.*
> *In beauty may our corn grow.*
> *In the trail of pollen may it rain.*
> *In beauty all around us, may it rain.*
> *In beauty may we walk.*
> *The beauty is restored.*
> *The beauty is restored.*
> *The beauty is restored.*
> *The beauty is restored.* (Tome 1983, 683)

The Diné Today

According to a Navajo creation story, after the joining of the last clan, "Henceforth the People were to increase their numbers and their strength from within. But their existence as a tribe was secure. They flourish on the surface of the fifth world to this

very day, it is said" (Zolbrod 1984, 339). Indeed, the Diné today are generally perceived by both Euroamericans and many other native peoples as the wealthiest
Native American nation because of the tribal income from natural resources. If the
yearly income from leases for oil, gas, and other resources were distributed annually to each Navajo person, however, the check would be only $200. Unemployment
today in Navajoland hovers near 50 percent. And the income from resource leases
will not last forever. As Tribal Chairman Peterson Zah put it in the early 1990s,
"Someday the coal, oil, and gas are going to be gone. What's going to happen to
the Navajo children then?" (Trimble 1993, 194).

A concern of many Navajo leaders is the demonstrable loss of economic self-
sufficiency among the Diné. One study showed that self-sufficiency declined
from 100 percent in 1920 to less than 5 percent in the 1990s (Churchill and
LaDuke 1992, 244–45). As anthropologists Klara Kelly and Peter Whiteley have
put it, "The Navajo Tribe is forced to beat the clock of dwindling natural
resources by cranking up a self-sustaining economy with one hand, while the
other is tied behind its back, dispensing welfare and jobs" (Trimble 1993, 194).

About half of the approximately 230,000 Navajo are youths (Page 1995, 50).
Navajo leaders have pinned hopes for the future of the Diné on education for
twenty-first-century jobs, and they have sought corporate support for educational programs to achieve that end. The need to improve opportunities for young
people is particularly urgent. Of concern in the last few years had been the
increase of crime associated with youth gangs on the reservation (see chapter 9).

Traditionalists believe that only through walking in *hozho* will the Diné live
in harmony with one another, with other peoples, and with the rest of nature.
Certainly, the ability of the Diné to honor tradition while adapting to changing
circumstances has been demonstrated in the past. Whether the majority of
Navajo can find the balance between the two in the twenty-first century remains
to be seen. As one Navajo leader put it, "Sure, we'd like to see a personal computer in every hogan on the reservation. We just want them programmed to think
Navajo" (Page 1995, 82).

More and more typical today are Diné who are like an administrator of the
college scholarship program for the Navajo nation. She appears to be thoroughly
assimilated, dressing in business clothes. Nevertheless, she is a committed traditionalist who knows and participates in ceremonials. She also attends Christian
church services from time to time and celebrates Christian holidays. When she
was asked by mountain climber Jim Whitaker to "stop" the windstorm that was
devastating his Mount Everest expedition in 1992, she replied that the wind could
never be stopped, but perhaps it could be moved. After her prayers, the skies
cleared over Everest just as a windstorm blew down huge trees at Whitaker's home
in Port Townsend, Washington (Page 1995, 141–46).

Some interpreters suggest that Navajo individualism, the respect for the freedom of individuals, will enable the Diné to find their own way in the future.

Others have focused on the communal and cooperative nature of the Diné as the key ingredient for future well-being. In fact, "both individualism and communalism operate in Navajo social organization, but they are more complementary than contradictory." The Diné are flexible and pragmatic and thus have been able to maintain their basic cultural values while adapting to changing circumstances (Witherspoon 1983a, 533; Cooper 1990).

One Navajo has recently compared the Diné to a tree that puts on a new growth ring every year: The tree has an essential, unchanging core, but it must react to external circumstances, absorbing what it must to continue and rejecting other influences which will harm it. Sometimes the rings show years of good growth; sometimes they show hardships. But the tree remains the same, in continuity with its roots. And it keeps on growing (Page 1995, 141–42).

Or as Harry Walters, curator of the museum at Diné College, put it, "You often hear: 'All the old ways are gone.' In some ways, this is true. Yet we are still Navajo. The language may be a little different, ceremonies a little different. We may use a pickup instead of a horse to carry the ceremonial wand on the first day of Enemyway. Nevertheless, we are still a unique people" (Trimble 1993, 122).

PART III

Pannational Movements and Other Issues

CHAPTER 6

The Ghost Dance: The Coming of a New World

When the sun died, I went up to heaven and saw God and all the people who died a long time ago. God told me to come back and tell my people they must be good and love another, and not fight, or steal, or lie. He gave me this dance to give to my people.

—Wovoka, Ghost Dance prophet (1890)

PEOPLE OF VARIOUS CULTURES when threatened with the destruction of their traditional ways of life have responded with enthusiasm to visionaries who offer hope of a "new age" in which they will return to the lost glory. Some twentieth-century anthropologists studying indigenous peoples have used the term "revitalization" to describe movements in these cultures that arise at times of extreme threat. For example, in the late nineteenth century in Melanesia in the South Pacific, so-called "cargo cults" developed. Colonial powers and missionaries had come to the area, and the traditional ways of life of indigenous peoples on Fiji and other islands were under pressure. The colonial trade goods introduced became known as "cargo." The word expanded to refer to the good life the people longed for, a "new age" in which they would enjoy the harmony and fullness of life they associated with the Europeans. The belief that the spirits would bestow goodness on the people, if they showed proper reverence for the spirits, was deeply rooted in the myths and rituals of these cultures. Often, a prophetic figure was associated with the revelation of the new age.

As noted in previous chapters, a number of Native American visionary prophets and prophecies have played important roles: Tenskwatawa, the Shawnee Prophet; Handsome Lake and his "Good Message" teaching among the

Hotinonshonni (Iroquois); Neolin, the Delaware Prophet; the prophets associated with the ghost dances of the Cherokee in the Southeast during the early decades of the nineteenth century; the prophecies among the Lakota and the Hopi; and the late-nineteenth-century prophet in the Northwest, Smohalla and his Prophet Dance (see Miller 1985).

In the late nineteenth century in North America a new movement arose among native nations. It was later called the "Ghost Dance" (or "Spirit Dance") by participants and those who observed and wrote about it.

This chapter first relates the history of the Ghost Dance movements of 1870 and especially 1890. The spread of the Ghost Dance throughout a number of native nations is noted, but the principal focus is on the Lakota adaptation of the Ghost Dance on their South Dakota reservations and the issue of the relationship between the Ghost Dance and the tragedy at Wounded Knee on 29 December 1890 (see chapter 4). This historical review concludes with the revival of the Ghost Dance in Canada, during the reoccupation of Wounded Knee in 1973, and again a year later on the Lakota Rosebud Reservation in South Dakota.

After the historical review are descriptions of the myth(s) underlying the Ghost Dance and several manifestations of the Ghost Dance ritual in various contexts. Turning to the extensive body of interpretation of the significance of the Ghost Dance, this chapter analyzes the following issues: James Mooney's perspective on the Ghost Dance, the relationship between the Church of Jesus Christ of Latter-day Saints (the Mormons) and the Ghost Dance movement, and the range of theories of the meaning of this pannational movement advanced during the past century.

Historical Overview

Wodziwob and the 1870 Ghost Dance

By 1870 the Northern Paiutes of Nevada were in a desperate situation. In 1867 a typhoid epidemic and other diseases wiped out one-tenth of the Walker River Paiutes. The next spring measles took a toll on children. The main food source was fish, and the lakes on which the people depended were nearly fished out. Furthermore, the game had been decimated. In 1869 a drought dried up the pine nuts and seeds the Paiutes gathered. Like many other native peoples during this period, the traditional way of life of the Northern Paiutes seemed to be vanishing.

That same year a twenty-five-year-old Paiute man known to Euroamerican settlers in the region as Fish Lake Joe, whose Paiute name was Wodziwob ("gray hair"), had a vision in which he was told that if Indians began round dances at night, the world would be renewed in the spring of 1871. He said he had been taken to another world where he was told that the dead would soon return, and that the disappearing animals would reappear and the old way of life among the Paiutes would be revived.

The movement spread throughout native peoples in California (see Du Bois 1939; and Beck and Walters 1977, 180–84), and possibly into Oregon or Washington. In California the dance enabled communities torn apart by the genocidal assault of the settlers to regroup and find a new basis for hope for the future. Many of the beliefs and practices that crystallized among California peoples as a result of the 1870 Ghost Dance movement continue to this day in communities of native peoples (Hultkrantz 1987, 545; Kehoe 1989, 32–34; Oesterreich 1991, xii–xiii).

Wovoka and the 1890 Ghost Dance

One of Wodziwob's apostles was Tavibo ("white man"), who was himself a full-blood Northern Paiute. Tavibo was a "weather doctor," which meant he had developed the ability to call on spiritual power to master the weather. His son, Wovoka ("The Cutter"), like many other Paiutes, as a young man went to work for a rancher who was settling in Mason Valley, Nevada. The rancher was a devout Presbyterian named David Wilson, and Wovoka was given the name Jack Wilson. He learned some English and had some exposure to the Christian views of the Wilsons.

In about 1880 Wovoka went to work in the hop fields of Oregon, Washington, and northern California, with Indians from scores of other nations. He learned about the customs of other native cultures, and probably heard of Indian prophets who had received visions of a new and glorious future. One was Smohalla ("The Preacher," see chapter 1). The themes of Smohalla's visions were typical of those received by earlier Native American prophets, namely that native peoples should not adopt the Euroamericans' ways. They should not plow and mine the living earth, but rather take only what the earth gave freely, he had been told. Smohalla started holding rituals in which he incorporated elements of Roman Catholicism with indigenous beliefs. He continued to receive messages from the Creator while in trance states (Kehoe 1989, 34–35).

By 1888 Wovoka had returned to Mason Valley, where he started a family and resumed work for the Wilsons. A series of earth tremors were felt throughout the year. During a solar eclipse (probably on 1 January 1889) Wovoka fell asleep and was taken to the "other world." A rancher said that Wovoka had the vision while he was very ill (Mooney 1965 [1896], 15).

Wovoka told ethnologist James Mooney, who visited him in 1892, that in his vision he had seen the Supreme God and all the people who had died long ago enjoying the old way of life. God told him to go back and tell his people to be good and love one another, "have no quarrelling and live in peace with the whites; that they must work, and not lie or steal; that they must put away all the old practices that savored of war; that if they faithfully obeyed his instructions they would at last be reunited with their friends in this other world where there would be no more death or sickness or old age" (Mooney 1965 [1896], 14).

This was the message Wovoka consistently gave to Euroamericans: that a reunion with ancestors would take place in heaven if the people lived moral lives consistent with Christian teaching. To Indians he said that the dead would return and the old way of life would be revived on earth, not in the "other world."

To both groups Wovoka said that God had given him a round dance to be performed for five days at intervals of about six weeks. This would bring happiness to the dancers and hasten the coming of the promised life. Wovoka adamantly denied that he taught hostility against whites, saying "his religion was one of universal peace." He said he himself thought it best for Indians to adopt white man's ways and civilization. He himself dressed like a white man and worked for a white rancher, and he was widely known by his "Christian" name—Jack Wilson (Mooney 1965 [1896], 14).

Despite these protestations, however, Wovoka was in fact dedicated to the traditional Paiute way of life. He lived in the traditional Paiute lodge called a *wickiup*, although he could have afforded a cabin. Though he wore "white" clothes, he minimized his own use of non-Paiute materials. Before his vision he had already become a "weather doctor" as his father was, leading traditional circle dances in which the Paiute people opened themselves to spiritual power (Kehoe 1989, 3–5).

As word of the new prophet spread to other native nations, hundreds of representatives began to come to his home to receive his instruction and experience the new dance themselves. Mormon settlers from the surrounding region also came, wondering whether Wovoka was the Messiah Joseph Smith had prophesied would appear in 1890 (see below).

Wovoka impressed the visitors with his ability to alter the weather. He is said to have caused ice to fall from the sky in July and water to appear in an empty container during a drought. He would also go into trances to receive new revelations in front of the visitors. Once he demonstrated his invulnerability by allowing his younger brother to shoot him with a shotgun shell full of dust and sand. His shirt was riddled with holes, but he was unhurt.

Some of the Indians who came to see Wovoka were skeptical, but most became devoted to Wovoka and his dance. They would join in dances that typically lasted four days, ending on the fifth morning, when the dancers shook out their blankets and shawls to rid themselves of evil. Using a familiar technique, during the dance Wovoka would often wave eagle feathers (symbolic of a flight to heaven) in front of a dancer's face to induce a trance.

Wovoka would typically send delegations back with some of the red paint he used in the dances he conducted, painted magpie feathers, pine nuts, and robes of woven strips of rabbit fur. From Indian Territory southern Arapaho and Cheyenne delegates made several visits. In August 1891 they received from Wovoka a message which has become known as "The Messiah Letter." In Mooney's free rendering, it reads as follows:

When you get home you must make a dance to continue five days. Dance four successive nights, and the last night keep up the dance until the morning of the fifth day, when all must bathe in the river and then disperse to their homes. You must all do in the same way.

I, Jack Wilson, love you all, and my heart is full of gladness for the gifts you have brought me. When you get home I shall give you a good cloud [rain?] which will make you feel good. I give you a good spirit and give you all good paint. I want you to come in three months, some from each tribe there [the Indian Territory].

There will be a good deal of snow this year and some rain. In the fall there will be such a rain as I have never given you before.

Grandfather says, when your friends die you must not cry. You must not hurt anybody or do harm to anyone. You must not fight. Do right always. It will give you satisfaction in life. . . .

Do not tell the white people about this. Jesus is now upon the earth. He appears like a cloud. The dead are alive all again. I do not know when they will be here; maybe this fall or in the spring. When the time comes there will be no more sickness and everyone will be young again.

Do not refuse to work for the whites and do not make any trouble with them until you leave them. When the earth shakes [at the coming of the new world] do not be afraid. It will not hurt you.

I want you to dance every six weeks. Make a feast at the dance and have food that everybody may eat. Then bathe in the water. That is all. You will receive good words again from me some time. Do not tell lies. (Mooney 1965 [1896], 23)

The Ghost Dance was embraced by Wovoka's own people, the Northern Paiutes. The movement quickly spread to neighboring peoples, including other Paiutes, the Utes, Shoshoni, and Washo in western Nevada. To the west it spread to native peoples in California and to the south to Arizona Mohave, Cohonino, and Pai (Dobyns and Euler 1967). To the east, in addition to the Arapaho and Cheyenne, the Ghost Dance was taken up by Assiniboin, Gros Ventre (Atsina), Mandan, Arikara, Pawnee, Caddo, Kichai, Wichita, Kiowa, Kiowa-Apache, some Comanche, Delaware, and Oto peoples. The Ghost Dance was embraced both in the Northern Plains and among those in these nations living by this time in Indian Territory. As discussed below, its adoption by the Lakota was the most famous and tragic development.

Although Wovoka never called himself anything but a prophet in his public statements or sometimes a messiah or messenger from God, as Jesus had been in his time, some of his disciples began proclaiming that he was the Son of God, Jesus Christ returned for the Indians (Kehoe 1989, 5–6; Hultkrantz 1987, 545). They said that he bore the nail prints on his hands and the spear wound in his side (Mooney 1965 [1896], 39–40).

Apart from the messianic implications, the core of the message Wovoka was trying to instill and manifest in the dance was to embrace "a clean, honest life." As the people moved in harmony in the dance, following the path of the sun, "so they must live and work in harmony." It broke down distinctions among people, as all regardless of age, gender, health, or material situation were "welcomed into a faith of hope for the future, consolation and assistance in the present, and honor to the Indians who had passed into the afterlife." At a time of intense suffering brought on by terrible epidemics and a campaign of cultural genocide, Wovoka's words were "a marvelous message" (Kehoe 1989, 7).

When Mooney visited Wovoka in January 1892, he found that despite rumors to the contrary Wovoka was "a mild tempered member of a weak and unwarlike tribe" and "his doctrine was one of peace." Sensational articles written by newspaper reporters who had never met him caused Wovoka to be denounced as an imposter and a lunatic by many Euroamericans, but Mooney found that Indians considered him "a direct messenger from the Other World" (Mooney 1965 [1896], 6–7). Mooney too was impressed by his sincerity and spirituality. (On Wovoka, see Bailey 1957; Dangberg 1968.)

The 1890 Ghost Dance (Wanagi Wacipi) among the Lakota

By 1890 there was widespread hunger, even starvation, on the six Lakota Reservations broken off from the Great Sioux Reservation (see chapter 4). Provisions, which had been cut since the mid–1880s in an effort to force the Lakota to take up farming, were not being delivered as promised. A summer drought was devastating. Epidemics of influenza, measles, and whooping cough swept through the reservations where the Lakota were confined like prisoners of war. At Pine Ridge up to forty-five Oglalas were dying each week in a population of 5,550 (Larson 1997, 264; DeMallie 1984, 265).

The Lakota may have already heard about the Ghost Dance from the Shoshones, who had picked it up from the Paiutes. In the fall of 1889 Good Thunder, Brave Bear, and several others went from Pine Ridge to the Pyramid Lake Reservation in Nevada, where Wovoka lived.

In the spring of 1890 a larger group from several Lakota reservations, including the above, journeyed to Nevada to meet Wovoka. They became his devoted disciples; upon their return they began to spread his message. Captain George Sword of the Oglala police, whose important role in the preservation of Lakota mythology is noted in chapter 4, recorded their account of the trip (see Overholt 1978). According to Sword's account, the Son of God had appeared to the visiting Lakota in a cloud of smoke, and said:

My grandchildren, when you get home, go to farming and send all your children to school. And on way home if you kill any buffalo cut the head, the tail, and the four feet and leave them, and the buffalo will come to live again. When the soldiers of the white people chief want to arrest me, I shall stretch out my arms, which will knock them to nothingness, or, if not that, the earth will open and swallow them in. My father commanded me to visit the Indians on purpose. I have come to the white people first, but they are not good. They killed me, and you can see the marks of my wounds on my feet, my hands, and on my back, but you will not take me home with you at this time. I want you to tell when you get home your people to follow my examples. Any one Indian who does not obey me and tries to be on whites' side will be covered over by a new land that is to come over this old one. (Mooney 1965 [1896], 41)

The way the Lakota and other Plains peoples heard Wovoka's message reflects their different situation. It had only been about a decade since their lands had, in their view, been stolen. Most desperately hoped for the destruction of the whites, not a life in harmony with them. On the way back the men claimed to Sword to have experienced several miracles, including a buffalo they had killed coming back to life, as the messiah said. They brought some of the buffalo meat home with them and shared it with others.

When they arrived back in South Dakota, Short Bull and the others began to proclaim the new revelation, and in the spring of 1890 the first Ghost Dance was held at the Pine Ridge Agency. As Leonard Crow Dog has observed, the message was "rain for thirsty souls" (Crow Dog 1995, 43).

It is estimated that about one-third of the Lakota embraced the Ghost Dance. Among the Plains nations, of the 20,000 people involved in the new movement, Mooney estimated that 16,000 were Teton Sioux (Lakota) (Mooney 1965 [1896], 61). Adapting the Ghost Dance to their own tradition, they put up a sun dance pole at the center of the dance circle. As in the sun dance, many danced to the point of exhaustion. They also gave it a "militaristic" twist, believing that specially painted cloth "ghost shirts" would make them impervious to bullets (see below) (Mooney 1965 [1896], 14).

Amidst the terrible drought of the summer of 1890, increasingly terrified settlers claimed they could hear Lakota dancing on the reservations through the day and night (Pfaller 1972). Red Cloud and other leaders at Pine Ridge were dubious, but dancers spoke of visions of their dead ancestors returning to earth and huge herds of buffalo, and the whites gone. So Red Cloud and other skeptical leaders quietly encouraged the dancing while not participating themselves (Larson 1997, 266).

The Ghost Dance was more popular among the southern Lakota reservations than the northern. At the Badlands plateau called the Stronghold on the Pine Ridge reservation, up to 3,500 believers gathered and danced. Most of them were Brulés from the Rosebud Reservation. The fact that women were dancing should have shown the concerned settlers that it was not a war dance (Larson 1997, 266).

At Pine Ridge, Little Wound told his followers, "My friends, if this is a good thing we shall have it; if it is not it will fall to earth itself. So you better learn this dance, so if the Messiah does come he will not pass us by but will help us get back our hunting ground and buffalo" (Larson 1997, 267). Some Lakota holy men linked the new ritual to the Lakota prophecy that the buffalo, having retreated to their subterranean world, would return (DeMallie 1982).

A political appointee with no experience working among Indians, Daniel Royer (given the nickname Young-Man-Afraid-of-Indians by the Lakota), came to Pine Ridge on 1 October to assume the post of agent. His predecessor had been more sanguine, saying as late as June that the "messiah craze" (as many Euro-americans were now calling the movement) would soon die down "possibly to be supplanted by something equally as silly" (Larson 1997, 269).

The principal dance ground on the Pine Ridge Reservation was at No Water's camp on White Clay Creek, about twenty miles from the agency. There ghost shirts had probably been worn for the first time in June 1890. In late August a dance with 2,000 participants was broken up.

By October 1890, according to Mooney, the Ghost Dance "was in full progress among the western Sioux and was rapidly spreading throughout the tribe" (Mooney 1965 [1896], 91). At Rosebud, Short Bull, Crow Dog, and Two Strike were the leaders. They stopped the dancing when warned, but amidst rumors of troops arriving, 1,800 Brulés left for Pine Ridge.

According to Mooney, in the same month Kicking Bear, "the chief high priest of the Ghost Dance among the Sioux," went to the Standing Rock Agency at the invitation of Sitting Bull to lead dances. Apparently, Sitting Bull himself was skeptical about the Ghost Dance, although he understood why his people were turning to it. In 1889 he had spoken to a white schoolteacher about his experience at the dances he had attended, in the context of his views on religion in general:

> Our religion seems foolish to you, but so does yours to me. The Baptists and Methodists and Presbyterians and the Catholics all have a different God. Why cannot we have one of our own? Why does the agent seek to take away our religion? My race is dying. Our God will soon die with us. If this new religion is not true then what matters? I do not know what to believe. If I could dream like the others and visit the spirit world myself, then it would be easy to believe, but the trance does not come to me. It passes me by. I help others to see their dead, but I am not aided. (Armstrong 1971, 128)

On the Standing Rock Reservation the main centers for the Ghost Dances were at camps of two old headmen, Big Foot and Hump. Sensing a potential explosion, Agent James McLaughlin of Standing Rock urged that Sitting Bull be removed to a military prison.

Meanwhile, at Pine Ridge Agent Royer was losing control of the situation. On 12 October he reported that 6,000 were dancing and that it was necessary to call out the military (Mooney 1965 [1896], 93). When Royer consulted General Miles, Miles said he thought the excitement would die out on its own, but Royer was soon sending requests for troops at a rate of one message per day.

In early November, Royer tried to get the chiefs to stop the dances, but they laughed at him. His calls for military intervention were now laced with near panic. Meanwhile, newspaper reporters and photographers were spreading the word of this "crisis" around the country, helping to arouse the public (Watson 1943). A *Chicago Tribune* headline ominously proclaimed "Indians Dancing with Guns," and pictures showed the Indians lying on the ground in trance states. "The Redskins are Dancing the Dreaded Ghost Dance" proclaimed the *Omaha Daily Bee* (Beasley 1995, 43).

On 13 November, responding to the growing public hysteria caused by such rhetoric and the portrayal of it in the press, President Harrison ordered that troops be sent, under the command of General Miles. On 19 November, the first troops arrived, including eight contingents from the Seventh Cavalry (under whose colors Custer and his men had been killed fourteen years earlier) led by Colonel Forsyth, and an African-American battalion of the Ninth Cavalry under Major Henry.

Very quickly 3,000 troops had gathered. In response, a large group of Lakota rushed to the Badlands Stronghold from both Pine Ridge and Rosebud. Soon there were 3,000 Lakota in the Badlands. According to Commissioner Morgan, they gave no indication of hostile intent. At most, only 700 of the 6,000 to 7,000 warriors among the 25,000 Sioux were involved.

By the beginning of December, the turmoil seemed to be quieting down. The agencies came under military control. Buffalo Bill Cody had been summoned to try to talk Sitting Bull into surrendering peacefully. The old medicine man, however, was still defiant in his refusal to accept the subjugation forced upon the Lakota. He had reportedly broken his "pipe of peace" and said he wanted to die fighting. McLaughlin learned that Sitting Bull was planning to go to Pine Ridge because "God" was about to arrive. Fearing what might happen if Sitting Bull reached the large group of warriors in the Badlands, a contingent of Lakota police, supported at a distance by soldiers, was dispatched on 15 December to arrest him. At first Sitting Bull agreed to go with the police, but then he refused and called for his followers to rescue him. Six police were killed, as were eight "hostiles," including Sitting Bull and his seventeen-year-old-son, Crow Foot.

When Hump surrendered with his followers, the last remaining prominent Lakota "Ghost Dance" leader outside the Badlands was *Sitanka*, Big Foot. Big Foot agreed to move toward the agency with his band of about 340, but when another army unit approached, the band apparently panicked and fled south towards the Badlands. At the same time the large group with Kicking Bear and

Short Bull in the Badlands was starting to move toward the Pine Ridge Agency under army pressure. Concerned about possible bloodshed, Red Cloud tried to discourage the continuation of the dances.

On 19 December, General Miles sent a telegram to the commander of the army saying that until the treaty obligations of the government were honored and the called-for provisions sent, his troops could do little to resolve the tense situation.

Chapter 4 describes the tragic events of the morning of 29 December 1890, when a force of 470 troopers, most from the Seventh Cavalry, opened fire on the totally surrounded camp of Big Foot's band (about 106 of the approximately 340 of whom were warriors) near Wounded Knee on the Pine Ridge Reservation. Mooney also gives a detailed account of what transpired, leading up to, during, and after what the army officially called the "Battle at Wounded Knee" (Mooney 1965 [1896], 114–40). Here is a portion of Mooney's description and evaluation of the actual massacre:

> At the first volley the Hotchkiss guns trained on the camp opened fire and sent a storm of shells and bullets among the women and children, who had gathered in front of the tipis to watch the unusual spectacle of military display. The guns poured in 2-pound explosive shells at the rate of nearly fifty per minute, mowing down everything alive. The terrible effect may be judged from the fact that one woman survivor, Blue Whirlwind, with whom the author conversed, received fourteen wounds, while each of her two little boys was also wounded by her side. In a few minutes 200 Indian men, women, and children, with 60 soldiers, were lying dead and wounded on the ground, the tipis had been torn down by the shells and some of them were burning above the helpless wounded, and the surviving handful of Indians were flying in wild panic to the shelter of the ravine, pursued by hundreds of maddened soldiers and followed by a raking fire from the Hotchkiss guns, which had been moved into position to sweep the ravine. (Mooney 1965 [1896], 117–18)

There can be no question that the pursuit was a massacre, where fleeing women, with infants in their arms, were shot down after resistance had ceased and when almost every warrior was stretched dead or dying on the ground.

In Mooney's assessment, because it was Black Fox, one of Big Foot's warriors, who fired the first shot, "the Indians were responsible for the engagement . . . but . . . the wholesale slaughter of women and children was unnecessary and inexcusable." He estimates that 300 Indians were killed; 31 soldiers died on the field, and several more of wounds. Only one settler was killed, in the several days of Lakota raids that followed the massacre (Mooney 1965 [1896], 119–20).

Mooney added to his assessment a comment on what he thought the incident said about the victors: "It is a commentary on our boasted Christian civilization that although there were two or three salaried missionaries at the agency not one went out to say a prayer over the poor mangled bodies off these victims of war" (Mooney 1965 [1896], 129–30).

Although the army commander on the scene was charged with misconduct, twenty-three members of the Seventh Cavalry unit at Wounded Knee were awarded the Congressional Medal of Honor, the nation's highest military honor, for their "heroic action" (Powers 1977, 122).

The soldiers involved expressed their sentiment by enthusiastically embracing a song written by W.H. Prather, a private in the "colored" Ninth Cavalry troop. The chorus of the song is as follows:

They claimed the shirt Messiah gave, no bullet could go through,
But when the Soldiers fired at them they saw this was not true.
The Medicine man supplied them with their great Messiah grace,
And he, too, pulled his freight and swore the 7th hard to face.
(Mooney 1965 [1896], 137)

The Ninth Cavalry was the one unit that served with distinction. Several days after the massacre at Wounded Knee, its troopers rode all night from the Badlands to relieve Seventh Cavalry soldiers who had been pinned down by angry Lakota warriors.

In his study of the relationship between the "Sioux Outbreak" of 1890 (as the government officially described the events leading up to the massacre at Wounded Knee), Mooney cites three underlying causes:

- unrest of the conservative element under the decay of the old life
- the repeated neglect of promises made by the government
- hunger (Mooney 1965 [1896], 69–74)

The Ghost Dance among the Sioux, he concludes, was not so much a cause as "a symptom of the real causes of dissatisfaction." He notes that the Ghost Dance was not linked to any other such outbreaks in other areas. He observes with obvious irony that the cost of responding to this avoidable "outbreak" was $40,000 per day for the thirty-two days of its duration, for a total of $1.2 million, with forty-nine soldiers and 300 Indians dead for no good reason (Mooney 1965 [1896], 88).

Mooney and the other reports he cites fail to mention another likely cause. The sun dance and other traditional Lakota rituals had just been outlawed. As Clyde Holler observed in his study of the Lakota sun dance, "it is unlikely that the Ghost Dance would have been as popular among the Sioux if the sun dance had not been banned." Among the Lakota the Ghost Dance took on the trappings of the sun dance, with the center pole, for example. It was, in effect, a substitute for the sun dance (Holler 1995, 135).

As noted in chapter 4, there is an apocalyptic story in Lakota lore about the current world pictured as a buffalo on its last legs. The buffalo starts out with four legs and thick hair. Over time the buffalo loses its hair and ultimately three of its legs. "When the buffalo is totally bald, and has lost its fourth leg, the world as we know it will come to an end." There is hope that this will lead to a spiritual regeneration in which the universe will start over once again and be more favorable to the Lakota. (Powers 1986b, 142–43). This prophecy may also have played a role in the enthusiastic reception of the Ghost Dance among the Lakota.

Ghost dances were held on the Lakota reservations after 1890. Horn Dance spoke of a Ghost Dance held in secret in 1909 "to prevent the government taking any more land." Guards were posted to warn of approaching police (Lewis 1990, 113).

Ghost Dance songs were still heard among the Lakota during the 1930s (Kehoe 1989, 8), and an attempt was made to revive the Dance during the tumultuous 1970s (see below).

The 1890 Ghost Dance among Other Nations

As we have noted, before the Ghost Dance had reached the Lakota, it was popular among other nations beyond its immediate area. By the spring of 1889, after delegates had visited Wovoka, the northern Arapaho and Shoshoni in Wyoming were holding Ghost Dances. By the summer word of the ritual had reached the southern Arapaho and Cheyenne in Indian Territory, as a result of letters written by pupils returning from eastern schools. At end of 1889 a large delegation including Sioux, northern Cheyenne, and northern Arapaho visited the messiah. The Ghost Dance allowed them to revive old dance styles which had been dormant for several years.

An Arapaho leader named Sitting Bull (not to be confused with the famous Sitting Bull of the Lakota) was particularly influential in the southern Ghost Dance. Some of the Arapaho called him the messiah. In September 1890 a huge dance of 3,000 was held on the South Canadian River, near Darlington, Oklahoma, including Arapaho and Cheyenne dancers as well as dancers from the Kiowa, Wichita, Caddo, and other nations. Sensationalized newspaper accounts warned of war dances and scalping parties. Settlers began to panic and call for troops. Lt. Hugh Scott of the Seventh Cavalry was assigned to investigate, and from December 1890 through February 1891 he visited camps and, despite what had happened among the Lakotas, he reported there was no danger posed by the dance.

In 1891 and 1892 delegations from Indian Territory visited Wovoka, and the dancing continued. The Ghost Dance was also popular among the Pawnee, Ponca, Oto, Missouri, Kansa, Iowa, Osage, and other nations in central Oklahoma. For example, the Pawnees were dancing in February 1892. In the dance they found a focus for an authentic cultural revitalization that enabled them to persevere during the difficult times of the early twentieth century (Kehoe 1989, 39; Lesser 1933).

Among other nations in Indian Territory, the dance was not as popular. The influential Comanche leader Quanah Parker opposed the dance, and, although there were Comanche dances, it did not take root. The Osage, who were better off economically than other nations, never adopted the dance (Mooney 1965 [1896], 75)

In general, among the nations of Indian Territory, as well as the northern nations beyond the Lakota, the Ghost Dance movement flourished then slowly died out as an active ritual, although its symbolism continued in the art of the peoples. This was in large measure because in most areas authorities did not allow themselves be stampeded into repressive action as a result of irrational fears. They allowed the dance to continue until it had run its course.

The Ghost Dance Revived

Isolated Ghost Dances occurred after 1890 and 1909. During the 1950s Ghost Dances were still occurring among the Canadian Dakota and the Wind River Shoshoni (Hultkrantz 1981; 1987, 545).

Alice Beck Kehoe found that the Ghost Dance was continuing in the 1960s in a movement called New Tidings (*Woyaka Teca*) in Round Plain, Saskatchewan, among the Wahpeton Sioux descendants of those who had fled to Canada after the 1862 "uprising" in Minnesota. The Ghost Dance had been introduced to this band at the same time it was being adopted by the Sioux in the United States in 1890, possibly by Kicking Bear and Short Bull. As the active Ghost Dance itself faded among the Saskatchewan Sioux in the late 1890s, a new form of the movement was created by incorporating Ghost Dance songs into the traditional Dakota Medicine Feast. The result was New Tidings, which drew in Christian symbolism to an essentially indigenous movement. Over the years New Tidings enabled this small band to reaffirm its Dakota heritage and to lead "clean, honest lives" while struggling against the stereotypes of the dominant society. It helped them to adapt to Eurocanadian culture without giving up their Dakota identity. Although the New Tidings movement itself faded with the decline in Dakota-fluency among the Wahpeton Sioux during the 1970s, it had fulfilled an important role (Kehoe 1989, 41–50).

The best known revival of the Ghost Dance occurred during the second siege of Wounded Knee on the Pine Ridge Reservation in 1973. As noted in chapter 4, in early 1973, the site of the Wounded Knee massacre was occupied by Oglala Lakotas and their American Indian Movement supporters. They were surrounded by federal forces, who placed the occupiers under a siege that lasted for more than two months.

In March 1973, on the first day of spring, the Lakota Ghost Dance was revived in a new, pannational context. Lakota medicine man Leonard Crow Dog was told in a vision by his great-great-grandfather, Jerome Crow Dog, a Ghost

Dance leader in 1890, to hold the dance once again. He emphasized the fact that the Ghost Dance transcended boundaries among Native American nations and united Indian people together.

According to his former wife, Mary, who was also at Wounded Knee in 1973, Crow Dog thought that in 1890 the people had misunderstood Wovoka and his message. The point was not that the dead would literally come back to life, but that the ancient beliefs and rituals would be revived (Crow Dog 1991, 153). Perhaps influenced by Black Elk's vision as related by John Neihardt in *Black Elk Speaks*, Leonard Crow Dog envisioned the dance as a way of mending the broken sacred hoop. In 1973, however, the sacred hoop was not just the hoop of the Lakota nation, but the circle of unity of all Indian peoples. The night before the dance, Leonard Crow Dog told those who would be dancing:

> Tomorrow, we're going to ghost dance. For eighty-three years it has never been danced. When they killed our people here so long ago, it was said that the nation's hoop was broken. We'll make the sacred hoop whole again. . . . We'll unite together as one tribe through the language of the Great Spirit. We're not going to divide. We're going to be brothers and sisters. Whether you're Mohawk, or Cheyenne, we'll be as one. (Crow Dog 1995, 153)

Crow Dog said that when they danced they would hold hands, and "if one gets into the power, if he's in a trance, if he falls down inside the ring, let him." The earth, he said, would be their drum and their feet would do the drumming. He would sing the Ghost Dance song of his grandfather. In their visions they would be elevated to another world where they would be able to see *Tunkashila* (Grandfather). They would see their relations who have died. They would see the buffalo coming up through Mother Earth. The dancers would wear painted ghost shirts made out of curtains or burlap bags or whatever could be found and upside-down American flags, like the ghost dancers of 1890. They won't wear "white man's clothes." "It's going to start here," he said, "at Wounded Knee, and it will continue. . . . We will dance for the future generations" (Crow Dog 1995, 126–27; Crow Dog 1991, 153).

A year later, in May 1974, Leonard Crow Dog and his father Henry held another Ghost Dance, this time at his family's allotment on the Rosebud Reservation. Native peoples from as far away as Alaska and Mexico had received word on the "moccasin telegraph" and came to take part (Crow Dog 1995, 130).

The Ghost Dance Myth and Ritual

The Ghost Dance Myth

In a section called "The Doctrine of the Ghost Dance," Mooney lays out the basic Ghost Dance myth, which he contended was common to the nations that adopted the ritual:

The time will come when the whole Indian race, living and dead, will be reunited upon a regenerated earth, to live a life of aboriginal happiness, forever free from death, disease, and misery. . . . [The whites are] left behind with the other things of earth that have served their temporary purpose. This will happen with no human action. (Mooney 1965 [1896], 19)

Each nation adapted this core narrative to its own myths. For example, the Cheyenne, Arapaho, Kiowa, and others in Indian Territory said that "the new earth, with all the resurrected dead from the beginning, and with the buffalo, the elk, and other game upon it, will come from the west and slide over the surface of the present earth, as the right hand might slide over the left. As it approaches, the Indians will be carried upward and alight on it by the aid of the sacred dance feathers which they wear in their hair and which will act as wings to bear them up." They will be unconscious for days and on waking will find themselves surrounded by former friends in the old-time surroundings (Mooney 1965 [1896], 28).

Some of the Sioux talked of a flood that would come when the earth trembled, filling the mouths of the whites with mud. When the time was at hand they were to gather at one spot and strip off their "white" clothing (Mooney 1965 [1896], 30).

And, as Mooney pointed out, "each apostle and believer has filled in the details according to his own mental capacity or ideas of happiness, with such additions as come to him from the trance [received during a dance]." Some native interpreters said that in the new world all racial distinctions would end, and whites and Indians would live in harmony together (Mooney 1965 [1896], 19, 27).

At first, apparently, the spring of 1891 was taken as the date at which the new world would begin. When that date passed it was assumed that "some time in the unknown future the Indian will be united with his friends who have gone before to be forever supremely happy, and that this happiness may be anticipated in dreams, if not actually hastened in reality, by earnest and frequent attendance on the sacred dance" (Mooney 1965 [1896], 20).

The Ghost Dance Ritual

Different names for the 1890 Ghost Dance were used among the various nations where it was adopted. The Paiutes called the ceremony the "dance in a circle." The Shoshoni name was "everybody dragging." The Comanches called it "the father's dance," with "father" a reference to Wovoka. The Kiowa used the phrase "dance with clasped hands"; the Caddos' name was "dance of all to the Father." The Prairie nations, including the Sioux, coined the phrase which was adopted by Mooney and other observers: Spirit or Ghost Dance (in Lakota, *Wanaghi wachipi*). For them the focus was on the the coming of the spirits ("ghosts") of the dead from the spirit world. (Mooney 1965 [1896], 35).

Early on, many ghost dancers were returning to traditional dress, buckskin if they could find it. In some nations the dancers wore "ghost shirts" made from cloth (probably because buckskin was not easy to obtain) but ornamented in Indian fashion. The shirts were especially popular among the Plains nations in the north, where memories of the battles with the army were more vivid and the possibility of renewed conflict a greater concern.

According to Mooney, the ghost shirts were worn as outside garments during the dance and under other garments at other times. They were similar in shape, fringing, and feather adornment but unique in painting and designs. Some shirts were simple; others were covered with symbols of sun, moon, stars, and visions of a trance the dancer had reported to a medicine man. Typically there were fringes on the shirts, sometimes painted red. The shirt was firmly believed to be impenetrable to bullets or weapons of any sort (Mooney 1965 [1896], 30–31). Mooney pointed out that the shirts may have been suggested by the "endowment robes" worn by ordained members of the Church of Jesus Christ of Latter-day Saints (Mooney 1965 [1896], 34). According to Mooney, Wovoka disclaimed responsibility for the shirts, probably because of their association with the "Sioux Outbreak."

Ghost Dances on the Pine Ridge Reservation (1890)

As noted, beginning in the spring of 1890 large Ghost Dances were held on the Lakota reservations. According to Mooney, before a typical Lakota Ghost Dance the men or at least the leaders fasted for twenty-four hours then entered sweat lodges at dawn. Dancers then were painted by a medicine man, with the designs determined by a previous trance vision of the dancer. At noon, the dance began. Priests sat around the base of the central tree. A woman shot sacred arrows in the four directions, which were then tied to the tree. The woman then stood by the tree with a sacred pipe pointed west. The dancers sat in a circle, sang a plaintive chant, then passed sacred food. At a sign from a priest, they stood, joined hands, and moved slowly from right to left while chanting the first song. Then came the frenzies, trances, and recitals of visions. The dances usually were held on Sundays (Mooney 1965 [1896], 66–68).

In 1932 Nicholas Black Elk described to John Neihardt one of his own visions that came to him during an 1890 Ghost Dance:

> All I saw was an eagle feather in front of my eyes at first. I felt as though I had fallen off a swing and gone out into the air. My arms were outstretched and right before me above I could see a spotted eagle dancing toward me with his wings fluttering and the shrill whistle he made. I could see a ridge right in front of me and I thought I was going to hit that ridge, but I went right over it. I did not move at all, I just looked ahead. After I reached the other side of the ridge I could see a beautiful land over there and people

During the "Ghost Dance craze," illustrated stories appeared in newspapers around the country to demonstrate that the "hysterical" dances might lead to a new Indian war, placing pressure on government officials to stop the dancing. (© CORBIS)

were camping there in circle[s] all over. I noticed that they had plenty, and I saw dried meat all over. I glided over the tipi. Then I went down feet first and lighted on the ground. As I was going down to the center of the hoop I could see a tree in full bloom with flowers on it. I could see two men coming toward me. They were dressed with ghost shirts like I was dressed. They came and said to me: "It is not yet time to see your Father, but we shall present to you something that you will carry home to your people and with this they shall come forth to see their loved ones." I could see fat horses all over and the wild animals ranging out over the country and hunters were returning with their meat. I was very happy to see that and I'm hungry for some of that meat right now. They told me to return at once and I was out in the air again and I glided the same as before back. (DeMallie 1984, 261)

In another vision, Black Elk saw a man with outstretched arms, with his body painted red and wearing an eagle feather, whom Black Elk believed was the "Son of the Great Spirit." The man said to him, "My life is such that all earthly beings that grow belong to me. My Father has said this. You must say this." The man's body changed into all colors, and all around him was light (DeMallie 1984, 263).

Dick Fool Bull, a relative of Leonard Crow Dog, who had witnessed Lakota Ghost Dances as a child, recounted as an old man what he had seen:

A man called Woman's Dress had been performing the dance and when the sun reached the center of the universe he ran into the middle of the dance circle, where the director was standing, and knelt down. Then he laid his body flat on the ground, face-down. He was lying there for a long time, like sleeping, and then, with the people still dancing, he woke up. The dance leader burned some sweet grass and smoked Woman's Dress up. When Woman's Dress stood up he was asked what he had seen and heard. Woman's Dress said, "I went to another world. It was beautiful and filled with good things. From there I brought back some *wasna*." (Crow Dog 1995, 43–44)

Ghost Dance Songs

Mooney collected hundreds of Ghost Dance songs during his research. The number of songs created was virtually limitless because every trance at every dance could produce a new one. A dancer who experienced a trance would typically be given a song by the leader to whom the dancer had described his or her vision. A single dance could result in as many as twenty or thirty songs. Some songs were repeated, in the opening and closing of the dance, but most were unique (Mooney 1965, [1896], 201).

Most of the songs Mooney gathered came from the southern Arapaho, where he witnessed and participated in dances (201–63), but he also gathered songs from the Cheyenne (263–79); Comanche (280–84); Paiute, Washo, and Pit River (285–92); Sioux (293–310); Kiowa and Kiowa Apache (310–24); and Wichita, Kichai, and Delaware (324–31) nations. The Lakota songs he gathered reflect the basic Ghost Dance myth but also elements from the traditional Lakota spirituality described in chapter 4. The two are blended together.

At the beginning of a typical Lakota Ghost Dance, the dancers stood motionless, with hands stretched to the west, country of the messiah and from whence the new spirit world will come (as well as the Black Hills, the home of the Thunderbirds). They then chanted the following song:

The father says so-E'yayo'!
The father says so-E'yayo'!
The father says so-E'yayo'!
The father says so-E'yayo'!
You shall see your grandfather ,
You shall see your grandfather.
The father says so,
The father says so.
You shall see your kindred-E'yayo'!
You shall see your kindred-E'yayo'!
The father says so,
The father says so. (Mooney 1965 [1896], 297)

A song referring to the sacred pipe brought by White Buffalo Woman clearly demonstrates the incorporation of Lakota tradition into the dance:

I bring you a pipe,
I bring you a pipe,
Says the father,
Says the father.
By means of it you shall live,
By means of it you shall live,
Says the father,
Says the father. (Mooney 1965 [1896], 297)

The Revived Ghost Dance Ritual (1973 and 1974)

When Leonard Crow Dog revived the Ghost Dance at Wounded Knee II in 1973 and on his ancestral land in 1974, he drew on the 1890 Lakota Ghost Dance as it had been described to him and other Lakota rituals (see chapter 4), but he was also inspired by his own vision and a new situation in which pan-Indian unity was needed. Although these were ad hoc occurrences that did not lead to a new Ghost Dance movement (Kehoe 1989, 102), they are certainly worth noting. Here is his description of the 1973 dance:

> We began with the sweat bath, one for the men and one for the women. We rubbed our bodies with sage and sweet grass. We prepared the dance circle. We put the evergreen, the tree of life, in the middle. We put tobacco ties and cloth offerings on it. We used sacred red face paint. We used magpie feathers. Every dancer wore an eagle feather in his hair. We danced in a circle, holding hands, from right to left, starting slowly and then going faster and faster, sometimes with arms upraised. We danced in the ravine where so many of our women and children had been killed by the Seventh Cavalry. . . . We had the young girl representing *Ptesan Win* standing in the circle, holding the pipe. She should have had an elk horn bow and four arrows with bone points to shoot toward the clouds in the four directions, but we did not have such a bow.
> . . . The earth trembled. I felt the ghosts dancing beneath the ground. And some of the dancers fell down in a trance, fell down like dead, receiving visions. So, at Wounded Knee, with a cold wind blowing, we reeducated ourselves. We had about thirty dancers. Many were barefoot, in the old ghost dance way, even though there was snow on the ground. (Crow Dog 1995, 128–29)

As noted, for Crow Dog, the purpose of the 1973 dance was to mend the broken hoop of the Lakota nation and all Indian people.

Leonard Crow Dog's former wife, Mary, has described the 1974 dance. Like the 1973 dance, it brought together Indians from around the country, but whites were not restricted from participating. A sixteen-year-old white girl danced alongside a Nahua and a Chihuahua Indian from Mexico dressed in their white campesino outfits. In the words of Mary Crow Dog:

> About a dozen dancers got into the power and received visions. One young Navajo with a red blanket wrapped around him suddenly began to dance with the movements of a bird. It seemed almost as if an eagle had taken possession of his body. The best thing that happened was the appearance of a flight of eagles toward the end of the dance. Nobody had even seen so many of these sacred birds together at one time. They circled with outspread wings over the dance ground and then flew off in an undulating line, like a long plumed serpent gliding through the clouds. It made us happy. (Crow Dog 1991, 213)

Interpretations of the Ghost Dance

The Mormons and the Ghost Dance

One issue raised by interpreters of the Ghost Dance was its relationship with the Church of Jesus Christ of Latter-day Saints (see Barney 1986). Mooney raised the question of Mormon influence on the Ghost Dance, without taking a definitive position. He suggested that the ghost shirt "may have been suggested by the 'endowment robe' of the Mormons, a seamless garment of white muslin adorned with symbolic figures, which is worn by their initiates as the most sacred badge of their faith, and by many of the believers is supposed to render the wearer invulnerable." He pointed out that "the Mormons have always manifested a particular interest in the Indians, whom they regard as the Lamanites of their sacred writings, and hence have made special efforts for their evangelization, with the result that a considerable number of the neighboring tribes of Ute, Paiute, Bannock, and Shoshone have been received into the Mormon church and invested with the endowment robe." An idea borrowed by the Shonshe from the Mormons, he suggested, could have found its way through the Arapaho to the Sioux and Cheyenne (Mooney 1965 [1896], 34–35).

He also cited a pamphlet published anonymously in Salt Lake City in 1892 entitled "The Mormons Have Stepped down and out of Celestial Government— the American Indians Have Stepped up and into Celestial Government." That pamphlet described Joseph Smith's 1843 prophecy that the messiah would reveal himself in 1890. The pamphlet claims that the messiah appeared at Walkers Lake, Nevada, in March 1890. The reign of the Gentiles over the American Indians came to an end in October 1892, it said. The atrocities visited by the government on the Indians (as at Wounded Knee) were, it said, a prelude to a war of extermination (Mooney 1965 [1896], 36–37).

Mooney then includes "Porcupine's Account of the Messiah." Porcupine reported that he saw whites performing the Ghost Dance (and Mooney notes he was traveling through Mormon country). In Nevada the whites and Indians were dancing together, Porcupine said, and he was told that "all the whites and Indians are brothers." At Walker Lake he saw the Christ (Wovoka), who was an Indian that wore white man's clothes except for moccasins. The next morning though he appeared as a white man. Porcupine saw a scar on the man's wrist and one on his face (Mooney 1965 [1896], 39–40).

The discussion of the relationship between Mormons and the Ghost Dance has continued to the present. Some see cross-fertilization. La Barre, for example, cites evidence that the "two revolutionary sects were syncretized" (La Barre 1970, 228). Some Mormons, he notes, accepted the Ghost Dance revelation, and some Bannock left Idaho to go to Utah and be baptized as Mormons.

Others emphasize the influence of the Ghost Dance on Mormons. Lanternari, for example, cites Mormon involvement in the 1870 dance. Many Mormons joined the Ghost Dance cult, he argues, as well as Smohalla's Dreamers. In 1892 Mormons believed that Wovoka was the messiah foretold by Joseph Smith in the 1840s (Lanternari 1963).

Other interpreters have suggested that too much has been made of the association. Coates has argued that despite efforts to "blame" the Ghost Dance on Mormons by Mooney, General Nelson Miles, and others, "close examination of the evidence shows that the Mormons did not conspire with the Indians in promoting the Ghost Dance." Some notions such as the end of the world, life after death of family and friends as well as self, special clothing came, he argues, from contact with the Shakers of California during the 1870 dance, not from the Mormons (Coates 1985).

Gregory Smoak argues that most of the accusations of Mormon responsibility for the Ghost Dance came from people who needed a scapegoat (e.g., General Miles). They did not want to acknowledge that the poverty and deprivation of the Indians could be the root cause. Mormons could have played a part (e.g., in the ghost shirt), but there is no clear proof (Smoak 1986).

James Mooney's Interpretation of the Ghost Dance

Between 1890 and 1893, Bureau of American Ethnology field researcher James Mooney, whose work among the Eastern Cherokee we have noted in chapter 3, travelled for twenty-two months, covering nearly 32,000 miles and spending time "with about twenty tribes" researching the Ghost Dance. As noted, he visited Wovoka in Nevada (see Moses 1987). He took part in the dance among the southern Arapaho and Cheyenne and made photographs of the dance with a Kodak camera. He also did extensive library research in preparing his monumental study. He believed it necessary to include accounts of previous prophets because the Ghost Dance was founded in "a hope common to all humanity" and "representative of a series of revival movements" (Mooney 1965 [1896], xii).

On the one hand, Mooney is remarkably free of the passions of the time. In one recent assessment, his work has been called "especially valuable in its objectivity," a "model of investigation for anthropologists, ethnographers and historians" (Oesterreich 1991, 9; cf. Kehoe 1989, ix). His study of the trauma of cultural change and loss of power in the Ghost Dance has been described as an exception to the rule that nineteenth-century anthropologists did not deal with the cultural changes among Native Americans resulting from contact with Euroamericans (Trigger and Washburn 1996, 99).

At a time when the Ghost Dance was being ignored, except as a potential threat, Mooney took it seriously as a religious phenomenon (Moses 1987). He considered Wovoka a true prophet and the Ghost Dance as legitimate as any other religious movement. Mooney's own background as the son of poor, despised Irish immigrants probably gave him sympathy for groups oppressed by English-speaking governments (Kehoe 1989, 30).

On the other hand, it might be argued that Mooney was ahead of his times. He recognized that in order to describe the Ghost Dance fully he would have to participate in it himself, which he did. He also played a role in perpetuating the movement, bringing back to the Arapaho and Cheyenne Ghost Dance items given to him by Wovoka, including sacred red paint (Mooney 1965 [1896], 20).

Woven throughout Mooney's description of the Ghost Dance, however, are judgments reflecting a bias that modern, educated people should regard aspects of the Ghost Dance such as the trances of the dancers as "humbug" (Mooney 1986 [1965], 199). He himself looks for rational explanations of the supposedly supernatural dimensions of the Ghost Dance. For example, Mooney writes that Wovoka "resorts to cheap trickery" like other Native American spiritual leaders to give the impression of miraculous powers (15). Speaking about the Lakota delegation to Wovoka and their reports about his "miracles," he concludes that they were not liars but were "laboring under some strange psychologic influence as yet unexplained" (66).

Mooney also accepted without question the dominant view of the time that Native Americans must move on from their "savage" ways to embrace Western civilization, including Christianity. Although he was not as enamored with an evolutionary understanding of human culture as some social theorists of his day (Kehoe 1989, 97), he did subscribe to the view that Native Americans needed to be "civilized." In his view, the Ghost Dance played an important role in that transition. He wrote that "[i]t is hardly possible for us to realize the tremendous and radical change which this doctrine works in the whole spirit of savage life." He assumed that "the thirst for blood and massacre" was in born in every Indian and that the Ghost Dance succeeded in "bringing the savage into civilization. It is such a revolution as comes but once in the life of a race." Mooney seemed to endorse the view of one of Wovoka's disciples that the Messiah "has prepared the way for their [the Indians'] final Christianization" (Mooney 1986 [1965], 25).

Mooney could also be condescending in his view of the Ghost Dance. In 1893 he was drafted by his friends among the southern Arapaho and Cheyenne to write a letter to Wovoka, inquiring as to the validity of a message they had received indicating that the prophet was tired of receiving delegations from other peoples and was instructing visitors to go home and tell others to stop the dance. He describes his feelings at the time that "[t]o one who knows these people their simple religious faith is too touching to be a subject of amusement" (Mooney 1965 [1896], 158). He also affirmed the stereotype of the Lakota which had circulated among Euroamericans throughout the nineteenth century, that they were "among the wildest and most warlike of all the western tribes" (61). Similarly, he accepted without comment the view that traditionalists such as Red Cloud and Sitting Bull were united in "wily disposition and hatred of the white man" (88–89).

Some interpreters contend that Mooney's early research on the Lakota sun dance actually contributed to the mood of suspicion that led to a military response and the tragedy at Wounded Knee. As noted, Omer Stewart, for example, contends that Mooney's reports had an effect on the military action taken and should therefore be criticized (Stewart 1980).

Finally, one should note Mooney's "universalism," linking the Ghost Dance to a common human impulse. It could be said that he wrote as a historian who sees themes that transcend particular tribes or nations (Oesterreich 1991, 71). It could also be argued, however, that this notion of universalism was part of Mooney's assumption that the Ghost Dance was part of a general human evolution toward a more rational approach to the problems of life.

Other Interpretations of the Ghost Dance

Mooney's relatively sympathetic view of the Ghost Dance was not echoed by other contemporary scholars. Writing soon after the massacre at Wounded Knee, Alice Fletcher echoed the common view in saying that the movement would have died out, without causing serious trouble, having been overcome "by the quiet, persistent influence of the progressive and educated part of the people." She accused "non-progressive and turbulent elements" of using the Ghost Dance movement to promote their own ends. As a result it "infected" a number of tribes (Fletcher 1891).

Some interpreters have suggested that the Ghost Dance was the last gasp of a dying Indian culture. Weston La Barre, for example, argues in his book on the nature of religion entitled *The Ghost Dance* that the Ghost Dance movements of

1870 and 1890 "represent the final catastrophe of Indian culture in the United States" (La Barre 1970, 226). He contends that ". . . the Great Ghost Dance of 1890 . . . provided the crashing climax to the collapse of American Indian culture" (229). The responses of other cultures to similar crises show, La Barre asserts, that the commonality of a spiritual response to cultural destruction is part of our human nature.

Historians have been particularly interested in the origins of the Ghost Dance movement. Leslie Spier broke new ground in attempting to demonstrate that the ultimate origin of the Ghost Dance movements of 1870 and 1890 was in the Northwest among tribes of the inner Plateau area. They had a belief indigenous to their cultures of impending destruction and renewal of the world, with return of the dead and a dance imitating the dances of the dead that would hasten the day. In this circular dance people would fall into trances and then give prophesies based on the visions they received. Spier describes pre–1870 movements extant in Nevada collectively as the Prophet Dance and suggests that they were the root of the later Ghost Dances. He points out that elements of Christianity had already been added to the indigenous Prophet Dance early in the nineteenth century decades before the Ghost Dance (Spier 1935; cf. Kehoe 1989, 97–98; Aberle 1959).

Subsequent study showed that the emergence of the prophetic dances Spier identified can be traced to reactions to disruptions in native cultures in the Northwest resulting from an increase in trade and epidemics introduced by the contact in the late eighteenth century (Walker 1969). The role of Protestant evangelists, who by the 1830s were active in promoting the expectation of a new age and an ecstatic form of worship in the Northwest, also needs to be considered (Miller 1985; cf. Kehoe 1989, 99–102).

Åke Hultkrantz synthesizes the research through the mid–1980s and identifies three roots for the Ghost Dance: (1) "earlier religious movements stimulated by Christian missions, (2) shamanic experiences, and (3) indigenous rituals" (1987, 545–46). The strongest evidence of Christian influence is reflected in the belief "that the Supreme Being had to introduce the new religious program through revelation to a prophet" as does the "hope for a new day of salvation, or the coming liberation," which implies "a linear view of history and an eschatological goal." The self-induced trances common to Wovoka and to the Ghost Dance participants, however, are more reflective of the shamanic pattern of communication with the spiritual. Perhaps the main root of the Ghost Dance is neither of these two factors, but the indigenous circular dance among native nations of the Great Basin, as Spier suggested. It is also sometimes called the "Father Dance" (Hittman 1973).

It is interesting to note that most anthropologists have favored the view that the Ghost Dance resulted from "readjustment to a new sociopolitical situation," while historians of religion have favored the view that "predominantly religious drives steered the development" (Hultkrantz 1987, 545). What you see does depend on the perspective from which you are looking!

Applying the perspective of "symbolic anthropology," DeMallie thinks that the assumptions often repeated about the Lakota Ghost Dance need to be re-evaluated on the basis of an understanding of the Lakota perspective. He empha-sizes that for the Sioux each individual was free to contribute to the overall understanding of religious power his own experience of that power. Thus each Sioux Ghost Dance leader adapted Wovoka's teachings on the basis of his own experience. Most studies of the Ghost Dance among the Sioux fail to take into account the Lakota perspective, which "was set in the interrelatedness of man, animals, earth, even plants which the white man either did not acknowledge or did not take seriously." The land, animals, and people were a "single system, no part of which could change without affecting the others." No unified body of Lakota Ghost Dance doctrinal teaching existed. The assumption that it was a political movement under the pretense of religion also needs to be challenged (DeMallie 1982).

Another focus of research has been the failure of the Diné to adopt the Ghost Dance, despite efforts to introduce the movement to them. Some interpreters have tried to find correlations between the loss of bison herds and the adopting of the Ghost Dance, pointing out that outside Nevada only those nations whose culture had been disrupted by the demise of the buffalo embraced the Ghost Dance. In addition, a correlation has been found between social solidarity (as reflected in firm matrilineages or patrilineages) to explain why some nations did not adopt the Ghost Dance (Carroll 1975; cf. Kehoe 1989, 105).

David Aberle contrasted the acceptance of the peyote movement in the 1930s after the stock reduction program with their failure to embrace the 1890 Ghost Dance movement when they had "relative" comfort, and developed the theory of "relative deprivation," that is, the discrepancy between legitimate expectation and actuality (Aberle 1962; cf. Worsley 1974 and Kehoe 1989, 107–9).

A simpler explanation was advanced by W.W. Hill (1944), who suggested that the major reason the Navajo did not accept the Ghost Dance, although they were exposed to it, was the fear of the dead that was fundamental to their culture. They did not want the "ghosts" to return! (Oesterreich 1991, 59; Kehoe 1989, 109–10).

Logan (1980) contrasts the Paiutes' adoption of the Ghost Dance with what occurred among the Lakota. The Paiutes were in an interdependent situation with the whites, and the whites took a laissez-faire attitude toward the dance. The Paiutes responded to the charisma of the prophet. The Lakota embraced the Ghost Dance less on the basis of the charisma of Wovoka than on the basis of their different relationship with Euroamericans. They were experiencing oppres-sion and deprivation, and the Ghost Dance offered much-needed hope for cul-tural revitalization (Oesterreich 1991, 85).

Thornton (1986) argues that the Ghost Dances of both 1870 and 1890 were not movements of mass hysteria but were deliberate religious efforts to confront dire demographic situations. They were attempted revitalizations in response to rapid population decline (in general for American Indians from 600,000 to 1800 to 228,000 in 1890). The twentieth-century growth in population would suggest that the movement was a success, not in the sense that the Ghost Dance literally brought back the dead, but that it encouraged the living to remain connected to a newly viable community (Oesterreich 1991, 75–79). Thornton has been criticized, however, for considering as solid data "too many arbitrary units, and too many estimates rather than firm counts" (Kehoe 1989, 106).

Basing his theory on the experience of the Hotinonshonni (Iroquois) and the development of the movement begun by Handsome Lake, Anthony Wallace (1956) developed the theory of "revitalization movements," which he defined as "deliberate, organized, conscious effort[s] by members of a society to construct a more satisfying culture." He suggested five stages in the development of such a movement in a culture:

- Steady state
- Period of individual stress
- Period of cultural distortion
- Period of revitalization
- New steady state

The parallels to the Ghost Dance movement in Nevada are evident. The first stage lasted until 1860, when aboriginal culture flourished. The second lasted from 1860 through the 1880s, when Euroamerican incursion began in earnest, with the incumbent stress. The third stage occurred during 1880s when the expansion of agribusiness in the Walker River Valley and the increased role of the U.S. government caused serious cultural distortion. The fourth began with the revelation to Wovoka and continued to about 1900. The fifth stage began in 1900, when agribusiness had completely dominated the area and the Paiutes had superficially assimilated to Euroamerican ways but maintained their own basic tenets for their culture. Alice Beck Kehoe argues: "By articulating a reformulated cultural pattern, Jack Wilson had forestalled the loss of Paiute culture." She suggests calling the movement in Nevada cultural "reformulation," while among the Lakota a more authentically cultural "revitalization" occurred (Kehoe 1989, 122–23).

Conclusion

From its first manifestations in the 1870s through its revival in the 1970s, the Ghost Dance has given Native Americans in desperate situations the spiritual courage to persevere in the face of seemingly insurmountable odds. It has been understood in different ways, based on the particular situation faced by the dancers.

As Peter Navakov has observed, prophetic movements such as the Ghost Dance give "Indians an important conceptual weapon in the power struggles between indigenous and invasive worldviews" (Nabakov 1996, 17–18). Rather than fomenting violence, the Ghost Dance enabled Native Americans at different times in different places to withstand—without resorting to force themselves—the physical and other forms of violence being perpetrated against them. Because efforts to destroy or undermine native cultures continue even in our "enlightened" era, although in more subtle forms than in the period between 1870 and 1890, it is likely that the Ghost Dance may yet again be revived.

CHAPTER 7

The Native American Church: Peyote and Pannationalism

The Native American Church is the only true Church of our people. It is an intertribal, multi-language network that joins hands to bring our people together.

—Robert Billie White Horse (Diné), president of
the Native American Church of Navajoland

PEYOTE (*Lophophora williamsii*) is a small, turnip- or carrot-shaped spineless cactus that grows in a limited area, principally in northern Mexico and southern Texas. It is a light green and segmented cactus, growing close to the ground from a taproot, singly or in clusters, one to two inches across (La Barre 1989, 11). Peyote is harvested by cutting off the tops of the clusters, leaving the root to produce more "buttons" (as the tops are called). After they have dried, the buttons may be consumed, either by chewing or by boiling to produce a drink, called "peyote tea," or by grinding to produce a powder.

Peyote contains various alkaloids, the most important of which is the psychoactive agent mescaline. Thirty peyote buttons contain about 500 milligrams of mescaline. According to those who have used peyote ritually, the first physical effects after consuming peyote are exhilaration, sometimes followed by nausea, vomiting, dizziness, sweating, and headaches. Thereafter, there is often "a warm and pleasant euphoria, an agreeable point of view, relaxation, colorful visual distortions, and a sense of timelessness . . . " (Stewart 1987, 3; cf. La Barre 1989, 7; Anderson 1980, 151–52). Acuity is sharpened. For example, the fire around which the worshippers are gathered may appear to be more beautifully colored. Changes in mood are experienced, for example, in a sense of being blessed. The experience may last up to ten hours (Smith and Snake 1996, 109–9; La Barre 1989, 19).

Called *peyotl* ("caterpillar," after the fuzzy appearance of the cactus) by the Aztec peoples of Mexico, peyote has been discovered by archaeologists in settings dating perhaps to 8000 B.C.E. (La Barre 1989, 291–92; Fikes 1996, 167). Historically, its religious use among the Huichol and Tarahumara peoples of northern Mexico dates to about 1600 C.E.

Use of peyote spread to Native American nations north of the border in the nineteenth century. Early in the twentieth century, a religious organization based on the sacramental use of peyote (the Native American Church [NAC]) was formed in Oklahoma, and "the gospel of peyote" was taken by missionaries to reservations and Indian communities throughout the country. Typically, each nation calls peyote "medicine" using a term in its own language (e.g., *unchela* in Lakota) (La Barre 1989, 15, 17, 105–9, 126–27). The Native American Church continues today in several branches as the most active pannational spiritual movement among American Indians.

According to experts, peyote is not habit forming and "in the controlled ambience of a peyote meeting it is in no way harmful." In the major study of the history of peyote use among Native Americans, Omer Stewart concluded that "peyotism has been a unifying influence in American Indian life, providing the basis for Indian friendships, rituals, social gatherings, travel, marriage, and more. It has been a source of comfort and healing and a means of expression for a troubled people. And it has resulted in one of the strongest pan-Indian movements in the United States" (Stewart 1987, xiii).

Since the earliest recognition of its use on Native American reservations in the 1880s, however, most Bureau of Indian Affairs officials and missionaries assumed it was a "dangerous drug." Many states passed antipeyote laws. Congress did not declare it a "controlled substance" until 1965, however, in response to the growing popularity of psychedelic drugs (Stewart 1987, 3). The legal and political debate over the ritual use of peyote continues today (see below).

This chapter presents an overview of the history of "peyotism": the earliest evidence of peyote use among native peoples; its spread among Native American nations; and the development of the Native American Church, the religious organization which considers peyote a sacrament amidst efforts to prohibit peyote use. It then considers the basic peyote myths and the rituals in which peyote is used sacramentally as well as the "theology" of the Native American Church. Also included are the testimonies of Native Americans who have found in the ritual consumption of peyote a source of meaning and purpose for their lives. Finally, the discussion turns to the situation of the Native American Church and issues surrounding use of peyote that have been prominent since 1990, focusing on the legal and political campaign to secure the freedom to use peyote in worship for members of the Native American Church, concerns over depletion of the supply of peyote, and the continuing discussion of the effects of peyote.

Historical Overview

Note: The most complete survey of the history of peyotism is Stewart's *Peyote Religion: A History* (1987). Other surveys can be found in La Barre 1989; Lanternari 1963, 63–100 and Slotkin 1956.

Prior to Contact with Europeans (ca. 8000 B.C.E.–1600 C.E.)

The native peoples of northern Mexico and southern Texas probably knew of the unusual properties of peyote for at least 10,000 years prior to their first contact with Europeans. Although not much is known about precontact peyotism, records show that in Mexico it was certainly used for centuries "as a medicine to be taken internally or as a poultice on sores; to foretell the future; to find lost objects; as a stimulant during strenuous activity, such as travel or war; and in group religious ceremonies when supernatural aid was sought through group participation." An annual festival involved the use of peyote in all-night rituals, preceded by a pilgrimage to gather the plant (Stewart 1987, 17; La Barre 1989, 7, 23–40, 109–10, 124–25, 131–37).

By the time of contact, ritual use of peyote had spread several hundred miles beyond the growth area. For the Aztecs *peyotl* was the "flesh of the gods." The Spanish missionaries who encountered the Aztecs called it "the devil's root," a name that has been applied ever since to peyote by those who consider it dangerous and demonic (De Ropp 1987, 46).

From Contact to the Formation of the Native American Church (ca. 1600–1918)

More than twenty-five groups indigenous to Mexico and Texas have been identified as using peyote before its introduction to the north. The Huichols, Tarahumaras, and Tepehuan peoples of Mexico still use peyote in rituals. Unfortunately, the use of peyote in contemporary Huichol spirituality has been misunderstood, even mocked, by anthropologists, who, for example, have erroneously reported that Huichols used peyote for enemas (cf. Fikes 1993).

The Huichol ritual hunt for peyote (400 kilometers northeast of their homeland) and Huichol peyote ceremonies have been carefully documented by sensitive researchers (e.g., Fikes 1985; 1996, 167–68; Myerhoff 1975; Furst 1972; La Barre 1989, 256–59). They point out that the Huichols consider peyote "the heart, soul, and memory of their Creator, Deer-Person." Healers and singers achieve union with their Creator through peyote, and peyote speaks through them (Fikes 1996, 167). The Tarahumara people's ceremonies have also been sympathetically described (cf. Artaud 1976).

The Catholic missionaries who were part of the Spanish conquest "found in peyote another evil to be rooted out of the New World." The first record of their contact with Indians who used peyote dates to 1560. By 1620 the Spanish Inquisition denounced it as diabolical and subjected Indian peyotists to torture and death (Fikes 1996, 169). Ironically, as the Roman Catholic Church spread, it inadvertently carried knowledge of peyote as missionaries used converted Indians from peyote growth areas to start new missions. By the end of the eighteenth century, peyote had spread west to the high Sierras and east to the Gulf coast, as well as to the north and south (Stewart 1987, 20–30).

Some evidence shows continuity between the ritual use of peyote among the Mexican native peoples and its use in the Native American Church: the gourd rattle; dedication to the four directions; cleansing in fire, smoke, and incense; all-night peyote meetings; cigarette smoking; and so on. In both contexts peyote is considered a sacred medicine that protects, allows one to see the future or find lost objects, and instructs users in how to live. In both there are pilgrimages to gather the plant. To a modern peyote roadman of the Native American Church, who participated in Mexican peyote meetings, they are the root from which the later movement sprang (Snake 1996, 231). Stewart asserts, however, that there are enough differences to conclude that peyotism in the United States is not simply a direct diffusion from Mexico (Stewart 1987, 41–42).

Some of the other native nations that settled in Indian Territory by 1890 had once lived in the peyote growth area in the previous 150 years, including the Lipan Apaches, Mescalero Apaches, Tonkawas, and Caddos. It is a 500 mile journey one way from Oklahoma to the "peyote gardens," as the growth area in southern Texas and northern Mexico is known. Lipan Apache and perhaps other traditional peyote users regularly made this trip as early as 1870. Those bringing peyote back introduced it to other peoples, including the Comanches and Kiowas.

Diffusion of peyote use accelerated in the 1880s, as the end of the "Indian wars" and the introduction of the railroads made the peyote growth area more accessible. By 1886 peyote was readily available in Oklahoma (at about $15 for 500 peyote buttons) and was gaining the attention of Bureau of Indian Affairs agents, some of whom suggested that peyote was similar to opium and should be outlawed. Opposition also came from some traditional spiritual leaders who considered it a threat to their status and the heritage of their people (Stewart 1987, 58–62; La Barre 1989, 109–12).

In Stewart's view, off-reservation boarding schools such as Carlisle School in Pennsylvania became a key means for spreading awareness of peyote. The English learned in the schools became a lingua franca for peyotists. Weston La Barre, however, sees the commonly held vision quest pattern as more important in the diffusion of peyote (La Barre 1989, 293). Another factor in the spread of peyote use was the Ghost Dance movement (Stewart 1972), which made a pannational spirituality that combined native and Christian elements attractive. The Ghost Dance was particularly strong between 1890 and 1893 in Oklahoma, with Indian agents, as noted in chapter 6, maintaining a hands-off policy. Ghost Dances increased visitation among the nations, and many who participated in the Ghost Dances also used peyote (Stewart 1987, 64–67; La Barre 1989, 113).

James Mooney documented a peyote ceremony among the Kiowa people that he first encountered in 1886 (La Barre 1989, 113) and then experienced during the time he spent in Indian Territory in the early 1890s (see below). His report is the first objective description of a peyote ritual, and it is remarkably similar to the contemporary ceremonies of the Native American Church (Stewart 1987, 34–39).

Most of the peyote roadmen (as the peyote ritual leaders are often called) had been educated in mission or Bureau of Indian Affairs schools and were active members of Christian churches. "Few found conflict in participating in shamanistic curing practices, ancient Indian ceremonials such as the Sun Dance, peyotism, and Christian Sunday schools." Some roadmen, however, gave up other practices and became avid missionaries for the use of peyote. Indeed, the decline of traditional tribal rituals, after many were outlawed, opened the door for acceptance of peyotism (Stewart 1987, 68–69; La Barre 1989, 113).

In about 1900 Caddo-Delaware medicine man John Wilson (ca. 1840–1901) developed the Big Moon Ceremony (later identified with the Cross Fire Ceremony), which he claimed to have learned from divine revelation (Hertzberg 1971, 243–45; La Barre 1989, 151–61). The major ceremonial difference between the Half Moon and Big Moon peyote ceremonies was the shape of the altar, with Wilson favoring a horseshoe shape (rather than the crescent shape of Half Moon rituals). The Big Moon ritual also included more complex symbols. It was somewhat less oriented toward Indian legend and lore and more toward Christianity. Theologically, however, the two branches of peyotism were quite similar: peyote was understood as being an emissary from God, a teacher who comes directly to a suppliant through individual revelation and who calls the person to commit to following the "peyote way." Both said the consumption of alcohol was not compatible with peyote use (Stewart 1987, 86–94).

One of the most important early roadmen in Oklahoma was the Comanche leader Quanah Parker (1845–1911). Parker was the biracial son of a white woman who had been captured as a twelve-year-old by Comanches in Texas in 1835. He claimed that he had been cured of a potentially fatal stomach ailment by peyote in 1885. Thereafter, he became an avid apostle of the Half Moon peyote ceremony and resisted innovations to it.

Although Parker was not a Christian himself, he maintained respect for Christianity. He could also contrast peyotism with Christianity, however, as when he said, "The white man goes into his church and talks about God. The Indian goes into his [peyote] tepee and talks to God." A successful businessman himself, Parker favored integration with Euroamericans and was a friend of and collaborator with white Christian missionaries and businessmen. Beyond the Comanche he conducted peyote meetings among the Cheyenne, Arapaho, Ponca, Oto, Pawnee, and Osage peoples during the 1890s. (Hertzberg 1971, 241–43; Stewart 1987, 70–79; La Barre 1989, 112–13; Cousineau and Rhine 1996, 91).

Nearly all of the nations arriving in Oklahoma after 1874 (e.g., Cheyenne and Arapaho, Osage, Quapaw, Seneca, Ponca, Kaw [Kansa], Tonkawa, Oto, Pawnee, Sac and Fox, Iowa, Kickapoo, Shawnee, and Delaware [Petrullo 1934]) incorporated peyote use to some extent. Typically, it was considered by these peoples "Indian Christianity" in contrast to the "white" Christianity associated with Euroamerican missionaries. Up to half of the members of the newly arriving nations typically adopted it (Stewart 1987, 97–127; La Barre 1989, 114–20).

With the growth of peyote use, the opposition of Indian agents and missionaries also increased. In 1888 one agent reported that "men went mad and killed their own people" (Stewart 1987, 128). That same year an attempt was made to apply the 1883 restrictions on Indian religions to peyote use on the Kiowa-Comanche Reservation in Oklahoma. An order was posted that read : "All Indians on this Reservation are hereby forbidden to eat peyote or to drink any decoction or liquor distilled therefrom" (Botsford and Echo Hawk 1996, 126). Those who disobeyed risked having their annuity goods and rations cut off.

By 1890 a general order forbidding the eating of "mescal beans" (erroneously associated with peyote during this period and used to designate peyote buttons) had been issued by the BIA. In 1899 the first statute specifically designed to control peyote was enacted in Oklahoma territory. Peyote was classified as an "intoxicating liquor," and its use, sale, exchange, gift, or introduction was made a misdemeanor. The law proved difficult to enforce (in part because peyote was available over the counter at drug stores because of its therapeutic value), however, and was eventually repealed in 1908 after extensive lobbying by Quanah Parker and other respected peyote leaders. Further efforts to enact antipeyote laws in Oklahoma failed in 1909 and 1927 (La Barre 1989, 223).

In 1903 a missionary complained to the BIA that after all-night peyote meetings, the people were "in such a state of stupefaction that it was utterly impossible to teach them anything from the word of God" (Stewart 1987, 132). Despite the campaign to suppress peyote, some BIA agents reported that peyote use did not lead to violence and was helping some Indians under their charge overcome alcohol abuse. The "compromise" policy was to limit to 500 the number of peyote buttons that could be purchased at one time, in the hope that this would cause its use to fade away (Stewart 1987, 143–45; La Barre 1989, 223).

By 1914 peyote had spread to a variety of other nations including the Bannock of Idaho; Lakota of the Dakotas (Spider 1987; Steinmetz 1990a, 87–96);

Prairie Potawatomi; Sac and Fox; Kickapoo; Ho Chunk (Winnebago); Iowa of Kansas, Nebraska and Iowa; Northern Arapaho; Wind River Shoshone; Cheyenne of Wyoming and Montana; Northern Ponca and Omaha of Nebraska; Menominee of Wisconsin; Anishanabé [Chippewa] of Minnesota; Utes of Colorado; and Taos Pueblo in New Mexico (cf. Stewart 1987, 148–208; Hertzberg 1971, 246–51). Wherever it spread, opposition developed among agents, missionaries, as well as traditional spiritual leaders who considered peyote a threat to the preservation of the nation's own traditions. In 1911 a federal Indian agent in South Dakota rounded up peyotists and jailed them without legal authority.

The response of contemporary Lakota holy man Leonard Crow Dog's grandfather, who first encountered peyote in 1918, is typical. He said, "a new power got hold of me, . . . It makes me understand myself . . . the peyote spirit is releasing me from what is binding me" (Crow Dog 1995, 94–95).

As peyote use spread there was an increasing distinction between the Wilson Big Moon (now known as Cross Fire) and the Comanche Half Moon (sometimes called the Tipi Way) rituals. In the former Christianity was emphasized. The basic all-night ceremony (see below), however, remained the same. Peyotists typically participated in either ceremony as the occasion arose. They also continued to take part in tribal rituals like the sun dance among the Plains nations as well as the ceremonies of Christian churches and traditional curing ceremonies (Stewart 1987, 208–9). The sentiment expressed by Leonard Crow Dog eighty years later reflects a perspective long held: "I see nothing wrong with holding onto my old Lakota beliefs while, at the same time, I also practice the peyote way together with my brothers and sisters from all tribes" (Crow Dog 1995, 91).

Attempts by Indian agents to promote a federal law prohibiting peyote failed in 1907 and again in 1910. In 1912 the Board of Indian Commissioners reported a "dangerous" spread of peyote use, "increased by its so-called religious associations" and urged swift suppression. A sum of $25,000 was designated annually in the federal budget for suppression of Indian use of peyote (Botsford and Echo Hawk 1996, 128). The same year the Society for American Indians, made up mostly of Native American leaders, announced their opposition to peyote.

In response, a strong lobbying effort was launched by supporters of peyote use. Cases were brought against a few peyote sellers on the basis of the 1897 law, but judges ruled that the law did not apply to peyote. These rulings encouraged opponents to mount an effort to pass a federal law. The attitude of most BIA superintendents was expressed by one who said, "I am of the opinion that the peyote is completely ruining the Indian people." There were supporters, however, even among missionaries. One said that he saw only a ritual to be admired and nothing reprehensible.

In 1918 Congressman Carl Hayden of Arizona introduced a bill that would have outlawed the use of peyote. The BIA reported that peyote was a fast-spreading harmful drug, that religion was being used as a subterfuge to promote its use, that peyote users also used whiskey, that claims that it helped combat alcoholism were ill-founded, and that most superintendents of agencies where it was used opposed it.

The secretary of the Society of American Indians charged that peyote excited "baser passions" and also that peyotists took money from Indians under false pretenses, drank alcohol, and were responsible for at least thirty deaths among the Utes. He warned that the drug would spread "like wild fire" among non-Indians if not suppressed.

These opposing voices were joined by General Richard Pratt, founder of the Carlisle Indian School, who attacked the Bureau of American Ethnology for misinforming Congress about the Indians and what was best for them. The testimonies of James Mooney, other anthropologists, scientists, and Indians, against the antipeyote bill proved decisive, though. Although the bill passed the House of Representatives, it was not enacted into law (Hertzberg 1971, 257–71; Stewart 1987, 213–18; La Barre 1989, 223).

Mooney had both observed and participated in peyote rituals in Oklahoma, so he spoke in his testimony from his own experience. His view of the rapid spread of peyote was that it reflected, rather than resisted, the assimilation of American Indians, and it certainly demonstrated the growth of a pannationalism that he considered positive.

Among the Native Americans who testified against the Hayden bill was an Osage named Arthur Bonnicastle who had studied at Carlisle School and fought in the American army during the Boxer Rebellion. He said,

> [Peyote] trains the mind to higher ideas in worshipping God. The principles laid down in the use of this peyote as it is taught in these meetings by the leader, teaches the Indians to do things that will lead to a better life in worshipping the Almighty; that is to train the mind to that end. I don't see any bad effects from its use. [To outlaw peyote would be] an injustice—because they don't use it to excess and use it to good advantage—use it in religion and their prayers and in times of sickness, and they don't use it between times of religious meetings. (Hertzberg 1971, 268)

The Formation of the Native American Church and Efforts to Restrict Peyote Use (1918–89)

In response to attempts to suppress peyote, supporters of peyote decided that the only way to secure protection for its continued use was to create a peyote "church." The first attempt to form such an institution came in 1914. In December, under the leadership of Jonathan Koshiway, an Oto, the First-born Church of Christ was formed. His intent was to amalgamate peyotism with Christianity so that it would become an accepted and institutionalized religion. He found parallels between peyotism and Biblical religion, for example, between the burning bush Moses saw and the peyote fire and between the wine and wafers of the Christian sacrament and the buttons and tea of peyotism (La Barre 1989, 167–70).

The Native American Church, however, was not established until October 1918 at a meeting in El Reno, Oklahoma, that brought together representatives from the Cheyenne, Oto, Ponca, Comanche, Kiowa, and Kiowa Apache nations. James Mooney provided advice, urging that such an institution be established. He was forced to make a sacrifice for his support, however; when his involvement became known, he was expelled by the Bureau of Indian Affairs from the Kiowa Reservation, and his study was halted. He died three years later, never having completed a report on peyotism, which could have rivalled his classic study of the Ghost Dance (Hertzberg 1971, 274).

The stated purpose of NAC was to

> foster and promote the religious beliefs of the several tribes of Indians in the State of Oklahoma, in the Christian religion with the practice of the Peyote Sacrament as commonly understood and used among the adherents of this religion in the several tribes of Indians in the State of Oklahoma, and to teach the Christian religion with morality, sobriety, industry, kindly charity and right living and to cultivate a spirit of self-respect and brotherly union among the members of the Native Race of Indians. . . (Hertzberg 1971, 271–74; Stewart 1987, 224; La Barre, 169–71)

After the incorporation of NAC there were no more serious attempts in Oklahoma to prohibit the ritual use of peyote. From that point on, NAC took the lead in national efforts to prevent antipeyote legislation.

Nationally, efforts to discourage or prohibit peyote use were rekindled in the 1920s. In 1922 a BIA study concluded that 13,345 Indians were active in "peyote religion" (4 percent of the total population of 316,008 Indians). The BIA printed an antipeyote pamphlet to discourage use. Once again, although bills to forbid peyote that were introduced in Congress did not pass, some states adopted prohibitions. By 1933, in addition to Utah, Colorado, and Nevada (which had enacted laws in 1917), the following states had enacted antipeyote legislation: Kansas (1920); Arizona, Montana, North Dakota, and South Dakota (all in 1923); Iowa (1924); New Mexico and Wyoming (1929); Idaho (1935); and Texas (1937). The state laws were "largely futile," however, because states had little jurisdiction over reservations. At best they slowed the traffic in peyote (Stewart 1987, 227–29; La Barre 1989, 224).

Missionaries continued to attack peyote use as ungodly. As a young boy at the school at Holy Rosary Mission (now Red Cloud School) near Pine Ridge, South Dakota, Emerson Spider was called a "dope eater" because his family was associated with the NAC. Times have changed. Today, some of the Lakota staff at Red Cloud School are members of NAC as well as active Catholics. In the early 1980s Spider went back to Red Cloud to explain the teachings of peyotism (Spider 1987, 197).

By 1920 there were active peyotists on the Navajo Reservation. In 1921 the "Peyote Church of Christ" was incorporated among Ho Chunk (Winnebago) peyotists in Nebraska. In 1922 the first NAC church was incorporated among the Lakota in South Dakota. To thwart state efforts to restrict the use of peyote, a separate church was incorporated in each county in South Dakota.

In many cases peyotists were also members of the Christian denominations represented on the reservations. This clearly shows that early on most Indians did not regard membership in the NAC or another peyote organization as incompatible with membership in a more orthodox Christian church.

Despite these efforts, disparaging remarks about peyote continued to appear in official reports. The Meriam Report of 1928, the basis of the reform movement in Indian policy in the next decade, called peyote addictive (although admitting that this had not been definitively determined) and said it was "probably harmful physically as well as socially" (Hertzberg 1971, 276).

When new BIA Commissioner John Collier led the sea change in Indian policy in the 1930s (see chapter 1), one of his objectives was to promote the religious freedom of American Indians. One of his initiatives was to change the BIA policy of resisting peyote use in ritual contexts. He withdrew the antipeyote pamphlet and replaced it with a circular directing BIA agents not to interfere with "Indian religious life or ceremonial expression" including rituals of the Native American Church (Botsford and Echo Hawk 1996, 128).

In 1934 the Native American Church of Oklahoma amended its charter to allow peyote organizations outside the state to affiliate with it. This new statement omitted distinctly Christian references in order to include non-Christian peyote groups (Hertzberg 1971, 283–84).

By this time peyote use had spread to Taos Pueblo in northern New Mexico. It was opposed by the Taos Pueblo government (La Barre 1989, 110–11), who won the support of the influential patron of Indian culture, Mabel Dodge Luhan. Luhan wrote to Collier's boss, Secretary of Interior Harold Ickes, in 1936, protesting the support for peyotists at Taos Pueblo: "Do you really mean that you are defending self-government when you take the side of a few drug addicts against the efforts of the pueblo officers to eradicate the usage of the peyote drug? . . . The Catholic Church does not recognize the 'Native American Church.' Would you stand for hashish, cocaine, or morphine and defend them on the grounds of religious liberty?" (Stewart 1987, 237). She was probably in part motivated by her concern that some in the group of artists and writers around her were taking peyote in addition to other, actually dangerous drugs.

Spurred on by such opposition, the U.S. Senate took up an antipeyote bill in 1937, but depositions and testimony by Franz Boas and other noted anthropologists helped defeat the effort. Indeed, by 1937 there was considerable expert opinion in support of the right of Native Americans to use peyote in rituals (Stewart 1987, 238).

Collier's support of peyote users was not uniform, however. In 1940 the Navajo Tribal Council passed a resolution intended to stamp out peyote use on the reservation because "its use was not connected with any Navajo religious practices" and it was "harmful and foreign to our traditional way of life." Collier approved the resolution, not because he thought peyote was harmful, but because he did not want to challenge the authority of the Navajo Tribal Council which he had worked so hard to create. A few arrests were made, but the resolution did not stop the spread of the NAC on the reservation (Stewart 1987, 296–97).

The publication in 1938 of Weston La Barre's Yale University doctoral dissertation as *The Peyote Cult* (now in its fifth edition [1989]) demonstrated the growing interest in peyotism. The book also served to regularize peyote meetings, as budding peyotists have turned to its descriptions of peyote rituals as a "manual" for how to conduct peyote meetings (much to La Barre's dismay!). La Barre had himself participated in meetings and had taken peyote during his field work (La Barre 1989, xi–xii; Farella 1984, 197). On the basis of his research, he concluded that "peyotism functions in all ways as a living religion: peyote christens the new-born and protects their early years, teaches the young, marries young men and women, rewards and punishes the behavior of adult years, and buries the dead–offering throughout consolation for troubles, chastening for bad deeds or thoughts, and serving as the focus for tribal and intertribal life" (La Barre 1989, 103).

In 1944 the Native American Church of the United States (later revised to the Native American Church of North America in 1955 in order to accommodate Canada) was formed. The preamble of the articles of incorporation of the body claims the right of native peoples to the protection of the First Amendment of the U.S. Constitution in the free exercise of religion and calls upon "all liberty loving people of our country for tolerance" (Slotkin 1956, 137–39; Stewart 1987, 239–46; La Barre 1989, 217).

An article in the *Journal of the American Medical Association* by a Mayo Clinic physician in 1949 condemned peyote use. This reflected the findings of an AMA committee that urged that peyote be outlawed as a habit-forming drug. The author did not interview any members of the NAC, however, and accepted uncritically hearsay from Indian agents and physicians who contended that peyote caused a deterioration in the morale of its users (Stewart 1987, 301; La Barre 1989, 195). Such antipeyote pronouncements were countered in a "Statement on Peyote" published in the respected journal *Science* in 1951 by La Barre and other scholars who had studied peyote use directly and who had taken it themselves (La Barre et al. 1951).

The last effort in Congress to regulate peyote directly occurred in 1963, but no law was passed. Although peyote was included in a list of forbidden psychedelic drugs in the 1965 Drug Abuse Control Act, the law was not aimed at peyotists, and the interpretation of the law by the Drug Enforcement Administration was that peyote when used in bona fide religious ceremonies was to be exempted. However, the law was used to harass NAC members. In 1978, for example, several Native American peyotists were arrested in Washington state for possession of a controlled substance when 100 peyote buttons were found in their car during a traffic stop. The case was thrown out by a judge who apologized to the defendants, but only after they had been held in jail for several months before the trial (Stewart 1987, 324).

Amid growing concern over drug use among young people and exaggerated claims for the benefits of drug use by academics such as Timothy Leary (La Barre 1989, 229–36; 268–70), state laws prohibiting use and possession of peyote continued to gain enough support to win approval. In 1965 New York passed a bill criminalizing peyote use. In 1967 the Texas legislature outlawed the possession of peyote, but, under pressure from NAC and its supporters, amended the law in 1969 to allow for peyote use by NAC (with members having to demonstrate that they had at least 25 percent Indian blood). Peyote dealers were required to keep records to show that their sales were to authorized purchasers (Stewart 1987, 246–47; La Barre 1989, 265).

Public awareness of peyote was enhanced by the publication of a description of a peyote meeting in the basement of the "Los Angeles Holiness Pan-Indian Rescue Mission" in N. Scott Momaday's Pulitzer Prize-winning novel *House Made of Dawn* (Momaday 1968, 110–14). He includes a speech based on one found in La Barre's *The Peyote Cult* (La Barre 1989, 266). Although there was no evidence of such gatherings in Los Angeles at the time, peyote meetings were becoming popular in Native American communities in San Francisco, Denver, Seattle, and other urban areas (Stewart 1987, 319–24). The excellent 1970 documentary film by Peter Furst, *To Find Our Life: The Peyote Hunt of the Huichols of Mexico,* also increased understanding of the role of peyote in its traditional cultural context.

As a result of intense lobbying by the NAC, in 1967 the Navajo Tribal Council voted to allow the NAC to transport and use peyote on the reservation, but only on a 29–26 vote (Stewart 1987, 310). The growth of peyote use on the Navajo reservation then increased dramatically. One-fourth of the membership of the NAC was Navajo. In 1976 51 percent of the peyote sold by dealers in Texas went to Arizona and New Mexico (Stewart 1987, 293).

By 1970, of the seventeen states that still had antipeyote laws, only five did not provide exemptions for Indians to use peyote ritually. South Dakota's law, amended in 1970, is typical. It stipulates that "[p]eyote when used as a sacrament in services of the Native American Church in a natural state which is unaltered except for drying or curing or slicing, is hereby excepted" (La Barre 1989, 265).

A series of highly publicized state cases in California, Arizona, and Oklahoma in the 1960s and 1970s confirmed the right of NAC members to protection of the First Amendment. For example, the Arizona Supreme Court ruled that "peyotism

[is] an established religion of many centuries' history . . . not a twentieth century cult nor a fad subject to extinction at a whim" (Botsford and Echo Hawk 1996, 132). A 1975 case in Oregon went against NAC, however. Clearly there was a need for clarification of the legal situation.

The attitude of missionaries toward peyotism was also changing. In the 1970s Father Paul Steinmetz, a Jesuit missionary on the Oglala Lakota Pine Ridge Reservation, began participating in NAC meetings. In 1975 he brought a papal blessing for NAC from Rome and read it during a peyote meeting (Steinmetz 1990a, 96–98).

The federal American Indian Religious Freedom Act passed in 1978 (see chapter 1) mentioned the need to protect peyote-users, but the law did not end unwarranted harassment. Writing in the mid–1980s, Omer Stewart observed that "NAC members were learning to be careful not to carry peyote around with them, to carry identification of membership in some NAC congregation, and to know the law" (Stewart 1987, 333). They could be arrested and detained for possession, but they would be cleared if it could be shown they were NAC members in good standing.

The involvement of non-Indians in the Native American Church has been and continues to be controversial. In 1984 a white couple was arrested in North Dakota for peyote possession by the FBI, although they had been NAC members for some years. They had been reported by NAC of North America President Emerson Jackson who claimed the couple could not be bona fide NAC members because they were non-Indians. He cited a 1982 NAC policy saying that NAC members had to be one-fourth Indian by blood quantum. The charges were dismissed, however, because the couple had legitimate NAC credentials.

This case reflects the divisions among peyotists and within the Native American Church. Most peyotists are not affiliated with the NAC of North America, although they consider themselves legitimate members of the NAC. In fact, each NAC congregation makes its own rules, including whether to accept non-Indians into membership (Stewart 1987, 333–34).

Efforts by Euroamericans to create their own organizations, such as the Neo-American Church, which uses mescaline as a sacrament, have proven thus far largely unsuccessful (La Barre 1989, vii, xiii). That has not stopped individuals and small groups from making their own trips to the peyote gardens or to find other ways to secure their own supply of the cactus illegally.

Peyote Myth, Rituals, and Beliefs

A Peyote Myth

Various myths of the origins of peyote have been documented. For example, James Mooney recorded the following myth from the Kiowa people; it was also common among other Plains peoples:

Two young men had gone upon a war expedition to the far south. They did not return at the expected time, and after long waiting their sister, according to Indian custom, retired alone to the hills to bewail their death. Worn out with grief and weeping, as night came on she was unable to get back to the camp and lay down where she was. In her dreams the peyote spirit came to her and said: "You wail for your brothers, but they still live. In the morning look, and where your head now rests, you will find that which will restore them to you." The spirit then gave her instructions and was gone. With the daylight she arose, and on looking where she had slept, she found peyote, which she dug up and took back with her to camp. Here she summoned the priests of the tribe, to whom she told her vision and delivered the instructions which she had received from the spirit. Under her direction the sacred tipi was set up with its crescent mound, and the old men entered and said prayers and sang the songs and ate the peyote–which seems to have been miraculously multiplied–until daylight, when they saw in their visions a picture of the two young warriors, wandering on foot and hungry in the far off passes of the Sierra Madre. A strong party was organized to penetrate the enemy's country and after many days the young men were found and restored to their people. Since then, the peyote is eaten by Indians with a song and prayer that they may see visions and know inspiration, and the young girl who first gave it is venerated as the "Peyote Woman." (cited in Stewart 1987, 36)

Peyote Rituals

Peyote rituals or meetings, as they are often called, are held for specific purposes, varying from nation to nation. Some reasons include celebrating a child's first four birthdays, curing an illness, recognizing a child's departure for or return from boarding school, asking for help during a time of economic stress, giving thanks for the healthy birth of a child or some success in life, celebrating a holiday such as Christmas or New Year's, solemnizing a marriage (after a Christian or traditional service), or memorializing the dead (La Barre 1989, 43; Aberle 1983, 559; Cousineau and Rhine 1996, 80–81).

What follows is a paraphrased and abbreviated version of La Barre's description of the Kiowa peyote meetings of the 1930s (La Barre 1989, 43–53), with additional information from other sources as noted, in order to draw a composite picture of a modern peyote meeting. Needless to say, not all the elements are found in all meetings, though the structure is fundamentally the same. Variations reflect the traditions of different nations, the Christian or non-Christian orientation, the "branch" of the NAC, and the preferences of the individual roadmen.

Oftentimes, there will be a "vow" to hold a peyote meeting, like the sun dance vow common among Plains nations (see chapter 4). Preparatory sweat baths are common. Today most ceremonies are open to men and to women over thirteen who are not menstruating, although women typically do not sing or handle the ritual objects. Among nations with matriarchal traditions (e.g., the Diné and Lakota), however, women may now participate as singers and even lead meetings. Traditional dress for the ceremony was buckskin, today replaced by blankets or folded sheets for men and shawls for women; many participants come dressed in their best clothes. Men may wear a silk handkerchief with a silver bola in the form of a peyote symbol. Some wear red bean necklaces or Indian jewelry and carry ceremonial feather fans and small gourd rattles (Stewart 1987, 328). Moccasins are typically worn. Men may paint themselves on the basis of visions they have received.

Meetings are often held in specially constructed tipis, lodges, or hogans (in the case of the Diné), but they may also be conducted in a house. The sponsor of the meeting selects a leader (often called the "road chief" or "roadman"), who has his own fire man and usually also a cedar man. In some contexts the sponsor approaches the desired roadman with tobacco, and if the roadman accepts it, he is agreeing to conduct the meeting. The sponsor is responsible for providing or paying for the peyote used, although some participants may bring their own buttons.

The leader provides the ritual paraphernalia: at least, a staff, gourd rattle, eagle bone (or reed) whistle, cedar incense, altar cloth, bundle of sage, water drum and drum stick, corn husks and tobacco (in a Half Moon Ceremony), peyote bags, water bucket, and fan of feathers (usually twelve) for doctoring. A satchel or case for the ritual items is also a necessity.

Each of the ritual objects is symbolic. For example, the staff may symbolize the Tree of Everlasting Life, the gourd rattle the mind and heart getting in tune with the creator and the rest of creation (Snake 1996, 230–32). The staff may also remind participants of the spear used to pierce Jesus in Cross Fire Ceremonies, or simply the staff of authority. Prayers pass up the staff and visions travel down from the peyote spirit. Eagle feathers may be tied to it.

A red horsehair top may be on the gourd, representing the rays of the sun. There may also be little stones in the gourd taken from any heaps, the voices of the spirits. The beadwork on the handle is in the shape of a rainbow. In Cross Fire Ceremonies there may be twelve strings in a fringe to signify the twelve apostles. The fans are made from the feathers of various birds. The twelve feathers of the fan may symbolize the twelve months of the year (Cousineau and Rhine 1996, 88). A roadman's fan may be made from eagle feathers, although, most desirable are macaw feathers, which have been used for more than a thousand years in Indian ceremonies.

The whistle connects the worshippers to the four directions and represents the sun. Individuals may bring their own staffs, gourds, and fans in a decorated box or pouch to use at specified points in the meeting (Crow Dog 1995, 99–102).

The drum, called a water drum, is traditionally a kettle with buckskin stretched over it. The drum is placed at the center of the room; it is the spirit of peyote. In a Cross Fire meeting a three-legged kettle is said to represent the Father, Son, and Holy Ghost and the skin across it the skin of Jesus beaten by the soldiers at his crucifixion. Or the skin may represent all the four-leggeds. The drum is filled about one-third-to-one-half-full with water, giving it a unique sound. Into the water live coals are dropped before the buckskin top is tied on with seven round pebbles or marbles. The kettle symbolizes thunder and rain, and the coals lightning. In a Cross Fire Ceremony the pebbles are the seven sacraments of the Church; in Lakota Half Moon Ceremonies they are the seven camp circles of the nation. The rope used to tie the head is made from twisted rawhide. When tied, the rope forms the design of the morning star on the bottom of the drum. The drumstick represents either the stick the government used to beat Indians or the stick used to whip Jesus. It also represents the growing things. Inside the drumstick are memories of loved ones who have died (Crow Dog 1995, 98–99).

The leader also provides a particularly large (often sixteen-segmented) peyote button (or satchel of buttons) known as "Father Peyote" (also called Peyote Chief, Chief Peyote, Old Man Peyote, Grandfather, the Interpreter, or the Holy Ghost in ceremonies with a Christian orientation). It may have been in the leader's family for generations. Participants often focus their gaze on Father Peyote throughout the ceremony.

In some Lakota ceremonies the roadman may bring a sacred pipe and place it in front of him on a rack made of two upright forked sticks and a crosspiece (Crow Dog 1995, 97; Steinmetz 1990a, 94–96). The pipe is smoked in place of the cornhusk cigarettes.

Another recurrent symbol is the water bird. Reuben Snake describes two kinds (Snake 1996, 227): one is an anhinga, a diving bird, and the other is a cormorant. In his ceremonies he used the feathers of the anhinga, for she is known (according to Creek legend) to dive beneath the water to bring up plants to feed to her sick young. The water bird is embroidered on shawls of women members and on their jewelry.

Any time after nightfall the ceremony begins when the participants follow the leader into the tipi (or other place), entering clockwise. The leader sits to the west of the fire, facing to the east. His drummer is to the south of him, to his right, and the cedar man to the north (left). The fire man has started the fire and tends it through the night. A tipi twenty-five feet in diameter can easily accommodate thirty worshippers.

A story told by NAC elders reflects the symbolism of the meeting place and the drum: "When you enter the tepee, it's like re-entering the womb of your mother. The tepee poles symbolize her ribs and the fireplace in the center signifies her blood that kept you warm and alive in her womb. The drum represents your mother's heart-beat, because that's the first sound you heard in her womb. . . . It also symbolizes the voice of God" (Snake 1996, 226).

The crescent altar (in the Half Moon Ceremony) of sand is at the west center, horns to the east. In the Cross Fire ritual the altar is in a horseshoe shape. The altar has a groove along it from horn to horn, with a flat place in the middle for Father Peyote, which rests on a bed of sage. The path represents the passage of a person from birth at the southern tip, to maturity and knowledge at the crest (where the peyote is), downward to death at the north. It also represents the unending cycle of life: when a person leaves this life he returns to the spirit world from which he came (Snake 1996, 229). For the Kiowa, the crescent also symbolizes the mountain range in the Kiowa story of the origins of peyote where Peyote Woman first discovered the cactus. With the ash from the fire the fire man creates another crescent or horseshoe-shaped altar between the fire and the mound. When there is no sand altar or fire, an altar cloth may be spread on the floor.

The fire is both physically and symbolically at the center. A family that honors the peyote way is said "to have a fire place." The fire represents the power of the sun, the spark passed from generation to generation. It is everlasting. The fire man shapes the fire into a half-moon (or horseshoe) design as the meeting is about to begin. The crescent signifies woman power. At midnight it may be shaped into a heart. At 4:00 A.M. it may be formed into a morning star, and at daybreak into a cross (for either the four cardinal directions or the Christian cross) (Crow Dog 1995, 102–3).

When the leader places Father Peyote on the altar, the ceremony has officially begun. In some nations Father Peyote stands for the button picked up by the woman in the legend of origins. In a Half Moon Ceremony the leader usually makes himself a cigarette from Bull Durham tobacco with corn husk papers and passes the material clockwise so that others can make their own. All light their cigarettes and the leader prays, asking that the power of peyote be present, that none get sick from the peyote. He also prays for the person for whom the ceremony is being held.

Next the cedar man sprinkles dried cedar on the fire to produce an aromatic smoke. The cedar is pleasing to the spirits. It stands for everlasting life, for only the cedar stays green while other trees lose their leaves. All the ritual objects are passed through the cedar smoke (an act called "cedaring") in order to purify them. The roadman takes out the peyote bag and passes it clockwise with each person taking out four buttons. He then rubs himself with crushed sage, as do the others. Sweet grass may also be used as an incense.

The buttons are now eaten, and from this point on anyone may call for the peyote bag without repeating the incense ceremony. Through the night a person consumes as few as four and as many as 75 or 100 buttons (some have claimed to have eaten more), but the average is from twelve to twenty. Some, especially older or ill participants, may take the peyote in a mush or a tea made from soaked and boiled buttons. If the peyote causes a person to vomit, it is assumed that the body is being purified.

More cedar is sprinkled on the fire, and the leader makes four motions with his staff in his left hand and gourd rattle in the right toward the rising smoke. Accompanied by the drummer, the leader begins the Opening Song, which comes from the peyote itself. The song is composed of syllables: *Na he he he na you witsi nai yo*, reflective of the Lipan Apache songs (Stewart 1987, 329). It means something like "The peyote recognizes you. It is going to give you a voice to use during the night" (Crow Dog 1995, 106). This is the first of four songs sung in every ceremony; the opening, midnight, morning water, and closing songs are the others. Each song is repeated four times.

Thereafter, singing, rattling, and drumming continue through the night, with intervals for prayers humbly (and often tearfully) invoking the aid of the spirit of peyote. These songs reflect the occasion of the ceremony: memorializing the dead, healing diseases, celebrating birthdays, and so on. Each person takes a turn drumming and singing four songs as the staff, fan, and rattle are passed in a meticulously prescribed manner. The purpose of the music is "to bring our minds together, to fuse our minds into one thought" (Snake 1996, 225). In meetings in which Christian themes are emphasized, the songs are often verses from the Bible. Some examples of peyote songs are offered below.

At midnight more cedar is placed on the fire, and the Midnight Water Call Song is sung. The fire man brings in a bucket of water, which is passed through cedar smoke. A little water is poured on the ground "for Mother Earth" (Stewart 1987, 329). The roadman goes outside and blows the eagle whistle to the four directions, which to some prefigures the angels blowing their trumpets at the end of the world (Steinmetz 1990a, 109). An altar cloth is laid out west of Father Peyote. The paraphernalia are placed on the cloth. The fire man makes a cigarette, and while he smokes offers a prayer. The leader and drummer follow. The bucket is passed so that worshippers may drink.

At this time people may leave to stretch. When they return, singing continues through the night. Up to two-thirds of a meeting is taken up with singing. More peyote may be passed, and participants may take out their own rattles and fans to use when singing. The cedar man may offer a prayer regarding the purpose of the meeting at the end of each round of songs. An example of such a prayer is "God the Father, have pity on me and have pity on these people. As we eat this medicine, have pity on us. God the Father, You will make it possible that my brother . . . will be able to pray. God the Father, You will see that his wife has good health. " (Steinmetz 1990a, 128).

At the first signs of dawn, the roadman sings the Morning (Dawn) Song. At this time the "peyote woman" (often the wife of the sponsor) brings more water. She represents the woman who first found peyote according to one tradition of the origin of peyote (see above). According to a Lakota peyotist, "The Morning Water Woman is like Mother Earth. She is mother of all. From her bosom came the water. She gave to all her children, the plants, the various species of animals, from the tiniest ant to the biggest elephant, the eagle" (Steinmetz 1990a, 107–8). The roadman may again blow his whistle to the four directions. This is the time at which "doctoring" is best done. The patient is fanned with feathers from the altar cloth by the leader or an older man. In some contexts a "baptism" ritual may be held at this time (although it may also be held at midnight).

While they wait for breakfast of water, parched corn in sweetened water, fruit, and dried sweetened meat, the roadman or an old man present may lecture the younger participants on proper behavior (although the talk may be given at midnight in some contexts). In Lakota ceremonies wasna, pemmican (dried buffalo meat), and chokecherries may be used (Crow Dog 1995, 98).

In a Cross Fire Ceremony passages from the Bible may be read and interpreted. When the full light of day has come and the food is ready, the roadman or fire man sings the Quitting or Closing Song. When Father Peyote is placed in the leader's satchel and the ritual objects are carefully put away, the ceremony has ended. As the participants emerge into the morning air they may raise their hands to the four directions in gratitude and greet each other with joy (Cousineau and Rhine 1996, 100).

The formal meeting ended, informal socializing continues, as worshippers share their peyote experiences. After lunch, people return to their homes, some having traveled long distances to reach the meeting site.

Although anthropologists and other observers have published many accounts of peyote meetings, the NAC has never made available written instructions. The ritual is to be learned by novice roadmen through apprenticeship and especially through attending ceremonies (Stewart 1987, 330). In addition to formal ceremonies, peyote songs may be sung at home and practice sessions may be held. Peyote may be used by individual believers outside the ritual context at times of special need (Stewart 1987, 330–31) (For a typical meeting followed by Navajo peyotists, see Aberle 1983, 559–62; 1991).

The Influence of Christianity

Daniel Aberle observed on the basis of his experience with Navajo peyotists that the language of peyote meetings was rich with Christian allusions. "Some of its [peyote religion's] symbolism is Christian, and God, Jesus, Mary, and the Heavenly Angels figure in prayers." He also noted that, however, "much more symbolism is Indian, and supernaturals of various tribes also appear in prayers; hence it may be called semi-Christian. It is nativistic in its stress on maintaining an Indian religion for Indians and in its ritual details. It is redemptive, rather than transformative, in seeking a major change in the soul of the believer, rather than in the social order" (Aberle 1983, 558).

The tension between Christian and traditional spiritual language was also observed by Father Paul Steinmetz in Oglala Lakota peyote meetings. While he concluded that "the Oglala Lakota in the Native American Church have explicit-ly Christian beliefs" and speak of God monotheistically, in Half Moon cere-monies the preferred form of address was the traditional *Tunkashila* ("Grandfather") (Steinmetz 1990a, 98).

Among the Ho Chunk the leader, drummer, and cedar man symbolize the "father, son, and holy spirit" (La Barre 1989, 64, 163). The Ho Chunk among oth-ers also use the Bible in the ceremony, placing Father Peyote on an open Bible (La Barre 1989, 73). The physiological effects of peyote are compared to the driving out of demons (La Barre 1989, 164). Bible passages such as Exodus 12:8 and Romans 11:16–18 are cited as references to peyote.

A typical Winnebago closing song is also Christian: "This is the road Jesus showed us to walk in," as is another song: "God, I thank you for all you have done for me through Jesus' name." Other songs with Christian influence include "When I die I will be at the door of heaven and Jesus will take me in," "God said in the beginning, 'Let there be light,'/ He meant it for you," and "Come ye to the road of the Son of God; come ye to the road" (La Barre 1989, 83–84).

Despite these indications of Christianity and peyotism synthesized, La Barre concluded that "the layer of Christianity on peyotism is very thin and superficial indeed" and that peyotism "is an essentially aboriginal American religion, oper-ating in terms of fundamental Indian concepts about powers, visions and native modes of doctoring" (La Barre 1989, 165–66, 199–200, 292).

Stewart, in contrast, has argued that Christian elements were "early, integral, basic and essential, and diffused with the rite itself" (Stewart 1948). J.S. Slotkin, who studied peyotism among the Menomini of Wisconsin, considered peyote rit-uals as Christianity adapted to traditional Indian beliefs and practices. He com-pared the empowerment experienced by the consumption of peyote with the power derived from the Christian consumption of consecrated bread and wine during the sacrament of Holy Communion (Slotkin 1952; 1956).

Åke Hultkrantz expresses the complexity of the relationship between pey-otism, Christianity, and traditional spirituality as follows:

> The peyote cult has its own theology, concentrated around the marvelous plant and with obvious traits of Catholic Christianity. On the other hand, the peyote movement tries to replace Christianity; God has sent Christ to the whites, peyote to the red man. At the same time the peyote movement has acted against the inherited, indigenous tribal religion, causing friction on reservations wherever it has appeared." (cited in La Barre 1989, 293)

He concludes that peyote gave an ideological foundation for opposing white supremacy in a way Christianity could not. If anything, in his view, it was an addition to rather than a fundamental change of the aboriginal ideological pattern.

Some peyotists have fully embraced Christianity. The Native American Church of Jesus Christ teaches adherents to give up traditional ways. The headman of the church in South Dakota in the late 1980s, Emerson Spider of Porcupine on the Pine Ridge Reservation, who calls himself a "born-again" Christian, said, "I'm not saying the traditional ways are bad, but it tells in the Bible, 'Choose you this day whom you will serve, whether the gods of Amorites our forefathers served; but as for me and my house, we will serve the Lord'" (Spider 1987, 191).

The tension between Christian and strictly indigenous beliefs will likely continue in the NAC. To this point, the tension has been largely healthy, giving Native Americans options in their adoption of the peyote way.

The Effects of Peyote

Serious studies of peyote have long shown that it is not a dangerous drug. It is not addictive. No evidence shows that it causes damage to chromosomes as had been alleged. No one has ever died as a result of ingesting peyote. In fact, reputable research has shown that behavior changes among peyote users have been overwhelmingly positive.

Emery Johnson, who directed the Indian Health Services for twelve years, wrote: "As a practicing physician for 38 years, I had patients who were active members of the NAC and in no instance did I find any evidence of abuse of peyote. . . Within the context of the Church, rather than a drug of abuse, peyote is actually used in the treatment of other substances." The noted psychiatrist Karl Menninger said, "Peyote is not harmful to these people; it is beneficial, comforting, inspiring, and appears to be spiritually nourishing. It is a better antidote to alcohol than anything the missionaries, the white man, the American Medical Association, and the public health services have come up with" (Smith and Snake 1996, 109–13).

Based on his career-long study, Weston La Barre concluded that "the alkaloids [in peyote] are only mildly toxic and have little or no untoward effect in the amounts used; the amount of mescaline is small and barely minimal pharamacodynamically; and peyote, I am certain, is in no sense addictive" (La Barre 1989, xiii; cf. 139–50, 218–22, 252–56, 288–90, 305–7 for a full discussion of research on the chemical nature and effects of peyote).

Peyote is certainly not a narcotic (La Barre 1989, 222–23), but the federal government and most states have defined peyote as a hallucinogen (like LSD and marijuana) with "a high potential for abuse." This classification has been vigorously challenged by the Native American Church, whose members contend that ingesting peyote does not cause hallucinations. The dispute continues, however (Smith and Snake 1996, 113–15). Father Steinmetz pointed out that the only outward effect he noted in taking peyote was increased fervor in prayer and singing (Steinmetz 1990a, 99).

Peyote "visions" are virtually always positive, giving instruction to the person on how to find healing. For example, a man with tuberculosis had a peyote vision in which he was wandering in a desert. Somebody instructed him to pray to his grandfather. At first he thought the voice meant his natural grandfather. Then he thought of his extended relatives and others who might also be addressed as "Grandfather." But the voice kept on repeating the instruction. Suddenly, he became aware that the voice was telling him to pray to the Great Spirit. He did, and when he left the meeting he was well (Steinmetz 1990a, 110–11; cf. 109–22).

Peyote Healings and Peyote's Protective Power

"Doctoring" as it is usually called is central to peyote rituals. Meetings are often called in order to heal a patient. Peyotists accept as an article of faith that the spirit of peyote has power to heal people. As noted above, peyote is often called "medicine." Accounts of healings have played a crucial role in the spread of peyotism. Stories of "miraculous" healings are common: a woman cured of cancer, a boy who had previously been unable to speak able to talk, a man with pneumonia healed, people with various mental disturbances made well. Weston La Barre witnessed successful "doctoring" with peyote for a crushed thigh, tuberculosis, and malnutrition (La Barre 1989, 85–88; cf. Steinmetz 1990a, 122–25).

Beyond the healing of specific maladies, the protective power of peyote is a source of comfort to believers. Through peyote believers gain support in facing the most serious personal problems. It frees users from anxieties. It enables them to withstand the pressures of the dominant society, particularly the dangers of the alcohol introduced to Native Americans by Euroamericans. Peyote meetings are often the occasion for the public admission of faults. Alongside faith in its protection is the awareness that peyote can also cause suffering to those who use peyote improperly or come to peyote for the wrong reasons (La Barre 1989, 93–104).

Some NAC members say there has been a decline in the healing power of peyote. Some of the problems they cite are as follows: use of alcohol by those also ingesting peyote, not having enough peyote to take, distractions in the meetings as people try to show off their medicine fans and generally try to outdo each other, arguments among people, increased use of hospitals, and the use of tape recorders in meetings (Steinmetz 1990a, 124).

The Testimony of Reuben Snake (1937–1993)

In the long debate over the legitimacy of the use of peyote, the voices least heard have often been those who have themselves been peyotists for most of their lives. That omission has been addressed through the publication of the memoirs of Native American Church leaders such as Reuben Snake (Snake 1996; Snake and Smith 1996, 15–37).

Snake, a Ho Chunk (Winnebago), whose Indian name is *Kikawa Unga* (To Rise Up), was baptized into the NAC as a two-year-old on Easter 1939. His commission at his baptism was to resurrect the heritage of his people. He was ordained as a roadman in the NAC on 26 October 1974. Snake was active in the struggle to protect the civil rights of Native Americans and to renew the culture of his own people. In 1977 he became the Winnebago tribal chairman. He also served as national chairman of the American Indian Movement and President of the National Congress of American Indians. In addition, he played a critical role in the fight to protect the freedom of religion of members of the NAC, which culminated in the passage, a year after his death, of the 1994 amendments to the American Indian Religious Freedom Act (see below). Although a powerful and accomplished leader, he was a gentle man. A member of the Snake Clan of the Ho Chunk people, he sometimes introduced himself as Reuben Snake, your Humble Serpent.

Snake, like other Ho Chunk NAC members, was comfortable participating in both the Cross Fire and Half Moon meetings. Both had been introduced to the Nebraska Winnebago people early in the century (Snake 1996, 254). According to Snake, "Everything we do [in the Native American Church]—our music, our dancing, our rituals—is done to honor the Creator and find our place in his creation" (Snake and Smith 1996, 16). For Snake, peyote "is the most powerful of all the plants because God endowed it with his love and compassion. . . . It enables us to treat one another tenderly, and with joy, love, and respect" (Smith and Snake 1996, 16, 18). The tipi in which peyote meetings are held is, he says, our mother's womb. Sitting in a circle, members look directly together into God's face, his fire (rather than at the back of each other's neck as in most Christian churches). Participants bare their souls to one another, asking for God's and their neighbors' forgiveness. They ingest the divine medicine in order to heal their souls.

By keeping their "ceremonial life intact down to its exact details," the native peoples can reverse the legacy of turmoil and confusion brought by Europeans to this continent, he says. At one ceremony he conducted, an astrophysicist guest remarked that the ancestors must have given excellent directions for orienting the tipi, because the first rays of the sun at dawn were aligned in the tipi's doorway and the main pole precisely. They were, the scientist said, "right on the mark." For Snake, if you keep the NAC's, teachings you will discover them to be "right on."

"The medicine is the teacher," he wrote, "and it teaches us all about life. So if you really want to understand life you have to come sit down around the light of this Holy Fire and eat this medicine and open up your mind to the Creation and to the Creator" (Snake 1996, 191). The most significant teaching he received from Peyote was a sense of humility, "that we can't be self-righteous, we can't be filled with pride and expect God to hear our prayers" (Snake 1996, 216–17).

For Snake, peyote is "the voice of God arising from the earth" (Smith and Snake 1996, 24). If Jesus was God incarnate in human form, Peyote is God incarnate in plant form. Like Jesus, Peyote teaches us to love our fellow men, he says. Snake distinguished the teachings of Jesus from what Christian people did in the name of Christ to indigenous peoples. He believed that "the core of Jesus Christ's teachings and the essence of traditional American Indian spirituality were compatible" (Snake 1996, 25, 210).

For Reuben Snake, spirituality and political activism were two sides of the same coin. In NAC meetings he prayed that the desperate needs of Indian people would be addressed, and then he went out and did his best to do just that (Snake 1996, 168). He liked to tell the story of a family whose home was being flooded by a rising river. A truck came by to offer to take them to safety, but they declined, saying that they trusted in the Lord to protect them. Their response was the same when a boat appeared, then, as the waters rose to the level of the roof of the house, a helicopter. They were swept away, and when they appeared in heaven before God, they asked, "Lord, we put our trust in you, why didn't you help us?" The Lord responded, "What do you mean? I sent you a truck, a boat, and a helicopter, but you didn't accept my help!"

Snake ingested peyote since his infancy and never, he says, did it cause him or any other church member he knew of to hallucinate; its directives have always been to live cleanly, with a loving heart. When he took peyote he sometimes saw his deceased relatives or those of the patient. These "visions" convinced him that human relationships extend beyond this life and that the ancestors are available to aid us in this world. Our lives on earth are only a portion of the cycle of life. That is symbolized in the half-moon altar, reflecting that our journeys are only partly visible to us, that the full circle of life extends beyond our earthly experience (Snake 1996, 31–32, 215).

The Native American Church and Peyotism Today

In the mid 1990s the Native American Church of North America had eighty chapters across the United States and Canada. Seventy different native nations were represented in its membership, which totalled about 250,000. Every state west of the Mississippi has at least one chapter. It is the largest single Native American religious organization. More Native Americans attend peyote meetings than any other Indian institution except for powwows (see chapter 9). The church has no paid, professional clergy (Fikes 1996, 172–73).

At the dawn of the twenty-first century, members of the NAC and other peyotists are addressing recurrent as well as new concerns. Some of the more important issues being faced are addressed here, as are the reasons for the great success of this movement.

The Ongoing Struggle for the Right of Native Americans to Use Peyote Ritually: The Smith Decision (1990) and Its Aftermath

The most important issue facing the various branches of the Native American Church today is, as it has been since 1918, protection of the right of NAC members to practice their spiritual traditions freely. The long struggle to secure this right is noted above. With the passage of the American Indian Freedom of Religion Act in 1978, most NAC members assumed that the battle had finally been won. Such was not the case, however.

In 1985 Al Smith, a Klamath Indian and a member of the Native American Church, was dismissed from his job in a private alcohol and drug abuse treatment program in Roseburg, Oregon, because he refused to give up using peyote in NAC ceremonies. Smith filed for unemployment benefits, and his claim, which was challenged by the state's Employment Division, was upheld in the state courts.

In October 1988 the Oregon Supreme Court ruled unanimously that the dismissal violated Smith's constitutional right to free religious expression. The state's attorney general appealed the decision in the federal courts, however, and the case went to the U.S. Supreme Court. On 17 April 1990 the Court announced its ruling in the case of *Employment Division, Oregon v. Smith*.

According to Lakota legal scholar Vine Deloria Jr., at issue was whether "the state of Oregon held a constitutional right to impose either civil or criminal penalties upon members of the NAC for their traditional use of sacramental peyote simply because use of the substance was legally denied to everyone else. The high court held that the state did in fact possess such rights." The effect was to void "long-settled interpretations of the constitutional protections extended over the free exercise of religion—not only with regard to Indians, but to everyone else as well—and throws them in the same 'community standards' arena covering pornography and other forms of obscenity" (Deloria 1992, 268).

With a stroke of the pen the justices of the U.S. Supreme Court had wiped out a test, established by more than 200 years of state and federal judicial decisions, that there must be a "compelling state interest" in order to restrict religious freedom. Writing for the majority Justice Scalia called religious diversity a "luxury" that a pluralistic society could no longer "afford." The Court ruled that the free exercise of religion was not protected by the First Amendment unless some other right protected by the amendment (such as speech or free association) was affected. The impact was, in the view of many constitutional scholars, to make religious freedom irrelevant (Botsford and Echo Hawk 1996, 136).

After the *Smith* decision, cases abridging the religious freedom of Amish people, Muslims, and Jews were directly affected, and many other groups feared they were next (Snake 1996, 183). A Catholic scholar expressed the view that under different circumstances the right of an underage member of the Catholic church to consume wine during the sacrament of Holy Communion could be challenged (Gaffney 1994, 6).

One of the dissenting justices in the *Smith* ruling characterized the situation well:

> The Court today—interprets the [Free Exercise] Clause to permit the government to prohibit, without justification, conduct mandated by an individual's religious beliefs, so long as the prohibition is generally applicable. But a law that prohibits certain conduct—conduct that happens to be an act of worship for someone—manifestly does prohibit that person's free exercise of his religion. A person who is barred from engaging in religiously motivated conduct is barred from freely exercising his religion. (Deloria 1992, 268)

In his dissent to the majority's ruling, Justice Blackmun wrote, "I do not believe the Founders thought their dearly bought freedom from religious persecution a 'luxury,' but an essential element of liberty—and they could not have thought religious intolerance 'unavoidable,' for they drafted the Religion Clauses precisely in order to avoid that intolerance" (Botsford and Echo Hawk 1996, 136–37).

The *Smith* ruling sent a chill through the Native American Church, and it also caused those concerned about the freedom of religious expression in the United States to take notice. As a result, a coalition, led by the Native American Church and its supporters, quickly came together to find a legislative remedy (which the Court's ruling suggested was a possible course of action). Reuben Snake and other NAC leaders took on the daunting task of overturning the high court's ruling. They formed the Native American Religious Freedom Project to educate the public on the ruling and the teachings of NAC and lobby for a change in the law. When asked how he planned to accomplish such a lofty goal, Reuben Snake said, "With a frequent flyer coupon and a prayer" (Botsford and Echo Hawk 1996, 140). One positive result of the otherwise disastrous ruling was to bring the various NAC factions together to speak with one voice. The project eventually broadened into the American Indian Religious Freedom Coalition to address issues other than the use of peyote. The work of the coalition is ongoing.

The first strategy was for NAC to join with other churches to secure passage of the Religious Freedom Restoration Act (RFRA) in 1993 in order to restore the "compelling state interest" test, even though the law did not address the right to use peyote in NAC ceremonies. In signing that bill President Clinton acknowledged that more legislative action was necessary in order to protect Native American religious practices (Smith and Snake 1996, 145).

In 1993 Senator Daniel Inouye introduced legislation to strengthen the 1978 law so that it would explicitly protect the right of NAC members to use peyote in their rituals, as well as to protect sacred sites, the use of animal parts in Native American rituals, and the rights of incarcerated Native Americans to have access to religious ceremonies such as the sweat lodge (Snake 1996, 185–86). A year later Congressman Bill Richardson of New Mexico introduced a similar bill in the House of Representatives. The Drug Enforcement Administration and Justice Department of the Clinton administration joined in support of the legislation. A documentary film entitled *The Peyote Road*, produced by Reuben Snake, also helped to make people aware of the injustice of the *Smith* decision.

The campaign came to a successful conclusion in 1994. Congress passed and on 6 October 1994 President Bill Clinton signed the American Indian Religious Freedom Act Amendments of 1994 (Public Law 103–344). The law effectively overturned the *Smith* ruling and legalized the ceremonial use of peyote by Indians in all fifty states. Congress recognized that "for many Indian people the traditional ceremonial use of the peyote cactus as a religious sacrament has for centuries been integral to a way of life, and significant in perpetuating Indian tribes and cultures" (Smith and Snake 1996, 146). The 250,000 members of NAC for the first time could practice their faith without fear of penalties or discrimination.

A related issue is whether non-Native Americans can claim a right to use peyote. As noted, a number of non-Indian "churches" have sprung up since the 1960s, each claiming that the exemption to the drug laws for the NAC discriminates against them. In 1991, however, the Fifth Circuit Court of Appeals "ruled that the U.S. government's trust relationship with tribal Native Americans places them in a special category that makes their exemption in order" (Botsford and Echo Hawk 1996, 129). Therefore, the government still may regulate the possession and use of peyote by non-Native Americans. This has troubled some NAC members who think that peyote is a medicine that should be available to non-Indians who are in need of its healing power.

The Depletion in the Supply of Peyote

The northernmost place peyote can be found today is Miranda, Texas, thirty miles north of the Mexican border. Peyotists must gather peyote in this area, because Mexico has outlawed its possession and export. The harvesting of peyote is controlled by Texas state law. To gather the plant the collector must have a state permit, which is granted only to someone who is registered as a custodian of peyote for the Native American Church.

The law treats peyote as a medicine; it has to be pure by FDA standards. A machine is used to "sanitize" the peyote, running hot and cold water over it. The peyote is then graded as large or small. One type has twelve spots on top. It is made into tea or mush. The other has ten spots and must be sun dried. After drying, the peyote button is the size of a silver dollar. The juice, the power, stays in it (Crow Dog 1996, 110).

One of the principal issues facing the Native American Church and other peyote users today is the depletion of the supply of peyote and the rapidly increasing cost. A substantial supply still remains in the peyote gardens in south Texas, but the increase in use, especially among Navajo peyotists, and the illegal harvesting of pey-ote by drug culture enthusiasts, has driven up the price substantially. Despite the regulations controlling harvesting, the gardens are essentially unprotected.

The price of peyote rose from $9.50 to $15.00 per 100 buttons in 1955 to $100 in 1984 and $135 in 1996 (Mesteth 1996). In the 1960s it was not uncommon for 1,000 buttons to be used at a meeting (Steinmetz 1990, 92). The dramatic rise in price has resulted in a significant reduction in the amount of peyote consumed at meetings; in many meetings only one-half to one-third of the peyote once con-sumed is available (Stewart 1987, 334–36).

Conclusion: Peyote and Pannationalism

As noted throughout this chapter, peyotism is an authentically pannational Native American spiritual tradition. During a period when national spiritual traditions were under active assault, the Native American Church and other forms of pey-otism served as a powerful spiritual force, uniting people from the 500 nations of Native North America. As Omer Stewart said, "Except for the Indian powwow, [the Native American Church] is the most pan-Indian institution in America" (Stewart 1987, 327). As Lakota medicine man and peyote roadman Leonard Crow Dog observed, "anything is good that brings our people together in a spiritual way, from the Yukon to the Rio Grande, from the Atlantic to the Pacific" (Crow Dog 1995, 91). According to respected scholar of religion Huston Smith, who support-ed the Native American Church in its most recent struggle for religious freedom, "The Native American Church is the spiritual bulwark of a quarter million of the original inhabitants of this continent" (Smith and Snake 1996, 9).

What have been and what will be the effects of the re-emergent spiritual nationalism sweeping across Native America? It is possible that it will lead some Native American traditionalists to withdraw from the Native American Church and other peyotist institutions because of their syncretistic nature. Indeed, as noted, as peyotism was spreading through native nations earlier in this century, some spiritual leaders spoke out against it. In the mid- to late 1990s, however, there was little evidence that this is the case. Most traditional spiritual leaders either follow the "peyote way" themselves, alongside their practice of the nation-al rituals, or are accepting of those who do.

CHAPTER 8

The Ecocrisis and Native American Spiritual Traditions

At the bottom of everything . . . is a religious view of the world that seeks to locate our species within a fabric of life that constitutes the natural world, the land and all its various forms of life. As long as Indians exist there will be a conflict between the tribes and any group that carelessly despoils the land and the life it supports.

—Vine Deloria Jr.

The white man thinks he owns the earth while the American Indian knows the earth owns him.

—Elwood Koshiway, Native American Church roadman

THE TERM *ecocrisis* refers to the present danger to the balance of life on planet Earth. It is an abbreviation of "ecological crisis" and a synonym for "environmental crisis."

The difficulty in accepting the reality of the ecocrisis is, of course, that, with some exceptions, it is not immediately visible to most of us. As I look out my window today at a sunny Missouri winter day, with clean white snow on the ground, a gorgeous blue sky above, clear water running in the stream behind my house, and a diversity of birds at the feeder in my backyard, it is tempting to be lulled into a sense of complacency about the state of the environment. My environment seems to be fine, so why should I be concerned? We must look beyond appearances, and beyond our own backyards, to see the ecocrisis facing all of us on planet Earth.

According to the current consensus of the world's scientific community, the ecocrisis is manifested in a number of areas. For example, the increasing carbon emissions in the world today are creating a "greenhouse effect" that threatens to alter the world's climate, with potentially disastrous consequences. In the past fifty years greenhouse gases have increased by one-third. More than 5 percent of the earth's protective ozone layer has been destroyed. More than one-third of the world's forests have been cut in this same period without replacing them. The world's deserts are also expanding as a direct result of the human impact on the environment.

Unless population growth is controlled, the carrying capacity of the earth may be exceeded in the next century. The world's population has exploded from about 500 million in 1600 to about 6 billion today, with 3.5 billion added in the past fifty years.

During the past half-century nearly one-fourth of the earth's topsoil has been wasted. More than one-fifth of the cropland has been ruined through excessive fertilization, urbanization, and irrigation. Natural resources are being consumed faster than they can be replenished.

Humans constitute only of one of 7 million species on earth, but we use about 45 percent of the food and oxygen supplied by photosynthesis. Human rapaciousness is already taking a toll on the planet's biodiversity. Together, the human disruption of the balance of life is causing a rate of extinction of species that exceeds anything the world has experienced in the past 65 million years.

As world leaders attempt to come to grips with the ecocrisis, many recognize that there is much to learn from the ecological perspectives of indigenous peoples. As Senator Daniel Inouye of Hawaii has said:

> Centuries before there was an environmental movement in the United States, the native people of this country expressed their reverence for the earth and all of its creatures on a daily basis. The conservation and preservation of natural resources were an unquestioned and integral part of everyday life. It is only in modern times that we as a nation have begun to realize how much we have to learn from the First Americans. (Smith and Snake 1996, 8)

This chapter explores the ecological implications of Native American spiritual traditions. Each tradition is, of course, unique, as is shown in previous chapters, but there are common ecological themes. Therefore, this chapter identifies five broad ecological themes in the spiritual traditions of American Indian nations:

- Interconnectedness: We are all related
- Reverence: All of life is spiritual
- Mother Earth: The womb of life
- Imbeddedness: We are the land and the land is us
- Reciprocity: Living in harmony

After addressing each of these themes, the chapter examines what happened when the Native American ecological perspectives collided with the worldview of the Europeans who came to the "New World." Then these questions are answered: What has been and what might be the impact of Native American ecological perspectives on efforts to address and resolve the ecocrisis? What might non-Indians learn from Native American teachings about their relationship with the rest of nature and how might they learn it? The chapter also examines how many American Indians have become ecological activists in recent decades.

First, however, the chapter confronts an issue at the heart of the attempts by non-Indians to understand the ecological teachings of Native Americans. A tendency has developed in recent decades to portray Native Americans as "ecological saints" who have always lived in a state of pure harmony with their environments. This image is yet another stereotype that distorts the reality. In order to appreciate the ecological insights of American Indians, one need not idealize their lifeways or freeze them in time. This issue is discussed in general, and an interesting case study is provided illustrating the phenomenon: the transformation of a now famous nineteenth-century speech given by the Duwamish Chief Seal'th (Seattle).

Native Americans as "Ecological Saints": A New Stereotype?

In the 1970s a popular public service announcement on television featured Cherokee actor Iron Eyes Cody paddling his canoe through polluted waters. As the camera focused in on his weathered face, viewers saw a tear running down his cheek. The television spot received a positive response because it played on the widely held image of American Indians as people who care deeply about the well-being of the environment.

As noted in chapter 1, the two most common stereotypes of Native Americans since first contact with Europeans have been those of "noble savages" "whose nobility, freedom, and spontaneity derive from their close association with the land" or "brutal savages" who manifest the unfeeling character of the natural world. In both cases Indians are imagined as "extensions of the environment." They "exist in the universe without appreciably changing it" (Vecsey 1980, 3–4).

Today, although both stereotypes continue, the most popular, exploited in the this television ad and in many other contexts, is that of Indians living in unadulterated harmony with nature. This is the image of Indians in most of the books on Native Americans to be found on the shelves of bookstores and that finds its way into the popular media. It is also an image perpetuated by some in the scholarly community, as well. In his thorough study entitled *American Indian Ecology*, J. Donald Hughes writes (Hughes 1983, 1–2) that "before Europeans arrived, American Indians lived throughout North America without destroying, without polluting, without using up the living resources of the natural world. . . . When

Former Georgia governor Zell Miller admires a poster featuring Cherokee actor Iron Eyes Cody, which has been widely used in public service announcements as a symbol of Native American concern for the environment. (AP/Wide World Photos)

Indians alone cared for the American earth, this continent was clothed in a green robe of forests, unbroken grasslands, and useful desert plants, filled with an abundance of wildlife. Changes have occurred since people with different attitudes have taken over" (Hughes 1983, 1–2).

We should not, however, romanticize the relationship of Native Americans with the rest of nature, before or after contact with Europeans. Native peoples are not and were not ecological saints who have always lived in a state of innocent harmony with their environments. Like all humans, Native Americans affected the environments in which they lived, as both conservers and destroyers. Fossil remains show evidence of abuse of nature by Native Americans centuries before contact with Europeans. As Hughes himself acknowledges, the collapse of the complex Native American urban society centered in Cahokia (near the Mississippi River, across from the modern city of St. Louis, Missouri), long before Europeans arrived in the area, probably resulted from exploitation and exhaustion of resources resulting in an ecological disaster (Hughes 1983, 99–100).

The "slash and burn" techniques of eastern woodlands peoples have also been cited to challenge the notion that Indians always lived in harmony with nature. In this method of farming, still practiced among some indigenous groups in the world, people moved their villages when the soil was depleted. Was this not abuse of the environment? In the context of societies that purposefully limited their populations and their technology, however, the techniques did not disrupt the balance of nature.

One of the most forceful challenges to the notion of Indians living in harmony with nature has been Calvin Martin's often cited study of the fur trade among Northeastern native nations (Martin 1978). Martin maintained that Indians hunted the beaver to near extinction because they blamed the beavers for the introduction of diseases, not merely because the Indians succumbed to the economic pressures of the white's fur market. In other words, he considers it anachronistic to call Native Americans conservationists, making the following assertion:

> Late in the 1960s, the North American Indian acquired yet another stereotypic image in the popular mind: the erstwhile savage, the drunken Indian, the "vanishing" Indian was conferred the title of ecological (i.e., conservation-minded) Indian. Propped up for everything that was environmentally sound, the Indian was introduced to the American public as the great high priest of the Ecology Cult. (Martin 1978, 157)

Martin chided nonnative environmentalists for looking to Native Americans as their "saviors," suggesting that "some day, perhaps [the environmentalist] will realize that he must look to someone else other than the American Indian for realistic spiritual inspiration" (Martin 1978, 188).

In response to Martin's views, however, other interpreters have argued that intense external pressures were the main factors in accounting for the overhunting and disappearance of the beaver. It was not the ecological ethic of Native Americans that failed them, but the assault on that ethic by the European invaders (Vecsey 1980, 28–29; Hughes 1983, 114; Cornell 1993, 342–37; Grinde and Johansen 1995, 29–30; for a full critique, see Krech 1981). Ironically, Martin himself has renounced most of his own conclusions in his earlier work, admitting he had never met an Indian when he wrote them, and become a passionate advocate of traditional Native American ways of relating to the earth and other beings (see, for example, his recent work, *The Way of the Human Being* [Martin 1999]).

In addition to Martin in his early work, other scholars have maintained that the idea of the "Native American ecologist" is a modern creation. Anthropologist William Starna has argued that it was Indian activists of the 1960s who invented the Native American environmental ethic in order to promote a pan-Indian pride and identity (Grinde and Johansen 1995, 30). Others have proposed that Indians, like other peoples, have a relationship with nature that is "thoroughly pragmatic or utilitarian, in the narrow sense that it is human interest, not love of, or respect for, 'the land' that explains the why and wherefore of [Native Americans'] intervention in the natural order" (Regan 1982, 215, 218–20).

Anthropologist Shepard Krech has provided the most thorough deconstruction of the "ecological saint" stereotype in his recent book, *The Ecological Indian: Myth and History*. Krech's carefully argued position is that

> At first a projection of European and European-Americans, [the image of the Indian as ecological saint] eventually became a self-image. American Indians have taken on the Noble Indian/Ecological Indian stereotype, embedding it in their self-fashioning, just as other indigenous peoples around the world have done with similar primordial ecological and conservationist stereotypes. (Krech 1999, 27)

This does not mean that the opposite image of Native Americans as abusers of nature is accurate. That too is a stereotype, one popular in the nineteenth century when Native Americans were being confined to reservations. Some of the points made to argue that Native Americans did not treat nature with respect are remnants of this racist attempt to portray Indians as "wasteful." For example, it is sometimes pointed out that Indians as well as Euroamericans shot buffalo, took their tongues and left the carcasses to rot. As Hughes properly observes, however, the native abuse of the buffalo came on the heels of the white slaughter of the animals, as young Indian hunters disregarded their elders' pleas not to kill buffalo indiscriminately, because these young hunters knew the whites would kill the buffalo anyway if they did not. In addition, some claims of wasteful hunting by Indians were nothing more than fabrications by Euroamericans intent on portraying the Indians as forfeiting their right to live freely. The objective was to justify the forcing of Native Americans off their traditional lands and onto reservations. Instances of waste by Native Americans were, in fact, extremely rare (Hughes 1983, 112–14, 41; cf. Vecsey 1980, 31).

The point has also been made that Native Americans did not abuse the environment because they lacked developed technology, and were thus incapable of harming nature very much. However, the indigenous technology of American Indians could actually have caused more damage than actually occurred (e.g., fish weirs could have been left closed rather than opened to let migrating fish through, and a stone axe could cut a tree as fast as a steel ax). "Even with a power saw in his hand there is reason to believe that the pre-Columbian Indian would have been environmentally responsible" (Nash 1972, 75).

Many Native Americans today are at the forefront of efforts to protect the earth and to promote ways of living in harmony with other creatures. Therefore, while we should reject as exploitative the narrow stereotype of Indians as "ecological saints" who can deliver the rest of us from our environmental sins, that should not keep us from developing an appreciation for the deeply engrained ecological teachings of Native American nations and drawing on these insights as we seek ways to confront and resolve the modern ecocrisis. As Christopher Vecsey observed, "Although American Indian actions have not always met their ideals, and although their ideals have not always been infallible in avoiding ecological errors, in large part there exists congruity between Indian ideals and actions" (Vecsey 1980, 27).

A Case Study: The Transformation of Chief Seal'th's Speech

On 29 October 1887 Dr. H.A. Smith published an article in the Seattle *Sunday Star* entitled "Scraps from a Diary—Chief Seattle." The article included Smith's alleged translation of a speech the Duwamish Chief Seattle (the anglicized version of Seal'th) had supposedly given more than thirty years earlier, as the chief was preparing to move his people across Puget Sound, away from the growing city named in his honor (Miller 1995, 325–26; cf. Vanderwerth 1971, 120–21).

Some scholars have questioned whether Smith's version of the speech accurately represents the words of Chief Seal'th, although its authenticity is defended by contemporary Native American scholars such as George Cornell (Cornell 1993, 26–27). To be sure, one of the themes of the speech, as recalled by Smith, sounds more Euroamerican than Native American: the inevitable demise of Native Americans in the face of advancing white civilization. The Chief's words (as expressed by Smith) reflect some fatalism that subtly endorses the taking of native lands by the the invaders. In addition, Smith's version of the speech expresses the view that all the earth is sacred to the Duwamish people, but in terms of past historical events more than the rhythms of nature (the more likely traditional Duwamish perspective). Furthermore, other versions of the speech circulated in the late nineteenth century are quite different from Smith's (cf. Armstrong 1971, 77–79). Nevertheless, some of the basic ecological themes of Native American spirituality discussed below (such as the sense of identity of the people with the land) are apparent in Smith's translation.

The speech as presented by Smith appeared in various anthologies of Indian orations, although, it was not particularly well-known. That changed in 1972 when Ted Perry, a University of Texas English professor, paraphrased portions of the Smith translation for the script of a film entitled *Home*. The film carried an environmental message. Perry's version of Chief Seal'th's speech underscores the ecological implications in Smith's version and takes some liberties with the facts in doing so. For example, Perry has Chief Seal'th talking about the white peoples' slaughter of the buffalo. The wholesale slaughter did not take place in earnest until well after 1854, and, in any event, it is not likely that a chief whose people subsisted on salmon and other fish would have waxed eloquent on the demise of the buffalo. In recent decades Perry's Chief Seattle has become an eloquent spokesperson for the philosophy of the environmental movement emerging in the 1970s. For example, Perry paints a lovely picture of ecological harmony, extrapolating on the images in Smith's version:

> Every part of this earth is sacred to my people. Every shining pine needle, every sandy shore, every mist in the dark woods, every meadow, every humming insect. All are holy in the memory and experience of my people.
>
> We know the sap which courses through the trees as we know the blood that courses through our veins. We are part of the earth and it is part of us. The perfumed flowers are our sisters. The bear, the deer, the great eagle, these are our brothers. The rocky crests, the juices in the meadow, the body heat of the pony, and man, all belong to the same family. (Campbell 1988, 34)

Perry's version of the speech also includes a stirring appeal to Chief Seattle's Euroamerican audience:

> Will you teach your children what we have taught our children? That the earth is our mother? What befalls the earth befalls all the sons of the earth.
>
> This we know: the earth does not belong to man, man belongs to the earth. All things are connected like the blood that unites us all. Man did not weave the web of life, he is merely a strand in it. Whatever he does to the web, he does to himself.

Unfortunately, there is no parallel in Smith's version to "the earth is our mother" or the "web of life," although by 1972 these had certainly become popular expressions in the environmental movement.

For the next twenty years Perry's version of the speech circulated in the environmental community as the authentic words of the Duwamish chief. It continues to be presented today as "Chief Seattle's Speech" with no explanation that it is actually, for the most part, a modern creation reflecting today's issues and sensibilities (Kaiser 1987). Some American Indian leaders even began to quote from the Perry version of the speech as evidence of the enlightened ecological ethic of earlier generations of Native Americans. In 1991 a children's book entitled *Brother Eagle, Sister Sky: A Message from Chief Seattle*, with the Perry version of the speech, was published and within a year sold more than one-quarter of a million copies. A chagrined Perry finally expressed regret for the misunderstanding, claiming he never intended to deceive people into thinking that his script contained the authentic words of Chief Seal'th (Grinde and Johansen 1995, 24–25).

The point of the transformation of Chief Seattle's speech is that turning earlier Native American leaders into ecological prophets or saints for our era may be as inappropriate as dismissing their words simply because they were spoken at times different from our own. Given the reality of the shaping of the statements of Native Americans by those who recorded and translated them, one should be careful not to place too much weight on any single utterance. Rather, one should look for patterns, ecological themes, in the words and, most importantly, the actions of Native Americans in the past and in the present.

Ecological Themes in Native American Spiritual Traditions

Despite the obstacles in trying to represent accurately the ecological teachings of Native American nations, several common themes emerge about the human relationship with the rest of nature. As Joseph Epes Brown has pointed out, Native American peoples have traditionally shared "a metaphysic of nature" in which is manifested "a reverence for the myriad forms and forces of the natural world specific to their immediate environment" (cited in Callicott 1994, 119).

Interconnectedness: We Are All Related

The traditional worldviews of the native nations studied in this volume all affirm that other beings are just as alive and conscious as humans, and with humans they form a single ecological community. A sense of kinship with all beings has caused native Americans to approach other beings as brothers and sisters. Other animals have been considered fellow "people" whose rights must be honored and who have a great deal to teach those who are attentive. Stones, trees, mountains, lakes, and all other "natural objects" also are alive and can educate those willing to listen to them.

As the Lakota Luther Standing Bear said, describing the worldview in which he was raised: "Everything was possessed of personality, only differing with us in form. Knowledge was inherent in all things. The world was a library and its books were the stones, the leaves, grass, brooks, and the birds and animals that shared, alike with us, the storms and blessings of the earth" (Standing Bear 1986, 194).

According to a Pawnee story, a tree being gnawed by a beaver screamed as she started to fall and turned into a woman. That night she said, "Brother, the timber you see are like people. Some are men and some are women. Be careful how you cut timber. You must first talk to the tree before you cut it" (Bierhorst 1994, 65–66).

From this perspective, humans are clearly not the only "people." The Zunis call everything, "whether it be a star, mountain, flower, eagle, or the earth itself, *hoi*, a "living person'" (Hughes 1983, 15). Or as the Lakota spiritual leader Nicholas Black Elk said simply, reflecting a perspective held in common among Plains nations, "With all beings and things we shall be as relatives" (Brown 1971, 105). In telling his life story Black Elk said, according to John Neihardt, that it would be not just his story but "the story of all life that is holy and is good to tell, and of us two-leggeds sharing in it with the four-leggeds and the wings of the air and all green things; for these are children of one mother and their father is one Spirit" (Black Elk 1972 [1932], 1).

Nonhuman animals have homes and villages, just like humans. For the Kwakiutl of the Pacific Northwest coast, the fish people live in a "rich country" on the other side of the ocean. The Anishinabé imagine the animal people living in villages under deep clear lakes. In the Pawnee cosmology animals have councils in river banks or deep within river islands. They have their own social organization, similar to that found in indigenous cultures (Bierhorst 1994, 31–37).

The principal image of this sense of interconnectedness in the Native American heritage, as it is universally, is the circle, or as the Plains people often say, the "sacred hoop" or "medicine wheel." The image expresses a "singular unity that is dynamic and encompassing." This means there is not the same distinction between the natural and supernatural as is assumed in the traditional Western worldview. In Native American cultures "every story, every song, every ceremony tells the Indian that each creature is part of a living whole and that all parts of that whole are related to one another by virtue of their participation in the whole of being" (Allen 1992, 56, 60).

In such an interconnected world, humans must understand their place. According to Vine Deloria Jr., "[r]ecognition that . . . human beings hold . . . an important place in . . . creation is tempered by the thought that they are dependent on everything in creation for their existence. . . . [T]he awareness of the meaning of life comes from observing how the various living things appear to mesh to provide a whole tapestry" (Deloria 1994, 88). "We are in one nest," is a Taos Pueblo saying (Hughes 1983, 15).

Luther Standing Bear said that according to Lakota belief humans do not occupy a special place in the eyes of *Wakan Tanka*. He learned that he "was only a part of everything that was called the world" (Bierhorst 1994, 86). Nicholas Black Elk said that humans must learn to humble themselves before the smallest ant, for they too are spiritual beings who may carry a message we need to hear (Brown 1971, 58).

The implications of this attitude of kinship with other living beings, no matter how seemingly insignificant, on the contemporary issue of protecting endangered species is clear. In testifying before a congressional committee against the construction of the Tellico Dam, which would flood historic Cherokee land and threaten the snail darter, Cherokee leader Jimmie Durham said:

> It is this incredible arrogance towards other life that has caused such
> destruction in this country. Who . . . has the right to play God and judge
> the life or death of an entire species of fellow beings which was put here by
> the same power that put us here? Who has the right to destroy a species of

life, and what can assuming that mean? Let me be emotional: To me, that fish is not just an abstract "endangered species" although it is that. It is a Cherokee fish and I am its brother. (Pisater 1979, 34–38)

We should not romanticize this sense of kinship, however. It does not mean that Native Americans are radical "animal rights" proponents who are interested in protecting each and every animal from being killed by humans. Emory Sekaquaptewa writes that when Hopi children were asked to bring in animals to a class, put them into a cage, and provide for them as part of an environmental project, they didn't seem interested in taking care of them. He points out that for Hopi people learning how to live with the environment "is not a matter of taking sides with one or some other living things; rather it is acceptance of the fact that if a certain living thing cannot survive on its own, that is a fact. . . . Learning to live with the environment is not a matter of taking sides, but of accepting facts" (Sekaquaptewa 1976, 42–43). In the harmony of the universe there is both life and death.

Reverence: All of Life Is Spiritual

According to Native American traditions, the world in which all things are living and all are interrelated is spiritual. As Intiwa, a Hopi, has put it, "The whole universe is enhanced with the same breath, rocks, trees, grass, earth, all animals, and men." Therefore, the proper response is reverence.

The Navajo goal of life, expressed in the word *hozho* (balance, harmony, beauty), expresses this attitude of reverence (see chapter 5 for a fuller discussion). In the words of the famous Diné prayer cited elsewhere in a different translation:

In beauty I walk,
With beauty before me, I walk.
With beauty behind me, I walk.
With beauty below me, I walk.
With beauty above me, I walk.
With beauty all around me, I walk.
It is finished in beauty. (Hughes 1983, 13)

The all-encompassing, all-pervasive spirit who inspires this awe and reverence, cannot be expressed in any one way. As noted, each nation has its own richly nuanced expressions for the spiritual, for sacred power, gods, and spirits. Today it is common, in the atmosphere of the pannational spirituality to which many Native Americans are attracted, to use such expressions as All Spirit, Great Spirit, or Great Mystery as a way of giving a name to which people can relate across boundaries. Paula Gunn Allen, for example, has written that "[a]s any American Indian knows, all of life is living—that is, dynamic and aware, partaking as it does in the life of the All Spirit and contributing as it does to the continuing life of that same Great Mystery" (Allen 1992, 56).

Both masculine and feminine images represent the deepest spiritual reality. At present, however, there is a reawakening to the feminine dimension. Drawing especially upon the traditions of his own Keres people of Laguna Pueblo, Allen writes imaginatively of

> a spirit that pervades everything, that is capable of powerful song and radiant movement, and that moves in and out of the mind. The colors of this spirit are multitudinous, a glowing, pulsing rainbow. Old Spider Woman is one name for this quintessential spirit, Spirit Woman is another. Corn Woman is one aspect of her, and Earth Woman is another. . . . At the center of all is Woman, and no thing is sacred (cooked, ripe, as the Keres Indians of Laguna Pueblo say it) without her blessing, her thinking. (Allen 1992, 13)

Mother Earth: The Womb of Life

Another commonly held belief among Native American nations is that the earth as a whole is alive and must be treated with respect. Although "sometimes male, or often sexless, the earth is indeed widely linked to femininity and motherhood" (Bierhorst 1994, 9). Balancing the earth as feminine, as mother, is the notion of the sky as masculine, as father. Much can be learned by examining the powerful, but controversial, image of the earth as mother, the womb of all life.

The image of the earth as mother seems pervasive in Native American cultures. In the words of Tahirussawichi, a Pawnee:

> *The signs of the dawn are seen in the east*
> *And the breath of new life is here . . .*
> *Mother Earth is the first to be called to awake . . .*
> *She moves, she awakes, she rises,*
> *She feels the breath of the new-born Dawn.* (Hughes 1983, vi)

This attitude toward the earth as mother caused Hopi farmers to resist the use of steel plows, because a plow "unnecessarily and cruelly tears the skin of the earth mother" (Loftin 1991, 9).

Appeals to Mother Earth by Native American leaders have been common in confrontations with Euroamericans since the Shawnee leader Tecumseh said to General William Henry Harrison in 1810: "The earth is my mother—on her bosom I will repose." In 1980 American Indian Movement leader Russell Means said, "Mother Earth will retaliate, the whole environment will retaliate, and the abusers will be eliminated" (Gill 1987, 1, 8).

Almost everywhere one looks, it seems, are found references to Mother Earth in Native American lore (Hultkrantz 1983). Joseph Epes Brown, for example, recorded a prayer of Nicholas Black Elk, in which the great Lakota spiritual leader addressed Mother Earth: "We are of earth, and belong to You, O Mother Earth from whom we receive our food. You care for our growth as do our own mothers. Every step that we take upon You should be done in a sacred manner; each step should be as a prayer" (Brown 1971, 12–13).

About 1885 the Native American prophet Smohalla, who helped inspire a renewal of traditional spirituality among the native nations of the Northwest in the 1860s (see chapters 1 and 6), is reputed to have said in response to efforts to confine the Indians of the region to reservations and take up Euroamerican agriculture:

You ask me to plow the ground! Shall I take a knife and tear my mother's bosom? Then when I die she will not take me to her bosom to rest.

You ask me to dig for stone! Shall I dig under her skin for her bones? Then when I die I cannot enter her body to be born again.

You ask me to cut grass and make hay and sell it, and be rich like white men! But how dare I cut off my mother's hair? (McLuhan 1987, 53)

It is also common to see references to plants as the dress of Mother Earth or as parts of her body. Like a mother, the earth gives birth to life. As noted, the teaching that life emerges from the earth is found in various Native American cultures. As the Nez Percé say simply, the people came "out of the ground" (Bierhorst 1994, 98).

Scholars of Native American spiritual traditions have long recognized the ubiquity of the image of Mother Earth. This consensus was questioned, however, in a controversial monograph published by Sam Gill entitled *Mother Earth: An American Story* (1987). Gill challenged the assumption of a commonly held Native American belief in Mother Earth on several grounds. On the basis of the uniqueness of Native American cultures, he questioned whether there was actually a shared belief in one such goddess. According to Gill, there is a rich diversity of feminine figures in Native American mythologies, but there is no one Mother Earth (Gill 1987, 153–54). He also contended that "while the scholarly discussions of Mother Earth uniformly considered her to be universal among tribes and to have existed since great antiquity, the majority of the evidence used as the basis for these claims was the statement made by Smohalla, with an occasional reference to [the] statement made by . . . Tecumseh" (Gill 1987, 5). In his search of ethnographic materials he could find no other meaningful references to Mother Earth.

Gill concluded that "Mother Earth has come into existence in America largely during the last one hundred years and . . . her existence stems primarily from two creative groups: scholars and Indians" (Gill 1987, 7). Mother Earth actually emerges from the Euroamerican's conception of "America, the nation, the land . . . as a dark-skinned woman, as an Indian, as a mother . . . [embracing] the expression of the potentiality, the fruition, the bounty, the productivity of the landscape and the people . . . [and] the mystery and enticing character of America" (Gill 1987, 155). Mother Earth was then embraced, Gill argues, by Native Americans who were losing their own connection to their particular lands and who found in this new concept a way to affirm their Indianness in a time of immense crisis, which continues to this day. According to Gill, "Mother Earth gives a primordial and spiritual base, and thus religious authority and responsibility to the Indian identity. She is the basis on which Indians articulate the superiority of their way of life over against 'white Americans' and from which they derive their responsibility to maintain their Indian identity" (Gill 1987, 148).

Gill's book set off a firestorm of protest, principally from Native Americans who considered it yet another in the long line of misinterpretations and exploitations of Indian spiritual traditions by nonnatives. Among the critics was Vine Deloria Jr., who reported that he had himself found numerous references to Mother Earth in the treaties he was researching. "Of course," he writes, "I did not find these references in ethnographic materials—I found them in minutes of councils and treaty negotiations. . . . Indians were not sitting around in seminar rooms articulating a nature philosophy for the benefit of non-Indian students, after all. They were trying to save their lands from exploitation and expropriation" (Grinde and Johansen 1995, 26). In fact, Deloria noted, General Oliver O. Howard heard Indians refer to their Mother Earth so often during a protracted treaty negotiation in the mid-nineteenth century that he said in frustration, "Twenty times over [you] repeat that the earth is your mother. . . . Let us hear it no more, but come to business" (Grinde and Johansen 1995, 32).

Indeed, the references to Mother Earth are just too frequent to dismiss them all as products of the interaction of Native Americans with Euroamerican scholars, although many do appear, as Gill notes, in the context of Native Americans speaking to Euroamerican audiences.

References to Mother Earth were also recorded early in the interactions between Native Americans and Europeans. For example, in the sixteenth century the *Penobscot Bedagi* (Big Thunder) said, "The earth is our mother. She nourished us; that which we put into the ground she returns to us, and healing plants she gives us likewise. If we are wounded, we go to our mother and seek to lay the wounded part against her, to be healed. Animals, too, do thus, they lay their wounds to the earth" (Miller 1995, 41).

Like other Native American concepts, the notion of Mother Earth has been distorted by modern interpreters who have often sentimentalized and oversimplified it. The image speaks not just of fertility and procreation in a warm and fuzzy way, as is often implied in its usage today. As folklorist Marta Weigle has put it, Mother Earth manifests "women's continuing strategies for creativity and empowerment" (cited by Bierhorst 1994, 92). For some Native Americans today Mother Earth has become so trivialized in modern usage, that the image has lost its deep and profound meaning and sense of mystery and power.

While controversy has swirled around Mother Earth, the counterpart, the sky as father, has not aroused as much interest. However, the sky is paired in most Native American traditions with the earth. Anishanabé scholar George Cornell describes their interaction: "The relationship between the earth mother and sky father is perceived as a continuous love affair, in which Native peoples are allowed to witness and participate. The power of the sun and the rains that impregnate the earth mother provide the necessities of life for Native peoples" (Cornell 1993, 22).

Imbeddedness: We Are the Land and the Land Is Us

Another ecological theme common in Native American spiritual traditions might be called "imbeddedness." From this perspective, humans are part of the land and the land is part of us. As Paula Gunn Allen has written: "We are the land. To the best of my understanding, that is the fundamental idea that permeates American Indian life; the land (Mother) and the people are the same. As Luther Standing Bear has said of his Lakota people, 'We are of the soil and the soil is of us'" (cited in Allen 1992, 119). Allen has also observed elsewhere that for Native Americans the land is "not a means of survival, a setting for our affairs, a resource on which we draw. . . It is rather a part of our being, dynamic, significant, real. It is ourself, . . . in a sense more real than any conceptualization or abstraction about the nature of the human being can ever be" (Allen 1979, 191).

Jimmie Durham, as he explained why he was resisting the building of a dam which would flood Cherokee land, said: "In *Ani Yonwiyah*, the language of my people, there is a word for land: *Eloheh*. This same word also means, history, culture and religion. This is because we Cherokees cannot separate our place on earth from our lives in it, nor from our vision and our meaning as a people" (Hughes 1983, 60).

It is important to realize that in the worldviews of Native Americans, concern for the earth has not been "vague or undifferentiated. . . Indians did not love the concept of nature; they loved particular locations, particular aspects of their environment." Here "their myths took place, . . . the heroes walked and their ancestors were buried, . . . the nature deities were helpful . . . conditions for subsistence were optimum" (Vecsey 1980, 25).

From this perspective, the world in which we live is a "sacred geography" in which the sacred history of a people is entwined with particular places. For example, according to Diné mythology a monster turned into a great winged rock (now known as Shiprock, outside the town of Shiprock in northeast Arizona) after being killed by the warrior twins (Hughes 1983, 58). Similarly, as noted in chapter 4, the Black Hills are a living being for the Lakota in their stories of origins.

Because of this attitude toward the land, it has been very difficult for Native Americans to adapt to the European point of view that land is a commodity to be bought and sold. The Wampanoag sachem Massasoit protested when his people were arrested for hunting on their land, which the Pilgrims claimed to have purchased:

> What is this you call property? It cannot be the earth. For the land is our mother, nourishing all her children, beasts, birds, fish, and all men. The woods, the steams, everything on it belongs to everybody and is for the use of all. How can one man say it belongs to him only? (Grinde and Johansen 1995, 30)

We have already encountered the difficulties the Lenape people had when approached by colonialists who wanted to purchase their lands. Like people in other native nations, the Lenape were willing to share use of the land, but they did not grasp that accepting payment for this privilege meant that they were giving up their right to use it as well (see chapter 2). The Native American attitude toward the land as shared inspired among Euroamericans the still-repeated pejorative phrase "Indian giver" to describe someone who tries to claim the right to continue to use something the person no longer "owns."

From the traditional Native American perspective, land cannot be owned individually; it is to be held in common, for the use of all, including both humans and nonhuman species. All living beings share the land. The Shawnee leader Tecumseh expressed a feeling deeply held by many Native American peoples when he rallied his allies to resist the westward expansion of the whites with these words (another famous reference to Mother Earth): "Let us unite as brothers, as sons of one Mother Earth. . . . Sell our land? Why not sell the air, the clouds, the great sea?" (Grinde and Johansen 1995, 31).

To Europeans who arrived in the "New World," much of the land was "'wild-deer-ness,' the place of wild beasts, not of men. Any who lived in it must be savages, not humans" (Hughes 1983, 2). The notion of the land as wild, however, has been foreign to most Native Americans. Luther Standing Bear has expressed a shared Indian perspective about "wilderness" in these now famous words:

> We did not think of the great open plains, the beautiful rolling hills, and winding streams with tangled growth, as "wild." Only to the white man was nature a "wilderness" and only to him was the land "infested" with "wild" animals and "savage" people. To us it was tame. Earth was bountiful

and we were surrounded with the blessings of the Great Mystery. Not until the hairy man from the east came and with brutal frenzy heaped injustices upon us and the families that we loved was it "wild" for us. When the very animals of the forest began fleeing from his approach, then it was that for us the "Wild West" began. (Standing Bear 1986, 38)

This is not to say that Native Americans had no concept of land ownership. That would be an inaccurate oversimplification. Indeed, claiming that Indians did not understand the idea of ownership was a technique sometimes used by unscrupulous Euroamericans to rationalize the taking of Native Americans lands. The notion that certain people have "title" to specific lands is deeply rooted in Native American cultures, not in the transactions of the marketplace, but in the sacred stories of the people. For example, the Kwakiutl and other northwestern coastal peoples believed that the use of specific resource territories was a right of family groups, descended in lineages from a mythic ancestor. Stretches of beaches and sections of streams and berry patches and forests for hunting were deemed family territories. They were willing to fight to defend them, not because they had bought them, but because the land was sacred to them. The Lakota can at the same time believe the Black Hills "belong" to them, both on the basis of the 1868 treaty and their own myths of who they are and where they came from, and also refuse to put a price on the hills (see chapter 4).

As noted elsewhere, the four cardinal directions are used in Native American rituals in various settings. In this context, it is important to point out that the four directions are not abstract but are embodied in a specific landscape. The home of the people is at the center, often guarded in each of the four directions by a sacred mountain with its own color, animal, bird, and mineral substance, as well as deity (Hughes 1983, 59). The Diné, for example, believe that if they move outside their homeland within the four sacred mountains, they will suffer, as they did when they were taken to Bosque Redondo (see chapter 5).

Reciprocity: Living in Harmony

According to another perspective common in Native American spiritual traditions, the world exists in a delicate balance. Therefore, humans must always act reciprocally, taking only that which is truly needed and replacing whatever is used. As contemporary Anishinabé scholar Winona LaDuke put it, "We give something in order to get something back from the creation" (Grinde and Johansen 1995, 16). In her study of nature religion in the Americas, Catherine Albanese expresses this basic Native American theme:

The well-being of Amerindian peoples depended in large measure on a correspondence between themselves and what they held sacred. The material world was a holy place; and so harmony with nature beings and natural forms was the controlling ethic, reciprocity the recognized mode of interaction. Ritual functioned to restore a lost harmony, like a great balancing act bringing the people back to right relation with the world. (Albanese 1990, 23)

Everything done is seen as part of a sacred interaction between humans and the rest of nature. One of the most important purposes of ceremonies is to maintain this harmony. By contrast, in the view of many Native Americans and others, the Western attitude of "dominance" over nature supports manipulation of nature. The famous Nez Percé leader Chief Joseph once said, "We were contented to let things remain as the Great Spirit made them. They [Euroamericans] were not, and would change the rivers and mountains if they did not suit them" (Reed 1986, 33).

From this perspective, if humans do not approach the natural world with reverence and respect, "if things are done wrongly, then there will be unfortunate consequences. Thus, the decision to cut even a single tree, or to kill a single animal, is a decision that cannot be made quickly or taken lightly. Continuance and balance are the primary considerations, not human comfort, or material or financial gain. Systems based on this 'circular logic' therefore tend to be self-sustaining and stable" (Bruchac 1993, 14).

In this world of reciprocity, harmony is not created; harmony and balance are present in the world as it is and must simply be observed and honored. Laguna author Leslie Marmon Silko describes how she was taught the way the world is by the stories she heard from her elders:

As Thought Woman and her sisters thought of it, the whole universe came into being. In this universe, there is not absolute good or absolute bad; there are only balances and harmonies that ebb and flow. Some years the desert receives abundant rain, other years there is too little rain, and sometimes there is so much rain that floods cause destruction. But rain itself is neither innocent nor guilty. The rain is simply itself. (Silko 1996, 64)

Reciprocity means that if humans show proper respect, the spirit beings will respond favorably and assist humans as they seek to live harmoniously. A Zia pueblo rain prayer exemplifies this attitude: "I send you prayer sticks and pay you sticks of office, kicksticks, hoops, shell mixture, various foods, that you may be pleased and have all things to wear and eat. I pay you these that you will beseech the cloud chiefs to send their people to water the earth that she may be fruitful and give to all people abundance of all food" (Hughes 1983, 76).

Sometimes the ethic of reciprocity can seem extreme when applied thoroughly and consistently. Silko writes about the elders in her pueblo community who would not kill flies even when they became bothersome, because once, long, long ago, when human beings were in a great deal of trouble, a Green Bottle Fly carried the desperate messages of human beings to the Mother Creator in the Fourth World, below this one. Human beings had outraged the Mother Creator by neglecting the Mother Corn altar while they dabbled with sorcery and magic. The Mother Creator disappeared, and with her disappeared the rain clouds, and the plants and the animals too. The people began to starve, and they had no way of reaching the Mother Creator down below. Green Bottle Fly took the message to the Mother Creator, and the people were saved. To show their gratitude, the old folks refused to kill any flies. (Silko 1996, 69)

N. Scott Momaday tells the story of a Navajo man who had no job and whose wife was pregnant. The man's family needed food, but he refused to hunt deer, saying, "it is inappropriate that I should take life just now when I am expecting the gift of life." According to Momaday, his attitude represents the principle of "appropriateness" observed by those who recognize that reciprocity operates in the harmony of the world (Momaday 1976a, 82).

The attitude of reciprocity is especially evident in the traditional farming practices of Native American communities (see Hughes 1983, 65–77). Traditional Hopi farmers have resisted steel plows because they tear the skin of the earth mother. Instead, they plant seeds with digging sticks made from greasewood. The Hopi were taught by Masauwu to revere the earth as a relative and to treat the earth as they would expect to be treated. It is not that reciprocity is looked upon mechanistically. Barre Toelken was told by a Hopi, when he asked if kicking the earth would cause a poor crop: "Well, I don't know whether that would happen or not, but it would just really show what kind of person you are" (cited by Loftin 1991, 9–10).

Reciprocity is also evident in traditional Native American hunting and gathering techniques. Hunting is conducted as a ritual intended to entreat the animals to allow themselves to be taken for the use of their human kin. The spirits of slain animals return to their own countries to report on their treatment by humans. If they have been treated with respect, they will return and/or encourage others to visit the humans. Or they will send sickness and accidents if the hunters do not behave properly.

The pueblo people who hunt antelope believe that "[t]he antelope merely consents to return home with the hunter. All phases of the hunt are conducted with love: the love the hunter and the people have for the Antelope People, and the love of the antelope who agree to give up their meat and blood so that human beings will not starve" (Silko 1996, 27).

The Menominee people of Wisconsin who gather wild rice always make sure some of the rice falls into the water so that there will be a crop the next year. While this might seem common sense, the practice is rooted in the basic ethical principle of restraint, implied by an ethic of reciprocity. Restraint is often combined with ritual, as when, for example, a Lenape healer not only passes by the first specimen of an herb he is hunting but makes a tobacco offering to the plant.

The native nations of the Northwest that traditionally depended on salmon maintain a similar reciprocal relationship. For these nations the salmon are also people, who have their own villages under the oceans to the west, from which they come each year to sacrifice themselves so that the native peoples may live. When the salmon arrive in their annual run, they are greeted with prayers of thanksgiving. The first salmon are either allowed to pass by or may be taken and ritually honored. After harvesting what they need, the peoples open their nets and traps so that most of the salmon can complete their spawning runs. Once caught, the flesh of the salmon is treated with respect, for the native fishermen know that, if they do not, the spirits of the fish will return home and not come back. Ceremonies are still held in association with the beginning of the salmon runs in native communities along the Columbia and other northwestern rivers. Their purpose is to honor the salmon and to express commitment to live in harmony with the life-giving fish people.

A Collision of Ecological Perspectives

The prevalent attitudes toward nature among the Europeans who came to the North American continent collided with the ecological perspectives of the native inhabitants, with catastrophic effect both on native peoples and on the land and other creatures (Callicott 1983). "It is the opposing—one might say the conflicting—views of nature, Indian and white, which help put the two groups into constant struggle with one another" (Vecsey 1980, 31–32). The tendency has been to portray this conflict as a stark contrast. Vine Deloria Jr, for example, has proposed that there are two kinds of people on the planet: natural peoples who "represent an ancient tradition that has always sought harmony with the environment" and hybrid peoples who view the planet as a place for our exploitation (Deloria 1994, 2). Native Americans were, of course, among the "natural" peoples, while the Europeans were emblematic of the "hybrid" group.

Kate Luckie, a Wintu elder from California expressed this dichotomy in 1925:

> The White people never cared for land or deer or bear. When we Indians kill meat, we eat it all up. When we dig roots, we make little holes. When we built houses, we make little holes. When we burn grass for grasshoppers, we don't ruin things. We shake down acorns and pinenuts. We don't chop down the trees. We only use dead wood. But the White people plow up the ground, pull down the trees, kill everything. The tree says, "Don't, I am sore. Don't hurt me." But they chop it down and cut it up. The spirit

of the land hates them. . . . Everywhere the White man has touched it, it is sore. (McLuhan 1987, 15)

According to the European heritage, nature is "a collective physical whole–an ordered cosmos comprising the animal and vegetable kingdoms on earth as well as the stars and other heavenly bodies. . . . Filtered through the lens of the eighteenth-century Enlightenment, . . . this understanding grew more systemic and more mechanistic, providing an overarching frame within which humans could comprehend themselves and their cultural pursuits and activities." This contrasts with the more "plural and personal" universe characteristic of Native American perspectives. As noted, "[i]nstead of the abstract and overarching 'nature' of Europe, [American Indians] saw a world peopled with other-than-human persons, often of mysterious powers and dispositions" (Albanese 1990, 20).

The European attitude toward the land and what was on it and under it is expressed in the now common phrase "natural resources," which was coined around 1500. This terminology implies that the environment is nothing more than material to be exploited by humans. Armed with this perspective, Euroamericans believed they were able to make more effective use of the land. This became a justification for removing Native Americans from their lands, for they were not as "productive."

As Commissioner of Indian Affairs Thomas Twiss put it in his 1859 report, from this perspective "the savage, the wild hunter tribes, must give way to the white man, who requires his prairie hunting grounds for the settlement and homes of millions of human beings, where now only a few thousand . . . rude barbarians derive a scanty, precarious, and insufficient subsistence" (Hagan 1980, 72).

The roots of the European perspective toward nature are at least in part found in the Jewish and Christian worldview (White 1967). Leaders of these religions have assumed, for example, on the basis of the traditional understanding of the story of creation in the book of Genesis in the Bible, that humans are separate from, rather than part of, the natural community. God also transcends nature, as nature's creator. God created humans in his image and gave them dominion over nature. God also directed humans to multiply and subdue the earth. Since nature is not in God's image, nature has no intrinsic value. It exists to be used for human ends (Young 2005, 328–29).

This understanding of nature, however, is not limited to religious people in the West. "Contemporary atheists and Christians alike have tended to define Western civilization as effective 'exploitation of the earth by man' and 'protection against the forces of nature.' To be civilized is to be free of nature, to rise above and transcend nature, to shield oneself from nature and exploit it." The terms given to Indians by Euroamericans (especially missionaries) closely associated them with nature: pagans (people of the countryside), heathens (people of wild, uninhabited places), and savages (people of the forests). "And since they were closely connected with nature, they had to be dominated like the rest of nature" (Vecsey 1980 36–37).

The Impact of Native American Ecological Teachings

For the first five centuries of European contact with indigenous peoples, the general assumption has been that the "burden" for Europeans and Euroamericans is to teach native peoples how to "survive" through assimilation into "civilization." Writing in the context of the relationship between Native Americans and Euroamericans, environmentalist and theologian Thomas Berry suggests that the process should be reversed. In his view, it is indigenous peoples who have the "lessons of survival" to teach:

> The Indian now offers to the Euroamerican a mystical sense of the place of the human and other living beings. This is a difficult teaching for us since we long ago lost our capacity for being present to the earth and its living forms in a mutually enhancing manner. This art of communion with the earth we can relearn from the Indian. Thus a reverse dependence is established. Survival in the future will likely depend more on our learning from the Indian than the Indian's learning from us. In some ultimate sense we need their mythic capacity for relating to this continent more than they need our capacity for mechanistic exploitation of the continent. (Berry 1988, 189–90; see Cornell 1985; Booth and Jacobs 1990)

More specifically, what might Euroamericans learn if they listened to the traditional Native American teachings about the environment? On most of the particular elements of the current ecological crisis, the Native American perspective could have an impact. For example, Native Americans have recognized the importance of keeping the human population in check. A Cherokee legend "represents the animals as worrying that people were becoming too numerous." Some evidence suggests that Native Americans observed various birth control techniques to limit population, ranging from sexual abstinence to the use of various plants and herbs as oral contraceptives or abortifacients (Hughes 1983, 95–98; Bierhorst 1994, 161–72). In the early nineteenth century, Thomas Jefferson acknowledged that Indians "have fewer children than we do" (Grinde and Johansen 1995, 32).

Not all Euroamericans have been oblivious to the potential of Native American teachings in helping them learn to live in harmony with nature. For example, Henry David Thoreau, although limited in his perception by the accepted stereotype of American Indians as "noble savages," "recognized Indians as people who had spent their lives in Nature and developed a knowledge of it that was superior to white men's" (Sayre 1977, x). In his journal Thoreau wrote, "The Indian . . . stands free and unconstrained in Nature, is her inhabitant and not her guest, and wears her easily and gracefully. But the civilized man has the habits of the house. His house is a prison." Thoreau believed that the "red men," as he sometimes called Indians, were important teachers of Euroamericans who, like him, were seeking to live in harmony with nature. He may have idealized Native Americans, but he was willing at least to try to attend carefully to their respect for nature.

Later in the nineteenth-century, John Wesley Powell, founder of the American Bureau of Ethnology, expressed admiration for the lifeways of Native Americans and sought to make their ability to live harmoniously in nature known to non-Indians.

John Muir, founder of the Sierra Club, who was himself adopted by a Tlingit band, admired the Native American understanding that "all nature was instinct with deity" and that animals have souls (Hughes 1983, 138; cf. Jacobs 1980, 56–57). (On both Muir's and Thoreau's experience with and attitude toward Native Americans, see Fleck 1985.)

In his famous essay, published in 1949, the naturalist Aldo Leopold called for a "land ethic" that recognizes that the earth and all its creatures, not just humans, have rights that humans must respect (Leopold 1949). In developing his land ethic, Leopold drew on the Western tradition of "rights" and argued they must be "extended" to the nonhuman world, but his perspective harmonizes well with the Native American understanding of the interdependence of all life (see Callicott 1989).

In recent decades a host of writers in the emergent field of "environmental ethics" have drawn on Native American perspectives. For example, J. Baird Callicott includes the Lakota and Ojibwa (Anishanabé) perspectives in his multicultural survey of ecological ethics, an attempt to find common ground amidst the diversity of ethical positions in the world's cultures. For example, he describes the Lakota tradition as envisioning "nature as a large extended family, and therefore mutual duties and obligations analogous to those governing family relations should also govern human relations with the earth and sky and with all other forms of life." These relations are characterized by "mutual care and mutual dependency." The Lakota, Callicott notes, "do not regard themselves in any way morally superior to or more spiritually advanced than other natural beings" (Callicott 1994, 121–22, 124). He finds both the Lakota and Anishanabé perspectives "capable of adaptation to the prevailing intellectual climate of the twentieth century, and thus relevant and useful in helping us deal with the contemporary environmental crisis" (131). For example, the Lakota view that other living things are the kin of humans is compatible with the fundamental insight of Darwinian evolutionary biology.

The movement known as Deep Ecology also has drawn heavily on Native American environmental insights. Deep Ecology "goes beyond a limited piece-meal shallow approach to environmental problems and attempts to articulate a comprehensive religious and philosophical world view" (Devall and Sessions 1985, 65; cf. Seed et al. 1988; Naess 1987). "Shallow environmentalism" is motivated by enlightened human self-interest and holds that nature exists primarily to serve human needs (Regan 1982, 210–11). The intent of Deep Ecology is to replace the Western view of nature with an "ecological egalitarianism" in which the "right to be" of every living thing is recognized. Deep Ecology calls people to be liberated from the manipulative understanding of the human relationship to the rest of nature characteristic of European civilizations and to reawaken to their place in the natural community.

The traditional perspective of Native Americans is often heralded by Deep Ecologists as a model of ecologically responsible living (Oelschlaeger 1994, 178), although the movement also draws on insights from Asian traditions. For example, the "poet laureate" of Deep Ecology, Gary Snyder, weaves together Native American and Asian (particularly Buddhist) imagery in his works to reawaken a sense of the sacrality of the land (e.g., Snyder 1974 and 1990).

As noted in previous chapters, the so-called New Age movement has attempt-ed to draw on Native American traditions in creating an eclectic approach to spir-ituality. Native American ecological themes have been particularly attractive to many New Age leaders. One of the most famous is Sun Bear, the son of an Anishanabé (Chippewa) man and a Euroamerican woman (Albanese 1990, 156–63). Sun Bear (born as Vincent La Duke) grew up on the White Earth Indian Reservation in Minnesota. In the 1960s he founded the Bear Tribe Medicine Society, an intentional community which he describes as a "group of native and non-native people sharing the same vision, philosophy, and direction toward the Earth and the Creation around us." The society holds gatherings it calls Medicine Wheel Gatherings. His followers have considered him a shaman, prophet, and teacher of exceptional wisdom. Critics (e.g., Deloria 1994, 40–41) have suggested that Sun Bear is trafficking on his native heritage, removed from its Anishanabé roots, and is taking advantage of a hot market for New Age gurus with eclectic, nondemanding teachings. Traditional Native American spiritual leaders do not create their own tribes!

A century ago it was assumed that if they were to survive, Native Americans would have to adopt the Western approach to relating to nature by subduing it. As the twenty-first century begins there is growing recognition that the opposite may be true. The survival of the culture that tried to assimilate American Indians may depend on a new willingness to incorporate Native American perspectives.

It is interesting that early in the history of interaction between the two ways of life, Euroamericans taken captive by Indians "often found Indian 'nature' ways alluring and refused to return to white society. To them and to the thousands of whites who ran away to live with and like Indians, Indian life represented a return to nature from which white civilization was alienated" (Vecsey 1980, 3). In a different form, this openness has returned.

The impact of the ecological insights of Native Americans has been important for centuries, even though it has not been widely recognized. In his popular and provocative book *Indian Givers: How The Indians of the Americas Transformed the World* (1988), anthropologist Jack Weatherford details all the benefits that European immigrants to this hemisphere received from the original inhabitants, who willingly shared what they had learned by closely observing the natural world of which they knew they were a part. Nowhere is this more evident than in the healing medicines. Tribal healers discovered the medicinal qualities of hundreds of plants (e.g., in relieving pain and suppressing ovulation). Hundreds of drugs currently used by physicians in standard medical practice are adaptations of substances used first by indigenous healers.

Some Euroamericans today are attempting to practice completely subsistence lifestyles, modelling themselves after what they assume to be the patterns of Native Americans before contact or indigenous people in other parts of the world today. Except for quite small communities, which can serve to inspire others, such "primitivism" is probably not practical, although many who have followed that path would debate the point. In general, "[t]he value of Indian environmental perspectives may lie not in advising a return to earlier ways of subsistence, but in helping to develop a new style of life that incorporates care and reverence for nature and understands the limits that must be placed on human actions affecting the natural environment within the context of present knowledge and capabilities" (Hughes 1983, 143).

Some Native Americans have expressed willingness to accept the challenge to share the ecological wisdom of their peoples with non-Indians. More than twenty years ago a group of Hotinonshonni (Iroquois) leaders issued a "call to consciousness" in which they said:

> The Native peoples of the Western Hemisphere can contribute to the survival potential of the human species. The majority of our peoples still live in accordance with the traditions which find their roots in the Mother Earth. But the Native people have need of a forum in which our voice can be heard. And we need alliances with the other people of the world to assist in our struggle to regain and maintain our ancestral lands and protect the Way of Life we follow.
>
> The traditional Native people hold the key to the reversal of the processes of Western Civilization, which hold the promise of unimaginable future suffering and destruction. Spiritualism is the highest form of political con-

sciousness. Our culture is among the world's surviving proprietors of that kind of consciousness. Our culture is among the most ancient continuously existing cultures in the world. We are the spiritual guardians of this place. We are here to impart that message. (Grinde and Johansen 1995, 268–69)

Other Native Americans, however, are uncomfortable with being put in the position of "saviors" of Euroamerican civilization. In Emory Sekaquaptewa's opinion, "what is happening here is that white man's technological methods of controlling the environment have begun to produce results which have become a measure of the quality of life. It is really the white man's own question about the quality of his life which leads him to search for potential alternatives in the Indian way of life." In other words, because whites created the problem, they must find their own answers, not look to Native Americans to solve them (Loftin 1991, 13).

In seeking to learn from Native American teachings how to live in harmony on earth, one must remember that although "Native America contributes to an understanding of the relationship between humans and the rest of nature. . . [n]o single idea, no set of rules, has yet been discovered that can prevent human society from overburdening the web of life that supports it" (Bierhorst 1994, ix).

Native American Ecological Activism

Native Americans have their own ecological battles to fight, to protect their own lands and the particular communities of living beings of which they are a part. Indeed, around the world today indigenous peoples are being "pushed to the edge of a cliff" by environmental crises. For example, the principal victims of the toxic waste dump listed first on the Environmental Protection Agency's Superfund list have been the Mohawks of Akwesasne (the St. Regis Reservation in New York, Ontario, and Quebec). The largest radioactive leak in the United States was not the result of the well-publicized disaster at the Three Mile Island nuclear power plant, but a little-known discharge on the Navajo Reservation in 1978.

For the sake of not only their own survival, but the future of the land and the community of life of which they are members, many American Indians are fighting back against such assaults on the environment. In this section are described some of the threats to the harmony of life faced by Native Americans on their own lands and examples of the ecological activism native peoples have undertaken not just to protect themselves, but to protect all peoples (human and other) and all life. As a Taos Pueblo leader said when the papers were being signed returning Blue Lake to the care of his people in 1970, "When we pray, it is for the betterment of the whole world. No distinctions are made" (Bierhorst 1994, 275).

As examples of ecological crises on native lands, one could examine the flooding of ancestral lands as a result of the building of dams, the clear-cut logging of

Native American nations must decide whether and how to allow the mining of coal and other natural resources on their land. Advocates point to the money to be earned from mineral leases, while opponents charge that such practices are an assault on Mother Earth. (© Buddy Mays/CORBIS)

forests on reservations, and the threats to water rights (Guerrero 1992, 189–216), among other challenges. Given the limitations of space, however, this chapter considers only the controversy over fishing rights in the Northwest and the Midwest, the pollution of the land and water as a result of the dumping of toxic waste on Mohawk lands in New York and Canada, and the damage caused by uranium mining on the Diné reservation in Arizona and New Mexico and Lakota lands in South Dakota. In each case we will describe the nature of the threat and the responses by Native Americans committed to defending the harmony of life.

The Fishing Rights Controversy

In 1854 and 1855 the first governor of Washington Territory, Isaac Stevens, forged treaties with Indians that took from them most of the land in what is now Montana, Idaho, and eastern Washington. The one point upon which the native peoples would not relent was their right to fish. Stevens acknowledged that fishing was essential to the Indians' subsistence; moreover, he did not think the continuation of traditional fishing by Indians would interfere with the advance of "civilization" (see Grinde and Johansen 1995, 145–69; Institute 1992, 217–39; Cohen 1986).

By 1900, however, Indians were being arrested for taking salmon under the terms of the treaties. As the century progressed, Euroamerican fishermen took an increasing percentage of the salmon, and new non-Indian settlements and the growing logging industry reduced the salmon runs. In the 1930s large hydroelectric dams on the Columbia River and its tributaries further reduced the salmon catch, by then less than one-sixth the size of the catch when the Native Americans alone were fishing.

Nonnative fishermen continued to increase in number and used the latest technology to take salmon in the open water, before they reached the river mouths where native fishermen had always harvested their catches. Native fishermen continued to be arrested, and state courts refused to enforce the treaty rights. While some defenders of native fishing rights took the case to federal courts, others ignored the threat of arrests and continued their traditional fishing practices. State fishery police were joined by vigilante sports fishermen in arresting or harassing the native fishermen. Celebrities such as Marlon Brando and Jane Fonda joined the Indian protesters, and the issue received national attention.

In 1965 the U.S. Supreme Court ruled that under the treaties Indians had the right to fish in "usual and accustomed places," but it also recognized the right of state authorities to regulate Indian fishing. Given the nature of state enforcement, little changed. The native "fish ins," as they were called at the time, continued.

The tide began to change in 1974 when a U.S. District Court judge ruled that under the terms of the nineteenth-century treaties, Indian fishermen were entitled to up to half the fish returning to off-reservation sites. In reality, they were able to take only a fraction of what the court said was rightfully theirs. Nonetheless, non-Indian fishermen and their supporters among state officials reacted with anger. Harassment of and even attacks on Indian fishermen escalated. Various legal and legislative strategies were attempted in an effort to undo the court ruling, even as it was extended to offer greater protection for the Indians. Restoration of treaty fishing rights contributed to renewal not only economically, but socially and spiritually, in Indian communities throughout the Northwest.

The antitreaty backlash continued into the 1980s and spread to other areas of the country where treaties protected Indian fishing rights. Members of the Anishinabé (Chippewa) bands of Minnesota, Wisconsin, and Michigan began to exert their rights to fish, and the federal courts supported them. In response, Anishinabé spearfishermen were harassed, and slogans such as "Save a walleye; spear a squaw" appeared on bumper stickers of cars and trucks driven by Euroamerican sports fishermen. Accommodations were reached, however, and although the fishing rights issue has not yet been resolved to everyone's satisfaction, tensions have eased in the Northwest and increasingly in Wisconsin. Contemporary state officials are more willing to work with Indians to resolve disputes than was the case with their predecessors.

In the 1990s, broader ecological concerns were joined with the fishing rights controversy, as dangerous levels of contaminants were discovered in some fish in the Northwest. Since Native Americans in the region consume, on average, a dozen times as much fish as nonnatives, they are at a greater risk. As a result, Northwestern nations have become increasingly involved in efforts to gain stricter enforcement of the Clean Water Act and other environmental legislation.

The principal motivation behind the campaign by these Native American nations to preserve fishing rights is not as much economic or political as it is spiritual. Clearly, however, all these are interrelated in indigenous worldviews. As noted, the peoples of the Northwest have sought to live in harmony with the salmon and other fish, whom they know not as a commodity to be exploited but as their brothers and sisters who willingly sacrifice their bodies for the good of their human relatives. They know as long as they show respect for the fish, the fish will continue to give to them. "For the Indians, . . . fishing is more than a job, more than a right, more than a way to make a living in a money economy. It is a way of life, a relation with the source of life, a means of identity as an Indian. For these Indians today, as for Indians in the past, their conceptions of, attitudes toward and relations with nature are essentially religious" (Vecsey 1980, 26).

Toxic Waste: The Case of Akwesasne

The Mohawks who established permanent residency at the confluence of the St. Lawrence and several other rivers in the mid-eighteenth century called the place Akwesasne ("land where the partridge drums"), because of the sound made by a male partridge during mating season. The area was rich in game, thickly forested, with rivers full of fish. The soil was fertile. Today, Akwesasne is one of the most polluted places in the United States and Canada. The fish and game are not safe to eat, and in some areas the waters are polluted and the soil unsafe to till (see Grinde and Johnasen 1995, 170–201).

Ironically, "Indian sovereignty" has been used by companies such as Alcoa, Reynolds, and General Motors as a way to avoid state, provincial, and federal antipollution laws and to create some of the worst toxic waste dumps in North America. This would be bad enough, but the dumps, many of which have been in use since the 1950s, have not kept polychlorinated biphenyls (PCBs) and other toxins from spreading. In one study, more than 500 contaminants were found in wildlife in and around Akwesasne. The traditional way of life of the Mohawks has literally been poisoned out of existence.

When public awareness of the environmental disaster spread in the 1980s, after a number of studies were published, the Mohawks filed suits against offending companies. The U.S. Environmental Protection Agency levied fines against companies. When turtles with high concentrations of PCBs began to appear,

Mohawk spiritual leaders recalled the creation stories of their people, which told how the world came into existence on the back of a turtle. As one leader put it, "the very underpinnings of the earth were coming apart."

Even while pressure increased to clean up the dumps, other entrepreneurs were coming to Akwesasne with proposals for municipal waste and medical waste incinerators. At this writing, these proposals have been rejected, although the ongoing dispute over the introduction of gambling at Akwesasne has threatened to deflect the Mohawks from their united resistance to the environmental assault.

Uranium Mining

The mineral resources on Native American lands have long been a target for energy companies and government agencies. The controversy over coal mining on Hopi and Diné lands, for example, is discussed in chapter 5. Another controversy is over the mining of uranium on reservations and other lands held in trust for or claimed by Native American nations (see Grinde and Johansen 1995, 202–18; Churchill and LaDuke 1992, 241–66).

A 1975 study revealed that two-thirds of the uranium on land under federal jurisdiction was to be found on reservation lands. The percentage rises when lands guaranteed to Native Americans by treaties are added. About 380 leases permitted mining uranium on reservations, compared to four on public lands. Although the extraction or use of uranium has affected indigenous peoples throughout the country and in U.S. protected areas such as the Marshall Islands in the Pacific, two of the worst situations have been in the Black Hills and on the Navajo Reservation. In both cases, some assimilated tribal leaders were willing to trade short-term economic gain for the long-term well-being of the land and people.

During the 1970s the discovery of uranium-rich rock in the Black Hills brought a rush of mining claims not unlike that which followed the discovery of gold in the 1870s (see chapter 4). It was the height of the Cold War and the "energy crisis," and demand for uranium both for nuclear weapons and nuclear power plants was high. By 1978 there were more than 5,000 uranium claims in the Black Hills National Forest. The underground water on the Pine Ridge Reservation near the hills was found to be polluted by waste leached from dumps created by the mines. During the 1970s the Air Force gunnery range in the northwest corner of the reservation, "borrowed" for use during World War II but never returned to the Lakota, was thought to be a dumping site for nuclear waste. About 3.5 million pounds of radioactive tailings were found dumped along the Cheyenne River on Lakota lands. Increased birth defects and cancer deaths on Lakota reservations have been linked to exposure to radioactivity. A secret government report in the 1970s recommended that land on the Lakota reservations (as well as an area on the Navajo Reservation) be designated "National Sacrifice

Areas" so that they could be made national dump sites for radioactive waste. These events were dramatized in the motion picture *Thunderheart*.

Uranium has been mined on the Navajo Reservation since the 1940s. Companies such as Atlantic Richfield, Continental Oil, Exxon, Humble Oil, Homestake Mining, Kerr McGee, Mobil Oil, Pioneer Nuclear, and United Nuclear have been engaged in mining the valuable ore. Many of the Navajos employed in these mines have paid a terrible price for the right to work in them. The rate of lung cancer among Navajo uranium miners has far exceeded that of the general Navajo population. In addition, the mining in the Southwest creates huge piles of radioactive tailings. Dust from the piles has blown into surrounding communities, and evidence of contamination has been found in water supplies. The risk of contracting lung cancer has been as much as twice as high for people living near mines as for the general population.

On 16 July 1978 an accident near Church Rock, New Mexico, unleashed a torrent of 100 million gallons of radioactive water. It remains the largest nuclear accident in the United States. Within several hours the radioactivity could be monitored fifty miles away in Gallup, New Mexico. The Rio Puerco River had 6,000 times the allowable standard of radioactivity. The accident was downplayed because it was in a "sparsely populated area," but for the Navajo and other residents it rendered unusable their major source of water.

In South Dakota, New Mexico, and Arizona, Lakota and Navajo protests against uranium mining have been supported by environmental groups and by nonnatives living in the areas, who are also concerned about the threats posed by the low-level radiation in waste materials. Indigenous peoples in other countries who are also threatened by uranium mining by multinational companies have joined with Native Americans in expressing outrage, taking legal action, and engaging in protests.

With the slowing of the arms race and the decline in the nuclear power industry in the 1980s, mining slowed down from the frenzied pace of the 1970s. By 1990 various studies had shown increased death rates among former uranium miners and those who lived near mines, and Congress passed legislation compensating the miners or members of their families. Compensation was slow and, however, like many other programs supposedly intended to help Native Americans, it was tied in knots by the federal bureaucracy. The threat posed by uranium mining is still present.

Cooperation in the Ecological Struggle

Native Americans have begun to come together to act on the basis of their commitment to Mother Earth and the interrelated community of life. In 1991 more than 500 participants from fifty-seven different tribes and reservations gathered in the Black Hills for a conference entitled "Protecting Mother Earth: The Toxic Threat to Indian Lands." It followed a similar conference the previous year on the Diné Reservation. The Black Hills conference was held near Bear Butte and was hosted by the Native Resource Coalition (from the Pine Ridge Reservation) and the Good Road Coalition (from the Rosebud Reservation). Many elders and spiritual leaders participated. The delegates formed the "Indigenous Environmental Network" as a clearinghouse for the activities of indigenous peoples who want to work together to protect the environment. They also wrote an "Environmental Code of Ethics" (Harvey and Harjo 1994, 270).

Native Americans have also joined with other concerned peoples to mount a campaign in defense of a way of life that does not destroy the balance of life. For example, also in 1991 a group of native and nonnative environmentalists met in Morelia, Mexico. Called the "Group of 100," they called for the creation of a "world court of the environment" to publicize "environmentally criminal activity" around the world. The goal to which they are committed is to reshape assumptions of the political economies of the world. One of its members, Jewell Praying Wolf James, a member of the Lummi nation, said: "Technology and science have 'objectively' separated care and consideration of the cumulative impacts of humankind's collective behavior away from social responsibility. The global community must discover an orientation that teaches the world to do with the minimal and not the maximum. We have to address our levels of consumption before the whole global community dies of ecocide" (Grinde and Johansen 1995, 39).

At the Earth Summit held in Brazil in 1992, Native American leaders joined with indigenous leaders from throughout the world to speak to the leaders of the so-called "developed" world so that in the discussions of how to address the environmental crisis the voice of Mother Earth would be heard. Following that meeting indigenous leaders have taken part in further gatherings of spiritual leaders of the world's religions to produce an "Earth Charter," a statement intended to inspire and guide efforts to respect the rights of the earth, even as the U.N. Human Rights Charter has served to foster great respect for human rights.

Concrete actions have also been taken cooperatively. For example, in 1991 the Anishinabé (Chippewa) of Lac du Flambeau set aside 1,000 acres of their land in northern Wisconsin as a wildlife preserve, working with the Nature Conservancy on the project. Such cooperation can be expected to continue and increase as trust grows between native leaders and environmental groups who are not merely trying to exploit Native American spiritual traditions. Some encouraging signs even suggest that federal and state governments are willing to respect the insights and leadership of Native American peoples in developing strategies to restore and protect the balance of life on native lands.

Sometimes, however, the interests of Native Americans and environmentalists have collided. For example, when the Makah nation of the Pacific Northwest coast sought to reassert its rights to hunt whales under an 1854 treaty, the proposal was vigorously opposed by a coalition of environmental groups. The Makah contended that the hunting of whales was an ancient tradition essential to the tribe's identity. The renewal of the whale-hunting tradition was critical, Makah leaders argued, to the revitalization of Makah culture at a time when the tribe faced a host of social and economic problems.

Environmentalists contended that if the Makah were allowed to hunt whales, other nations such as Japan and Norway would assert that whale hunting was essential to their cultural traditions. The door would be opened, they argued, to the restoration of the wholesale slaughter of whales, which had brought this noble animal to the brink of extinction.

The International Whaling Commission, however, agreed to allow the Makah to take five whales a year for four years, beginning in 1999. On 17 May 1999, after a period of ritual preparation, Makah hunters harpooned a twenty-foot grey whale off the coast of Washington. It was the first whale hunted by the Makah in more than seventy years. On the day of the hunt a Makah elder observed, "the whale presented himself to the hunters, as though he were offering himself to them." After the hunt, the whale was cut up and divided among the members of the tribe, in keeping with Makah tradition. A member of one of the environmental groups that sought unsuccessfully to disrupt the Makah hunt said angrily, "Those people should be ashamed of themselves! They have savagely taken the life of another sentient being for no good reason. We will not let this brutality continue!"

Conclusion

The single most important question facing humans at the beginning of a new millennium is whether we will learn to construct just and environmentally sustainable societies before it is too late. Surely the way to create such societies is to replace the fundamentally materialistic, myopic ethics that have dominated human affairs for most of the past five hundred years and which have brought us to the brink of ecological catastrophe with ways of acting rooted in a deeper sense of the interconnectedness of all life. While Native American spiritual traditions do not provide the only such ethical teachings, they can provide valuable insights into the contours of ways of living in harmony with all of nature. (On the environmental teachings of other spiritual traditions, see Young 2005 and Callicott 1994.)

From some native perspectives there is a certain inevitability about the process now unfolding, and what is called for is not furious activity to "protect the earth" as much as quiet patience as the earth preserves her own balance. Leslie Marmon Silko has pointed out that some pueblo prophecies speak of the arrival and disappearance of the Europeans, not the people themselves but their customs and their values. "The old people say this has already begun to happen, and that is is a spiritual process that no armies will be able to stop. So the old people laugh when they hear about the 'desecration' of the earth, because humankind, they know, is nothing in comparison to the earth. Blast it, dig it up, or cook it with nuclear explosions: the earth remains. Humans desecrate only themselves. The earth is inviolate" (Silko 1996, 125).

Other elders, however, are trying to communicate to the young people in their nations a sense of urgency and responsibility. Charles Yazzie Morgan, a Diné elder of the Towering House clan, posed this challenge to young people: "What we do to the land can destroy what give us life. Even now there are springs that no longer run. I am talking not only for myself, but for those who may be born tonight. We have to think of them. How will they drink? How will they live? What kind of life are we giving them? . . . I say to you, my children: Study! Prepare for a job! Plan for the future! But don't forget the land and the people who went before you. They will be your blessing and will make you strong" (Trimble 1993, 122).

In 1980 Onondaga Faithkeeper Oren Lyons issued a challenge to nonnatives which remains relevant decades later, exhorting us all to learn the basic principle taken for granted in Hotinonshonni (Iroquois) tradition, that we must evaluate all our actions on the basis of their consequences for the seventh generation beyond our own:

> We are facing together, you and I, your people and my people, your children and my children, we are facing together a very bleak future. There seems to be at this point very little consideration, minimum consideration, for what is to occur, the exploitation of wealth, blood, and the guts of our mother, the earth. Without the earth, without your mother, you could not be sitting here; without the sun, you would not be here. . . . In one rationalization upon another, you continue the exploitation for wealth and power. But you must consider in the process and in choosing the direction of your life: how will this affect the seventh generation? (Lyons 1980, 173–74)

CHAPTER 9

Native America in the Twenty-First Century: Looking to the Future with Hope

It is time for the people to gather and perform their old ceremonies and make a final effort to renew the earth and its peoples—hoofed, winged, and others.

—Vine Deloria Jr., Lakota

IN THEIR STUDY OF NATIVE AMERICAN HISTORY, Karen Harvey and Lisa Harjo concluded:

> A renaissance is taking place among Native American people. This renaissance is not of a material nature. It is a spiritual renaissance, a retrieving and reviving of our original covenant with the Creator. We are reaffirming our relationship and stewardship with our Mother Earth. (Harvey and Harjo 1994, 285)

Their theme of a hopeful future rooted in an unfolding Native American spiritual renaissance is supported by this study of four individual native nations and pan-national movements such as the Native American Church. This final chapter, considers some of the primary indications that, despite continuing serious challenges, hope is blossoming forth across Native America. First, it examines broad issues such as population, health, education, language, the powwow movement, economic empowerment, treaty rights and other legal issues, art and literature, and challenging stereotypes. Then, it focuses on the range of concerns related more directly to the resurgence of Native American spiritual traditions: protection of religious freedom and sacred sites, return of sacred items, confronting the exploitation of traditional spirituality, and the emergence of a common "Native American spirituality."

Native American Population: An Amazing Resurgence

A dramatic turnaround has occurred in Native American population. As noted in chapter 1, by 1900 the number of Native Americans had fallen to about 250,000. By 1980 the U.S. Census listed 1,423,043 American Indians and Alaskan Natives (Inuit and Aleuts) living in the United States. A decade later the census enumerated 2,025,143. In ten years the total number of Native Americans in the United States had risen by more than one-half million, an increase of about 40 percent. These numbers do not include those who identified themselves in the U.S. Census as having Indian ancestry (nearly 9 million in 1990). Estimates of the number of U.S. citizens with some known Native American ancestry today run as high as twenty-five million (Wilson 1999, xxiv).

In 1990, of the 2 million Native Americans in the United States, 62.3 percent lived off reservations, mostly in urban areas, with the remaining 37.7 percent on Indian lands. Nearly 300 Indian reservations in the United States included a total of 56.2 million acres of reservation and trust lands. By the end of the decade there were 554 federally recognized tribes, including 200 Alaskan village groups.

Behind the raw statistics, however, lies a continuing controversy: how should membership in Native American nations be determined? The "degree of Indian blood" (or blood quantum) as a method of determining "Indian identity" traces to the 1887 General Allotment (Dawes) Act (see chapter 1). By creating this "blood quantum" criterion and allotting land on its basis, considerable "surplus" Indian lands were qualified for distribution to "non-Indians." As Vine Deloria Jr. has observed, "Indian tribal membership is a fiction created by the federal government, not a creation of the Indian peoples themselves" (Deloria 1994, 243). The absurdity of "blood quantum" designation is captured well by Cherokee writer Jimmie Durham, who observed that "the question of my 'identity' often comes up. I think I must be a mixed-blood. I claim to be male, although only one of my parents was male" (Jaimes 1992a, 123).

From the perspective of most Native American interpreters, determination of "Indian identity" should be a matter decided solely according to each people's traditions of decision making. Each nation has its own methods of bringing into the people "outsiders" from other native peoples or even nonnatives through marriage, birth, adoption, and naturalization. Whether Indian nations can recover these inclusive traditions is a critical issue for the future (Stiffarm and Lane 1992, 45).

Another cause of concern is intermarriage. By 1990 roughly half of the marriages of Native Americans were with nonnative spouses (as compared with 1 percent of Euroamericans and 2 percent of African Americans). At this rate, according to one estimate, "the number of Native Americans with 50 percent or more of 'Indian blood' . . . will decline from around 87 percent in 1980 to only about 8 percent in 2080" (Wilson 1999, 424).

Healing the People: Health and Health Care

As demonstrated in chapter 1, the principal factor causing the drastic reduction in the population of the original inhabitants of the Americas was the introduction of diseases from Europe. Five hundred years later, although there are encouraging signs, American Indians are still paying the price for the changes in lifestyle resulting from the European invasion of the continent.

Some signs are positive. Life expectancy at birth for Native Americans has increased in recent decades, from 51 years in 1940 to 71 in 1980, four years less than the figure for the Euroamerican population. Infant mortality, more than twice the national average in 1955, was actually lower than the national average by 1985. The number of American Indian physicians is increasing, up 63 percent between 1980 and 1990 (although the total is still less than 1,000). In that same period the number of American Indian registered nurses grew by 92 percent.

Increasing numbers of Native Americans are also turning to traditional healers, who draw on the accumulated knowledge of natural medicines and/or the ritual cures deeply rooted in their peoples' traditions. In many cases, both traditional healers and modern medicine are utilized. Fortunately, more medical professionals are willing to recognize the efficacy of traditional healing methods than ever before. For example, on the Diné (Navajo) Reservation medicine men and

women are welcomed at Indian Health Service Hospitals. At one hospital a "healing room" has been designed in the shape of a traditional hogan. In her recent autobiography, Diné surgeon Dr. Lori Arviso Alvord describes how she learned to draw on traditional Navajo healing (see chapter 5) in combination with Western medicine in her practice (Alvord and Van Pelt 1999).

Still, there is cause for serious concern. The poverty common on reservations forces too many Native Americans to depend on substandard, non-nutritious foods high in fat and sugar. The occurrence of diseases associated with diet are disproportionately high among American Indians. Diabetes, a disease often related to diet and lifestyle, poses a grave risk to the health of many Native Americans.

Substance abuse, especially alcohol addiction, is almost certainly the most seri-

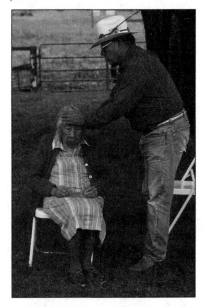

Today many Native Americans turn both to modern medicine and to traditional healers. (© Peter Turnley/CORBIS)

ous health issue among Native Americans. Due probably to both environmental factors (poverty, despair, unemployment) and genetic predisposition, American Indians have a higher rate of alcoholism than do other national or ethnic groups. In the 1980s deaths due to alcohol dependence syndrome, alcoholic psychoses, and chronic liver disease and cirrhosis were four to five times higher among Native Americans than among the general population (Washburn 1996, 462). It must be noted that the most successful programs to fight substance abuse among Native Americans have been those rooted in the indigenous spiritual traditions studied in this work.

Suicide is another significant health-related issue among American Indians. Substance abuse is one form of subintentional suicide, but the rate of intentional suicide is also high among Native Americans. In 1990 the suicide rate for Native Americans was 15 per 100,000 (down from a peak of 29 per 100,000 in 1975), compared with 11.7 in the general population.

Educating the People: The Role of the Tribal Colleges

In the late 1990s half of the more than 2 million Native Americans in the United States were under the age of eighteen, a percentage twice as high as that of the general population. A recent survey shows that more than 96 percent of today's American Indian youth identify with their Native American nations. The survey also finds them, on the whole, optimistic about the future, though they recognize the serious problems facing Native American peoples (Ewen 1998, 26).

One of the biggest challenges facing Native American leaders in the future will be to provide meaningful education for these young people, and older people as well, education that prepares students for the complex, technological world of the future while enabling them to keep and nurture roots in their own traditional cultures.

As has been shown, for too long traditional spirituality was attacked rather than taught in schools attended by Indians. Today that has largely, if not totally, changed. Important developments have occurred in education for younger Native Americans in tribally sponsored and/or supported private and public schools, which lie outside the scope of this discussion. The focus here is on the role of the tribal colleges in the development of education with a native perspective and in creating hope for the future.

According to Paul Boyer, author of a Carnegie Foundation study on Native American tribal colleges published in 1997, "[m]ore than any other single institution, [tribal colleges] are changing lives and offering real hope for the future" (Boyer 1997, 1; see Garrod and Larimore 1998). As James Shanley, president of one of the tribal colleges, Fort Peck Community College in Montana, put it: "If there is a force that can help Indians survive and escape the global homogenization, it is the tribal college" (Harris 1998, 33). The willingness of tribal colleges to combine opportunities for Native Americans to study their own language, culture, and spirituality along with education for meaningful jobs in today's society is central to this critical role.

The Navajo Community College (now called Diné College) opened in 1968 as the first tribal college. By the mid–1990s twenty-seven tribally controlled colleges in eleven states had opened, with more on the way. Enrollment has grown from about 10,000 students in 1989 to about 20,000 from over 200 hundred nations and indigenous groups in 1995. Diné College remains the largest tribal college, with about 1,500 students. Today there are more women than men taking classes at tribal colleges, and most have at least one child. The median age for students is the early thirties. At present, the enrollment of the existing colleges is growing fast, from 10 to 100 percent a year.

Without question, tribal colleges are helping to improve the economic situations on the reservations on which they are located. A recent study showed that "[w]hen you look at growth in income and reduction in poverty, tribal college reservations far outstrip those that have not made this investment in human capital and technological capacity" (Harris 1998, 32).

Of particular interest in this discussion is the role the tribal colleges are playing and will continue to play in preserving and renewing traditional Native American spirituality. The colleges typically view the traditional spirituality of the nation sponsoring the college as the center of their educational mission. Aware that many students have not been exposed very fully to the tribal traditions and that the future well-being of the people will depend on their spiritual vitality, the colleges are making a commitment to grounding students in their tribal spiritual heritages. They offer, and in some cases require, courses, many taught by elders or traditional spiritual leaders, in "native languages, history, philosophy, and the arts, botany, astronomy, and more" (Boyer 1997, 5). As discussed, all of these areas encompass "spirituality" in a native context. In some classes Western concepts are being combined with traditional knowledge. For example, at Diné College a course in Navajo astronomy mixes insights from Harvard physicists and Diné elders (Boyer 1997, 66).

Beyond classes there is a commitment by tribal college leaders "to make their colleges as fully reflective of their cultures as other colleges are of western culture" (Boyer 1997, 65). For example, at Oglala Lakota College on the Pine Ridge Reservation in South Dakota, college leaders claim they want the governance as well as the curriculum of the college to reflect a "Lakota perspective."

The tribal colleges are also growing stronger in their commitment to "rebuilding respect for traditional ways of knowing." As Boyer notes, "American Indian cultures find strength through their language, kinship, and a strong sense of connection to nature and the cosmos—and these subjects may be more satisfactorily investigated and understood through forms of scholarship distinctly Indian" (Boyer 1997, 6). In some colleges students are sent into their communities to spend time with traditional elders to gain an appreciation of their way of looking at the world.

The principal challenge the tribal colleges face as they seek to create a more hopeful future is financial. They have depended heavily on federal support because their tuitions are necessarily low and they do not have significant endowments. As part of the trend toward a smaller federal government, however, funding for tribal colleges has not kept pace with growing enrollments. The establishment of the American Indian College Fund in 1989 has helped stimulate more private giving, and each college does its own fund raising, seeking its own government and foundation grants as well as engaging in direct mail campaigns. Another private agency, the American Indian Graduate Center, provides scholarships for Native American graduate students at tribal and other colleges. Rapid enrollment growth has outpaced the colleges' and private funds' capabilities to raise money, however, and a number of the colleges are never more than a semester away from closing. Greater financing of the private funds and individual colleges is critically needed from concerned supporters beyond the reservations.

Some critics believe that despite their assertions of commitment to traditional culture, the tribal colleges are actually part of the long campaign to assimilate Native Americans into Euroamerican civilization. One Native American traditional leader has called the tribal colleges "just more of the same old BIA activities done for the colonial purposes of the larger culture" (Harris 1998, 32). Some traditionalists have withdrawn support previously given for the colleges and have refused to teach courses in language, culture, and spirituality because they seem to be only window dressing on an essentially Euroamerican curriculum. Other traditionalists, however, continue to cooperate with the colleges in seeking viable education in these areas.

This tension will probably continue in the years ahead and will require open and honest dialogue among college leaders and tribal elders and other spiritual leaders. The American Indian College Fund has shown awareness of this special need and may become the source of primary support for strengthening the "cultural" component of the tribal colleges through its Fund for Cultural Preservation. On Lakota reservations tribal college leaders support the movement to re-create a political system rooted in extended family units (tiyospaye) on the Lakota reservations (see Chapter Four). As Fort Peck Community College, President James Shanley has pointed out, rather than undermining a renewal of tradition, "[a] resurgence of interest in Sioux ceremonial culture in the past 20 years has often paralleled the development of tribal education, including the tribal colleges" (Harris 1998, 32).

In addition to the tribal colleges, three government-supported institutions of higher education have been established for Native Americans, and these will continue to play important roles in creating a more hopeful future. Operated by the Bureau of Indian Affairs, they are Haskell Indian Nations University in Lawrence, Kansas; Southwest Indian Polytechnic Institute in Albuquerque; and the Institute of American Indian Arts. These institutions are allied with the tribal colleges in the American Indian Higher Education Consortium. While their ability to instruct students in traditional spirituality is more limited than the in tribally controlled colleges, they still offer valuable courses and programs in this area. In addition, Native American studies programs at public and private colleges and universities throughout the country are offering an array of courses on Native American spirituality.

Naming the World: Keeping Languages Alive

According to the 1990 U.S. Census, about 250 separate tribal languages were being spoken by Native Americans. In the view of virtually all Native American leaders, the preservation of these traditional languages is crucial to the cultural survival and spiritual vitality of Indian nations. Without fluency in their own languages, Native Americans seem inevitably to lose touch with their heritage, their stories, their songs, and their rituals. In the 1990s only 23 percent of Indians spoke their native language at home (Wilson 1999, 424). Native American cultures are oral cultures; oral tradition is essential to cultural continuity and renewal. When the people lose their language, they begin to lose touch with who they are.

As noted, taking away traditional languages from Native Americans was for too long part of a strategy to "civilize" Indian people. Children at boarding schools were routinely punished for speaking their native tongues. Even when day schools replaced boarding schools, students were forbidden to use their own languages. For well more than 100 years, American Indian children grew up in an atmosphere that discouraged and often prohibited them from learning their own languages. Now parents and even grandparents have lost touch with the language as a viable mode of expression and are therefore unable to teach it to their children.

Another factor contributing to the decline in traditional languages has been the movement off reservations. In search of employment (and encouraged during the 1950s and 1960s by government relocation programs; see chapter 1), thousands of Indians left their reservations and moved to cities. Their survival depended on their fluency in English. The spread of television has also taken a toll, especially with satellite technology. The languages of relatively small indigenous cultures are only a generation away from irrelevancy, even extinction. Some Native American languages have died, and most today are threatened.

Again, there are hopeful signs. The policy of forbidding the speaking of native languages has changed. Now schools on reservations are introducing the teaching of traditional languages into their curricula. For example, one of the tribal colleges, Fort Peck College in Montana, is sponsoring an immersion program for Native American children ages three to five. The greatest success is achieved at the earliest level, so the teaching of native languages in Head Start and other preschool programs has been emphasized. Older people who did not have the opportunity to learn their own languages as children are undertaking the immensely difficult task of learning as adults in ever greater numbers. Special audio tapes and even programs are now available on the Internet for those trying to learn native languages (although this practice is opposed by some traditionalists who resist using modern technology to transmit the languages). Radio stations, and even some television stations, with programming in native languages have opened on reservations and are popular.

The renewal of traditional spirituality has brought many Indians into contact with stories and songs in their own languages. A few decades ago Native Americans who were fluent in their own languages were often looked down upon or ignored by younger Indians. Now those elders who do speak traditional languages as their primary languages are again being honored and sought out as mentors.

Bringing the People Together: The Powwow Movement

Although, like the tribal colleges, the spreading powwow movement does not seem at first glance to be spiritual, its important role in the revitalization and renewal of Indian nations gives it a spiritual dimension. "Powwows" are gatherings in which American Indians from different nations meet to perform and observe stylized social dances. They may or may not be sponsored by a particular tribal group, but they are almost always pannational gatherings. Powwows also attract nonnative audiences, usually drawn by the colorful dances.

Powwow derives from an old Algonquian term for a spiritual leader or medicine man. As part of their ceremonies, the holy men would perform dances, and early European observers, as often was the case, misunderstood what they were seeing and called the dances by the name for the leaders: *pau wau.* Therefore, in origin powwows were indeed ritual dances, performed in the context of the quest for harmony now recognized in so many different settings among Native American nations.

In prereservation days native peoples from different nations gathered at annual trade fairs, at first among native nations and then incorporating the Europeans who brought new goods. As noted, among Plains nations there were annual camp circles that brought the various nomadic bands together for the sun dance and for socializing. With trading posts and government agencies replacing the trading fairs and with traditional rituals like the sun dance outlawed, however, a vacuum was created. It was filled in part by powwows, which over the years have continued to grow. In addition to serving as places of gathering for native peoples, they have functioned as the principal way for nonnatives to experience in a nonintrusive manner the richness of traditional American Indian cultures.

A Cherokee teacher expressed the reason powwows are so popular among Native Americans and will undoubtedly remain so: "We go to powwows to make us happy" (Parfit 1994, 91). She clearly did not mean "happy" in the superficial sense expressed by people going to a typical weekend party, but rather "happy" in the deeper sense of the Diné term *hozho*–fulfilled, harmonious, aware of beauty, at peace (see chapter 5).

By the mid–1990s more than 1,000 powwows were being held each year throughout the United States and Canada. It is estimated that up to 90 percent of the more than 2 million Native Americans in the United States attend at least one powwow each year (Parfit 1994, 98).

Typically held on weekends, powwows revolve around competition in dances such as the Men's Fancy, Grass, or Traditional Dances and the Women's Fancy Shawl, Jingle Dress, or Traditional Buckskin Dances. The dances are all tied to spiritual rituals, including dances once carried out in preparation for hunting or combat, as well as in ceremonies of healing, or in celebration of success in battle or the hunt.

In addition to the competitive and social dancing there are occasions at pow-wows when families or other groups will hold honor dances for a son or daughter who has returned from the armed services or has graduated from college. Sometimes the honor dance is in response to a tragedy, such as the death of a child or grandchild in an automobile accident. In association with honor dances there will often be giveaways, in which the proud family or group will bestow gifts on those who have come to support them. As noted, these giveaways also have their roots in the spiritual traditions of various Native American nations

Most Native Americans today call powwows simply celebrations. Whether held in a small community deep in a rural reservation or in a convention center in a major city, powwows are ringing reaffirmations of pride in being Indian and expressions of commitment to living unashamedly as members of separate nations who are nonetheless willing to come together as one Indian people. Only if one thinks of "spiritual" in a narrow sense, which would certainly be inappropriate for Native American cultures, should powwows be called nonspiritual or strictly social or secular events. Although powwows are not now and will not become substitutes for the traditional rituals of each nation or the rituals of pannational movements as the Native American Church, they are spiritual in the fullest sense of the term. They are modern ceremonies.

The Powwow Trail is one name for the path that takes dancers and spectators from one powwow to another, sometimes from one corner of the United States and Canada to another. Symbolically, it is also a path in search of harmony for those who walk it with an attitude of reverence, respect, humility, and joyful spontaneity. It is a path with deep roots in the traditions of the past, but also a trail that is fundamentally oriented toward the experience of happiness and pride in the present, and hope for the future.

Providing for All the People: Economic Empowerment

Poverty continues to plague Indian reservations and off-reservation Native American communities. As noted in the discussions of particular nations, the American government has fallen far short in its treaty commitments to provide for the welfare of native peoples (see Hoxie 1993). Moreover, appropriations for programs on reservations have been cut in recent years, and the available funds often disappear into a bureaucratic hole before they reach the people for whom they are ostensibly intended.

Tribal governments, imposed on native nations during the reform efforts of the 1930s (see chapter 1), are still plagued by corruption and inefficiencies, although there have been successful reforms in recent years. Today unemployment rates on reservations are as high as 80 percent and often are in the 40–60 percent range. Although the gap between median family income for Native Americans and Euroamericans narrowed between 1980 and 1990, it is still significant.

Many Native American leaders now clearly understand that the future economic well-being of Native Americans will not be sustained, much less enhanced, simply by reliance on government programs administered by federal and/or tribal bureaucrats. The keys will be self-reliance and self-determination rooted in the contemporary spiritual renaissance. These values depend on Native American leaders with a combination of practical skills and commitment to the well-being of all the people and the wider community of life.

The gambling industry has been a boon to some Native American peoples. For example, by 1998 unemployment on the Gila Bend Reservation in Arizona had been cut from 40 to 15 percent due to the opening of a casino along Interstate 10 close to Phoenix. In Minnesota and South Dakota, the number of Indians on welfare has also declined significantly since the introduction of casino gambling. In one year (1992) the budget of the Oneida Tribe of Wisconsin grew from $5 million to $85 million as a direct result of gambling revenue. Faced with declining federal support, some Indian nations have been able to draw on gambling income to support education, health care, housing, business development, land acquisition, and retirement benefits for their members.

The success of a few casinos, however, is creating the unfortunate impression, fostered by the media, that American Indians are awash in a sea of gambling money. People who seem to know little else about Native Americans, have heard about the 300 Mashantucket Pequots in Ledyard, Connecticut, who earned $600 million in

Casinos on reservations are regarded by many Native Americans as an economic boon generating much-needed revenue for worthwhile projects, but others see in the gaming industry a rejection of traditional spiritual values. (© Phil Schermeister/CORBIS)

one year from the Foxwoods Casino. In an effort to regulate the fast-growing gambling industry on reservations and trust lands, Congress passed the Indian Gaming Regulation Act in 1988. This Act created an Indian Gaming Commission and charged the Bureau of Indian Affairs with the responsibility for enforcing strict rules regarding non-Indian involvement and ensuring that gaming benefitted Indian people. State efforts to regulate Indian gaming have so far met with only limited success.

In fact, only a relatively few Native American nations have benefited from the burgeoning tribal gaming industry, and those that have must share their earnings with the companies hired to administer the casinos. In addition, many Indians live on reservations too far from densely populated areas to benefit from the gambling boon, or in urban areas cut off from the casinos.

Of particular concern for the future is the potential spiritual cost of dependence on income from gambling for those nations that have reaped significant profits, especially those who have simply allocated the income to individuals rather than community projects. In this respect, casinos may be "the most disruptive force since the allotment policy" (Wilson 1999, 417). That is an issue Native American leaders and communities will continue to face in the years ahead.

Beyond the casinos, there are hopeful signs that more stable economic opportunities created by and for Native Americans will provide meaningful and dignified jobs on and off reservations. For example, the Mississippi Choctaws have become one of the twenty top employers in the state, with five auto-related electronics factories and a greeting card operation (Washburn 1996, 441).

Lending programs for small businesses on reservations, modeled after successful efforts to fund such enterprises in developing countries in Asia, Africa, and Central America, are also promising. The First Nations Development Institute, begun in 1981 and headquartered in Virginia, is providing and will continue to make available resources and guidance for the funding of small, often home-based, ventures. In part as a result of its efforts, the number of Native American-owned businesses grew fivefold to 102,234 (and eightfold in receipts to more than $8 million) in a five-year period between 1987 and 1992 (Casey 1998, 12). Businesses range from selling traditional Native American arts and crafts on the World Wide Web to selling Indian fry bread at a newly opened restaurant in a county court house. The Institute calls its program "culture first" capitalism.

"Microenterprises" supported by loan funds such as the Lakota Fund on the Pine Ridge Reservation hold out perhaps the greatest hope for a more secure economic future for Native Americans. Programs such as the Center for Tribal Entrepreneurial Studies at Haskell Indian Nations University and the National Center for American Indian Enterprise Development in Mesa, Arizona, have greatly assisted in this effort (Chuckluck 1998; for other supportive programs and agencies, see Olson-Crawford 1998).

Native leaders in this effort subscribe to a model of economic development for the sake of the well-being of the community as a whole rather than merely the creation of wealth for individuals. According to this model, "business growth becomes part of a larger agenda for social renewal, encompassing issues as diverse as housing, the environment, cultural renewal and political sovereignty" (Boyer 1997, 48).

Under the terms of the Personal Responsibility and Work Opportunity Reconciliation Act of 1996 (the so-called Welfare Reform Act), Native American nations are empowered to contract to administer new welfare programs, bypassing the state governments. Theoretically, this will enable Native Americans to assume greater control over how federal funds are spent on the reservations. Only a few of the native nations, however, will be able to provide the typical 45 percent of the matching funds required under the law to implement control. The Navajo nation would have to create 2,500 new jobs in the first year alone in order to meet the work participation requirements of the law. Therefore, some experts think the pattern of federal paternalism is likely to continue, and even more misery on the reservations will follow (Shanley 1998).

Moreover, although the Welfare Reform Act is intended to decrease poverty by emphasizing "personal responsibility," "its punitive nature . . . attacks the symptoms of poverty instead of the root causes." Tribal College leaders point out that they have taken another approach to decreasing welfare dependency: community responsibility. "Instead of focusing exclusively upon 'personal responsibility,' they promote their communities' capacity to help students reach their full potential. Using their traditional values as a foundation, they have created models that should be studied by anyone interested in reducing dependency and despair in this country" (Ambler 1998, 8).

The law does have supporters among Indian leaders. For example, John Bushman of the Turtle Mountain Band of Chippewas is an attorney who directs the Division of Tribal Services of the U.S. Department of Health and Human Services, which is responsible for implementing welfare reform among the tribes. He points out that the Welfare Reform Act "provides an opportunity for tribal governments to reclaim and exercise sovereignty" and for "the federal, state, and tribal governments to reshape how each conducts business with the other" (Bushman 1998, 22).

Regardless of what happens as a result of welfare reform, according to growing numbers of Native American leaders, economic development not rooted in traditional spirituality will not serve the whole community and will fail the individuals it intends to help. Whether Indian nations will be able to maintain the ideals of their spiritual heritage while becoming players in the emergent world economy is one of the most significant issues facing Native Americans at the beginning of the twenty-first century.

Defending the People: Treaty Rights and Other Legal Issues

Among the most important issues facing Native Americans today are reclamation of treaty rights and the proper exercise of the trust responsibility of the federal government. In the case of the latter, the struggle to reform the Bureau of Indian Affairs is critical. Identified by many observers as the most inefficient and corrupt federal agency, critics charge that the BIA still wastes millions of dollars appropriated by Congress to be spent for the welfare of Indians. Despite the growing number of Native Americans hired as BIA employees, the BIA seems to resist all efforts to make substantive changes. The suggestion that the BIA be eliminated and funds be given directly to Indian nations for administration is gaining support. As Chief Claude Cox of the Creek Nation observed, "Reforming the BIA is like rotating four bald tires on an old car. The net result would be no change" (Mankiller 1993, 168).

For Native Americans defense of treaty rights is tantamount with maintaining their own integrity. Nearly 400 treaties were negotiated between the United States and sovereign Native American nations before Congress stopped the practice in 1871. The struggle to force compliance with these treaties has resulted in victories, but much work remains to be done.

The most divisive area of recognition of treaty rights deals with land. It has been estimated that American Indian nations today occupy approximately 2.5

percent of their original land basis (Churchill and LaDuke 1992, 243). Up to 35 percent of the continental United States should be in native hands according to the last known judicial ruling or legislative action. Today a number of native nations are actively pursuing land claims against the federal government.

Another of the principal legal issues for Native American nations today is federal recognition. Nations that had been terminated under the ill-fated federal policy of the 1950s and 60s (see chapter 1) and other groups that had not been recognized are involved. Among the nations or groups that have recently gained or regained federal recognition are the Lenape (Delaware) of Oklahoma (see chapter 2), the Micmac of Maine, the Mohegan of Connecticut, the Catawba of South Carolina, and the San Juan Southern Paiute of Arizona.

For many Native Americans and others the imprisonment of Leonard Peltier is a potent symbol of the injustice Native peoples continue to experience in the United States (see Matthiesen 1983; Vander Wall 1992). Peltier, an Anishinabé-Lakota, was convicted on a murder charge resulting from the death of two FBI agents in a shooting on the Oglala Lakota Pine Ridge Reservation in 1975 (see chapter 4). Peltier's supporters believe that his conviction was based on fraudulent evidence and that his incarceration was as a result of his political views and his role as a leader in the American Indian Movement. They view him as a prisoner of war in the ongoing struggle to liberate Native Americans from colonial oppression. At this writing efforts to win his release or at least a new trial have proven unsuccessful.

Many of these legal battles are being fought by "warriors with attaché cases," including the lawyers of the Native American Rights Fund (NARF). Created in 1970, the NARF is the principal defender of Indian sovereignty today (Sanders 1990). It was founded to provide competent and ethical legal representation for Native Americans and to protect the traditional ways of life of Native peoples.

The most radical interpretation of the current political/legal situation is that indigenous nations are still in a state of "colonization." From this perspective, most "tribal governments" (elected according to provisions of the Indian Reorganization Act of 1934) are little more than puppets of the federal bureaucracies and big corporations. As in other colonial situations, these leaders, it is alleged, enrich themselves at the expense of their people. Nothing less than "revolutions," in which the people who are rooted in the traditional ways of the nation seize control from the assimilated leaders, will meaningfully change the situation.

Others point out that this analysis is rooted in a radical ideology that does not always respect or recognize cultural traditions. Not all elected leaders have "sold out," they assert, and a posture that splits native peoples simply continues the "divide and conquer" approach that has plagued Indian nations since the Euroamerican invasion. According to this perspective, it is possible to build coalitions among sensitive elected leaders and traditionalists and chart a course that truly benefits the people.

Inspiring the People: The Renewal of Native American Art and Literature

At the onset of a new century an artistic and literary renaissance is well underway among Native Americans. Virtually all artists and writers draw heavily for inspiration from their own spiritual traditions, even as they engage the contemporary situation of native peoples. Unfortunately, because of limited space only a few of this immensely talented group are mentioned here.

Some of the more prominent contemporary artists include Kevin Red Star (Crow), Randy Lee White (Lakota), Virginia Stroud (Cree-Cherokee), Richard West Sr. (Cheyenne), Fritz Scholder (Luiseno), T.C. Cannon (Caddo-Kiowa), R.C. Gorman (Diné), and George Longfish (Seneca-Tuscarora). Native American literature is also enjoying great success. Beginning with the publication of Kiowa author N. Scott Momaday's Pulitzer Prize–winning novel *House Made of Dawn* in 1968, there has been a series of acclaimed works by American Indian writers. Momaday was followed by writers such as poet Simon Ortiz (Acoma), novelist James Welch (Blackfeet-Gros Ventre), and Gerald Vizenor (Anishinabé [Chippewa]). Today many of the most widely read and admired Native American authors are women: Leslie Marmon Silko (Laguna), Wendy Rose (Hopi-Miwok), Paula Gunn Allen (Laguna), Roberta Hill Whiteman (Oneida), Joy Harjo (Creek), Linda Hogan (Chickasaw), and Louise Erdrich (Anishinabé). Sherman Alexie (Spokane-Coeur d'Alene) is another young author whose prose and poetry are highly regarded.

The contemporary artistic and literary flowering has been enhanced by the increasing importance of Native American scholarship. Growing numbers of Native American scholars have taken positions at colleges and universities and have been instrumental in the development of Native American studies programs across the continent.

Naming the People: Challenging the Stereotyping of Native Americans

One of the cultural issues with which Native Americans still contend is the continued stereotyping of Indian peoples in American life. As noted, the names by which many Native Americans are known reflect the use of pejorative labels. Across Native America, the people are reclaiming their right to be known by their own names.

Beyond tribal names, the best-known example of this issue is the use of stereotypical images of Native Americans as mascots for professional and other sports teams. For a number of years a campaign has been under way to convince the owners of professional teams such as the Cleveland Indians, the Washington Redskins, the Kansas City Chiefs, and the Atlanta Braves, and the boards of universities whose teams use Indian names (such as the Florida State Seminoles or the Fighting Illini of the University of Illinois) to change them. The debate has aroused strong emotions. Team loyalists frequently express the view that such names are meant to honor Native Americans. The Cleveland Indians are so named, it is pointed out, to pay tribute to Francis Sockalexis, a Penobscot, who played for the Cleveland baseball team from 1897 to 1899, as one of the first Native Americans to play for a professional team. Atlanta Brave fans contend that their "tomahawk chop" is meant to honor Indian courage in battle.

In the view of those challenging such stereotyping, at a time when Indian nations are working hard to develop their own sense of pride and to instill in young people positive images, the pervasiveness of such images is one more obstacle that must be overcome. How, they ask, would Italian Americans respond to the contention that a naming a major league baseball team the "Dallas Dagos" is intended as a tribute to the contributions of Italians to American life? Or would Hispanic Americans remain silent if there were a football team called the "Spokane Spics"? Would Jewish Americans not challenge the naming of a team the Jacksonville Jewboys or African Americans a team called the Boston Buck Niggers (roughly equivalent to Redskins)? As William Means of the International Indian Treaty Council has said: "If we can't get white America to understand the basic issue of human respect, how can we get them to understand more substantive issues like sovereignty, treaty rights and water rights?" (cited in Hauptman 1995, 82).

The common contemporary stereotyping of Native Americans as "ecological saints" is analyzed in chapter 8. There is, however, another type of stereotyping with which Native Americans must contend. It is rooted in the centuries-old image of the Indian as "brutal savage," long perpetuated in movies and today revived in the context of Indian militancy. As long as Indians are engaged in acts of defiance, as in the occupation of Wounded Knee in 1973, the general public can place them in a known framework. They are "acting Indian." Images of Indians as vicious warriors have been used in other settings as well. In a 1990 *Time* magazine article, the American "total war" in the Persian Gulf was compared to Plains Indian societies in which "the passage to manhood . . . required the blooding of the spear, the taking of a scalp or head" (cited in Jaimes and Halsey 1992, 315). It is harder for non-Indians to "imagine Indians who identify themselves with native cultural and tribal values as energy entrepreneurs, as doctors, as lawyers, as business executives, as computer programmers, and as government officials" (Hauptman 1995, 110).

The Quest for Harmony: The Renewal of Traditional Spirituality

Among the issues that will affect the ability of Native Americans to practice their traditional spirituality, the most pressing include the continuing struggle for religious freedom for Native Americans; protection of sacred sites; return of sacred items taken from burials or sold to museums and other collectors; the struggle against exploitation of traditional beliefs and rituals by self-appointed, non-Indian and in some cases Indian, advocates of so-called New Age spirituality; and the emergence of a common "Native American spirituality."

Protection of Religious Freedom

The American Indian Religious Freedom Act of 1978 was intended to guarantee the same right to free expression of religion for Native Americans as has been enjoyed by all in the United States. Just what practices are covered under the law, however, has been the subject of legal conflict ever since.

In 1988, in a 5–4 vote, the U.S. Supreme Court ruled (in *Lyng* v. *Northwest Indian Cemetery Protective Association*) that members of the Yurok, Karok, and Tolowa Nations in northern California could not halt construction of a paved U.S. Forest Service road (known as the G-O Road) through Six Rivers National Forest because it was in and around a sacred area known to them as High Country. These nations had reserved this area for centuries for vision quests, gathering medicine roots, and other ceremonial purposes. The majority decision held that government activities cannot be disrupted by religious claims because of the variety of religious beliefs in American society. One justice compared these native peoples' relation to the land to the religious feeling that some have when they gaze on the Lincoln Memorial, linking traditions held for hundreds if not thousands of years with a momentary sentiment! The dissenting opinion in the case pointed out that the ruling "sacrifices a religion at least as old as the Nation itself, along with the spiritual well-being of its approximately 5,000 adherents, so that the Forest Service can build a 6-mile segment of road" (Deloria 1992, 286). Ironically, the road construction was later abandoned. The *Lyng* ruling, however, in effect derailed the efforts of other indigenous nations to seek judicial support in their efforts to protect sacred sites.

As noted in the discussion of the Native American Church (chapter 7), in 1990 in *Employment Division, Department of Human Resources of Oregon* v. *Smith*, the Supreme Court ruled that individual states had the power to regulate and declare illegal the ceremonial use of peyote by members of the church. This ruling sent a chill not only throughout the Native American Church, but also among all concerned about religious freedom and the constitutional provision of separation of church and state. As a result of the courageous struggle of leaders and supporters of the Native American Church, federal legislation was enacted in 1994 protecting the freedom of Native Americans to use peyote ceremonially. As Native Americans have learned, however, efforts to restrict their right to practice their traditional spirituality will reappear in new forms.

In 1996, for the first time, the United States was formally investigated by the United Nations in response to a charge of violation of the religious freedom of indigenous peoples. Abdelfattah Armor, U.N. Special Rapporteur on Religious

Intolerance, went to Arizona to investigate the claims of the Sovereign Diné Nation of Big Mountain (see chapter 5). Senator Jesse Helms, chairman of the Senate Foreign Relations Committee, called the investigation a waste of money, claiming that there was no religious intolerance in the United States. The International Indian Treaty Council responded, however, by pointing out the long history of repression of the spiritual practices of Native Americans in the United States. The willingness of Native American leaders to call international attention to their campaign for religious freedom can be expected to continue. The religious freedom of Native Americans is now on the international agenda.

Protection of Sacred Sites

It is difficult for most nonnatives to understand why Indians must conduct certain ceremonies only on sacred sites they rarely visit and which are not visibly sanctified. Moreover, the secrecy that surrounds these sites and the rituals conducted at them arouses suspicion. For outsiders to understand, they must be willing to try to hear the sense of sacrality of the land found among American Indians.

Vine Deloria Jr. has identified four ways in which land is sacred to Native Americans:

1. Lands are sacred because an event of great importance occurred there. For example, Wounded Knee on the Pine Ridge Reservation in South Dakota is such a site because of the massacre there in 1890 and the reoccupation of the site in 1973 (see chapter 4). These sites are sanctified when ceremonies are held there. They create a "sense of social cohesion" among the people.

2. Other lands are sacred because of some specific spiritual significance is associated with them. For example, the San Francisco Mountains west of the Hopi Reservation are associated with the story of the Hopi migration and the *katsinas* (spirits) who help the Hopis live in harmony. Buffalo Gap at the southeastern edge of the Black Hills of South Dakota marks the place where buffalo emerged each spring to initiate the Lakota cycle of yearly ceremonies (see chapter 4).

3. Still other lands are sacred in and of themselves because they are sites at which holy beings revealed themselves. For the Taos people of New Mexico, Blue Lake is such a site. For various Plains nations Bear Butte, north of the Black Hills, is another (see chapter 4).

4. Native peoples are always open to the possibility that a site not yet known to be sacred will take on sacred significance. In a sense, then, all land is potentially sacred (Deloria 1994, 272–77).

According to Deloria, the importance of sacred sites for Native Americans (and others in the modern world) cannot be overestimated. They are, he writes, "the foundation of all other beings and practices because they represent the presence of the sacred in our lives. They properly inform us that we are not larger than nature and that we have responsibilities to the rest of the natural world that transcend our personal desires and wishes" (Deloria 1994, 281).

Beginning with the restoration of Blue Lake in New Mexico to the Taos People in 1970, there have been some victories in the struggle to protect sacred sites. Numerous setbacks have occurred, however, and the struggle will continue in the twenty-first century.

Return of Sacred Objects

Repatriation is the term applied to return of an object taken from its original location without just cause. For centuries objects sacred to Native American peoples have been stolen, expropriated, or purchased in situations of duress. In the case of stolen objects (such as a Hopi shield stolen from the village of Oraibi and later returned by the Heard Museum in Phoenix where it had been donated), there is no doubt that repatriation is the proper course. In cases of "cultural patrimony," however, when theft cannot be proven and the object is "owned" by the nation as a whole, not any particular individual or group, the case for repatriation has proven harder to make. Collectors of such items typically consider them "works of art" and are often reluctant to turn them over to tribal authorities. Such cases can often be negotiated, but the process is usually slow. For example, a Zuni war god donated to the Denver Museum of Natural History in 1968 was finally returned to the Zuni nation in 1991.

Another "repatriation" issue is the return of human remains taken by archaeologists from native burials for study and display. The Native American Rights Fund has taken the lead in promoting legislation and filing suits to force the return of identifiable skeletal remains. For example, the 1990 Native American Graves Protection and Repatriation Act (NAGPRA) forced federal agencies and private museums receiving federal funds to survey their collections of Native American human remains and burial objects, notify the appropriate tribes, and, if the tribes so requested, return the remains and objects for reburial or other proper disposition. The agencies and museums also had to inventory their sacred and cultural objects and return them to the appropriate tribes. The act also stipulated that Indian nations have ownership of cultural items discovered on their lands and that trafficking in such items is strictly prohibited.

Under the provisions of NAGPRA, when archeologists excavate burials, any human remains unearthed must be returned to Native American nations when the cultural affiliation of the person(s) can be determined. Some scientists have challenged the unlimited implementation of NAGPRA as a threat to the public's right to knowledge of the American past. They claim the act is poorly written and should be amended to protect valid research. In response, Native American leaders have asked why digging up the graves of Euroamericans is a crime, while excavating Native American burials is seen as research. They say NAGPRA's protections of their sacred traditions are long overdue.

The discovery of an apparently 9,000-year-old skeleton with allegedly Caucasian features (called Kennewick Man) in 1996 along the Columbia River in the state of Washington and a NAGPRA claim by several tribes in the area has engendered a particular heated controversy (see Thomas 2000). A coalition of scientists has sued to block return of the remains to area tribes for burial, after tribal leaders invoked the NAGPRA provisions and demanded the skeleton be returned.

Exploitation of Traditional Spirituality

The rapid growth of interest in Native American spirituality among nonnatives has led to a great deal of exploitation. Some Native Americans have taken advantage of this interest. As Vine Deloria has observed, "whites . . . pay hundreds of dollars for the privilege of sitting on the ground, having corn flour thrown in their faces, and being told that the earth was round and all things lived in circles" (Deloria 1994, 41).

Euroamerican entrepreneurs have also been willing to take advantage of this marketing opportunity. In a novel entitled *Hanta Yo* author Ruth Beebe Hill claimed to have discovered the "original" Dakota language and to know the truth about Dakota/Lakota culture, which has been lost by Dakota/Lakota people themselves. The movie entitled *Mystic Warrior* is based on the book. Lynn Andrew's works (including *Medicine Woman* and a host of others) claim to reveal secrets for living revealed by two Cree medicine women (with Lakota names).

Hopi scholar Wendy Rose has characterized and interpreted the typical setting in which a nonnative "whiteshaman" presents himself/herself as a legitimate Native American spiritual leader:

> during performances whiteshamans typically don a bastardized composite of
> pseudo-Indian "style" buckskins, beadwork, headbands, moccasins, and
> sometimes paper masks intended to portray native spiritual beings such as
> Coyote or Raven. They often appear carrying gourd rattles, eagle feathers,
> "peace pipes," medicine bags, and other items reflective of native ceremonial
> life. Their readings are frequently accompanied by the burning of sage, "pipe
> ceremonies," the conducting of chants and beating of drums of vaguely
> native type, and the like. One may be hard-pressed to identify a particular

indigenous culture being portrayed, but the obviously intended effect is American Indian. The point is that the whiteshaman reader/performer aspires to "embody the Indian," in effect "becoming" the "real" Indian even when actual native people are present. Native reality is subsumed and negated by imposition of a "greater" or "more universal" contrivance. (Rose 1992, 405)

New Age enthusiasts have been especially drawn to traditional spirituality. On reservations around the country, "seekers" show up at the doors of spiritual leaders asking to have rituals such as the vision quest conducted for them. Some have claimed to have become "pipe carriers," an office with "hazy historical and cultural antecedents" (Deloria 1994, 43).

As Deloria observes, "[i]n the 1990s, Indian religions are a hot item. It is the outward symbolic form that is most popular. Many people, Indian and non-Indian, have taken a few principles to heart, mostly those beliefs that require little in the way of changing one's lifestyle. Tribal religions have been trivialized beyond redemption by people sincerely wishing to learn about them" (Deloria 1994, 43).

Particularly popular today is the appropriation of prophecies emerging from the traditions of various Native American nations. For example, the recent birth of a white buffalo calf in Wisconsin has been linked to Lakota tradition as a prophecy of the last chance for humans to learn to live in harmony (see chapter 4). The interpretation of that prophecy is the legitimate domain of recognized traditional spiritual leaders; nevertheless, the publicity about the birth of "Miracle," as her owners named her, caused a host of nonnative self-appointed interpreters to make claims about the prophecy.

Today many Native Americans sincerely believe that their spirituality "is more in touch with reality than is that of the questing, questioning, and never satisfied EuroAmericans. This attitude explains both the ease with which Indians are willing to absorb the rituals of outsiders, if they can be incorporated into their own scheme of belief, and why in other cases they feign ignorance of their own traditions or are uncooperative toward those seeking to 'study' their religion" (Washburn 1996, 461–62).

The attitude among many Native Americans toward such exploitation is expressed well by Margo Thunderbird:

They came for our land, for what grew or could be grown on it, for the resources in it, and for our clean air and pure water. They stole these things from us, and in the taking they also stole our free ways and the best of our leaders, killed in battle or assassinated. And now, after all that, they've come for the very last of our possessions; now they want our pride, our history, our spiritual traditions. They want to rewrite and remake these things, to claim them for themselves. The lies and thefts just never end. (Rose 1992, 403)

According to Osage-Cherokee scholar Grant Tinker, as white Christian spirituality withers for many modern Euroamericans and they seek to fill their own spiritual void, they turn to Indian spirituality. But they can only come to Native American rituals from their own Euroamerican cultural contexts. As a result, in this environment of adaptation, ". . . native traditions can only be understood by analogy with white experience." This serves to dilute the very traditions the Euroamericans claim to be seeking to honor, and this dilution affects Native Americans (Tinker 1993, 121).

The first casualty in this new cultural imposition, according to Tinker, is "the strong deep structure cultural value of community and group cohesion. . . . [D]ancing in a ceremony in order 'that the people may live' gives way to the New Age Euroamerican quest for individual spiritual power." He warns that many younger Indians are learning to see their ceremonial traditions "through increasingly individualist eyes." Another trend is "the temptation . . . to convert spiritual tradition into career and economic development opportunities." Traditional people begin to shift, often without realizing it, the traditional rituals to accommodate the participation of whites.

The result, according to Tinker, is that "Indian people are all too ready to participate in our own oppression and continuing conquest. Craving the approval of white acquaintances and hoping for a broader understanding of and appreciation for the validity of traditional ceremonial life, Indian people often rush to invite this new European invasion, the invasion of what remains of tribal ceremonies." It is also harmful to the Euroamericans, who erroneously believe they can fill their own spiritual vacuums by superficial ventures into Native American spiritual traditions (Tinker 1993, 120–23).

The Emergence of a Common "Native American Spirituality"

One interesting and important question to be considered for the future is whether a common "Native American spirituality" that transcends the spirituality of any particular nation is emerging and gaining strength.

The pannational Native American Church is examined in chapter 7; another trend is the spread of the Plains complex of traditions (especially the sweat lodge, vision quest, and sun dance). Some interpreters think it has become the basis for a contemporary transnational Native American spirituality. On my visits to Lakota reservations in South Dakota in recent years, I have met Native Americans, such as a young Apache man living in California, who had rediscovered their native spiritual roots through attending, then participating in, Lakota sun dances. Especially for American Indians whose own national spiritual heritage has faded, these originally Plains rituals have become their own.

While this trend has contributed to unity among Native Americans as they cooperate in facing challenges such as those described in this chapter, the "homogenization" associated with it has been "criticized by some [Native Americans] as diluting tribal differences into a generic pan-Indian culture almost as harmful as assimilation" (Smith and Warrior 1996: 279).

Whether the traditions of particular nations can be renewed, while commitment to a shared Native American spirituality grows, is a question that will remain for the foreseeable future.

Conclusion

In contrast to the hopeful signs stressed above, there are, to be sure, indications of a less hopeful future. In the late 1990s, for example, a growing problem on Native American reservations was the growth of youth gangs. Experts trace the introduction of the gangs to the spread of cable and satellite television on the reservations in the 1980s and 90s, exposing Indian youth to the urban gang culture. Native American young people living in urban areas have also experienced directly ethnic gangs, and they introduced the phenomenon when they visited relatives on reservations. One of the effects has been an increase in serious crime on reservations in recent years. For example, the rate of homicide increased 87 percent in five years on the Navajo Reservation.

The "gang problem" is one example of a serious dilemma with which many Native Americans must contend. As one Navajo leader put it, Indian youths turn to gangs because of the spiritual vacuum in their lives. They are cut off or alienated from their traditional cultures and their spiritual traditions and turned off by the Christian piety taught them by missionaries and, in many cases, by their parents and grandparents. It appears that the "gang problem" is just one of a number that will be solved not by more federal programs and more dollars alone, but by authentic spiritual renewal.

The spiritual renewal is under way, and it has the *potential* to transform Native American gang members into modern warriors for their people, willing to fight not with bullets but with knowledge and pride, connecting not just to other gang members but to all the people and all of life. It also has the potential to transform Native Americans who continue to fill the spiritual vacuums in their lives with alcohol or other drugs. The only question is whether it will spread far enough, fast enough, deeply enough to renew not only individuals but the people as a whole.

It may even be that the power of a reinvigorated Native American spirituality will spread in meaningful ways beyond the reservations, beyond the descendants of the first inhabitants of this continent, to touch the nonnative population. As Grant Tinker has observed:

Not only do Indians tell the stories, sing the songs, speak the prayers, and perform the ceremonies that root themselves deeply in Grandmother, the earth, they are actually audacious enough to think that their stories and their ways of reverencing creation will some day win over the immigrant conquerors and transform them. Optimism and enduring patience seem to run in the life blood of Native American peoples. Such is the spirit of hope that marks the American Indian struggle of resistance in the midst of a world of pain. (Tinker 1996, 129)

*　　　*　　　*

IT IS FITTING to end this look into the future and the entire reflection on the quest for harmony in Native American spiritual traditions with the words of Alfonso Ortiz (Tewa), whom we cited in the Introduction:

"We shall tell you of our struggles," they said.
"We are all the People of this land.
We were created out of the forces
of earth and sky, the stars and water.
We must make sure that the balance of the earth be kept.
There is no other way." (cited in Harvey and Harjo 1994, 8)

Bibliography

ABERLE, DAVID F. 1959. "The Prophet Dance and Reactions to White Contact." *Southwestern Journal of Anthropology* XV: 74–83.

————. 1962. "A Note on Relative Deprivation Theory as Applied to Millennarian and Other Cult Movements." In *Millennial Dreams in Action*, edited by Sylvia L. Thrupp. The Hague: Mouton & Co., 209–14.

————. 1982a. *The Peyote Religion among the Navajo*. 2d ed. Chicago: University of Chicago Press. 1st ed., 1966.

————. 1982b. "The Future of Navajo Religion." In *Navajo Religion and Culture*, edited by David M. Brugge and Charlotte J. Frisbie. Santa Fe: Museum of New Mexico Papers in Anthropology. No. 17, pp. 219–31.

————. 1983. "Peyote Religion among the Navajo." In *Handbook of North American Indians: Southwest*, vol. 10, edited by Alfonso Ortiz. Washington, D.C.: Smithsonian Institution, 558–69.

————. 1991. *The Peyote Religion among the Navajo*. 2d ed. Norman: University of Oklahoma Press. First published in 1966.

Adams, Richard C. 1904. *The Ancient Religion of the Delaware Indians*. Washington, D.C.: Law Reporter Printing Co.

————. 1905. *Legends of the Delaware Indians and Picture Writing*. Washington, D.C.

Albanese, Catherine L. 1984. "Exploring Regional Religion: A Case Study of the Cherokee." *History of Religions* 23 (1984), 344–71.

————. 1990. *Nature Religion in America: From the Algonkian Indians to the New Age*. Chicago: University of Chicago Press.

Albers, Patricia, and Beatrice Medicine, eds. 1983. *The Hidden Half: Studies of Plains Indian Women*. New York: University Press of America.

Allen, Paula Gunn. 1979. "Iyani: It Goes This Way." In *The Remembered Earth*, edited by Geary Hobson. Albuquerque, N.M.: Red Earth Press.

————. 1992. *The Sacred Hoop: Recovering the Feminine in American Indian Traditions*. Boston: Beacon Press.

Alvord, Lori Arviso and Elizabeth Cohen Van Pelt. 1999. *The Scalpel and the Bear: The First Navajo Woman Surgeon Combines Western Medicine and Traditional Healing*. New York: Bantam.

Ambler, Marjane. 1998. "A Community Responsibility for Welfare Reform." *Tribal College: Journal of American Indian Higher Education* 9 (3): 8–11.

Ambrose, Stephen. 1975. *Crazy Horse and Custer: The Parallel Lives of Two American Warriors*. New York: Doubleday.

————. 1996. *Undaunted Courage: Meriwether Lewis, Thomas Jefferson and the Opening of the American West*. New York: Simon and Schuster.

Amiotte, Arthur. 1987. "The Lakota Sun Dance: Historical and Contemporary Perspectives." In *Sioux Indian Religion: Tradition and Innovation*, edited by Raymond J. DeMallie and Douglas R. Parks. Norman: University of Oklahoma Press, 75–89.

Anderson, Edward F. 1980. *Peyote: The Divine Cactus*. Tucson: University of Arizona Press.

Anderson, William, ed. 1991. *Cherokee Removal: Before and After*. Athens: University of Georgia Press.

Andrist, Ralph K. 1993. *The Long Death: The Last Days of the Plains Indian*. New York: Macmillan. First published in 1964.

Arden, Harvey. 1987. "The Fire That Never Dies." *National Geographic* 172 (3): 370–403.

Armstrong, Virginia. 1971. *I Have Spoken: American History through the Voice of Indians*. Chicago: Swallow Press.

Artaud, Antonin. 1976. *The Peyote Dance*. trans. Helen Weaver. New York: Farrar, Strauss, and Giroux.

Axtell, James. 1985. *The Invasion Within*. New York: Oxford University Press.

————. 1988. *After Columbus: Essays in the Ethnohistory of Colonial North America*. New York: Oxford University Press.

————. 1992. *Beyond 1492: Encounter in Colonial North America*. New York: Oxford University Press.

Bailey, Garrick, and Roberta Glenn Bailey. 1986. *A History of the Navajos: The Reservation Years*. Santa Fe, N.M.: School of American Research Press.

Bailey, Lynn. 1970. *Bosque Redondo: An American Concentration Camp*. Pasadena, Calif.: Socio-Technical Publications.

Bailey, Paul. 1957. *Wovoka, the Indian Messiah*. Los Angeles: Westernlore Press.

Baldridge, William. 1993. *New Visions for the Americas*. Philadelphia: Fortress Press.

————. 1996. "Reclaiming our Histories." In *Native and Christian: Indigenous Voices on Religious Identity in the United States and Canada*, edited by James Treat. New York: Routledge, 83–92.

Barney, Garold D. 1986. *Mormons, Indians, and the Ghost Dance Religion of 1890*. Lanham, Md.: University Press of America.

Beasley, Conger, Jr. 1992. "The Return of the Lakota." *E Magazine* (September/October): 37–42, 65.

————. 1995. *We Are a People in This World: The Lakota Sioux and the Massacre at Wounded Knee*. Fayetteville: University of Arkansas Press.

Beck, Peggy, and Anna Walters. 1977. *The Sacred: Ways of Knowledge, Sources of Life*. Tsaile, Ariz.: Navajo Community College Press.

Begay, Keats, et al. 1977. *Navajos and World War II*. Tsaile, Ariz.: Navajo Community College.

Benedek, Emily. 1992. *The Wind Won't Know Me: A History of the Navajo-Hopi Land Dispute*. New York: Alfred A. Knopf.

Bergman, Robert. 1973. "A School for Medicine Men." *American Journal of Psychiatry* 130: 663–66.

Berkhofer, Robert F., Jr. 1978. *The White Man's Indian: Images of the American Indian from Columbus to the Present*. New York: Knopf.

Berkhofer, Robert K. 1976. *Salvation and the Savage*. New York: Atheneum.

Berry, Thomas. 1988. "The Historical Role of the American Indian." *The Dream of the Earth*. San Francisco: Sierra Club Books, 180–93.

Bierhorst, John. 1994. *The Way of the Earth: Native America and the Environment.* New York: William Morrow and Company.

——. 1995. *Mythology of the Lenape: Guide and Texts.* Tucson: University of Arizona Press.

Bingham, Sam and Janet. 1984. *Between Sacred Mountains: Navajo Stories and Lessons from the Land.* Tucson: University of Arizona Press.

Biolsi, Thomas. 1992. *Organizing the Lakota: The Political Economy of the New Deal on the Pine Ridge and Rosebud Reservations.* Tucson: University of Arizona Press.

Black Elk, (Nicholas), as told to John G. Neihardt (Flaming Rainbow). 1972. *Black Elk Speaks. Being the Life Story of a Holy Man of the Oglala Sioux.* New York: Pocket Books. First published in 1932.

Black Elk, Wallace H., and William S. Lyon. 1990. *Black Elk: The Sacred Ways of a Lakota.* San Francisco: Harper & Row.

Boly, Peter. 1984. "Ethnic Identity and Cultural Resistance: Oglala-Sioux of the Pine Ridge Reservation Today." *North American Indian Studies* 2 (Göttingen: Edition Herodot), 204–24.

Booth, Annie L., and Harvey M. Jacobs. 1990. "Ties That Bind: Native American Beliefs as a Foundation for Environmental Consciousness." *Environmental Ethics* 12 (1990): 27–43.

Botsford, James, and Walter B. Echo Hawk. 1996. "The Legal Tango: The Native American Church versus the United States of America." In *One Nation Under God,* edited by Huston Smith and Reuben Snake. Santa Fe, N.M.: Clear Light Publishers, 125–41.

Bowden, Henry Warner. 1981. *American Indians and Christian Missions: Studies in Cultural Conflict.* Chicago: University of Chicago Press.

Boyer, Paul. 1997. *Native American Colleges: Progress and Prospects.* Princeton, N.J.: Carnegie Foundation for the Advancement of Teaching.

Brave Bird, Mary, with Richard Erdoes. 1994. *Ohitika Woman.* New York: HarperPerennial.

Brinton, Daniel. 1884. *The Lenape and their Legends: with the Complete Text and Symbols of the Walam Olum.* New York: AMS Press.

Brown, Dee. 1981. *Bury My Heart at Wounded Knee: An Indian History of the American West.* New York: Holt, Rinehart, and Winston. First published 1972.

Brown, Joseph Epes. 1982. *The Spiritual Legacy of the American Indian.* New York: Crossroad.

——, ed. 1971. *The Sacred Pipe. Black Elk's Account of the Seven Rites of the Oglala Sioux.* New York: Penguin Edition. First published 1953.

Bruchac, Joseph, III. 1993. "The Circle of Stories." *Buried Roots and Indestructible Seeds,* edited by Mark A. Lindquist and Martin Zanger. Madison: University of Wisconsin Press, 9–20.

——. 1993. *The Native American Sweat Lodge: History and Legends.* Crossing Press.

Brugge, David M. 1983. "Navajo Prehistory and History to 1850." In *Handbook of North American Indians: Southwest,* vol. 10. , edited by Alfonso Ortiz. Washington, D.C.: Smithsonian Institution, 489–501.

——. 1985. *Navajos in the Catholic Church Records of New Mexico, 1694–1875.* Tsaile, Ariz.: Community College Press.

——. 1994. *The Navajo-Hopi Land Dispute: An American Tragedy.* Albuquerque: University of New Mexico Press.

Brugge, David M., and Charlotte J. Frisbie, eds. 1982. *Navajo Religion and Culture: Selected Views.* Papers in Honor of Leland C. Wyman. Santa Fe: Museum of New Mexico Papers in Anthropology, No. 17.

Bucko, Raymond A. 1999. *The Lakota Ritual of the Sweat Lodge: History and Contemporary Practice.* Lincoln: University of Nebraska Press.

Burnett, Robert, and John Koster. 1974. *The Road to Wounded Knee*. New York: Bantam.

Bushman, John. 1998. "Welfare Reform in Indian Country: Crisis or Opportunity?" *Tribal College: Journal of American Indian Higher Education* 9 (3): 22–23.

Callicott, J. Baird. 1983. "Traditional American Indian and Traditional Western European Attitudes towards Nature: An Overview." In *Environmental Philosophy: A Collection of Readings*, edited by Robert Elliot and Arran Gare. University Park: Pennsylvania State University, 231–59.

———. 1989. *In Defense of the Land Ethic: Essays in Environmental Philosophy*. Albany: State University of New York Press.

———. 1994. *Earth Insights: A Multicultural Survey of Ecological Ethics from the Mediterranean Basin to the Australian Outback*. Berkeley: University of California Press.

Campbell, Janet, and Archie Sam. 1975–76. "The Primal Fire Lingers." *The Chronicles of Oklahoma* 53: 463–75.

Campbell, Joseph, with Bill Moyers. 1988. *The Power of Myth*. New York: Doubleday.

Carlson, Leonard. 1981. *Indians, Bureaucrats, and the Land: The Dawes Act and the Decline of Indian Farming*. Westport, Conn.: Greenwood Press.

Carroll, Michael P. 1975. "Revitalization Movements and Social Structure: Some Quantitative Texts." *American Sociological Review* 40: 389–401.

Casey, Carolyn. 1998. "Entrepreneurs Stimulate Tribal Economies." *Tribal College: Journal of American Indian Higher Education* 9 (3): 12–14.

Catches, Pete, Sr., and Peter Catches. 1997. *Oceti Wakan = Sacred Fireplace*. Pine Ridge, S.D.: Oceti Wakan.

Catlin, George. 1996. *North American Indians*. New York: Penguin (reprint of 1903 edition).

Champagne, Duane. 1988. "The Delaware Revitalization Movement of the Early 1760's: A Suggested Reinterpretation." *American Indian Quarterly* 12: 107–26.

———, ed. 1994a. *Chronology of Native North American History: From Pre-Columbian Times to the Present*. Detroit: Gale Research Inc.

———, ed. 1994b. *The Native North American Almanac*. Detroit: Gale Research Inc.

Charleston, Steve. 1996. "The Old Testament of Native America." In *Native and Christian: Indigenous Voices on Religious Identity in the United States and Canada*, edited by James Treat. New York: Routledge, 68–80.

Chuckluck, Cheryl Foley. 1998. "Haskell Builds upon Old Skills." *Tribal College: Journal of American Indian Higher Education* 9 (3): 15.

Churchill, Ward. 1992. "The Earth Is Our Mother: Struggles for American Indian Land and Liberation in the Contemporary United States." In *The State of Native America: Genocide, Colonization, and Resistance*, edited by M. Annette Jaimes. Boston: South End Press, 139–88.

———, ed. 1989. *Critical Issues in Native North America*. Copenhagen: International Work Group on Indigenous Affairs.

Churchill, Ward, and Winona LaDuke. 1992. "Native North America: The Political Economy of Radioactive Colonialism." In *The State of Native America: Genocide, Colonization, and Resistance*, edited by M. Annette Jaimes. Boston: South End Press, 241–66.

Churchill Ward, and Jim Vander Wall. 1988. *Agents of Repression: The FBI's Secret Wars against the Black Panther Party and the American Indian Movement*. Boston: South End Press.

Clemmer, Richard. 1995. "The Hopi-Navajo Land Dispute: 1958–1993." In *Roads in the Sky: The Hopi Indians in a Century of Change*. Boulder, Colo.: Westview Press, 232–72.

Coates, Lawrence G. 1985. "The Mormons and the Ghost Dance." *Dialog: A Journal of Mormon Thought* 18 (4): 89–111.

Coffer, W.E. 1978. *Spirits of the Sacred Mountain: Creation Stories of the American Indian*. New York: Van Nostrand Reinhold.

Cohen, Faye G. 1986. *Treaties on Trial: The Continuing Controversy over Northwest Fishing Rights*. Seattle: University of Washington Press.

Cooper, Guy H. 1984. *Development and Stress in Navajo Religion*. Stockholm: Almqvist and Wiksell.

———. 1990. "Individualism and Integration in Navajo Religion." In *Religion in Native North America*, edited by Christopher Vecsey. Moscow: University of Idaho Press, 67–82.

Cordell, Linda S., and Bruce D. Smith. 1996. "Indigenous Farmers." In *The Cambridge History of the Native Peoples of the Americas*, vol. 1, part 1, edited by Bruce Trigger and Wilcomb Washburn. Cambridge: Cambridge University Press, 201–66.

Cornell, George L. 1985. "The Influence of Native Americans on Modern Conservationists." *Environmental Review* 9 (1985), 105–17.

———. 1993. "Native American Perceptions of the Environment." In *Buried Roots and Indestructible Seeds: The Survival of American Indian Life in Story, History, and Spirit*, edited by Mark Lindquist and Martin Zanger. Madison: University of Wisconsin Press, 21–41.

Cornell, Stephen. 1988. *The Return of the Native: American Indian Political Resurgence*. New York: Oxford University Press.

Correll, J. Lee. 1979. *Through White Men's Eyes: A Contribution to Navajo History*. 6 vols. Window Rock: Navajo Heritage Center.

Cousineau, Phil, and Gary Rhine. 1996. "The Peyote Ceremony." In *One Nation under God*, edited by Huston Smith and Reuben Snake. Santa Fe, N.M.: Clear Light Publishers, 77–101.

Crosby, Alfred W. 1986. *Ecological Imperialism: The Biological Expansion of Europe, 900–1900*. New York: Cambridge University Press.

Crow Dog, Leonard, with Richard Erdoes. 1995. *Crow Dog: Six Generations of Sioux Medicine Men*. New York: HarperCollins.

Crow Dog, Mary, with Richard Erdoes. 1991. *Lakota Woman*. New York: HarperPerennial.

Curtis, Edward S. 1907–30 *The North American Indian*. ed. Frederick W. Hodge. 20 vols. Norwood, Mass.: Plimpton Press. Reprinted: Johnson Reprint, 1970.

Dangberg, Grace M. 1968. "Wovoka." *Nevada Historical Society Quarterly* 11: 1–53.

Danker, Donald F. 1981. "The Wounded Knee Interviews of Eli S. Ricker." *Nebraska History* 62: 151–243.

De Ropp, Robert S. 1987. "Psychedelic Drugs." In *Encyclopedia of Religion*, vol. 12, edited by Mircea Eliade. New York: Macmillan, 46–57.

Dean, Nora Thompson. 1978. "Delaware Indian Reminiscences." *Bulletin of the Archaeological Society of New Jersey* 35: 1–17.

Dean, Nora Thompson, and Jay Miller. 1977. "A Personal Account of the Unami Delaware Big House Rite." *Pennsylvania Archaeologist* (1977): 39–43.

Debo, Angie. 1984. *And Still the Waters Run: The Betrayal of the Five Civilized Tribes*. Norman: University of Oklahoma Press. First published in 1940.

———. 1989. *A History of Indians of the United States*. Norman: University of Oklahoma Press.

Deloria, Ella C. 1929. "The Sun Dance of the Oglala Sioux." *Journal of American Folklore* 42: 354–413.

———. 1931. *Dakota Texts*. Publications of the American Ethnological Society, vol. 14. New York: Ge. E. Stechert and Co.

———. 1944. *Speaking of Indians*. New York: Friendship Press.

———. 1988. *Waterlily*. Lincoln: University of Nebraska Press.

Deloria, Vine, Jr. 1969. *Custer Died for Your Sins: An Indian Manifesto*. New York: Avon Books.
———. 1970. *We Talk, You Listen: New Tribes, New Turf.* New York: Macmillan Company.
———. 1978. "A Native American Perspective on Liberation Theologies." In *Is Liberation Theology for North America? The Response of First World Churches*, edited by Sergio Torres et al. New York: Theology in the Americas, 12–20.
———. 1985. *Behind the Trail of Broken Treaties*. Austin: University of Texas Press. First published in 1974.
———. 1992. "Trouble in High Places: Erosion of American Indian Rights to Religious Freedom in the United States." In *The State of Native America: Genocide, Colonization, and Resistance*, edited by M. Annette Jaimes. Boston: South End Press, 267–90.
———. 1994. *God is Red: A Native View of Religion*. Golden, Colo.: Fulcrum Publishing. Updating the 1973 edition.
———. 1997. *Red Earth, White Lies: Native Americans and the Myth of Scientific Fact*. Golden, Colo.: Fulcrum Publishing.
———, ed. 1985. *American Indian Policy in the Twentieth Century*. Norman: University of Oklahoma Press.
Deloria, Vine, Jr., and Clifford M. Lytle. 1984. *The Nations Within: The Past and Future of American Indian Sovereignty*. New York: Pantheon Books.
Deloria, Vine, Sr. 1987. "The Establishment of Christianity among the Sioux." In *Sioux Indian Religion: Tradition and Innovation*, edited by Raymond J. DeMallie and Douglas R. Parks. Norman: University of Oklahoma Press, 91–111.
DeMallie, Raymond J. 1982. "The Lakota Ghost Dance: An Ethnohistorical Account." *Pacific Historical Review* 51: 385–406.
———. 1987. "Lakota Belief and Ritual in the Nineteenth Century." In *Sioux Indian Religion: Tradition and Innovation*, edited by Raymond J. DeMallie and Douglas R. Parks. Norman: University of Oklahoma Press, 25–43.
———, ed. 1984. *The Sixth Grandfather: Black Elk's Teachings Given to John G. Neihardt*. Lincoln: University of Nebraska Press.
DeMallie, Raymond J., and Douglas R. Parks, eds. 1987. *Sioux Indian Religion: Tradition and Innovation*. Norman: University of Oklahoma Press.
Densmore, Frances. 1931. *The Peyote Cult and Treatment of the Sick among the Winnebago Indians*. Bureau of American Ethnology Bulletin No. 3205. Washington, D.C.: Smithsonian Institution.
———. 1918. *Teton Sioux Music*. Bureau of American Ethnology. Bulletin No. 61. Washington, D.C.: Smithsonian Institution.
Devall, Bill, and George Sessions. 1985. *Deep Ecology: Living As If Nature Mattered*. Salt Lake City: Peregrine Smith Books.
Dickens, Roy S., Jr. 1979. "The Origins and Development of Cherokee Culture." In *The Cherokee Indian Nation*, edited by Duane H. King. Knoxville: University of Tennessee Press, 3–32.
Dobyns, Henry F. 1983. *Their Numbers Became Thinned*. Knoxville: University of Tennessee Press.
Dobyns, Henry F., and Robert C. Euler. 1967. *The Ghost Dance of 1889 among the Pai Indians of Northwestern Arizona*. Flagstaff: Prescott College Press.
Dolaghan, Thomas, and David Scates. 1978. *The Navajos Are Coming to Jesus*. South Pasadena, Calif.: William Carey Library.

Dooling, D.M., ed. 1990. *The Sons of the Wind: The Sacred Stories of the Lakota*. San Francisco: HarperCollins. First published in 1984.

Dorris, Michael. 1989. *The Broken Cord*. New York: Harper & Row.

Dowd, Gregory. 1992. *A Spirited Resistance*. Baltimore: Johns Hopkins University Press.

Drinnon, Richard. 1987. *Keeper of Concentration Camps: Dillon S. Myer and American Racism*. Berkeley: University of California Press.

DuBois, Cora. 1939. "The 1870 Ghost Dance." *Anthropological Records*, University of California, 3 (1).

Dyk, Walter, recorder. 1967. *Son of Old Man Hat: A Navaho Autobiography*. Lincoln: University of Nebraska Press. First published 1938.

Eastman, Charles Alexander. 1911. *The Soul of the Indian: An Interpretation*. Lincoln: University of Nebraska Press. Reprinted in 1980.

———. 1916. *From the Deep Woods to Civilization: Chapters in the Autobiography of an Indian*. Lincoln: University of Nebraska. Reprinted in 1977.

Echo-Hawk, W. 1991. "Loopholes in Religious Liberty: The Need for a Federal Law to Protect Freedom of Worship for Native People." In *NARF Legal Review*. Boulder: Native American Rights Fund.

Ehle, John. 1988. *Trail of Tears: The Rise and Fall of the Cherokee Nation*. New York: Anchor Books.

Erdoes, Richard. 1972. *The Sun Dance People*. New York: Random House.

Erdoes, Richard, and Alfonso Ortiz, ed. 1984. *American Indian Myths and Legends*. New York: Pantheon Books.

Ewen, Alexander. 1998. "Generation X in Indian Country: A Native Americas Youth Survey." *Native Americas: Akwe:kon's Journal of Indigenous Issues* 14 (4): 24–29.

Farella, John R. 1984. *The Main Stalk: A Synthesis of Navajo Philosophy*. Tucson: University of Arizona Press.

Faris, James C. 1990. *The Nightway: A History and a History of Documentation of a Navajo Ceremonial*. Albuquerque: University of New Mexico Press.

Feher-Elston, Catherine. 1988. *Children of Sacred Ground: America's Last Indian War*. Flagstaff, Ariz.: Northland Publishing.

Fenton, William N., and John Gulick, eds. 1961. *Symposium on Cherokee and Iroquois Culture*. Bureau of American Ethnology. Bulletin No. 180. Washington, D.C.: Government Printing Office.

Feraca, Stephen E. 1963. *Wakinyan: Contemporary Teton Dakota Religion*. Browning, Mont.: Museum of the Plains Indians.

Fikes, Jay C. 1985. *Huichol Indian Identity and Adaptation*. Doctoral Dissertation. Ann Arbor, Mich.: University Microfilms International.

———. 1993. *Carlos Castaneda, Academic Opportunism and the Psychedelic Sixties*. Victoria, B.C.: Millenia Press.

———. 1996. "A Brief History of the Native American Church." In *One Nation under God*, edited by Huston Smith and Reuben Snake. Santa Fe, N.M.: Clear Light Publishers, 167–73.

Finger, John R. 1984. *The Eastern Band of Cherokees, 1819–1900*. Knoxville: University of Tennessee Press.

Fishler, Stanley A. 1953. *In the Beginning: A Navaho Creation Myth*. University of Utah Anthropological Papers. No. 13. Salt Lake City: University of Utah.

Fixico, Donald L. 1986. *Termination and Relocation: Federal Indian Policy, 1945–1960*. Albuquerque: University of New Mexico Press.

Fleck, Richard F. 1985. *Henry Thoreau and John Muir among the Indians*. Hamden, Conn.: Archon Books.

Fletcher, Alice. 1891. "The Indian Messiah." *Journal of American Folkore* 4 (12): 55–57.

Fogelson, Raymond. 1961. "Change, Persistence, and accommodation in Cherokee Medico-Magical Beliefs." In *Symposium on Cherokee and Iroquois Culture*, edited by William N. Fenton and John Gulick. Bureau of American Ethnology. Bulletin No. 180. Washington, D.C.: Government Printing Office, 219–20.

———. 1978. *The Cherokees: A Critical Bibliography*. Bloomington: University of Indiana Press.

Fogelson, Raymond, and Paul Kutsche. 1961. "Cherokee Economic Cooperatives: The Gadugi." In *Symposium on Cherokee and Iroquois Culture*, edited by William N. Fenton and John Gulick. Bureau of American Ethnology. Bulletin No. 180. Washington, D.C.: Government Printing Office, 83–124.

Fox, Matthew. 1983. *Original Blessing: A Primer in Creation Spirituality*. Santa Fe, N.M.: Bear & Co.

———. 1988. *The Coming of the Cosmic Christ: The Healing of Mother Earth and the Birth of a Global Renaissance*. San Francisco: Harper & Row.

Frisbie, Charlotte J. 1967. *Kinaalda': A Study of the Navaho Girl's Puberty Ceremony*. Middletown, Conn.: Wesleyan University Press.

———. 1987. *Navajo Medicine Bundles or Jish: Acquisition, Transmission, and Disposition in the Past and Present*. Albuquerque: University of New Mexico Press.

Furst, Peter T., ed. 1972. *Flesh of the Gods: The Ritual Use of Hallucinogens*. New York: Praeger.

———. 1976. *Hallucinogens and Culture*. San Francisco: Chandler and Sharp.

Gaffney, Edward. 1994. "How Free Is Religion in America?" *U.S. Catholic* 59 (4): 6, 8.

Gagnon, Greg, and Karen White Eyes. 1992. *Pine Ridge Reservation: Yesterday and Today*. Interior, S.D.: Badlands Natural History Association.

Garrod, Andrew, and Colleen Larimore, eds. 1998. *First Person, First Peoples: Native American College Graduates Tell Their Life Stories*. Ithaca, N.Y.: Cornell University Press.

Geertz, Armin. 1994. *The Invention of Prophecy: Continuity and Meaning in Hopi Indian Religion*. Berkeley: University of California Press.

Gill, Sam D. 1979a. "Whirling Logs and Coloured Sands." In *Native Religious Traditions*, edited by Earle H. Waugh and K. Dad Prithipaul, eds. Waterloo, Ontario: Wilfrid Laurier University Press, 151–64.

———. 1979b. *Songs of Life: An Introduction to Navajo Religious Culture*. Leiden, Netherlands: E.J. Brill.

———. 1981. *Sacred Words: A Study of Navajo Religion and Prayer*. Contributions in Intercultural and Comparative Studies. No. 4. Westport, Conn.: Greenwood Press.

———. 1982. *Native American Religions: An Introduction*. The Religious Life of Man Series. Belmont, Calif.: Wadsworth.

———. 1983a. "Navajo Views of Their Origin." In *Handbook of North American Indians: Southwest*, vol. 10, edited by Alfonso Ortiz. Washington, D.C.: Smithsonian Institution, 502–5.

———. 1983b. *Native American Traditions: Sources and Interpretations*. Belmont, Calif.: Wadsworth.

———. 1987. *Mother Earth: An American Story*. Chicago: University of Chicago Press.

Goddard, Ives. 1978. "Delaware." In *Handbook of North American Indians: Northeast*, vol. 15, edited by Bruce Trigger. Washington, D.C.: Smithsonian Institution., 213–39.

Gore, Rick. 1997. "The Most Ancient Americans." *National Geographic* 192 (4): 92–99.

Green, Michael D. 1982. *The Politics of Indian Removal*. Lincoln: University of Nebraska Press.

Greene, Jerome A. 1970. "The Sioux Land Commission of 1889: Prelude to Wounded Knee." *South Dakota History* 1 (1): 41–72.

———, ed. 1994. *Lakota and Cheyenne: Indian View of the Great Sioux War, 1876–77*. Norman: University of Oklahoma Press.

Griffin-Pierce, Trudy. 1992. *Earth Is My Mother, Sky Is My Father: Space, Time, and Astronomy in Navajo Sandpainting*. Albuquerque: University of New Mexico Press.

Grinde, Donald A., Jr. 1982. *The Iroqouis and the Founding of the American Nation*. San Francisco.

———. 1992. "Iroquois Political Theory and the Roots of American Democracy." In *Exiled in the Land of the Free: Democracy, Indian Nations, and the U.S. Constitution*, by Oren Lyons et al. Santa Fe, N.M.: Clear Light Publishers, 227–80.

Grinde, Donald A., Jr., and Bruce Johansen. 1991. *Exemplar of Liberty: Native America and the Evolution of Democracy*. Los Angeles: American Indian Studies Center of UCLA.

———. 1995. *Ecocide of North America: Environmental Destruction of Indian Lands and People*. Santa Fe, N.M.: Clear Light Publishers.

Grumet, Robert S. 1989. *The Lenapes*, edited by Frank W. Porter III. New York: Chelsea House Publishers.

Guerrero, Marianna. 1992. "American Indian Water Rights: The Blood of Life in Native America." In *The State of Native America: Genocide, Colonization, and Resistance*, edited by M. Annette Jaimes. Boston: South End Press, 189–216.

Hagan, William T. 1980. "Justifying Dispossession of the Indian: The Land Utilization Argument." In *American Indian Environments : Ecological Issues in Native American History*, edited by Christopher Vecsey and Robert W. Venables. Syracuse: Syracuse University Press, 65–80.

Haile, Berard. 1938a. *Origin Legend of the Navaho Enemy Way*. Yale University Publications in Anthropology. No. 18. New Haven: Yale University Press.

———. 1938b. "Navaho Chantways and Ceremonials." *American Anthropologist* 40: 639–52.

———. 1943. *Origin Legend of the Navaho Flintway*. Chicago: University of Chicago Press.

———. 1947. *Prayer Stick Cutting in a Five Night Ceremonial of the Male Branch of Shooting Way*. Chicago: University of Chicago Press.

———. 1950. *Origin of the Gateway Ritual in the Male Branch of Shooting Way*. St. Michaels, Ariz.: St. Michael's Press.

———. 1981a. "Women versus Men: A Conflict of Navajo Emergence." *American Tribal Religions*. Vol. 6. Lincoln: University of Nebraska Press.

———. 1981b. "The Upward Moving and Emergence Way." *American Tribal Religions*. Vol. 7. Lincoln: University of Nebraska Press.

———. 1984. "Navajo Coyote Tales." *American Tribal Religions*. Vol. 8. Lincoln: University of Nebraska Press.

Hall, Suzanne, ed. 1992. *The People: Reflections of Native Peoples on the Catholic Experience in North America*. Washington, D.C.: National Catholic Educational Association.

Hargrove, Eugene, ed. 1986. *Religion and Environmental Crisis*. Athens: University of Georgia Press.

Harrington, Mark R. 1913. "A Preliminary Sketch of Lenape Culture." *American Anthropologist* 15: 208–35.

Harrington, Mark R. 1921. "Religion and Ceremonies of the Lenape." In *Indian Notes and Monographs*. *Indian Notes and Monographs*. Series 2, No. 19. New York: Museum of the American Indian, Heye Foundation.

Harris, David D. 1998. "Survival in Our Own Way: Tribal Colleges and Indian Communities." *Native Americas: Akwe:kon's Journal of Indigenous Issues* 14 (4): 30–33.

Harrod, Howard L. 1987. *Renewing the World: Plains Indian Religion and Morality.* Tucson: University of Arizona Press.

———. 1995. *Becoming and Remaining a People: Native American Religions on the Northern Great Plains.* Tuscson: University of Arizona Press.

Harvey, Karen D., and Lisa D. Harjo. 1994. *Indian Country: A History of Native People in America.* Golden, Colo.: North American Press.

Hassrick, Royal B. 1964. *The Sioux: Life and Customs of a Warrior Society.* Norman: University of Oklahoma Press.

Hauptman, Laurence M. 1986. *Iroquois Struggle for Survival: World War II to Red Power.* Syracuse: Syracuse University Press.

———. 1995. *Tribes and Tribulations: Misconceptions about American Indians and Their Histories.* Albuquerque: University of New Mexico Press.

Heckewelder, John. 1876. *History, Manners and Customs of the Indian Nations Who Once Inhabited Pennsylvania and the Neighboring States*, edited by William C. Reichel. Philadelphia: Historical Society of Pennsylvania.

Heizer, Robert F., ed. 1974. *The Destruction of the California Indians.* Santa Barbara, Calif.: Peregrine Smith.

Hendrix, Janey E. 1983. "Redbird Smith and the Nighthawk Keetoowahs." *Journal of Cherokee Studies* 8: 22–39, 73–86.

Hertzberg, Hazel W. 1971. *The Search for an American Indian Identity: Modern Pan-Indian Movements.* Syracuse: Syracuse University Press.

Hill, W. W. 1944. "The Navaho Indians and the Ghost Dance of 1890." *American Anthropologist* 40: 523–27.

Hillerman, Tony. 1978. *Listening Woman.* New York: HarperCollins.

———. 1989. *Talking God.* New York: HarperCollins.

Hittman, Michael. 1973. "The 1870 Ghost Dance at the Walker River Reservation: A Reconstruction." *Ethnohistory* 20 (3): 247–78.

Holler, Clyde. 1984a. "Black Elk's Relationship to Christianity." *American Indian Quarterly* 8 (1): 37–49.

———. 1984b. "Lakota Religion and Tragedy: The Theology of Black Elk Speaks." *Journal of the American Academy of Religion* 52 (1): 19–45.

———. 1995. *Black Elk's Religion: The Sun Dance and Lakota Catholicism.* Syracuse: Syracuse University Press.

Hoxie, Frederick E. 1984. *A Final Promise: The Campaign to Assimilate the Indians, 1880–1920.* Lincoln: University of Nebraska Press.

———. 1993. "Why Treaties?" *Buried Roots and Indestructible Seeds*, edited by Mark A. Lindquist and Martin Zanger. Madison: University of Wisconsin Press, 85–105.

———. 1996. "The Reservation Period, 1880–1960." In *The Cambridge History of the Native Peoples of the Americas*, vol. 1, part 1, edited by Bruce Trigger and Wilcomb Washburn. Cambridge: Cambridge University Press, 183–258.

———, ed. 1988. *Indians in American History: An Introduction.* Arlington Heights, Ill.: Harlan Davidson.

Hudson, Charles. 1976. *The Southeastern Indians.* Knoxville: University of Tennessee Press.

———. 1984. *Elements of Southeastern Indian Religion*. Leiden, Netherlands: E.J. Brill.

Hughes, J. Donald. 1983. *American Indian Ecology*. El Paso, Tex.: Texas Western University.

Hultkrantz, Åke. 1981. "The Changing Meaning of the Ghost Dance as Evidenced by the Wind River Shoshoni." In *Belief and Worship in Native North America*, edited by Christopher Vecsey. Syracuse: Syracuse University Press, 264–81.

———. 1983. "The Religion of the Goddess in North America." In *The Book of the Goddess, Past and Present*, edited by C. Olsen. New York: Crossroad, 202–16.

———. 1987. "Ghost Dance." In *The Encyclopedia of Religion*, vol. 5, edited by Mircea Eliade. New York: Macmillan, 544–47.

Hurtevant, William C. 1979. "Southeastern Indian Formulas." In *Native North American Spirituality of the Eastern Woodlands*, edited by Elisabeth Tooker. Mahwah, N.J.: Paulist Press, 282–93.

Hyde, George E. 1975. *Red Cloud's Folk: A History of the Oglala Sioux Indians*. Norman: University of Oklahoma Press. First published in 1937.

Indiana Historical Society. 1954. *Walam Olum or Red Score: The Migration Legend of the Lenni Lenape or Delaware Indians—A New Translation, Interpreted by Linguistic, Historical, Archeological, Ethnological, and Physical Anthropological Studies*. Chicago: Lakeside Press.

Institute for Natural Progress, The. 1992. "In Usual and Accustomed Places: Contemporary American Indian Fishing Rights Struggles." In *The State of Native America: Genocide, Colonization, and Resistance*, edited by M. Annette Jaimes. Boston: South End Press, 217–39.

Interpress Columnists Service, ed. 1993. *Story Earth: Native Voices on the Environment*. San Francisco: Mercury House.

Iverson, Pete R. 1981 *The Navajo Nation*. Westport, Conn.: Greenwood Press.

———. 1990. *The Navajos*. New York: Chelsea House.

Jackson, Donald. 1972. *Custer's Gold: The United States Cavalry Expedition of 1874*. Lincoln: University of Nebraska Press.

Jackson, Helen. 1886. *A Century of Dishonor: A Sketch of the United States Government's Dealing with Some of the Indian Tribes*. Boston: Roberts Brothers.

Jacobs, Wilbur R. 1980. "Indians as Ecologists and other Environmental Themes in American Frontier History." In *American Indian Environments: Ecological Issues in Native American History*, edited by Christopher Vecsey and Robert W. Venables. Syracuse: Syracuse University Press, 46–64.

Jahner, Elaine A. 1987. "Lakota Genesis: The Oral Tradition." In *Sioux Indian Religion: Tradition and Innovation*, edited by Raymond J. DeMallie and Douglas R. Parks. Norman: University of Oklahoma Press, 45–65.

Jaimes, M. Annette, ed. 1992. *The State of Native America: Genocide, Colonization, and Resistance*. Boston: South End Press.

Jennings, Francis. 1975. *The Invasion of America: Indians, Colonialism, and the Cant of Conquest*. Chapel Hill: University of North Carolina Press.

Jennings, J.D. 1994. *Prehistory of North America*. 2d ed. New York: McGraw Hill.

Jensen Richard E., R. Eli Paul, and John E. Carter. 1991. *Eyewitness at Wounded Knee*. Lincoln: University of Nebraska Press.

Johansen, Bruce E. 1982. *Forgotten Founders: Benjamin Franklin, the Iroquois and the Rationale for the American Revolution*. Ipswich, Mass.: Gambi Publishers.

Jorgensen, Joseph G. 1969. "Ghost Dance, Bear Dance, and Sun Dance." *Handbook of North American Indians*, vol. 11, ed. Warren L. D'Azevedo. (Washington, D.C.: Smithsonian Institution), 660–72.

———. 1972. *The Sun Dance: Power for the Powerless*. Chicago: University of Chicago Press.

Josephy, Alvin M., Jr. 1961. *The American Heritage Book of Indians*. New York: American Heritage.

———. 1971. *Red Power: The American Indians' Fight for Freedom*. New York: American Heritage Press.

———. 1985. *The Indian Heritage of America*. Rev. ed. New York: Alfred A. Knopf, 1985. First published 1968.

———. 1993. *America in 1492: The World of the Indian Peoples before the Arrival of Columbus*. 2d ed. New York: Vintage.

———. 1994. *500 Nations: An Illustrated History of North American Indians*. New York: Alfred A. Knopf.

———. 1990. *Wounded Knee: Lest We Forget*. Cody, Wyo.: Buffalo Bill Historical Center.

Jumping Bull, Calvin. 1996. Presentation at seminar on Lakota history, culture, and spirituality. Oglala Lakota College. Kyle, South Dakota, May 16–17.

Kaiser, P.L. 1984. "The Lakota Sacred Pipe: Its Tribal Use and Religious Philosophy." *American Indian Culture and Research Journal* 8: 1–26.

Kaiser, Rudolph. 1987. "Chief Seattle's Speech(es): American Origins and European Reception." In *Recovering the Word: Essays on Native American Literature*, edited by Brian Swamm and Arnold Krupat. Berkeley: University of California Press, 497–536.

Kammer, Jerry. 1980. *The Second Long Walk: The Navajo-Hopi Land Dispute*. Albuquerque: University of New Mexico Press.

Kehoe, Alice Beck. 1981. *North American Indians: A Comprehensive Account*. Englewood Cliffs, N.J.: Prentice-Hall.

———. 1989. *The Ghost Dance: Ethnohistory and Revitalization. Case Studies in Cultural Anthropology*. New York: Holt, Rinehart, and Winston.

Kelly, Lawrence C. 1983. *The Assault on Assimilation: John Collier and the Origins of Indian Policy Reform*. Albuquerque: University of New Mexico Press.

Kilpatrick, Jack F., and Anna G. Kilpatrick. 1964. *Friends of Thunder: Folktales of the Oklahoma Cherokees*. Dallas: Southern Methodist University Press.

King, Duane H., ed. 1979. *The Cherokee Indian Nation: A Troubled History*. Knoxville: University of Tennessee Press.

Klah, Hasteen. 1942. *Navajo Creation Myth, the Story of Emergence*. Recorded by Mary Wheelwright. Santa Fe, N.M.: Museum of Navajo Ceremonial Art.

Kluckhohn, Clyde. 1938. "Participation in Ceremonials in a Navaho Community." *American Anthropologist* 40: 359–69.

———. 1962. *Navaho Witchcraft*. Boston: Beacon Press. First published 1944.

Kluckhohn, Clyde, and Dorothea Leighton. 1974. *The Navaho*. Rev. ed. Cambridge: Harvard University Press. First published 1940.

Kluckhohn, Clyde, Willard W. Hill, and Lucy Wales Kluckhohn. 1971. *Navaho Material Culture*. Cambridge: Harvard University Press.

Kopper, P., ed. 1986. *The Smithsonian Book of North American Indians: Before the Coming of the Europeans*. Washington, D.C.: Smithsonian Books.

Krech, Shepard, III. 1981. *Indians, Animals, and the Fur Trade: A Critique of "Keepers of the Game."* Athens: University of Georgia Press.

———. 1999. *The Ecological Indian: Myth and History*. New York: W.W. Norton & Company.

La Barre, Weston. 1970. *The Ghost Dance: Origins of Religion*. Garden City, N.Y.: Doubleday & Co.

———. 1989. *The Peyote Cult*. 5th ed. New York: Schocken Books. First published in 1938.

La Barre, Weston, et al. 1951. "Statement on Peyote." *Science* 114: 582–83.

Lame Deer, Archie (Fire), and Richard Erdoes. 1992. *Gift of Power: The Life and Teachings of a Lakota Medicine Man*. Sante Fe, N.M.: Bear & Co.

Lame Deer, John (Fire), and Richard Erdoes. 1972. *Lame Deer, Seeker of Visions*. New York: Simon and Schuster.

Lanternari, Vittorio. 1963. *The Religions of the Oppressed: A Study of Modern Messianic Cults*. New York: Alfred A. Knopf.

LaPointe, James. 1976. *Legends of the Lakota*. San Francisco: Indian Historian Press.

Larson, Robert W. 1997. *Red Cloud: Warrior-Statesman of the Lakota Sioux*. Norman: University of Oklahoma Press.

Lazar, Jerry. 1995. *Red Cloud: Sioux War Chief*. New York: Chelsea House Publishers.

Lazarus, Edward. 1991. *Black Hills, White Justice: The Sioux Nation versus the United States, 1775 to the Present*. San Francisco: HarperCollins.

Leacock, Eleanor, and N.O. Lurie, eds. 1971. *The North American Indian in Historical Perspective*. New York: Random House.

Leopold, Aldo. 1949. *A Sand County Almanac and Sketches Here and There*. New York: Oxford University Press. Reprinted in 1981.

Lesser, Alexander. 1933. *The Pawnee Ghost Dance Hand Game: A Study of Cultural Change*. New York: Columbia University Press.

Lewis, Thomas H. 1987. "The Contemporary Yuwipi." In *Sioux Indian Religion: Tradition and Innovation*, edited by Raymond J. DeMallie and Douglas R. Parks. Norman: University of Oklahoma Press, 173–87.

———. 1990. *The Medicine Men: Oglala Sioux Ceremony and Healing*. Lincoln: University of Nebraska Press.

Limerick, Patricia Nelson. 1987. *The Legacy of Conquest: The Unbroken Past of the American West*. New York: Norton.

Lincoln, Kenneth. 1983. *Native American Renaissance*. Berkeley: University of California Press.

Lindquist, Mark A. and Martin Zanger, ed. 1993. *Buried Roots and Indestructible Seeds*. Madison: University of Wisconsin Press.

Littlefield, Daniel F., Jr. 1971. "Utopian Dreams of the Cherokee Fullbloods, 1890–1934." *Journal of the West* 10: 404–27.

Locke, Raymond Friday. 1992. *The Book of the Navajo*. 5th ed. Los Angeles: Mankind Publishing Company.

Loftin, John D. 1991. *Religion and Hopi Life in the Twentieth Century*. Bloomington: Indiana University Press.

Logan, Brad. 1980. "The Ghost Dance Among the Paiute: An Ethnohistorical View of the Documentary Evidence 1889–1893." *Ethnohistory: The Bulletin of the Ohio Valley Historic Indian Conference* 27 (3): 267–88.

Lone Hill, Karen. 1996. Presentation at seminar on Lakota History, Culture, and Spirituality. Oglala Lakota College, Kyle, South Dakota, May 16–17.

Looking Horse, Arval. 1987. "The Sacred Pipe in Modern Life." In *Sioux Indian Religion: Tradition and Innovation*, edited by Raymond J. DeMallie and Douglas R. Parks. Norman: University of Oklahoma Press, 67–73.

Lopez, Barry. 1976. *Desert Notes: Reflections in the Eye of a Raven*. Kansas City: Sheed, Andrews, and McMeel.

———. 1978. *Of Wolves and Men*. New York: Charles Scribner's Sons.

———. 1979. *River Notes: The Dance of Herons*. Kansas City: Sheed, Andrews, and McMeel.

———. 1986. *Arctic Dreams: Imagination and Desire in a Northeastern Landscape*. New York: Scribner.

Luckert, Karl W. 1975. *The Navajo Hunter Tradition*. Tucson: University of Arizona Press.

————. 1977. *Navajo Mountain and Rainbow Bridge Religion*. American Tribal Religions. Vol. 1. Flagstaff: Museum of Northern Arizona Press.

————. 1978. *A Navajo Bringing-Home Ceremony: The Claus Chee Sonny Version of Deerway Ajilee*. American Tribal Religions. Vol. 3. Flagstaff: Museum of Northern Arizona Press.

————. 1979a. *Coyoteway: A Navajo Holyway Healing Ceremonial*. Flagstaff: Museum of Northern Arizona Press.

————. 1979b. "An Approach to Navaho Mythology." In *Native Religious Traditions*, edited by Earle H. Waugh and K. Dad Prithipaul. Waterloo, Ontario: Wilfrid Laurier Univrsity Press, 117–32.

Lyman, Stanley David. 1991. *Wounded Knee 1973: A Personal Account*, edited by Floyd A. O'Neil, June K. Lyman, and Susan McKay. Lincoln: University of Nebraska Press.

Lyons, Oren. 1980. "An Iroquois Perspective." In *American Indian Environments: Ecological Issues in Native American History*, edited by Christopher Vecsey and Robert W. Venables. Syracuse: Syracuse University Press, 171–74.

Lyons, Oren, et al. 1992. *Exiled in the Land of the Free: Democracy, Indian Nations, and the U.S. Constitution*. Santa Fe, N.M.: Clear Light Publishers.

MacDonald, Peter, with Ted Schwarts. 1993. *The Last Warrior: Peter MacDonald and the Navajo Nation*. New York: Orion Books.

Macgregor, Gordon. 1946. *Warriors without Weapons: A Study of the Society and Personality Development of the Pine Ridge Sioux*. Chicago: University of Chicago Press.

Mails, Thomas. 1972. *The Mystic Warriors of the Plains*. Garden City, N.Y.: Doubleday.

————. 1978. *Sundancing at Rosebud and Pine Ridge*. Sioux Falls, S.D.: Augustana College Center for Western Studies.

————. 1979. *Fools Crow*. New York: Doubleday.

————. 1991a. *Plains Indians: Dog Soldiers, Bear Men, and Buffalo Women*. New York: Promontory Press.

————. 1991b. *Fools Crow: Wisdom and Power*. Tulsa: Council Oaks Books.

Mander, Jerry. 1991. *In the Absence of the Sacred: The Failure of Technology and the Survival of the Indian Nations*. San Francisco: Sierra Club Books.

Mankiller, Wilma, with Michael Wallis. 1993. *Mankiller: A Chief and Her People*. New York: St. Martin's Press.

Markowitz, Harvey. 1987. "The Catholic Mission and the Sioux: A Crisis in the Early Paradigm." In *Sioux Indian Religion: Tradition and Innovation*, edited by Raymond J. DeMallie and Douglas R. Parks. Norman: University of Oklahoma Press, 113–47.

Martin, Calvin. 1978. *Keepers of the Game: Indian-Animal Relationships and the Fur Trade*. Berkeley: University of California Press.

————, ed. 1987. *The American Indians and the Problem of History*. Oxford: Oxford University Press.

————. 1999. *The Way of Being Human*. New Haven: Yale University Press.

Matthews, Washington. 1887. *The Mountain Chant: A Navajo Ceremony*. Washington, D.C.: Bureau of American Ethnology.

————. 1897. *Navaho Legends*. Boston: American Folklore Society.

————. 1902. *The Night Chant: A Navajo Ceremony*. Memoirs, Vol. 6. New York: American Museum of Natural History.

————. 1907. "Navaho Myths, Prayers and Songs." Edited by Pliny E. Goddard. University of California Publications in American Archaeology and Ethnology. Vol. 5, pp. 21–63.

Matthiessen, Peter. 1992. *In the Spirit of Crazy Horse*. New York: Penguin. First published in 1983.

McCracken, Horace L. 1956. "The Delaware Big House." *Chronicles of Oklahoma* 34: 183–92.

McCutchen, David, trans. 1993. *The Red Record (The Wallam Olum): The Oldest Native North American History.* Garden City Park, N.Y.: Avery Publishing Group.

McGregor, James H. 1940. *The Wounded Knee Massacre from the Viewpoint of the Sioux.* Baltimore: Wirth Brothers.

McLoughlin, William G. 1984a.. *The Cherokee Ghost Dance: Essays on the Southeastern Indians, 1789–1861.* Macon, Ga.: Mercer University Press.

————. 1984b. *Cherokees and Missionaries, 1789–1829.* New Haven: Yale University Press.

————. 1986. *Cherokee Renascence in the New Republic.* Princeton: Princeton University Press.

————. 1990. *Champions of the Cherokees: Evan and John B. Jones.* Princeton: Princeton University Press.

McLoughlin, William G., and Walter H. Conser Jr., eds. 1994. *The Cherokees and Christianity: Essays on Acculturation and Cultural Persistence.* Athens: University of Georgia Press.

McLuhan, T.C. 1987. *Touch the Earth.* New York: Promontory. First published in 1971.

McNeley, James Kale. 1981. *Holy Wind in Navajo Philosophy.* Tucson: University of Arizona Press.

McNickle, D'Arcy. 1973. *Native Tribalism: Indian Survivals and Renewals.* New York: Oxford University Press.

Means, Russell, with Marvin J. Wolf. 1995. *Where White Men Fear to Tread: The Autobiography of Russell Means.* New York: St. Martin's Press.

Medicine, Beatrice. 1987. "Indian Women and the Renaissance of Traditional Religion." In *Sioux Indian Religion: Tradition and Innovation*, edited by Raymond J. DeMallie and Douglas R. Parks. Norman: University of Oklahoma Press, 159–71.

Messerschmidt, Jim. 1984. *The Trial of Leonard Peltier.* Raritan, N.J.: South End Press.

Mesteth, Wilmer (Stampede). 1996. Presentation at seminar on Lakota history, culture, and spirituality. Oglala Lakota College, Kyle, South Dakota, May 16–17.

Mesteth, Wilmer, Darrell Standing Elk, and Phyllis Swift Hawk. 1995. "Declaration of War against Exploiters of Lakota Spirituality." Updated 4 March.

Meyer, William. 1971. *Native Americans: The New Resistance.* New York: International Publishers.

Michaelsen, R.S. 1983. "'We Also Have a Religion': The Free Exercise of Religion among Native Americans." *American Indian Quarterly* 7: 111–42.

Mihesuah, Devon A. 1996. *American Indians: Stereotypes and Realities.* Atlanta: Clarity Press.

————, ed. 1998. *Natives and Academics: Researching and Writing about American Indians.* Lincoln: University of Nebraska Press.

Miller, Christopher. 1985. *Prophetic Worlds: Indians and Whites of the Columbia Plateau.* New Brunswick, N.J.: Rutgers University Press.

Miller, David H. 1986. *Ghost Dance.* Lincoln: University of Nebraska Press. First published in 1959.

Miller, Lee, ed. 1995. *From the Heart: Voices of the American Indian.* New York: Alfred A. Knopf.

Mitchell, Frank. 1980. *Navajo Blessingway Singer: The Autobiography of Frank Mitchell.* Edited by Charlotte J. Frisbie and David McAllister. Tucson: University of Arizona Press.

Mohawk, John. 1992. "Indians and Democracy: No One Ever Told Us." In *Exiled in the Land of the Free: Democracy, Indian Nations, and the U.S. Constitution*, by Oren Lyons et al. Santa Fe, N.M.: Clear Light Publishers, 43–71.

Momaday, N. Scott. 1968. *House Made of Dawn.* New York: Harper & Row.

————. 1976a. "Native American Attitudes to the Environment." In *Seeing with a Native Eye: Essays on Native American Religion*, edited by Walter Capps. New York: Harper Forum Books, 79–85.

————. 1976b. "A First American Views His Land." *National Geographic* 15 (July): 13–18.

Mooney, James. 1891. *Sacred Formulas of the Cherokee.* Washington, D.C.: Bureau of American Ethnology. 7th Annual Report. Reprinted in Nashville, Tenn.: Elder Booksellers, 1982.

————. 1900. *Myths of the Cherokee.* Washington, D.C.: Smithsonian Institution, Bureau of American Ethnology. 19th Annual Report. Reprinted in Nashville, Tenn.: Elder Booksellers, 1982.

————. 1965. *The Ghost-Dance Religion and the Sioux Outbreak of 1890,* abridged with an introduction by Anthony F.C. Wallace. Chicago: University of Chicago Press. First published in 1896 in *Fourteenth Annual Report of the Bureau of American Ethnology, 1892–1893,* Part 2. Washington, D.C.: Government Printing Office, 641–1110. Reprinted in 1973 by Dover Press and in 1991 by University of Nebraska Press.

Mooney, James, and Frans M. Olbrechts. 1932. *The Swimmer Manuscript: Cherokee Sacred Formulas and Medical Prescriptions.* Bureau of American Ethnology. Bulletin No. 99. Washington, D.C.: Smithsonian Institution.

Morison, Samuel Eliot. 1971. *The European Discovery of America: The Northern Voyages, A.D. 500–1600.* New York: Oxford University Press.

————. 1974. *The European Discovery of America: The Southern Voyages, A.D. 1492–1616.* New York: Oxford University Press.

Morris, Glenn T. 1992. "International Law and Politics: Toward a Right to Self-Determination for Indigenous Peoples." In *The State of Native America: Genocide, Colonization, and Resistance,* edited by M. Annette Jaimes. Boston: South End Press, 55–86.

Moses, L.G. 1985. "'My Father Tells Me So': Wovoka: The Ghost Dance Prophet." *American Indian Quarterly* 9 (3): 335–51.

————. 1987. "James Mooney and Wovoka: An Ethnologist's Visit with the Ghost Dance Prophet." *Nevada Historical Society Quarterly.* 30 (2): 131–46.

Moulton, Gary E. 1985. *John Ross, Cherokee Chief.* Athens: University of Georgia Press.

Müller, Werner. 1968. "Supreme Being and Big House: The Delaware and Algonquian of the Atlantic Seaboard." In *Pre-Columbian American Religions,* trans. Stanley Davis. New York: Holt, Rinehart, and Winston.

Myerhoff, Barbara. 1975. *Peyote Hunt: The Sacred Journey of the Huichol Indians.* Ithaca, N.Y.: Cornell University Press.

Nabokov, Peter. 1996. "Native Views of History." In *The Cambridge History of the Native Peoples of the Americas,* vol. 1, part 1, edited by Bruce Trigger and Wilcomb Washburn. Cambridge: Cambridge University Press, 1–59.

————, ed. 1991. *Native American Testimony: A Chronicle of Indian-White Relations from Prophecy to the Present: 1492–1992.* New York: Viking Press.

Naess, Arne. 1987. *Ecology, Community, and Lifestyle: Outline of an Ecosophy.* Cambridge: Cambridge University Press.

Nash, Gary. 1992. *Red, White, and Black: The Peoples of Early North America.* 3d ed. Englewood Cliffs, N.J.: Prentice-Hall.

Nash, Roderick. 1988. *The Rights of Nature: A History of Environmental Ethics.* Madison: University of Wisconsin Press.

————, ed. 1972. *Environment and Americans: The Problem of Priorities.* New York: Holt, Rinehart, and Winston.

Neihardt, John G. 1973. *When the Tree Flowered: An Authentic Tale of the Old Sioux World.* New York: Pocket Books. First published in 1951.

Newcomb, Franc Johnson. 1964. *Hosteen Klah: Navajo Medicine Man and Sand Painter.* Norman: University of Oklahoma Press.

Newcomb, Franc Johnson, and Gladys Reichard. 1975. *Sandpaintings of the Navaho Shooting Chant*. New York: Dover Publications.

Newcomb, William W., Jr. 1956a. *The Culture and the Acculturation of the Delaware Indians*. Ann Arbor: University of Michigan Press.

————. 1956b. "The Peyote Cult of the Delaware Indians." *Texas Journal of Science* 8: 202–11.

Noriega, Jorge. 1992. "American Indian Education in the United States: Indoctrination for Subordination to Colonialism." In *The State of Native America: Genocide, Colonization, and Resistance*, edited by M. Annette Jaimes. Boston: South End Press, 371–402.

O'Brien, Sharon. 1989. *American Indian Tribal Governments*. Norman: University of Oklahoma Press.

O'Bryan, Aileen. 1956. *The Diné: Origin Myths of the Navaho Indians*. Bureau of American Ethnology. Bulletin No. 163. Washington, D.C.: Government Printing Office.

Oelschlaeger, Max. 1994. *Caring for Creation: An Ecumenical Approach to the Environmental Crisis*. New Haven: Yale University Press.

Olson, James C. 1965. *Red Cloud and the Sioux Problem*. Lincoln: University of Nebraska Press.

Olson-Crawford, Shawn. 1998. "Resources on American Indian Economic Development and Entrepreneurship." *Tribal College: Journal of American Indian Higher Education* 9 (3): 36–37.

Ortiz, Alfonso. 1991. "Origins." *National Geographic* (Oct. 1991): 6–7.

————, ed. 1983. *Handbook of North American Indians: Southwest*, vol. 10. Washington, D.C.: Smithsonian Institution.

Osterreich, Shelley Anne. 1991. *The American Indian Ghost Dance, 1870 and 1890*. Biographies and Indexes in American History. Number 19.Westport, Conn.: Greenwood Press.

Overholt, Thomas W. 1978. "Short Bull, Black Elk, Sword, and the Meaning of the Ghost Dance." *Religion* 8 (2): 171–95.

————. 1979. "American Indians as 'Natural Ecologists,'" *American Indian Journal* 5: 9–16.

Page, Susanne and Jake. 1995. *Navajo*. New York: Harry N. Abrams Publishers.

Paper, Jordan. 1988. *Offering Smoke: The Sacred Pipe and Native American Religion*. Moscow: University of Idaho Press.

Parezo, Nancy. 1983. *Navajo Sandpainting: From Religious Act to Commercial Art*. Tucson: University of Arizona Press.

————. 1996. "The Diné (Navajos): Sheep Is Life." *Paths of Life: American Indians of the Southwest and Northern Mexico*, edited by Thomas E. Sheridan and Nancy Parezo. Tucson: University of Arizona Press, 3–34.

Parfit, Michael. 1994. "Powwow: A Gathering of the Tribes." *National Geographic* 185 (6): 88–113.

Parman, Donald L. 1976. *The Navajos and the New Deal*. New Haven: Yale University Press.

Paul, Doris. 1973. *The Navajo Codetalkers*. Philadelphia: Dorrance.

Peithmann, Irvin M. 1964. *Red Men of Fire: A History of the Cherokee Indians*. Springfield, Ill.: Charles C. Thomas.

Perdue, Theda. 1979. *Slavery and the Evolution of Cherokee Society, 1540–1866*. Knoxville: University of Tennessee Press.

————. 1989. *The Cherokee*. New York: Chelsea House Publishers.

Perdue, Theda, and Michael Green, ed. 1995. *The Cherokee Removal: A Brief History with Documents*. New York: Bedford Books of St. Martin's Press.

Persico, V. Richard, Jr. 1979. "Early Nineteenth-Century Cherokee Political Organization." In *The Cherokee Indian Nation*, edited by Duane H. King. Knoxville: University of Tennessee Press, 92–109.

Petrullo, Vincenzo. 1934. *The Diabolic Root: A Study of Peyotism, the New Indian Religion, among the Delawares*. Philadelphia: University of Pennsylvania Press.

Pfaller, Louis. 1972. "The Indian Scare of 1890." *North Dakota History* 39 (2): 7–17.

Philbrook Art Center. 1993. "The Big House Religion of the Delaware Exhibit." Opened November 1993. Tulsa, Oklahoma.

Philip, Kenneth R., ed. 1986. *Indian Self-Rule: First-Hand Accounts of Indian-White Relations from Roosevelt to Reagan*. Salt Lake City: Howe Brothers.

Pickering, Robert B. 1997. *Seeing the White Buffalo*. Denver: Denver Museum of Natural History Press.

Pisater, Edwin. 1979. "Endangered Species: Costs and Benefits." *Environmental Ethics* 1 (4): 34–38.

Poor Man, Mercy. 1987. "Christian Life Fellowship Church." In *Sioux Indian Religion: Tradition and Innovation*, edited by Raymond J. DeMallie and Douglas R. Parks. Norman: University of Oklahoma Press, 149–55.

Powers, Marla N. 1986a. *Oglala Women: Myth, Ritual, and Reality*. Chicago: University of Chicago Press.

———. 1990a. "Mistress, Mother, Visionary Spirit: The Lakota Culture Heroine." *Religion in Native North America*, edited by Christopher Vecsey. Moscow: University of Idaho Press, 36–48.

———. 1991. *Lakota Naming: A Modern Day Hunka Ceremony*. Kendall Park, N.J.: Lakota Books.

Powers, William K. 1977. *Oglala Religion*. Lincoln: University of Nebraska Press.

———. 1982. *Yuwipi: Vision and Experience in Oglala Ritual*. Lincoln: University of Nebraska Press.

———. 1986b. *Sacred Language: The Nature of Supernatural Discourse in Lakota*. Norman: University of Oklahoma Press.

———. 1987. "Lakota Religion." In *The Encylopedia of Religion*, vol. 8, edited by Mircea Eliade. New York: Macmillan, 434–36.

———. 1990b. "When Black Elk Speaks, Everybody Listens." *Religion in Native North America*, edited by Christopher Vecsey. Moscow: University of Idaho Press, 136–51.

Prewitt, Terry J. 1981. *Tradition and Change in the Oklahoma Delaware Big House Community: 1867–1924*. Tulsa: University of Tulsa Contributions in Archaeology. No. 9.

Price, Catherine. 1996. *The Oglala People, 1841–1879: A Political History*. Lincoln: University of Nebraska Press.

Prucha, Francis Paul. 1976. *American Indian Policy in Crisis: Christian Reformers and the Indian, 1865–1900*. Norman: University of Oklahoma Press.

———. 1986. *The Great Father: The United States Government and the American Indians*. 2 vols. Lincoln: University of Nebraska Press.

Rafinesque, Constantine S. 1836. *The American Nations; or, Outlines of Their General History, Ancient and Modern*. Philadelphia: C.S. Rafinesque.

Redhouse, John. 1985. *Geopolitics of the Navajo-Hopi Land Dispute*. Albuquerque: Redhouse/Wright Publications.

Reed, Gerard. 1986. "A Native American Environmental Ethic: A Homily on Black Elk." In *Religion and Environmental Crisis*, edited by Eugene Hargrove. Athens: University of Georgia Press, 25–52.

Regan, Tom. 1982. "Environmental Ethics and the Ambiguity of the Native Americans' Relationship with Nature." In *All That Dwell Therein: Animal Rights and Environmental Ethics* (Berkeley: University of California Press), 206–39.

Reichard, Gladys. 1944. *The Story of the Navaho Hail Chant*. New York: Columbia University.

————. 1970. *Navaho Religion: A Study of Symbolism.* 2d ed. New York: Pantheon. First published 1950.

————. 1977. *Navajo Medicine Man: Sandpaintings and Legends of Miguelito.* New York: Dover. First published 1939.

Rice, Julian. 1991. *Black Elk's Story: Distinguishing its Lakota Purpose.* Albuquerque: University of New Mexico Press.

————. 1992. *Deer Women and Elk Men: The Lakota Narratives of Ella Deloria.* Albuquerque: University of New Mexico Press.

Roessel, Robert A., Jr. 1983a.. *Dinetah: Navajo History.* Vol. II. Edited by T.C. McCarthy. Chinle, Ariz.: Navajo Curriculum Center, Rough Rock Demonstration School.

————. 1983b. "Navajo History, 1850–1923." In *Handbook of North American Indians: Southwest,* vol. 10. , edited by Alfonso Ortiz. Washington, D.C.: Smithsonian Institution, 506–23

Roessel, Ruth, ed. 1973. *Navajo Stories of the Long Walk Period.* Tsaile, Ariz.: Navajo Community College.

Rose, Wendy. 1992. "The Great Pretenders: Further Reflections on Whiteshamanism." In *The State of Native America: Genocide, Colonization, and Resistance,* edited by M. Annette Jaimes. Boston: South End Press, 403–21.

Rossman, Douglas. 1988. *Where Legends Live: A Pictorial Guide to Cherokee Mythic Places.* Cherokee, N.C.: Cherokee Publications.

Sale, Kirkpatrick. 1990. *The Conquest of Paradise: Christopher Columbus and the Columbian Legacy.* New York: Alfred A. Knopf.

Salisbury, Neal. 1996. "Native People and European Settlers in Eastern North America, 1600–1783." In *The Cambridge History of the Native Peoples of the Americas,* vol. 1, part 1, edited by Bruce Trigger and Wilcomb Washburn. Cambridge: Cambridge University Press, 399–460.

Sanders, S. 1990. *Our First Twenty Years.* Boulder: Native American Rights Fund.

Sandoz, Mari. 1992. *Crazy Horse: The Strange Man of the Oglalas.* Lincoln: University of Nebraska Press. First published in 1942.

Satz, Ronald. 1975. *American Indian Policy in the Jacksonian Era.* Lincoln: University of Nebraska Press.

Sayre, Robert F. 1977. *Thoreau and the American Indians.* Princeton: Princeton University Press.

Schultes, Richard E. and Albert Hoffman. 1979. *Plants of the Gods.* New York: McGraw-Hill.

Schultz, Paul and George Tinker. 1988. *Rivers of Life: Native Spirituality for Native Churches.* Minneapolis: Augsburg Press.

Seed, John, and Johanna Macy, Pat Fleming, and Arne Naess. 1988. *Thinking Like a Mountain: Towards a Council of All Beings.* Philadelphia: New Society Publishers.

Sekaquaptewa, Emory. 1976. "Hopi Indian Ceremonies." *Seeing With a Native Eye,* edited by Walter H. Capps. New York: Harper & Row, 35–43.

Seton, Ernest Thompson. 1936. *The Gospel of the Red Man.* New York: Doubleday Doran.

Shanley, James. 1998. "Welfare Reform Will Create More Misery." *Tribal College: Journal of American Indian Higher Education* 9 (3): 19–21.

Silko, Leslie Marmon. 1986. *Ceremony.* New York: Penguin Books. First published in 1977.

————. 1996. *Yellow Woman and a Beauty of the Spirit.* New York: Simon and Schuster.

Slotkin, James S. 1952. "Menomini Peyotism. A Study of Individual Variation in a Primary Group with a Homogenous Culture." *Transactions of the American Philosophical Society* 42: 571.

————. 1956. *The Peyote Religion: A Study in Indian-White Relations.* Glencoe, Ill.: Free Press.

————. 1973. *Regeneration through Violence: The Mythology of the American Frontier, 1600–1800.* Middletown, Conn.: Wesleyan University Press.

————. 1985. *The Fatal Environment: The Myth of the Frontier in the Age of Industrialization, 1800–1890.* New York: Atheneum.

Smith, Bruce D. 1996. "Agricultural Chiefdoms of the Eastern Woodlands." In *The Cambridge History of the Native Peoples of the Americas*, vol. 1, part 1, edited by Bruce Trigger and Wilcomb Washburn. Cambridge: Cambridge University Press, 267–323.

Smith, Huston, and Reuben Snake, ed. 1996. *One Nation under God: The Triumph of the Native American Church.* Santa Fe, N.M.: Clear Light Publishers.

Smith, Paul Chaat, and Robert Allen Warrior. 1996. *Like a Hurricane: The Indian Movement from Alcatraz to Wounded Knee.* New York: New Press.

Smoak, Gregory. 1986. "Mormons and the Ghost Dance of 1890." *South Dakota History* 16 (3): 269–94.

Snake, Reuben. 1992. *The Peyote Road.* Documentary film. Executive Producer: Reuben Snake. Directors: Fidel Moreno, Gary Rhine, and Phil Cousineau. Kifaru Productions, San Francisco, Calif.

————. 1996. *Reuben Snake: Your Humble Serpent*, as told to Jay Fikes. Santa Fe, N.M.: Clear Light Publishers.

Snow, Dean R. 1994. *The Iroquois.* The Peoples of America Series. Oxford, U.K.: Blackwell.

————. 1996. "The First Americans and the Differentiation of Hunter-Gatherer Cultures." In *The Cambridge History of the Native Peoples of the Americas*, vol. 1, part 1, edited by Bruce Trigger and Wilcomb Washburn. Cambridge: Cambridge University Press, 125–99.

Snyder, Gary. 1974. *Turtle Island.* New York: New Directions.

————. 1990. *The Practice of the Wild.* San Francisco: North Point Press.

Speck, Frank G. 1931. *A Study of the Delaware Big House Ceremony.* Vol. 2. Harrisburg: Pennsylvania Historical Commission.

————. 1937. "Oklahoma Delaware Ceremonies, Feasts and Dances." *Memoirs of the American Philosophical Society* 7: 1–161.

————. 1945. *The Celestial Bear Comes Down to Earth.* Reading, Pa.: Reading Public Museum and Art Gallery. Scientific Publication No. 7.

Speck, Frank G., and Leonard Broom, in collaboration with Will West Long. 1983. *Cherokee Dance and Drama.* Norman: University of Oklahoma Press. First published in 1951.

Spencer, Katherine. 1947. *Reflections of Social Life in the Navaho Origin Myth.* Albuquerque: University of New Mexico Press.

————. 1957. *Mythology and Values: An Analysis of Navaho Chantway Myths.* American Folklore Society Memoirs. Vol. 48. Boston: American Folklore Society.

Spicer, E.H. 1969. *A Short History of the Indians of the United States.* New York: D. Van Nostrand.

————. 1982. *The American Indians.* Cambridge, Mass.: Belknap Press of Harvard University Press.

Spider, Emerson, Sr. 1987. "The Native American Church of Jesus Christ." In *Sioux Indian Religion: Tradition and Innovation*, edited by Raymond J. DeMallie and Douglas R. Parks. Norman: University of Oklahoma Press, 189–209.

Spier, Leslie. 1935. *The Prophet Dance of the Northwest and Its Derivatives: The Source of the Ghost Dance.* American Anthropological Association, General Series in Anthropology. No. 1.

Standing Bear, Luther. 1986. *Land of the Spotted Eagle.* Lincoln: University of Nebraska Press. First published in 1933.

Stannard, David E. 1992. *American Holocaust: Columbus and the Conquest of the New World.* New York: Oxford University Press.

Stead, Robert. 1987. "Traditional Lakota Religion in Modern Life." In *Sioux Indian Religion: Tradition and Innovation*, edited by Raymond J. DeMallie and Douglas R. Parks. Norman: University of Oklahoma Press, 211–16.

Steinmetz, Paul B., S.J. 1970. "The Relationship Between Plains Indian Religion and Christianity: A Priest's Viewpoint." *Plains Anthropologist* 15: 83–86.

———. 1984. "The Sacred Pipe in American Indian Religions." *American Indian Culture and Research Journal* 8: 27–80.

———. 1990a. *Pipe, Bible, and Peyote among the Oglala Lakota: A Study in Religious Diversity.* Revised edition. Knoxville: University of Tennessee Press. First published in 1980.

———. 1990b. "Shamanic Images in Peyote Visions." In *Religion in Native North America*, edited by Christopher Vecsey. Moscow: University of Idaho Press, 104–16.

Steltenkamp, Michael. 1993. *Black Elk: Holy Man of the Oglala.* Norman: University of Oklahoma Press.

Stewart, Irene. 1982. *A Voice in Her Tribe: A Navajo Woman's Own Story.* Socorro, N.M.: Ballena Press.

Stewart, Omer C. 1948. "Ute Peyotism." University of Colorado Studies, Series in Anthropology. Vol. 1, pp. 1–42.

———. 1972. "The Peyote Religion and the Ghost Dance." *Indian Historian* 5 (4): 27–30.

———. 1980. "The Ghost Dance" and "The Native American Church." In *Anthropology on the Great Plains*, edited by W. Raymond Wood and Margot Liberty. Lincoln: University of Nebraska Press, 178–96.

———. 1986. "The Peyote Religion." In *Handbook of North American Indians*, vol. 11, edited by Warren L. D'Azevedo. Washington, D.C.: Smithsonian Institution, 673–81.

———. 1987. *Peyote Religion: A History.* Norman: University of Oklahoma Press.

Stewart, Omer C., and David F. Aberle. 1957. *Navajo and Ute Peyotism: A Chronological and Distributional Study.* Boulder: University of Colorado Press.

Stiffarm, Lenore A., and Phil Lane Jr. 1992. "The Demography of Native North America: A Question of American Indian Survival." In *The State of Native America: Genocide, Colonization, and Resistance*, edited by M. Annette Jaimes. Boston: South End Press, 23–53.

Stolzman, William. 1986. *How to Take Part in Lakota Ceremonies.* Pine Ridge, S.D.: Heritage Center, Red Cloud Indian School.

———. 1992. *The Pipe and Christ.* 4th ed. Chamberlain, S.D.: Tipi Press.

Strickland, Rennard. 1982. *Fire and the Spirits: Cherokee Law from Clan to Court.* Norman: University of Oklahoma Press.

Takaki, Ronald. 1993. *A Different Mirror: A History of Multicultural America.* Boston: Little, Brown and Company.

Tantaquidgeon, Gladys. 1972. *Folk Medicine of the Delaware and Related Algonkian Indians.* Anthropological Series. No. 3. Harrisburg, Pa.: Pennsylvania Historical and Museum Commission. First published in 1942.

Terrell, John Upton. 1979. *The Arrow and the Cross: A History of the American Indian and the Missionaries.* Santa Barbara: Capra Press.

Thistlewaite, Susan Brooks, and Mary Potter Engle, eds. 1990. *Lift Every Voice: Constructing Christian Theologies from the Underside.* San Francisco: Harper & Row.

Thomas, David Hurst. 2000. *Skull Wars: Kennewick Man, Archeology, and the Battle for Native American Identity.* New York: Basic Books.

Thomas, Robert K. 1961. "The Redbird Smith Movement." In *Symposium on Cherokee and Iroquois Culture*, edited by William N. Fenton and John Gulick. Bureau of American Ethnology. Bulletin No. 180. Washington, D.C.: Government Printing Office, 159–66.

Thompson, Gerald E. 1976. *The Army and the Navajo: The Bosque Redondo Reservation Experiment, 1863–68*. Tucson: University of Arizona Press.

Thornton, Russell. 1986. *We Shall Live Again: The 1870 and 1890 Ghost Dance Movements as Demographic Revitalizations*. Cambridge: Cambridge University Press.

———. 1987. *American Indian Holocaust and Survival*. Norman: University of Oklahoma.

———. 1990. *The Cherokees: A Population History*. Lincoln: University of Nebraska Press.

———. 1999. *Studying Native America: Problems and Prospects*. Madison: University of Wisconsin Press.

Tinker, George. 1993. *Missionary Conquest: The Gospel and Native American Cultural Genocide*. Minneapolis: Augsburg/Fortress Press.

———. 1996. "Spirituality, Native American Personhood, Sovereignty, and Solidarity." In *Native and Christian: Indigenous Voices on Religious Identity in the United States and Canada*, edited by James Treat. New York: Routledge, 115–31.

Todorov, Tzvetan. 1982. *The Conquest of America*. New York: Harper & Row.

Tome, Marshall. 1983. "The Navajo Nation Today." In *Handbook of North American Indians: Southwest*, vol. 10. , edited by Alfonso Ortiz. Washington, D.C.: Smithsonian Institution, 679–83.

Tooker, Elisabeth, ed. 1979. "Delaware Big House Ceremonial." In *Native North American Spirituality of the Eastern Woodlands* (Mahwah, N.J.: Paulist Press), 104–24. (Excerpts from Speck's 1931 study [retranslated by Ives Goddard] and from Harrington's 1921 study.)

Towner, Ronald H., ed. 1996. *The Archaeology of Navajo Origins*. Salt Lake City: University of Utah Press.

Trafzer, Clifford E. 1982. *The Kit Carson Campaign: The Last Great Navajo War*. Norman: University of Oklahoma Press.

Treat, James, ed. 1996. *Native and Christian: Indigenous Voices on Religious Identity in the United States and Canada*. New York: Routledge.

Trigger, Bruce, and William R. Swagerty. 1996. "Entertaining Strangers: North America in the Sixteenth Century." In *The Cambridge History of the Native Peoples of the Americas*, vol. 1, part 1, edited by Bruce Trigger and Wilcomb Washburn. Cambridge: Cambridge University Press, 325–98.

Trigger, Bruce, and Wilcomb Washburn, eds. 1996. *The Cambridge History of the Native Peoples of the Americas*. Vol. 1, part 1. Cambridge: Cambridge University Press.

Trigger, Bruce, ed. 1978. *Handbook of North American Indians: Northeast*. Vol. 15. Washington, D.C.: Smithsonian Institution.

Trimble, Stephen. 1993. "The Navajo." In *The People: Indians of the American Southwest*. Santa Fe, N.M.: School of American Research, 21–94.

Underhill, Ruth. 1953. *Here Come the Navaho!* Indian Life and Customs. No. 8. Lawrence, Kans.: United States Indian Service.

———. 1956. *The Navajos*. Norman: University of Oklahoma Press.

Utley, Robert M. 1963. *The Last Days of the Sioux Nation*. New Haven: Yale University Press.

———. 1993. *The Lance and the Shield: The Life and Times of Sitting Bull*. New York: Henry Holt and Co.

Van der Wall, Jim. 1992. "A Warrior Caged: The Continuing Struggle of Leonard Peltier." In *The State of Native America: Genocide, Colonization, and Resistance*, edited by M. Annette Jaimes. Boston: South End Press, 291–310.

Vanderwerth, W.C., ed. 1971. *Indian Oratory: Famous Speeches by Noted Indian Chieftains*. Norman: University of Oklahoma Press.

Vaughan, Alden. 1979. *New England Frontier: Puritans and Indians, 1620–1675*. 2d ed. New York: Norton.

Vecsey, Christopher. 1980. "American Indian Environmental Religions." In *American Indian Environments: Ecological Issues in Native American History*, edited by Christopher Vecsey and Robert W. Venables. Syracuse: Syracuse University Press 1–37.

Vecsey , Christopher, and Robert W. Venables, eds. 1980. *American Indian Environments: Ecological Issues in Native American History*. Syracuse: Syracuse University Press.

Venables, Robert W. 1992. "American Indian Influences on the America of the Founding Fathers." In *Exiled in the Land of the Free: Democracy, Indian Nations, and the U.S. Constitution*, by Oren Lyons et al. Santa Fe, N.M.: Clear Light Publishers, 73–124.

Vestal, Stanley. 1957. *Sitting Bull: Champion of the Sioux*. Norman: University of Oklahoma Press. First published in 1932.

Viola, H.J., ed. 1990. *After Columbus: The Smithsonian Chronicle of the North American Indian*. Washington, D.C.: Smithsonian/Orion Books.

Voget, Fred W. 1968. "Review of the Peyote Religion among the Navaho." *American Anthroplogist* 70: 118–19.

Vogt, Evon Z. 1961. "Navaho." In *Perspectives in American Indian Culture Change,* ed. Edward H. Spicer. Chicago: University of Chicago Press.

Wahrhaftig, Albert L., and Jane Lukens-Wahrhaftig. 1979. "New Militants or Resurrected State? The Five County Northeastern Oklahoma Cherokee Organization." In *The Cherokee Indian Nation*, edited by Duane H. King. Knoxville: University of Tennessee Press, 223–46.

Waldman, Carl, ed. 1985. *Atlas of the North American Indian*. New York: Facts on File.

Walker, Deward E., Jr. 1969. "New Light on the Prophet Dance." *Ethnohistory* 16 (3): 245–55.

Walker, James R. 1917. *The Sun Dance and Other Ceremonies of the Oglala Division of the Teton Dakota*. American Museum of Natural History. Anthropological Papers. Vol. 16, pp. 50–221.

Walker, James R. 1980. *Lakota Belief and Ritual*. Edited by Raymond J. DeMaillie and Elaine A. Jahner. Lincoln: University of Nebraska Press.

———. 1982. *Lakota Society*. Edited by Raymond J. DeMallie. Lincoln: University of Nebraska Press.

———. 1983. *Lakota Myth*. Edited by Elaine A. Jahner. Lincoln: University of Nebraska Press.

Wallace, Anthony F.C. 1949. *King of the Delawares: Teedyuscung, 1700–1763*. Philadephia: University of Pennsylvania Press.

———. 1956. "Revitalization Movements: Some Theoretical Considerations for their Comparative Study." *American Anthropologist* 58: 264–81.

———. 1999. *Jefferson and the Indians: The Tragic Fate of the First Americans*. Cambridge, Mass.: Belknap Press of Harvard University Press.

Warner, Michael. 1970. "Protestant Missionary Activity among the Navajo, 1890–1912." *New Mexico Historical Review* 45: 209–32.

Warrior, Robert Allen. 1996. "Canaanites, Cowboys, and Indians: Deliverance, Conquest, and Liberation Theology Today." In *Native and Christian: Indigenous Voices on Religious Identity in the United States and Canada*, edited by James Treat. New York: Routledge, 93–104.

Washburn, Wilcomb E. 1989. "Anthropological Advocacy in the Hopi-Navajo Land Dispute." *American Anthropologist* 91. 738–43.

———. 1995. *Red Man's Land/White Man's Law: A Study of the Past and Present Status of the American Indian*. Rev. ed. Norman: University of Oklahoma Press. (1971)

————. 1996. "The Native American Renaissance, 1960–1995." In *The Cambridge History of the Native Peoples of the Americas*, vol. 1, part 2, edited by Bruce Trigger and Wilcomb Washburn. Cambridge: Cambridge University Press, 401–73.

Watson, Elmo Scott. 1943. "The Last Indian War, 1890–91—A Study of Newspaper Jingoism." *Journalism Quarterly* 20: 205–19.

Waugh, Earle H., and K. Dad Prithipaul, eds. 1977. *Native Religious Traditions*. Waterloo, Ontario: Wilfrid Laurier University Press.

Weatherford, Jack. 1988. *Indian Givers: How the Indians of the Americas Transformed the World*. New York: Fawcett Columbine.

————. 1991. *Native Roots: How the Indians Enriched America*. New York: Crown.

————. 1994. *Savages and Civilization: Who Will Survive?* New York: Crown.

Welch, James, and Paul Stekler. 1994. *Killing Custer: The Battle of the Little Bighorn and the Fate of the Plains Indians*. New York: W.W. Norton.

Welsager, C.A. 1972. *The Delaware Indians: A History*. New Brunswick, N.J.: Rutgers University Press.

————. 1978. *The Delaware Indian Westward Migration*. Wallingford, Pa.: Middle Atlantic Press.

West, Richard. 1996. "Indian Spirituality: Another Vision." In *Native and Christian: Indigenous Voices on Religious Identity in the United States and Canada*, edited by James Treat. New York: Routledge, 29–37.

Weyler, Rex. 1984. *Blood of the Land: The Government and Corporate War against the American Indian Movement*. New York: Vintage Books.

Wheelwright, Mary C. 1956. *The Myth and Prayers of the Great Star Chant and the Myth of the Coyote Chant*. Santa Fe, N.M.: Wheelwright Museum of the American Indian.

White, Lynn. 1967. "The Historical Roots of Our Ecological Crisis." *Science* 155: 1203–7.

White, Richard. 1978. "The Winning of the West: The Expansion of the Western Sioux in the Eighteenth and Nineteenth Centuries." *Journal of American History* 65: 319–43.

————. 1984. "Native Americans and the Environment." In *Scholars and the Indian Experience*, edited by William Swagerty. Bloomington: Indiana University Press, 179–204.

————. 1991. *"It's Your Misfortune and None of My Own": A History of the American West*. Norman: University of Oklahoma Press.

Wilkins, Thurman. 1986. *Cherokee Tragedy: The Ridge Family and the Decimation of a People*. 2d ed. rev. Norman: University of Oklahoma Press.

Willink, Roseann S., and Paul G. Zolbrod. 1997. *Weaving a World: Textiles and the Navajo Way of Seeing*. Santa Fe: Museum of New Mexico Press.

Wilson, James. 1999. *The Earth Shall Weep: A History of Native America*. New York: Atlantic Monthly Press.

Wisecarver, Charmaine White Face. 1990. "Wounded Knee: Mending the Sacred Hoop." *Native Peoples* (Spring): 8–16.

Wissler, Clark. 1912. *Societies and Ceremonial Associations in the Oglala Division of Teton Dakota*. New York: American Museum of Natural History.

Witherspoon, Gary. 1975. *Navaho Kinship and Marriage*. Chicago: University of Chicago Press.

————. 1977. *Language and Art in the Navajo Universe*. Ann Arbor: University of Michigan Press.

————. 1983a. "Navajo Social Organization." In *Handbook of North American Indians: Southwest*, vol. 10, edited by Alfonso Ortiz. Washington, D.C.: Smithsonian Institution: 524–35.

————. 1983b. "Language and Reality in Navajo World View." In *Handbook of North American Indians: Southwest*, vol. 10, edited by Alfonso Ortiz. Washington, D.C.: Smithsonian Institution: 570–78.

Witthoft, John. 1946. "The Cherokee Green Corn Medicine and the Green Corn Festival." *Journal of the Washington Academy of Sciences* 36: 213–19.

———. 1948. "Will West Long, Cherokee Informant." *American Anthropologist* 50: 355–59.

Wollock, Jeffrey. 1998. "Protagonism Emergent: Indians and Higher Education." *Native Americas: Akwe:kon's Journal of Indigenous Issues* 14 (4): 12–23.

Wood, John. 1982. "Western Navajo Religious Affiliations." In *Navajo Religion and Culture: Selected Views*, edited by David M Brugge and Charlotte J. Frisbie. Museum of New Mexico Papers in Anthropology, No.17.

Woodward, Grace Steele. 1963. *The Cherokees*. Norman: University of Oklahoma Press.

Worsley, Peter. 1974. *The Trumpet Shall Sound*. New York: Schocken Books. First published in 1957.

Wyckoff, Lydia Lloyd, and Curtis Zunigha. 1994. "Delaware: Honoring the Past and Preparing for the Future." *Native Peoples: The Arts and Lifeways* 7 (3): 56–62.

Wyman, Leland C. 1957. *Beautyway: A Navaho Ceremonial*. Bollingen Series LIII. New York: Pantheon Books.

———. 1965. *The Red Antway of the Navaho*. Navajo Religion Series, Vol. 5. Santa Fe, N.M.: Museum of Navajo Ceremonial Art.

———. 1970. *Blessingway*. Tucson: University of Arizona Press.

———. 1975. *The Mountainway of the Navaho*. Tucson: University of Arizona Press.

———. 1983a. "Navajo Ceremonial Systems." In *Handbook of North American Indians: Southwest*, vol. 10. , edited by Alfonso Ortiz. Washington, D.C.: Smithsonian Institution, 536–57.

———. 1983b. *Southwest Indian Dry Painting*. Santa Fe and Albuquerque: School of American Research and University of New Mexico Press.

Wyman, Leland C., and Clyde Kluckhohn. 1938. *Navaho Classification of Their Song Ceremonials*. American Anthropological Association Memoirs, No. 50. Menasha, Wis.: American Anthropological Association.

Young, William A. 2005. *The World's Religions: Worldviews and Contemporary Issues*, 2nd. ed. Upper Saddle River, N.J.: Prentice-Hall.

Zimmerman, Bill. 1976. *Airlift to Wounded Knee*. Chicago: Swallow Press.

Zinn, Howard. 1995. *A People's History of the United States*. Rev. ed. New York: Harper Perennial. First published in 1980.

Zolbrod, Paul G. 1984. *Diné Bahane': The Navajo Creation Story*. Albuquerque: University of New Mexico Press.

Zunigha, Curtis, elected chief of the Delaware Tribe of Indians. 1997. Interview with the author, Bartlesville and Dewey, Okla., 21 October.

Index

ESTE LIBRO HA SIDO POSIBLE POR EL TRABAJO DE

COMITÉ EDITORIAL Silvia Aguilera, Mario Garcés, Luis Alberto Mansilla, Tomás Moulian, Naín Nómez, Jorge Guzmán, Julio Pinto, Paulo Slachevsky, Hernán Soto, José Leandro Urbina, Verónica Zondek, Ximena Valdés, Santiago Santa Cruz **PRODUCCIÓN EDITORIAL** Guillermo Bustamante **PROYECTOS** Ignacio Aguilera **DISEÑO Y DIAGRAMACIÓN EDITORIAL** Leonardo Flores **CORRECCIÓN DE PRUEBAS** Raúl Cáceres **DISTRIBUCIÓN** Nikos Matsiordas **COMUNIDAD DE LECTORES** Francisco Miranda, Marcelo Reyes **VENTAS** Elba Blamey, Luis Fre, Marcelo Melo, Olga Herrera **BODEGA** Francisco Cerda, Pedro Morales, Carlos Villarroel **LIBRERÍAS** Nora Carreño, Ernesto Córdova **COMERCIAL GRÁFICA LOM** Juan Aguilera, Danilo Ramírez, Inés Altamirano, Eduardo Yáñez **SERVICIO AL CLIENTE** Elizardo Aguilera, José Lizana, Ingrid Rivas **DISEÑO Y DIAGRAMACIÓN COMPUTACIONAL** Nacor Quiñones, Luis Ugalde, Jessica Ibaceta **SECRETARIA COMERCIAL** Elioska Molina **PRODUCCIÓN IMPRENTA** Carlos Aguilera, Gabriel Muñoz **SECRETARIA IMPRENTA** Jasmín Alfaro **IMPRESIÓN DIGITAL** William Tobar **IMPRESIÓN OFFSET** Rodrigo Véliz **ENCUADERNACIÓN** Ana Escudero, Andrés Rivera, Edith Zapata, Pedro Villagra, Eduardo Tobar **DESPACHO** Matías Sepúlveda **MANTENCIÓN** Jaime Arel **ADMINISTRACIÓN** Mirtha Ávila, Alejandra Bustos, Andrea Veas, César Delgado.

LOM EDICIONES